A HISTORY OF
AUSTRALIAN LITERATURE

PURE AND APPLIED

A critical review of all forms of literature produced in Australia from the first books published after the arrival of the First Fleet until 1950, with short accounts of later publications up to 1960

H. M. GREEN

Sometime Librarian of the University of Sydney and President of the Australian Institute of Librarians

VOLUME II

1923–1950

REVISED BY DOROTHY GREEN

ANGUS & ROBERTSON PUBLISHERS

By the same author in this series
A History of Australian Literature
Volume I
1789-1923

ANGUS & ROBERTSON PUBLISHERS
London · Sydney · Melbourne

First published by Angus & Robertson Publishers, Australia, 1961
Reprinted, with corrections, 1962
Reprinted 1966, 1968, 1971, 1974
This revised edition 1985

National Library of Australia
Cataloguing-in-publication data.

Green, H. M. (Henry MacKenzie), 1881-1962
A history of Australian literature. Volume 2.

Rev. ed.
Includes index.
ISBN 0 207 14335 8 (set).
ISBN 0 207 14255 6 (v.2).

1. Australian literature—History and criticism.
I. Title.

A820'.9

Typeset in 12pt Bembo by Graphicraft Typesetters Ltd., Hong Kong

Printed in Shenzhen, China

Volume Two

FOREWORD TO THE SECOND EDITION OF VOLUME II

THE INTRODUCTION to this History and the Foreword to the second edition as a whole will be found in Volume I. The purpose of this Foreword is simply to inform the reader of the kinds of revision to be expected here, as a result of the changes made to the original plan.

It was at first intended to rewrite the sections on a number of writers discussed in the original volume in order to take in work which they had produced since 1950, without departing too far from the original text. For example, by the closing date of this volume such a major poet as A. D. Hope had not published the manuscripts of his poems which were available to H. M. Green, and Judith Wright had published only two books. Because of the delay in printing the History it became clear in the nineteen-sixties that the original assessments of poets who were at the beginning of their careers when the book went to press, would not suffice: first, because in some cases writers had changed their direction; second, because problems of style and outlook in treatment became more difficult as time passed. A further difficulty was that, for personal and professional reasons, progress with the revision was intermittent, except during the years 1969, 1971, and for the three years from 1973 to 1976. During the latter period, time was occupied by a work which arose out of a reconsideration of material in Volume I; this has now become a source-book in its own right. After the revision had to be suspended again at the end of 1976 because of teaching commitments, the publishers decided to abandon the plan to bring Volume II up to date to 1973, and to publish it with its original closing date of 1950, thus eliminating the final chapter. It was decided to remove the new material to a third volume, with a closing date of 1980, which would be the sole responsibility of the present writer.

Volume II will therefore retain its character as the work of a man with a consistent point of view of the growth of Australian literature for more than fifty years. There are fewer alterations than might be expected in a work dealing with a complex Period, though some minor writers have been omitted.

The alterations are of three kinds:

1. Factual errors, misprints, slips of various kinds have been corrected as far as possible.

2. Death-dates have been supplied where these are obtainable for authors

who have died since Green wrote. This task is not always an easy one and consumes a great deal of time. Few authors attract much attention from newspapers, and minor writers hardly any at all. Libraries do not keep records unless there is an obvious obituary published in the press, and Registries of Deaths cannot help unless an approximate date and place of death are known. This fact alone places a restriction on the generous help afforded since 1966 by the staff and the publications of the *Australian Dictionary of Biography*. Again, some writers have disappeared overseas after publishing one or two Australian books, and their movements have been impossible to trace. What is surprising and saddening, in fact, is the general failure to keep track of modern writers, to notice their deaths or to take any responsibility for this sort of record, even among institutions which might be supposed to value literature.

An effort has been made to check death-dates up to 1984, but writers who die while this volume is in the press will be mentioned in the third volume.

3. Significant changes in point of view, or facts recently come to light which qualify what Green had written have been marked in the text by interpolations or alterations in square brackets and by the use of footnotes indicated with an asterisk. In a few instances where interruptions to the text were impracticable, emendations will be found in the Appendices.

For the convenience of overseas readers daunted by the difficulty of obtaining a book dated, for example, 1852, a select list of reprints of books considered important has been added. The list is restricted mainly to authors whose work is hard to obtain, though there is a general reluctance in Australia to keep in print even books that sell readily, and a similar reluctance of booksellers to stock them in any number. At the moment it is comparatively easy to find one edition or another, or one selection or another of Henry Lawson's short stories. It is not at all easy to find copies of Harris's *Settlers and Convicts* which, after its second printing in 1852, was not published again until 1953. Australian literature is afflicted grievously by the fact that there is no concerted policy to keep its significant books in print. Not only are books printed once later lost to sight, but there is an appreciable number of books still in manuscript which ought to see the light of day: Arthur Davies's study of the God-King in poetry, for example, and Hilton Barton's critique of psycho-analysis, to name only two. If the whole range of Australian literature suddenly became visible and accessible, the limited canon now considered respectable would have to be considerably enlarged and might look very different from the one which too many of us take for granted.

FOURTH PERIOD

(1923-1950)

*

WORLD CONSCIOUSNESS AND DISILLUSION

CHAPTER I

INTRODUCTION

THE BEGINNING and ending and the primary characteristics of the fourth of the Periods into which Australian literature has been divided in this volume are much less easily determinable than those of any of the others. The earliest books that could reasonably be considered Australian formed a natural starting point for the first Period; the second may as reasonably be considered to open with the gradual settling down and consolidation that followed the ridge between two Periods, the gold-rushes; the third had also an obvious natural beginning, though since it merged in its successor only gradually its ending and therefore the beginning of the present Period are more debatable. The ruling characteristics of the three preceding Periods are also much more marked than those of the fourth: each of them possessed a unity that ours does not. As Yeats said:[1] "Nations, races, and individual men are unified by an image, or bundle of related images", and in the first and third Periods of Australian life and the literature that arose from it certain national images stand out clearly: in the first Period it was freedom and in the third nationhood; but in the second there is no easily discernible unifying image, and so far as there existed any general aim it seems to have been merely the acquisition of wealth. In the present Period also the acquisition of wealth is an easily discernible national aim, but perhaps this distinction may be made: that whereas during the second Period wealth was desired as a means to position and authority and as something to be handed down to a succeeding generation, it seems now to be desired, generally speaking, as a means to individual comfort and security. In other characteristics however the present Period differs widely from any of the others. In spite of the lack of any sharp line of demarcation between this and the Period which it immediately succeeded, there is no doubt that something new and different began to take shape not long after the first World War. In part, it had come into existence earlier: for example the self-sufficient isolation of the third Period came to an end on the outbreak of that war; and the romantic idealism that had inspired it was unable to survive the early German victories, the retreat from Gallipoli and the enormous losses in Flanders and on the Somme. But the revival of confidence and the short-lived prosperity that followed the final

[1] In "The Trembling of the Veil" (*Autobiographies*, London, 1955), pp. 194-5.

victory carried on some of the principal motives of the third Period until it became evident that the new world that victory had seemed to promise was not after all just round the corner. The year 1923 or thereabouts has been assumed here to mark the turning of the tide: not the full tide by any means, for there was yet the Depression to follow, and further disillusions, and the second World War, but a turning-point. And if there is a comparative vagueness about the beginning of this final Period there is still more about its ending: we seem to be somewhere near it now, but that is almost all that can at present be said. One is reminded of Bergson's ingenious paradox about the possibility of altering the past; the underlying element of truth in this paradox being of course that the nature of a historical period will seem to differ according as it is regarded as part of a larger whole: as, let us say, the beginning of bad or worse times or as a mere precursor of the good or better times that have arrived. So the present age of the world in general and Australia in particular will no doubt to our successors alter its appearance according as present doubts, indeterminacies and lack of confidence in the future, complicated by our ostrich-like tendency to bury our heads in the comfortable present, are followed by a third World War, or by scientific annihilation, or on the other hand by a continuance of peace and a gradual improvement in conditions generally.

Still, certain facts about the age in which we live are evident enough. Whenever exactly it may be taken to begin, in it realism has gradually replaced romance, and there has been a swing over from hope and confidence towards doubt and disillusion. These changes were by no means wholly the direct effects of the first World War, but it soon became clear that the world was not after all safe for democracy, and there were growing doubts whether democracy was worth saving; it became clear that economic security was as far off as ever and dissatisfaction with the capitalistic system became comparatively widespread, along with a general distrust, except in fascist Italy, in nazi Germany and in communist Russia, of any substitute that had yet been devised for it. And presently, out of the diversity of national thought and ideal as well as out of an individual desire for power arose the second World War, which also left an unhappy wake after it had been won. Apart from our fear of that one of the conflicting ideal systems which still survives, something of the regimentation that war had made necessary remains, as it always does, in time of peace, at least in the shape of an authoritarianism that tends to become a real danger. All these changes have been reflected in Australia, now that it has become quite clear that she can no longer isolate herself in either war or peace from affairs in Europe, or Asia either. They have all been factors in the substitution of something approaching cosmopolitanism for the extreme nationalism of the preceding Period, at the same time that self-satisfaction has been replaced by a desire to learn from abroad; the average Australian, so far as there is such a person, instead of being consciously and rather blatantly nationalistic, tends nowadays to look overseas, and in particular to America, for ideas and ideals. Other factors have been the natural tendency at the end of a Period to swing over to an opposite extreme, and also the growth and influence of the comparatively cosmopolitan cities: these now contain nearly half the population, or, if the country towns are added, about three-fifths.

As one crisis after another has loomed and faded, fear of attack from without or of another Depression have lately tended to slip into the background, and, what with the growth of the country's wealth[2] and its more even distribution, the fear and disillusion that ruled during the first part of the Period have weakened, and there has been lately a tendency to forget, except at periodical crises, the shadows behind the curtain. Yet there are domestic shadows also, quite apart from those which stretch towards us from overseas: the danger, on which our own economists are practically unanimous but against which our politicians seem unable to take action, that the country's constantly increasing support of industries unable to support themselves may raise the costs of Australian manufactures to a point at which they can no longer be exported; and the danger of the vicious circle of prices and wages that constantly threatens inflation and its consequences. Besides these, there are two other domestic shadows that are even less seriously regarded than the rest because their effects are less material: the authoritarian tendency that has been mentioned, which already threatens to circumscribe expression of ideas in literature as well as in politics; and, what is even more serious from a literary point of view, the degradation of standards that necessarily attaches to the growth of a class of readers whose notion of literary entertainment is primitive and largely physical, to whom it has not occurred that to get the best out of a book the reader must give as well as take, and who have in any case a quite undeveloped taste and judgment. This last does not of course apply to Australian readers only or to all Australian readers, but the class to which it does apply seems to be comparatively larger in Australia than in older and more civilized countries. Nevertheless the community as a whole seems lately to have settled down to enjoy the material comforts of life with a modified optimism, concentrating upon the foreground and ignoring what lies behind it; more or less convinced that since it is manifestly in the interests of the newspapers to emphasize a crisis, all crises are no more than newspaper creations. And, thanks to short hours, high wages, plenty of

[2] The value of Australian production was in 1950 more than three and a half times as great as at the end of the preceding Period.

work and provision by the community for the aged and other unfit, this is now, so far as Australia is concerned, a comfortable age, and has sunk back into the general flatness that results from the lack of any but a material ideal. The earliest Period, with all its hates and envies, critics and cruelties, having freedoms to fight for and the determination to attain them was by no means flat and unidealistic; the third Period had also ideals to fight for, social and political, and a determination to attain them, though the bulk of the population was, as it always is, stirred out of itself only at times. But with the present Period it is different. The objects that Labour had set before it in the nineties have been realized to the extent that it is the average citizen, and, most of all the worker with his hands, for whom the laws are made, who builds the customs that supplement the laws, and of whom the politicians think first, though the great commercial interests come a good second. Labour, therefore, has no longer troubled itself much about national indebtedness, costs of production or anything else whose threat is not immediate; and the employing classes have been concerned almost wholly with preserving the large share of the general prosperity that still remains to them: though they cannot help being more conscious of social and industrial difficulties, they can apparently suggest no practical remedy except that labour should work longer and harder than it does.

All this appears, directly or indirectly, in even the pure literature of the Period, and especially in that part of it which most closely reflects the national life: its prose fiction. Writers as well as readers are affected by the national disinclination to look beneath the surface of things. The Australian novelist and short-story writer have always, since the nineties at least, considered it their business to present a picture of Australia, of Australians and their way of life, and in this they have succeeded: the countryside and the men and women who have grown out of it possess a distinct individuality, and this has been often vividly displayed. But our novelists and short-story writers seem to assume even now that with this their business ends; concentrating upon the superficial qualities that distinguish Australians as such from Englishmen, Americans, Europeans, and life in Australia from life overseas, they tend to ignore, except in so far as these are implied within their picture, what is after all of greater fundamental importance: the qualities that Australia and Australians share with man as man and life as life. Vivid descriptions of a man, a scene, an action: Australian fiction abounds in these; but just as the average man or woman, in Australia as elsewhere, lives along the surface, so the average Australian novelist or short-story writer is satisfied to display a superficial aspect of character and life. This is true of the average writer anywhere, but of the writers that really matter it is not true; and that is probably one reason why there are so few Australian novels and short stories that really matter. Of Australian poetry, at its best again, this is not true: Hope, McAuley, Judith Wright and in their different ways Slessor and FitzGerald do ask what life is underneath; what it is about; they do trace some of the underlying springs of thought and action: but as a general rule the novelists do not; and if they probe beneath the surface they sometimes, like Penton or Herbert, do so with a particular purpose in mind, which, however important, has nothing to do with fundamentals or with the purpose of the novel as a reflector of life. Christina Stead was an exception, and so is Leonard Mann, and, except in her latest novels, Katharine Prichard; but the most talented of the younger writers, and, in her own line of country, the most experienced, Kylie Tennant, though she does fairly often dip beneath the surface, always lifts her head again in a hurry, as though to take breath after even so short an absence from her usual sphere: she does this either because she is afraid of the fundamental forces whose skirts she has just brushed, or of her ability to handle them, or perhaps she may be afraid that they will not interest her readers.* The average Australian writer of fiction is seldom inclined to weave even into his backgrounds anything that is not intimately connected with the surface life of this generation or the last, or with the conditions that brought it into being. This defect is accentuated by another in which the influence of journalism upon literature, which has been referred to more than once in this History, is evident: the writing of a particular novel is too often regarded as though it had been a journalistic assignment:[3] to write up, let us say, circus life and the wandering of a circus over the Australian countryside, or the life of a fishing village, or of opal miners, or of the dwellers in a city slum, or of "travellers" in the days of the Depression. The writer's subject in such circumstances is not life itself or some particular aspect of life as such, but some kind of life that illustrates Australian types and scenes and occupations; it is not merely that he sets his story against a particular kind of background, the background becomes the foreground and the story is built out of it, so that one is continually conscious of a restriction of purpose to something different from and less than the proper purpose of prose fiction: this of course breaks through at times and may redeem the story, and it says a good deal for the talent of the novelists so handicapped that they are often at such times able to enlarge journalism into literature. But it must not be imagined that the Australian novelist is concerned to present the national life in which he specializes as beyond reproach; on the contrary a current of criticism flows through the fiction as well as the rest of the literature of the Period, either underground or rising to the surface in what is sometimes hard and bitter satire; or, in history as well as

[3] I owe this, as well as many other suggestions, to my wife.

* [*Tell Morning This* is an exception.]

fiction, in a determination to expose past errors and inherited misunderstandings. In this may be observed, alongside an inherited national pride and desire for self-expression, the age's tendency to disillusion and its revulsion from the romanticism of its fathers and grandfathers, combined with a determination to discover and set out the bare truth, particularly if what is conceived as finally true tends to expose the falsity of a belief that had been formerly found pleasant.

If Australian literature and in particular Australian fiction has still its parochial aspect, it is nevertheless true that compared with the literature of the preceding Period it might almost be called cosmopolitan; at least it may be said to look in the main overseas for its ideas, its art and its methods generally. And yet this has not meant so much as might have been imagined: modern influences, especially in the matter of construction and psychology, are evident, but except among minor writers there have been few actual imitations, and scarcely any writer of prose or verse can be said to belong to an oversea school; this is however the less surprising in that, as has been already remarked in this History, Australian writers seldom coalesce into schools. The strongest poetic influence, here as in Britain, has been that of the early Eliot and his successors, but no Australian poet of any real importance[4] can be said to be a follower of Eliot, and the defeatism for which he stands, or used to stand, is as far as possible from striking any Australian note: of the two most prominent poets of the day, FitzGerald is as far from Eliotism as the north pole from the south; and Slessor, though Eliot among others affected his early work, has developed a style and manner that are entirely his own. There are traces of one or two other modern English poets, but they are no more than traces; Freud and Joyce have done no more than contribute to the general literary atmosphere;[5] Lawrence has opened up new fields and points of view in Australian fiction, and has also helped to free our writers from certain conventions and inhibitions, but he has had no actual followers here, and his "dark forces" never appealed to Australian writers. Dostoevsky had, as will be seen, some effect upon an early novel of Katharine Prichard's and Hardy is no doubt among her literary ancestors; Hemingway and Dos Passos have, with one exception,[6] affected only minor writers who are not mentioned in this History; a few of our dramatists have evidently studied O'Neill, Synge and Shaw, but none of these have had anything like the effect that might have been expected. Of local influences, on the other hand, one at least is strong: the Australianism of the nineties still helps to mould the novel, particularly the novel of the countryside, and, to a

[4] Unless we include Bertram Higgins.

[5] Though one Australian novelist, early in the Period, introduced to Australia the "stream-of-consciousness" method (see pp. 1154-5).

[6] Dal Stivens.

lesser extent, the short story. However, country or city, and there are far more city novels than there used to be, today's novelists have learnt a great deal in workmanship and especially in construction; yet, though their talent is undeniable, they have not produced a Furphy, let alone a Henry Handel Richardson; this may be partly owing to the double handicap that has been mentioned, or it may be that, as in the past, the tallest poppies have grown naturally in the field of verse.* Christina Stead seemed at first to have it in her to reach as great a height as any Australian novelist, but of her eleven novels only two have an Australian setting and one a substitute for an Australian setting. From 1928 to 1974 she lived abroad, in England, the United States and Europe, and her novels reflect her cosmopolitan status. She illustrates more strongly than any other Australian novelist the tendency already suggested towards the revelation of character and mood and motive by means of psychological analysis rather than action, as well as a preference for such a revelation over action itself. This tendency runs across all fictional groups today: it is shown clearly in Eleanor Dark's non-historical novels; in all Barnard Eldershaw's novels except the first; in the novels and short stories of Vance Palmer, and to some extent in those of Frank Davison; even Prichard and Tennant, though they cannot be described as psychological novelists, are by no means always content to allow their characters to present themselves through action: indeed one of the finest pieces of psychological analysis in Australian fiction occurs in Prichard's *Working Bullocks*, when Red's amorphous mental processes, the driftings of his half-conscious mind, are translated into something that is far more definite to the reader than to himself.[7] And the action that occupies a great part of Brian Penton's two novels is intimately connected with the mental or more often emotional states of which it is always an outcome and illustration; it is never there for its own sake or for the sake of the purpose which the story does not conceal. However this may be, in the present Period a far higher standard has been reached in poetry than in prose. It is true that the same may be said of all the Periods, but the difference is the more marked today in that there has been so great an increase in the number of novels, some of them by writers of considerable talent; yet not even the best work of Prichard, Tennant, Penton, Dark, Eldershaw, Mann, Davison, let us say, can stand comparison with the best work of, for instance, FitzGerald, Slessor, McAuley, Hope or Judith Wright. These poets have scarcely anything in common except that they mix brains with their emotions: on the one hand in Slessor they sometimes approach the border of journalism, and on the other, perhaps on account of their precision of thought and expression, Hope

* [Patrick White's great achievements were to come after 1950.]
7 Something will be said about this later.

and McAuley are accused of being academic; FitzGerald writes like what he is in fact, a poet who has been trained in science and sails sometimes close to the flat coastline of prose; and Judith Wright draws her life from the countryside: none of them is restricted by his inclinations or his literary origins, or by any underlying bent or purpose or native or foreign influence. FitzGerald began as a follower of Brennan, but soon set off on a voyage of his own; and Slessor in his beginnings owed something, not only, as has been remarked already, to Eliot, but to the art of Norman Lindsay. And, if we look further across the field of poetry, the work of Douglas Stewart has a good deal in common with the English and Scottish folk-ballad, and that of David Campbell with the bush ballad as well: yet there is no imitation here but kinship, which has provided a stimulus and helped these two poets to find and enlarge themselves; and the Chinese art and thought upon which Harold Stewart has built have opened out a new and individual world for him and perhaps for other Australian poets. In the remaining forms of pure literature the achievement has been much smaller than in poetry or prose fiction. In 1950 the drama depended largely upon a writer who is Australian only by adoption; the short story, though it has put on a modern dress, has, with a few marked exceptions, mostly the work of writers who are better known as novelists, little underneath it; sometimes it reminds one of the South African Campbell's remark about the curb and the bloody horse. There are more competent essayists than in the preceding Period, but none of the calibre and range of Murdoch, though the comparatively unknown E. T. Brown is worth judging by more than merely local standards. In criticism, Douglas Stewart, who is also the foremost Australian playwright, stands out, by reason partly of his editorship of the Red Page of the *Bulletin* but much more of his own talent, as the natural successor of A. G. Stephens; but Stewart does not stand as Stephens stood, almost alone, for the critical work of Barnard Eldershaw and several others cannot be left out of account. In what may be called literary scholarship, to distinguish it from the scholarship that is involved in for instance history, there has been, largely no doubt owing to the growth of the universities and their staffs, a real advance in the work of native scholars. Waldock, the first in this kind who was Australian born and bred, had won a European reputation before an early death that cut short his work half done; and there is Chisholm, a specialist in French symbolism, a couple of whose old students now in France have been referred to as "the Australian School of Mallarmé". There have been few classical scholars of a kind of which this History takes account, but among them the English-born Woodhouse is also known abroad, particularly for his work on the *Odyssey*. In philosophy and psychology, so far as concerns publications in book-form there has not been the advance that might have been expected from the establishment of additional university chairs; but in the religious sphere the work of Samuel Angus on Christianity and the mystery religions in Greece and Rome opened new ground so far as Australia was concerned.

In applied literature the developments in History and Economics have been at first sight surprising: the difficult problems that have arisen with the growth of the country's wealth and industries and the governmental control of wages and prices have stimulated Australian economists; and in history there has been the tendency, at the close of an age of political and military action, to take stock of the past; fresh sources of information have been discovered, and there has also been the tendency, in an age whose fundamental ideals have radically changed, to develop fresh historical points of view. The works of economists and historians often overlap, not only because history has nowadays broadened its base and because Australian economics is concerned more with practice than with theory, but because at modern universities the teaching of each subject involves something of the other, and most of the leading writers on both are university graduates, if not lecturers or professors. In history it is a matter for argument whether Wood and Scott and Henderson have been surpassed by their successors, some of whom were their pupils, but there is no doubt that in the historico-economic fields there are a far greater number of competent scholars than there were in the preceding Period; on the other hand the close connection in this country between literature in the narrower sense and journalism is sometimes again evident, in that here and there a piece of fine scholarship is half spoilt by the adoption of methods of expression that belong properly to the second-rate journalist. In economics the alliance with journalism is less evident; here also something like an Australian school has developed, whose work is based largely upon local statistics, upon the effects of economic laws on local political projects and policies, and upon regional and industrial surveys. Evatt's *Labour Leader* is, in spite of some lapses in impartiality, among the ablest political or historical biographies of this or any other Australian Period; but there are other biographies only less able, or less informed by the personality of the writer. There are several notable constitutional histories, and one, whose author is Australian only by adoption, on jurisprudence. It may be noted that almost all the writers on these subjects were Australian-born, but one of the best biographies of the Period was the work of the English-born A. L. Sadler, during his more than twenty years' occupancy of a chair of Oriental Studies at the University of Sydney. In scientific literature the developments have been comparatively small, except in anthropology, in which a great amount of good work has been done: this has sprung out of the establishment at the University of Sydney of a Chair of Anthropology, at which most of the field workers have been trained; out of the provision, in the periodical *Oceania*, of a means of expression for those research workers who were not yet ready for publication in book-form; out of the existence in the Australian interior of still unexhausted sources of anthropological material and of much more in Papua and the Pacific Islands; and out of Commonwealth and American subsidies. Anthropological workers have provided much that must be of considerable value to the administrator as well as to the student of social anthropology, and from the point of view of this History it may be noted that most of the anthropological work is well written and that some of the descriptions are extremely vivid. But perhaps as marked as any of the literary developments in the Period has been that of journalism. There have not been so many good literary magazines as during the preceding Period, but it had nothing comparable with *Oceania* or the *Economic Record*, and *Meanjin* and also *Southerly* have gradually become literary magazines that stand by themselves in the periodical literature of Australia and are highly regarded abroad. As for the newspapers, a few of them can hold their own, technically, with the leading papers of the modern world; from a purely literary point of view their place is not quite so high, but they reflect very capably the attitude and desires of the Australian community, or, at any rate in some instances, of its less cultured sections.

It is as hard to summarize the literary achievement of this present Period as to define its temporal limits, and harder still to compare it with that of the last; such a comparison would be almost as difficult, on its infinitely smaller scale, as a comparison of the literatures of the Victorian and Elizabethan ages. For instance, recent developments in fiction may alter the comparisons between poets and prose-writers. It may be said, however, that in spite of the lack of such commanding figures as three or four that stood out in the age that was based upon the nineties, this, take it all round, can stand up to any such comparison: not so strongly, however, as to justify what seems to be a tendency nowadays to belittle the literary achievement of our parents and grandparents.

CHAPTER II

VERSE

THE INTELLECTUALS

Slessor; FitzGerald

IN SPITE of the comparative lack in Australian literature of schools, in the sense of groups of writers animated by common principle or practice, there are of course lines of natural cleavage and relationship by observing which it is possible to get a clearer perspective of the general field; there then appear a number of groups, though they overlap so that it may be now and then a matter of opinion to which group a particular writer properly belongs. Of the field as a whole, regarded from a distance sufficient to allow of generalization, three things are immediately evident: first, that as the poetry of the previous age was, with all qualifications, lyrical or lyrically descriptive, so the poetry of the present age is predominantly reflective; and second, that there nevertheless exists today a broad line of demarcation between the majority, who are reflective to the point of being definitely intellectual, and the minority, who are predominantly lyrical, or lyrically descriptive again. Of course a lyrist will often mix brains with his emotions, as indeed most lyrists do, to a greater or lesser extent; and an intellectual may be passionate enough, though the object of his emotion will often be an idea rather than a person; as a matter of fact the intellectuals have produced some of the finest of our love poems: but these facts do not affect the general conclusions as stated. Naturally the field of poetry here referred to is not coextensive with the field of verse; it is an oasis within that wider field. The ephemeridae who flutter about the boundaries of that oasis, and indeed about the boundaries of literature generally, are slow to reflect the variations between age and age: today therefore they are mostly lyrical, or lyrical-descriptive, but whereas among the more important writers of this type there are naturally some who link this Period with the last, exhibiting characteristics of both, among its lesser writers a few carry the characteristics of the preceding Period almost unaltered into this. The reflective quality that has been observed to attach to the poetic field as a whole does not stand by itself; it is no more than an important constituent in a complex which we may for the moment be satisfied to call modernism. But other constituents of this complex, and in particular those which attach to form rather than content,[1] appear in

[1] For critical purposes it is sometimes, as here, convenient to assume a distinction which, ideally at least, does not exist.

some of the most lyrical poetry of the day; and apart from that, allied in some ways to both the intellectuals and the lyrists, there is, or was, a small but extremely vocal group in which some of the characteristics of modernism are carried to an extreme. On the whole then, it seems well not to apply the terms "modernist" or "reflective" to any particular group of poets, but to refer to the two main groups as intellectuals and lyrists or lyrically-descriptive poets, subdividing each wherever it may seem advisable. In differentiating the one group from the other the test applied has been what is considered the essential quality of the poetry, quite apart from its subject-matter, and the few borderline poets who even on this basis cannot be definitely assigned to either of the two main groups are dealt with separately as linking them.

At the head of the intellectuals stand four poets[2] who can be taken together only on the basis here adopted, for their ideals and methods differ widely and they by no means form a school: two are disillusioned romantics, whose attitudes find frequent expression in satire that is sometimes extremely bitter; the third is a classic, who has produced incidentally a satire that is no less overwhelming in that its weapon is sheer ridicule; the last is an indomitable optimist. These four are the most notable Australian poets of today; taken together, they are also in different ways among the most modern, though only one of them is modernist in manner and expression: because of this and because he has played the leading part in bringing modernism into Australian poetry, as well as because he is one of its leaders, Kenneth Slessor (Orange, New South Wales, 1901-71), may be considered first. He left school direct for journalism and has remained in that profession since; some may still remember the series of fancifully humorous articles, more entertaining than anything of the sort in the Australia of his generation, that suddenly brightened his first newspaper, the Sydney *Sun*, and the hit they made within as well as without the ranks of professional journalism. As "special" writer and later as editor he worked on several other newspapers in Melbourne and Sydney; foı three years he was Australian Official War Correspondent with the Second A.I.F.; in 1944 he returned to Australia and became literary editor and leader-writer on the Sydney *Sun*; in 1958 he joined the staff of the Sydney *Daily Telegraph*. Slessor began verse-writing early; after leaving school, mainly through Edith Sitwell's annual anthology, *Wheels* (1916-21), he discovered the "new poetry"; he met the Lindsays and, with Jack Lindsay, edited the periodical *Vision* (1922), and the anthology *Poetry in Australia* (1923), of which the first is discussed elsewhere.[3] His publications

[2] [Green wished later to include Judith Wright here; his reasons are given in Appendix 1, p. 1485.]

[3] See p. 1326.

include *Thief of the Moon* (Sydney, 1924); *Earth-Visitors* (a reprint of the other, with illustrations by Norman Lindsay, London, 1926); *Cuckooz Contrey* (Sydney, 1932); and *Five Bells* (Sydney, 1939); all the poems written up to that time that Slessor considered worth reprinting[4] were afterwards collected in *One Hundred Poems* (Sydney, 1944). Since then he has published only occasional poems, though he edited the annual anthology *Poetry in Australia* for 1945; all the references here are to *One Hundred Poems*.

Slessor's poetical life may be divided into three phases, in the first of which the influences of Norman Lindsay and Hugh McCrae are evident, and in the second that of Eliot and the moderns generally; in the third he is, with one or two unimportant qualifications, himself alone. The first phase lasted from 1919 to 1926,[5] including poems that had not yet appeared in book-form, and ending with *Earth-Visitors*. The title-poem of this book is dedicated to N(orman) L(indsay) and the poem "Realities" to Lindsay's etchings. It is Lindsay's artistic work, more especially his paintings, and the spirit behind it that are suggested by the poems of this phase, and they suggest even more strongly the poems of McCrae, or rather not the poems themselves but the spirit in which they are written: the careless freedom, the zest for life, especially the life of the senses. McCrae is also suggested in occasional specific lines and phrases, notably that of "some god on a stone pedestal"; and "the statues dance" is an actual phrase of McCrae's. Yet the impression one gets of Slessor in this phase of his poetic development is not in the least of an imitator of Lindsay, or of McCrae either, but rather of McCrae and Slessor[6] working in the studio of a common master, though in a different craft, using a phrase or so which may be taken as common, whoever happened to be the first with them; sharing, though in different degrees, the master's enthusiasm for the life of the flesh, and developing his attitude in directions each of his own: Jack Lindsay purely sensual; McCrae more fanciful, more delicate, more imaginative, and yet with much of the master's vital force; Slessor the more serious, the more thoughtful, the least sensual, the only real romantic among them. These early poems of his are limited, adolescent sometimes, but sometimes in their own manner splendid; mostly visual imaginations, concrete, clear-cut and coloured, but without McCrae's extraordinary mastery of sound-effects; a free rush of sensuous imagery whose rhythms are less conventional than McCrae's but by no means in essence modern. And though these poems are inspired by the studio's common zest for life, they are not quite so deeply occupied with the life of mere sensation,

---

[4] Of the 35 poems in *Earth-Visitors*, eleven were omitted from *One Hundred Poems*.

[5] The dates are Slessor's; see the table of contents to *One Hundred Poems*.

[6] And Jack Lindsay, in his early poems.

with the realism of the moment, regarding it sometimes with dissatisfaction, even sadness, feeling beyond it after something better, with the antennae of the imagination. Occasionally, as in "The Night Ride" and "A Sunset" there is a foretaste of the disillusion that was to mark Slessor's succeeding stage, and here and there even a faint reflection of the Eliotism in which it was more than once to find expression; for example,

> . . . now there is nothing,
> Wind gone and men gone, only the water
> Stumbling over the stones in silence;

but the last line is reminiscent of a well-known cadence of de la Mare's. As a rule Slessor's enthusiasm, essentially romantic, looks outward and backward, sometimes into the world of myth, as in "Earth-Visitors", in which the pagan gods come down to visit earthly women, or "Pan at Lane Cove", in which not only Pan but Chiron and his centaurs figure, though by no means as McCrae would have handled them. Or sometimes the vision is directed, more realistically, down slopes of past time, transfiguring historic characters with a romantic imagination, as in "Nuremberg", or "Marco Polo", or "Heine in Paris"; or, a queer mixture of romance and satire, "The Man of Sentiment". Slessor is nearest to McCrae when he celebrates

> Good roaring pistol-boys, brave lads of gold,
> Good roistering easy maids, blown cock-a-hoop
> On floods of tavern-steam;

or in the lines in which

> . . . country-girls, in hats of straw,
> Take kissing as a natural law,

though even here if the spirit is McCrae's the form is Slessor's and in this poem too there is a hint of the later attitude, in the cynicism of the conclusion:

> I didn't notice her till we kissed.
> How pleasant, a sentimentalist!

If Slessor had continued to develop along these lines we might have had another poet of something of the same type as McCrae, though reflective and more serious; but the likeness would have extended no farther than the type, for, studio influence and all, this early poetry of Slessor's is markedly individual: in its rhythms, for example,

> In this house, there is anger, in the forest, night,
> But love is under my laughter, and under my cloak, flight,

and in its images, which are not in the least like McCrae's. The two poets meet, and differ, in the line

> Cold stars are bubbling round the moon,

where, in spite of the resemblance in type of conception, the adjective and the mood it helps to represent are the contrary of what would have been likely to come from McCrae; and the two are poles apart when Slessor says,

> Cold, cold are the birds that, bubbling out of night,
> Cried once to my ears their unremembered tune.*

The second phase in Slessor's poetic development occupies the years 1927-32,[7] from a year after the publication of *Earth-Visitors* to the publication of *Cuckooz Contrey*: between these two phases there is a great gap; at first sight it would seem that the poetry they produced had scarcely anything in common. Slessor has now abandoned the Lindsay studio for good; just as out of it he had occasionally looked forward, so he may now give it an occasional backward glance, as in "Rubens' Hell" or "La Dame du Palais de la Reine"; but the "shaft of irritation", in that poem, in which

> . . . serious doubts occur of Love
> That spoils the Peacock, sours the Dove,
> And mixes up the lower classes
> So hopelessly with those above

is much more characteristic of the phase the poem belongs to than of the phase towards which it looks back. The zest for life, never furious as with McCrae, now dips for the most part underground, like an outback Australian river, though it is still perceptible beneath the prevailing waste of irony and bitter disillusion, qualities which have arisen, it should be noted, not so much from any literary influence as from the poet's own experience of life. But it would be as hard for any representative of a young and vigorous and on the whole extremely lucky and prosperous country, with a history of real though mostly material achievement, to be thoroughly disillusioned, as it would be unusual for him to be entirely lacking in the national characteristic of irony; and now and then, but most notably in "Five Visions of Captain Cook",

> . . . that captain with the sad
> And fine white face, who never lost a man
> Or flinched a peril,

and also in the related "Captain Dobbin", from which these lines are taken, enthusiasm breaks through the crust that has formed over it.

* [Slessor's fondness for "bubble" images does not always find exact referents.]

[7] The dates are again Slessor's own.

In a more picturesque manner along with something of the humour that used to be so marked a characteristic of Slessor's journalistic "specials", but that never finds free and unmixed outlet in his poetry, enthusiasm comes to the surface in the "Atlas" series; and one extremely amusing poem, "Country Towns", which however is not quite characteristic of Slessor, tells of

> Verandahs baked with musky sleep,
> Mulberry faces dozing deep,
> And dogs that lick the sunlight up
> Like paste of gold—or, roused in vain
> By far, mysterious buggy-wheels,
> Lower their ears, and drowse again.

"Captain Dobbin" and the Cook and Atlas series represent an imaginative escape from the life of the present day; but they differ essentially from the poems of the previous phase in lacking their rich sensuous quality and in reflecting activities of the mind rather than of the senses, in being comparatively dry, astringent, and in that a strand of irony is entwined much more strongly in the rope of their enthusiasm. In the poems that deal with character and adventure Slessor's backward-looking tendency objectivizes itself, throws off the medieval and mythopoeic, and becomes realistic in treatment though still romantic in feeling; from them has started a movement which, with the co-operation of FitzGerald, has, as will be seen later, spread amongst younger writers and become one of the literary currents of the day. In the Atlas poems there is a nearer approach to the now almost deserted land of myth, in for instance the lines in which the poet spies

> . . . by moonlight
> Behind a royal bamboo

the King of Cuckooz Contrey riding in a curricle drawn by ninety virgins and drinking milk from a snow-white elephant; it is still nearer in the reference, an outstanding exception to the poetry of this phase, to the mermaids

> With wet and scarlet lips
> And fish-dark difficult hips,

who mocked the vessels that sailed those waters, delighting their crews, but for singing outside their captains' port-holes

> . . . fiercely reprehended
> By the governors of the P. & O.

It has been seen how the young man's fascination by fresh sensuous experience, raised to an imaginative plane, was half spoilt, in the poetry of the previous phase, by a not always fully conscious perception that the pleasures of sense were short and shallow, and a feeling that for anything better one must look beyond the real world; and how this feeling deepens and is intellectually realized at the same time that purely sensuous pleasures cease to appeal. And when, instead of looking backward down the slopes of time at history and the ornaments of geography, the poet has to do with the world that actually surrounds him, he finds that he has come to a pass from which he views a country where the human mind cannot live permanently and retain its sanity. It is, for the most part, a country in which, transmuting Eliot's waste land to that of the Australian outback, there are

> . . . gullies that no longer flow
> And wells that nobody can find,
> Lashed by the screaming of the crow,
> Stabbed by the needles of the mind;

it is an Australian version of the country in which Swift lived, the country of Glubbdubdrib, a horror that makes the flesh creep; the country in which man is without power or hope, lashed down, like Gulliver, with innumerable cables: his desires, his limitations, his accidents, his vices, his diseases. From all this the poet's only refuge is in his art: apart from excursions into the past, in which the ideal finds some opportunity, there is only the imaginative crystallization of impressions of a reality that has lost its savour. In this art Slessor continually experiments, producing novel and characteristic effects by means of "a considered breaking of rules":[8] rules which he had however first to master, and of which he had shown his mastery in the early poems. Slessor followed therefore a road opened up by other poets of today, and in particular by Eliot, to whom he was, in the circumstances, naturally attracted: even in the Cook poems there is the image of the fog and the window pane, with its reminiscence of the famous image in "The Waste Land"; there are the lines, in "Elegy in a Botanic Gardens",

> In the autumn I came
> Where spring had used me better,
> To the clear red pebbles and the men of stone;

and in "The Old Play",

> It is not like this at all,
> Never, never like this.

A few reminiscences, possibly deliberate,[9] of other poets are traceable

---

[8] See "Writing Poetry: The Why and The How", an A.B.C. wireless talk reprinted in *Southerly*, vol. ix (1948), no. 3, p. 169.

[9] But it is possible, for Slessor always knows exactly what he is doing, that all these reminiscences are deliberate, and also that the weaving into his own verses of lines, or at least phraseology, in order to produce particular effects, was itself adopted from Eliot, though Slessor does not carry the practice far.

in the poems of the phase that follows this: of Donne, in the question,

> . . . where's the lust a skull has for a bone?;

of Housman, in the lines,

> I, too, from clods of aching thought,
> Have turned up sharper knives;

and Slessor even uses a phrase, "the talons of the rain", that occurs also in FitzGerald's "Essay on Memory".[10] But, though these reminiscences are worth noting, it would be easy to draw an entirely wrong inference from them; the fact that Slessor touches two or three other modern poets here and there is not essentially more important than that he shares a disillusion felt, at least until lately, by modern poets generally. What really matters is that Slessor's is a highly individual disillusion, informed by a personality that is also individual, and expressed in a markedly individual manner. In addition, few poets are animated by an energy such as that with which Slessor expresses the bitterness of his conception of life; his attitude is at the farthest extreme from Eliot's, in that about it there is no weariness or submission, but indignation rather: his is a bitterness that is savage with anger and contempt.

Of Slessor's third phase, the date limits given are 1933-39: that is, from a year after *Cuckooz Contrey* to *Five Bells*. Since *One Hundred Poems* did not appear until 1944, five years are left unaccounted for; in those years therefore Slessor wrote nothing that he considered worth collecting, at least as it then stood; and he has published so little since *One Hundred Poems* that it is impossible to form an opinion whether his third phase still continues, or whether it is to be succeeded by a fourth. There is no such sudden and striking gap between the third and second phases as between the second and first; the third phase represents merely a natural development out of the second. Yet there are definite differences between them: historic excursions no longer afford a respite from life as it is today, or an outlet for an idealism that nothing can quite subdue; indeed the only glance back into history is the "Vesper Song of the Reverend Samuel Marsden",[11] which is a savage and sardonic character-sketch. Disillusion is indeed intensified in this third phase; in place of history there is a curious preoccupation with Time, a preoccupation which also has infected several of the younger poets, unless it again is among the offspring of a general disillusion: Time, the enfolding wave, the bony knife, the

---

[10] But FitzGerald tells me that he took this image over from an early poem that was printed in a Victorian literary periodical; Slessor also may have seen it there, and reproduced an unconscious memory.

[11] Unless we include the short poem, "The Knife", by reason of the reference to primitive man.

. . . . hundred yachts
That fly behind the daylight;

the crier of farewells; the opener and closer of doors, who

Over the edges of dead Nows and Heres,
Blindly and softly, as a mistress might,
. . . keeps appointments with a million years.

This preoccupation; the caustic analysis of certain aspects of modernity; a couple of poems for friends; a further development of the experiments with word and rhythm which culminate in that fascinating *tour de force*, "Sleep"; one or two more country satires, and, for the first time, some poems upon aspects of city life: these, with the title-poem, make up the bulk of the work of this phase. Most of the city poems are satires, but one contains the admission that the poet is attracted to the life that he at the same time despises; that he finds loveliness not only in

Smells rich and rasping, smoke and fat and fish
And puffs of paraffin that crimp the nose,
Or grease that blesses onions with a hiss,

but even in

The dips and molls with flip and shiny gaze
. . . .
Ranging the pavements of their pasturage.

Above all the rest stands a poem in which Slessor at last achieves himself and his full powers. "Five Bells" is an elegy on a friend of his youth, who, like Lycidas, was drowned; the work is good enough to encourage comparison with the great English elegies, but what stands out in such a comparison is not the likenesses but the differences: setting aside "Adonais" and "In Memoriam" as insusceptible of comparison, "Five Bells" is far shorter than "Lycidas" or "The Scholar-Gipsy" or "Thyrsis"; it is not a pastoral; and it lacks Milton's massive and elaborate dignity and Arnold's quick and flowing charm: instead of being deliberate or sad, it is a fiery outburst, a protest, angry and despairing, at a real and agonizing personal loss, and not merely at the death of an old friend but at death itself, at the cold impenetrability of the window panes at which the dead man is visualized as knocking,[12] as striving in agony to pierce. And the

[12] This type of image seems to have haunted Slessor. "The Ghost" (p. 31) ends with the lines:

So the ghost cried, and pressed to the dark pane,
Like a white leaf, his face . . . in vain . . . in vain . . .

In "The Atlas" (p. 57) there is a reference to

The world of dead men staring out of glass.

In the last of the "Music" series (p. 46) a "shining Guest" presses his face, "like a strange wafer"

Secret and starry, at thy pane.

And there are several other references (pp. 17, 46, and 53) to windows or panes.

[The ultimate source of this image is Hardy's poem, "The Face at the Window"; see Slessor's short story in *Vision*, no. 1, "The Dark Garden".]

man as well as the loss is made real, his "Gaunt chin and pricked eye"; his

> . . . raging tales
> Of Irish kings and English perfidy,
> And dirtier perfidy of publicans;

his stories of girls brown or white, and angry-tongued: all are so real that we realize the more keenly his drowning agony:

> I felt the wet push its black thumb-balls in,
> The night you died, I felt your eardrums crack,
> And the short agony, the longer dream,
> The Nothing that was neither long nor short.

In no Australian poem have thought and sensation more closely blended with their natural music; it is lit all through by flaring images, of

> . . . the moon's drench, that straight enormous glaze,
> . . . the scraping squeal
> Of seabirds' voices,
>
> . . . .
>
> The naphtha-flash of lightning . . . ,
> Knifing the dark with deathly photographs;

and through it all rings the recurrent knell of

> Five bells, the bumpkin calculus of Time.
>
> . . . .
>
> *Five bells.*

The masterly restraint, the scholarly dignity, that mark for example "The Scholar-Gipsy" are lacking, but Slessor did not aim at these, and there is the same deliberate completion of a predetermined aesthetic purpose, and with it a fiercely tragic emotion, a hot sincerity, a realistic power and frantic energy at which Arnold did not aim.

Slessor's work, like that of any other writer who helps to introduce a new literary phase, has two values, historical and absolute, which are independent and best considered apart. It might be contended that Brennan, in his adoption of French symbolistic principles, and in his use, particularly in the Lilith poems, of the "free association" of images, was a forerunner of surrealism in Australian literature; but Brennan has had in this as in other respects scarcely any direct influence and until quite lately none at all. Wilmot was definitely a poet of the transition between this age and the last, and his "Melbourne Odes" are in spirit almost wholly modern; but these, even in their first appearance, in pamphlet form, were not published until the early thirties. There are traces of modernism in even the early poems of Macartney; and other poets had, as will be seen, shown the influence of Eliot by 1931; but it was Slessor who in 1932, with the publication of *Cuckooz Contrey*, introduced into Australian poetry modernity in both attitude and technique. This of itself would give his poetry a historical value; but that is of course a secondary matter. To begin with, considering its comparative smallness in quantity, for *One Hundred Poems* contains little more than 4000 lines, in scope it is, as will have been seen, extraordinarily rich and varied. And it is also extraordinarily individual; without suggesting an equality of literary values it may be said that "Five Bells" stands out, a thing in itself, as much as "Lycidas" or "The Scholar-Gipsy"; and it sticks in the memory, not merely by reason of its striking passages, but, as a whole, more persistently than any but the greatest of its kind. To say that there has been nothing comparable with it in Australian poetry is to say little, for the only previous Australian elegies that matter are Dyson's "Poems in Memory of a Wife" and Zora Cross's "Elegy on an Australian Schoolboy", both of which are slight by comparison. And there are plenty of other illustrations of Slessor's individuality: a typical line or even a typical phrase of his later poetry could not be ascribed to any other poet, and it would be hard to find a verse, typical or no, that was not easily distinguishable as his. One factor in making Slessor's poetry so easily distinguishable is his technique; based on the study of the poetry of today, and perfected by continual experiment, it is not only quite his own and superior to that of any other Australian poet of his generation, but comparable at its best with that of any contemporary in England or the United States: in this matter Slessor stands out as McCrae did a generation earlier. The outstanding example in this respect is "Sleep"; the internal and final half-rhymes and assonances, the novel and elaborately constructed medley of vowel and consonantal music, the elaborate onomatopoeia, with its inseparable alliance of idea, mood and sound; the detailed elaboration of the parallel between sleep and the womb make the poem a fascinating *tour de force*, the last two verses especially:

> And you shall cling and clamber there
> And slumber there, in that dumb chamber,
> Beat with my blood's beat, hear my heart move
> Blindly in bones that ride above you,
> Delve in my flesh, dissolved and bedded,
> Through viewless valves embodied so—
>
> Till daylight, the expulsion and awakening,
> The riving and the driving forth,
> Life with remorseless forceps beckoning—
> Pangs and betrayal of harsh birth.

Another example is "The Country Ride", the fascination of whose first two lovely verses is due in part to novelty of form:[13]

[13] There is perhaps a reminiscence of D. H. Lawrence's "The Cypress", but this is probably no more than a coincidence.

Earth which has known so many passages
Of April air, so many marriages
Of strange and lovely atoms breeding light,
Never may find again that lost delight.

In the sharp sky, the frosty deepnesses,
There are still birds to barb the silences,
There are still fields to meet the morning on,
But those who made them beautiful have gone.

Of course much more than technique, in the sense of mere craftsmanship, or even of the particular methods used by Slessor in his verse-making, are involved in this sort of thing: the effect produced depends first on the poet's recording apparatus, his senses; next on his conception, the purpose for which he proposes to employ them; next on the way in which his records are assembled and transmuted by the imagination; and finally on the manner in which the material is resolved into an appropriate music, which itself is the result of the imagination playing upon memories of recorded verbal sounds and by selection creating a sequence which has about it much more of the hearer than of the heard. By these means the poet can not only convey appropriately a conception which is more or less novel, as with "Sleep", but can confer novelty upon a theme which is by no means novel, as with "The Country Ride", provided only that he feels it as novel and can impregnate it with his own personality: from that impregnation a new life arises. But technique, however individual, is no more, if we must, as for critical purposes we must, regard it separately, than the poet's vehicle; the individuality of his poetry depends in the last resort on something wider and deeper than that, or even than the eye and ear of his imagination; in the last resort we arrive at his whole mental and emotional complex: not merely his philosophy, formulated or unformulated, or even the outlook on life upon which that philosophy depends, but all that makes him different from other men; there, of course, we can do no more than show how the poetic personality has developed. Considering Slessor's poetry as a whole, but with more particular reference to that of his second and third phases as representing his fuller development, we are conscious of dealing with an attitude which, though not novel in type is novel within that type, and with a method which, though it also has its typical relationships, is even more novel; at its best it appears about as new and striking as any poetry can be, setting aside the work of such a genius as must by its very nature transform whatever it touches into something transcendently rich and strange. Here, however, words which have been used deliberately point in the direction of a defect which, like the nature of Slessor's poetry generally, is well illustrated by a consideration of his images. Readers of this History will have perceived the importance that is here attached to the poetic image; it is indeed of the essence of poetry, a fact that by no means however implies agreement with the surrealist doctrine that a poem should or may consist of a series of unrelated images. Slessor is, like McCrae, prolific in images: most are sad or bitter, as when he speaks of "trees winged with death"; of "The rat Pain, biting with bloody teeth"; of "The sodden ecstasies of rectitude"; of the "dark Star-Chamber of the soul". There are exceptions of course, as in the charming description of the "bee-sweet ancient words" of Chinese sages; or in the cheerful

> Sophie's my world . . . my arm must soon or later
> Like Francis Drake turn circumnavigator;

or their loveliness may outweigh their sadness, as in the lines,

> Time, you must cry farewell, take up the track,
> And leave this lovely moment at your back!

But sad or glad, these images are always not merely novel but striking: there is the highly individual reference in an early poem to "the quiet noise of planets feeding"; there is the rather far-fetched reference to the confidence of his young officers in Cook,

> Men who ride broomsticks with a mesmerist
> Mock the typhoon;

there are the startling descriptions of

> . . . darkness flying with crystals;
> And the great Miser, Night,
> Rubbing a mountain's breast-bone
> With an old rind of light;

and of how

> The naphtha-flash of lightning slit the sky,
> Knifing the dark with deathly photographs.

This quality is so general in Slessor's images as to suggest that there is something deliberate, something purposive about it: some of them fairly leap out of their context; but it is the business of an image to be an ordered part of its context, to enlighten it; not to flare so strongly as to make that context fade; it would appear that Slessor's capacity for producing original and striking effects has tempted him to be as original and striking as he can. This temptation may well have been encouraged by his lifelong pursuit of journalism, one of whose principal objects is to catch the reader's eye, almost at all costs; some of the images appear to have been heightened a little, so that they arouse a faint and far-off suggestion of artificiality. And there is one more defect: Slessor has not, as Virginia Woolf puts it, distinguishing in this respect Jane Austen from

Charlotte Brontë, "consumed his impediments". A poet, like any other artist, presents, whether he will or no, a view of life or of some aspect of life, an attitude towards life, and to be of value, it must be an individual view or attitude: but in this connection individual and personal are not entirely the same thing, and the attitude should not be so personal as to be biased by private experience; such experience must of course contribute to the formation of the attitude, but it should not be allowed to twist it in any particular direction. Or, looking at the matter in a slightly different way: to say that a work of art must be individual must not be taken to imply that it should be influenced by idiosyncrasies that are not fundamental. The material out of which a work of art is composed includes of course the observer as well as the observed, but it should no more contain fortuitous elements of the one than of the other; there would in that case be about it an element of the photographic, which would detract from its absolute value, and in this respect Slessor's work as a whole falls short of the highest artistry: he does not stand sufficiently apart from it to allow it to appear distinct. But it must be added, first, that this last is a defect from which scarcely any Australian poets and few poets anywhere are free; and second, that such a test is not worth while except with a writer whose individuality and art are quite out of the common and whose work is wide in range: Kenneth Slessor is such a writer, and in the qualities that characteristically mark him he has no rivals in Australia today.

The work of Robert David FitzGerald (Sydney, 1902–) blows like a fresh wind across today, exhaling a courage and confident aspiration, a sense of wonder and mystery that are strange in a world which is bored and afraid and sorry for itself, and a poetry in which this attitude was intensified under the shadow of the early work of T. S. Eliot. FitzGerald represents in fact a life and an interest in life that wars and depressions have dammed back after the upwelling of the nineties; that upwelling had found its most characteristic expression in the ballad revival in Britain and the dominions, but FitzGerald's poems have none of the qualities of the ballad, Australian or other, except vigour and an adventurous spirit which had until lately almost evaporated from the poetry of the Old World. Looking back along the stream of English poetry, this aspect of FitzGerald's work seems to have most in common with that of the poets of the romantic revival in the early days of the French Revolution, or, better perhaps, of the early Elizabethans; but, unlike so many romantics, he is never sentimental or vague or in love with scenery, nor is he word-drunk like the early Elizabethans: what he has to say matters more to him than to most poets, and after that its precise expression. In this respect he resembles Alec Hope, but he is not so concise, or, largely because of his subject-matter, so perspicuous;

like Hope again, he has his occasional prosy passages, and, more often, passages of what may be called poetic record, and he also has his narrow escapes from prose, to which however he has fairly often a companionship, usually far off but sometimes close; but, apart from the images into which that record sometimes heats and melts and glows, they take the form, not, as with Hope's "Damnation of Byron", of a rich slow-moving march of verbal music, but, especially in the later and more characteristic poems, of a rush and fiery outbreak of free enthusiasm. This free enthusiasm and an accompanying zest for life in which he differs utterly from Hope would be enough in themselves to constitute him a romantic, but in his later and more characteristic poems he is a romantic of today and not of yesterday, and the sphere to which his later poems belong is quite different from any that one might have imagined congenial to a romantic poet: it is essentially an intellectual sphere, for FitzGerald is of all things an analyst, a psychologist, a metaphysician, who, beginning with and seldom entirely abandoning his own emotions and ideas, has gradually moved outward from them and away even from the present day. Yet there is nothing of the ivory tower about the vantage ground from which he attempts his analytic explorations of character and of the ultimate nature of life: its purpose is not refuge, but avoidance of distractions from an object more important to him than the problems of the present moment. In his most important and most characteristic poems, on the one hand he presents us with historical characters at a crisis; on the other he feels back beyond history and through geologic periods towards the processes of life's becoming, towards the force that lies behind them and that reveals itself in the succession of changing shapes that it throws off, as it were in a succession of experiments. Yet FitzGerald is by far the simplest, the least subtle or sophisticated of the poets of the group in which he is here placed; he is indeed naïve at times, and yet again some of his poems are harder to fathom than any except one or two of McAuley's. FitzGerald's occasional obscurity is however by no means deliberate or due to indifference or lack of craftsmanship, though he is not so consummate a craftsman as Slessor or McAuley; it is due in part to his manner of expressing himself, which is extremely allusive and symbolic, and in greater part to the difficulty of the task he has undertaken: this involves once or twice, as in "The Face of the Waters", the expression of what cannot except symbolically be expressed. Now that science meets philosophy in a metaphysics that is permeated by the imagination, it is not so surprising that poetry should have become a third member of the partnership; what is surprising is that a new and culturally half-developed country should have provided the first notable example: the first two examples, it might even be contended, thinking of Baylebridge; but ethics was an important member of that firm, and its principal business was assembly and organization rather than analytical research. This is not however to suggest that there is anything profoundly original about FitzGerald's leading idea: the virtue of his poetry consists not in the novelty of what he has to express, but in the intensity and individuality with which he has reconceived it, worked it out for himself instead of merely rearranging it, and also in his method of expression, about which more later.

FitzGerald is a nephew of the late Professor J. Le Gay Brereton, with whose verses his have however nothing in common. By a queer coincidence, since the very essence of his work is adventure, he was born and still lives in the steady, old-fashioned Sydney suburb of Hunter's Hill. He was educated at the Sydney Grammar School and the University of Sydney, which he left to become a land surveyor, after two years' study of science, without taking a degree; for five years he worked in Fiji, determining tribal boundaries for the Native Lands Commission; during the second World War he was engaged in New South Wales on engineering surveys for the construction of aerodromes; after the war he joined the staff of the Property and Survey Branch of the Department of the Interior: largely an office job. FitzGerald had published by 1950 three books of verse: *The Greater Apollo:*[14] *Seven Metaphysical Songs* (Sydney, 1927), a booklet whose contents were included in *To Meet the Sun* (Sydney, 1929); and *Moonlight Acre* (Melbourne, 1938); this includes "Essay on Memory", a poem which won an Australia-wide competition held during the 150th Anniversary Celebrations in Sydney. But FitzGerald is less to be judged by his printed work than any of the "intellectuals" except Hope. Some of his best poems had not in 1950 been collected in book-form, and in the evenings, or sometimes in the middle of the nights after professionally busy days, he used to write regularly verse only some of which appeared in the magazines. At the date when this History closed he was at work upon a long poem, a short extract from which, under the title "Said the Don", was included in *Australian Poetry 1945*; in the meantime a collection of poems, whose provisional title is, appropriately, *This Night's Orbit*, was being held back for the sake of any poems, excursions from the longer work in progress, that might be added to it. In the preface to this History it was noted that though no work would be discussed that had not been published by the end of 1950, an exception would be made in a few instances in which I had been allowed to see the manuscript of a work that seemed too important to omit; one of these instances is *This Night's Orbit.*[15]

[14] The god, it may be noted, not merely of poetry but of oracular wisdom; here, of metaphysical poetry.

[15] *This Night's Orbit* was published in Melbourne in 1953, and the long poem previously referred to, under the title *Between Two Tides*, in Sydney in 1952. For the convenience of the reader all references

FitzGerald's work may be divided into three phases, of which the second and that part of the third which was seen in typescript represent a marked advance upon the other. In the first phase the poet as such is dominant, in the second and third the thinker as such; yet there is thinking enough in the early poems to fit out quite a number of first volumes of poetry, and the poetry is the better for the thinking, as it is likely to be the better for anything that feeds the mind and stimulates the imagination, provided the thought has become an integral part of the poetry, does not overburden it and change instead of increasing its life, so that it becomes prose. There are indeed several passages of sheer prose in *To Meet the Sun*, though curiously enough they are not in the "seven metaphysical poems" that were taken over from *The Greater Apollo*; the prosiness seems to be due, not to any burden of thought that has proved too difficult to resolve into poetry, but simply to the poet's habit of thinking in verse, along with an occasional inability to discriminate between prose and poetry; an excellent example of this,[16] though by no means the most extreme, is the first verse of "Tradition":

> Great praise I give, the full praise that is due
> To him whom most I envy among men
> And most fear; I shall not hold back praise
> Although my heart is slow to assent thereto.

To Meet the Sun is the work of a man who is, except in the quality of his thought, younger than his years, which were at the time of its publication twenty-seven: the attitude here is of a thoughtful youth not long emerged from adolescence, still to all appearance unacquainted with Eliot and the other moderns, and, unlike Slessor, unaffected by the Lindsay-McCrae influence;[17] he builds upon the foundations of the romantic tradition, and repeats, though in a context that is his own, outworn romantic words and phrases[18] that seem strange today and that he has since almost entirely abandoned. And he is beset by reminiscences of his favourite poets, who have not yet been entirely digested: of these the most noticeable is Brennan, whose influence reached well into FitzGerald's second phase; it is evident not so much in the first-personal method which he still prefers as a rule, as in his feeling that he is to be a wanderer along a road that is "lonely and aloof", past "windows staring out into the dark", in the lines about "kindly-speaking friends", and in

to the collections of poems contained in *This Night's Orbit* are made to the book as published instead of to the typescript; *Between Two Tides*, not having been seen in manuscript, is not discussed here. FitzGerald has since published *The Wind at your Door* (Sydney, 1959).

[16] See also *To Meet the Sun*, "very tired" (p. 2), "Is most unworthy art" (p. 17), "I have not found one" (p. 40), "I greatly regret" (p. 51), "Although I greatly wish" (p. 52).

[17] FitzGerald was represented in Jack Lindsay's *Poetry in Australia*, but he has nothing in common with the tone of that anthology except enthusiasm and dislike of convention.

[18] Knights, fays, a castle keep, a herald's bugle, rapiers, dim dreams, yea, thereof, adown, agleam, and so on.

"My years are built at tragic cost". But Yeats is almost as evident as Brennan: for example where the poet thanks his friends "for the folly of your good word", and in the references to "Riders of Air", and to the "ten crying hounds";[19] one or two other reminiscences might be traced if it were worth while. But out of all this emerges the impression of a young poet whose talent is as unmistakable as its unripeness: quite as much as most young poets he is preoccupied with his own desires and mental processes; but, which is less usual, the processes sometimes yield results, and he is never mawkish or sentimental. FitzGerald is, with a temporary lapse or two,[20] quite sure of himself, confident, not merely of ultimate achievement, but that the achievement will be poetic, and the poetry metaphysical; moreover, a good sign with a youthful but serious poet, he can laugh, and puts life above books: he hates the thought of poring

> . . . all day long in the museum of years
> over a manuscript;

and he declares that

> The wisdom of the greybeards, long-of-tooth,
> Is wisdom of dust and death, say what you will.

There is achievement as well as promise in the poetry of this first phase, and not least in the earliest part of it: in "The Greater Apollo" series, in a fine and characteristic poem in which Swinburnian rhymes are combined with an internal rhyme in a fashion which suggests some of the Irish poets, FitzGerald emphasizes the idea of permanence through change, of the survival of the type, through the death of the individual, in the eternal type;[21] here he is feeling after what was to become the leading principle of his later poetry:

> Time is a fool if he thinks to have ended
> One single splendid thing that has been:
> Though much has changed what is expended
> Of all that the youthful earth has seen?
> To-morrow and yesterday are cheated
> While undefeated one cliff still stands,
> For the one could speak for all cliffs long vanished
> Till Time himself were destroyed or banished
> From the uncompleted work of his hands.

---

[19] See also "Lethe" (p. 25), "When You Are Sitting" (p. 4), and the whole of "Pursuit" (p. 6).

[20] See "The Future" (p. 9) and, in spite of the line quoted from this poem, "Sindbad" (p. 13).

[21] The same idea appears in the last section of "The Greater Apollo" series (p. 39) and in the lines referring to

> . . . the dusk of time
> Whence loveliness like rhyme
> Must echo itself, re-surge
> (p. 50).

The Greater Apollo series contains also one of FitzGerald's most pregnant images, which, incidentally, represents an alteration, a re-invention, much for the better, from the original in the booklet, in the lines in which he speaks of

> . . . this street where, little of ease,
> The death bound multitude
> Fends back the threatening silences
> With straws of livelihood.

Outside this series there is the rather fascinating and rather fairytale-like "Castle in the South", with its cliffs that

> . . . watch the wrinkled waste of waves
> Through the proud unhurrying hours;

and, not least, there is "Calm", with its symbolical reference to the "sole star" that

> . . . falters and dips
> Along the line of the mast.

Boats, with

> The torn wash flaring at the bow,

"seas to be adventured yet", "the quay-side thronged with magic ships", castles in the south, "strange impossible islands" sufficiently indicate FitzGerald's adventurous spirit; but by this time he has decided that it is "wide seas of the mind" that he is to explore, "tacking into a gale that the heart feels".

The gap between the poetry of the first and second phase, between *To Meet the Sun* and *Moonlight Acre*, lasted nine years. More than half those years were spent in Fiji, to which there are a number of references in the poems,[22] and for some time FitzGerald was, except for the natives, alone. There is not, as with Slessor, an almost clean break with the poetry of the first phase; *Moonlight Acre* consists of two series and two longer poems, and the first in order, the title-series, reads as though it had been written not long after the publication of *To Meet the Sun*, with which it has a good deal in common: FitzGerald's development has therefore been gradual and it continued throughout this phase. Taken as a whole, however, *Moonlight Acre* is the work of a man who is now grown up, so far as FitzGerald will ever grow up. In the title-series there are still a number of romantic survivals embedded in the style,[23] and Brennan is still apparent in the references to "the hearths" and the "little homes in the dusk"; but even from this series the spirit and mannerisms of the early Yeats have evaporated, and any other reminiscences, a cadence

[22] pp. 23, 35, 43, 44.
[23] Scimitars, a scabbard gleam, shoon, cark (adopted, probably from Brennan), high roads of jeopardy, and a few others.

of Housman's and a suggestion of Emerson, or is it Baylebridge?, are perhaps coincidences and in any case unimportant. In the rest of the book there are a couple of deliberate imitations of Pope, but only one influence,[24] and that not literary but scientific: at this stage of his development FitzGerald read A. N. Whitehead's *Science and the Modern World*; and the recognition that so distinguished a philosopher shared something of his own point of view was both a reinforcement and a stimulus. Whitehead's reference to his endeavour "to give a record of a great adventure in the region of thought" would appeal naturally to FitzGerald; Whitehead's remark about the

> . . . union of passionate interest in the detailed facts with equal devotion to abstract generalisation which forms the novelty in our present society

might have been directed to FitzGerald himself; and the approach in "The Hidden Bole" and "Essay on Memory" may well have been affected by Whitehead's reference to "the concept of the real world as exhibiting the evolution of an idea", and by his assertion that

> . . . the full scientific mentality instinctively holds that all things great and small are conceivable as exemplifications of general principles which reign throughout the natural order.

There are also in the title-series two or three prose passages of the sort that has been discussed already; but in the bulk of the poetry of FitzGerald's second phase, along with outworn romanticisms, prosiness and on the other hand lyrism also disappear: the poet passes

> . . . outward, and beyond
> thought's reckoning, where time's a pond
> unrippled by any stone
> knowledge has thrown.

All except those who insist upon the lyric at any cost will here discover a finer as well as a much more vigorous and individual beauty, even though it is of a more uniformly intellectual cast. This, however, is not to say that the title-series does not contain some of FitzGerald's best work; there are for instance the fascinating fragments that begin "Dark trees beset the moonlight acre" and "Life, toss up your florin"; there is the delightfully whimsical family reminiscence that begins, "Now Doctor Bell's portrait is hung in tall Trinity"; and there is the beautiful love poem that repeats the survival idea already referred to; here are its last three verses:

> So when I clasp you here I keep
> all that dead lovers have desired,

---

[24] Unless one likes to add Bergson, but what FitzGerald perceives at the back of all living forms is something more than Bergson's *élan vital.*

waken their bodies from long sleep
and their dreams, changeless and untired.

Held thus, you become drawn breath of any
who have been loved—once named, once known;
and the brief lives of that white many
you hand on, deathless and your own.

There is only this embrace at last
anywhere: others touched you once,
but I touch all the present and past
and the wide sky's uncounted suns.

Still, it is in the rest of the book, the "Copernicus" series, "The Hidden Bole", and "Essay on Memory" that FitzGerald first reaches his full powers and their characteristic expression. The disappearance of reflections from an earlier literary age does not mean that he has adopted either the outlook or the methods of the new, even to the comparatively small extent to which these have affected Australian poetry: on the contrary he dislikes its attitude and most of its methods very strongly; dislike is indeed too mild a word for his feeling towards Eliot's "hatred of life, and passion, and desire". And Eliot and the other modernists[25] are trying, FitzGerald contends,[26] not merely to introduce new ideas and methods into poetry but to change its nature by destroying the continuity of its form and the coherence of its thought; he admits however the service they have rendered in insisting that no subject is unsuitable for verse and in introducing an approximation to the language and rhythms of prose; and he does not object to their obscurity, provided it is not due to discontinuity of thought or to allusiveness of a sort that is comprehensible only by the writer or a few initiates. To obscurity as such FitzGerald could indeed hardly object, seeing that he is himself at times obscure, though he is clear enough as compared with many of the English moderns. On this subject he says:[27]

> . . . any new idea, any old idea not tarnished by the money-changers, any thought rising above the commonplace, will generally be obscure to the hasty and indolent: where thought is expressed, or emotion projected, with the utmost economy and effectiveness, obscurity there may be, and a dark fault it is indeed, but one that must be corrected in the reader, not the writer.[28]

---

[25] But he prefers to call them "recent" rather than to use the wider term, "modern".

[26] In "An Attitude to Modern Poetry", in *Southerly*, vol. ix (1948), no. 3, pp. 148-55. Curiously enough, he objects to the Sitwells, though Edith Sitwell's efforts to extend the scope of poetry have surely a value. And he approves of Day Lewis, some of whose work has certainly the sort of obscurity to which he objects.

[27] See the article in *Southerly* that has been already referred to.

[28] Yet in *To Meet the Sun* he had said:

> Alas! that black words, penned,
> Oft bring an end
> To the sincerest thought. . . .
> There's much I truly meant
> I now not understand.

He adds the reminder that obscurity is not especially new; but it does not follow that it is always justifiable. Its origin was natural enough: to suggest that romantic poetry was without intellectual content would be absurd, but that content often consisted of generalizations, and there was often, at least among the later and lesser romantics, a willingness to sacrifice some of their implications in the interests of a melody and clarity that were assumed to be of primary importance; against such characteristics the moderns have as a body both consciously and subconsciously rebelled, even those who, like FitzGerald, will have nothing to do with extremism. Among most moderns it is the intellectual appeal that is of primary importance, and in any case the general desire to enlarge the sphere of poetry and the special interest in the subconscious have made melody and clarity harder to attain, in spite of the modern freedom of technique. So that whereas with FitzGerald's immediate poetic predecessors it was "think by all means, provided you keep within the traditional limits of the sphere of poetry and remember that a poem is not born until it has been communicated to the reader", to FitzGerald, along with modern poets in general, apart from the extremists, it is "think as deeply and as subtly as you like", or even "as you can; there are no bounds to the poetic sphere and interpretation is the reader's responsibility, provided you have made it humanly possible to him", and the extremists would omit the qualification; however today the pendulum seems to have entered upon its backward swing, away from obscurity, and also from defeatist gloom. It would appear then that in one respect at least FitzGerald's attitude and practice were ahead of as well as behind his time, which is not surprising in the representative of a community that is slow to accept new fashions, literary and other. It cannot be said that FitzGerald's love of adventure extends into the domain of poetic form: he may best be described as a traditionalist who has yet adopted some of the freedoms of modernity and is affected by the urge of its rebellious rhythm, though it has not swung him to an extreme. Like Hope, but without Hope's bias and limitation, he writes as a scientist who is a poet also, and as a result of the difficulty of his metaphysical task he has to some extent availed himself of the modern doctrine of the reader's responsibility. The language and rhythms of FitzGerald's later poetry are, at least from "Essay on Memory" onward, almost invariably those of the ordinary speech of an educated man. About the rhythms there is otherwise nothing particularly modern: they depend on beat, not syllable, but that is no new thing in English poetry; and they run more freely than was usual in the days of our fathers and grandfathers, but they would have been quite acceptable to Brennan; nor are they, in themselves, particularly individual, though constituents in a style that is strikingly so. FitzGerald uses any metre that comes handy, preferring as a rule the five-beat line, rhymed as a rule, but irregularly; but of free verse, in the sense of lines of varying lengths and unrhymed, there are no examples in *Moonlight Acre*, though there had been two or three in *To Meet the Sun*.[29] In *This Night's Orbit* there is one poem, the fascinating "Face of the Waters", whose verse may be considered free, for the lines are irregular and there are sometimes exact rhymes, sometimes half-rhymes and sometimes no rhymes at all; *Between Two Tides* was written in blank verse. In the matter of rhyme FitzGerald's poetry is increasingly modern. In both *To Meet the Sun* and *Moonlight Acre*, except for such liberties as have been not uncommon in English poetry since the days of the Pre-Raphaelites,[30] the rhymes are with one exception[31] regular until we come to "Essay on Memory"; but in this poem, from the opening couplet,

> Rain in my ears: impatiently there raps
> at a sealed door the fury of chill drops—

half-rhymes are introduced infrequently but systematically, and in *This Night's Orbit* they are sprinkled, though still rather sparingly, among regular rhymes not only in the two longer poems but in about half the shorter poems as well. The introducer of the half-rhyme, Wilfred Owen, and a few of his successors, have used it with a deliberate artistic purpose, in order to produce a particular sort of effect, but as a general rule the object of those who use it today seems to be merely freedom, convenience; this is true sometimes of FitzGerald, but at other times, as in "Essay on Memory", the half-rhymes are used with an aesthetic purpose: consciously or unconsciously, in the second half-rhyme the vowel is with FitzGerald almost invariably broader, fuller than in the other, producing an effect of strength[32] which is in keeping with the style in general; FitzGerald is modern also in that after *To Meet the Sun* he does not begin a line with a capital, except when it follows a full stop.[33]

As one would expect of a poet whose intellectual outlook is that of a scientist, or rather of a scientific philosopher, FitzGerald's method also is scientific, so far as is consistent with that of poetry. It is always logical and precise, and it is also concise, in that words are very seldom wasted,[34]

---

[29] "The Insignificant Meeting" (p. 10), the last verse of "Banishment" (p. 31), "When You Speak" (p. 52).

[30] In *To Meet the Sun*: enough—thereof (p. 18), abyss—is (p. 36), feel—real (p. 34); in *Moonlight Acre*: once—suns (p. 22), tuft—rebuffed, impress—head dress, down—own (p. 24), else—citadels (p. 48).

[31] Sentry—country (p. 13).

[32] There is an interesting discussion on half-rhymes in R. G. Howarth's *Notes on Modern Poetic Technique* (Sydney, 1949), pp. 50-61.

[33] It might have been supposed that he was here following Brennan, who had introduced the practice to Australia; but the Brennan influence is most marked in FitzGerald's first book, in which he still follows the old convention in this matter.

[34] There are occasional exceptions, as in "light of old suns long given to the dead" (*Moonlight Acre*, p. 51).

but as to the conciseness there is what may be regarded as a qualification: in a sense, FitzGerald often repeats himself, though in a different manner, as if the climber of a mountain were to try first one way of approach and then another. Of one or two Australian poets it has been here remarked that they think naturally in images; but images are the wheels and also the machinery by which FitzGerald's poetry moves forward; and in his metaphysical poems he feels his way gradually towards the complete statement of what he wishes to convey by means of a succession of images, of which several may be used to explain and illustrate the same idea, though usually from different points of view: the images are however more than explanatory and illustrative; FitzGerald may be said to tell his story in pictures, which flow one out of the other, so that we are able not only to perceive but to see with the eye the gradual unfolding of the theme. FitzGerald's poetry is therefore copious, and may seem at first sight to be diffuse; but given the method adopted it would be hard to find another so well fitted to convey the processes and the results of what is both a poetic and a scientific investigation: such a conveyal could scarcely be condensed. In this succession of images "Essay on Memory" in particular resembles the poetry of the surrealists, but it differs in everything else, for its images are not drawn from the subconscious, and they are all closely and logically connected; indeed the continuity of the thought is so close, the images on which the thought is carried forward are so interwoven, the development of the thesis, for it is a thesis, is so gradual, that, in spite of the immense energy and along with it the clarity of the utterance and of the spirit behind it, the pictorial succession often flashes past too smoothly and swiftly to allow the mind to see behind any particular image, to grasp its relationship and import; it is this that makes some of the poetry hard to follow on a first reading. It is true that all poetry worth reading needs rereading, perhaps many times, if its full import is to be grasped, but this applies more strongly to some of FitzGerald's poetry than to that of others whose makers regard communication as important. FitzGerald's poetry may therefore seem at first sight in one way more difficult and in another way easier than it is; and since his characteristic movement is from thought to thought rather than from one aspect to another of emotion, and since his images themselves are concise by any reckoning, it is not surprising that a large proportion of them should be epigrammatic, as in

> . . . Caesar is now a purse. . . .
>
> . . . .
>
> and bankers rule us, all at odds with thieves,
> and humped attorneys have us in their hold
> who press us dry between dead parchment leaves;

and

The fall of evening is the rebirth of knowing.

But it is "Essay on Memory" that is richest in images of this kind; for example:

... life would perish on its pavement-flags
but that we clasp about us cast-off rags
and robes of dead kings. . . .

. . . .

Foresight is but a bargain that we make,
which, even should life keep it, death will break;

. . . .

Wherefore all good is effort, and all truth
encounter and overcoming. . . .

The immediately preceding poem, "The Hidden Bole", which might have been entitled "Essay on Beauty", contains an image that is perhaps even more packed with thought, the Shakespearian

We ask no more than let our joy be frail,
Since its whole wisdom is its passing hence.

This poem also and most appropriately contains two images of another kind, in which beauty is uppermost: the lovely description of the dancer in the ballet Giselle,[35] as

. . . the prisoned sunshine that became
delicate contour of escaping fire;

and, at the conclusion of the poem, the magnificent

Fade twilight; bird give over: the immense
murmur of night halts at your edge of air.

In "Essay on Memory", as also, with a slight shift of interest, in "The Hidden Bole" and "The Face of the Waters", FitzGerald is at his most metaphysical. "The Hidden Bole", which reminds one here and there of O'Dowd's "Alma Venus", though unlike that poem it is closely wrought and has a definite structure, examines the nature of beauty: distiller of magics that, as

One above other writhe the wrestling dooms

it appears for a moment and is gone; it puts us

. . . in bond
to moonlight, the charmed circle of your will;

and though in its temporal manifestations momentary, it is in a sense eternal, as an aspect of the "fertile force within this mud" about the roots of life. Here the poem links with "Essay on Memory", whose theme is the unity and continuity of life, of being: memory is for the

[35] This may be compared with the description of Taglioni in Brennan and Brereton's *Mask*. (See pp. 749–50.) [The poem is in fact an elegy for Pavlova and celebrates the concept of beauty as motion.]

purpose of this poem neither record nor human history, nor the long preceding "sky-old story" that science tries to outline, nor the "composite mind whose cells are men"; it is the impression that the past has left upon the present, that far-off past whose voice is heard in rain and wind, two of the oldest things in the world,[36] changers and fertilizers not only of the earth but of the imagination. With their stimulus it is possible to explore the past, and find life to be

> . . . one wavering inward flame
> unquenched through change and time,

although the forms in which it expresses itself are continually changing: the lamp, the spark, the individual life or form of life, flickers out, but life itself, the flame, remains. Or, to put it in another way, life is the shaper of things, and individual lives may be regarded as

> . . . forms worked over
> in one huge bulk ere each is lost for ever,
> not as reality but its escape
> in impress after impress of pure shape.

From this point of view "all is become action"; it is the creative force that matters, not the passing forms that it creates: the bird, for instance, is nothing apart from the motion that is proper to it, the force that has brought it into being. "This," says the poet, "heart denies", fastening naturally upon the concrete; and it is true, to hark back for a moment to the previous poem, that

> . . . even boughs the plan rejects
> shed at the outmost fringe, are of the whole—
> sheltering, share the life their loss protects,
> the main line of ascent, the hidden bole.

And the forms which are life and which life throws off are all connected and interdependent; ourselves among them, for we too are Memory, in the sense in which FitzGerald uses the term,

> . . . and retain
> so much of those gone, the little death can gain
> is found a cheat of the senses; change and birth
> convulsive writhing of autophagous earth.

And then the poem concentrates upon the present, upon the hour that is but "a gulp in the long throat of the past", so that

> now must decision be brief, must jump or perish
> under the feet and fury of stampede;

[36] There is a penetrating analysis of "Essay on Memory" by Professor A. R. Chisholm in the *Australian Quarterly* (vol. x, no. 3, September 1938, pp. 65-71), to which I am at several points indebted.

so that we must

> . . . knot this hour's activity as a rope
> in strength of climbing hands; for still our hope
> best clings to shoulders swarming.

Finally, in a burst of confident enthusiasm, the poem swings towards the poet's own people and their task:

> We whose scope
> clasps the tremendous leagues of summer-south,
> thunder-oppressive with curbed energies,
> least of all folk need question our day's worth
> or think its turmoil twitchings of spent earth.
>
> . . . .
>
> Whatever the task, it lies in front: we must
> build upward though we guess not to what skies,
> and though the eruptive Babels that we thrust
> vital in air will fritter back to dust;
> else we betray the lamp behind our eyes,
> the quickening in our veins, both held in trust
> since long before the scumming of the germ
> upon first seas. We will serve out our term;
> not yet the impetus flags whose course began
> when at the blank mouth of our stinking lair
> we saw night's infinite curtain shake with grey,
> and so went forth determined to be Man,
> standing at last erect, and watched new day
> wrap back the dark and strip the valley bare.

The tone of the poems in FitzGerald's third phase is soberer, the analyst more in evidence as such. The enthusiasm which is perhaps his most marked characteristic is evident enough, but it is now comparatively restrained and runs often beneath the surface; youthful exuberance has given way to a conservation of the energy of which there is however still no lack; there are again a few prosy passages and even poems;[37] the intellect burns throughout with a drier light. The collection in *This Night's Orbit* is uneven: it consists of a number of short poems, most of which are self-analyses again; the rather longer metaphysical poem, "The Face of the Waters", and the two long historical poems "Heemskerck Shoals" and "Fifth Day": these are focal points in the collection. There is still the tendency to advance along a succession of images, but there is nowhere so rich a flow of them as helped to give its characteristic quality to "Essay on Memory"; and there is still the same epigrammatic tendency about the images, for example:

> . . . You could not hide in a bag
> Thousands of miles of trafficable seas;
>
> . . . .

[37] "Standpoints" for example, and "In Personal Vein".

who had taken age's shilling and complete
grey uniform though not its grey eclipse;

and

only the one-eyed man walks straight through his brain.

There is the extraordinary alive and graphic

. . . old scenes are blown
like sand across these hillocks

and, from the metaphysical poem, an image that gains much however from its context,

There is no release from the rack
Of darkness for the unformed shape.

In one image, from "Heemskerck Shoals", FitzGerald returns to the subject and repeats the note of the last part of "Essay on Memory":

Then, because
room hungered there for greatness, gaped in demand,
men could give greatness gladly to that land.

In a few of the shorter poems analysis seems to have dried up the juice of poetry; but this is by no means true of all of them, and, taken in the lump, if they do not add to FitzGerald's reputation, they do not detract from it. In considering the personal poems there is one point that it is important to remember: FitzGerald resembles Brennan in this, that his personal poems have a significance wider than that of the merely personal; but the reason is different. In "The Wanderer" Brennan is, perhaps designedly, Everyman, and his shorter personal poems, for almost all his poems are personal, acquire their more general application by reason of the universality of their emotion, which, though intensely individual, reaches below the surface to something kindred in very many. FitzGerald attains a similar result along another line: even his personal poems are, unlike Brennan's, in a sense impersonal, in that they are straight analyses without strain or bias of any kind; it is almost as though he were analysing someone else. Incidentally, that is one reason why the transition from self-analysis to analysis of a historic character comes so easily and naturally with him; his personal poems may therefore be read as impartial analyses of a particular and today unusual type of person. And since these personal poems contain, like Brennan's again, characteristics which in spite of their poetic significance are primarily moral and have a particular value for humanity, especially today, they possess an importance unusual in their kind. But their moral importance is different from Brennan's. Brennan's poetry at its best exudes not only an indomitable courage and determination, but a kind of royalty that compels allegiance, as it were to a king in exile; FitzGerald's personality is not overwhelming like Brennan's, and in any case it is too simple and modest to produce such an effect; but all his work exudes a courage that is quite as indomitable and that is undimmed by memories of past misfortune, taking us back to that of confident youth. Brennan's courage is in one sense splendid, in that it triumphs over a foreknowledge of material defeat; FitzGerald's is splendid in another sense, for it involves a refusal to acknowledge the possibility of defeat, an assured confidence in ultimate victory. Brennan shines out of a murky and tormented gloom; FitzGerald shines with a light that is clear and unvarying, and to him, unlike Brennan, in spite of difficulties and trials that are real enough though not of his making, this is "a glad world to know". But FitzGerald has become aware that life is not nearly long enough for achievement that is worth while; he says:

> I use this life to live in; I need eight more
> for learning and ambition and to explore
>
> where necessary haste
> went by so fast
>
> that there was only a vision, never proved,
> of wider living.

Still, he declares, in a manner that recalls the older Yeats, that

> Though here is evidence
> that years burr as they go
> the edge-tool of sense,
> I will not have it so.
> And surely that is enough
> to preserve the temper still;
> softening or wearing rough
> being failure of will;

and in a lighter mood, with a burst of bravado:

> What Time has raked up he can have—
> his scavengings and thievings;
> however he may hook and shave
> he only gets my leavings.

"The Face of the Waters",[38] the one metaphysical poem in *This Night's Orbit*, links up with "The Hidden Bole" and "Essay on Memory"; it attempts, by means of a transparent and extremely vivid symbolism, to probe deeper than either of these did, to convey, pictorially as it were, the poet's conception of the ultimate force of life in operation, or rather of the spirit in which it may be imagined as working: the force from which proceeds all that is and all that fails to be. It is an attempt

[38] *This Night's Orbit*, p. 28.

> . . . to twang the string which is not a string but silence
> plucked at the heart of silence;

it is therefore, as FitzGerald admits, an attempt at the impossible; there can be no

> . . . floor to the bottomless;
> except in so far as conjecture must arrive,
> lungs cracking, at the depth of its dive;
> where downward further is further distress
> with no change in it; as if a mile and an inch
> are equally squeezed into a pinch,
> and retreating limits of cold mind
> frozen, smoothed, defined.

Yet this poem has an extraordinary fascination, in "The tension of silence", "the agony of not being", the "tentative migration" of the unformed or half-formed shapes,

> . . . the scurry of feet—those myriads
> crossing the black granite; and again
> laughter cruelly in pursuit; and then
> the twang like a harpstring or the spring of a trap,
> and the swerve on the polished surface: the little soft pads
> sidling and skidding and avoiding; but soon caught up
> in the hand of laughter and put back . . .
>
> . . . .
>
> feet running fearfully out of nothing at the core of nothing:
> colour, light, life, fearfully
> becoming eyes and understanding: sound becoming ears . . .

And at last,

> Worlds that were spun adrift re-enter
> that intolerable centre;
>
> . . . .
>
> The eggshell collapses
> in the fist of the intolerable instant;
> all is what it was before.
> Yet is that eternal instant
> the pinpoint bursting into reality
>
> . . . .
>
> the struggle to magpie-morning and all life's clamour and lust;
> the part breaking through the whole;
> light and the clear day and so simple a goal.

This poem is FitzGerald's most striking adventure, even farther than in "Essay on Memory", along what had been hitherto his most characteristic line; but in "Heemskerck Shoals" and "Fifth Day" it is a new line that he opens out: new for FitzGerald that is, though Slessor had shown the way and perhaps suggested the expedition. In these two poems FitzGerald projects himself outward as in the three metaphysical poems he had turned inward; but the first three are just as much adventures as the last two, and the last two are just as much analyses as the first three. As Whitehead had in one way or another affected the metaphysical poems, so Browning may have had some effect upon one at least of the historical; but here also the influence was probably in the nature of a stimulus, in showing that the sort of characterization FitzGerald had in mind could be carried out, more directly and in more detail than with Slessor, in poetry: there were also of course Browning's exemplifications of a method that might seem the most effective possible; but in the sort of characterization that FitzGerald here attempted there would probably be a far-off likeness to Browning even if the poet had not read him. "Heemskerck Shoals" is a third-personal monologue in irregular rhymes and half-rhymes, in which Tasman muses over lost and possible opportunities and the Australia which he has never seen but towards which he feels an extraordinary attraction: it is an extremely lifelike and human characterization, of the man who dreams imaginatively into the future, while at the same time he keeps insisting that he dislikes dreaming, being "a practical man". Now and then the method of exposition approaches that of prose, but it approaches it on the side of poetry, does not reach it, and produces an effect to which prose could not attain. Direct and forcible, not so concise as the other historical poem, but without wasting words, "Heemskerck Shoals"[39] possesses a strong and convincing individual life and reads better each time one reads it; FitzGerald has taken full advantage of his superior situation in time, and from that point of view his own enthusiasm finds vent through Tasman:

It was unthrift
of the faculties to dazzle them on a glitter
of wishes that dulled the mind; men would do better
to ask of the southern land in sober terms
what could be made of it that they could put
their strength and skill in making. Think of farms
growing into the hills and foot by foot
driving the wastes before them; cities, unbuilt,
only awaiting builders; shipyards bursting
with vessels on the slips about to be spilt
into the stream of trade; and a harbour mouth
crammed with those vessels bringing home to the south
wealth fairly won, not milkers come from thirsting
ports of the foreign north

. . . .

[39] *This Night's Orbit*, p. 21.

. . . perhaps the ground
was not all barren; it would be one task
to learn its needs and fill them; good was not found
but by that ache of striving which might ask
too much of ordinary men. Though that
was what the thought in his mind was biting at:
the necessity in men, deep down, close cramped,
not seen in their own hearts, for some attempt
at being more than ordinary men,
rising above themselves. It was an urge
that swung from wars to follies, being the purge
of stagnation from the veins, and violent when
there was little to work it off against; but was
man's only greatness also. Then, because
room hungered there for greatness, gaped in demand,
men could give greatness gladly to that land.

"Fifth Day"[40] is a descriptive poem, much more dramatic than the other, in seven-line verses running *ababbcc*, which deals with part of the trial of Warren Hastings:

. . . history hooks
the observer into its foreground while he looks.

It is not Hastings but the trial, the "swarming of motives and intrigues", that is the subject, the trial in its setting projected vividly before the eye and ear along with a running accompaniment of critical thought: of the persons who appear, Burke is given as much space as Hastings; Francis is shown, poisonous in the background; Pitt is just mentioned, and Fox, asleep until the finish; even Gurney the reporter has his couple of verses, rounding the whole act. This poem does not run easily like the other; it is tight, dry, compact; every phrase is pointed and not a word could be left out: this is perhaps the most concise and vivid of all FitzGerald's poems. Few phrases or passages rise above their context, but the level is high, from the opening verse onward:

In William Rufus's hall the galleries reached
half to the rafters like a roost for lords,
perching the fashion of England; back seats fetched
more than a nabob's bribe. The season affords
nothing so sought as these hard boards;
so rustling ladies, crush your muslin frocks . . .
There's Mrs Fitzherbert in the royal box.

Hastings is there in front of us, kneeling at the bar, like life, "infirm, staggering a little, with steady eyes and voice",

Undersized, spare, licked dry by tropic heat;
one, with severe forehead and hard lips,
who had taken age's shilling and complete

---

[40] The same, p. 31.

grey uniform though not its grey eclipse—
with movements like commands, like whips:
here is the centre, whether for applause or loathing,
when evidence and acquittal alike mean nothing.

Burke, the tool of Francis, Burke whose

. . . heavy features liven with that magic
under them and their spectacles, which turns
knowledge to vision, and vision to strategic
marshalling of words and march of logic
through illustrations like landscapes and up steep
Quebec heights of statistics—

Burke is nevertheless farther from us; he is suddenly ill, and Fox wakes up to hurry to his aid; and then,

The court adjourned.
Gurney stoppered his inkhorn, wiped his pen . . .
Poor Mr Burke! But it was money earned
lightly and sweetened labour, for lesser men,
to go home early now and then.
Tuck today under an arm—though Hastings bent
that frown, there remained but shorthand. He bowed and went.

This poem also reads better each time one reads it, but in its close and pointed analysis it is of quite a different kind from "Heemskerck Shoals". What is more, in it FitzGerald avoids, with all its close reporting, what is his greatest danger, though so far it has been only here and there, in patches, that he has run into prosiness.

For FitzGerald, like Brennan once more, Australian comparisons are inadequate; how he will ultimately compare with Brennan must depend upon the quality of his later work. It is certain that he stands above all other Australian poets, by reason, to borrow from Arnold, of his sincerity and strength. In these qualities, and also in the scarcely less important courage, freshness, balance and sanity of his outlook it is hard to find any poet of today who can compare with him. There is of course Roy Campbell, the "tremendous South African", to quote FitzGerald's own words, who is so different in every other way; but after all there is more substance in FitzGerald: his eye is always entirely on his object, and even when, as in so many of his shorter poems, that object is himself and his own mental processes, they are never sentimentalized. He is the only Australian poet who has entirely, to quote Virginia Woolf again, "consumed his impediments", who can observe both the world without and the world within from a point of view that is quite uninfluenced by self-regard or inessential idiosyncrasy. The mind and temperament revealed in his poetry are of an unusual type, combining as they do the reflective with the adventurous, the poetic with the analytical, the psychologist with the metaphysician. His work is the more tonic for the world as it is today in that in it he looks not over but through its evils and disappointments, seeing beyond them, and the more again in that what he has to say is neither didactic nor even as a rule critical except by inference; it is presented as a poetic image, which resembles the touchstone of Stevenson's fable, in whose light truth and falsity appear as they are.

CHAPTER III

VERSE

THE INTELLECTUALS CONTINUED

Hope; McAuley; McKellar; Mann; Rosemary Dobson; Hart-Smith. The Eliotites: Higgins; O'Dwyer; Others. Ethel Anderson; Betty Riddell; Thompson; Others. Younger Writers: Webb; Others

HOPE'S DISILLUSION* is different in kind from Slessor's, and the two poets have nothing else in common, except romanticism and a sense of humour which is usually more or less submerged. Generally speaking, it is about life that Slessor is disillusioned, about the conditions in which man is set, conditions that crucify him; Hope is disillusioned about man himself, about his nature and possibilities. Slessor retains a sensuous delight in certain aspects of Nature, an intoxication, even, with their loveliness, and he finds keen pleasure in the attempt to translate them into poetry; but to Hope all is pain and ugliness, and it is only now and then that he gets an obvious pleasure from the poetic expression of what he sees and feels, or that a fantastic humour relieves him. Hope's range is narrower than Slessor's: he is concerned almost solely with man, and incidentally woman, as affected by sex in its various aspects. And on the side of form, whereas Slessor depends upon imagery at least as much as upon rhythm, Hope's work is not remarkable for images, though it is by no means without them; its character depends far more upon the power and individuality of its rhythms. But neither Hope's rhythms nor his images are the obvious results of experiment, and Hope is not, like Slessor, occupied with the analysis and manipulation of poetic form: it is the facts that he analyses, and his efforts are concentrated almost wholly upon the discovery of what is for him exact truth, and upon its expression with perfect exactness and clarity. He is therefore in the first place, like FitzGerald, with whom however he has nothing else in common, fundamentally a scientist as well as a poet: but to suggest that he uses verse merely as a medium for the conveyal of the results of his analyses would be a bad mistake, for though sometimes only secondarily he is yet a poet essentially; and this appears not merely in the nature of his verse, but in the attitude that always strongly underlies and sometimes impregnates his scientific analyses.

Alec Derwent Hope, (Cooma, N.S.W., 1907-) was educated at Bathurst and Sydney High Schools and the Universities of Sydney and Oxford, to which he won a travelling scholarship. After teaching for some years in State schools in up-country New South Wales, he became

* [This disillusion may be less pronounced in the later poems, but it never ceases to be present.]

a lecturer in English at the Sydney Teachers' Training College: during this period he was lent to the Department of Labour and Industry as a vocational psychologist, and he also gave regular and highly successful broadcasts, including a number in the A.B.C. Children's Session; he then lectured in English at the University of Melbourne, after which he was appointed Professor of English at the Canberra University College (later the Australian National University) from 1951 to 1967. Although Hope has published a considerable amount of poetry in *Southerly*, *Meanjin*, and other Australian periodicals, it was long before any of it was collected in book-form,[1] though typescript collections have been circulated among his friends; nevertheless, in his case as in FitzGerald's it has been considered advisable to break the general rule restricting the scope of this History to books already printed. The typescript of *The Wandering Islands* was prefaced by the following lines from canto IX of the *Inferno*:

O voi, che avete gl'intelletti sani,
mirate la dottrina, che s'ascende
sotto il velame degli versi strani![2]

There are three other references to the *Inferno*, all in a poem that describes the development of child into man: the title of this poem is "Ascent into Hell"; it begins with the line, "I, too, at the mid-point, in a well-lit wood"; and it ends with part of the inscription on the gate of hell, "'*per me si va tra la perduta gente*'".[3] It is clear that this poet, like the other, means to deal with a nation of the lost. The motto conveys that the author wishes the reader to pay special attention to the subject-matter of the poems; it might be contended that he thereby, like some other poets, transgressed the first law of poetry, that it should be its own object; but of course such a direction to the reader must not be taken to imply that the poet thinks of nothing but what our grandfathers would have called his "message", any more than that the conclusions of the analyst are not integral constituents of the poems that contain them. But regarding the quotation from the *Inferno* there is another point. Upon the circumstances in which Dante speaks, and he is speaking to the reader, a commentator[4] provided the following gloss:

---

[1] After the closing date of this History he published *The Wandering Islands* (Sydney, 1955), which however omits some of his best poems, perhaps because they would not have accorded with the atmosphere of the collection. As with FitzGerald, for the reader's convenience, quotations from poems included in this book are referred to it; other poems are referred to publications in which they have appeared.

[2]
O you who are of sane mind,
Consider the wisdom that appears
From beneath the veil of these strange verses.

In the book itself these lines are substituted by the following:

Men must either bear their guilt and weakness
Or be a servile instrument to powers
That darken knowledge and corrupt the heart.

[3] Through me you enter among the nation of the lost.

> The words compel us to . . . ask what the mystic meaning is which is to be read between the lines . . . the pilgrim is brought into contact with the mystery of evil and its punishment. . . . The three Erinnyes, types of the remorse of conscience . . . strike terror into the soul. . . . There remains a more terrible experience, the despair and unbelief that petrify the soul and make it callous. . . . There is a point at which the contemplation of evil becomes fatal to the soul's life.

If we assume that Hope had in mind either the words of this commentator or ideas similar to those which he expresses, it would seem to follow that the evils and uglinesses that are discovered are considered blameworthy, that the poet is haunted in fact by a sense of sin, and indeed he does in many places appear not merely to analyse but to blame;[5] and also that he realizes the danger of the continual contemplation of such evils as he continually discovers. The title of the collection has also a certain significance in that it draws attention to the title-poem. Its theme is that of the best known of Arnold's Marguerite poems, but there could be no better illustration of the part played by individuality and convention when two poets handle the same theme: here we have on the one hand the disillusioned romantic of today, who stands at close quarters with life as he sees it and reports it without reticences; and on the other hand the Victorian romantic, who, saddened but not disillusioned, stands a little apart, ignoring all that he regards as unaesthetic or inessential, and creates a calm and quiet though nevertheless impassioned beauty in which life is idealized. Setting aside passages of deliberate beauty on the one hand, and of deliberate ugliness on the other, as reflecting, more or less, the fashion of the poet's day, the beginnings and the endings of the two poems may be contrasted; Arnold's

> Yes! in the sea of life enisled,
> With echoing straits between us thrown,
> Dotting the shoreless watery wild,
> We mortal millions live *alone*.
> The islands feel the enclasping flow,
> And then their endless bounds they know,

with Hope's

> You cannot build bridges between the wandering islands;
> The Mind has no neighbours, and the unteachable heart
> Announces its armistice time after time, but spends
> Its love to draw them closer and closer apart;

and Arnold's

> Who order'd, that their longing's fire
> Should be, as soon as kindled, cool'd?
> Who renders vain their deep desire?—

---

[4] See *The Commedia and Canzoniere of Dante Alighieri*, translated by E. H. Plumptre (London, 1886), vol. i, "Hell", canto IX, p. 45, note 61.

[5] For example there is the reference in "Flower Poems" to "dirty mind", and in "Easter Hymn", the statement that "there will be no forgiveness"; and there are examples in "Australia" and in other poems.

A God, a God their severance ruled!
And bade betwixt their shores to be
The unplumb'd, salt, estranging sea,

with Hope's

And then in the crash of ruined cliffs, the smother
And swirl of foam, the wandering islands part,
But all that one mind ever knows of another,
Or breaks the long isolation of the heart

Was in that instant. The shipwrecked sailor senses
His own despair in a retreating face.
Around him he hears in the huge monotonous voices
Of wave and wind: "The Rescue will not take place."

To the modern poet man is, with few exceptions, no figure for romantic pity, but a vulgar, lonely, sex-obsessed insignificance, who seeks escape from an utterly trivial and monotonous world in a comic adventure strip, with its

Commercial travellers' tales of a slick Munchausen,

though he himself is no more adventurous than a sheep; or he finds his escape in the daily dope of the radio, which saves him from thinking of his troubles—or anything else. If he is a little more literate he finds vicarious satisfaction in feeding "grublike" on the flowers of literature which some expert analyses for him with his "scalpel of reason":

Only transfusion of a poem's blood
Can save [him], bleeding from [his] civilisation.[6]

Even at the best, man is no more than "the thinking plant", tearing at the dirt to which he is inescapably fastened, feeling the pull at his skull of the mass of other men, feeling his

. . . red sap of thought
On mansoil bleed—
And still the wounded root
Of will unfreed

By its own act of life
Chained to the ground.
Love itself twists a knife
Hard in that wound.[7]

Man loves only himself, eats himself, and thus destroys himself, and the child's development into man is, as in the poem already referred to, an "ascent into hell"; it is noteworthy that this was the title given to an

[6] "Flower Poem", *The Wandering Islands*, p. 11; compare with this poem the description of "the feelies" in *Brave New World*.

[7] "Lying on the Lawn", typescript.

earlier collection of Hope's poems.[8] Outside man and his immediate flock, there is the larger flock, the nation to which he belongs, and here we find the same disillusion; partly in revulsion against the exaggerations of the "patriot"[9] and partly out of a determination to emphasize aspects commonly glossed over, in "Australia",[10] one of his finest poems, Hope sees his country as

> A woman beyond her change of life, a breast
> Still tender but within the womb is dry;
>
> without songs, architecture, history:
> the emotions and superstitions of younger lands,
>
> Her rivers of water drown among inland sands,
> The river of her immense stupidity
>
> Floods her monotonous tribes from Cairns to Perth.
>
> . . . .
>
> And her five cities, like five teeming sores
> Each drains her; a vast parasite robber-state
> Where second-hand Europeans pullulate
> Timidly on the edge of alien shores.

Still, he admits the far-off possibility of hope:

> Yet there are some like me turn gladly home
> From the lush jungle of modern thought, to find
> The Arabian desert of the human mind,
> Hoping, if still from deserts the prophets come,
>
> Such savage and scarlet as no green hills dare
> Springs in this waste, some spirit which escapes
> The learned doubt, the chatter of cultured apes
> Which is called civilisation over there.

But man's and his analyst's main preoccupation is with love, and with that, largely as the manifestation of sex in its most primitive aspect: thought, passion, will, everything else are a "huge irrelevance" to the purpose of the phallic god. All the young lover can think of is the act, and yet it means death to himself, who had hoped to find fruition in love, and to his beloved, who is in a sense his creation; she yields nothing to him, but on the contrary does her best to transform him into a domestic chattel. In "The Invocation"[11] the relations of modern educated man and woman are analysed without symbolism or satire: first, the man's

[8] This is also the title of a poem in the printed collection.

[9] And in particular the literary patriot; it is worth while comparing Furphy in this respect.

[10] Printed in *Australian Poetry 1944* (Sydney, 1945), p. 21, and in *Modern Australian Poetry* (Melbourne, 1946), p. 18. The text is that of the second (1952) edition of the anthology; it differs from the other mainly in punctuation.

[11] In the printed book, "Pygmalion"; in this book "Invocation" is a different poem.

arrogant assumption that the woman will become what he wills her to become:

Now woman, if you have it in you to live,
This is your living body's prerogative. . . .
                    This guess of mine,
all my invention, my superb design. . . .
I built you out of nothing; now build for me.

. . . .

And in myself this man I have willed to know
wakes at long last: Although I planned it so
I did not know I had so much to bring,
so much I could not give, and dared not lend,
into these hands my spirit I commend . . .
O take it, for it is a precious thing.

And then, the man's indignant astonishment; she is changed, but not in the direction in which he had wished her to change:

I cannot summon you as once you were;
You come with a new movement; the surprise
of unaccustomed hands, reluctant eyes,
menstrual, remote.
                    Unsummoned, you are still
there; a cancer ripening in the will. . . .
        . . . O God! What do you want? . . .
This is my room, my mind: Get out of here!

Hope's attitude has much in common with that of Strindberg, or of Swift. He himself says that he is not a satirist, but a recorder of life as he sees it; whether his assertion is correct or no depends on what one means by satire: the greater part of his work certainly holds humanity up to "hatred, ridicule or contempt", the legal definition of defamation, which comes close to being also a definition of satire; and for one or more of these purposes it as certainly accentuates the defects it discovers, both negatively, by presenting them unrelieved, and positively, by accentuation. But if it is required of satire that it be humorous, even though the humour be bitter, then a large proportion of these poems are not true satires, for they are as serious as they could be; and if the purpose of the satirist is assumed to be reform, then it is doubtful whether Hope is a satirist at all, for to him analysis is almost invariably its own end and purpose; it is a devastating analysis, which seems to carry with it an implication that the evils his scalpel exposes are inseparable from the nature of the creature on the dissecting table. But such an assumption would surely go too far: did Swift for instance believe that the yahoo was reformable?; and some of Swift's satires would scarcely conform with the first assumption either. It would probably be agreed that about three-fifths of the poems in *The Wandering Islands* were satires, and that another fifth were doubtful, but a few would comply with any reasonable definition, and these include a couple of the best, "Conquistador"[12] and "Return from the Freudian Isles".[13] The former is a delightful burlesque, however serious the intention, of the relationship of the insignificant male and the possessive female:

I sing of the decline of Henry Clay
Who loved a white girl of uncommon size.
Although a small man in a little way,
He had in him some seed of enterprise.

Each day he caught the seven-thirty train
To work, watered his garden after tea,
Took an umbrella if it looked like rain
And was remarkably like you or me.

He meets the lady in a hotel lounge, and at closing time she asks him home; at last,

. . . in her quiet room they were alone.
There, towering over Henry by a head,
She stood and took her clothes off one by one,
And then she stretched herself upon the bed.

Her bulk of beauty, her stupendous grace
Challenged the lion heart in his puny dust.
Proudly his Moment looked him in the face:
He rose to meet it as a hero must;

Climbed the white mountain of unravished snow,
Planted his tiny flag upon the peak,
The smooth drifts, scarcely breathing, lay below.
She did not take the trouble to smile or speak.

And afterwards, it may have been in play,
The enormous girl rolled over and squashed him flat;
And, as she could not send him home that way,
Used him thereafter as a bedside mat.

"The Return from the Freudian Isles" satirizes Freud and his followers by means of a *reductio ad absurdum*; it is a pity there is not space to quote both these poems in full. Unusual attention has been paid here to the analyses themselves, apart from the poetry from which they have been roughly and incompletely quarried out, in part because of their declared importance to the poet, and in part because what he has to say constitutes so large a proportion of what he has to convey. But if there had been

---

[12] Printed in *Meanjin*, vol. vi (1947), no. 3, pp. 174–5, and in *Modern Australian Poetry* (2nd edition, Melbourne, 1952), pp. 82–4.
[13] *Australian Poetry 1943* (Sydney, 1944), p. 21.

no more about Hope's work than the analyses and their results, it would have been better done in prose; actually, some of the poems in which the analyses are embodied are among the most notable and are certainly the best of their kind that have come out of the Australia of today. The principal characteristics of Hope's poetry as such are its simple, outspoken sincerity, its individuality and its power; at its best, as in "The Damnation of Byron", it appeals to mind and emotions at once: it appeals through the ear rather more than through the eye, for though there are some impressive pictures, they are as a rule representational, generalized, as far as possible from being literal reproductions of the observations and imaginative visions upon which they are based. In Hope's work in general, the intellect has charge of the imagination, controlling and directing it towards purposes that are consciously willed; yet the results are not by any means artificial, for at the same time the imagination kindles the intellect, fusing emotionally the results of analysis. Hope is an academic in the broader sense, in that his work carries with it an air of wide and systematic reading, and shows a determination to find and use only the word that is exactly right, from a scientific as well as from a poetic point of view; but he is most unacademic in the blunt outspokenness of his realism. He is modern in that his language is that of prose; but it is a prose that is always correct, precise, and its vocabulary is that of a cultivated man, except that at times it is more colloquial than that of even the young intellectual of today, at least when he writes for print.[14] Hope is modern also in his use of near-rhyme and assonance:[15] beyond that, he will occasionally use even dissonance, as in senses—voices. And in his use of "free rhythms" he is modern again, omitting syllables when it suits him, as in the second line of the following,

> As the professor snips the richest bud
> For his lapel, his scalpel of reason;

or adding them, as in the first line of the two following,

> Till his heart, leaping in ecstasy from her stream
> Died on the bank, threshing in silver death:

here we have, incidentally, one of the most living images in the Australian poetry of today. All Hope's images are highly individual, but there is never about them any air of strain or artificiality: it is true that a large proportion are obviously directed to a particular purpose, come as illustrations to a particular thesis, but one feels that come they do, that

[14] Hope says not only "it used to be exciting", "the islanders were very much impressed" and "for the island climate is often extremely cold", but "one hill was the dead spit of the rest". He even speaks of "lovely frails", but there is a *double entendre* here.

[15] For example: motion—amputation, sailor—call or.

they have not been constructed deliberately. Many, of course, are connected with the poet's main preoccupation, for example:

> . . . the grinning girls
> Sit spinning the bright fibre of their sex;
>
> Her Old Boys' Union . . .
> Danced round the bonfire of his burning sex;
>
> . . . squeezing under rubber foundations
> Giggles the uneasy blood;

and

> The mouth repeating its own rich circumflex.

Some are purely intellectual, but none the less forcible for that; "the haemorrhage of rent" for instance, and

> . . . that sly
> Anus of mind the historian.

Most of these have a modern colouring, but some, including many of the best, are not tied down to today; one it would be a pity to dig out from its matrix:

> There, in the clear night still I listen, waking
> To a crunch of sulky wheels on the distant road;
> The marsh of stars reflects a starry croaking;
> I hear in the pillow the sobbing of my blood.

Others are

> that huge succulent, twisting dark;
>
> . . . .
>
> Adventure opened wide its grisly jaws;
>
> . . . .
>
> The ache of its mysterious event;
>
> . . . .
>
> . . . the light that pours
> a tarnished glory on the soil of death.

Some of the best of Hope's images depend mainly upon rhythm, and many of these, and others also, are to be found in "The Damnation of Byron",[16] from which one of two of the above have been taken. In this poem Hope rises above the limitations that have been imposed by his purpose and his method upon his poetry; here, more than in most of his poems, form and content are, as ideally they always should be, one; here his poetic as distinct from his analytical gift, finds free scope; his mind is not tied down closely, though it is never tied down absolutely, to investigation and record, with the result that the imagination runs

[16] Printed in *Modern Australian Poetry*, 2nd edition (Melbourne, 1952), pp. 148-51.

freer; the poem marches forward with a slow and solemn dignity, through a series of generalized but none the less vivid images, upon waves of rhythm that are individual and sometimes splendid:

> When the great hero, adding to the charms
> of genius and his scandals, left the light
> stamped with the irresistible trade of arms,
> the Hell of Women received him as their right.
>
> Through the Infernal Fields he makes his way
> playing again, but on a giant stage
> his own Don Juan; pursuing day by day
> Childe Harold's last astonishing pilgrimage.

We see the "landscape of erotic dreams", the innumerable bodies of women whose beauties stir,

> mysterious like the freshening of a rose;
> as, the incomparable connoisseur,
> pale and serene across their world he goes.

Every type of woman is there, and he has all of them,

> drowned in the brute somnambulism of sex;

but he is the more alone, and gradually he begins to feel

> the deep significance of his solitude;

even his own society becomes a horror, and

> . . . he descends
> simply to treat them as The Enemy,

exhausting himself in the delights of a torture that his victims adore. At last,

> . . . neurotic, hounded by strange fears,

his journey changes to a flight;

> Delirious, broken, fugitive, he hears
> Marching and countermarching in the night,

and there approaches

> the Eternal Goddess in whose placid hand
> are all the happy and all the rebellious dead.

He prays her for oblivion; but in a terrible passage the body of the divinity is invitingly revealed:

> slowly she smiles at him . . .
> And the great hero, mad with the terrible
> madness of souls turns fleeing, while the dim
> plains heave with the immense derision of Hell.

James Phillip McAuley (Lakemba, N.S.W., 1917-76), though by far the youngest of the four, and though he has written, or rather preserved, less than any of them, is extremely mature, and seems to belong to an older world; the others are obviously poets of a young country: FitzGerald almost disregardful of the atmosphere of modernity; Slessor and Hope with their indignant protest against what the poets of older civilizations, looking out from the tumulus of the ages, accept as established, however bitterly they may attack it. McAuley also accepts what he criticizes, but he is too self-possessed for his criticism to be bitter, though it is exceedingly sharp; as compared with the other three he is restrained, controlled; he does not possess FitzGerald's free enthusiasm, but unlike Hope and Slessor he is not so much disillusioned as unillusioned, and he is quieter in attack. He is much more academic, in all senses of the word, than any of the other three: in attitude conservative, looking back to the age of Dryden and Pope and before that to the Latin and Greek classics, he is as widely read as any of the others, and likes an occasional out-of-the-way word:[17] not that, like Furphy, he wants to show off his knowledge, for he was brought up where knowledge is common, but because he writes for people to whom such words are not so strange. Yet he is unconventional, even rebellious, as academics go; and though as much as FitzGerald he dislikes ultra-modernism in attitude and practice, he is sometimes, like the modernists, neglectful of the need for communication, writes occasional "private" verses, and admits, like Eliot, that some of his poems need notes. Unlike Slessor, he does not deliberately experiment with sound and rhythm, but he shows himself, in all except his very early poems, like Hope, a master craftsman, and has developed a technique, based on those of the ancient classics and the English classicists, which is, in a broad sense, modern, though far from being modernistic.

McAuley's parents were Australian-born; he was educated at Fort Street High School, Sydney, and the University of Sydney; afterwards he coached, taught in several schools, and was during the second World War a member of the Army Education Service, stationed for a time in New Guinea. He later lectured in Colonial Administration at the Australian School of Pacific Administration, edited *Quadrant* magazine and became Professor of English at the University of Tasmania. His interests were wide: he was an accomplished musician and a fine executant on organ and piano, and an authority on New Guinea; his first collection of verse, *Under Aldebaran*,[18] was published in Melbourne in 1946. The outstanding characteristics of McAuley's poetry are brooding power and a highly individual music; its leading idea is that of rhythmic change throughout

---

[17] For example: haruspicate (p. 11), gnosis (p. 39), synecdoche (p. 61), chiasma (p. 61), saprophyte (p. 48).

[18] He has since published another book of verse, *A Vision of Ceremony* (Sydney, 1956).

the ages, as brought about by the creative imagination: this crops up continually as a theme and is latent almost everywhere. In "The Blue Horses" (a comparatively youthful poem which fascinates, in spite of technical defects, because of its energy and bright revealing images) the hooves of imaginative passion trample the conventions into a chaos out of which other conventions will emerge:

> Progeny of winds, sea-forms, earth-bestriders,
> From the blue quarries of their natal hills
> Terribly emerging to their riders,
> Blue Horses lift their neighing trumpets to the moon!
> They stamp among the spiritual mills
> That weave a universe from our decay:
> The specious outline crumbles at the shock
> Of visionary hooves, and in dismay
> Men hide among the tumbled images.

"The Incarnation of Sirius" deals with a similar but vaster rhythm, in which

> . . . the millennial instinct of new flight
>
> . . . .
>
> . . . echoing in the troubled soul of Earth,
> Quickened a virgin's womb, to bring to birth,

the heresiarch, the supreme rebel,

> The monstrous form of God's antagonist;

revolution flares, and fades, and

> The stars that with rebellion had consorted
> Fled back in silence to their former stations.

In "Chorale" the "dance and counterdance" of rhythmic change are referred to again, and the translation of the creative energies of the age into poetry, that "seraph in the soul" that "teaches, when it does not seem to teach", and whose business it is,

> When the delirium swirls within the gyre,

to

> Hold the lamp steady, though creation shake.

All these poems are symbolic; so indeed are almost all the best of McAuley's poems; most of his symbols are reasonably transparent, but not all of them: "The Family of Love" certainly requires, though it seems scarcely to deserve, its explanatory note. In addition to the poems on the primary theme, there are a couple of excursions into history and myth, for McAuley also has been affected by the historical trend already

with fairly frequent images, unrolls smoothly and evenly, but the suggestion of the eighteenth century, which arises largely, though by no means wholly, out of the poet's lucidity and poise, besides being qualified by a freer scansion which is yet by no means ultra-modern, is offset by the fact that the lines are not end-stopped, so that the smooth evenness extends to whole paragraphs and pages. There is nothing particularly novel about McAuley's rhythms, though like his friend Harold Stewart he has a fondness for the spondee with its two strong successive beats, and even for three strong beats running,[21] as in "O clear day" and "in bright dry air". But he is extremely sensitive to verbal music; and just as the simplicity of his style is broken at times by the introduction of out-of-the-way terms, so his general coolness and self-possession often warm or deepen into a lovely or a penetrating image; occasionally they blaze up in a pyrotechnic and orchestral brilliance, almost as though Dryden were to have plunged for a moment into early Elizabethanism: this occurs, for example, in the magnificent "Incarnation of Sirius",[22] in which

> Anubis-headed, the heresiarch
> Sprang to a height, fire-sinewed in the dark,
> And his ten fingers, bracketed on high,
> Were a blazing candelabra in the sky.

There is an almost sensual fascination in the "texture" of the style of this poem, in which consonants play a part whose importance was often neglected by the smooth melodists of the later romantic age, specialists in vowel music. Even such outbursts are felt to be deliberate, but this does not imply any element of artificiality about them; McAuley is far too much of an artist for that. Comparable with the last quoted is a much quieter passage that has already been referred to:

> O seraph in the soul, who singing climb
> The orders of creation as a stair,
> And hold a silver lamp above the time
> And places of our deepening despair:
>
> When the delirium swirls within the gyre,
> And comets die, and iron voices wake,
> Be witness to the sun; and mounting higher
> Hold the lamp steady, though creation shake.

But more characteristic of McAuley are the two love poems which have been quoted already, in whole or in part, and the beautiful "Autumn", a translation from Rilke. Among McAuley's images are those of the

> Women from the Arabian Nights, that wore
> The sunlight and the moonlight as a dress;

[21] Technically, a molossus. [22] p. 15.

of the earth,

> . . . as the sun beheld it on creation
> Green, with rivering silver, like brocade;

and, bringing into Australia a whiff of the eighteenth century,

> Those sober citizens of Sweet Content,
> Koalas. . . .

But more characteristic again are some of the images from the love poems:

> Five senses build
> A pentagon of pleasure:
> But mind, exceeding common measure,
> Is unfulfilled;
>
> . . . .
>
> For by continual growth love keeps us strangers,
>
> . . . .
>
> Imperfect in imperfect, love
> Grows within music;

and, this, from "Philoctetes", of the gods:

> —Rarely do they appear,
> Who move behind the invisible curtain,
> And every showing-forth is partial, turning
> A broken mirror to ourselves.

In a scholar, and a classical scholar at that, one would expect to find, as in Brennan, many reminiscences of the great writers of the past; but in McAuley they are no more than reminiscences: there is no such unconscious imitation as one finds occasionally in Brennan. Apart from the classical and classicist contributions to the style and atmosphere of his work, there are a couple of folk-ballad reminiscences,[23] and a few of later writers; there are one or two reflections of Yeats,[24] and an occasional suggestion of Donne and Rilke, and a couple of lines in "Henry the Navigator"[25] may have been suggested by Slessor's "Atlas" poems; there are also a few deliberate imitations, as of Blake,[26] and

---

[23]
> The blossoms have their will;
> I would that I had mine.
> (p. 33)

and the ballad imitation in "Dialogue" (p. 41).

[24] In the lines about the "seraph in the soul", and in
> For seven days I could be
> Married to a mountain or a tree,
> In love with swan, or cat, or antelope
> (p. 19).

[25]
> His bright designs of puff-cheeked cherubims
> Blowing wind-spokes over continents
> (p. 12).

[26] "He who himself will not forgive" etc., (p. 44).

Eliot:[27] but all these are no more than exemplifications of the continuity of literature. McAuley is an extremely individual poet, who makes whatever he has to say his own; occasionally he conveys it in a manner that, as with Brennan, though less often, suggests the "grand style", but except in being a scholar-poet he is not in the least like Brennan: he is much less withdrawn within his own centre, and his humour finds full expression in some of his verses; on the other hand he has not Brennan's representational capacity, or his overwhelming personality. His comparative youth, the variety of his subjects, and the fact that he has written far more than what he has thought worth preserving, suggest that further development may reasonably be expected from McAuley; *Under Aldebaran* has already placed him among the leading poets of the Australia of today, or of any other day.

The four leading intellectual poets might have been five but for the cutting short of one of the most promising of all Australian youthful poetic talents. John Alexander Ross McKellar[28] (Dulwich Hill, N.S.W., 1904-32) was educated at the Sydney Boys' High School, which he left at fifteen to become a bank clerk. His energy and ability were so unusual that he received promotion after promotion, at the same time that he was writing verse, reading widely in French as well as English, and, in translation, in the Greek and Latin classics, playing cricket and grade football and helping in the affairs of his old school; but overwork weakened a strong constitution and he died of pneumonia at twenty-seven. His book of verse, *Twenty-Six* (Sydney, 1932),[29] appeared in the last year of his life: a prolific year, for his talent was ripening fast and it was stimulated by the preparation of the book and its publication. Slessor selected the poems, which are the best that were then available; McKellar for his part read the proofs of *Cuckooz Contrey*, and suggested several amendments: it says much for his taste that Slessor found all of them "justified and excellent".[30] In spite of favourable reviews and the book's extraordinary promise it was long before McKellar's talent made any impression, and his *Collected Poems* (Sydney, 1946) were not published for fourteen years. As with McAuley, McKellar's principal literary interests were in the poetry of the eighteenth century and in the Latin and Greek classics; also ideas play a considerable though a smaller part in his poetry, and, considering his more emotional temperament, he also was self-possessed though far less mature. But these resemblances

[27] "So I called out: Please" etc. (p. 45).

[28] For a number of biographical details I am indebted to a memoir by McKellar's friend and old schoolmaster, J. W. Gibbes, introductory to a collection of McKellar's poems in *Southerly*, vol. v (1944), No. 4, pp. 3-10, and to a biographical note by Mr Gibbes, in the *Collected Poems*.

[29] On the title-page 1931. The book was so named because its contents were written before McKellar was twenty-six, and because it was originally to have contained twenty-six poems. The references here are however to the *Collected Poems*.

[30] In a letter to me, 11th August 1947.

are only superficial, even so far as they go: it was in choice of subject that the classics influenced McKellar, which was natural enough, seeing that he did not read them in the original; and though an eighteenth-century influence is evident in the clearness, directness, conciseness of his style, his is a warmed classicism, which merely clothes a youthful and romantic enthusiasm. Yet McKellar's poetry is almost free from romantic sentimentalities and tag-ends, and his attitude is that of a modern, as distinct from a modernist, though he is drawn to and dwells upon the past. The attractiveness, even charm of a fresh and sympathetic personality are reflected in all he wrote; like many other young poets, McKellar was possessed by the transience of beauty, of the ideal, of things in general, and this is the theme of many of his poems, usually with an ironic touch at the conclusion. It is not surprising to find a strong reflection of Housman in his earlier and now and then in his later poems, and here and there of Cabell, though of no other writer of today; there is something of Cabell in McKellar's preoccupation with the idea of Helen, of whom he has the beautiful image,

> . . . ere Time grew old
> Destiny bruised his brow against her breasts.

McKellar's poetry is not particularly rich in images, though he can write, in "On Reading a Catalogue of French Prints",

> The fading margins of a page confine
> A century of golden candleshine;

and he has a couple of delightful humorous images:

> The goose's quill is mightier than the sword
> If this be—not uncomfortably near;

and, of poets,

> That irritable race, begot by wind
> Upon the belly of futility.

Yet his poetic imagination is sharply visual, and he has a number of real and sympathetic pictures, as this, from eighteenth-century France:

> The Marquis looks towards the lighted stage;
> One hand is his; the lover's lips engage
> The other, while the lady stands between,
> Calm in her beauty, smiling and serene.
> Like figures poised a moment in the dance,
> They stay, the living monument of France,
> Nor seem to hear, beneath the 'cello's whine,
> The snarling mongrel pack of 'Eighty-nine;

or this, from "Oxford Street—The Five Ways", of the young Italian who drew him in imagination back to ancient Rome:

> A young Italian, dangling lazy feet
> From a precarious pile of silver beet,
> Pillared upon a cauliflower's heart,
> Surrendered to the jolting of the cart,
> And whilst his father's horse drew lumbering on,
> Slept in the sun's luxuriance and was gone. . . .

McKellar's imagination had in it a marked element of dream, of fantasy: this is strikingly apparent in "The Ribbon and the Rose",[31] a fascinating playlet in which he harks back on the one hand to his Scottish ancestry and the romance of the Bonnie Prince, and on the other to the equally romantic story of Troilus and Cressida, presenting all three on the stage with a sympathetic sentiment which is redeemed from sentimentality by realism and a touch of irony; it may be seen also in the plot of "Fourth Napoleon", in which an Australian sergeant of the first World War deserts in Italy and becomes in the end despot over a great part of western Europe; as it stands, this poem is not, in spite of its promise and some fine lines, among McKellar's best, but it was not revised or even finished. Among the fantasies, "The Retreat from Heaven"[32] is a little masterpiece, suggested probably by the meeting of Napoleon and the Tsar Alexander on a raft in the Niemen in 1807, by the burning of Moscow and the great retreat, and by the supposed betrayal of Ney by Napoleon, but founded upon the idea of the loyalty to lost causes by followers after the desertion of their leaders,[33] and upon a feeling of the emptiness or unattainability of ideals. Jesus and Napoleon meet at the gates of Heaven:

> The armies joined; I saw the Prince of Peace
> Desert his Staff of twelve, and then advance,
> Beneath the swirling snow that would not cease,
> To greet the waiting Emperor of France.
>
> The soldiers laughed, unloosing belt and pack;
> Now was the fighting done, the end in sight.
> For comrades left to wolves along the track
> They sighed, who'd rest in Heaven's beds that night.

But Heaven is empty, deserted:

> Napoleon turned, and Jesus called his name;
> They paused, and then fled headlong down the street. . . .
> The waiting armies marked a distant flame,
> Then heard the bugles sounding the retreat.

---

[31] p. 41.
[32] p. 63.
[33] Compare in "The Ribbon and the Rose" the loyalty of the Highlander who dies at Culloden and refuses to believe that his prince fled from that field.

They saw their leaders' carriage thunder past,
And Rumor whispered, until Panic cried;
A musket cracked; defiant, scornful, last
Stood Michel Ney, with Peter at his side.

In this poem, and in two or three others, for example "Res Publica" and "Twelve O'clock Boat", conception and craftsmanship are well matched, and these at least should be included in any Australian anthology. Pure fantasy, romantic reflections of classical themes and of eighteenth-century France, old books, Debussy, Newton, Jacobitism, the first World War, a "Counterblast to the Press from a Bank Teller": McKellar's range was so wide, his enthusiasm was so strong and so sincere that there is no saying how far he might have travelled; as it is, he takes a place in Australian poetry that corresponds in some ways with that in English poetry of Rupert Brooke.

Of all the Australian poets of today, Leonard Mann, (Melbourne, 1895-1981) is the most obviously a child of this age of war, depression and fear of war. He was educated at Melbourne State schools and the University of Melbourne, but for some time he had to work as a clerk by day and attend lectures of an evening. He broke off a law course to enlist in the first A.I.F., in which he served as infantryman and gunner; he finished his law course after the war, and became Organizing Secretary of the Victorian Employers' Federation, and, during the second World War, Industrial and State Manager of the Department of Aircraft Production.[34] Besides novels, which will be discussed in a later chapter, he has published three books of verse: *The Plumed Voice* (Sydney, 1938), *Poems from the Mask* (Melbourne, 1941), and *The Delectable Mountains* (Sydney, 1944).[35] Mann is a humanist and a destructive critic of a world order that allows of wars and of a social system that allows of depressions: not that he is by any means a propagandist, but this attitude is implicit in his verse as in his prose. Nothing has been able to crush his ideal enthusiasm, but it has become covered with a rough dark crust like that of a hot coal exposed to the cold air; yet its heat can still be felt, and it glows out sometimes. The tone of his poetry is not so much gloomy as sombre; there is nothing about it of dejection, still less of despair; it is solemn, at times grim, with outbreaks of grave beauty that may extend over a whole poem. Mann is the most honest of artists; he accepts and refuses to romanticize the hard facts of experience, but though they weigh him down they do not overwhelm him, because to him life is still worth while; one of his most sombre and also one of his finest poems, "At Manly", whose theme is the nervous strain of modern life, is lifted out

[34] For some of these biographical details I am indebted to "Leonard Mann—Humanist", an article by Nettie Palmer in *Book News*, April 1947.

[35] And since the closing date of this History, *Elegiac and Other Poems* (Melbourne, 1957). For Mann's novels, see pp. 1137-43.

of what appears at first to be despair by the last verse, in which life triumphs over the conditions of life:[36]

Down below the combers drape
Rocks with bridal finery,
To the northward cape on cape
Thrusts a slavered snout to sea.

Peace, is there no peace?
On the beach
The waves are breaking
Without cease,
In the glare
The roofs are shaking.

. . .

Peace, is there no peace?
At the nerves
The mind is tearing
Without cease,
On the man
The world is wearing.

Peace?
Who will to live
They wish no peace
That death can give.

This poem is not typical of Mann; it conveys the shake and shuddering of the nerves with an artistry that he does not show elsewhere; more characteristic is "The Dark Dominions", in which

The dark age triumphs. Yet lights at distance
Show here and there, solacing each other
With knowledge of like hope, of resistance
Within that the conqueror fails to smother.

Here it is the exceptions, the seeds of hope, that redeem what would otherwise be sheer gloom; elsewhere it is the enduring energy that pervades Mann's poetry and is quite incompatible with anything like despair, and the images of the beauty that may glow from a facet of evil, of disaster: examples are the description of the exhausted earth in "Summer Pastoral",

Only the tiger snake
Chilled by its blood's own cold
Flows slowly through the dust
From its innermost fold;

in "Before the Crash",

---

[36] *Plumed Voice*, p. 24.

> . . . when the plane loses its speed and rolls
> Into a spin the stars swim by in shoals;

and in "The Garden",

> Here a green shield abates
> The javelins of heat.

In spite of his lack of illusion, Mann stands, not with the

> Older men who have no hope beyond death,
> Robing themselves in tattered memories,

but with the young men who

> . . . will pursue
> Mirage, drink heavenly dew
> While the lost body's thirst
> Laps on a sand accursed:

with them he can say,

> The imperishable now
> Is ours. We pluck the bough
> Golden within the grove
> And walk in light with love;

and now and then, as in another of his best poems, "The Earth", the vision itself is of beauty:[37]

> Minute made visible and heard,
> Fact born of space by lust of time,
> The aftermath of the first word,
> Mote dried from a drift of slime;
>
> Earth 'tis enough to know but this,
> You give such beauty to our eyes
> And all our senses, here love is
> And the dream-stuff of Paradise.

Mann faces life with as great a courage and ultimate confidence as FitzGerald; but instead of adopting a point of view from which things as they are represent only an incidental moment in the ocean of change, of becoming, he stands amidst the strain and weariness of the struggle, and yet refuses to allow them to warp his point of view: his flag flies indomitably even above defeat; he is indeed a more vigorous and outspoken opponent of defeatism and the "death-wish" of Eliot and his followers than any other Australian poet.[38] This finds literal expression in the title-poem of *The Delectable Mountains*: unfortunately

---

[37] *Plumed Voice*, p. 22.

[38] See p. 961, note 26.

renderings of ballet scenes have obviously influenced her work; she taught art and art appreciation at Frensham; was engaged on cipher work with the R.A.N. during the second World War, and was, before her marriage, on the editorial staff of a well-known firm of Sydney publishers. Apart from an early and privately printed collection of poems, she has published *In a Convex Mirror* (Sydney, 1944) and *The Ship of Ice* (Sydney, 1948);[44] the title-piece of the second book won the *Sydney Morning Herald's* poetry prize in 1946. Love of pictures and of the making of pictures; interest in design and in humanity, a little remote; interest in the painters of pictures; grace, delicacy and lightness and precision of touch: some of the elements in Miss Dobson's poetry are clearly derivative from or at least allied with her inheritance or training. But this is not true of all of them: her mind is of a predominantly intellectual cast; she sees persons, scenes and actions against a background of universals, into which they fade; she is haunted by the dream and drift of time, and by the clock, its minister and symbol; her first book especially is sprinkled thickly with references to these,[45] and, less frequently, to silence and dream. She searches through time,

> Moving in mist down unfrequented pathways;

finding scenes, images, storm, a ship

> Becalmed in Time and sealed with a cork of ice;

or through revelations of old legends:

> Time was a dream, and I could raise
> The ghost of that gold-crested bird
> Who lit the morning sky with flame
> When Helen slipped from Paris' arms
> And all the ships set sail for Troy.

She looks forward in time as well as backward, so that

> Time in [her] ticking clock becomes
> A desperate traveller of the night,
> Heard hooves down highways of the mind
> Beating with midnight urgency.
> Past quiet pools pricked out with stars,
> Crusted with bright autumnal mire,
> He rides, with fire from flint and iron;
> Past leaning darkness fenced apart
> By hedges white with final dust.
> He needs no sign, but wheels and turns
> Obedient to the wheeling sky,
> And rides to warn—but whom he warns
> I know not, and I fear to know;

[44] She has since published another book of verse, *Child With a Cockatoo* (Sydney, 1955).
[45] In the two books together there are a couple of score of such references, explicit or implicit.

or she slips into the

> . . . silence between tick and tock,

set, as it were, in a frame of timelessness. Her world approaches the world of magic, of fairy-tale, as when she tells how her "Godmother in a crooked hat" taught her how "To spin good thread to pass the time", and how by the pricking of a finger to "plunge the whole world into sleep"; at least, as Miss Dobson truly says,

> She taught me how to spin a tale;

even the realities, or pseudo realities, of her second book, *The Ship of Ice*, are mixed with fairy-tale. The cream of this book is not the playlet but the series of pictorial dialogues in which Devil and Angel compete for the souls of painter, poet, cartographer, a scarecrow, Methuselah and a dying king: they are witty, amusing and sometimes fascinating, even if now and then their conclusions do not come as a surprise. Indeed, here as elsewhere, in construction, in character-creation, in rhythm even, Rosemary Dobson touches occasionally the edge of formula: each poem has its central idea, each character its summary conception, upon which the mind of its creator seems just a little too fixed; it may be that there is something lacking in her range of experience, so that she does not always find it easy to round out a conception, even within the narrow limits that she sets herself, to embody it fully with material that only the real world can provide.

Rosemary Dobson is a fine but not a perfect craftsman; she is at her best in the exact definition of her moods and impressions by means of phrase and image. Her rhythms, though in particular cases individual enough, tend rather often towards the conventional; in her smooth, slow four or five-beat lines the beats recur so often without variation that they become at times just a little monotonous;[46] it is true that the monotony helps towards the predominant dream-like effect, and may therefore be to some extent deliberate, but it becomes nevertheless a defect, which occurs even in some of her best poems. In the second book the rhythms are freer, easier, and there is a characteristic use of the feminine ending; the wording also is less concise, more easy-going, sometimes a little verbose even: now and then one wonders whether the need has not been felt to fill up some of those free and easy lines, a need which is just not made evident.[47] But the occasional weakness of the rhythms

---

[46] See, for example, the first two lines of "In a Convex Mirror", the first seven of "Over the Hill", the first four of "In a Cafe" (*In a Convex Mirror*).

[47] For example:

> Pardon me if the story reads obscurely
>
> ("The Dutch Tavern Portrait");

is more than balanced by the originality of the images, most of which seem to arise quite simply and naturally in their maker's mind: the still room is "brushed with dusk"; the eyes of the homeward-bound workman are

> . . . facing west
> To take the lemon-coloured light
> While the day slowly drains away;

the brows of the plotters are "cross-hatched with evil". Some of the images are more striking, as of the girl who

> . . . leant on the iron railing
> In a parroty dress with eyes on the tipsy soldiers;

or of the branch broken from the plum-tree,

> The white foam running like light along the bough;

or of the whale that

> Outstrips their chase in a bubbling worry of foam;

or of the scarecrow

> With a hat full
> Of bird's song
> And a heart of gold straw:

or they pierce a little deeper, as

> I suppose if you kill what you hate you kill yourself;

or in the description of death as

> . . . the most naked journey.

The best and most characteristic of the first collection, for example the title-poem, and "The Rider", which has been quoted, are little cameos, facets of a reflective fancy, whose defects are merely incidental and scarcely visible except under the critical glass; more obviously and deliberately individual, "Cockerel Sun" is an attractive little *tour de force*. In the second collection reality is still at a first remove: here, the most characteristic as well as the best of the poems are contained in the Devil and Angel series, in which we perceive, according to the point of view, angelic or diabolic, either

---

> I kept a memo folded in my garment;
> Having a slight forgetfulness to combat
> I arm myself against it
> ("Methuselah")
>
> . . . a Southerner's invention
> ("Painter of Antwerp").

All these are from *The Ship of Ice*.

A cornucopia of falling brilliance,
Light trembling from the chandelier and music,
Rustle of talk and laughter, flame on silk,

or

. . . a shell, its hollows filled with shadows
Where spiders plot devices in the corners
And dust dries up the dregs from fallen glasses.

In these and the other short sketches in this book Rosemary Dobson shows an insight into character that was possessed by the old Dutch masters of painting, though it does not go so deep, and is not expressed with such realistic effect. Besides human insight, there are in these Devil and Angel poems a quiet humour and a rich and individual fancy: the result is a series of sparkling dramatic miniatures, and more than miniatures, seeing that they contain movement, action; something of Browning is traceable at the back of them, but only if one looks for it, and then only as an element in their ancestry: light, fanciful, now and then extravagant if you like, one can come back to them again and again. If some of their themes are by no means novel, by conception and treatment all have been individualized: the cartographer for example, who is not satisfied with either heaven or hell but wants both of them to explore; the poet who wants only time for the completion of his great epic; give him a year or two and he will, to the half-concealed satisfaction of devil and angel both, immortalize them in his poem:

"Hold, hold," the poet said. "Stand thus a moment,
It wants a phrase here—there, that's your description
Neatly wrote up against Eternity.
Thanks, gentlemen, the door awaits behind you . . .
Forgive me for not rising;
I have an ode conceived that waits delivery."

And thus we found ourselves upon the doorstep.
"Well—!" said the Devil,
And "Well—!" I said upon the self-same instant.

Apart from local influences,[48] the most evident influence in the poems of the first book is that of De La Mare, in "Moving in Mist".[49] In one poem[50] there is a touch of Eliot and, in a single line, a touch of Hopkins.[51] In connection with the second book Browning has already been mentioned, but at the back of much of it stands Slessor, whose Atlas poems

[48] And such a deliberate reflection as appears in "The Tempest" (*In a Convex Mirror*, p. 9).
[49] And perhaps also in a couple of lines of "The Idlers":

The soul divides the darkness
In haste to be gone.
(*In a Convex Mirror*)

[50] "In a Cafe" (the same).
[51] "Look close at the wavering, stayed now, coralline branches" ("Moving in a Mist"; the same).

are obvious in "The Cartographer" and "Traveller's Tale"; the tendency towards the dramatically historical has obviously affected Rosemary Dobson in these and in "The Ship of Ice" and one or two other poems. An individual line recalls FitzGerald[52] and another recalls Judith Wright:[53] but there is nothing illegitimate in any of these echoings; it would be unnatural for a writer to be unaffected by his reading either of the classics or of his contemporaries. Rosemary Dobson's reading has been digested and absorbed, she reflects for herself, and, if enlarged experience of life should carry her outward into a deeper and more realistic synthesis, that will not detract from the quality of the work she has done already.

William Hart-Smith (Tunbridge Wells, England, 1911-) is another example of the catalytic effect upon a young migrant writer of the impact of this so new and different country; he came to Australia via New Zealand and has returned there, but he served in the A.I.F. and Australia has had a considerable influence on his poetic work. The Australian influence has been canalized in two channels: Hart-Smith was caught up first by the Jindyworobak movement[54] and then by the historico-dramatic movement that has been mentioned, and he has written some of the most interesting of the poems that this movement has produced. Generally speaking his attitude is modern, except in the importance he attaches to clarity; most of his verse is in irregular unrhymed lines and he is among the few who understand the art of making free verse: occasionally however the lines are regular and occasionally he uses a suggestion of rhyme, or half-rhymes, or straight-out rhymes, which are introduced as a rule at crucial points, to hammer down an effect;[55] as a rule he uses capitals only as they are used in prose, but there are exceptions in his earlier books. Hart-Smith has published four small books of verse: *Columbus Goes West* (Adelaide, 1943), *Harvest* (Melbourne, 1945), *The Unceasing Ground* (Sydney, 1946), and *Christopher Columbus* (Christchurch, N.Z., 1948); of these the last is by far the best. His work is so distinctive that none of it is likely to be taken for another man's; not that it is entirely free from reminiscences: in "We are the Elders",[56] the verse about the children of the aborigines, "Young old men with dry tongues", suggests Eliot. There are also echoes of Francis Thompson in "Spider" and "The Fugitive", which were probably written with an unconscious recollection of "The Snowflake" and "The Hound of Heaven"; and the free verse may owe something to Pound;[57] but even these influences have been more or less translated into Hart-Smith's

---

52 "Here's my Tom Tiddler's Land of danger" ("In My End is My Beginning", *The Ship of Ice*).
53 "Night draws his convoys in" ("The Dancing Ships", the same).
54 See pp. 1069-70.
55 This is seen especially in the Columbus poems.
56 *Columbus Goes West*, p. 4.
57 See, on this point and on others, an excellent article in the Red Page of the *Bulletin*, 30th June 1948.

own idiom and are anyhow negligible in the mass of his work. Without the force, the intensity of Mann's poetic personality or the free imaginative vision of Rosemary Dobson, he is almost as individual as either. He observes and analyses with a patient, scrupulous exactness, reflects and synthesizes and transmits his results almost in skeleton form, with a dry, clear-cut conciseness that is yet pictorial and dramatic. A good example of the earlier work in which he writes as a Jindyworobak is "Nullarbor", in which he analyses simply, directly and most conscientiously a characteristic impression of the empty, rimless, red Australian desert, and of a figure in whom its essence is concentrated and given life. It is a striking record, but it is no more than a record, addressed to the rational rather than to the imaginative understanding, and lacking in the illuminating fusion which produces poetry; yet it gets there, or almost there, by virtue of the poet's individuality, of his honesty and indefatigable determination, and of a freshness that no labour can entirely overlay. This, and the character-study "Moondeen" are among the best of those Jindyworobak poems which attempt to capture the spirit of Australia or of the Australian aborigine, and to give appropriate expression to either without the help or hindrance of elements from overseas. But even in his first three books only one aspect of Hart-Smith's talent was occupied with Jindyworobakism; other aspects, psychological, intellectual, analytic, and more and more historical found at the same time a quite different expression, and his last book is concerned with a different world. His vision has its limits and qualifications, so that sometimes the central idea is by no means novel, and sometimes the results of his meditations are obvious: a number of such poems are merely sketches not far removed from the commonplace. But elsewhere, as in "Said Those Hands" or "Flame the Cat", these defects almost disappear; in an occasional image, as in that of the stone that

> repeats what the sky is saying
> as the sun goes down,

he achieves the poetic fusion whose lack elsewhere has been noted; and "Spider"[58] is, for all its reminiscence of "The Snowflake" and its slightness, a glimpse of delicate beauty which, incidentally, owes much of its crystalline quality to its rhyme. Hart-Smith takes the greatest pains to form a clear conception and to communicate it exactly and in full: communication is with him of the essence of poetry, and in the art of communication he has a high degree of proficiency; if he cannot sound the well to the bottom, he makes it clear how far he has gone. On the other hand, in the bulk of his work, though not so much in the Columbus poems, he tends to concentrate first on the idea and then

[58] *Columbus Goes West*, p. 12.

upon its expression, instead of upon the making of a poem of which the idea should be an indissoluble part: his determination to sound as deeply as possible is accompanied by a determination to make the most of what he finds, and these together give some of his poems an air of effort, of artificiality even. But in *Christopher Columbus* many of these limitations are transcended; some of the best of this series of poems had been published in the preceding collections separately, but they gain very greatly from their appearance as parts of a sequence: we now see Columbus, if not quite in the round, at least as a character as well sketched as Slessor's Cook or FitzGerald's Tasman, though the poems are not comparable as poems. We get glimpses of the attitude of the time; of the ignorance and religious and philosophical prejudices Columbus had to face; of his ideals and his long struggle to obtain the means of realizing them before it is too late:

Elbows in wine-shops, news of the ocean isles
they tell in taverns under a stinking lamp.
Madre de Dios, here is evidence!

And once a swollen corpse, a woman's,
naked, tattooed, face-down in a scum
of jellyfish and weed . . .

And bits of wood to Santo sometimes come,
most strangely carved.

The woman drowned, they say, had almond eyes.
Masters, a ship, a ship, for my youth dies!

And then we are led on to the actual voyages, with their doubts and dangers and betrayals and loneliness; and finally to the strange wonder, the fearful triumph of the first to attain[59] the legendary unknown. We begin with a felicitous and individual expression of the warm tranquillity that follows upon the resolution of preliminary difficulties and the opening of the way towards the goal; and then, the central and finest poem of the series, "Space":[60]

Columbus looks towards the New World,
the sea is flat and nothing breaks the rim
of the world's disc;
he takes the sphere with him.

Day into night the same, the only change
the living variation at the core
of this man's universe;
and silent on the silver ship he broods.

---

[59] From Europe, that is, and excepting the Norsemen.

[60] p. 23.

Red gouts of weed, and skimming fish, to crack
the stupefying emptiness of sea,
night, and the unimpassioned gaze of stars. . . .

And God be praised for the compass, oaths
bawled in the fo'c'sle,
broken heads and wine,
song and guitars,
the tramp of boots,
the wash and whip of brine.

"Time", "Sargasso Weed and a Crab", "Westward, Seven Hundred and Fifty Leagues", "Landfall [3]", "The Land of Mangon": each is a sharp little etching in a psychological frame, fine things, even torn out of their context; and finally there are the subsequent voyages, their disappointments, and their ultimate reward. A succession of glimpses, a skeleton epic in psychological pictures, *Christopher Columbus* is yet impressive and revealing by reason particularly of those illuminative images which had occurred only occasionally before:

the Lord sent a drowsiness upon us;

he wound up the ravel of the wind
on the rod of his arm,
and in the calm set a current of the sea
to twist our ship towards the shore;

and there is the fascinating spectacle of the waterspout, with the ejaculation, so appropriate as to be inevitable:

They saw a rope of cloud twist down
and a tongue of sea drawn up as the whirlwind blew,
drinking the ocean up in a plume of foam.
'Santa Maria, look! . . . how far is home!';

there is the poem "Time", which is a single image; and the image of the savage who

. . . walks as if he had no body
and had no thought therefore
to clothe it.

Hart-Smith is still a comparatively young man; if in his next book he can make in range and quality as great an advance on *Christopher Columbus* as that did on his other books, he will be among the leaders in the poetic world on this side or the other of the Tasman.

"The Waste Land" was first published[61] in 1923, but Eliot's influence was not strongly evident in Australia until the early thirties; *Cuckooz Contrey* appeared in 1932, though there were, as has been said already,

[61] In book-form.

suggestions of Eliot in Slessor's earlier work, and about the same time other young Australian poets showed that they had been reading Eliot. Bertram Higgins (Melbourne, 1901-74) had his schooling in Melbourne, but afterwards took a degree at Oxford and was for a while on the staff of the *Spectator*; he served in the R.A.F. during the second World War, returned to Australia and then lived in Melbourne. During 1931 he contributed to *Stream*,[62] working at the same time upon "Mordecaius Overture", which was published separately in Melbourne in 1933. Outside a small coterie Higgins is almost unknown, but it includes several prominent writers and critics and within it he has been magnified above Eliot himself.[63] Higgins's is one of those divided talents in which a predominant interest in the world of thought is accompanied by a genuine and individual poetic ability devoted largely though not wholly to its service; in such cases the unity which is of the essence of poetry, and which implies a sublimation of thought in emotion, must be comparatively rare. There is also a risk of so close a concentration upon the development of the idea and its formulation as part of the poet's mental landscape that insufficient attention is paid to objectivizing it in the world outside the poet and his associates and admirers, and into this defect Higgins, like others of the tribe of Eliot, has fallen: it is as though the maternal activities were concentrated upon the development of the foetus without bothering much about its delivery. Of "The Confrontation", a poem included in a volume that was never published, even so acute and sympathetic an admirer as Professor Chisholm declared that it was "really too obscure";[64] Higgins himself must have realized that the poem needed a great deal of explanation, for he supplied[65] a prose commentary of more than 3000 words. It is an interesting and in some respects a beautiful poem and contains one or two memorable images, notably that of the voice that speaks "an octave higher than the ears"; and there are some interesting but unsuccessful experiments in rhyme. "Mordecaius Overture" is longer and more ambitious, though still a short poem; it seems shorter still because it is so tightly packed with meaning: it is, in the main, a soliloquy between the Judaeo-Roman world in which Mordecaius is deeply rooted and the new order that is represented by Christ and Christianity. He has watched the Crucifixion and is now watching the volcanic eruption that overwhelmed Pompeii, from which he with difficulty escapes. The Crucifixion has always haunted him, and the Pompeiian disaster revives it in his mind, as he works his way with

---

[62] See pp. 1331-2.

[63] Professor A. R. Chisholm thinks that "in the poetic quality of 'The Confrontation' and the metaphysical range of the 'Mordecaius' Higgins surpasses T. S. Eliot" (letter to me, 21st January 1930): but some of Higgins's admirers have gone much farther.

[64] *Australian National Review*, Dec. 1, 1938.

[65] At the request of the editors of *Stream*, in which the poem first appeared.

difficulty towards safety through falling cinders and lightning-split darkness. But all this has a mental and spiritual reference also, for Mordecaius is at the same time trying to work his way through the moral and intellectual problems of his own life, towards some settled decision between the opposing calls upon him by the old faith and order and the new:

> Go where the lightning points? Or where the penumbra glows?
> Madness, to tempt new lands by a forked and fitful path
> While the old House, split to its hearth, still stands.
> Down the long slope I go. . . .
> There where the calm clouds pile, how softly unrolls
> The Past in a white fume of waving scrolls!

The title of the poem seems to suggest that the theme is to be developed along musical lines, touching upon one section after another and interweaving them; but it might also indicate that it was intended as a prologue to a longer poem on the subject, or to Mordecaius's subsequent decision, which has not been reached when the poem ends: quite possibly all three are intended. The soliloquy is interrupted by three other voices, which are indicated in different ways: the Paschal angel, the angel of the Jewish Passover, whose speeches are set in inverted commas; a "lout", who merely interjects, and whose remarks are italicized; and, in single inverted commas, what may be intended to represent a stratum of Mordecaius's consciousness, or of his unconscious mind. And, if this were not complicated enough, a number of sentences, apart from the lout's italicized words, are bracketed. It is possible that all the voices, even the Angel's, may represent diffeient levels in Mordecaius's conscious or unconscious mind, and it seems likely that the lout at least represents a vulgar element in Mordecaius, or in man, for Mordecaius seems to be not merely an individual but also man in general: this poem shadows forth beauty, and power also, but both are so heavily veiled that even their contours are obscured and it is impossible to grasp them in detail. The verse is free and for the most part unrhymed, but there are occasional rhymes, some of them complete, some incomplete and some internal, in a manner that is effective though not novel; this is illustrated in the dramatic close of the poem. Some fine phrases, touches of drama, an obvious appreciation of verbal music, a feeling throughout of poetry under a self-imposed cloud; a general attitude, intellectual, moral and aesthetic, that reminds one of Eliot, as well as numerous echoings of Eliot: Higgins is never likely to be much more than a name and an example of talent obstructed and confined; but even as such he has his place in Australian poetry. Of the work of the other members of the group, *Lilacs Out of the Dead Land* (Melbourne, 1932), a youthful production by Edgar George Holt (Burnley, Lancashire, England, 1904-), who was educated in Brisbane and became editor of *Smith's Weekly*, reflects a number of the later romantic poets as well as Eliot, but it contains also one or two striking images. *Outside Looking In* (Melbourne, 1933), a collection of poems which first appeared in *Art in Australia* as early as 1930, combines an even more Eliotean attitude and manner and a youthful and satiric energy to such an incongruous effect as to suggest a mask; its author, Stanley Clive Perry Turnbull (Glenorchy, Tas.,[66] 1906-75), was Acting Editor of the *Argus*, was attached to the Ministry of Munitions and was later Public Relations Officer to the University of Melbourne; he also published a number of historical biographies. The third member of the group, Joseph (Henry) O'Dwyer (Melbourne, 1912-), published nothing in book-form until much later, but his verse, though in matter and manner indebted to Eliot, shows nevertheless a marked individuality. He took an Arts degree at the University of Queensland, has been public servant, school-teacher and farmer, and now lives in Melbourne. The theme of his principal poem, "The Trojan Doom",[67] is the decay of society and the individual, the emptiness of life and its disillusion, the world's unrest, the mind's uncertainty. The poem is included in O'Dwyer's *Poems* (Melbourne, 1941), and its thesis underlies the rest of the book also, and is the basis of his second book, *The Turning Year* (Melbourne, 1944), though that is in form a series of poems on the seasons. O'Dwyer has a preference for free verse with a few rhymes, but in his principal poem and in his second book the verse is more regular; he is a strictly meditative poet, and all his meditations are in a mood of gloom. "The Trojan Doom" was obviously written with "The Waste Land" in mind, and here and elsewhere there are many echoes of "The Waste Land",[68] but these echoes are after all subsidiary and the verse as a whole is individual; earnest, ironic, dignified, and expressed with a sometimes rather rugged force: Man, says O'Dwyer, has

---

[66] Turnbull afterwards published a better and less Eliotean book, *Fourteen Poems* (Melbourne, 1944).

[67] It was awarded the C. J. Dennis Memorial Prize for 1941.

[68] See, for instance,

> When the garbage tins are ravaged
> in the privacy of alleys
> ("The Trojan Doom");
> the no more toil of foetid afternoon
> with stalebread smells
> ("The Schoolboys");

and

> What can we hope for in our generation
> but the hair greying about the temples of an old frustration
> ("Pilgrimage").

> . . . blighted for the body's ends
> the spirit's pledge
> pleading necessity;

this and "the monstrous city" and "the swift infection of the commonwealth", reflect "the jerry-building of our universe". Sometimes O'Dwyer is prosy, sometimes the results of his meditations are rather obvious and his irony rather cheap, and he has a queer fondness for out-of-the-way words; but he can brighten into a sharp image, and at his best he shows a feeling for slow, sonorous and rather heavy rhythms, as

> May it not happen that in the dark night,
> though the earth seem confident of her sombre power
> to hold one's feet, when the cocks crow dimly near
> and the cows, alone on a low wide plain,
> bassoon their urge, or the fleeting cars
> sprinkle their nervous trumpetings below,
> the soul may be released from labouring
> the pitiful prayer, and wholly take her charge
> into the unthreatened peace of contemplation.

There remain a number of intellectuals, who conform to no natural grouping; of those who have presumably though by no means inevitably realized their full powers, three women and a couple of men stand out by reason of their individuality of manner and outlook. Ethel (Louise) Anderson (*née* Mason, Leamington, England, 1883-1958); was of Australian parentage and was educated in Sydney, where she lived, except that she spent the first ten years of her married life in India. She published, besides essays and short stories, two books of verse: *Squatters' Luck* (Melbourne, 1942) and *Sunday at Yarralumla* (Sydney 1947).[69] Mrs Anderson's is a sophisticated and eccentric talent, twisted and variegated by euphuisms and playful conceits; nevertheless it finds expression sometimes in interesting experiments with sound and rhythm and sometimes in an unexpected freshness and sincerity. Her first book contains a number of ballads which will be discussed later;[70] in her second book the sophisticate is for the most part at play, but here and there, as in "Love in Age", the sincere and unaffected poet shows through, creating a thing of beauty:

> Where the fountain murmurs in the shade
> Gilds the leaning lily stems with dew
> Lovelier than the mystery of birth,
>
> Stars the drooping iris hearts with light
> Brighter than the radiances of life,
> Two old lovers speak of love in age.
>
> . . . .

---

[69] And, since the closing date of this History, *The Song of Hagar* (Sydney, 1957). For Mrs Anderson's short stories, see p. 1255; for her essays, p. 1279.

[70] See pp. 1062-3.

Still, the fountain, murmurous in shade,
Still, the leaning lilies, wet with dew;
Gone the lovers to a longer night.

Betty (Elizabeth Richmond) Riddell (Mrs E. N. Greatorex, Napier, N.Z., 1909-), a Sydney journalist who has travelled in Europe and the United States, has published *The Untrammelled* (Sydney, 1940) and *Poems* (Sydney, 1948). Her verse is bitter sometimes but always restrained, clear-cut and definite, and some of her imagery is full of colour, as in the poem about the old sailor who

... dreams of a little island
Rolling like an apple in the wide green sea.

The third member of this group, (Olive) Mary Finnin (Mrs J. J. Connellan, Geelong, Vic., 1906-) was educated at the University of Melbourne; before her marriage she was a teacher of art; her vision is seldom penetrative, and she has seldom anything very notable to say, yet there is sincerity and depth of feeling about her austere and rather formal verses, so that one continually expects from them what somehow never appears. She is at her best in a few images, as in

Thought spins in pin-point light—
the thief of time.[71]

The poems in *Ritual Dance* (Melbourne, 1939) and *Blue Prints* (Melbourne, 1944), by Donovan (Charles) Clarke (Bristol, England, 1907-), are terse, dry, analytic, with occasional romantic touches; Clarke, who has been teacher, critic and lecturer in Australia, has one memorable image, that tells how some day

... the past will rise with the sweet, sharp smell of camphor,
As a moth comes fluttering out of a fold in Time,

but he has been unable to rise to its level again. John (Joseph Meagher) Thompson (Melbourne, 1907-68), was a graduate of the University of Melbourne, served in the second A.I.F., and then worked on the senior staff of the A.B.C., where he was well known for his "Quality Street" and other broadcasts. In his principal book, *Sesame* (Sydney, 1943),[72] he also is at his best in a memorable image, in which he tells how

... everlasting moments cry
like golden trumpets in my blood;

---

[71] "Watch Tower" (*Alms for Oblivion*, Melbourne, 1947); this is one of a number of small collections of verse, but she has since published a book of verse, *The Shield of Place* (Sydney, 1958).

[72] After 1950 he published another book of verse, *Thirty Poems* (Sydney, 1954), and, with Slessor and Howarth, compiled *The Penguin Book of Australian Verse* (London, 1958).

but he has also other good images, as of the

> . . . clock in the half gloom
> chipping the moments from the day,
> snicking them leaf by leaf away,
> yet mesmerising Time himself
> till each particular hour distends
> infinitely, and never ends.

Thompson's verse is more vigorous and in its leftist feeling more outspoken than Clarke's, and one gets the impression that there is more in him than has been yet expressed.

Of the younger intellectuals, Francis (Charles) Webb (Adelaide, 1925–73) became, on the release of his first book, along with David Campbell,[73] the most promising of today's Australian poets. He went to school in Sydney, served in the R.A.A.F. in England and Canada and worked mainly as a clerk. [In later years he spent some time as a patient in psychiatric hospitals.] "A Drum for Ben Boyd",[74] which was published in book-form in Sydney in 1948 after appearing in the *Bulletin* as a serial, is a historical poem of about 500 lines; it takes a high place in the movement towards historic narrative and depiction of historic characters that followed upon the poems of this type by Slessor and FitzGerald: its form may have been suggested by Slessor's "Five Visions of Captain Cook", and in its sinewy line and masculine directness and vigour it has something in common with FitzGerald, though nothing of his youthful and confident spirit. For a poem written, as it was, when the author was only twenty-two, this is an extraordinary performance; the grasp of character is especially surprising in so young a writer. The people through whose eyes we catch prejudiced and conflicting glimpses of the central character: a disgruntled journalist, a half-drunken whaler, an old Norwegian boatshed-owner, a marine artist whom Boyd had brought out with him, a Papuan native, a malevolent pioneer of the district that Boyd had made almost his own, a politician, the commander of the vessel that had been sent out to search for Boyd, an old sea-captain stranded on an office chair: all these are real and striking, with a touch of satire; and if Boyd himself is less solid and definite, that fits in well enough with his legendary as well as his historic qualities, with their invitations to discordance and imaginations. Webb's poetic gift is unmistakable; for example in the Author's Prologue,

> It is in the dawn-watch, picked clean of colour and star,
> That the giants of the past gird on forgotten power;

---

[73] See pp. 1059–62.

[74] This was awarded the Grace Leven Prize for the year's best book of poems; Webb later published *Leichhardt in Theatre* (Sydney, 1952), which also had first appeared as a serial in the *Bulletin*, and *Birthday* (Sydney, 1953).

in the marine painter's

> Sometimes a tale
> Lags about like smoke on the sluggish wharves;

and in the old pioneer's

> I have loved two things deeply: the earth and silence,
> Two giant bulks furrowed by cold harmony.

John (Streeter) Manifold (Melbourne, 1915-) had his schooling at the Geelong Grammar School, graduated at Cambridge and in the second World War served in the British army, in which he became a captain in the Intelligence Corps. Manifold is a passionate lover of music, and has published editions of English and French instrumental chamber works of the seventeenth century: his *Selected Verse* (New York, 1946), shows an extremely versatile talent, ranging over ballad, lyric, song, sonnet and satire, always vigorous and aggressive, but handicapped by a bitterness that is for the most part political, and by journalistic carelessness; he has imagination and feels deeply but is at his best when he canalizes his bitterness in sheer satire. The third of the younger poets, Frederick John Blight (Unley, S.A., 1913-) was trained as an accountant, worked on an orange orchard and at ringbarking and kangaroo shooting, and became an administrative officer with the Commissioner of Prices, Brisbane, and then a member of the Queensland State Timber Industry Enquiry Commission. In *The Old Pianist* (Sydney, 1945)[75] he shows himself, by comparison with the other two, quiet, calm, restrained; a ruminative poet, who approaches his subjects in a manner that is quite his own and rather fascinating. His images are of an unusual type: there is the hurricane lantern, the bush slattern, which dances of nights

> . . . with lambent flame,
> In a shawl of lace, her flying-ant mantle.
>
> . . .
>
> With her pungent smut
> She filled the room till, putting her out,
> The barman swore and the customers choked.

And, in "To a Farmer, Fencing", there is the vision of the spiderweb of wires with which the farmer enmeshes his stock, and with which he himself is enmeshed by some city spider, who

> Lurks out of sight of web upon a thread
> That links a telephone beside his bed;
> He sets his net and seldom after toils,
> But sleeps and smiles and feasts upon the spoils.

---

[75] He has since published *The Two Suns Met* (Sydney, 1954).

Blight is one of those who, to use his own words, which recall those of Brennan's Wanderer, strives

> . . . to lead the mind's procession
> Out of the town, beyond the last house, through the woods,
> Till the soul comes through the wilderness, and the world's fires
> Expire on their last hearth.

[Both Blight and Manifold have more than fulfilled their early promise, though they have had less attention from critics than they deserve, and have exercised less influence on younger poets than Webb, perhaps for reasons which have nothing to do with literature. Manifold's "The Tomb of Lt. John Learmonth, A.I.F." from *Selected Verse* is one of the finest of Australian elegies.]

CHAPTER IV

VERSE

LYRICAL AND LYRICALLY DESCRIPTIVE POETS

Debatable Ground: Macartney; Vrepont; Grano. Judith Wright. Poets of Love: Mackenzie; Moore; Lesbia Harford; McCuaig. Folk-ballad Affiliations: Douglas Stewart; Hopegood

IN THE debatable ground between the two main groups into which the poets of today have been roughly and for convenience divided are three poets who may therefore be taken together, though they were quite unlike one another. Frederick Thomas Bennett Macartney (Melbourne, 1887-1980), the most firmly established and also the most accomplished of the three artists, linked not only two different kinds of poetry but, like his friend Wilmot, the poetry of two Periods. He was only six years younger than Wilmot, but the tone of his work as a whole is definitely more modern: its reflections, in attitude and phraseology, of the poetry of the later romantic age do not stand out like Wilmot's; they take the shape rather of a light sentiment that is sometimes sentimental than of those outbreaks of romantic emotion which characterize Wilmot and are almost unknown in the English and Australian poetry of today. Macartney has less poetic fire than Wilmot, and when he burns it is usually with a drier and more regulated flame; his emotional expression is not only less forcible but much less outright, and it is reined and guided by a rational and dispassionate intelligence. He was educated in Melbourne, and worked as a clerk, a shorthand reporter, a freelance journalist, and bookkeeper on a Riverina sheep station, and for some years he was employed as Clerk of Courts, Sheriff and Public Trustee in the Northern Territory; as well as lecturing for the Commonwealth Literary Fund in several universities, he also edited and rearranged Miller's *Australian Literature* and prepared the article on literature for the new edition of *The Australian Encyclopaedia*. Macartney published a number of booklets of verse, which were collected in *Preferences*[1] (Sydney, 1941), and followed by *Ode of Our Times* (Melbourne, 1944), *Gaily the Troubadour* (Melbourne, 1946), and *Tripod for Homeward Incense* (Sydney, 1947). He is a lightweight by comparison with the leaders of Australian poetry, but it would be easy to lay too much emphasis upon this fact: he handles his material with so graceful an artistry that there is a danger of assuming that the result must lack substance; of the best of his work such an

[1] To this volume all references here are made, unless stated otherwise.

assumption would be quite mistaken, but a proportion of it has some affiliation with the old-fashioned album verse, in that it achieves a rather facile prettiness upon some subject that does not matter very much to the poet or anybody else; examples are "Colours of Love" and "Passenger", but even the dainty "Veronica"[2] would not be out of place in a Victorian album whose contributors included poets as well as poetasters. To this aspect of Macartney's poetry belong the romantic reflections that have been referred to; for example the couplet,

> You that love roses, now the rose is dead
> What garland can I give you but a song?;[3]

on the other hand even the most trifling of Macartney's verses have usually about them a certain distinction and a perhaps faint but still evident astringency that differentiate them from what they may superficially resemble. But he is often rambling and diffuse; in his brain fancies flicker here and there like butterflies,[4] which he follows gracefully but indiscriminately through verse after verse; and his rhythms are often so conventional that one prepares immediately to be bored: it is a preparation doomed happily to disappointment, but in his verse the regular five-beat line is worked to death. And finally, there is about almost all of it a smoothness, a restraint that sometimes gives the impression of not being very difficult, and that especially handicaps his satires: this would not matter so much but that for those who read Macartney's verses the satires seldom break new ground; for those to whom they would be better addressed a more appropriate instrument than a rapier would be a sharp spike dipped in corrosive sublimate. Nevertheless at their best the delicate allusive wit of these satires is a delight; almost all of them are collected in *Gaily the Troubadour*, which incidentally shows a quite unusual mastery of such medieval poetic forms as the virelai, rondel, kyrielle and the rest, which were revived in England by Lang, Dobson and others in the seventies and eighties, and in the Australia of the nineties by Stephens, who introduced them to readers of the *Bulletin's* Red Page. A couple of satires are addressed to the politician:

> The Country Member has his say
> (Nymphs and shepherds, come away!);

and, from the "Hymn to Canberra":

> And this is where the books are banned:
>   Was it for girl-guide and boy-scout
> Our nation's leaders fitly planned?

---

[2] p. 49.

[3] Others are "the arches of this Austral night" (*Preferences*, p. 37) and "a lilt of lilies" (*Ode of Our Times*, p. 12).

[4] See *Tripod For Homeward Incense*. Unfortunately the pages of this little book are not numbered. The page mentioned contains the line, "White butterflies flicker, as in me these fancies."

One should pink some university lecturers:

> The blowfly comes again
> To lecture in a small
> Slow academic drawl;

there is also the Press, whose

> picture pages sublimate
> . . . aspects of the nearly great
> To please the nearly literate;

and the radio, by whose devices

> Silence, the hell of fools, is conquered too.

Macartney's verse has sometimes that rare quality, charm; this is exemplified especially in "Bargain Basement",[5] which in its own kind would be hard to equal:

> Not there, my dear, not there:
> this way—down the stair.
>
> Have you a line of hillocks and some white
> absurd young lambs, all wool, and light
> as leaping air?
>
> No, sir—sorry! . . .
> Alright, don't worry.
>
> You keep, perhaps
> some inexpensive scraps
> of early green
> springtime sateen,
> with colour partly lost
> in folds of frost,
> prinked with those flowers that smell
> so sweetly?—I know them well
> but can't recall the name:
> I saw them somewhere a month ago.
>
> Unfortunately, madam, no. . . .
> Ah, what a shame!
>
> . . . .
>
> Then, do you stock
> that delicate sort of frock
> now worn by blossoming orchards, thin,
> wide and airy, like a crinoline?
>
> No, madam, no; but I might find . . .
> O, never mind.

---

[5] p. 114.

Come on, my dear:
there's nothing for us here.
Thank goodness, we still have, in the Lay By
(for what it's worth
when we two die)
that remnant double-width of damaged earth.

Similar qualities combine with gentle reminiscence in "Tripod for Homeward Incense", a poem in which an Australian wanderer in China is lured by an old incense tripod from the "indolent golden girl" who is "Dusting its flame with sandalwood" to the ancestor to whom it is dedicated,

Old Father Yi, whose thoughts were swans
Floating upon his lilied mind;

thence to the ancient and accomplished civilization which both represent; and thence again to the "hard, bare splendour" of the wanderer's own country. Macartney's poetry has other aspects, one of which is reflected in "Ode of Our Times," a philosophic poem about whose substance there is little that is particularly new or so stated that it presents itself as new, but which contains an aphorism that might be a useful irritant,

Philosophy is a serious simpleton
Wondering why children play upon a hill;

and a definition whose relevance is obvious:

A freedom of blind cogs.

Another section of Macartney's poetry reflects his experiences of black and yellow and white in the far north, in which

Hard light cuts clear the edges of all shapes:

some of the poems in this section may have pointed the way for the Jindyworobaks. There remain the more overtly serious poems that are scattered sparingly through his work; one of the most effective of these is "You'll Know Love", at whose conclusion Macartney breaks out for once into forcible and outright statement:

You'll know love when it has taken
Body and soul and left both shaken.

Macartney's poems, being a mixture of opposites, retain the power to surprise; it is hard to form an accurate idea of his position in the world of Australian poetry, but it is certainly neither low nor among the highest.

The other two poets who stand in the debatable ground between the intellectuals and the lyrists have certain circumstances and characteristics in common: both were born in Victoria but moved to Queensland

and have done their best work there, beginning under the stimulus of the poetic renascence that centred on *Meanjin* in the early forties, a renascence which they helped to create; both have also been fairly regular contributors to the Jindyworobak anthologies. Both, again, developed late: Brian Vrepont (Benjamin Arthur Truebridge, Melbourne, 1882–1955) did not find his way into print until he was fifty,[6] and his only book of verse, *Beyond the Claw* (Sydney 1943), did not appear until he was sixty-one; Paul (Langton) Grano (Ararat, Vic., 1894–1975) wrote little until he was thirty-five, and is at his best in *Poems New and Old* (Melbourne, 1945), which was published, therefore, when he was fifty-one.[7] And both poets are marked illustrations of the fact, apparent in every Australian literary category, that local writers draw something from this country which distinguishes their work from that of writers of corresponding talents overseas. Vrepont was educated at a State school and privately; he became Chief Study Teacher of the violin at the Melbourne University Conservatorium, and also a freelance journalist, a book reviewer and a masseur; he has wandered about Australia on foot, horse, and bicycle, and has had some gold-mining experience in North Queensland; it is probable that the varied nature of his experience both reflects and has contributed to his poetic individuality. Vrepont's style in particular has certain bizarre characteristics that in another might appear artificial, even exhibitionistic, but in him they seem natural, if a little eccentric: prominent among such characteristics is an abruptness of diction, a fondness for a succession of monosyllables that produces a staccato effect; sometimes this may have an onomatopoeic value, as in the description of crabs eating,

> Pincering microcosms from the scaly rocks,
> Timed to split-second mouth shutterings
> Like Chinamen with chop-sticks;

but sometimes it amounts to a mere choked cacophony, as in another line from the same poem, which tells how man, "suicided from his home, the earth",

> Shall see no lord sun spray gold on wave.[8]

Vrepont also uses verbs as nouns and intransitives as transitives, and he invents words or verbal conjunctions, some of which are extremely effective; he speaks for instance of

> . . . the thrip-thrush silky music of my feet,

---

[6] But he wrote a great deal of verse as a youth, and Grano had previously published several little books of verse.

[7] *Poems New and Old* contained, however, the substance of previous booklets.

[8] Other examples: "Bite big, nip small or sting" (p. 80), "Past thundered, masked travellers flash'd" (p. 25).

of

> Sispering sistering sounds,

and of the

> Hop-flighting of birds.

Apart from their choppy nature, his rhythms, though free are not particularly modern, and his rhymes are usually regular, though he does use half-rhymes and assonances on occasion, and will rhyme a light with a strong syllable; and he has a pronounced liking for internal rhyming, as in the lines,

> There was a great heat on the land,
> But crackle-dry as wing of a dragon-fly.

Vrepont's queer and rather attractive idiosyncrasy excludes outside influences, though there seems to be an affinity here and there with a method sometimes employed by L. H. Allen,[9] whose work belongs to the previous Period; his poetry has, largely owing to its method of expression, that quality of unexpectedness which is usually a mark of exceptional talent; he tells of larks that "uprise"

> With a whistling run of feet;

of

> A flapping Chinese music of fat hands' clapping;

and, really beautiful, of

> Water-cool tone-drops, in a warm half dark.

There is thought in every one of the poems, but there is not about any of it the quality of surprise that attaches to the style; "One" has a certain impressiveness as a reflective poem, but almost all the best poems are essentially lyrical, the lovely "Heron" for instance, and "The Apple Tree", which has a sweet freshness that appears also, though rarely, elsewhere: "The Fishers" links the two aspects of his poetry. It may be noted that in all but one of Vrepont's best poems the style is uncharacteristically simple: the single exception is the long poem, "The Miracle",[10] which has a compulsive force that almost succeeds in lifting its theme, soil erosion, to the height of world tragedy;[11] "The Miracle" opens well:

---

[9] Compare, for instance, parts of "Invictus" (p. 23) with Allen's "Curse of Cain" (*Phaedra*, p. 25).

[10] This was awarded the C. J. Dennis Memorial Prize for 1939.

[11] Of course it might conceivably come to that, but man seems to be, in this respect, awakening out of his stupidity.

Great fear was on the cities—
The obscene dread of war,
But Earth, that nothing pities,
And nothing answers for,
Fired the first and deadly shot
Against her enemy;

and it ends with one of Vrepont's best passages:

Still on the mountains stands the peerless one,
Still slinks in jungle depths the changeless ape,
On the vast loom of time's unhaste is spun
A creature conscious of its final shape.

Grano's is a lighter talent, but it also is markedly individual, partly for similar reasons. His family was on his father's side West Indian and ultimately Spanish; he took a Law degree at the University of Melbourne but after a few years' practice became in turn insurance salesman, advertising writer, theatrical advance-agent, mine storeman, commercial traveller, freelance journalist, and a member of the staff of the Queensland Main Roads Commission. Like Vrepont, he creates words of his own, some of which are very effective: swallows

wisping hither, thither,
slithing, slancing, glithing, glancing;

leaves that go "skattle, skittle, skattle"; jarring windows that "jattle", and sheets that go "schlop"; there are others, but all these are collected in a single poem, "Windy", which is among the curiosities of Australian poetry, but is also rather more than that. Like Vrepont once more, Grano can strike home at times, as in "Man has grown fearful of silence"; or, from "Song of the Butcher Bird",

He is in the rung tree,
high, high as can be,
and below him and about
the morning's spread out
shining on bush-and bough;

or when in "Romance and Business" he tells how the business man, dead to the loveliness of an old house and garden, can find nothing to say but

. . . a splendid site . . . so near the tram, and that's
A big advantage to a block of flats.

Unlike Vrepont however, Grano is an extremely uneven poet; his reflections run usually along the surface, and what with this and an inclination to diffuseness, some of his longer poems thin out to almost nothing: "Invocation", which begins by capturing something of the fresh spaciousness of the high air, is very disappointing for this reason.

Freshness often characterizes those of his poems that deal with open-air subjects; and Grano knows how to give full effect to the sonorous aboriginal names of his native woods and hills, winds, birds, little townships: Chalambar, Langi Ghiran, Coot-tha and Moormbool. Except in a fondness for free verse, which suffers from his inability to be sharp and concise, and in an avoidance of initial capitals, Grano is not particularly modern; there is nothing unusual about his rhymes or rhythms. Religious enthusiasm has inspired some of his best poems, and with one exception the few influences that one can trace in his work are of Roman Catholic poets; several lines in "Jude, Look Down" seem to represent deliberate imitations of Hopkins.[12] The exception[13] is Eliot, whose influence is apparent in only one poem, "A Word for the Innkeeper", which may owe something to "The Journey of the Magi", though its immediate inspiration was the overcrowding of Brisbane in wartime: this is however a fine poem, simple, sincere, and so real that one sees it all and is impressed. There are a number of short satiric pieces, amusing but not quite sharp and succinct enough to strike home: "Churchill" is a partial exception. [Grano and Vrepont were interesting examples of retention of vigour in a late development, but neither progressed further. Vrepont died soon after the end of the present Period; Grano, except for the odd magazine poem, fell silent long before his death.] Others who hold an intermediate position between the intellectual and the lyric and descriptive poets will be discussed in dealing with three other groups: the Jindyworobaks, the Angry Penguins, and the Poets of War.

Judith (Arundell) Wright (Mrs J. McKinney, Armidale, N.S.W., 1915-) is even more pre-eminent among the lyrists than FitzGerald among the intellectual poets; the reasons for including her in this rather than in the other group are easier to appreciate than to specify: almost everything she writes is charged with thought, yet compared with any of the intellectuals she is seen to be of a different kind. The difference is very evident in a comparison with another woman poet, Rosemary Dobson, who has nothing like her passionate intensity; but take FitzGerald: he can be intense enough, but the object of his intensity is always an idea or connected with an idea; so it is, almost always, with Hope and Slessor, though with them the idea becomes much oftener than with FitzGerald a personal matter. Just as with those poets who have been here grouped together as intellectuals, however strong the emotion, the general mental attitude is not only reflected in it but has often given

---

[12] For example, "brown-dappled-softness-swaying rest".

[13] "Day of the Kingfisher" (p. 57) might appear to be another exception, but it appears that the resemblance between the openings of the two poems is merely coincidental, since when he wrote this poem Grano had not read Arnold's "Philomel". Grano's poems have been collected in *Poems New and Old*. He also published an anthology of Roman Catholic verse, *Witness to the Stars* (Sydney, 1946).

birth to it; so with those who have been here grouped as lyrists, however strongly their verses may be charged with thought, it is the emotion that has come first and given birth to it. Broadly speaking it may be said that the lyrists feel, and think; that the intellectuals think, and feel. By all these tests Judith Wright is essentially lyrist rather than intellectual; or, and this goes nearer to the root of the matter, it may be said that she is a lyrist because life sings through her veins in music. She is on her father's side an Australian of the fifth generation, and all the generations have been on the land; she was born and brought up in New South Wales, and to the days and scenes of her New England childhood she frequently returns; she was educated at the New England Grammar School and at the University of Sydney, and worked as stenographer and private secretary in Sydney and in Brisbane, where she helped in the production of the early *Meanjin* and was employed by the Universities Commission, and also, while her brothers were at the war, on the land: she has published two books of verse: *The Moving Image* (Melbourne, 1946) and *Woman to Man* (Sydney, 1949).[14] Judith Wright has to a very unusual extent the power of entering into the objects of her experience, of becoming part of them and of making them part of herself; moreover she perceives each object with an imaginative vision that relates it to other objects, so that it becomes part of a unified experience, a world, her world;[15] beyond that, she conjures up each object's past and sometimes also its future; and since her own past remains to her almost as real and interesting as her present, though not so interesting as her future,[16] her vision appears independent of time as well as of space. She tells of herself when she tells how two ancient voices say to her:

> 'The world is my heart, the world is love or hate. . . .'
> 'The world is my body;
> is what my eyes can see and my hands hold;'

and she says:[17]

> Many roads meet here
> in me, the traveller and the ways I travel.
> All the hills' gathered waters feed my seas
> who am the swimmer and the mountain river;
> and the long slopes' concurrence is my flesh
> who am the gazer and the land I stare on;
> and dogwood blooms within my winter blood,
> and orchards fruit in me and need no season.

---

[14] And, since the closing date of this History, *The Gateway* (Sydney, 1953), *The Two Fires* (Sydney, 1955) and a couple of anthologies.

[15] See the second of the following quotations.

[16]
> And yet, the lovelier distance is ahead,
> I would go farther with you, clock and star,
> Though the earth break under my feet and storm
> Snatch at my breath and night ride over me.

[17] *The Moving Image*, p. 31.

But if she listens to voices out of man's far-off past, she likes also to tell of what lies about her: of the lover, the unborn, the child and childhood; of the hawthorn hedge she planted long ago, of the brother and sisters who are nothing but memories, of midnight and a flame-tree in a quarry; of the bull, the winter kestrel and the small blue Arab stallion dancing on a hill; of the returned soldier, married to his farm as well as to his wife; of the bullocky, Moses of a promised land; of the little half-caste girl who is tired of being dead and wants to dance in the sunlight, "and beat with a waddy on the bright moon like a gong"; of mustering in the Bogongs and driving for Cobb and Co; of cycads whose "smooth dark flames flicker at time's own root"; of the metho drinker; of the surfer; of the city asleep; of song in a wine-bar, the old prison and the convict shepherd; of the country dance. She tells how Mrs McClarty went off with twenty cows to milk,

> . . . the music stinging
> like sixty wasps under her best dress;

and how Eva Callaghan

> . . . whose boy died in the army
> sat under the streamers like a house to let
> and went alone, a black pot brimming with tears.
> "Once my body was a white cedar, my breasts the buds on the quince-tree,
> that now are fallen and grey like logs on a cleared hill.
> Then why is my blood not quiet? what is the good
> of the whips of music stinging along my blood?"

This is a wide range: and yet in another way Judith Wright's range is not so wide, for it is through her own mind, emotions, personality that all this world is seen; it is through her veins that it sings in music. Therefore, though in a sense the world is laid out before her to observe, it is yet to a greater or a lesser degree as a part of herself that she observes it; in a sense she stands apart, the maker of time and fear, to which she refuses to yield, knowing that "to yield to either is to be dead", yet she is

> . . . caught in the endless circle of time and star
> that never chime with the blood:

indeed it could not be otherwise, since she herself is her world; sometimes indeed time and the world spin faster and faster about her, until

> mind cannot grasp them now, or heart take hold.

Time and the clock haunt her as they haunt Rosemary Dobson;[18] it is almost all that these two poets have in common: time is a spider that

[18] There are a score or two of references to one or the other in Judith Wright's two books.

"binds us helpless till his sting goes in", a rat that gnaws away her beauty; it is as though time and space stood still for Judith Wright while her attention was fixed upon the world of her experience, but that whenever she lifts her mind towards its two tyrants, they spin dizzyingly. In the circumstances it is not surprising that there should be an element of mysticism[19] in her work; what is surprising is that her method of expression, her whole attitude is essentially simple, sensible, matter-of-fact; with all her passionate intensity of vision, her feet are firmly based upon the ground: this is perhaps best seen in her conception and treatment of love, for a number of her poems are love poems. But to say that in this matter especially her feet are firmly based upon the ground by no means implies a mere materialism; it is simply that her attitude is far removed from that of the conventionally romantic poet: women are fundamentally much less romantic than men, more matter-of-fact, and when they write romantically about love, that is, as a rule, because they have adopted something of the conventional attitude of the romantic poets through the ages, most of whom have been men. The fact that this is also the attitude of many women who are not fully awakened, so to speak, is not in point here, nor is the fact that the attitude of many men towards love is by no means romantic, though this will be in point a few pages farther on. Judith Wright's is in this matter what may therefore be called the woman's point of view: she is not concerned with the romance of love, or even with the man as the prime object of passion: with her he is in the main the instrument, the collaborator in the creation of the child. Not that he is to her by any means an abstract or an unregarded instrument, or an instrument merely: he is beloved and she laments his loss; he is, what she also is to him, though more incidentally, a refuge from loneliness; but it is the child or the child to be on which her passionate thought is set. Her attitude on this subject is illustrated in two of her finest and most characteristic poems. The first, "The Company of Lovers",[20] differs radically from that of the love poetry even of today, in which the masculine point of view though modified is still paramount; at the most it represents only one aspect of that point of view:

> We meet and part now over all the world,
> We, the lost company,
> take hands together in the night, forget
> the night in our brief happiness, silently.
> We, who sought many things, throw all away
> for this one thing, one only,
> remembering that in the narrow grave
> we shall be lonely.

---

[19] See, for instance, "Dream" (*Woman to Man*, p. 18) and "Blind Man's Song" (the same, p. 57).

[20] *The Moving Image*, p. 10.

Death marshals up his armies round us now.
Their footsteps crowd too near.
Lock your warm hand above the chilling heart
and for a time I live without my fear.
Grope in the night to find me and embrace,
for the dark preludes of the drums begin,
and round us, round the company of lovers,
Death draws his cordons in.

The other, "Woman to Man",[21] is feminine wholly:

The eyeless labourer in the night,
the selfless, shapeless seed I hold,
builds for its resurrection day—
silent and swift and deep from sight
foresees the unimagined light.

. . . .

This is the maker and the made;
this is the question and reply;
the blind head butting at the dark,
the blaze of light along the blade.
Oh hold me, for I am afraid.

"Woman's Song" and "Woman to Child"[22] develop the same theme and would be well worth quoting if there were space enough; this series, for it is really a series, is completed later by a terrible poem, "The Unborn", of which the first part deals with the woman who must deny, and deny that she has denied

that bubble of sunlight broken and thrown away.

In the second part of this poem it is the unborn who cries out of the darkness:

Not even tears were mine,
not even death;
not even the dazzling pain
of one first breath.

I never knew the sleep
of the warm womb.
The end of my beginning
was dumb; was dumb.

Only the foot of the stair
I felt, being blind.
Then came the touch of fear
time now can never mend.

---

[21] *Woman to Man*, p. 1.
[22] The same, pp. 2, 3.

My name was a dark sound
that made no word.
Terror alone spoke it
and nothing heard.

Neither awake nor asleep
on the rack of dark I lie,
hearing my own not-voice,
"What was I? I? I?"

This last poem, in its two parts, is unique: it could scarcely have been written by a man, the women poets of the past could scarcely have handled such a theme, and it has not been handled, to my knowledge, by a woman poet of today. Connected with the same series are a number of poems that deal with "the green world of a child", but for them there is no space here.

Judith Wright's style is a style of today, but with few exceptions, it is independent of modern fashions: her lines begin without initial capitals except after a full stop, and she uses half-rhymes as well as regular rhymes, and a freedom of rhythm that is not however carried to extremes; free verse is rare with her, but she is one of the few poets of today who understand how to use it; she writes here as elsewhere with economy and precision, and she knows how to get the full effect out of the contrast between the long and the short lines;[23] one interesting characteristic of her rhythms is that she ends two or three of her lines with three strong beats in succession, and once at least with three strong beats followed by a weak.[24] Free-moving, independent, her eye focused closely upon some particular object, she almost always uses, not necessarily what used to be called the "inevitable" word or phrase: if indeed there can be such a thing, but the word or phrase that is inevitable for her in its particular context: this applies not merely to the most notable of her expressions, but to all of them; she tells of "the hard inquiring wind", of a river "drunken with rain"; of the "quiet sea-noise"; of

Blue blowing smoke of twigs from the noon fire,
red blowing dust of roads where the teams go slow;

of the clock that "leaked the year away". She observes and records easily and naturally; her all-pervading individuality never seems to require stimulating, and if her attitude towards love is entirely feminine, that can scarcely be said of her attitude towards life as a whole, and certainly

---

[23] For instance,

To be alone in a strange place in spring
shakes the heart.

(*Woman to Man*, p. 11).

[24] "Eyes stride far" and "whole day full" (*Woman to Man*, p. 18; a molossus), and "heart laid quiet" (the same, p. 19; an epitrite). As will be seen, Harold Stewart makes a practice of this kind of rhythm (see p. 1054).

not of her style: except on the one subject, she writes neither as woman nor as man, but as an individual person, though this is not to say that her sex is not evident. Few masculine, let alone feminine poets are capable of the power that glows through the title-poem of *The Moving Image*, where for instance she tells how, in a world that is

> . . . evil and small
> like a dried head from the islands with a grin of shell,

there is nothing for it but to wait

> Till the tide of life come back, till time's great tide
> roar from our depths and send us mad again
> with a singing madness;

towards the end of the poem she has another immense image:

> Over the airfield looms the idol of night.
> In its shadow the earth is spun by a stellar wind
> in an eddy of spiral stars.

She speaks of "a doom of planes", of "the breakers' cold continual thunder", of "summer's bubble-sound of sweet creek-water", and, drawing upon a source that Australian poets have only lately discovered, she tells of

> . . . parrots exploding in green and scarlet.

In a burst of ecstasy, she cries out:

> But look, oh look, the Gothic tree's on fire
> with blown galahs, and fuming with wild wings;

and there are the two unforgettable lines in which, from the "star-struck darkness" about the bullocky's camp-fire,

> . . . centuries of cattlebells
> rang with their sweet uneasy sound.

A few literary reminiscences are scattered about Judith Wright's work, but most are faint and some may be due to affinity or coincidence; they are such as might be expected of a poet who is conscious of a world of poetry as well as of life, but also of an individuality too strong to need the building of a careful wall about it: far-off suggestions of the re-creation of the drowning in Slessor's "Five Bells";[25] a possible echo of the theme, the unity and continuity of life, of FitzGerald's "Essay on Memory",[26] and another perhaps of a passage in his "Face of the Waters";[27] a trick of expression that may have been caught from Douglas

[25] "Night ride over me" (*The Moving Image*, p. 1), "we know the agony we do not know" (the same, p. 16), "The night comes up over you" (*Woman to Man*, p. 50).
[26] The first passage on p. 3 of *The Moving Image*.
[27] "Amoebae doubling from the acid" (*Woman to Man*, p. 6).

Stewart;[28] an image that may have been consciously or unconsciously borrowed from Housman[29] and a slight suggestion of Housman in another poem.[30] There is also a phrase that carries with it a suggestion of Eliot;[31] but Judith Wright is as far from Eliot as FitzGerald in her attitude to life: "All that is real," she says, "is to live, to desire, to be"; and, in the last line of "The Unborn", there may be an unconscious memory of the last line of a poem of De La Mare's.[32] But all these are unimportant, except as illustrations of the unity and continuity of literature.

A couple of lines that certainly and several whole poems that probably belong to world literature; half a dozen poems that are among the best of their kind in the present day: it is an amazing production for a woman of thirty-five, and it fixes Judith Wright's position, alongside those of FitzGerald and Slessor, among the first of living poets, in Australia or elsewhere.

Most of the other lyrists also have written love poems, but love is by no means always the centre of their poetic worlds, nor does it always mean the same thing to them. Kenneth (Ivo) Mackenzie (Perth, 1913–55), is the complete amorist, and because of the fundamental differences between the aspects of love that mean most to her and almost everything to him, he and Judith Wright may be considered complementary, at least to the extent that her attitude is in a sense typically feminine, whereas his represents one variety of the typically masculine. Mackenzie's parents were Australians; he was educated at a Perth Grammar School and at the University of Western Australia, where he studied Law and Agriculture; he moved to Melbourne and then to Sydney, married and became a newspaper and radio journalist; he served in the second World War and in 1948 he was awarded a Commonwealth Literary Fellowship for the writing of a book on garrison life in Australia. Mackenzie began verse-making as a schoolboy, and published, besides a couple of novels which are discussed elsewhere,[33] and several others that appeared too late for this History, two books of verse: *Our Earth*, which was illustrated by Norman Lindsay and published in Sydney in 1937, and *The Moonlit Doorway* (Sydney, 1944). The first is a long lyrical-pastoral poem, written in free

[28] "Only the mad old girl from the hut on the hill" (*The Moving Image*, p. 22) and "say the old sisters on the veranda" (*Woman to Man*, p. 8).

[29] "the steepled cone of night" (*The Moving Image*, p. 25); compare "the vast and moon-eclipsing cone of night".

[30] "Woman's Song" (*Woman to Man*, p. 2).

[31] "Where do the roads lead? It is not where we expected" (*The Moving Image*, p. 21).

[32] The poem is "Who" (*Poems 1919 to 1934*, London, 1935, p. 83). It ends:

2ND STRANGER: *Who walks with us on the hills?*
WILD BIRD: Ay! . . . Aye! . . . . *Ay!*

[33] See pp. 1170–2.

but fairly regular five-beat iambics, with occasional interpolations of passages with six beats; it deals with the fertile earth, the succession of the seasons and the progress of country love, all as against the mechanical life of the cities. Smooth, dignified, rich in sensuous imagery, it is unimpassioned, and, lacking sufficient impetus to carry the reader forward, becomes monotonous; it is in fact, except for its lack of passion and the excellence of its verbal craftsmanship, a young man's work, full of poetic materials that have not been synthesized into an organic unity. In the second book, a collection of short poems, promise becomes achievement in a particular kind: rather more than half its contents deal with love or with woman from a lover's point of view; all are rich, sensuous, and if not exactly impassioned, though the poet speaks of passion, yet sensitive and intense. To Mackenzie as to most poets, love centres upon its fundamental act, but with him the act is not in any way romanticized: there is no element of mysticism or even of symbolism about it; its importance is simply sensual, though the sensuality is of the most refined and sophisticated kind. The woman is to Mackenzie essentially even more an instrument than the man is to Judith Wright: so to him the woman is in essence the means to the gratification of desire, just as to her the man is in essence the means towards the creation of the child. This is not to imply that with Kenneth Mackenzie any more than with Judith Wright the lover is regarded from a single point of view: his concentration upon her is by no means invariably physiological though it is so as a rule and mainly; it extends to all the circumstances: the poetic illumination that begins and glows brightest at the centre spreads on all sides until it reaches the outer world. The feeling that Mackenzie celebrates is not without tenderness; he can say:

> You are my Helen and my child as well,
> my little sleeping love; and in this rhyme
> whatever words can say, these words must tell
> of love to outwear usage, outlast time
> and leave a mark upon my heart and spirit;

but this is not characteristic, and may owe something to the fact that in the sonnet-sequence of which this is the seventh there is a definite reminiscence of Shakespeare. Mackenzie's is a self-regarding attitude to love; he is after all not much interested in his lover, or lovers, except as representing the lovely trappings of a rapturous act; at least not interested deeply enough to sketch any of them except as figures of physical allurement and acquiescence: indeed they are not lovers but a lover, who is neither individualized nor understood. It is true that he speaks of

> all I have learned here of myself and her
> in many an hour of rich and leisured silence;

but he does not really seem to have learnt much, and these lines from "The Moonlit Doorway" seem always applicable:

> "She was a pale woman lying there
> whom you have never seen, whom you have known
> well at night only—never well by day."

"Alas!" he says in another place, "How well I knew you"; but the fact is that he never has known her, except in a particular aspect, and that entirely superficial. He can describe

> your burning face and soft, defensive hands,
> the helpless salutation of your breasts,
> your opened eyes and mutely opened lips,
> and all your hot brown body's eagerness;

and he can say, very characteristically,

> Of what spices, what perfumes,
> what virtues and delicate parts
> is she compounded!
>
> How excellent her face, her person,
> natural and well for love's arts
> shaped, smoothed, rounded!
>
> If I could not love these, I could not
> love at all ever again;

but he can go no farther than that. As a poet of love, he is in fact the consummate egoist; the idea that love involves an element of surrender, of sacrifice, is entirely foreign to him: of course egoism need not damn a poet, but it defines a limitation. Mackenzie's attitude in this matter has its points of contact with McCrae's, but it is lacking in the immense and simple gusto in love as an essential part of life and the living and delightful world that characterizes McCrae's poetry, and lacking even more in its breadth and spaciousness. Mackenzie's love poetry is that of a warm curtained room whose atmosphere becomes after a while oppressive: reading it, one is not surprised that he should have said[34] that almost all his poems had been written in bed. But if this is his most characteristic attitude, it is not that of all his poetry: the first two lines of "Norman's Place",

> Blessed by the mountain sun, kissed by that air
> Of cool blue height, the house is half asleep,

have open-air freshness enough; and elsewhere he speaks of

> you up there among your many mountains
> where the sweet air's like water in a glass.

[34] In *Southerly*, vol. ix (1948), no. 4, p. 217, "Writing Poetry: The Why and The How".

His description of the coming of rain[35] is full of freshness and action:

Then when December stands upon the threshold
wearing the bleached garment of late summer,
golden and glowing like a wedded woman,
it rains. . . . Incredible clemency despaired of,
dispensed at last: *it rains, it rains, it rains!*
I went and jumped and danced and shouted in it,
naked and streaming, somewhere before midnight,
chilled by the south-east wind grown suddenly cold.
Up from south and east, out of the ocean,
out of the heavy forest country marching,
out of the opal mountains, out of the sky,
out of the conscience of repentant gods
this liquid benison, this profound deliverance
from half a death;

and there is a fine burst of early morning radiance in the poem in which, after a night of wandering "westward, seaward, moonward",

Watching, we saw
the hill crest crowned with a white garland of girls
bearing upon their shoulders light and morning,
risen knee-deep out of the southern sky.

But sometimes even when Mackenzie's subject belongs to the open air the atmosphere is not that of out-of-doors; for example, in "The tree at Post 4" the soldier's vision of his beloved, imaged for him in the white and shining trunk of a gum-tree, recalls a "warm room's velvet depth of night", and this gives its atmosphere to the whole poem. And Mackenzie is at his best when he is most characteristic, as in the book's title-poem, in which the lover tells of the dark room whose doorway,

. . . beautiful in its silky moonlit splendour,

opens upon

The peacock-eye of the half-moon long since up;
the peacock-blue of the iridescent sky
moonlit to starless pallor;

and of the "imperial peacocks" that "scream out their scornful warning":

Beware of you [they say], your man's fallibility
in keeping faith. Beware of moons and midnights
lest the white body of the beloved suffer
a sad sky-change, and through that moonlit doorway
pass headlong into the hell of discontent,
the double hell of conscience and of scorn,
the final hell of hate. Beware, beware. . . .

---

[35] pp. 42–3, "It rains".

"Tell me now," the poet asks, watching his beloved asleep,

what you think lazily about, stretched here at ease
across my arm and shoulder and my heart;

but this is a rhetorical question: what she thinks about does not really concern him; what really concerns him is

. . . the dark entry of this blood and flesh
into that younger and more innocent
flesh and blood, when the night was not far worn;

and how

This was my fortune, that her breasts
should stand upright and for an hour or more
tell me this body warmed and tensed and turned
with love to mine.

In spite of its restriction, this is however an extremely beautiful poem. One of the most remarkable of Mackenzie's poems, "Going upstairs", deals however not with love-making but with the sudden and for the lover amazing death that is its consequence; the would-be midnight murderer is himself killed suddenly by a shot out of the darkness, and we get the last workings of his mind as he lies dying:

Why need they stand so long?
Why does not either laugh, or weep, or shout
while I lie here upon the landing floor
in blood and death, and now can hope no more
to celebrate her triumph with a song?

The candle withers to a point in space,
and darkness comes downstairs with lazy tread:
first I have lost her figure, then her face,
and now her name is blotted from the night
by one long bloody snore without respite—
like some gross drunkard's in a narrow bed.

Some rhyme, with a little half-rhyme; mostly five-beat blank verse,[36] rhyme free only in respect of extra syllables and often with a soft feminine ending: all this Mackenzie has at his fingers' ends. His work is extraordinarily even, never sinking and seldom rising above a certain level; this is truer however of lines and phrases than of poems and passages; he speaks of "Beauty's eternal quality, surprise", but his work contains comparatively few surprises, thus suggesting a considerable element of conscious craftsmanship: a few images stick in the mind however, as,

I heard the music of your faithful heart
enter the orchestra of my desire;

---

[36] ". . . I consider the five-foot line—call it iambic pentameter or blank verse, as you choose—the ultimate line in the writing of English poetry".

and

> The sorrowful velvet ribbon of the bugle notes
> winds round my heart, and wraps away the day
> with its repeated call for sleep. . . .

What Mackenzie aims at, that he attains: warm, velvety-smooth, seldom striking, never surprising, each poem moves forward not slowly but deliberately, giving the impression always of complete control; his poetry is that of an artist so accomplished that except for the air of control and deliberateness it might almost seem to have to come into being on its own account. It is highly individual, and its only affiliations are with the Pre-Raphaelites, and, in the sonnets, with the sonnets of Shakespeare; there has been nothing like it in Australia hitherto, and within its marked limitations it would be hard to match.

Tom Inglis Moore (Camden, N.S.W., 1901–78) differs from Kenneth Mackenzie almost as much as both differ from Judith Wright. Moore is a lover but not an amorist, though he does not neglect but on the contrary emphasizes the physical aspect of love: his attitude is thoroughly romantic; his approach is not sophisticated and deliberate like Mackenzie's, but simple, direct and joyous, and there is about his poetry in general, in spite of some artificialities, an air of freshness and the out of doors. To him the beloved is an individual and also an ideal, not merely an object of desire; even when, as in "White Hawthorn", both face and name are quite forgotten the ecstasy remains ideal in memory. Moore was a graduate of Sydney, and Oxford, to which he won a scholarship; after lecturing in English in the United States and as Associate Professor of English at the University of the Philippines, he returned to Australia, became sub-warden of St Paul's College, the University of Sydney, and wrote reviews and leaders for the *Sydney Morning Herald*. Though married, he enlisted as a gunner in the second A.I.F., but transferred to the Army Education Service; at the closing date of this History he was lecturer in Pacific Studies at the Canberra University College, and was also a member of the Advisory Board of the Commonwealth Literary Fund, for which he lectured at several universities; he won the *Sydney Morning Herald*'s poetry competition in 1949.[37] Moore published, besides critical work, two books of verse: *Adagio in Blue* (Sydney, 1938), and *Emu Parade* (Sydney, 1941); the second consists of war poems and is discussed elsewhere.[38] The essential romanticism of his poetic attitude extends beyond his love poems, and yet he is conscientiously modern, though without pushing his modernity to extremes; there is a definitely intellectual quality in his raptures, which one feels

[37] Moore became Senior Lecturer in Australian Literature, Canberra University College, and afterwards, until 1966, Associate Professor of Australian Literature, Australian National University, Canberra.

[38] See pp. 1066–7; Moore's critical work is discussed on pp. 1286–7. After the closing date of this History he published *Bayonet and Grass* (Sydney, 1957).

to be partly natural and partly imposed, yet they remain raptures, because of the strength and sincerity of the emotion expressed: it is a fundamentally simple emotion, in which the thought is in part dissolved, in part held in suspension, but seldom developed. One is conscious also of an effort to attract, and the result of all this is a queer combination of the natural and the artificial which sometimes arrests the attention in a manner that was not desired. Although Moore's eye is thus not always and entirely on his object, he has a bright, candid and almost boyish ardour that can be very engaging; it is rather naïve however, and sometimes it runs away with his aesthetic judgment in a manner that a keener sensitivity would have restrained, as in the stressed and repeated references to "the blood's wild singing" and the burning or lusting loins: the emotional element in Moore's work is more interesting than the intellectual, being deeper and more real. Except in the nature of some of his images, and in his occasional use of half-rhymes, there is nothing particularly modern about Moore's actual style, though both these characteristics become more marked in his second book: he has a good many romantic tag-ends, and can even sing "hosannas to the morn";[39] but he has a real gift of imagery, though he sometimes forces it a little, as in:

> . . . obelisk moments, carved by hammering passion.

In

> Now does the moon, night's golden hind,
> Wear on her bright, uplifted brow
> Fresh antlers of the forked and spreading gum-twigs,

the poetic imagination may have been urged a little; and

> . . . when the full-breasted moon
> Suckles a nestling cloud

may perhaps be a little obvious, but

> . . . the undertone of the far surf
> Beating soft as the drowsed heart

is natural and unforced. Moore is not so accomplished a craftsman as Mackenzie, and his work is far more uneven; but just as much of his poetry falls far below the average level of Mackenzie's, so once or twice he is better than Mackenzie's best. His rhythms are mostly conventional, and though he does occasionally attempt free verse, it is not successful because it is insufficiently clear-cut and concise: the main fault in Moore's style is a rambling diffuseness that combines in some of his deliberately thoughtful poems with a tendency to the intellectually obvious to produce work that is

---

[39] *Adagio in Blue*, p. 77. Other examples are: "shallop of self" (the same, p. 78), "limbs of lovers,

prosy and monotonous.[40] But except for a possible reflection of Neilson in "Song for Lovers", and for one or two reminiscences of FitzGerald,[41] Moore is himself alone, and in several poems, of which the most typical is "Druidic Gums", an epithalamium set in the bush, he reaches a fairly high level. Much less characteristic but reaching perhaps a higher level is the lovely "Song for Lovers", from the first book,[42] without which any good Australian anthology would be incomplete:

Love needs no pondered words,
No high philosophy;
Enough the singing birds
In the green tree.

Enough the touch of hand,
Whose trembling worship tells
Faiths deeper than command
Cathedral bells.

Blood sings fresh truths that wise
Old Plato never knew;
Dimmed are thought's evening eyes
By sun on dew.

Come rainbow or the rose,
Vision shall find new birth:
With love more lovely grows
Beauty on earth.

Darkly death waits, yet we
In a wild hour shall know
Bright immortality,
Before we go.

Lesbia (Venner) Harford (*née* Keogh, Melbourne, 1891-1927), who gave up her health and the greater part of her life to social work, was a pure lyrist, and almost half her collected poems deal with love; in a sense indeed they all do, for she differs from many other social reformers in that the motive of her enthusiasm was love, in its largest sense, and not hate: she loved especially the factory girls alongside whom she worked, and even in the few poems in which she attacks rather than sympathizes, what she says is quiet, restrained, implicit rather than expressed in set terms.[43] She was a Melbourne graduate in Law, and, with honours, in Philosophy; she coached, taught Art, and worked in a solicitor's office, and, less to earn her living than to get to understand the living

[40] See "Monists" (*Adagio in Blue*, p. 90), "Let Us Smash the Clamps" (the same, p. 86), "In Hospital" (the same, p. 82), "Men Never See the Sky" (the same, p. 78).

[41] Compare "Ghosts" (*Adagio in Blue*, p. 37) with FitzGerald's "Envy goes groping for the kisses" (*Moonlight Acre*, p. 21); and compare the passage about "cataloguing scholars" (*Adagio in Blue*, p. 77) with FitzGerald's references to "greybeards, long-of-tooth" (*To Meet the Sun*, p. 19) and to books and learning (the same, pp. 15-16).

[42] p. 25.

[43] See, for example, XXXV, XXXIX, XLVIII, XLIX.

conditions of factory girls, in a clothing factory; she was also an organizer of sweated women and at one time edited a furniture trades magazine; but she had always been delicate, and she overworked and died at thirty-six. All her life she was writing verses, which flowed from her naturally, with an artless charm: poetry represented to her the frank and simple expression of every side of a nature that was sensitive, gentle, unselfish, supremely sympathetic, and capable of passionate devotion, and all these qualities are reflected in her poetry. She was quite careless of the conventions, of domesticity, sex or anything else; with work waiting for her, she could lie reading or writing on an unmade bed:

> Wide-open window, wide-open door,
> Books on the floor.
>
> . . . .
>
> But what's the hell of a mess to me
> When I am free,
>
> And wind blows in and a delicate song
> Flickers along!;

and in "Periodicity" she could be as outspoken as Judith Wright in "The Unborn"; incidentally in this poem there are some beautiful lines:

> Women, I say,
> Are beautiful in change,
> Remote, immortal, like the moon they range.

She is indeed quite as feminine a poet as Judith Wright, but in a different way, for with her love and the child are quite separable: her child is the future, the revolution, the freeing of the down-trodden. And whereas Judith Wright's ranging over a whole world of thought and experience is inseparable from a creative imagination in whose light it takes upon itself an inevitably poetic form, Lesbia Harford was not much of an artist, and not much of a poetic craftsman; not that she had not a genuine poetic gift, but she did not take it seriously: her serious business was with life, not poetry,[44] and with the amelioration of the conditions of life. Poetry was to her no more than a casual though inevitable reflection of herself; and every passing shade of thought or emotion, carelessly fanciful, humorous, serious, slipped into verse that was always fresh and natural but often slight in the extreme. The result was a collection of poems that constitute in the mass a charming unconscious portrait of a charming person: individually they are light, easy, graceful verses that have sometimes no more substance than a breath of air, but sometimes again they crystallize into genuine poetry. Lesbia Keogh had neither the will nor, perhaps, the power to criticize what she wrote, and the poems collected

[44] See II, "Deliverance Through Art".

after her death by Nettie Palmer and published[45] as *The Poems of Lesbia Harford* (Melbourne, 1941) represent only a fraction of her actual poetic output; her social verses, of which the published collection contains comparatively few, are extremely human and deal more with her fellow workers against the background of their everyday conditions than with her own aims and ideals, though these are implicit. In the mass she regarded her "little factory girls" with a gently critical affection:

Blind as moles:
You are crude,
You are sweet,—little girls,
And amazingly rude.

But so fine
To be gay,
Gentle people are dull
At the end of the day.

As individuals, working beside her at the machines, she sketches them lightly, chattering of "last week's picnic and this week's joys", making her their innocent but by no means ignorant confidences. She also deals with the "dawn-struck" boys who also are her companions, with prison gates and with the revolution that is to come; for

She has all Ireland in her blood—
All Ireland's need of sword and tears,
With memories dim before the flood,
And conflicts of a thousand years.

Sexual love is therefore by no means of first importance to Lesbia Harford, though her lover may think so:

. . . he thinks of my heart as a mirror clear
To reflect the image I hold most dear.
But my heart is much more like a stream, I think,
Where my lover may come when he needs to drink.

. . . .

While the hidden waters run strong and free,
Unheeded, unguessed at the soul of me.

Her love is deep enough, but, like everything else in life to her, it is nothing without freedom: in spite of possessive moods of her own, she enjoins her lover,

Oh, make no woman of me, you who can,
Or I will make a husband of a man!

By my unwomanly love that sets you free
Love all myself, but least the woman in me;

---

[45] Under the sponsorship of the Commonwealth Literary Fund.

and again,

No loveliness of mine
That comes and goes
Wild-fuchsia-like,
Need blind you to the rose.

So I who bless
Your hot and passionate ways
Still need the starry loves
Of virgin days.

Even love itself is a prison to her, so that she tries to escape from it, as in one of the most beautiful of her poems:

I have golden shoes
To make me fleet,
They are like the wind
Underneath my feet.

When my lover's kiss
Is overbold,
I can run away
In my shoes of gold.

Nay, when I am shod
With this bright fire,
I am forced to run
From my own desire;

indeed she goes so far as to say:

Sometimes I think the happiest of love's moments
Is the blest moment of release from loving.

. . . .

For no two lovers are a single person
And lovers' union means a soul's suppression.

Curious in a way, and yet not curious, seeing that her poetry is of the most lyrical, that the best of it should arise, not out of what was her life's object and ideal, but out of her own private and personal experience. As with most poets and lovers, beauty has called strongly upon her: natural beauty, as in the poems about the trees, of which she says,

Lovely, lovely, lovely the sapling sighing,
Lovely the dead tree lies;

and beauty itself, in "Beauty and Terror", which may however contain a reflection of her revolutionary aspect:

Beauty does not walk through lovely days,
Beauty walks with horror in her hair;
Down long centuries of pleasant ways
Men have found the terrible most fair.

Youth is lovelier in death than life,
Beauty mightier in pain than joy,
Doubly splendid burn the fires of strife
Brighter than the brightness they destroy.

Lesbia Harford's contribution to Australian poetry, and in particular to Australian love poetry, is small, but real.

Almost all the poems of Ronald McCuaig (Newcastle, N.S.W., 1908-), deal with women, and most of the women are young and described from the point of view of a young man who finds them at least attractive, so that it is near enough to the truth to say that he also is, more or less, a poet of love, if we give the term a rather wide application. He is a curious compound of a witty and outspoken poetic virtuoso and a sophisticated, ironic and equally outspoken observer of one aspect of modern life, who is also capable of flashes of insight. In another way again he is a curious compound, for about a third of his poems carry one back to the seventeenth century and to the old French verse-forms, while the rest owe something to Eliot and Pound, though McCuaig's attitude to life is by no means Eliot's, and he believes that "poetry which cannot be spoken, and understood at the speed at which it is spoken is to that degree less than the best";[46] he has published[47] two booklets of verse which were brought together in *Quod Ronald McCuaig* (Sydney, 1946). McCuaig, born of a Scottish-Irish father and a Welsh mother in 1908, was educated at Newcastle and Sydney; at seventeen he was sweeping warehouse floors, and at twenty he became a radio journalist and later worked on various Sydney newspapers, with an interval as a labourer in a cardboard-box factory; later he joined the *Bulletin*, married, travelled round the world and, after his retirement, wrote children's books. Beginning with attempts to write verse in the forms of music, he went on to cultivate some of the metrical forms that Macartney also practised in the satiric verses collected in *Gaily the Troubadour*.[48] But most of McCuaig's poems are of all things musical, and satiric only in an undertone; his strong satiric tendency finds direct expression mostly in the second section of his book: it is in this that there appears the influence of the moderns, whom he "first endured, then pitied, then embraced"; but these different influences "boiled together in one pot". Pound and Eliot showed McCuaig how to write about personal experiences in the ordinary language of today; he tried also "to write so simply that the poem would appear to be ordinary conversation and yet take the reader

[46] *Southerly*, vol. ix (1948), no. 4, p. 208, "Writing Poetry: The Why and The How".
[47] Besides sketches that are discussed on p. 1260.
[48] See p. 1016.

by surprise".[49] He is not always sucessful in these attempts: in "The Commercial Traveller's Wife" he tries to convey by means of broken rhythms "the intonations and reflections" of the barber who told him the story while cutting his hair; most readers will probably agree that the purpose of the broken rhythms is not evident without McCuaig's explanation, though they are then seen to be appropriate. And perhaps in this and certainly in one or two of the other poems the surprise endings seem a little forced; but sometimes they are both natural and beautiful, with a flash of tragedy: in what may appear at first an amusing trifle, "The Proposal", a young man, after a circumlocutory advance upon "the virgin visit" to his flat, "removing the bandages of beauty's wounds",

> Saw naked, like a deft
> "I told you so",
> The quivering-lipped love I left
> Two years ago;

and "Beauty and the Beast" ends with the moon shining

> . . . with the wan
> Wavering smile of a plain woman
> Who feels that love is not enough
> And knows she has no more than Love.

The lyrics in the first section of *Quod Ronald McCuaig*, which was published originally, in 1941, as *The Wanton Goldfish*, are madrigals, triolets, and a romanticized chanty; some of them are merely delicate and fanciful poetic exercises, pretty trifles, but at their best they are charming; "Love Me and Never Leave Me" for instance:

> Love me, and never leave me,
> Love, nor ever deceive me,
> And I shall always bless you
> If I may undress you:
> Which I heard a lover say
> To his sweetheart, where they lay.
>
> He, though he did undress her,
> Did not always bless her;
> She, though she would not leave him
> Often did deceive him;
> Yet they loved, and when they died
> They were buried side by side;

or "The Hungry Moths", or "Chanty": one would like to print all of them. The second and longer section of the book, most of which appeared originally as *Vaudeville* in 1938, seems at the first glance an extraordinary contrast to the other, since it deals mainly with clerk

[49] See the article in *Southerly* that has been referred to.

and typist and office and flat life in the Sydney of today, described with a satiric sympathy. But apart from a free and careless outspokenness that is sometimes ribald, and an apparently free and careless flow of words that is actually calculated to the last decimal, though the old French forms have been abandoned, there runs through most of the poems in this section a strong undercurrent of music and a freshness that, city and all, suggest the pastoral aspect of seventeenth-century English poetry. This is particularly evident in a couple of the best of the poems, "The Passionate Clerk to His Love", with its reminiscence of Marlowe, and "Music in the Air", which combines in an unusual manner sardonic realism and a ballad-like music, as may be seen from the poem of which the following is an extract:

> There was music in the air
> And the moon shone bright
> When Jack had his girl
> On Friday night.
>
> . . . .
>
> They went to a cafe;
> The soup was cold;
> The beef was scraggy,
> The prunes full of mould:
> *There was music in the air*
> *And the moon shone bright*
> *As they ate their dinner*
> *On Friday night:*
>
> . . . .
>
> They closed the door;
> Mary hung
> Lax in his arms;
> His fierce lips stung:
> *There was music in the air*
> *And the moon shone bright*
> *When they closed the door*
> *On Friday night.*

Almost all the poems in this part of the book are or at least involve impressions of women; they are usually light sketches, often of one aspect only, but clear-cut and effective so far as they go: the bank typist, the surfer, the waitress, the artist's model, the "pick-up", "The Old Girl", and the middle-aged woman, from whom

> The kindly sun has drained away
> Her life, like suds on washing day.

There is no doubt about McCuaig's poetic and satiric gifts, and of the charming or dramatically effective use that he has made of them now and then; but it seems that he did not rise beyond this level.

The next two lyrists have scarcely anything in common with the rest, but with one another they have one thing in common: that their verses are impregnated, though with quite different results, with the spirit of the folk-ballad. Douglas (Alexander) Stewart (Eltham, N.Z., 1913-) is another example of the crossing of the Australian and the New Zealand literatures, and like two of his predecessors[50] he was brought over from New Zealand by the *Bulletin* to edit its Red Page; he was educated at the New Plymouth Boys' High School and at the Victoria University College, and worked on the staff of several New Zealand newspapers; he travelled with a merry-go-round and worked his passage to England, at the same time contributing to the *Bulletin*, whose staff he joined in 1938. His books of verse include, besides two that do not concern us here[51] and two that are mentioned in the section dealing with poems of war,[52] *The Dosser in Springtime* (Sydney, 1946) and *Glencoe* (Sydney, 1947).[53] No Australian writer has possessed a more varied talent, for besides being one of the principal Australian lyrists of the day and its principal critic, as a playwright for the stage and for the air he stands by himself in this country. No writer who is aware, as Stewart is, of the literary currents in the oversea world, not even FitzGerald, could be less affected by them; from his verse alone, except for a modern freedom of rhyme and rhythm and language one might imagine that he had never heard of Eliot and his successors: at its best it has a gay freshness that reminds one of sunlight on spring water, and that, dashed with irony, enlivens and reinforces his tragedy; humour is as important and indissoluble a constituent of it, and indeed of his work generally, as it is of McCrae's: he even goes so far as to remark, in the character of a crow it is true, but there is a good deal of Stewart in all his animal characterizations, that "the best of love is its laughter". His verse has a casual easiness that is not so careless as it may seem at first glance, and indeed it is often deliberate; but sometimes it becomes discursive and a little longwinded, so that the freshness that is never absent tends a little to fade. It has a whimsical exuberant fancy that is often delightful, as in the description of the billygoat that the mason rode over the mountain tops "with his beard spread out like a sneeze"; but sometimes it is merely flippant, and sometimes, with a carelessness that is more than merely apparent, Stewart can slip into prosiness or mere journalese: this sort of

[50] Arthur Adams and David McKee Wright.

[51] *Green Lions* (Auckland, 1936) and *The White Cry* (London, 1939), though a few of the poems in the first were written during a six months' visit to Sydney. On the other hand there are some nostalgic reminiscences of New Zealand in *Elegy For an Airman* (Sydney, 1940). For Stewart's plays, see pp. 1264-9, and for his critical work, pp. 1288-92. His short stories, collected in *A Girl With Red Hair* (Sydney, 1944), seem on the whole to belong to New Zealand rather than to Australian literature.

[52] See p. 1065.

[53] He has also published since the closing date of this History, *Sun Orchids* (Sydney, 1952) and *The Birdsville Track* (Sydney, 1955).

thing[54] amounts to more than an incidental defect when in a poem as good as "Lady Feeding the Cats" there are references to a "bonnet much bedraggled" and meat that "demands attention"; and it is a serious matter when "The Bishop",[55] a poem that is dignified and basically serious, however light and free its treatment, is sprinkled with cheap journalistic colloquialisms. It might be argued of course that these were an inseparable part of the conception of the poem; but dignity, though compatible with freedom and lightness, is surely not compatible with so much flippancy as this: beyond a certain point the mingling of opposites in poetry is incompatible. The following verses may give an idea of the qualities that make and disfigure the poem:

> Robed and mitred the bishop stands and hard by his ear a pigeon
> Preens in the sun on the top of his head and tells him about religion.
>
> Oh, Time has struck the bishop stiff with its eye as cold as a gorgon's,
> His body is bronze and his heart is too (if a statue contains such organs);
>
> . . . .
>
> No one has heard him shudder and clank when free at last from the ship
> Bill goes rolling to Palmer Street with a bottle parked on his hip. . . .
>
> . . . .
>
> Smith of the suburbs reading his paper, escaping by tram from the boss,
> The trim little bits with their scarlet nails homing to flats at the Cross;
>
> The rich and the poor, the strong and the weak, the priest and sinner and sot
> Whether they like it or whether they don't the bishop blesses the lot.
>
> . . . .
>
> Solid in space, secure in time, defiant he takes his stand,
> The whole of life goes blessed on its way beneath the sun of his hand.

Connected with these other qualities is a desire to flout the literary conventions and the trivialities and pseudo-profundities of the academics and the intelligentsia: like FitzGerald, Stewart has a hit at the professors, or some of them:

> A kind of seagull, a closer view discloses,
> A twinkling people, eager in legs and beak;

and at the critics, or some of them,

> Stabbing the dancer's back for [their] conscience' sake.

He has an unusually individual and vivid imagination: he can "walk on the stars like stepping-stones" and he can enter into beings so far apart as the old lady who feeds the cats; the cats themselves; the white

---

[54] Examples include: "They'll come with handcuffs and no compunction" (*The Dosser in Springtime*, p. 15), and

> Life was scarcely convenient
> Dragging a ball and chain
>
> (the same, p. 20).

[55] The same, p. 59.

old dosser in the cave who dreams of the girl he has seen bathing in the creek; those of his Highland race who were concerned in the massacre of Glencoe; a cricket; a lizard; and even a bunyip: to the extent at least of making them all seem exceedingly real; and occasionally, though uncharacteristically, his imagination realizes itself in pure beauty, as in "The Jacaranda", in which this matter-of-fact and yet whimsical humorist approaches a mystic world. In his tribute to the unknown soldier, "whose name is Man", true as it is and with all its perfection of workmanship, Stewart's creative imagination seems to have flagged a little, so that this is not among his best work; and in the *Elegy for an Airman* his talent was not yet mature, in spite of the fine symbolism of

> the city is lost in a wind of autumn leaves,

and the beautiful image of the vessel far out at night,

> the starry city that wheels its course in the darkness.

Stewart's second Australian book, *Glencoe*, is a ballad-sequence which has much of the force and freshness and vivid colouring of the old Scottish folk-ballad, together with an individuality which the typical folk-ballad does not often possess because of its grinding smooth in the stream of constant repetition by word of mouth. The Glencoe series are not imitations of the old ballads however, but use their form and conventions in the creation of a series of hard little thumbnail sketches and swift dramatic actions, all moving, bright and vivid, to the gay as well as tragic lilt of folk-song; there could never be any doubt, as there may be with some of Scott's ballads, about their modernity: their deliberate half-rhymes, for instance, contrast strongly with the rhyme or broken rhyme of the folk-ballads. Towards the end we are made to feel that the sharp edges of the hate and murder with which the story deals have been blunted by time and the mingling of clans, and the hate that survived for a while at least appears after all to have been real only in spasms, since bottle-nosed Jock, who has refused to drink with a Campbell, admits that he himself is a Campbell on his father's side; yet the facts and feelings are shown as real and strongly remembered in the lovely poem of which these are the first and last verses:

> Sigh, wind in the pine;
> River, weep as you flow;
> Terrible things were done
> Long, long ago.
>
> . . .
>
> Sigh, wind in the pine,
> Cover it over with snow;
> But terrible things were done
> Long, long ago.

Stewart thinks, as naturally as any poet, in images: some of them are bizarre, as in the description of the goat's beard already quoted; or roughly realistic, as in

> The broken ridge like a bullock's ribs lies crumbling under the blue;

or fresh and sweet, as in that of the girl washing:

> When the cool bush-water kisses her face in greeting
> It is not girl and water but sisters are meeting;

and there is Hobbs's vision of

> . . . the city
> He would lie beside of nights,
> Like a white girl sleeping
> In her glittering bed of lights;

and the Bunyip's pool in which

> . . . the stars are laid
> Like stone by silver stone;

and

> the bullfrogs groaning like trombones
> And the frogs that shrilled like a bell.

Like most strongly individual styles, Stewart's contains marked mannerisms: he is fond of the refrain, and his principal mannerism is a particular use of it: "Said the white old dosser in the cave" and so on. FitzGerald had used before him the "conceit" of the poet's having stolen for his own purposes pieces and qualities of the real world;[56] but that may well be a coincidence, and anyhow the idea is not novel and the treatments are quite different; but there are no other reflections in Stewart's poetry. The best of it stands high among Australian lyrics, and, taking into account the extraordinary range of his creative accomplishment, for his criticism also is creative, he is one of the most notable writers in Australia of the nineteen-fifties.

The second of these two lyrists is (Cedric) Peter Hopegood (Billericay, Essex, England, 1891-1967); he is definitely an intellectual, though an eccentric one, but he has been placed in this group because it is mainly as a lyrist that he matters. He approaches even closer than Stewart to the folk-ballad: indeed some of his poems are not imitations but re-creations, which are almost as hard to distinguish from true folk-ballads as some of Scott's. Like Stewart, he is not Australian by birth; but he lived in Australia for nearly thirty years, and all that matter of his

[56] Compare Stewart's "The Stolen Mountain" (*The Dosser in Springtime*, p. 46) and pt iii of FitzGerald's "Greater Apollo" (*To Meet the Sun*, p. 34).

verses have been written as well as published in this country. It is typical of him that he got part of his education at an agricultural college and part at an art school; it was finished in war and wandering; after five years' roughing it in Canada, he served in The Essex Regiment in the first World War, from which he emerged with gassed lungs, a commission and a pension. Followed a few years teaching commercial art and what in Australia would be called "swagging it", after which for health reasons he came out to Australia, working as a journalist, as a freelance artist, as shell-opener on a pearl lugger, and on stations in the north-west of Western Australia. Later he became, in the intervals of what he regarded as his main job, a freelance journalist. Almost all his best poems are contained in his latest book, *Circus at World's End* (Sydney, 1947), which also contains an introductory essay on his theory and his purpose in writing; but there are a few of the best in *Thirteen from Oahu* (Sydney, 1940), and in particular "Free Martin", which is quoted later; in a previous book he had not yet found himself.

Hopegood was extraordinarily well read in comparative ethnology, philology, symbology, mythology and folklore, and he was convinced that all myths, all symbols, originate in dream, and trace back ultimately, in some mystic way, through archetypes, to the earth-mother, the only real dreamer; he believed that these archetypes are all symbolical statements of the supreme problem of life, "the process of Regeneration or Rebirth into a larger sphere of awareness", and he said that it was with the object of promoting this that he wrote his verses. They are therefore deliberately propagandist, and it is pertinent that in the Canadian backwoods Hopegood began to work out his ideas in verse instead of prose because he ran out of paper and pencil and verse is easier to remember, and that afterwards he found prose too slow and cumbrous in recording his deepening experience.[57] There is, therefore, a world of thought and theory behind Hopegood's poems; the theory gains as well as loses by being expressed in verse, and the verse gains as well as loses by being the vehicle of theory. The theory is obviously handicapped, because in the compression and allusiveness that belong to the nature of poetry much of it is lost or becomes exceedingly difficult to follow out; yet it gains by the exemplification and illustration which are of the nature of poetry, though they help the understanding of the theory along imaginative rather than intellectual lines. As for the verse considered as such, the theory too often overburdens it: some of the allusions demand both reading and thought that absorbs the whole of the attention; also, in the

[57] For the facts here mentioned, see the introductory essay referred to; Hopegood's autobiography, *Peter Lecky by Himself* (London, 1935); and an article of his in the series, "Writing Poetry: The Why and The How", in *Southerly*, vol. x (1949), no. 1, pp. 44–8. A two-part article by Donovan Clarke, "The Poetry of Peter Hopegood", in *Southerly*, vol. viii (1947), no. 2, pp. 75–88; and no. 3, pp. 161–9, is also worth reading.

attempt at exposition the verse sometimes flattens into prose and sometimes degenerates into sheer doggerel, especially where there is an attempt at humour, always a difficult job with a fundamentally serious poet. On the other hand when the poet in Hopegood takes charge, when he is carried away by the spirit as distinguished from the material of his treasury, the theory becomes implicit only, and, no longer sedimental, is borne along in solution: the poet then approaches near to the essentials of the folk-ballad with whose form his verses are so closely associated, and absorbs from it elements, mystical, magical, or of gnomic wisdom, which accord closely with his own temperament and experience, and what he writes becomes more than a mere vehicle of theory or the imitation of a particular kind of poetry. For Hopegood has himself certain characteristics that bring him close to the folk-balladist in two different aspects: he is not only essentially a man of action, and of adventurous action, with which, whatever their original authors, so far as they had individual authors, the folk-ballads are usually in the main concerned, but he is also a mystic, and certain personal experiences have reinforced the mystical element in him, so that it is easy for him to approach the ballad on that side also. Both of these characteristics in Hopegood appear in, for instance, "Sir Godfrey's Good Neighbour"; in this poem, whose subject is taken from a legend given in Scott's *Minstrelsy of the Scottish Border*, the folk-ballad combines, sometimes incongruously, with the romanticism of Scott's day. It is a tale of magical adventure which contains also touches of poetic magic; they are derived obviously from the folk-ballad, but they appear naturally, and have, in their context, an individuality that prevents one from regarding them as mere borrowings: there are for instance the lines in which Sir Godfrey

> . . . looked to the east and he looked to the west
> and he peered a little below the day;

and there is the passage in which

> a bearded rider in weeds of grey
> with a crane-wing hat by way of crest
> came riding out of the east, or west,
> or maybe a little below the sun,

though these lines are followed by modern and colloquial expressions that almost destroy the atmosphere of the poem. In a different manner the two elements in Hopegood the poet combine in such poems as "The Clam's Dream" and "The Protagonist": symbolic poems, though all Hopegood's poems are symbolic, whose object is to convey a kind of almost allegorical wisdom, but which are at the same time full of movement and change. But it is when Hopegood follows the form of the folk-ballad most closely, as in "Free Martin", that his re-creations are closest; in this extract, for example:

When the chase has dwindled,
  Martin, says the roe;
Ask for what you will . . .
  it is yours before I go.

. . . .

I would like a mantle
  deep and dark and blue;
I would like a sharp arrow
  to sever it in two.

. . . .

Yet I charge you answer
  this before I go:
Who shall wear a cloak shent
  by a sharp arrow?

Martin gives for answer:
  Just before the dawn
comes a naked fellow
  and lays him on the lawn.

Bloody are his limbs and crown;
  bloody is his track;
and cold . . . cold . . . cold
  blows the wind from off the lake.

I would share my mantle
  dark and blue and deep
with that bloody cold one
  who troubles all my sleep.

He is close, again, to another quality that belongs to the folk-ballad only in a very wide sense of the term, in such a poem as "The Nicorn's Dower"; here we have an example of a vision which is not the less acute than when it takes an intellectual form, as in "The Clam's Dream" or "The Protagonist", and also a sparkling freshness, even if in this instance it may owe something to De La Mare; the poem begins:

Only the nicorn knows
what hides behind the hills
only the crownéd snow-white haunter
of snow-hushed rills,
that fumbles with eager lips
at the tingling breast of the snow. . . .

Hopegood is at his best, then, when he is at his simplest and when his theories are implicit merely, and also when he is closest to the folk-ballad; and besides what his poems owe to the theory which also often overburdens them, they owe something also to his own temperament and experience, and more to a genuine poetic faculty which can never be entirely overwhelmed.

CHAPTER V

VERSE

LYRICAL AND LYRICALLY DESCRIPTIVE POETS CONTINUED

Description and Atmosphere: Harold Stewart. Links with the previous Period: Devaney; Winifred Shaw; Others. A Link with America: Moll. Poet Balladists: Campbell; Ethel Anderson; Others. Younger Poets. Poets of War. Groups: Angry Penguins; Jindyworobaks; Others. General and Periodical Anthologies

WITH Harold (Frederick) Stewart (Sydney, 1916-) the descriptive element in modern Australian poetry becomes much larger: so far as his published work is concerned he might almost be described as a painter of verbal pictures, with the effect of crayon or watercolour; yet he could not possibly be called a "nature poet"; there is too large an imaginative element in his pictures, and they are never derived at first hand from the real world. He was born of Australian parents, and educated at Fort Street Boys' High School, at the State Conservatorium of Music and at the University of Sydney; during the war he was attached to the Directorate of Research and Civil Affairs. He gives his profession as "poet and art critic", lives more or less isolated from society,[1] though he engages in a little wireless and newspaper journalism, and is a friend of Hope and of McAuley, whose collaborator he was in the "Ern Malley" experiment.[2] Though Stewart has written, or rather preserved, for his standards are high, comparatively little, his poetry may be said to have already passed through three phases: the first two are represented in *Phoenix Wings* (Sydney, 1948), the only book of verse he had published when this History ended, and the third by a long poem, "Orpheus",[3] which was awarded a prize in the *Sydney Morning Herald's* 1949 verse competition. The poems of Stewart's first and second phases may best be considered together, for they are written in the same style and their principal differences are in the adoption of a new set of pictorial conventions and in the ripening of the poet's powers. The poetry of the first phase consists, besides some capable translations from Mallarmé and Valéry, of the poems grouped together under the heading "The Annunciation", and also of "Give Me New Phoenix Wings" and "The Phoenix Palm" from the group headed "The Ascension of Fêng";

[1] [For the last fifteen years or so, Stewart has lived in Kyoto, feeling that Japan is his spiritual home.]

[2] See pp. 1072-3.

[3] "Orpheus" was published in book-form in Sydney in 1956, along with a number of short poems, some of them allied to "Orpheus" and others Chinese, as in *Phoenix Wings*.

all the rest belong to the second phase; this however does not agree with Stewart's own grouping, in which he brings together for his particular purposes earlier and later poems and poems that are different in kind. The poems of the first phase, are, except for the translations, purely subjective; in them Stewart, to vary slightly one of his own lines,

> Wanders [his] own dream's lonely shore:

the two finest of them, "The Annunciation" and "Phoenix Wings", are beautiful things, translucent, crystalline; but their themes, of the first, the coming of inspiration to the dreaming poet, and of the second, the frustration of his attempts at the unattainable, are overlaid and almost hidden by imagery; it is not that they are vague, but simply that all that is at first visible through their luminous atmosphere is a series of figures of cut crystal. The poems of the second phase are still pictorial, but the pictures are not essentially of Stewart's own creation: they are based upon actual paintings, or at least paintings of a particular kind, usually landscapes, or landscapes with figures; and it is a point of importance that these landscapes are Chinese. Other Australian poets have felt the influence of the Orient,[4] but it has been a passing influence; they have turned to it, and turned away again; but Stewart appears to have found in the Orient a natural affinity: in Chinese literature, in the Zen philosophy, in Chinese culture generally and most of all in Chinese landscape painting, he has become so absorbed that an important part of his work is based, not, as with most poets who have written in English, upon the culture of Britain and perhaps France or Italy or Germany or Greece and Rome, but upon the culture of Ancient China.[5] These Chinese poems approach reality more nearly than the others: because they are concerned with a world which is, basically, outside the poet's mind; because the landscapes on which they are based are detailed and as realistic as the conventions of Chinese art allow; and because they involve human beings and their relationships, though these are stylized. And the wild geese, in the finest of all the poems, closely as they and their treatment blend with all the rest, are extremely realistic; one feels that the poet must have watched wild geese, as indeed he did: nevertheless it is after all paintings and not nature upon which these poems are ultimately founded, and ideals and imaginations rather than actuality with which they are concerned, so that they are still at one remove from the real world. Stewart is by no means a mere imitator; apart from the personal observation with which he supplements that of the Chinese painters, there could be no question of the Occidental origin of these poems:

[4] Macartney for instance, in his *Tripod for Homeward Incense*.

[5] "What Greece has been, from the Renascence on, to English poets, Ancient China and the East in general are to me" (Letter to me, 17th April 1943).

material, manner, conventions may be Chinese, but it is always an Occidental who is using them, and an Occidental with his own way of putting things; there remains about Stewart's Chinese poems the atmosphere of their subject, but it is blent with a general indebtedness to the English poets of the eighteenth century and with rhythmic innovations and other factors of his own.

Harold Stewart is among the two or three most painstaking, elaborate and accomplished verbal artists in Australian verse. He never wastes a word, though he does sometimes waste a passage and become definitely long-winded; it is as though he could not bear to waste good material. His critical self-judgment is otherwise so good that it is worth pointing out a few lapses: there is for instance the "quartered quartz" in which the desire for onomatopoeia has led him into an infelicity; and occasionally, but very seldom, a full stop comes in towards the beginning or end of a line, producing the effect of a sudden bump;[6] Stewart always knows exactly what he is attempting, but these appear to represent slips in taste, such as may well happen now and then, when long working over a line or passage may temporarily blind one to the difference between an effect that is aesthetic and one that is not. And, connected with the occasional longwindedness that has been mentioned, there is, even, and indeed especially, in his best poem a tendency to dwell so long upon a note that it becomes monotonous. Stewart's attitude and method are those of a sophisticated and painstaking simplicity: what he wishes to convey is in its essence simple, but he uses the most elaborate and conscious art to keep it simple and to make it crystal-clear. And since his poetry, or rather his published poetry, is all of the same kind, he uses many artifices to avoid monotony; one or two he took over from the eighteenth century:[7] the iambic pentameter which constitutes his principal metre is constantly varied by the inclusion of a hexameter. He is an enthusiast, an expert, and to some extent an innovator in rhythm, and this and his bright imagination and command of epithet make all the difference; but here also there is a weakness: he has an extremely strong feeling for balance, also apparently inherited from the eighteenth century, and his use of it becomes a little monotonous. Some examples are beautiful, as in

Cerulean content and clear delight;

some are at least striking, as in

This senile courtesan and impious nun,

. . . .

Sensual lava and volcanic lust,

[6] For example: "Coil like sleeping dragons. Fog fills." But in this matter he is by no means alone among poets of today.

[7] Or possibly Brennan may have influenced him here.

and

> . . . restless rubies among rough-cast gold;

but there are so many that they tend to become mechanical, especially when, as with

> The soft forewarning of a hovered hand,

the phrasing is itself mechanical; but there are not many such examples as this. Sometimes the balance is carried over a couple of lines, as when, this time an Elizabethan reminiscence, Stewart speaks of

> Its golden ball of quintessential fire,
> Its fiery sphere of elemental gold;

or

> Cheekbones in haggard creases of decay
> And mummy-puckered parchment of the skin;

these also are at any rate striking, but some can barely pay their passage, and there is one,

> Arise, and soar into the breathless realms
> And rarest altitudes of paradise,

that is merely wind. Another characteristic of Stewart's is his fondness for double or even treble epithets, as

> Over a pale serene turquoise sky,

and

> This solitary sovereign silver star:

these are extremely effective, but the most interesting element in Stewart's style is his use of rhythm. He is fond of manipulating accent, or quantity, for some of his lines will scan both accentually and quantitatively, the words being dwelt upon as well as stressed, and to the same extent; this of course is true also of other poets, but they are as a rule poets who depend more than Stewart, in his published work, upon the Latin and Greek classics: an example is the first of the two lines quoted above. Lines of the same weight, lines that take the same time to say, need not of course contain the same number of syllables; if they contain a comparatively large number of syllables the line has usually to be hurried, as in the often-quoted examples from Tennyson; if on the contrary the line contains comparatively few syllables, the pause, or the stress, on some of the syllables has to be increased: most poets use this fact in order to vary their rhythms and to produce desired effects. Stewart is particularly fond of omitting syllables in order to make his lines run jointless, as though they were cast of some smooth and running water—not built of separate units; by this means he produces novel as well as beautiful effects, in which however his choice of epithet plays an important part; for the epithets give the lines their tone, and he is able in this way to dwell upon them as well as to reinforce their effect, as in the following lines:

> To wander her own dream's lonely shore;
> . . . .
> With a rose haze, paler below;
> . . . .
> With pale citrine tone, the watery light;
> . . . .
> And five pearls are in her youthful hair;
> . . . .
> His smooth shoulders dominate the whole.

Another characteristic rhythmic effect of Stewart's is the ending of a line not merely with two final stresses, or long quantities, but sometimes, a very unusual practice among poets with three,[8] as in

> And space as to a vast kiss thrill;
> . . . .
> Into the Ocean, time since past;
> . . . .
> Like pine-ink, tracing on to warm brown silk;
> . . . .
> Nothing will ever break that fierce soul down;
> . . . .
> Gone with the echo of a far high cry.

There might conceivably be differences of opinion as to the scansion of some of these lines, but on the other hand there are many other instances in which it would be legitimate to scan a line of Stewart's as having three final stresses; still more of Stewart's lines end with a cretic, a strong-weak-strong, or long-short-long, in which the intermediary weak, or short, is so nearly strong, or long, as to produce an effect almost the same as in the lines quoted above.

"Orpheus" is an entirely different kind of poetry. It deals with the myth of Orpheus's descent into Hell to recover his wife Persephone, but it makes of the myth an elaborate psychological allegory on modern lines; for example the Sybil whom Orpheus consults "lives within the cranial cave", and she tells him that

> That poet who would most excell
> On earth, must first descend to Hell,
> To rescue from the night's control
> And bring to light his bride, the soul.

---

[8] Technically, a molossus. As has been seen, Judith Wright and one or two others use this rhythm, though they do not make a practice of it (see p. 1027).

Orpheus in his descent is represented as a victim of the mother-complex, and Eurydice, in her farewell to him, declares that he

> . . . loved the past, and looked behind;
> Yet he who seeks will never find
> Full-grown Anteros if he yields
> to yearning for maternal fields.

The poem is written throughout in five-line tetrameters, in which the first three lines and the last two rhyme with one another, or the first two and the last three; this is the only variation in the verse-form, and the rhythm is smooth and unvaried throughout. As a result, though the poem is lucid, terse, compact and almost perfect in workmanship, and though there are passages of wisdom and some fine lines, for instance

> For Music rules the atoms' round,
> And in the air at dusk is found
> Her bright astronomy of sound;

and though the applications of the allegory are interesting, the poem as a whole is monotonous. Monotony, indeed, is a danger that Stewart has always to avoid: in "Orpheus" he does not seem even to try to avoid it; in the Chinese and earlier poems, though their range is small and their subjects slight, and though there is a constant repetition of effects, rhythmic and other, he takes pains to avoid it, and on the whole, though not invariably, he succeeds. The earlier poems in his first book are luminous with a clear crystalline beauty such as had not previously been attained in the poetry of this country at any rate; here he reminds one sometimes of Mallarmé, but there is this essential difference, that Stewart describes where Mallarmé suggests. And in the later poems in the same book, the Chinese poems, the clear crystalline beauty passes into a beauty that is less ethereal but not less delicate and more subtle; it is also more human, even to the extent of having humorous touches sometimes, and contains a little more substance: here is a passage in which Stewart is somewhere near his best; it is from "A Flight of Wild Geese", and it has about it something of the feeling, the atmosphere, of a painting by a Chinese master upon silk; but the passage quoted can give only a faint and partial idea of the whole poem, which is in its kind a masterpiece: Wu Tao-tzŭ, the greatest of Chinese artists, has entered into his own landscape roll, and meets there an old fisherman, Chang Chih-ho; as they are talking, "skeins" of wild geese arrive and "span the sky"; but Chang Chih-ho declares that

> ". . . they have been here since time began."

The poem goes on; it is impossible to give any real idea of it without a long quotation:

Down the sky in file the wild geese tack,
Slanting their obliquely angled track
Toward the estuary's bank of sand
With blocks of basalt strewn along the strand.
The leader there comes skidding in, to sit
On a long splash, for the sheer sport of it:
His tail-feathers fan to brake the flight;
And webbed feet and red legs alight,
As if fixed in a clear aquamarine,
So still the surface-water is, and green.
There he stands upright in the water-rings,
Throws out his breast, and flaps his wide wings;
There ducks, to ladle over back and head
Wingfuls of water; shakes his tail to shed
Superfluous drops; and washing over, grooms
Down smooth and trim his toilet-ruffled plumes;
And then into a comfortable unrest
Worries the pin-plumage of his breast.
More glide in after him. The others land
Pinions aloft, and settle on the sand,
Where flat snapping bills hiss and contest
Scraps of aquatic weed that one possessed.
Pushing a fold of glass against the stream,
One paddles in pursuit of his own gleam.
Another stoops his pliant neck to sip
This running ripple with the glassy lip,
And elevates it after every dip.
A third, whose bill tugged at the wavering weeds,
Lifts their dripping ribbons up, and feeds.
Riding its undulating ebb, the fleet
Of geese sets sail upon the glaucous sheet;
But a snapped stick startles one among
Them. Instantly the floating flock is sprung.
Low over the water skims each pair:
The downbeat of the wing-tip in the air
Touching the upbeat of its image there.
Once in the central air, they travel south
Beyond the sandspit at the river's mouth,
Beyond the dim horizon. All are gone.
But, like a flock of feathers dropped upon
The refluent air after their motion's flown,
A soft flocculence of cloud is strown;
And hovers, as invisible waves of wake
Diverge, and on the mountains sprayless break.

Wu Tao-tzŭ:
"They have migrated to a warmer clime".

Chang Chih-ho:
"They will be here now till the end of time."

It has been already noted that among the lesser lyrical and descriptive poets there are several who carry the characteristics of the preceding

Period into this; the most interesting of them is James (Martin) Devaney (Bendigo, Vic., 1890-1976), whose work, though he was three years younger than Macartney and nine years younger than Wilmot, has about it little trace of modernity. Devaney's parents were Australian and Irish; he was teacher, tutor and freelance journalist, concentrating largely on "nature" subjects and Aboriginal lore, and the greater part of his life was spent in Queensland; he wrote short stories, novels and also a biography of Shaw Neilson which is mentioned elsewhere,[9] and his verse was collected in *Poems* (Sydney, 1950). Devaney is essentially a romantic poet, a sensitive observer and seeker for beauty in nature, in which he finds reflected his own moods; and he conveys what he discovers in sweet and simple melody; thus both his aim and his method are those of a previous generation, but they are pervaded by a quiet and unaffected personality and a deep sincerity that redeem them from mere echoing: in one of his later poems, "Winter Westerlies", he breaks into a freer rhythm and speaks with an unaccustomed force; and in another, "The Evening Gleam", he achieves at last fitting expression for the calm loveliness that he has been pursuing for so long. A couple of women poets, Elsie (Clarice) Cole[10] (Mrs A. H. Angel, Melbourne) and Myra (Evelyn Sydenham) Morris,[11] (Boort, Vic., 1893-1966), who belong to the beginning of this Period, have much in common with the poetry of the last, and in particular with the poems of Dorothea Mackellar, though their talents are smaller. They too are poets of colour and light: Elsie Cole tells of

> The clouded pink of apples crisp with frost,
> And grey-blue grapes, mysterious with bloom;

and Myra Morris of

> Black-boughed old plums with azure caught between,
> Tall plum-trees pearled with soft, effulgent light,
> Spattered with drifts of snow;

yet there is no essential likeness between the work of these two. Elsie Cole is the richer in images, but they are not so striking as Dorothea Mackellar's; her themes are slight, and one feels that they do not matter to her so much as the images in which they are bodied forth. Myra Morris's themes are also slight, but her best verse, as in "White Magic", has a creamy richness, along with a certain daintiness and charm; she has the wider range of the two, but her easy irregular rhythm and her slow, smooth running movement, as against Elsie Cole's joyous dance,

---

[9] See p. 1360.

[10] Her best book is *Children of Joy* (Melbourne, 1928).

[11] Her best book of verse is *White Magic* (Melbourne, 1929); she has also written novels and short stories.

encourage a wordiness to which she is in any case inclined. A generation later, less striking and colourful but more modern, except for the survival in her verses of a number of romantic tag-ends, was Norma (Lochlena) Davis (Whitemore, Tas., 1906-45); in her one book of verse, *Earth Cry* (Sydney, 1943), her romantic love for Tasmanian earth and all that grows and moves upon it found expression in little pictures that are closely observed and often revealing. At the farthest possible extreme from all these is Charles Rischbieth Jury (Adelaide, 1894-1958), who served in the first World War and became Professor of English at his own university. His *Galahad, Selenemia and Poems* (Adelaide, 1939) and his verse play, *Love and the Virgins* (London, 1929), are reminiscent of the Romantic Age in English Literature, and of Keats's Greece, but they contain chords of beauty.

At the beginning of the Period three young poets, after publishing a book each, left Australia, not to return. Jack Lindsay (Melbourne, 1900-), eldest son of Norman Lindsay, is a graduate of the University of Queensland. His only Australian book,[12] *Fauns and Ladies* (Sydney 1924) is a vigorous but monotonous celebration of Aphrodite Pandemos and her rites; in Australia he also helped to found and edit the periodical *Vision*,[13] and, with Kenneth Slessor, an anthology, *Poetry in Australia*. The second poet, Raymond (Herbert) McGrath (Sydney, 1903-77), a leading British architect, when a student in architecture at the University of Sydney published in *Seven Songs of Meadow Lane* (Sydney, 1924) some light verses full of grace and fancy. The third and by far the most interesting of the three, Winifred (Maitland) Shaw (Mrs R. M. Taplyn, Singleton, N.S.W., 1905-), was working in a government office in Singapore when she was captured by the Japanese and interned in Changi prison camp; since the war she has been living in England. She has published three little books of verse, of which the first was written when she was only fourteen: this, *The Aspen Tree* (Sydney, 1920), is a marvellous production for so young a girl; but the two others that followed it repeated the note, and not so well. Winifred Shaw had read a good deal of classical as well as English literature, and was deeply interested in ancient Greece and in the English ballad; her short lyrics, light but exquisitely carved, suggest a young romantic's impression of the folk-ballad and of the Greek anthology: one or two of the best are like statuettes of rose-coloured marble.

Among the established lyric and descriptive writers there is a curious link with America in Ernest George Moll (Murtoa, Vic., 1900-): he had his schooling in Australia, but proceeded to the University of

---

[12] But since this was written he has published an autobiography, *Life Rarely Tells* (London, 1958), which deals with his life in Australia. Jack Lindsay's English novels are referred to on p. 1232.

[13] See p. 1326.

Harvard and has been Professor of English at Oregon since 1928; nevertheless he retains and is proud of his Australian citizenship, has made several recent visits to Australia, and has published four books of Australian verse.[14] Of these, the most interesting is the first, *Cut from Mulga*, for Moll's range is narrow, and he tends to repeat his effects; but his is a genuine talent, though not a considerable one: he has a pleasant, easy style, a sincere affection for the beasts and birds of the bush, and a tender sympathy for the victims of the cruelty of man and nature, though it tends to run into sentimentality, and a gentle, humorous satire. Essentially Australian, Moll's verses have yet a curiously hybrid tone, with their occasional Americanisms and the obvious influence of Frost; he shows also a sympathetic kinship with his old friend, the late Professor Brereton. Other established lyrists are Clement Christesen and R. G. Howarth, of both of whom there will be more to say later in dealing with the literary magazines they edit, *Meanjin*[15] and *Southerly*.[16] Christesen's descriptive lyrics[17] are short, light, bright, mainly of the bush and its birds, with glimpses of femininity; Howarth's[18] are love poems, simple and sensuous, a little in the manner of the seventeenth century.

Earlier in this History it was said that the bush ballad had died with the disappearance of the conditions that gave it birth, but its spirit is very much alive in the poems of David (Watt Ian) Campbell (Ellerslie station, near Adelong, N.S.W., 1916–79). Yet Campbell scarcely ever uses the ballad form; he is essentially a poet, and is indeed, along with Francis Webb, the most considerable of all the younger Australian poets of today. He was educated at The King's School, N.S.W., and at Cambridge, to which he won a scholarship; at both school and college he distinguished himself in athletics, especially football, in which he represented England against Ireland and Wales, and in 1938 he returned to Australia. When war broke out he joined the R.A.A.F. and ended as a Wing-Commander, with a D.F.C. and Bar, and later he became a Squadron Leader; his life after the war was spent as a farmer in and around the Australian Capital Territory. His first book to be published was *Speak with the Sun* (London, 1949),[19] but there has been nothing in verse more distinctively Australian since *The Man from Snowy River*. Campbell was born and bred in that south-east corner of New South Wales which is an important part of Paterson's country, his Australia is Paterson's, or rather part of Paterson's,

[14] *Cut from Mulga* (Melbourne, 1940), *Brief Waters* (Sydney, 1945), *Beware the Cuckoo* (Sydney, 1947), *The Waterhole* (Sydney, 1948); also, after the closing date of this History, *The Lifted Spear* (Sydney, 1953), and a collection, *Poems, 1940–55* (Sydney, 1957).

[15] See pp. 782, 1328.

[16] See p. 1330.

[17] Collected in three small booklets: *North Coast* (Brisbane, 1943), *South Coast* (Brisbane, 1944), and *Dirge and Lyrics* (Melbourne, 1945); also a prose anthology, *Australian Heritage* (see p. 1261).

[18] Collected in *Spright and Geist* (Sydney, 1944) and *Involuntaries* (Sydney, 1948).

[19] But Campbell has since published *The Miracle of Mullion Hill* (Sydney, 1956) and a book of short stories, *Evening Under Lamplight* (Sydney, 1959).

and though it is reflected in poems, not ballads, they are definitely in the ballad tradition; the range of his Australia is much narrower than Paterson's, and he has nothing like Paterson's multiplicity of outback types and scenes, but what he brings before us is permeated and reinforced with mental and imaginative elements which for Paterson scarcely existed and for most of the bush balladists did not exist at all. A verse-craft, an arrangement of poetic effects, a type of imagery, an intellectual background and quality and a definite element of mysticism: all these elements Campbell adds to the bush ballads, besides departing from its form, producing something that is as new as it is old. And just as Paterson opens his small but occasionally unforgettable windows upon the country-side, so Campbell also has his glimpses, his little pictures, less concise, less realistic, less strongly outlined, but more imaginative, more artistic and not less real, and striking below the superficial layers of consciousness. In "The Stockman" for example, where Paterson might have flashed a moment of vision, not new in kind but new in intensity and focusing a simple aspect of truth, Campbell gives us something that if it lacks Paterson's primitive force, goes deeper and means more: with Paterson it is a stockman's vision that is given us; with Campbell it is the vision of an imaginative poet of a later and a more intellectual society who retains the stockman's eye but can perceive what the stockman cannot perceive. It is necessary to quote the whole poem[20] to make clear what has been said:

The sun was in the summer grass,
The coolibahs were twisted steel:
The stockman paused beneath their shade
And sat upon his heel,
And with the reins looped through his arm
He rolled tobacco in his palm.

His horse stood still. His cattle dog
Tongued in the shadow of the tree,
And for a moment on the plain
Time waited for the three.
And then the stockman licked his fag
And Time took up his solar swag.

I saw the stockman mount and ride
Across the mirage on the plain;
And still that timeless moment brought
Fresh ripples to my brain:
It seemed in that distorting air
I saw his grandson sitting there.

[20] Other examples are "Spring Hares" and "Winter Stock Route", and there are several in "The Possum and the Moon".

And as the spirit of the bush comes naturally to Campbell, so, following the example of a poet with whom he has nothing whatever in common, he deliberately embodies names and phrases from the poets, in this case from the old bush balladists, so that the ghosts of those who haunt that part of Australia's past speak through him and enrich him with their echoes. For him the magpie sings, with Souter,

"Tan-tan tara, boys!"

on old John Bax's horn; with him Ogilvie's skewbald dingo sleeps at Brigalow Gap; he deliberately recalls, in his "Conroy's Gap", Paterson's ballad of the same name, with its references to the racehorse, "The Swagman", to the grog shanty, "Shadow of Death", and to the rider who "rode as mountain horsemen ride"; and Paterson's Clancy calls to his dog in another poem. Campbell introduces also real as distinct from literary bush characters of the ballad days to reinforce his effects; and he introduces much else that was foreign to the tradition of the bush balladists: he translates parts of Shakespeare's songs into Australian idiom, as in "Summer" and still more obviously in "Winter", of which here is the first verse:

When magpies sing in sky and tree
And colts like dragons snuff the air
And frosts paint hollows white till three
And lamp-lit children skip their prayer;
Then Meg and Joan at midnight lie
And quake to hear the dingoes cry
Who nightly round the white church stone
Snap at their tails and the frosty moon.

Much of Campbell's imagery draws upon his war experience: the hawk is on convoy duty and the crow a paratrooper and there is a "morse-key cricket"; speaking generally it is unlike the imagery of the bush ballad: the grass is "bleached like a barmaid's hair"; there is the fluttering of "starling emotions", the bookmaker is a "marsupial man"; and

Spinster pines
Complain continuously, sigh their set lines,
Knitting white socks of cloud or patching sunlight.

And if Campbell covers only a part of the ballad country, he ranges far outside it, as indeed Paterson does sometimes: one or two of his war poems[21] are among the best that the second World War has produced in this country, and some of his bush poems, as for example, "Humping a Bluey" stand quite outside the bush ballad tradition. But even where he stands well within that tradition, Campbell imports into it not merely thought and perception that are beyond the balladists, but something of

[21] See pp. 1065-6. [It should be noted that Campbell's poetry underwent continual renewal until his untimely death; he became one of the most versatile of poets.]

modernity in general, though little of its sophistication; his style is quite different from anything that could be imagined of a bush balladist: it is full of sound and rhythmic effects in which they were not interested, and of which they were in any case not capable, though Souter is to a certain extent an exception here. The influence of Douglas Stewart is obvious, particularly in "Humping a Bluey"; there may also be something of the later Yeats; Time and half-mystical twists and reversions in Time haunt him as they haunt Rosemary Dobson and Judith Wright; and his feeling of the continuity of life through its constant changes sometimes recalls FitzGerald. But this is not intended to suggest that Campbell's style is not individual; it is indeed markedly so: he is fond of contrasts of colour and light:

Ants in the red earth,
Red ants in red stone;

Though the snake writhes in the dust of noon
It will not die
Till black night brings the white moon;

On the grey blue bough
Of the blue grey tree
The magpie now
Works alchemy;

The granite air is golden;

and

The hare leaps in the bright green morning,
Pirouettes in rainbow light.

And though he plays with words as the balladists did not and could not, he is essentially simple and natural and on occasion colloquial; in spite of the mystical quality that is strong within him Campbell is always a bushman, even a typical bushman, though a bushman plus.

There are also a few writers who stick bravely to the old ballad tradition, refusing to admit that what belongs to an earlier age cannot, generally speaking, be revived; their verses, though sometimes vigorous enough, lack distinction and are not memorable. But Lex McLennan (Taree, N.S.W., 1909-) and Charles Shaw[22] (Melbourne, 1900–55) deserve mention: both McLennan's *Spirit of the West* and Shaw's *Warrumbungle Mare* were published in Sydney in 1943. In these two balladists simplicity survives into modernity, but in a third writer of ballads, or pseudo-ballads, sophistication metamorphoses a past simplicity. Ethel Anderson, whose poems are discussed elsewhere,[23] in *Squatters' Luck* (Melbourne, 1942) takes the bush ballad and bush verses generally and plays with them,

[22] Shaw has also written prose "sketches" in something the manner of Steele Rudd.

[23] See p. 1010.

embroidering and working them up in a manner of her own, yet with a sympathetic understanding that enables her to preserve a good deal of their spirit as well as some of their scenes and dramatis personae. The result, though extremely artificial, has yet an underlying sincerity, and is curiously attractive. Mrs Anderson's Silas and Eustace are, in spite of their most uncharacteristic names, true to the old types, real and characteristic as far as they go, and her handling, in "Flood", "Fire" and "War", of outback nomenclature is masterly; here are the first and last verses of "Fire":

From black clouds over the lost Warrumbungles,
Thick-hazed, invisible Tambourine Mountains,
Scarred Picton Razorbacks, burnt-out Jugiongs,
Dour and waterless slopes below Kosciusko
   Bush fires, blazing, obliterate the landscape.

. . . .

The frantic black swan covering her cygnets,
The Wonga pigeon, cowering on her nestlings,
The red foal, the fawn calf, myriads of butterflies
—Moonbeams, jewels, jezabels, and wood whites—
All the bright, wild tribes of the bushland perish.

Yet, surprisingly, Mrs Anderson is perhaps at her best in what is in form the most original of buckjumping ballads, and among the most striking of them in other respects; here is part of it:

Jack Brady tit-tit-tup-ped once into Bourke,
On his thoroughbred stallion he soon set to work
   To give a display
   In a negligent way
Of what a good buckjumping rider could do.
            (*Hup! Knickerbockerbuckaroo!*)

. . . .

Then out spoke a jackeroo newly come west,
"*Your beast is a beauty, but mine is the best,*
   His name is well known
   From Gilgandra to Scone,
As the king bucking brumby this side the Barcoo."
            (*Hup! Knickerbockerbuckaroo!*)

. . . .

For sixty true seconds he held his head high,

and so on, true to tradition in story at least. Several other young poets in this section are also promising; the most likely seem Nan (Nancy May) McDonald (Eastwood, N.S.W., 1921-74), and also Peter (Keith) Miles (Toowoomba, Q., 1921-). Both are good craftsmen with a feeling for rhythm and a gift of imagery: Miles (*Pacific Moon*, Melbourne, 1945) can tell of "lost gulls of paper boys" and of his liking

> . . . to lie in the sun discovering
> the texture of the wind and its pure pattern
> like a blind man in great folds of pure silk;

and Nan McDonald (*Pacific Sea*, Sydney, 1947)[24] can tell of

> The yellow, cat-eared lamp-flame,

and of

> the vast shining freedom of the sea;

but neither has found very much to say as yet. And, *Songs of the East Coast* (Sydney, 1947), by Val (Valentine Thomas) Vallis (Gladstone, Q., 1916–), with its wharves and ships and nets and fishing and the varied, life, human and other, where land meets sea have a fresh and individual interest that suggests possibilities for the future.

The second World War gave rise to much more poetry than the first. As a collection, Gellert's war poems remain unapproached, but at least one individual poem can take its place among the best that have arisen out of either war; several others, one by a combatant poet and two or three by non-combatant poets of established reputation, reach a high standard; and many young men received a genuine poetic impulse from experiences in the fighting line in New Guinea or the Middle East. Very little poetry dealing with the first World War appeared even at the beginning of the present Period; but the whole of the poetry of Leonard Mann was affected by his war experiences, though he wrote few war poems: one of them, "The Delectable Mountains",[25] has been already alluded to in a different context. And Henry Weston Pryce (Wulwye station, Monaro, N.S.W., 1891–1963), a Sydney journalist who served with the first A.I.F., published in *Your Old Battalion* (Sydney, 1926), a not otherwise remarkable collection of war verse, a couple of poems that are above the average, and one memorable passage:

> But here one sees the souls of men from cant and creed win free,
> Here Christ with eyes and cap of steel is known to such as need . . .
> In your dark hour you'll find him there; although your eyes but see
> A comrade with a cigarette, stooping to give Godspeed.

By far the finest of the second series of war poems was Slessor's "Beach Burial",[26] which was based on his experience as Commonwealth War Correspondent at El Alamein; it would be hard to find anything more pitiful than the lament for an unknown seaman, one of so many, washed up on the beach, of which these are the first two stanzas:

---

[24] Nan McDonald has since published two other books of verse, *The Lonely Fire* (Sydney, 1954) and *The Lighthouse* (Sydney, 1959).

[25] See pp. 996–7.

[26] Printed in *Australian Poetry 1944* (Sydney, 1945), and in Slessor's *Poems*, 1957.

Softly and humbly to the Gulf of Arabs
The convoys of dead sailors come;
At night they sway and wander in the waters far under,
But morning rolls them in the foam.

Between the sob and clubbing of the gunfire
Someone, it seems, has time for this,
To pluck them from the shallows and bury them in burrows
And tread the sand upon their nakedness.

Not pity but bewilderment was the burden of FitzGerald's "1918-1941",[27] with its

Distant the guns are and no wind veering
has brought them into hearing, nor yet in these lands
do they bawl between hills as between a pair of hands;
but there's what we were bred to . . . and strange it is then
to be lifting our sons up to watch the marching men.

Tattered the bewilderment I pull across my shoulders . . .
with eyes but no thought in them to mark the way I tread
and a thought without eyes that runs lost in my head.

Of the work of other non-combatant poets of established reputation, there was Douglas Stewart's[28] *Elegy for an Airman* (Sydney, 1940) and *Sonnets to the Unknown Soldier* (Sydney, 1941); Moll and Mackenzie also wrote several war poems, and so, as with Mary Gilmore in the first World War, did one woman, Elizabeth Riddell; in particular there was her "The Children March",[29] which tells how

Nightly turning their thoughts to the forsaken hearth,
The wandering, wondering children of the world
March on the sea and land and crowded air—
The unsmiling sons, the sad bewildered daughters.

But after "Beach Burial" one of the two most notable of the second series of war poems is David Campbell's "Men in Green", a mystic fantasy based on jungle fighting in New Guinea. It has been remarked in the discussion of Campbell's other poems,[30] that in him the spirit of the bush ballad has survived, though in another form, but it is the European folk-ballad that this poem recalls;★ it is given extra fascination by the imaginative twist in time that appeals to Campbell; here are some of the verses:

---

[27] Printed in *Australian Poetry 1941* (Sydney, 1941).

[28] For Stewart's poems, see pp. 1043-6; his plays, pp. 1264-9; his critical work, pp. 1288-92.

[29] See *Australian Poetry 1943* (Sydney, 1944); this poem was not included in any of Betty Riddell's printed collections. For Moll's and Mackenzie's poems, see pp. 1058-9 and 1029-34 respectively. For Betty Riddell's other poems, see p. 1011.

[30] See pp. 1059-61.

★ [There is, however, a direct reference to Paterson's "The Man from Ironbark" in the last stanza quoted on page 1066.]

Oh, there were fifteen men in green,
Each with a tommy-gun,
Who leapt into my plane at dawn;
We rose to meet the sun.

. . .

We climbed towards the distant range
Where two white paws of cloud
Clutched at the shoulders of the pass;
The green men laughed aloud.

. . .

And when on Dobadura's field
We landed, each man raised
His thumb towards the open sky;
But to their right I gazed.

For fifteen men in jungle green
Rose from the kunai grass
And came towards the plane. My men
In silence watched them pass;
It seemed they looked upon themselves
In Time's prophetic glass.

. . . .

They had not feared the ape-like cloud
That climbed the mountain crest;
They had not feared the summer's sun
With bullets for their breast.

Their eyes were bright, their looks were dull,
Their skin had turned to clay.
Nature had met them in the night
And stalked them in the day.

[Equally impressive is John Manifold's elegy, "The Tomb of Lt. John Learmonth, A.I.F." (in *Selected Verse*), a vigorous celebration of "courage chemically pure". At the end of the struggle for Crete, Learmonth took to the hills, saying he would not be captured alive. The poet sees him as a legendary figure, from a line of Australian heroes who refused to surrender. The last few lines are:

. . . Let others mourn and feel
He died for nothing: nothings have their place.
While thus the kind and civilized conceal

This spring of unsuspected inward grace
And look on death as equals, I am filled
With queer affection for the human race.]

Emu Parade (Sydney, 1941), by Tom Inglis Moore, whose other poems have been previously discussed,[31] consists entirely of war poems.

[31] See pp. 1034-6.

The poems in this collection, carefully up to date and sometimes carefully Australian, cannot approach the best of those in Moore's first book; and some of his images here seem a little too ingenious, as in the elaborate passage about "the clanking separator of this war" and the way in which it operates; but some, as for instance "war's bushfire", and "unpaddocked plains of space" are natural enough, so far as that goes, and the description of a soldier's final leave as

> . . . a close, silent fight between
> The thrust-back shadow and the snatched-at joy

comes very near succeeding.

In the work of the younger poets there is little mental background; they crystallize without illumination; they are poems of youth that is fine and frank and genuine, but in whom the shock of war has not been a springboard to the mind or the imagination; it has been an emotional rather than an imaginative or intellectual stimulus: all have felt deeply and what they feel each has tried to express without heroics; each has some poetic gift and a greater or lesser degree of poetic craftsmanship; but none stands far above the rest. Shawn (Hamilton) O'Leary (Ipswich, Q., 1916-), a graduate of the University of Queensland and in peacetime a journalist and afterwards a farmer, served in the Middle East, New Guinea and Borneo; he wrote in *Spikenard and Bayonet* (Melbourne, 1941), one poem, "The Olive Trees", that is often quoted, and another, "The Bayonet", that is terrible and hard to forget. Maurice (Edward) Biggs (Kadina, S.A., 1915-), a man of very varied occupations and, when this History closed, a shipping clerk, served in Palestine, Egypt, Greece, Crete, Syria and New Guinea; his *Poems of War and Peace* (Sydney, 1945) shows a keen observation, a feeling for colour and an instinct for the telling phrase, and he has one or two memorable passages, as

> I saw Death, once, sprawled in the sunny grass,
> His bullets spilled, his rifle flung away,
> Oblivious of the chattering Vickers guns . . .

and

> He came from where the Murrumbidgee runs
> Through golden paddocks of obeisant hay,
> And grass more sunny than this Cretan pass.

A Soldier's Miscellany (Sydney, 1945), by Eric Irvin (Sydney, 1908-), in peacetime a country journalist, is pervaded by a quiet thoughtfulness, as well as a simplicity and definiteness of observation that makes the description of the cattle in "Homeward Journey" the best piece of work in this book, but a later poem, "Midnight Patrol"[32] is even

[32] Printed in *Poetry*, No. 12 (September, 1944), and *Australian Poetry 1944* (Sydney, 1945).

better. In *Battle Stations* (Sydney, 1944), John Quinn (Toronto, Canada, 1915-65)—who served in the Middle East and Darwin—became a war correspondent and later Feature Editor on the Adelaide *News*, showed talent that he did not realize, though in "Argument" he came near to doing so. A few poets dealt with war at sea, notably Michael (Rayner) Thwaites (Brisbane, 1915-); he won a Rhodes scholarship to Oxford, became a Lieutenant-Commander, lectured in English at the University of Melbourne, [worked for A.S.I.O., and later the Parliamentary Library, until his retirement]. The title-poem of *The Jervis Bay* (London, 1943), tells how the old liner heroically held off a German battleship long enough to enable a convoy to escape: this poem is of the clan of "The Revenge", not comparable with that poem, but in no way an imitation. In the same book, "Milton Blind", which won the Newdigate Prize at Oxford, is thoughtful and dignified, far superior to most university prize poems. An anthology, *Poets at War*, (Melbourne, 1944), compiled by Ian Mudie,[33] is better mentioned here than with the other anthologies: most of the combatant poets above mentioned are represented, though not always by their best work, and there are no discoveries. The quality of the collection is handicapped by its limitation to poems by men who actually served with the fighting forces and there are one or two omissions for which it is hard to account;[34] but within the given range the poems are generally well chosen.

There remain these poets who are members or supporters of the only actual schools existing in mid-century Australian poetry, as distinct from those groups of poets who in this History have been taken together for convenience and because they have certain characteristics in common. The views and aims of the Jindyworobaks and the Angry Penguins are at opposite extremes: the Jindyworobaks were an extreme development of Australianism in literature; and the Angry Penguins were an outpost of the British and American surrealists and of their outgrowth, the New Apocalyptics. Both were in effect youth movements: most of their followers were youthful and their founders were respectively twenty-five and eighteen; both movements have the vigour and confidence and enthusiasm of youth, and beneath the narrowness, exaggeration and mistaken assumptions of the Jindyworobaks and the pose and clamour and artificiality of the Angry Penguins both are sincere. The Jindyworobaks had a wide influence, especially upon the younger Australian writers of verse, and more than one established writer has sympathized with at least their fundamental purpose and contributed to their annual anthology[35] poems that comply with their

---

[33] For Mudie's poems, see p. 1071.
[34] Thwaites, for example.
[35] *Jindyworobak Anthology* (1938-53).

requirements, more or less; the Angry Penguins also found contributors to their magazine[36] who did not belong to their school. Two or three members of each school wrote poems worth inclusion in anthologies of modern Australian poetry, but no actual member of either, not even their leaders, is among the outstanding poets of their country today, and the rank and file are of small individual importance.

In favour of the Jindyworobaks it may be said that they occasioned more controversy than any other body of writers in Australian literature. Their fundamental principle, that Australian culture must be based upon the Australian environment, would be accepted by most Australian critics; but this is by no means a new principle, and many of its applications as well as many of the Jindyworobaks' assumptions are unacceptable even to some of their strongest admirers.. "Jindyworobak" is an Aboriginal word, meaning to annex, to join, and the school and its anthology were founded in 1938, with the object of bringing Australian writers, and in particular Australian poets, into intimate contact with their environment. The founder, Rex (Reginald Charles) Ingamells (Orroroo, S.A., 1913-55), a graduate of the University of Adelaide, worked and wandered over a considerable part of South Australia and Victoria, and was a tutor for the Workers' Educational Association and a high school teacher in South Australia. Justifiably provoked by the wet-blanketing of Australian literature in an ill-advised article by an English-born Melbourne professor[37] and stimulated by P. R. Stephensen's *Foundations of Culture in Australia*,[38] by a holiday in Central Australia and an acquaintance with the anthropologist T. G. H. Strehlow,[39] Ingamells decided, apparently without a very wide reading of either Australian or modern English literature, that Australian writers had not been Australian enough; that Paterson and Lawson had written larrikin verses, sometimes in incongruous English idiom, and that because of his misleading associations Kendall was "practically valueless as an Australian poet". And in a pamphlet, *Conditional Culture* (Adelaide, 1938), from which these assertions are taken, he urged that Australian culture depended not merely upon a clear recognition of environmental values, but upon the use of only such imagery as was "truly Australian", and upon an understanding of Australian history and traditions, including those of the aborigines, from whose art and song "we must learn much of our new technique". It is true that he added that some of the best Australian literature must deal with universal themes and might have no local colour at all; but this has the air of having been an afterthought, a saving proviso ignored in practice; in the early numbers of his anthology

[36] *Angry Penguins* (see pp. 1072-3).
[37] G. H. Cowling, in the *Age*, 16th February 1935.
[38] See pp. 1438-9.
[39] For Strehlow's work, see pp. 1452-4.

Ingamells deliberately and admittedly rejected "poetically better non-Australian verse in favour of mediocre Australian".[40] It is clear that Ingamells could not have known his bush balladists very well, or understood Kendall in relation to his surroundings, and he ignores O'Dowd's "The Bush", Lawson's short stories, and Furphy's *Such is Life*, and all the other founders or precursors of Australianism in Australian literature; moreover, many of the idioms and images that Ingamells grouped as English were in fact worn-out tag-ends of Victorian romanticism, of which few traces were left by that time in English or for that matter Australian poets of standing. He was therefore flogging a dead horse, or, as he would probably have preferred to say, shooting a dead kangaroo; he was also using a weapon that must recoil on the wielder, since though a writer is foolish to use worn-out or inappropriate images, he must be free to write what he likes. And finally Ingamells ignored the fact that the culture of the Aborigines is farther from us, more alien than any European culture could be.* Yet, with all this, Jindyworobakism was valuable in several respects: it helped to keep the current cosmopolitan tendency, itself in part a revulsion from the parochialism of the Australian nineties, from going to extremes; it encouraged young poets to try to give expression in their own ways to their own feelings, their own moods, in surroundings with which they were familiar; and it emphasized a very important fact, that, in the words of a Jindyworobak supporter,[41] "we have to let the sunshine of this land into our souls". Ingamells' own verse may be judged from his *Selected Poems* (Melbourne, 1944), in which his love for the Australian outback and his admiration for the Aborigine and his legends find expression by means of a poetic talent that is genuine and not without individuality, but not great. He can give bright little glimpses, in rhyme or free verse, of birds and beasts and moods and incidents of the bush, and he can tell an adventurous story; but except where, as in such cases, his material is given him, he fails. In his longer poems especially there is little substance; his ideas are neither new nor profound and he is unable to develop them in poetry; with an exception to be mentioned, he is at his best in his glimpses and in a few episodes from early Australian history, in which atmosphere as well as subject is provided, as in "Ship from Thames" and "Macquarie Harbour". But he has a fine line or phrase here and there, as

> . . . in the Bight
> rollers will bring the stars ashore at night;

and

[40] See Editor's Note to the *Jindyworobak Anthology 1939*.

[41] Victor Kennedy, in a Jindyworobak pamphlet, *Flaunted Banners* (Adelaide, 1941) p. 6.

* [Nevertheless, the attempt to come to terms with aboriginal culture was long overdue and valuable in itself.]

The sun, with shattering bird-bright shout,
tears star-dusk's glittering gloom,
and all day long goes walkabout
from Botany to Broome.

And there is one outstanding exception to what has been said about Ingamells' longer poems; in "Memory of Hills",[42] of which here are a couple of verses, he surpassed himself:

There are rock-rooted ranges to dominate
the ways of man with peace, enforced but healing;
there are crows settling on the boundary gate,
or poised in the sky, or wheeling.

Slowly the sun moves over the red land, slowly
over the dust-puff silence that never changes
except for crow caws that suddenly, wholly
envelop those random ranges.

. . . .

The old hills are obstinate in my mind,
and I thank them now for the long familiarity.
Merely I shut my eyes to find
their reflex of moonlight, their kind
wrinkled acknowledgment of the moon's clarity.

After Ingamells, and quite as enthusiastic a Jindyworobak, is Ian (Mayelston) Mudie (Hawthorn, S.A., 1911-76), who obtained his life's education at Scotch College, Adelaide, "and carrying a swag"; he worked at freelance journalism, among other occupations, and his verse was collected in *Poems: 1934-1944* (Melbourne, 1945).[43] Mudie's verse has many characteristics in common with Ingamells', but his talent is smaller and less varied and he is even less able to develop an idea, so that except in very short poems he tends to grow monotonous and dull; a couple of these however, almost perfect little cameos, reach at least a formal level to which Ingamells does not attain, though unfortunately after them there is a great gap, the same note being repeated and repeated. In one of these little cameos, "Underground", Australianism is traced in short and telling lines to the underground river that is to Mudie at least the main legitimate source of Australian culture; in the other, "Resurgence", appears a second facet of extreme Jindyworobak theory, that all oversea influence is alien and disturbing. Mudie carries Jindyworobakism further than any other of its votaries, declaring[44] that

. . . beauty we shall not find
till Europe fades from the mind.

[42] This was published twice in the *Jindyworobak Anthology*. After the closing date of this History Ingamells published a long poem, *The Great South Land* (Melbourne, 1951), and an Aboriginal story, *Aranda Boy* (Melbourne, 1952).

[43] Mudie published two more books of verse: *The Blue Crane* (Sydney, 1959) and *Selected Poems* (Sydney, 1976).

[44] "Skull" (*Poems: 1934-1944*, p. 47).

Of the other Jindyworobaks, none stands out; this is by no means to say that nothing stands out in the *Jindyworobak Anthology* except a few of the best poems of Ingamells and Mudie; it contains a fair proportion of good verse, some of which is quite out of the common, but almost all of this is the work of established poets who were not members of the Jindyworobak Club: such poets as Hart-Smith, Mann and Judith Wright. Of much less ability but still deserving mention is (Wilfred Frank) Flexmore Hudson (Charters Towers, Q., 1913-), who though not such a member edited several of the Jindyworobak Anthologies; he is a graduate of the University of Adelaide, and the best of his verses are collected in *As Iron Hills* (Melbourne, 1944). Hudson has the Jindyworobaks' simple and intense affection for the Australian countryside with a strong dislike for "suburban creeds of stone" and "cities that spread like sores";[45] but though capable of a striking image his inspirations are short: he seems unable to produce a whole poem that shall do his talent justice. Something of the same attitude is shared by Paul Hasluck (*Into the Desert*, Claremont, W.A., 1939), who has however no Jindyworobak connections. He also turns from civilization to where

> The desert, full of seeds, lies waiting for the rain,[46]

and his talent also shows more possibility than achievement. Hasluck's more important work on the Aborigines is referred to elsewhere.[47]

The Angry Penguins, so called from a line in a poem[48] by their founder and leader, Max Harris, specialized in the image and in the liberation of the subconscious, mainly in an emotional form. But though their principles were imported, Harris's personality gave them, at least in his own poetry and in the general atmosphere of the magazine of the group, which was named after it, a quality that marks it off as individual, and even, in its defects as much as its merits, Australian. Max (Maxwell Hemby) Harris (Adelaide, 1921-) is again an Adelaide graduate, and while a university student he founded both the school and its magazine;[49] he has published two books of verse, *The Gift of Blood* (Adelaide, 1940) and *Dramas from the Sky* (Adelaide, 1942).[50] Harris and his magazine, though not all its contributors, carried to an extreme some of the essential characters of unbroken youth; they were self-conscious and arrogant as well as vigorous and rather crude, often angry and always clamorous. They became for a while widely known, as the victims of a hoax inflicted on them by James McAuley and Harold Stewart;[51] this

[45] Compare Hope's "five cities, like five teeming sores" ("Australia").

[46] Compare again Hope's "Australia".

[47] See pp. 1451-2.

[48] "Drunks, the angry penguins of the night" (*The Gift of Blood*, p.60).

[49] It had the same title as the school.

[50] And, since this History closed, another, *The Coorong*, (Adelaide, 1955).

[51] For the poems of McAuley and Stewart, see pp. 985-91 and 1050-6 respectively.

was actually designed as an experiment, to see whether the Angry Penguins, as representing surrealism, would accept as true surrealist poetry "a collection of garish images without coherent meaning and structure," which its makers attributed to an imaginary poet. Harris himself, and a number of members of the intelligentsia, overseas as well as in Australia, accepted the sham poetry as work of genius, and Harris published it as such, even after its authors had exposed the trick in the Press. Of course though McAuley and Stewart had proved that fashion was capable of hypnotizing readers into accepting what was mainly, though not wholly, rubbish, as poetry of a high order, that does not prove that every surrealist poem is rubbish, and some of even the Angry Penguin productions are by no means rubbish; however, Harris's own poems are at their best when least surrealistic, as in "Lullaby"[52] and "Mad Jasper", and this applies to his images, as "the crackling haste of the bushfire", "the village air weighted with solemn bells", "drunks, the angry penguins of the night" and

O darling now that I have seen you again
watch the minutes bombing and tomorrow slain!

Pretentious, full of obvious effort after novelty of effect, clumsy at times and lacking in substance and definiteness of idea and expression: with all these faults of a talented adolescence which has followed marsh-lights and boasts because it is not sure of itself, there is yet a suggestion about these verses that, given ripeness of talent and judgment, Harris may yet be found among the really worthwhile poets of the day. Of the other members of this school, Dutton's and Kershaw's verses are much closer to the original model than Harris's: they are also more adult, more sophisticated, and superior in craftsmanship, though at least in Kershaw's case they are not more suggestive of future possibilities: they belong obviously to the Old World rather than to the new, though many of them were written in this country and published in *Angry Penguins*, and though both poets were Australian-born. Geoffrey (Piers Henry) Dutton (Kapunda, S.A. 1922-) was born on a South Australian sheep station and educated in Victoria; he was a Flight Lieutenant in the R.A.A.F., and lectured in English at the University of Adelaide before turning to writing and publishing: his only book of verse[53] so far is *Night Flight and Sunrise* (Melbourne, 1944). Alister (Nasmyth) Kershaw (Melbourne, 1921-), was educated in Melbourne and has published two books of verse, *The Lonely Verge* (Adelaide, 1943) and *Excellent Stranger*

[52] Printed in *Australian Poetry 1948* (Sydney, 1949); the rest of the quotations are from one or other of Harris's two books of verse.

[53] He has also published a novel, *The Mortal and the Marble* (London, 1950), which is discussed elsewhere (see pp. 1168-9), several descriptive works and a book of verse covering a kind of Grand Tour, *Antipodes in Shoes* (London, 1958).

(Melbourne, 1944); he is a journalist and a wanderer, but has now settled in France, so that later work of his will probably not concern us. His poems are delicate, subtle, accomplished, possessed of a sensitiveness and grace that are almost feminine; but they are slight: he has very little to say. His images are parts of himself: "leaves, ghosts in the hunted August", "the blades of rain", "the traveller, the strangler of immense regrets", and so on. Dutton is a far stronger and intenser poet than Kershaw, and lives more in a world of action; he is the most obscure of these three Angry Penguins, and sometimes his obscurity seems to arise deliberately, almost, one would say, out of perversity rather than out of carelessness of communication. Though he observes surrealist principles, he has an individual way of perceiving and putting things, as in the first verse of "The Hero",

> The hero slid the landscape round his wing,
> Won his soft love
> By sentiment of violin,
> Tore fabric from eight deaths above;

or in another poem, "The Mountain",

> The mountain he flew over did not want him,
> Loose with age, the shaggy cliffs looked down
> While webbed in fire the angels' right was lent him
> To pass the mighty without fear and frown.

In the same poem, he says that

> . . . being alive sufficed
> To see death powerless in the waste of snow.

And elsewhere,

> Desire roars through the unmoving trees.

There were far more anthologies than in the previous Period, and one or two of the best were far superior to any of their predecessors; there now came into existence for the first time a good and representative periodical anthology; and beyond that there are a number of special anthologies, which explore in some detail most of the currents in the Australian verse of the day: these serve a useful purpose, but they are rather indiscriminate, and remarkable more for enthusiasm than for judgment. Considering the anthologies of the Period as a whole, in spite of the advance upon those of the previous Period, it may be said that if there is any Australian critic of the present generation capable of illustrating in a one-volume anthology what the poets of his country have achieved or attempted, he has not yet shown himself in print.[54] Easily the best of Australian historical anthologies is *An Australasian Anthology: Australian and New Zealand Poems* (London, 1927), by Percival Serle (Elsternwick, Vic., 1871-1951); he was educated at Scotch College, Melbourne, and became Chief Clerk and accountant at the University of Melbourne, from which position he retired to devote himself to literary research, mainly in verse. Serle's outlook is not quite that of today, but this has not affected his anthology, because it scarcely touches the present Period: its first two editions appeared when the Period was just beginning, and the "short supplementary section" which was added to the third Australian edition, in 1946, was by another hand. The first two editions, in which Serle had the assistance of Wilmot and of Robert Henderson Croll, a well-known Melbourne man of letters, stood, and, within the limits of its range, was, when this was written, far above other historical anthologies of Australian verse; by its means it became possible to get a summary impression of the course Australian poetry had followed up to the beginning of the present Period: Serle's taste was catholic and had a background of wide reading, Wilmot was among the leading critics of the day, and their idiosyncrasies more or less cancelled one another out. It is of course possible to disagree with some of their selections and in particular with the inclusion of a number of poets who are now deservedly forgotten, and also with the omission of Baylebridge's "I Worshipped When My Veins Were Fresh", Gellert's "In the Trench", Boake's "Where the Dead Men Lie", and Ada Cambridge's "On Australian Hills", which last every anthologist has somehow missed; but this anthology maintained for the first time a proper perspective, so that the more important poets stand out as they should; what is more, it was introduced by a short summary of the development of Australian and New Zealand poetry which was among the best of the forerunners of today's historical criticism. Unfortunately the section that was added[55] to deal with current poetry cannot compare with the main collection: there are some strange omissions;[56] the choice of the work of those poets who are included is often poor;[57] and, worst of all, perspective is lacking. It is not possible to infer from it who are the leading Australian poets today; indeed several others are given more space than for instance Slessor, Wright and FitzGerald; incidentally, the omission of New

---

[54] This was written before the publication of Judith Wright's *Book of Australian Verse*, or the *Penguin Book of Australian Verse*, compiled by John Thompson, Kenneth Slessor and R. G. Howarth. But neither of these anthologies can be considered complete.

[55] "After consultation with Mr Serle and with the valuable advice of Mrs Vance Palmer" (Publisher's Preface). Serle was unavailable for the work itself, and both his collaborators were dead.

[56] For instance, A. D. Hope, Harold Stewart, William Hart-Smith, Kenneth Mackenzie, and Rosemary Dobson.

[57] As in the cases of Wright, McAuley, FitzGerald, and Hopegood.

Zealand poets seems to imply that there are none worth inclusion; since the word "Australasian" is still included in the title. The latest (1945) edition of Murdoch's anthology,[58] which after the first edition had dropped the misleading "Oxford" and was now entitled *A Book of Australasian Verse*, is far inferior to Serle's; the main collection has been much improved by the omission of a number of unimportant writers and the inclusion of several who had been unavailable before, but perspective is still lacking: for example Brennan is represented only by four short poems, which include nothing from "The Wanderer", McCrae by three poems and Mary Gilmore by two, in neither case their best, as against eleven by Archibald Strong, who would have been the first to acknowledge such an absurdity.[59] But as to the modern additions and omissions it is far worse: there is nothing by Hope, McAuley, David Campbell or Douglas Stewart, and incredible as it may seem, nothing by Slessor or Judith Wright; that there is nothing by FitzGerald or Baylebridge either may not have been Murdoch's fault, for it is understood that in these cases permission was refused. The most popular of today's anthologies is *Poets of Australia* (Sydney, 1946), by George Mackaness, whose more important work in history will be mentioned later.[60] The popularity of this anthology is probably due to its principal defect: it covers a far wider range than any of the others, so that almost every reader can find what he wants in it; this however has involved the inclusion of many poems whose literary interest, if they ever had any, evaporated long ago, and of a good deal that is mere rubbish. There was also the present writer's *Modern Australian Poetry* (Melbourne, 1946). Of the other general anthologies, one, *The High Road of Australian Verse* (Oxford, 1929), was compiled by Jeremiah Joseph Stable, (Gawler, S.A., 1883-1953) who was Professor of English Language and Literature in the University of Queensland; *The Bond of Poetry* (Oxford, 1924), by the same compiler, anticipated Wilmot in placing English and Australian poems side by side, with similar results: Stable published another anthology whose object was to illustrate the development of verse in Queensland during the first century of its settlement, but such a collection has small literary if some sociological value.[61] Popular anthologies for children of varying ages were compiled by George Mackaness, and by Stable again, though Stable's readers were confined mainly to Queensland; and there were the group anthologies, which have been considered along with the groups they

---

[58] Latest so far as the scope of this History is concerned; another edition appeared in 1951.

[59] Also, Gordon is still given seven poems (13 pages), O'Dowd eight (14 pages), and Wilmot six (17 pages).

[60] See p. 1369.

[61] *A Book of Queensland Verse* (Brisbane, 1924). A much better mixed anthology was *In Fealty to Apollo* (Melbourne, 1932), by Ian Maxwell and A. A. Phillips.

represent. Of the general periodical anthologies, one of the most interesting is *Poetry* (1941–7), whose editor was the poet Flexmore Hudson: this, like so many of the other publications of the day, is an example of the literary awakenings, in verse especially, that have occurred in the smaller Australian States. *Poetry*, first published in Adelaide, but transferred, like *Meanjin*, to Melbourne, was a quarterly, originally of Australian verse, which later drew also from Britain, Ireland and America; but though its scope is thus wide, in another sense it is limited, for it contains little by the leading poets[62] and much that is almost negligible. The principles on which it is compiled seem rather vague, and this impression is deepened by the handing over, as with the Jindyworobak anthologies, of occasional issues to poets of varying points of view; it may however be taken to represent youth, with its enthusiasms and disdain of conventions and a tendency to iconoclasm which is particularly noticeable in the reviews that are sprinkled among the poems. *Australian Poetry* (Sydney, 1941–73),[63] is by far the most important of the periodical anthologies: it ranges over the whole field of current Australian poetry, without regard to movement or group; its editors are chosen from the leading critics and poets of the day; there is a different editor every year, and each is free to select poems of a year or so before his own, if they have been passed over by previous editors, so that idiosyncrasies of taste tend to be cancelled out: the result is a periodical anthology that reflects pretty closely the best verse of the current year, and by whose means it is possible to glance over recent developments in Australian poetry. There is however one drawback to this anthology: the range of selection seems to depend very largely on the results of circularization among known writers; the selections are however well made, and though the standards of the volumes vary a good deal, that is inevitable as the stream of poetry varies.

[62] Judith Wright is a prominent exception.

[63] This is an annual publication, except that there were single volumes for 1949–50 and 1951–52. [The anthology ceased publication after 1973.]

CHAPTER VI

THE NOVEL

Novels of the Countryside. The Lawson-Furphy Tradition: Katharine Prichard; Kylie Tennant; Eve Langley

DURING THE early part of the Period most young writers turned naturally to the novel as a form of literary expression, just as their immediate predecessors had turned naturally to the short story or to verse. This was largely though by no means wholly a matter of markets, home and oversea. A contributing cause may well have been the *Bulletin's* growing interest in the novel, as exemplified in the competitions that it initiated, and its publication of prize-winners as serials; yet though the fairly frequent newspaper and other competitions that sprang up later, and especially those of the *Sydney Morning Herald*, with its far larger prizes, have been both an encouragement and an advertisement and have brought out some capable new novelists and one or two that are more than capable, they have not introduced any who can be called first-rate, in prose or verse either, and some of the best novelists of the Period[1] do not appear to have been brought out by the competitions. An important factor in the increase of novel-writing has been the increased attention to British and American readers in Australian novels that began after the first World War, and that increased, so far as America was concerned, with her closer relations with Australia during the second; but it does not seem to be Australian novels as such that have attracted oversea readers, so much as the information about life in Australia to be obtained from them, for the oversea interest in Australian verse has been comparatively small. All this has found of course a reflection in the willingness of local and oversea publishers to accept novels by Australians; so far as local publishers are concerned this willingness has been helped and accentuated by the twenty-five per cent adverse exchange, which has operated as a corresponding tariff in favour of locally published books. Another cause has been the creation of new readers of fiction as a result of the spread of general education and of civilization generally and of the extension of leisure and comfort among all classes; but the desire of the greater number of these new readers has been for entertainment in the narrower sense, and this is true largely, though by no means wholly, even of the products of university and other higher education;

[1] For example, Stead, Dark, Penton, and Herbert.

so that the new conditions have made largely for quantity rather than for literary quality. Still, the general average of the Australian novel of today, though not its best examples, is higher than it was a couple of generations ago, and in formal competence the improvement has been great, even in work that is otherwise negligible. The literary defect that corresponds today to previous novelists' comparative neglect of form is slickness, writing smoothly to a recipe that is commercial rather than aesthetic, putting a shiny polish upon a piece of deal rather than taking the trouble to find a better wood and bring out its grain; the deal will fetch as much, more, probably, and its purchasers won't know the difference. But the peaks of the novel of today are no higher than those of the novel of the nineties, and they are lower than those of today's poetry; except Christina Stead, who became an expatriate, Katharine Susannah Prichard, Kylie Tennant and a couple of writers of historical fiction, no modern Australian novelist reaches the not so very high standards of England or the United States, as a number of Australian poets do. Again, in spite of the increased intellectual background and "fundamental brainwork" in the better Australian novels of today, few of them appeal to the mind or the imagination like the best English novels or the best Australian poetry. Scarcely any of their characters are thinking people, and any thought-content is usually implicit or flows over from the author; the Australian novelist prefers as a rule to deal with ordinary men and women, whose motives, even when they are comparatively complicated, are fundamentally simple and clear-cut, and who are concerned as a rule with action rather than thought: there are some important exceptions, but as to the Australian novel in general this marks a definite limitation. Still the Australian novels of today are not therefore less interesting or important than those of yesterday, nor does it follow that they are not for cultivated readers; for the principal concern of the novel is after all with life, and the fundamentals of life are simple: if there is any type of novel that is superior to other types it is certainly not the philosophical, and novels about the intelligentsia are as limited as any other kind; unless their writers possess unusual talent they are apt to be extremely dull. As one would expect, then, few Australian novelists are concerned with the ideas and problems of the day: sometimes, as with Prichard or Mann or Tennant, they set out and illuminate such problems, and allow ideas to show through the life they describe; but with few exceptions neither they nor their characters reflect upon them. Barnard Eldershaw and Dark deal with men and women who think and imagine and have definite attitudes towards current problems; but these authors are by no means typical, although in their work a fiction that is much more cosmopolitan than its predecessor comes closest to the fiction of the modern civilized world.

The Australian novelist is now at least a member of a world-profession; he is by no means obsessed, like most of his predecessors, by a narrow nationalism, and can be critical, sometimes bitterly critical, of some of his own country's institutions and of aspects of its life and thought: the disillusion that ruled the larger part of this Period and which still to some extent persists, has crystallized in the deliberate showing-up, with Penton of the romantic idealization of the pioneers, and with Herbert of the cruel treatment of the Aborigines in the Northern Territory. It is true that the work of even the leading novelists is still in subject and often in tone also essentially Australian, but today's is a comparatively sophisticated Australianism, more aware of the world without: we are no longer allowed to feel that as a community we need attend only to our own concerns in a kind of static isolation; on the contrary we perceive ourselves to be afloat upon a current of world-change. Yet on the whole, in spite of the strong and obvious contrasts between the novels of today and yesterday, they still have important characteristics in common: not only nationalism, however metamorphosed today, and an ultimate dependence upon action and the simpler aspects of human nature and its conditions and surroundings, but also a characteristic that traces back as far as the immigration novel of the beginnings: the Australian novelist is still something of a publicist; he seems unable to get away from the feeling that it is his business to tell about his country, its inhabitants, their characteristics, their kind of life. He no longer, as did the immediate successors of the early "immigration agents",[2] sets out to explain to English readers less directly and a little less crudely the beauties and opportunities of this new and generous country; he no longer, as in the nineties, though their writers at least addressed themselves to their fellow countrymen, aims at emphasizing aspects and qualities that he considers preferable as being typically Australian. But he does seem to feel that his subject is and ought to be closely connected with Australia and Australian life rather than with the world and life in the world.[3] As regards choice of subject, such an attitude is perfectly justifiable in so far as it involves merely the commonsense principle of writing about what one knows best, but local characteristics and distinctions may surely nowadays be taken in the stride, no more sought out than avoided; and in any case a colouring, national or other, may be made effective without spending a great deal of space upon detailed description and illustration.

By far the greater number of the Australian novelists of today concern themselves wholly or mainly with the countryside, though most of them have little else in common. These may be considered first, not merely as most characteristic but because they include some of the best

[2] See, for instance, pp. 90, 248, 249.

[3] On this point something has already been said, in the introduction to the present Period.

Australian fiction writers of the day; and first among them five who belong to the main stream of the "Australian" tradition, deriving from Lawson, or, in one case, from Furphy; some of them have written city as well as country novels, but all these writers will be taken together here. Probably after Henry Handel Richardson the most notable of all Australian novelists and the most representative without qualification, is Katharine Prichard. Historically, Furphy has a higher place, because he began a line of progression which is extremely important in Australian fiction; Prichard is of the tribe of Lawson, and, individual as she is, she cannot be called an originator in the sense that Furphy and Lawson are originators. Again, most critics would probably agree that if we must we could better spare *Working Bullocks* or *Coonardoo* than *Such is Life*; on the other hand, an author's literary value depends upon the quantity as well as quality of his work, and Furphy must stand by a single book: even *Rigby's Romance* is far inferior to several of Prichard's novels; also her work is as "Australian" as Furphy's, or Lawson's either, and her field much wider than Furphy's at any rate. On the whole, then, it is reasonable to say that the size and scope of her work place Katharine Susannah Prichard next after Richardson, in spite of her stylistic defects. In one or two respects, indeed, she is superior: Richardson's lack of humour, at least its submergence in her general seriousness, has been pointed out already; but though Prichard is in her own way quite as earnest, her work contains a good deal of quiet humour, which is often used to enforce and illustrate her purpose. In the second place, though Richardson is by no means without poetic vision, as may be seen in some of her short stories and in *Maurice Guest*, poetic expression is comparatively rare with her; in Prichard on the other hand a stream of poetry runs strong: it is one of the main strengths of *Coonardoo*. But such qualities as these, though important enough, are not after all the qualities by which a novelist stands or falls. Richardson depends finally not only upon her literary talent, but upon her comparative largeness, breadth of vision, grasp of life as a whole: it is these that separate out the few writers who come first into our minds when we think of the drama or the novel at its highest range, and in them Richardson is among Australian novelists supreme. It may also be said that Katharine Prichard's overmastering aim to represent Australia has had the effect of circumscribing her faculties, though this is open of course to the rejoinder that it is her nature and faculties that have dictated that aim. "It is true, I think," she wrote once,[4]

> . . . that I know thoroughly every phase of life in Australia, I write of; that I absorb the life of our people and country with love and an intense and intimate sympathy; I strive to express myself from those sources.

---

[4] In a letter to me, 4th November 1929.

But she added something that opens up a large question:

> My defect as a writer is probably that I am too much of the soil. But I'd rather be that and fall from universal standards than be less the medium for expression of this place and people.

The answer to the question thus opened up, whether a writer can fall from universal standards through being too occupied with what is local, is, I think, only if it is local merely. The life described in what is one of Prichard's best novels, certainly her most "Australian", *Working Bullocks*, is by no means entirely so restricted: Red, Deb and the rest, Australian as they are, are also representative of a class that stretches all over the world; Tessa, Mrs Colburn, Mrs Pennyfather, Neil and Wally might be seen in any country, and Mark is an international type. On the other hand, the life in *Coonardoo*, in which in another way Prichard is also at her best and at least as individual, is comparatively isolated from the wider world, except in the pain of its tragedy. It cannot be said that even here Prichard contemplates Australian life and types and scenes *in vacuo*; but she certainly does, not merely here but in her work in general, focus the best of her powers upon them. She spends more space on their elaboration, illustration and emphasis than is justified in the interests of her stories as such; and, what is perhaps even more important, she scarcely ever, and never in her best and most characteristic work, draws, except for purposes of contrast, a character that is not distinctively Australian,[5] though it may also belong to a type that is world-wide. On the whole then it is fair to say that her insistence upon nationality does detract from her world-value as a novelist.

Katharine Susannah Prichard (Levuka, Fiji, 1884-1969) was, therefore, like Boldrewood, born outside Australia, though she was brought to Tasmania when only three years old; with oversea excursions, she has spent the whole of her life here, and is more Australian than most Australian-born writers, as Boldrewood also was, by the standards of his time. Her mother was born in Australia of Irish and Scotch parents; her father was a Welshman, brought here as a child of four; he edited newspapers in Fiji, Tasmania and Melbourne, and also wrote prose fiction and verse. For some years Katharine ran wild in much the same fashion as the little girl in her *Wild Oats of Han*, which is indeed largely autobiographical; part of her schooling was under the poet J. B. O'Hara, who encouraged the literary gift that had already begun to appear; she taught in outback schools in Victoria and New South Wales and contributed short stories to Australian periodicals; at twenty-four she went off to England on several journalistic commissions, and on her return she edited the Women's Section of a Melbourne newspaper.

---

[5] Mark (*Working Bullocks*) and Rocca (*Haxby's Circus*) are exceptions.

Then, after a trip to the South Seas and America, followed six years' freelancing in London, where what she saw of conditions among the poor in the great cities, as well as what she read of sociology, economics, and the class struggle gave her a broad-based sympathy with the oppressed among the workers: she became, like Lawson, an apostle of extreme democracy, and in particular of mateship. After publishing her first two novels she returned to Australia, where she married the late Captain Hugo Throssell, V.C., and she lived afterwards in Western Australia, with excursions to the other States and to the East. The Russian novelists, Flaubert, Theocritus, the Greek dramatists, Anatole France, Gustav Frenssen, as well as English and Australian authors and Marx, Jung and Lenin: she most probably read as widely as Henry Handel Richardson; and she published, apart from political pamphlets, nine novels, two volumes of short stories, several plays[6] and some verse, all well spaced over a period of thirty-six years. Her work may be divided into three periods:[7] during the first, from 1914 to 1921, she was learning her trade as novelist; during the second, to 1933, she produced her best work; the third was, from a purely literary point of view, a period of decline. Her first novel[8] was notable only for its evidence of her sympathy with the down-and-out in London; it was followed, in date of publication preceded, by *The Pioneers* (London, 1915), which possesses some individuality in a conventionally romantic framework and is written with a certain amount of distinction: it is set in the early colonial days and won £250 for the Australian section in an all-British novel competition. So far she had not emerged from the ruck, simply because she had not even begun to understand herself or to realize her possibilities, or even where her fundamental interest lay. Her next book, *Black Opal* (London, 1921), represents a long step forward; it is clearly the work of a writer who thinks and reads as well as feels, who possesses a definite literary individuality, and who takes her profession seriously, though she is not yet a master at it; in preparation for this novel she lived for some months at Lightning Ridge, a well-known opal field in northern New South Wales.[9] Involved with the story in *Black Opal* is a study of social relationships, for the opal-mining community in which the scene is set is actually a tiny commonwealth, simple, friendly, unorganized, upon which we see impinging the greater world that attempts to engulf it. And the novel embodies two distinct elements: in the first place there is an underlying idea or principle, for it is more than a theme, of social service,

---

[6] For her plays, see p. 1273; for her short stories, pp. 1241-4.

[7] Measuring by dates of publication.

[8] *Windlestraws* (London, 1916).

[9] Similar preliminary studies were made in preparation for all those of her later novels with whose types and background she was not already well acquainted; on this point, see the introduction to this Period, p. 935.

co-operation, self-sacrifice for the common good, which resembles Lawson's mateship intellectualized; in the second place, the leading characters carry with them symbolic elements, so that one gets the impression, as with some of Dostoevsky's characters, that they are, at least in part, reflections of something greater that stands dimly perceptible behind them. Unfortunately these suggestions and implications are not invariably well handled, and there is something inconsistent, even nebulous, about several of the characters that carry them; they do not seem to have been completely realized:[10] the book is therefore not entirely a success; it may best be described as a failure of marked individuality and promise. The promise was to be fulfilled, but along rather different lines. In *Working Bullocks* (London, 1926), which opens her second phase, Katharine Prichard has found herself. Again she concentrates upon a small community, though much larger than that in *Black Opal*, of workers who earn their living up country and mainly in the open air; but this time the community is larger, the conditions harder, more relentless, because the greater world has taken charge. Here also a philosophical background exists, but it is not so developed and the element of philosophico-poetic fantasy has disappeared; on the other hand, all the characters are fully realized, and they draw a vigour and richness from the soil and the great trees which are a part of their lives. There is in this community the same strong spirit of mateship as in *Black Opal*, but it is never organized, though there is an attempt at its organization. There is lacking the singleness and unity of the smaller community, partly because of the closer contacts in *Working Bullocks* with the modern industrial world; it has no natural leaders, and its principal characters represent a much more primitive stage of human development than the opal miners: they are human cattle, who compare, so far as any Australians can compare, with the peasants of Europe. They possess a comparative quickness and a careless independence that Australian conditions have brought out, but they also are yoked to the pole of the world's waggon and must pull for their lives. The book deals with the great karri forests of Western Australia and with the timber-getters who, like the huge trees among which and by whose deaths they live, are a primary outgrowth of the soil, filled with its simple, rich and vigorous life; the underlying idea is that of the vigour and fecundity that spring from the intimate relationship of man with the earth, and of the way in which that vigour and fecundity are harnessed to the relentless purposes of organized industry. But this is not the whole story, for an inseparable

[10] Sophie seems at once a little too simple and too theatrical, the Joseph-and-Mary-like ending between her and Potch fails to convince, and Snowshoes is not much more than an idea. Michael however is undoubtedly a success, except for a blurring in his symbolization.

part of it concerns the little bush township that is the timber-getters' centre, the sawmill in which some of their friends and relations work, the horse-racing, wood-chopping and so on that are incidental to the general life, and the attempt at concerted action by the mill-hands which affords an opportunity to show how even the bush worker is drawn into the class struggle. Yet although Katharine Prichard's sympathies are obvious, the artist in her did not at this time allow her to preach; there is an agitator from outside who preaches, but though he is presented as an extremely human and sympathetic character, and though his philosophy, for he is a travelled and educated man, is undoubtedly that of his creator, he is not a mere mouthpiece, and an adventurous and wandering man of his type might well have found his way to this little bush community, and have acted as he did. The book also represents a conflict between life and an ultimately victorious fate; but in spite of its tragic episodes, by and large the conflict is by no means a gloomy or even a monotonous one, for the strong life shown rejoices in exercising its vitality, to whatever result. Prichard's next novel, *Coonardoo* (London, 1929) shows an aspect of her talent that had not appeared before. The book is a far-west symphony, through which the little song at the beginning about the kangaroos dancing, and the patient, submissive, graceful little figure that sits crooning the song to the clicking of two sticks haunts like a lyric motif: it is the story of a far-out north-west station, of white and, at the beginning, unspoilt black; a story of loneliness and monotony and incessant effort on the one hand and of selfless devotion on the other; a story filled with dust and vibrating heat and the dry horizonless plains, but also with the "faint incense of paper daisies and sandalwood". Through all this; through Hugh's marriage with the shallow and selfish woman who deserts him for the softer life of the coastal town; through the happier time when his daughter has come up to live with him; and through the loneliness during the interval, Coonardoo is quite unconsciously drawing him, both herself and as symbolizing the spirit of the place:[11] the end is bitter and cruel tragedy, but in spite of sordid elements that are not hidden, the story remains beautiful, and every aspect of it appears inevitable. There is however a defect of structure in *Coonardoo*. Life on a far-out back station at the time with which the story deals was extraordinarily monotonous. Writers of station life of those or earlier days have usually therefore, in the effort

[11] [The idea of a romance between a white man and an Australian black woman seemed absurd to most readers and outraged many of them when the book was serialized as a prize-winning novel in the *Bulletin* in 1928. It shared the prize with Barnard Eldershaw's *A House is Built*. But Coonardoo belonged to a tribe not yet degraded by civilization; she was drawn from life, though characteristics acceptable to whites were emphasized. The photograph of the original shows a fine-looking woman.]

to collect material for their plots, crammed together into a story that might cover only a year or two incidents that would actually occur if at at all only seldom and over long periods; if falsification of this sort is to be avoided, station novelists who set their stories in the past must depend largely upon psychological analysis, and the action must take place largely in the minds of the characters.[12] Katharine Prichard tries to avoid such falsification without attempting any elaborate psychological analysis, which indeed is outside her line, and as a result the trajectory of the story is rather flat; when it first appeared as a serial in the *Bulletin* it seemed broken-backed, though the defect[13] is not nearly so marked when one reads it in book-form. And there are other defects, some of them also resulting from an attempt to avoid monotony: with the death of Hugh's mother a principal character drops out before the story is half through, and after another third of it new characters are introduced, in particular Hugh's daughter, now grown up; one feels here that there has been interference from without, in order to prop up a structural weakness.

The last novel of this phase, *Haxby's Circus* (London, 1930)[14] is the story of a small family-owned circus, of its travels over many of the country districts of New South Wales and Victoria, of the self and family-sacrificing devotion to it of the proprietor, and of what followed. The underlying idea is again, as in *Black Opal*, and, incidentally, in *Coonardoo*, devotion to a possession that represents an ideal; but here there is neither poetry nor philosophy but an atmosphere of the ordinary and matter of fact: it is the atmosphere of the circus itself, not of the romance that is deliberately thrown about it by its proprietor, partly for business purposes; yet, curiously enough, there is more humour about this than about any other of Katharine Prichard's novels. The story itself might conceivably be translated to England or the United States, but as told it could not be anything but Australian: it illustrates one of Prichard's essential qualities, that she can take a theme, a conception that is not new and so handle it that it acquires an individuality that is marked, deriving in part from herself and in part from the country in which it is set. There are several tragic episodes, and the end is more tragic than any of them: the transformation, primarily as the result of an accident, of a fine young bareback rider into a fat, sensual, hunchbacked old woman, at once clown and circus manager, who is fond

---

[12] Vance Palmer attempted something of the kind in *The Man Hamilton* (see p. 1110).

[13] It might of course be contended that a story that is actually monotonous ought to produce a monotonous effect. But, though the reader must of course be allowed to appreciate the monotony of the life described, the story must not be allowed to become monotonous. In describing a bore it is not necessary to be boring, though it is a nice question whether even Jane Austen gets over this difficulty with Miss Bates.

[14] The American edition was called *Fay's Circus* (New York, 1931) and includes an account of a fight which is omitted in the English edition; from the latter all quotations here are taken.

of nothing so much as "garlic . . and beer, and a bit of fresh bread and cheese". To this phase belongs also *The Wild Oats of Han* (Sydney, 1928), which comes in between *Working Bullocks* and *Coonardoo*. The nearest oversea parallel to *Han* would be *Tom Sawyer*, with a touch of *Huckleberry Finn*; but it is a far-off parallel, even apart from the fact that here the principal character is a little girl. The story belongs to a world that is entirely real; there are no excursions into a world of satire, there are no sentimental interludes, and, though there is plenty of high spirits, there is no humour. Nevertheless *Han* is as delightful as it is true to life; there has been nothing like it in Australia and little anywhere, and if it cannot rank with *Huckleberry Finn*, that is partly because it accepts the limits of its kind instead of transcending them.

In Prichard's third phase her social sympathies assume more and more a political form and finally override the artist in her, so that her work becomes part social history, part sheer propaganda. In the first book of this phase, *Intimate Strangers* (London, 1937), the change is only beginning. The story moves in a world almost entirely different from those of her other novels; without quite abandoning the primitive, or comparatively primitive, Prichard here superimposes upon it a stratum that represents suburban society on holiday: basking, swimming, love-making in one of those seaside suburbs or townships that are scattered around the Australian coasts, within the reach of the large towns and capital cities. The story centres upon a cultivated, sensitive and attractive woman, who is worn down by the vagaries of an inconstant though fundamentally devoted husband, the difficulties of the Depression and a sympathy with its victims, to say nothing of two extremely lively children; finally, just in time to save her from a rather piratical adventurer who has about him a faint reminiscence of the films, these two intimate strangers are reunited, not quite credibly, in "the fire of a regenerating idea in which it seemed they would attain freedom and unity".[15] There are some rhetorical speeches in support of the fight of the worker for a better world, but all the characters except the pirate and perhaps to some extent the husband, are real; and there are bright kaleidoscopic panoramas that catch the spirit of the surfing crowds and the beaches. The last three books[16] are a trilogy which tells the story of the life of the Western Australian goldfields, in the old prospecting days and in the days of the great mining companies: they were based very thoroughly on searches through the files of old newspapers, on wanderings with prospectors, and on the reminiscences of pioneers, particularly two whom Katharine Prichard calls Dinny Quinn and Sally Gough. Their personal

[15] p. 410.

[16] *The Roaring Nineties* (Sydney, 1946), *Golden Miles* (London and Sydney, 1948) and *Winged Seeds* (Sydney, 1950). There was also a thriller, *Moon of Desire* (London, 1941), which need not be discussed here.

story runs through the whole, but it is no more than a bright streak that winds through a great sheaf of documentary; a thin living stream that keeps fading into and submerging beneath the sands of a fictionized but heavily documented history of the miners and their wrongs: some of the conversations read like reports of speeches at a strike meeting or vernacularized passages from a leading article in a Labour paper or extracts from evidence given before a royal commission; for example,[17]

> "Looks like as if this bloke was sayin' stabilise the gold producin' industry and you stave off revolution," Dinny remarked.
>
> "And that the value of gold is a problem only socialism can solve," Tom said quietly. "For us that means strengthening the organisation of the workers: the trade unions and the political representation of the working class. We're going to have a tussle here presently."
>
> "It was a great fight the lumpers put up against a scab union on the wharves," Dinny reminded him.
>
> "You've said it Dinny," Tom agreed. . . .

Just once or twice however we are reminded of the old Katharine Prichard, as when Sally says of De Morfé,[18] "He's a devil, and I hate him. . . . But I wish we had been lovers, years ago. . . ." Typically Australian, comparatively primitive, country types and ordinary people: most of Prichard's characters are all these: they represent in Prichard's mind, as they did in the minds of so many people in the nineties, the period during which she got all her early and most lasting impressions, a complex which was also and still largely remains a national ideal; even now if we, who are mostly city-born, think of an Australian, there rises before our minds a picture, not of someone walking down Pitt or Collins Street, but of a man in some small country town or township or station or small farm, or perhaps glimpsed for a moment out of a car or a railway carriage at a siding in the West. Such people are ordinary in the sense that they do not stand out from the crowd as the possessors of unusual qualities, of mind at any rate; yet they are not ordinary in the sense of being average: on the contrary they may be comparatively hard to find in the community nowadays, though how common they were in the nineties may be seen from Bean's history of the first World War, and especially from its carefully documented notes. None of them, as Katharine Prichard draws them, is merely ordinary; they are ideal persons and the means by which may, she hopes, be created an ideal community: and finally they are comparatively primitive, or sometimes, as with Red and Deb in *Working Bullocks*, primitive entirely. To Prichard civilization often spoils human beings; it is in the survival of the primitive

---

[17] *Golden Miles*, p. 287. See also *The Roaring Nineties*, pp. 345, 351, and *Winged Seeds*, pp. 220-1, 366; but instances are everywhere.

[18] p. 112.

in the civilized world that she, like several other thinkers, finds the world's best hope.

From the characteristics of the types and scenes and actions with which Katharine Prichard deals, the method of their presentation naturally follows. Take the two extreme instances that have just been mentioned: no "stream of consciousness", in the ordinary sense of the phrase, could be used to reveal the states of mind of Red or Deb. Their thoughts are feelings and their feelings are sometimes inchoate, confused; that, no doubt, is true of most of us sometimes, though civilized people are much more definite in their thinking than primitive people. But even if civilized people always thought in words, Red and Deb had not the words to think in; it would be impossible even to adumbrate their states of mind except by general description: only a film could do the job properly; that indeed is the weakness of the stream-of-consciousness method, that it attempts to do what only a film could do, just as its strength lies in removing from the description of mental processes the conventional literary forms that were used formerly. Prichard is however a poet, though only in prose,[19] and this helps her to convey an impression, an atmosphere, an inference; to make clear and real, for instance, a state of feeling that has no definite edges and may drift across the mind like a cloud across the sky. In what follows we see, in part, how Red first realized the state of his feelings for Deb; he and Deb and her father are lying, tired, under the great trees in a midday haze, and the other two drop off to sleep:[20]

> Sun-dazed and sleepy himself in the heat and stillness, Red saw Deb lying on the dry leaves, an arm's length from him. She had turned her back and flung an arm over her face. Her limbs twined over each other, brown legs and long brown arms, bare from under her blue cotton dress.
>
> Red thought of a young tree fallen there beside him as he took Deb in. His sleep-stricken brain tore the blue rags of dress from her young strong body, and it gleamed against the dark foliage and through the haze of the forest, as trunks of the karri gleamed, mellow ivory, with the glamour of parchment, the lustre of silk. Dreaming, afraid to stir, disturb or change the half-waking, strange soaking joyousness he lay in, Red wondered vaguely whether he was asleep or awake.

The objection to this method is that it is apt to carry the writer beyond the limitations of his subject; it will be noted that what Prichard has here given us is not entirely a representation of Red's state of mind, but in part a translation of it to the writer's and the reader's level: "mellow ivory, with the glamour of parchment, the lustre of silk" would have been far beyond Red's experience; so of course would the words used, but they are not supposed to be Red's. The representation becomes much less subjective as it goes on, though here and there,

---

[19] Her verse is negligible.

[20] *Working Bullocks*, pp. 113-14.

and especially when Red thinks that he will "fold with" Deb, the words in which he is made to think are not the words that would have come into his mind if any words came, because these would have been misleading:

> He saw old Colburn asleep beside the dead tree, and Deb lying there across the sheening leaves.
>
> . . . .
>
> Deb! It was as if he had shouted to himself away at the back of his brain. . . . Deb! Red communed with himself, vaguely, sleepily, comparing her with women he had known, other men's wives he had made up to when they were willing, women in brothels, and Tessa. Tessa with her tricks, the scent she put on her clothes. . . . Red had never had a woman to himself. He had never wanted one. Marriage he had always regarded as the price of a woman to himself. He did not want to think of marriage now. He was a brumby, Red told himself. He would take his mares when he wanted them, when and how.
>
> He remembered the Boss and the way he had gone to his mate, and she had stood to him, tremulous, eyes dilated, squealing with delight as he bit her flanks.
>
> . . . .
>
> When he took a mate he would bite her flanks and she would spring to his passion, cry with delight as he held her. And she would be a woman like this girl, strong, with animal instincts undaunted. Why not this one? Why not Deb?
>
> . . . .
>
> Through the hot stillness, the sweet breathing of the forest, Red lay and gazed at her, afraid to wake, to break the pleasant drowsing of his blood and brain . . . Presently he would move over and fold with her, he told himself. 'And if the old man wakes, I'll kill him and throw him behind the dead tree there', his brain clicked to the ticking of the tree crickets.
>
> . . . .
>
> 'My, have I been asleep?' Deb looked at Red, wide eyes smiling sleepily.
>
> Tom Colburn sat up too, stretching and yawning.
>
> Dream and passion fell from Red. As if he had been caught in an attempt to ravish the girl and murder her father, a sense of guilt and rage, sombre, implacable, inundated him.*

It would have been even less possible to represent directly what went on in the mind of Coonardoo. She is less articulate than even Red or Deb; her feelings, though strong enough, are even farther from emerging into clear and definite consciousness; so, when Mrs Watt tells her as a little girl that she wants her to learn to look after the house for Hughie's sake, her reaction is not to be conveyed except by a glance and an inference:[21]

> "What's the good of trying to teach you, if you don't want to learn?" Mrs Bessie asked irritably. "And goodness knows who's to look after Hugh when I'm gone!"
>
> Coonardoo's eyes slanted in her direction, and away, at that.
>
> "Of course," Mrs Bessie said, "that's why I want to train and teach you, all I can. Meenie and I can't live for ever. And who's to look after Hugh then? He'll marry

* [This and other passages suggest a complex sexuality in the author herself for which the novels as a whole form a pattern of self-expression.]

[21] *Coonardoo*, p. 26.

some day, I suppose; but even so, I'd like to think he had some good faithful soul to look after him. Meenie's been that to me. If you're only half as good to Hugh . . ."

As if they had made a new compact, Coonardoo went steadily about her jobs after that. . . .

With her other novels, in which the men and women are not so primitive, a more modern method might no doubt have been adopted, but Prichard continues as before, though she is modern enough in other ways. The short sketches that with her usually precede the revelation of a character's mental processes are not mere descriptions but are themselves revealing, in modern fashion: typical examples are the vignettes of Red and Deb and Mrs Colburn in *Working Bullocks*.[22] But the introductory vignette of Coonardoo, as she sits, singing to herself and waiting for Hugh to come out of the house, on the last day before his departure for boarding school, is developed and carried forward on a stream of romantic poetry.[23] It is a beautiful passage, handicapped though it is by the staccato effect of the succession of short paragraphs.

Coonardoo was singing. Sitting under dark bushes overhung with curdy white blossom, she clicked two small sticks together, singing:

"*Towera chinima poodinya,*
Towera jinner mulbeena . . ."

Over and over again, in a thin reedy voice, away at the back of her head, the melody flowed like water running over smooth pebbles in a dry creek bed. Winding and falling, the words rattled together and flew eerily, as if she were whispering to herself, exclaiming [at], and in awe of, the kangaroos who came over the range and made a dance with their little feet in the twilight, before they began to feed.

. . . .

It was no more than a twitter in the shadow of dark bushes near the veranda; a twitter with the clicking of small sticks. Coonardoo was not supposed to be there at all. Everybody was asleep in the long house of mud bricks and corrugated iron, and under the brush-wood sheds beyond the kala miah. But Coonardoo did not want to sleep.

A little aboriginal girl about nine years old in a faded blue gina-gina, she sat there, part of the shadows, with her dark skin, fair hair, and brown eyes shadowed across the cornea. Clicking and singing, she watched the plains, the wide shallow pan of red earth under iron stone pebbles which spread out before her to the furry edge of the mulga, grey-green, under pale blue sky.

. . . .

Yellow moths drifted down from the white gum blossom. Its fragrance of dry grass and honey made Coonardoo feel sleepy. And she had decided not to sleep, but to watch the plains for first sight of the horses and buggy coming from Nuniewarra.

Her eyes fluttered after the moths. She could see low brown huts down there beside the well, a deep narrow well, the Gnarler had dug long ago, at a little distance from the creek. Coonardoo they called it, the dark well, or the well in the shadows. Coonardoo had been named after the well near which she was born. The huts were the huts of her people.

---

[22] *Working Bullocks*, pp. 8, 9–10, 13.
[23] *Coonardoo*, pp. 11–12.

There is poetry also in the glimpse in *Haxby's Circus*, most uncharacteristic in a book that is largely filled with prosaic detail and in which even the tragedy is for the most part prosaically expressed, of Gina's state of mind after her brother's death:[24]

> Gina did not know where she was going that night, she walked out across the plains back towards the town she had come from. The earth stretched far and wide beneath a sky glimmering with the first light of day. Sky and plains rocked and wavered before her, so that she did not know which was plain and which sky. She seemed to be floating through the sky, drifting over the earth, falling through darkness.

Besides such analyses, Prichard is good in descriptions of scenery, as in the pictures of surfing beaches in *Intimate Strangers*, or the glimpses of the countryside through which Haxby's Circus passes; better where action is involved, as in the taking of the brumby stallion in *Working Bullocks*, or in the log-chopping contest; better again where these are blent with personality, as in the pages in which Red sees to it that his horse shall be disqualified. But she is best, with a qualification to be mentioned later, in tragic episodes, and particularly in the pages describing the death of Coonardoo.

Katharine Prichard was, after Richardson, the first Australian woman writer to realize that fiction-writing is a trade that must be taken seriously and that requires a long apprenticeship,[25] and her method of construction is not only professional in its competence, but modern, in that plot has been influenced in her by pattern. Take *Working Bullocks* for example. There is a plot: Red Burke's attempt to work himself out of the ruck, to attain the comfort and security represented by the possession of a bullock team of his own; his failures, and finally his seizing of something that he must have at all costs, a second possession that will almost certainly involve the first, though it also involves the acceptance of the sugar-coated pill of his destiny. But there is also a definite element of pattern, for many of the characters and incidents of the story are off the main road of the plot as outlined, and yet they are felt to belong to the book's structure: the whole business of the sawmill and the strike; of Tessa and her string of interferences with Red; of the catching of the brumby stallion; of Deb's story, apart from her linking up with Red; and many other characters and incidents: the plan of this novel represents a map rather than a road; an arrangement on a plane surface rather than a succession, even a branching succession, in line; a closely woven piece of cloth rather than a rope, however coiled and knotted. An example of the closeness with which the texture of the book is woven is the careful linking up of the present with the future: as for instance Deb's

[24] *Haxby's Circus*, (London, 1930), p. 135.

[25] Some years ago a not so young writer, annoyed at my criticism of a story of his, complained that I had spoken as if writing was a mere trade, "like a plumber's or a lawyer's". That, of course, was what I had been trying to get into his head, though I should not have used the word "mere".

happiness, closely entwined with her brother's happiness, which is so great that it almost forebodes disaster, just before that brother is smashed to death by the breaking of the wire rope; and her momentary horror of the great trees and dread of their vengeance, just before her second brother's death in the sawmill. Other examples of this closeness of weave are the series of gratuitous occurrences that keep Red and Tessa apart so long, and the elaborate involvement of the Tessa motif: these last also reinforce the moving current of the story. In *Haxby's Circus* there are several breaks, but apart from these the texture is woven quite as closely; with *Coonardoo*, as has been seen, it is different. There is also the art, in which journalism and literature meet, with which the eye of the reader of each book is caught at its very beginning by some picture or image, almost always an image of action, and such as to suggest that there is something interesting to come, sometimes even to hint at the sort of story that lies ahead: this suggestive quality is of course allied with that by which the characters are introduced. Prichard was also one of the first women writers in this country to observe and to record in a manner that is not limited by sex, or the conventions of sex: there are for instance in *Working Bullocks* Wally's views on marriage, and there are the fights in this novel and in *Haxby's Circus*. There are also the fairly numerous colloquialisms, chosen obviously because they are typically Australian, which are however masculine as a rule, or at any rate they are used in a masculine fashion: examples are Wally's "my intentions is honourable, and my prospeks—a ticket in Tat's"; Gina's "I'm as hard as goat's knees"; Billy Gale's "rough as bags"; and Mrs Pennyfather's "Got a face on you like a wet week". And Katharine Prichard is never afraid of an epithet or an adjective because of what some readers might think of it; of this there is a good example in *Working Bullocks*, when Deb is speaking of her mother's idea of the reason for her attraction to Red: "Mum says I'm bulling—and that's all there is to it."[26] Allied with such expressions are the phrases or sentences in which her quiet humour sometimes finds characteristic expression; they are never there purely on their own account, and are as a rule vehicles for character-revelation: in reply to Mrs Haxby's remark that "Dan never made as much of one of his children as he's made of that pony",

> "Aw, go on Mum," Dan protested, "a man can have half a dozen kids—but there's not another pony like Phil."[27]

One of the objects of such remarks is of course to emphasize the devotion of every member of the circus to the circus itself and all that is closely

---

[26] *Working Bullocks*, p. 292.
[27] *Haxby's Circus* (London, 1930), p. 178. See also Max's exclamation on the death of the old mare, p. 232.

connected with it; the outstanding example occurs when old Haxby is dying:[28]

> "Don't let me die here, Gina," he gasped, when he realised his strength was failing, with a flare of his old spirit. "Get me back to Sydney. . . . Let's do the thing in style. . . . Like Max's wedding. . . . It'll be . . . a good ad. for the show."

But in the matter of style Prichard is not so professional, so competent, as in the matter of construction. She has a real gift of style, but certain defects have prevented it from coming to full fruition, of which the most obvious is a shortness of sentences and paragraphs whose jerky effect handicaps some of her best pages. In the passage that has been quoted from the opening of *Coonardoo*, a rhythm of thought, a rhythm of vision is conveyed by means of language whose rhythm is broken; it is as though a beautiful little picture had been smashed and roughly pieced together, with small gaps between the pieces. As important, almost, is a tendency to cliché, which is surprising in a writer of Prichard's individuality, and beyond that an occasional lapse into contentedness with the ordinary, the second- or even the third-rate, so that she will use a phrase or description that might have come from a writer of imperfect taste and minor talent. As to clichés, there are for instance "the slain giants", in a description of the great logs brought to the sawmill, and Red's "sleep-stricken brain" in the passage quoted from *Working Bullocks*; next door to this, "tore the blue rags of dress from her young strong body" illustrates the other defect. Again in *Working Bullocks*, the dramatic description of Mrs Colburn's frantic and exciting dramatic outburst on the death of her second son is in part spoiled by defects of both kinds; the passage[29] begins:

> Mrs Colburn went to the bed and knelt beside Billy, caressing the straight sturdy limbs of his young body with her toil-worn hands, kissing his hands and head and feet.

"Toil-worn hands" might conceivably be excused on the ground that it is the only possible phrase, but there can be no excuse for "the straight sturdy limbs of his young body". In all this Prichard's early journalistic apprenticeship was no doubt a factor, but to allow it to produce a continuing effect there must have been a weakness in her sense of rhythm, and, what is surprising in a writer whose work as a whole is so careful, a lack of continuous solicitude in revision. Nevertheless a realization of these defects must not be allowed to overshadow the merits of Prichard's style. Its ruling characteristics, which have been already exemplified, are simplicity, idiomatic colouring, and realism combined with poetic feeling; it is usually though not invariably concise, though some of

[28] *Haxby's Circus* (London, 1930), p. 333.
[29] *Working Bullocks*, p. 241.

its best descriptions are a little scattered; even in its poetic passages it is based strongly upon fact and never vague; it is direct and seldom relies upon suggestion, in spite of the occasional symbolic references that have been mentioned; and, without the least suspicion of artificiality, it is individual. Prichard has been called a disciple of Lawrence: she admires him and for her as for others writers of her period "he lifted horizons and gave us a confidence of attack", but there is no other resemblance, except perhaps in a couple of passages that were written before she had read any of his books. She has been also accused of modelling herself upon Sheila Kaye-Smith, one of whose books she had read at the time, but there is nothing between them either, except that both are of the tribe of Hardy, and that both have used the theme of the devotion to property; a comparison of these two novelists will show how much an author can gain by working in new fields and a new atmosphere.

Katharine Susannah Prichard has been translated into a number of foreign languages, French, German, Danish, Hungarian and Russian; and letters of appreciation have reached her from such far-off places as Persia, China and the South American republics. And it is well that her novels as well as Richardson's should be known abroad: if the one writer reaches a standard such that the world cannot do without her work, the standard reached by the other is in her best work very high; and it represents a vision, real and ideal, of her country and her countrymen which they should keep before them, and which may have also a value for a world that is losing sight of some of the primitive virtues.

Kylie Tennant, a generation younger than Katharine Prichard, has a good deal in common with her, but there are also radical differences. Tennant also is of the tribe of Lawson, and, like Prichard, she combines with his friendliness and width of sympathy something of Furphy's immense vitality and zest for life. She has not Furphy's weight of personality, but then she is still far younger than he was when he wrote his masterpiece. She is at least as rich in character and incident as Prichard, as much in love with her country and its people, and as interested in its national types, but she is franker than Prichard about their faults. Also, like Lawson but unlike Furphy or Prichard, she writes about city as well as country. Her sympathies are as emphatically with men and women who work, when they are in work, with their hands, but at her best she concentrates not upon those who are regular members of a working society, but upon those others who wander about the fringes of society, either workless or drifting from job to job or job to idleness.

Not that they are drawn as such outcasts as Gorki's; in the mass they are shown to stand for qualities that are extremely important to society: for freedom, independence, courage, even heroism; in fact, it is for the adventurous and vagabond element in society that Kylie Tennant stands, the element with which society has as little as possible to do, because it will not meet the demands of society; the element that traces back towards the primitive and at the same time forward in the direction of the millennium. And, since her methods are in accordance with her subject-matter, Tennant's novels are essentially picaresque. Like Prichard again, she makes before each story a careful preliminary study of the life and conditions with which it is to deal,[30] unless she happens to be acquainted with them already. On the other hand she is not a professional novelist in the sense in which Prichard and Palmer are professional novelists; she says she does not take her novel-writing seriously but writes for the fun of the thing and also to make enough money to enable her husband to retire from teaching. Prichard's novels have always a framework, not merely artistic but also philosophic, social, sometimes even political, but Tennant's can scarcely be said to have a framework at all: this constitutes her great defect as a novelist. Again, Prichard, though by no means without humour, is, in her attitude to life as well as in her underlying purposes, not only earnest but essentially serious: it may be said that to her life is a tragedy redeemed but also reinforced by humour; to Tennant, on the other hand, life is tragi-comedy dressed as comedy; it is so rich in amusing people and situations that the harshness, the pain and even tragedy, which are never hidden though they are never emphasized, tend to be submerged for the reader in their light-hearted context. And whereas Prichard's is a quiet and intermittent humour, Tennant's is all-pervading and sometimes hilarious: where there is a discoverable absurdity she emphasizes it, and her emphasis takes often the shape of satire, a quality that is quite absent from Prichard's work; but Tennant's satire is always humorous, never bitter unrelievedly, as with several of our principal poets. And whereas Prichard is a romantic, though a realistic one, Kylie Tennant is best described as a humorous realist, though with an undercurrent of romance that is conveyed as a rule by implication only. Finally, Tennant's career as a writer is not marked, like Prichard's, by a gradual development followed by a decline: after her first book there is a fairly steady level of performance, except that her city novels are inferior to the others, and that one of them is very slight.

[30] *Tiburon* is said to have been modelled on Canowindra, where Kylie Tennant lived for a while, but the preface declares that it is "a composite of many Australian places". *The Battlers* reflects her own experiences "on the track", and *Lost Haven* was founded on certain aspects of the country township in which she once lived. Before writing *Foveaux* she lived for some time in a Sydney slum district, and the other city novels are based, again, on experiences of her own

Kylie Tennant (Mrs L. C. Rodd, Manly, N.S.W., 1912-), had her schooling in Manly, and then hitch-hiked to Melbourne, where for some time she sold newspapers, soft drinks and tobacco in a railway kiosk. In Sydney again, she did a year's psychology and economics at the University, supporting herself by journalism and selling typewriters. She has tried also chicken-farming, reviewing and speaking over the radio, and she has been Assistant Publicity Officer to the A.B.C.; then on a tramp about the country districts of New South Wales she met and married a school-teacher at Canowindra. She has published so far three country novels: *Tiburon* (Sydney, 1935), which won the *Bulletin's* S. H. Prior Memorial Prize for that year; *The Battlers* (London, 1941), which shared the *Bulletin* prize for 1940 with *The Pea Pickers*,[31] and won the Australian Literature Society's gold medal for the best book of 1941; and *Lost Haven* (New York and Melbourne, 1946); her city novels are *Foveaux* (London, 1939); *Ride on Stranger* (London, Sydney, and New York, 1943); and *Time Enough Later* (New York, 1943). She has also written short stories, which have not been collected.[32] *Tiburon* has the characteristics one would expect in the first novel of a writer of talent; everything seems to have been poured into it without regard to relevance:[33] it is a series of pictures of the out-of-work fringe of a country town during the Depression, and of its relations with the local police and "society"; intertwined with this is the fragmentary and insubstantial romantic relationship of a "literary" lady schoolteacher and a member of the fringe. With *The Battlers* it becomes clear that there is plenty more left in the basket that had filled *Tiburon* with plums; this novel has the advantage of movement, and it is rather more than a succession of incidents strung together upon the principal characters: the men and women are of the types that constitute the fringe in *Tiburon*, though they are different individuals, but here what is shown is their wanderings from town to town, after the dole and any jobs they can come across, provided they do not have to work too hard at them. There is an obvious parallel with Steinbeck's *The Grapes of Wrath*, but except that both books deal with the wanderings of the landless, it is the contrasts that are most striking: *The Grapes of Wrath* is almost undiluted tragedy; in *The Battlers* there is much less tragedy, and it is kept mainly in the background. To this three causes contribute: the humorous personality of the author; the cheerful heroism of the down-and-outs and their stubborn refusal to be really down and out; and the attitude towards

---

[31] See pp. 1105-7.

[32] Since the closing date of this History, she has also published *The Joyful Condemned* (London, 1953), and *The Honey Flow* (London, 1956), as well as a play, *Tether a Dragon* (Sydney, 1952) and a work of history, *Australia: Her Story* (London, 1953).

[33] For example, Jingo's amusing play (pp. 210-29) has no logical connection with the rest of the story; indeed Jingo himself has scarcely any.

them of most of the police and at least the less "genteel" members of society. The nomads are certainly not welcomed, but they meet as a rule with patience, with a good deal of kindness and with scarcely any cruelty; also, these Australian nomads have no bitter memories of dispossession, for they have never possessed any property of which they could be dispossessed. *Lost Haven* is even more static than *Tiburon*; it contains neither structure nor story, and the tragedy with which it ends has not been prepared for and has evidently been clapped down upon it like the old-fashioned candle-extinguisher, simply because its author thought it was about time to stop. The book is a large, rich slab of the life of a lazy little fishing township, into which have been introduced for no apparent reason two city visitors, a rather dull lady librarian and her scarcely credible suitor. The city novels share the high spirits and sardonic humour of the others, but they run thinner, and it is clear that the cities do not provide Kylie Tennant with the wealth of idiosyncrasy, the "humours", the novelty that are to be found on the countryside. The most serious or at least the most earnest of the city novels, *Foveaux*, is a crowded study of the "progress" of a Sydney slum district with which is entwined a thread of story: this book does not quite come off; either its author did not live long enough in the slums to enable her to breathe their life easily and naturally; or perhaps the dirt and drabness, though they could not subdue her humour, so far as character and incidents were concerned, had an effect upon her general outlook of fresh hopefulness. *Time Enough Later* is a slight thing, and reminiscent of the next novel to be mentioned, but it is entertaining, and the episode that gives rise to the title, Rabelaisian in matter but quite otherwise in treatment, is delightful. *Ride on Stranger* is a city as *The Battlers* is a country picaresque. It tells of the wanderings of a "difficult" but extremely capable young woman from job to job, as an underpaid waitress in an unpleasant restaurant, as a miscellaneous handyman in a broadcasting station, as a private secretary and handyman again to an "Abbot" of a once well-known order of theosophists, and in a leftist club and leftist politics. Many characters and several "movements" are satirized with a quietly ribald humour; it has been said that the characters are reminiscent of Dickens's, and there is some truth in this; at least they are humorously exaggerated, and they belong to no particular place or time.

Few Australian writers have sketched such a range and variety of characters as Kylie Tennant, and none except Furphy has given her characters more vigorous life. The most interesting, the most deftly touched in are by no means always the principals; certainly Jamaica is more interesting than Alec Suderman, Lucy Rossingdale than Shannon, and practically everybody else than Jessica Daunt in *Tiburon*; and in *The Battlers* it might be argued that Dancy is more interesting than

Snow: here however personal preferences come in. In *Tiburon*, the only novel in which the better-off classes are represented as a group, some of the best effects are got by bringing members of these classes into contact with members of the nomadic fringe. There is for instance the episode[34] in which Mrs Malloy, a richly built and dressed old lady, who had made herself the council's curse for many years by her generosity to that undesirable element, the wandering unemployed, gives Blue and Dutch a lift in her car, to the fury of her snobbish daughter:

> "How far y' going?" she called. "Give y' a lift out to the shelter-shed?"
>
> "Thank you, lady, but we won't bother you, thank you all the same," Blue began, as he saw the look on the young woman's face.
>
> "Hop in," the old lady ordered in a cracked, harsh voice, "and not so much talk about it. Now, Bella"—to her daughter—"move over."
>
> They noticed that the old lady had taken off her patent-leather shoes and was nursing them in her lap. They drove off uncomfortably.
>
> "I'm Mrs Malloy," she said, as though that explained everything. "I s'pose"—she looked severely through her steel-rimmed glasses—"you've both got children to support."
>
> They agreed nervously that they had.
>
> "Six of them," Blue said, "but I had to leave them in Sydney with the mother-in-law when me wife died."
>
> "Not six," the old woman reproved, shaking her head. "You won't get anythin' out of 'em with six. They'll be saying 'Wicked, depraved wretch havin' all them kids an' not able to support 'em. Ought to be shot!' Three's quite enough."
>
> "Mother!"
>
> "Three's too many," she amended. "I got three." Blue and Dutch were feeling more and more uneasy. "What're you doin' out this way? Napthaline faking?"
>
> "We was thinkin' of havin' a go," Blue responded with a grin, but we left our stock lyin' about an' the moths ate it."
>
> . . . .
>
> The chauffeur had stopped the car.
>
> "Well, there's the shed," Mrs Malloy said regretfully. "'The Flea Bag', the boys call it. Sorry I can't ask you home."
>
> "That's all right with us, lady," Blue responded with a glance at the furious face of the old woman's daughter. "Thank you for the lift. I don't suppose you know of anyone who 'as arf a day's gardenin'—"
>
> "No," snapped the young woman, slamming the door.
>
> "That's all right, lady. They're always tellin' us to put by for a rainy day."
>
> "Here." The old lady leaned out of the window as the car moved off. "To buy napthaline," she called. A ten-shilling note lay in Blue's hand.

And there is the dialogue between Denny the Magsman and the local clergyman, known generally as Bill Sorrell, who has come to see him in hospital,[35] and the description of the Whites in their home-built hovel.[36] The Whites are quite the toughest of the fringe, rather too

---

[34] pp. 20–2; the dialogue between Blue and the vague, kind-hearted, rather sentimental doctor's wife (pp. 35–6) is almost as good as that quoted here.

[35] *Tiburon*, pp. 266–9.

[36] The same, p. 31.

much even for Blue, and Kylie Tennant pulls few punches in describing them. Snow, in *The Battlers*, is as close to life, as little exaggerated, as any of Tennant's characters, and interesting partly because of the position he occupies, tying the book together and literally bearing most of the burden on his shoulders:[37]

> Snow's face had no notable handsomeness, resembling closely the countenance of a particularly sleepy shark. His little, light-coloured eyes, each side of a huge, jutting nose, were half shut, just as his mouth—he breathed through it—was half-open to a gape of big, yellow teeth above an almost imperceptible chin. His forehead did not count in an assembly of features, as it was either hidden by an old felt hat or by a growth of straw-coloured hair which had earned him the usual bush name for fair-haired men: "Snow". His words were few and his speech slow. If he became excited, he stuttered. He seldom spoke a sentence without three "bloodys" in it, but he never knew he was swearing. It was as natural as his stutter.

Unlike the nomads in general, Snow was not naturally disinclined to work; he had "got a sickener of it" when he was a youngster, from his father, a half-starved wheat-cocky, but nowadays "a married man, when he can get work, he's got to take it". Snow was also different from the other nomads in that he preferred as a rule to travel alone, yet either as a substitute for the family from which he was cut off at the beginning of the story, or because he had something of the ambition of Patsy MacCann in James Stephens's *Demi-Gods*, to gather to himself a clan, he allowed a small group to collect round him; perhaps however it may have been just that he didn't feel able to turn them away, for he was, in spite of his toughness, "a weak man and kind-hearted, except when he was drunk". Dancy, "The Stray", the first and only permanent follower of Snow's, except when his small son joins the party later, is an even more striking example of Kylie Tennant's refusal to idealize the people in whom she is most interested, at least on their introduction to the reader. At first sight, when Snow discovers her, trying to steal food from his tucker-box, she scarcely seems human: she is toothless, she uses the foulest of foul language, and she hates everybody, man or woman; later, she turns out to be loyal and kind and even willing to work hard, at a pinch, and, when at last with a present of five pounds she gets herself a set of teeth, she is "almost handsome"! There is something of Lawson in what would nowadays be called a sentimental contrast of this sort; and there is something of Lawson again in the case of the delightful Miss Phipps, if only one could believe in her, who, after an unbroken record of sometimes crude and now and then extremely cunning selfishness, returns three fifty-pound notes to the father of a young wastrel who has given them to her when he is drunk. The book is full of "characters", a number of whom are quite as interesting as any of those mentioned, except that they are

[37] *The Battlers*, p. 9.

more lightly sketched. Again, in *Lost Haven*, there are, not so much Alec Suderman, whom the author seems to prefer, but Kelly Starbrace and his legal wife Jamaica, who is now the *de facto* wife of Alec, and about the only person who can get the better of Kelly in an argument or in any other way:[38]

> Jamaica had once been a beauty, a big blonde with a marble-white body and chilly blue eyes. Even now, in the fat of middle age, she conveyed an impression of strength and cleanliness; but there seemed to be several acres of coloured print dress around her frame. The kitchen was spotless and shone with polish. Its cedar framework had been painted a bright green. The dresser, the sink, the cupboard, were hung with chintz patterns in orange and purple. Pink artificial roses in gilt vases stood at either end of the mantlepiece, and the walls were adorned with pictures of her son Len as a baby, an enlarged snap-shot of Alec standing on the deck of the *Sea Eagle*, a studio portrait, villainously coloured, of Tessie and her mother. Several calendars showing English cottages bowered in flowers hung between the photographs. Jamaica liked her colours raw.

Of the men and women in the city novels, Lucy Rossingale in *Ride On Stranger* stands out, the idol of her women's session, the dear, rather pathetic baby who needs so much petting and looking after, the utterly unscrupulous egoist, whose "genial natural manner had always a little wistful accent, as if she said: 'I do so want you to like me' with every word"; for we don't really and entirely believe in Southwell Vaughan-Quilter, Abbot of the Order of Human Brotherhood, which is so amusingly satirized: as for Shannon, in the same book, she strikes one as an invented character, sharing some of the author's all-round ability and a little of her all-round experience; we cannot quite accept her either, and don't want to.

Several facts about Kylie Tennant's character-portrayal emerge. In the first place, allowing for touches, or in some cases, deep digs, of humorous exaggeration, they are almost all credible; all of them give the impression of having been based on life, but developed, or at least amplified, in one direction or another by means of a vigorously creative imagination. This is true of their settings also, and Tennant seldom makes any attempt to hide her sources: it is said that a character in one of her stories was deeply touched when he read of his own death. In the second place, about them all, with very few exceptions, there is an atmosphere of Lawsonian mateship: Shannon, in *Ride on Stranger*, and to a lesser extent Bessie in *Time Enough Later*, exemplify a dogged and lonely courage as well as kindness of heart, and there is something of the same sort in the principal characters in *Foveaux*, as indeed there is in all her "battlers", though as a general rule it is the humorous side of their difficulties that is emphasized. Apart from such underlying motifs as this and the heroism of the nomads, or those who refuse to be nomads, in

[38] p. 17.

Tiburon and *The Battlers*, none of Tennant's characters and none of the communities to which they belong stands for anything at all. Tennant is not, in her novels, a theorist about life; she observes with an eye like a hawk, and records with a humorous and often sardonic pen; but she does no more than that; she illuminates the surface of life and shows it up in high relief, but if she goes beneath the surface it is only by implication: such an implication is however strong in *Foveaux* and *The Battlers*, and there is of course the satire in *Ride on Stranger* and the implicit tragedy in Shannon, so far as Shannon can be accepted as real. There are plenty of opportunities for tragedy elsewhere, but they are never developed.[39] The thoughts and feelings of Kylie Tennant's characters are conveyed almost entirely by means of conversation and action: indeed the books consist very largely of conversations, though some of these are dynamic in the extreme, and there is plenty of condensed action in the intervals between them.

Kylie Tennant's style is simple and direct; but almost all Australian literary styles possess these qualities; it is easy, free, colloquial; but most possess these qualities also, though not to so great an extent. Her sentences are short, and her paragraphs are as a rule short also; but this is largely the result of the great proportion of conversation in the novels: not entirely however; there are examples, as will be seen in the passage to be quoted about Snow's sheep-duffing, or paragraphs whose shortness may represent a lapse into journalistic practice, as with Prichard; but this is a lapse, not, as with Prichard, a habit. Unlike Prichard, Tennant has a good ear for rhythm and seldom uses a cliche, and except for her images and an occasional short passage, the poetic element in her style is comparatively small: her principal object is clearly efficiency and common sense. And her style is more than concise, it is condensed, so that it is unusually difficult to shorten a passage for the purpose of quotation; she follows closely the old journalistic rule, which is also a good rule for most kinds of literature, taking the term in the narrower sense: say what you have to say and then stop. Her imagination is visual and she sees in images and often expresses herself by their means, but she never introduces an image for its own sake, or spends unnecessary space upon it; almost all her images are humorous, ironically humorous as a rule, and a number of them are extremely witty: they are outright, vigorous, and highly individual, in these respects recalling the images of H. G. Wells. She uses an Australian colloquialism now and then, but prefers as a rule to invent her own expressions: Miss Daunt, the long, slim, fastidious, half-hearted schoolteacher in *Tiburon*, "had started out as a greyhound of the spirit and ended up half water-spaniel"; and of Mrs

[39] For example, The Apostle in *The Battlers* and Alec in *Lost Haven*. [The Apostle indeed, like David Aumbry in *Tell Morning This* (Sydney, 1967), can be regarded as a vehicle of the author's view of life, which is far more precise than simple Lawsonian mateship.]

Claufield, *Tiburon's* snobbish social leader, Kylie Tennant says that "the lace about her throat always gave her the look of an aristocrat faced with something unfortunate and smelly"; in *The Battlers*, there is a description of a westerly wind "biting with all the malice of the thousands of miles of barbed wire over which it had blown";[40] and the Stray has a "talent for eking out the bare bones of truth into a tasty stew". In *Ride On Stranger*, "if God was to issue white wings to every genuine working-class leader, the whole damn lot of them would be footsore"; and Mr Litchin, the unpleasant restaurant proprietor, "rolled in his own emotions like a dog who has found a particularly odorous and enjoyable patch in the road". In *Time Enough Later*, Maurice "had expended enough energy to cut through a battleship with a blow lamp", and in *Foveaux*, Mr Bross "doddered through the dancers in the manner of a hen walking over an ants' nest": these are a few of the plums, but the taste of the pudding as a whole is of course better judged by complete slices. A few have been served out to the reader already, but as illustrations of Tennant's style rather than of her revelation of character, here is Snow, in *The Battlers*, duffing a sheep; incidentally, the passage with which it opens is one of the very few in which, apart again from the images, there is poetry in Kylie Tennant's prose:[41]

> Snow cared little for the wind, as it hushed his fire sideways like a mother soothing a rowdy child in its cot . . . at sundown there would be a breathless, tranquil silence, as the world turned over on its side for the night, with the sky like a translucent bubble of pale green glass, so fragile you would think that, at the tap of a finger-nail, it would ring and shiver the first stars down in trails of fire like water-drops on a window-pane.
>
> . . .
>
> As he listened for the faint bleating that betrayed the presence of the flock, and moved, with a low word to Bluey, towards that uneasy sound, Snow's big, loose, slouching body knitted into the swift decision of the born hunter. . . . In sheep-stealing . . . he took the quiet pleasure of an artist exercising his skill. Returning with a plump yearling over his shoulders, he had something of the benevolent aspect of a good shepherd in a church window. . . . As he cut his find's throat and flung the entrails to Bluey, he was thinking that life "on the track" was not so bad, with good places to camp and "cockies' sheep to knock over".
>
> . . . .
>
> He hung the carcase in a tree removed far enough from the clearing to escape the notice of any inquisitive visitors. Snow had been "in for meat" several times, and another gaol term was something he did not welcome. It was different in Queensland, where a man could always take a sheep for food as long as he left the skin hanging on the fence.

But life on the track could be hard enough, when "night after night they . . . huddled shivering round the fire . . . [and afterwards] the aching

[40] For a telling description of this wind and its effects see James Devaney's poem, "Winter Westerlies".

[41] pp. 8–9.

cold kept them awake"; or when, in another part of the country, the conditions were more characteristic of outback Australia:

> . . . there had been little rain for nine years, and now the heat of the summer was upon the place again. Already, the trees, the grass, had a dusty, ashy look, and the earth was but an anvil upon which the light beat and beat. It was a hard country, worn bare by winds as hot as a furnace blast, only the jagged flints jutting above the surface; and the people in the same way were worn bare, grated down until only the hardest parts of them were left showing.

[This vivid picture is followed by an episode which reveals that life on the land is almost as precarious for the small farmer as it is for the nomads, but neither the nomads nor the settlers show any inclination to return to the cities.] Some of the descriptions in the city novels are as lifelike, though not as individual or striking: they might have been written anywhere, but they show Kylie Tennant's range: *Foveaux* contains[42] a picture of a fish shop in a slum district that is as good as anything of the sort in *Jonah* or *Seven Poor Men of Sydney*, and in *Ride on Stranger* there is the extract from Bleeby Peverill's "Roses Are Blooming" broadcasting session and the Rabelaisian glimpse of what is said to have actually happened during the playing of a twelve-inch record.

But for one fundamental defect Kylie Tennant would be among the leading novelists of the English-speaking world today. It is not that she does not go in for psychoanalysis, for about this there is an element of mere fashion, and we get to know her men and women without it; nor is it that she turns her back upon all but Australian types, for some of her country and most of her city characters might have lived anywhere in western Europe or in the United States, though it is true that her universal types are not so good as the others: we should come nearer the mark if we were to say that she does not penetrate deep beneath the surface of her men and women, though she does penetrate to the bottom of some of them, Dancy and Snow for instance, so far as they go. The test of literature, it has been said, is whether we live more intensely for the reading of it, whether it quickens and vitalizes our faculties, and this test Kylie Tennant's novels pass easily, up to a point, though there are faculties, some of them among the most important, that she never touches at all. Her fundamental limitation consists in her utter carelessness of structure. It is not a novelist's business merely to present us with a slice of life, a snapshot or series of snapshots, however good; he should be an artist, not merely an accurate observer and recorder; it is his business to impose a form upon the aspect of life with which he is concerned; or, if you like, to uncover the form that lies concealed within it; to make a pattern out of life, or to reveal the pattern that lies

[42] p. 110.

latent there, obscured by chance occurrences. Whether such a form or pattern exists or not may be a matter for the metaphysicians; at any rate the mind cannot properly appreciate anything, least of all so complicated and heterogeneous a thing as life, or an aspect of life, unless it is arranged, organized; and such arrangement, such organization, is one of the principal objects of any art. But except in the selection and depiction of particular characters and incidents who appeal to Kylie Tennant and the fitting of them together into a society, and in her style within its limitations, there is scarcely any art about her novels. *The Battlers* is something of an exception: here there is a definite story, though sometimes it sits down for a while and looks at something that is in itself interesting, but has little really to do with it: there are even traces of a plot. And since in richness and vitality *The Battlers* is little inferior to the almost purely episodic *Tiburon* and the static and quite structureless *Lost Haven* it is the best novel that Kylie Tennant has written so far.

Here also may best be considered Eve Langley's one novel,[43] *The Pea Pickers* (Sydney, 1942), because of its richness in character and incident, its picaresque adventurousness and its abundance of life; but it has scarcely anything else in common with Kylie Tennant's work, even with *The Battlers*, to which it comes nearest: it shared with that novel the *Bulletin's* S. H. Prior Prize for 1940. Eve Langley (Mrs Hilary Clark, Forbes, N.S.W., 1908-74) was educated at Forbes, but her family took her to Molong and then to Gippsland and the Dandenongs; she migrated to New Zealand, after an attempt at bean- and pea-growing which was frustrated by bad seasons; she became a proof-reader, a freelance journalist and a librarian, and published verse and short stories, which have not been collected. *The Pea Pickers* is a long, crowded, undisciplined, self-conscious and highly fanciful fictionized autobiography. It tells of the wanderings of the narrator and her sister, dressed as men and calling themselves Steve and Blue, apple-packing, hop-picking, pea-picking on the Victorian countryside. Earning little and that precariously, they are sometimes so hungry that they are grateful for a gift of "a lot of stale bread lying around 'that might be all right for your little dorg'"; they "convey" as much as they can from their fellow workers and acquaintances, live excitingly, and have on the whole the time of their lives. Eve Langley has a natural instinct for story-telling and a perfect control of her instrument. She has, like Kylie Tennant, the sharpest of eyes for the picturesque and the absurd, but in her, humour runs parallel to and intermingles with a self-centred, melancholy and often hysterical frustration. Everything she observes, though not everything she feels, she makes interesting; but, as with Tom Collins, it is her personality that after all makes her book, as well as sometimes

[43] Since this History closed she has published another, *White Topee* (Sydney, 1954).

marring it: her romantic and self-conscious egotism, which merges often in sentimentality, at first repels; but as we grow better acquainted with her, the repulsion fades, and the reader is absorbed. Largely through the personality of its author the book becomes an image of romantic and adventurous youth, possessed by a double longing, to be loved and to be famous, especially to be loved; but at the same time overflowing with high spirits and finding a wild humour in everything. What with this longing of Steve's, which becomes quite reckless in its search after an embodiment of the ideal, the beauty of the more normal Blue, and their enterprising explorations after work and something to eat, the sisters run risks of several sorts. They know how to look after themselves, with laughter, a bucket of dirty water, a billy-lid of hot stew, and even a knife and a stiletto, but one at least of Steve's temporary idealizations must have possessed unusual self-restraint if he was real. Probably imagination played a large part in his making; but it is hard to imagine any man replying in such a cheaply "literary" manner as this to Steve's appealing accusation of coldness and self-sufficiency:

> "No, Steve. My love for you is pure. I do not need to touch you. I am with you; that is enough. From other women coarse self-satisfaction may be obtained, but you give the uncloying cleanliness of your mental passion to me, and I am satisfied."

Eve Langley's romanticism sometimes runs her into this sort of thing, and some of her emotional interludes read like early Keats in his worst manner or like the worst patches in *My Brilliant Career*; nevertheless she has a genuine and individual poetic gift; here is an imaginary farewell from her first lover:

> It was a look, and then a kiss, that said, "I am the earth of Gippsland, and while I endure I shall bring to me and send from me, lovers, wives, sons and daughters unending. But you, I do not need." Then he stepped back lightly and silently on his insect feet that trod the ground as though tapping it for honey wells.

There are certain marked resemblances between Eve Langley and the Russian diarist, Marie Bashkirtseff, whose temperament was, as her translator has pointed out,[44] violent and full of stress and tumult, and her personality "a singular mixture of untutored instincts joined to an ultra-modern subtlety of brain and nerves". Through the veins of both life burned like a fever, and the ambitions of both were for fame and a lover, though Marie Bashkirtseff had by far the greater and more varied talent and to her fame meant much more; the following extract from her diary[45] might have been written by Eve Langley, except that the style is sober and logical rather than romantic:

[44] See *The Journal of Marie Bashkirtseff*, translated, with an introduction, by Mathilde Blind (London, 1870), p. ix. The translator ascribes this mixture of qualities to barbaric blood and a cultured upbringing.

[45] Monday, 21st February 1876 (p. 58).

I seek, I find, I invent a man; I stake my life on him; he becomes part and parcel of all my sensations; and then when my head, open to all the winds of heaven, is full of him, it will perhaps only bring me suffering and tears.

Something about Eve Langley's egotism reminds one also of the heroine of *My Brilliant Career*, and so does the naïvety of, for instance, the rejection of her appeal to her second lover, though the mere idea of making any such appeal would have infuriated the heroine of Miles Franklin's novel. And in the whimsical quality of Eve Langley's invention there is some resemblance to that of Hugh McCrae as a writer of prose: this is particularly evident in the names the girls give to men, animals and places: Diddlie Herkits; Mrs Beesknees; Pricie-ole-man; Tomcatto, the Italian operatic star; Seldom-Fed, Avadrink, and, best of all Borreler-worreloil! Except for Steve's two lovers when they are talking intimately to her, all the characters in the book are self-consistent inhabitants of the world that *The Pea Pickers* creates, strange as it is; but there is about all of them, in varying degrees, an element of fantasy, so that though one might meet and recognize them they would not be quite the same: they would lack something. And there is at least as much fantasy in Eve Langley's mannered and formal style, in whose epithets and images there is again some resemblance to McCrae's; for instance:

"Kelly kissed me with the furtive whiskery kiss of youth, smelling of the sun and feeling like a blow from a hairbrush"; "Poor old Jim; he attached himself to us like a tick to a well-wooled lamb before shearing time"; Marriage is a "procession of perambulators"; "Mooney, the youngest boy, was all black and white like a mourning envelope".

Sometimes the image extends over a whole paragraph, as in the glimpse of Steve's first love; but perhaps the following is more characteristic; Leep Singh, "the prince of India", wishes to join them in their room; he does not know that they have just been fumigating it with sulphur:

"What you got to sell?" he asked with a crafty smile. "You," I responded, "and in this wise. Come, enter, thou gorgeous and voluptuous gourmet of the East. O, that Solomon had seen thee in thy purple before he went to the tents of Sheba! Thou, with the baldrics of Calcutta scarlet, with thy shoulder-knobs of string and tar, made by the craftsmen to dazzle all time: thou of the painted cheek (the rouge of the methylated spirit jar), thou of the breath given by the glorious goddess Pyorrhoea. . . . Come then, into my chamber, fall, and be in Elysium."

And with a hasty look to see if the room was dim with sulphur I pushed him in and locked the door.

He got out after an uproar and fled vomiting across the fields, and I had to nail a piece of wood over the window to take the place of the glass he had broken in his agony to escape.

The Pea Pickers has been called the most original novel since *Such Is Life*. This is probably true, though by no means all its originality has a literary value.

CHAPTER VII

THE NOVEL

The Lawson-Furphy Tradition Continued: Palmer; Davison; Others. Other Novels of the Countryside: Lowe; Hatfield; White; Blunden; Velia Ercole; Cecil Mann; Casey; Edwards; Morrison; Others

VANCE PALMER has in common with the other three followers of the Lawson-Furphy tradition only those characteristics which make him a member of the same group; he lacks their exuberant vitality, but none of them possesses his systematic and unvarying craftsmanship. And, from a general literary point of view, his range has also to be taken into account: novels, short stories, plays, verse; studies, literary, historical and biographical; no Australian writer except Douglas Stewart has so varied a talent. And since, during the forties and fifties, he was a widely known writer, he was able to exert an influence upon the younger generation in the direction in which it was most needed. Like Prichard and Tennant, he belongs to the tribe of Lawson rather than Furphy, and his preference for the life and scenes of his own country has persisted in spite of a wide acquaintance with the rest of the world; when he introduces exotic types it is either, as with Kloss in *Golconda*, because they are necessary to his general purpose, or, as with Besanck in *Legend for Sanderson*, in order to bring out the flavour of the others, like a spoonful of condiment in a simple dish, and of such characters it is only of Besanck that we get more than a glimpse. As with the other members of the group, Palmer's subject is the ordinary man, but in the creation of character he depends much less than they do upon description, action, and spoken words, specializing in psychological analysis, though he does not use the stream of consciousness. Like Prichard and Tennant, he makes his preliminary studies of type and scene, regarding the one as inseparable from the other; but one of his characters, or sometimes a pair, always stands out above the rest, and, unlike Tennant, he has always a story to tell. (Edward) Vance Palmer (Bundaberg, Q., 1885-1959) was educated at Ipswich, Queensland; his mother was Irish, his father Australian. There was a literary atmosphere about the family: his grandfather had contributed to Sydney *Punch* away back in the sixties and had been a friend of Wentworth, Kendall and Deniehy; his father, who wrote himself, told him stories about these men and made them familiar to him. Vance had always wanted to write about the men and scenes among which he grew up, and the discovery of Lawson stimulated him greatly, giving his surroundings a new significance; at seventeen or eighteen he broke into a couple of English magazines, and at nineteen he went off to try his luck in London. After a couple of years of fair success there, he returned to Australia by way of Finland, Russia, Siberia and the East, and was for some years tutor, book-keeper, drover and overseer on outback Queensland stations. A little later he was writing in London, the United States and Australia again; he married Janet Higgins ("Nettie Palmer") and published two books of verse, a book of one-act plays[1] and several romances; he enlisted in the A.I.F., and after the war he helped to establish the Pioneer Players. Apart from the early romances, which were published under a pen-name, and a novel[2] that also need not concern us, he has published the following novels, spread out over twenty-four years: *The Outpost* (London, 1924), *The Man Hamilton* (London, 1928), *Men Are Human* (London, 1930), *The Passage* (London, 1930), *Daybreak* (London, 1932), *The Swayne Family* (Sydney, 1934), *Hurricane* (Sydney, 1935), *Legend for Sanderson* (Sydney, 1937), *Cyclone* (Sydney, 1947), and *Golconda* (Sydney, 1948). *Hurricane* is a rewritten version of *The Outpost*, about both of which there will be something to say later.

Like several other Australian writers, of prose and verse, Palmer belongs to two historic Periods and two quite different literary worlds,[3] and his work shows this in a curious way. There appears to have been a conflict in his nature between the nineties and modernity as represented respectively by his temperament and his will: temperamentally he is a romantic idealist; but recoiling from the emotionalism, the vehemence of romanticism in its decline, he has in all his later work cultivated detachment, restraint, an unillusioned realism; the result, in a sensitive nature, has been a marked self-consciousness, which has been transferred to most of Palmer's leading characters, and to some of the others as well. All this may have something to do also with a deep-seated brooding melancholy that has been ascribed to Palmer's work in general: the melancholy certainly exists, subduing the zest for life of some of his principal characters, casting a shadow over the story and transposing it into a minor key; nevertheless it is always found compatible with a quiet, sardonic humour. Palmer's determination to transfer to modernity

[1] For Palmer's ballads, see pp. 450–1; for his plays, pp. 743–5; for his short stories, pp. 1244–5; for his historical sketches, p. 1382. Since the closing date of this History he published *Legend of the Nineties* (Melbourne, 1954), which is referred to on p. 387, note 1, and two novels: *Seed Time* (Sydney, 1957) and *The Big Fellow* (Sydney, 1959), and a collection of short stories, *Let the Birds Fly*. Another collection, *The Rainbow Bird* (Sydney, 1957) was an anthology.

[2] *Cronulla* (Sydney, 1925).

[3] This sort of thing is likely to happen whenever the Periods into which a history of literature have been divided are short. As a rule it is not difficult to attribute a writer's work as a whole to one particular Period, but in Palmer's case and in two or three others, it has seemed here advisable to divide earlier and later work between two Periods.

goes beyond a mere change-over; it has involved an attempt even to eradicate from the only one of his early novels that he has thought worth preserving[4] all traces of the romantic idealism in which it was conceived and written. It is worth contrasting *The Outpost* with the revised version that was published eleven years later as *Hurricane*: in both, the principal character, Faulkner, resident magistrate at a Papuan outpost, allows his feeling for a woman to delay his suppression of a native outbreak, with the result that lives and also his position are lost; but whereas in the first version Faulkner is in love with the girl, in the second the attraction is sensual merely, and there is no marriage or desire for it on either side. Unfortunately the alteration has weakened the motive past credulity: Faulkner, who is shown as an extremely strong character, without any hankering after women, and determined to make a success of his job, would scarcely in the circumstances have delayed with the girl for a purely sensual reason. It is clear that Faulkner's motive was altered in order to avoid giving the story a conventional romantic ending; but the whole scheme of the story is romantic, so that even in the revised version a romantic ending was an artistic necessity. In the result then, a story that was a good one,[5] though of a kind now unfashionable among serious writers, becomes distorted, and so does the character of the hero. In none of the novels of Palmer's that are here discussed do we find a romantic story on the old conventional model, with a predestined happy ending; of the characteristics that carry through them all, the first, a romantic survival that is still common among the rank and file though it has almost faded out among standard writers, is a sympathy with the principal character which is often coloured by idealization; the second is the embodiment of an attitude which has nowadays, largely as the result of wars and the politics that have produced them, been abandoned: it consists in an admiration of the power that arises out of personality, though the admiration is by no means naïve. From these two factors springs the dominant motif in Palmer's novels: the hero as strong man engaged in a struggle with fate. This motif is most obvious in *The Outpost-Hurricane*. In *The Man Hamilton*, psychological analysis becomes important, and in contrast with *The Outpost-Hurricane* there is little action, except in the minds of the characters: Hamilton, married to a half-caste by whom he has a son of fourteen, falls in love with a governess on a neighbouring station; they decide not to go off together because the boy is handicapped enough already and because the life Hamilton has made for himself would be broken. In spite of some

[4] It certainly was worth preserving, though whether the original version should not have been retained is another matter.

[5] Except for some naïveties natural in an early novel, particularly in connection with the drawing of the hero's character; see, for example, the remark about "the Panjandrum" on p. 7 and Faulkner's reply to the taunt about his romanticism on p. 14.

sharply conceived and sketched minor characters, the book as a whole fails because the hero is insufficiently realized; we are never brought into intimate contact with Hamilton, and he does not bear out his description as a man of "inflexible will", much less what he says of himself, that "it's always been neck or nothing with me". This book has however its place in the history of Australian fiction by reason of its attempt to provide a psychological plot for the station novel instead of relying upon a forced collection of old properties.[6] The next two books are a great advance; indeed they represent Palmer's highest achievement: *The Passage* is almost invariably considered the better of the two, but with it, at least, must be ranked *Men Are Human*, which has been much underrated.[7] This is a far stronger and richer book than *The Man Hamilton*; we get to know intimately the principal as well as the minor characters, and it is the characters who, in their strength and weakness, make the story. The relationship between Roger McCurdie, the old station-owner who is unable to surrender control to the son to whom he is devoted; between Roger and the old half-caste stockman, his "dark shadow", who suffers as Roger suffers by the loss of a loved son; and between Boyd McCurdie and the woman he loves and on the other hand the old stockman's daughter, with whom he has become entangled: all these are naturally and inevitably interwoven; the book is actually a study in human weakness and fate working through apparent accident. Here the hero is divided; his principal characteristics are possessed by old Roger, a man of intense driving energy, bursting with vitality, rather coarse in fibre, kind-hearted and likeable, but pigheaded, unconsciously selfish and bounded wholly by the material. More than any other of Palmer's characters, except Faulkner and the sketch of Sanderson, a man of action and shown in action, he is the least characteristic of any of them, but the most real, impressive and interesting. Here Roger is arranging for Boyd, on his return from the first World War, to be brought home in style from the railway siding; he could not drive the seventy miles himself because he had broken his collarbone in a fall from a horse:[8]

> There was a smell of crushed corn, of hides, and of old leather at the stables. Old Duncan and his son Jim, a lively, bright-eyed boy of fifteen, had caught the horses and were making ready for the road. Near the open door of the saddle-room stood a bay mare having her feet trimmed, her groomed skin shining like satin, and the sun scintillating from her nickel-plated harness. . . . The light buggy had been hauled

[6] On this point, see pp. 233, 1085-6 and note 12.

[7] Partly, perhaps, because it was awarded only third prize in a *Bulletin* competition (1929), whereas *The Passage* was awarded a first (1930). But *Men Are Human* would have won in an ordinary year: in 1929 the judges had to decide between three of the best novels that have been submitted for an Australian competition; *Coonardoo* and *A House is Built* were bracketed first, by a narrow margin, which left only the third place for *Men Are Human*.

[8] *Men Are Human*, pp. 12-13.

out and washed the day before, and McCurdie stood looking at it critically, blinking a little in the morning light with his pale-blue eyes that were set so closely together. A big man, with heavy shoulders, he looked impressive even with his hat on, but when he stood bareheaded, as now, his high-domed forehead, bald as an egg, gave him an added suggestion of power. At sixty-seven he was still filled with an explosive vitality, and both men and dogs moved quickly out of his way when he roared; but so well were his little quirks and humours known that he did not often need to test the full strength of his lungs.

"Where are the other horses?" he asked.

Duncan glanced up from beneath the bay mare's belly with a hint of surprise.

"The others? Jeff told me to take Bunny and Storm. They're used to the buggy, like."

"Well, and don't you want a couple of leaders?" snapped McCurdie. "Good God, man, you don't mean to crawl in there like a lame dog sneaking into a dark corner! There's any quantity of young horses on the place broken into harness."

The other half of the hero, in the sense that he seems to possess the author's sympathies and to be intended to attract ours, is Roger's son, Boyd, a returned soldier with a Military Cross and a fine record as a strong man, who is however conscious of a weakness known only to himself. In his sensitiveness and self-consciousness he is much more characteristic of Palmer's principal characters than his father; he has harder luck than most, and fate, in the form of accidents which strength and efficiency might have got the better of, frustrates and finally overwhelms him. *The Passage* is at least as rich in character and event, but everything about it is much more restrained; there is plenty of life and colour and motion, but nothing so vital and forthright as old McCurdie; it is a study of power that is slow of both development and acceptance. The story is set in a Queensland fishing village, and it tells in particular of a family which Lew, the eldest son, has to carry on his shoulders; of the failure of his bright but shallow younger brother, for whom so much has been sacrificed; Lew has indeed to carry the whole village, and redeems it from decline. Interwoven with this is Lew's relationship with two women, of whom he lets the right one slip and marries the other, light and flashy, but comes back to the first in the end. Lew is to all appearances a slow-minded old plugger, who will never achieve much; but he is the possessor of a quiet strength, drawn from the earth and water about him, though at first he is scarcely aware of it himself; it is aroused, suddenly and not perhaps altogether credibly, after his brother's failure and the village's decline, by the obvious need for him, by an expression of confidence from the mother who has never appreciated him, and by a meeting with the woman he had let slip. About the other novels less need be said. In *Daybreak* the hero is again doubled: an idealized war leader who goes to pieces in civil life, and a rather humdrum young fellow who is pulled two ways between loyalty to his former leader and to his family; the book ends rather inconclusively with the dissolution of one set of loyalties by death and "an assurance that life was not so broken and inconsecutive as it seemed". In *The Swayne Family*[9] Palmer turns to the cities; here he owes a good deal to *The Forsyte Saga*; there are even some similarities in detail;[10] the protagonist is even more than with Galsworthy a whole family, for none of the characters stand out as many of Galsworthy's do, yet this is not so much an imitation as an Australian parallel. In *Legend for Sanderson* we have the hero as ghost, an overshadowing ghost, a legend that comes alive; making everything else seem pale and thin. He is dead by the time the story really opens:[11] a hard, jovial, conscienceless old buccaneer, who has progressed from scrub work to cabinet minister, and undischarged bankrupt; the principal living character is his son, a self-conscious, ineffectual young fellow who seems always about to do something important; but he never does, and the story ends like that, flat with a hill in the background: this might be well enough if we were brought into fuller contact with old Sanderson, but he is after all only sketched, though in strong lines. *Cyclone* deals, in a manner slightly reminiscent of that in *Daybreak*, with divided loyalties, but setting and treatment are quite different: the principal character is undistinguished; there is an attempt to represent him as heroic in his struggle with the storm, in which "authority was flowing to him naturally by virtue of his newly-charged will", but when he has emerged as victor we cannot accept the picture of him as "life itself that was driving on through the sand; blind, battered, yet moving to some pulse in its secret core". *Golconda* is the story of a silver-lead Mount Morgan, and the life connected with it; Macy Donovan, two-up school proprietor, union organizer, member of parliament and future cabinet minister, stands out over the other characters, a man of guts and drive; and next to him old Mahony, the man without the driving energy and with a secret flaw: there is some similarity in scene and types to those of Katharine Prichard's last three books, but Palmer's is not spoilt by propaganda.

The other qualities that run throughout Palmer's work are not always quite consistent with one another or with the ruling motif that has just been considered. Most important is the tendency to concentrate upon the ordinary man which he shares with the other members of his group: with Palmer however the term ordinary is elastic; it will have been noticed how it includes a self-consciousness and sensitivity which are abnormal, in that the ordinary man does not possess them to anything like the same extent as Palmer shows them. Palmer's heroes are notable

[9] This tied with F. S. Hibble's *Karangi* (see p. 1133) for first place in the Melbourne Centenary novel competition in 1934.

[10] For instance, Ernest's visit to the family's place of origin (Chapter XXIII); Digby's collection of etchings (p. 329); "Moderately, yes that's the word, I suppose" (p. 166); Digby in the police court (pp. 233-4); and at the cricket match (p. 93).

[11] We do get one glimpse of him in life, but that is in his last days, which fade out in accidental death.

as the possessors not of faculties that are beyond the experience of the ordinary man, but of drive, organizing power, personality with which the ordinary man is familiar on a small scale, though he may not possess them himself. The mental processes of Palmer's heroes, like those of his minor characters, are simple; they may be aware of a wider world as the minor characters are not, but they are not endowed with, for instance, imaginative vision; there is nothing subtle or even unexpected about any of them, and though some of them are comparatively sophisticated, it is after all a simple sophistication: in fact, Palmer's exceptional characters are exceptional only in that they represent the ordinary raised to a higher power. In these circumstances his treatment of them is not entirely appropriate: he is devoted to the analytical method, yet there is scarcely anything in their mental processes that might not be conveyed by action or conversation; the result is that we have often a fairly elaborate analysis of the nature of something that does not need it: this state of affairs is contributed to by one of Palmer's outstanding merits, a logic and clarity of perception and expression that makes what is not in any case difficult seem obvious. In their concentration upon the normal, the ordinary, the members of the "Australian" group run a danger of conveying an atmosphere of undistinguished mediocrity, a danger from which only the novelty of types and settings and their extraordinary vitality saves them. To this danger Palmer is not so liable because of the set of unusual attributes with which he endows at least his leading characters, and also because of his accomplished craftsmanship; but the prevalence of these unusual attributes, a self-conscious sensitiveness, an awareness of the critical attitudes of others, and a tendency to analysis, and the uniformity of the methods by which they are presented exposes Palmer to a corresponding danger, that of monotony, and this he does not always escape. There is also something about Palmer's characters' awareness of critical attitudes, even those who are drawn as strong and self-reliant, which suggests that after all they are not quite sure of themselves; and there is always something to be aware of, for in each of Palmer's novels there is at least one more or less mildly malicious onlooker, of whose disapprobation or even mere amusement the principal character is uneasily conscious. A typical example is where Boyd, in *Men Are Human*, who has been carrying a bucket for Josie, the half-caste girl with whom he afterwards becomes entangled, notices his mother-in-law watching him:[12]

> Over on the other verandah he saw Ada standing in a flowered wrapper, eating a ripe fig, and the inscrutable smile in her eyes made him feel a raw boy again. The woman always seemed to see the comic side of every encounter!

---

[12] p. 35.

Boyd was a particularly sensitive person, but it is the same with Nina and even Hamilton in *The Man Hamilton*, Lew in *The Passage*, and even Mahony in *Golconda* and Faulkner in *Hurricane*; once, in *Legend for Sanderson*, it is people in general who are conscious of a malicious onlooker:

> Yet his entrance created a secret uneasiness, put people on their guard. They could never be quite sure of being armed against the penetration of those agate eyes, the malice of that barbed tongue.

Connected with Palmer's dislike of romantic extremes is an ingrained preference not only for understatement but for avoidance of the outright, for indirectness of approach, for conveyal by implication: this is sometimes carried so far as to result in a disinclination for action. Hence another paradox, in that not merely Palmer's principal characters but even others whose means of expression are largely confined to conversation and action appear too often as contemplative of past action, or of the possibilities of action to come, or of imagined action, rather than as actually acting. What is more, when Palmer does describe action, he often prefers to record it indirectly, through the mouth of some witness; it is true that by this means he kills two birds with one stone, since the witness is made to help describe himself as well as what he has observed: nevertheless the practice makes the story seem less real. Not that Palmer is incapable of reproducing action directly; on the contrary some of his descriptions of it are full and vivid, as for example the account of the fight between Rossiter and Axel in *Daybreak*, most of the scenes in which old McCurdie, in *Men Are Human* are concerned, and Lew's long dive in *The Passage*;[13] and, as one would expect, there are many instances in *Hurricane*. But as a rule when he does describe action he compresses it into as short a space as possible: it would be hard to defend the summary nature of the three lines in which it is told how Lew carried the body of his small son down to a dinghy and rowed out to bury him at sea.[14] But the most outstanding instances are Palmer's love scenes: here he seems always to omit everything that he can possibly leave to the imagination: when, in *The Passage*, Clem and Lew at last come together we get merely a bare sketch of what happens; when Boyd meets Barbara in Sydney, although it is later made quite clear that matters had then come to a head between them, there are no more than four words of conversation and a short highly generalized description, and these only as recalled later in Boyd's mind. This is indeed an example of action that is merely reported, and of that there are innumerable other examples: it is only by a few words from Boyd that we are made aware that he has just had a verbal encounter with Mace, and given him the sack;

[13] Quoted on pp. 1117–18.

[14] There is also the short though dramatic summary of Boyd's death in *Men Are Human*.

yet it was the feeling aroused largely by this encounter that was ultimately to lead to Boyd's death. And there is a strong tendency in Palmer to convey even conversation indirectly, or to imagine it altogether; apart from the loss of realism, one can scarcely believe that so many people would be able to imagine so clearly and correctly what others might say or do in particular circumstances. And it is not only Palmer's introspective characters who behave like this; old McCurdie, who is, except Sanderson, the least imaginative of Palmer's principal characters, pictures himself meeting his son in style, so that all the hotel loungers will nudge one another and say:

> "Hullo! There's McCurdie in from Abernethy. Come out of his shell again, hasn't he? That son of his must be coming home."

And here is another speech that McCurdie imagines:

> "You left me a long time. How am I to know you won't leave me again? Better for me to keep with the one who seems fixed:"

the imagined speaker is his dog![15]

In the matter of construction and style Palmer is a master of his craft; everything is in place and every incident fits into the general design; not only is there neither carelessness nor waywardness—sometimes indeed one is inclined to wish for something a little wayward—but everything is conceived and written with formal correctness; even the conversations are formalized: indeed what one is shown is often not so much life in the raw as a crystallization of life into a form in which there is a loss in realism and vitality. In the matter of plot Palmer is straightforward, though he seems to have been influenced by the doctrine of pattern, in that the scheme of a book sometimes fans out into a number of lines of progression, lets one observe a landscape rather than a succession of events in one or in alternate directions. With the qualification that the style is the man and that a writer cannot climb beyond himself, Palmer's style is about as good as it could be; he has forged and filed it into the perfect implement—for him. As has been noticed with Katharine Prichard, he realizes the importance of being quick off the mark, striking a clear note at the outset of each novel: "The anchored dinghy rocked gently on the long swell"; "McCurdie awoke before it was dawn"; "There was an air of subdued excitement around Cayley's"; "Through the drowsy afternoon the plane droned on like a deliberate hornet, lost in upper air", and so on; Palmer follows the same practice even in the openings of many of his chapters. Such qualities as restraint and indirectness of approach that have been already noted in another connection are everywhere evident in Palmer's style, and also a laconic

[15] There is another example in which a jackass is imagined as speaking.

precision and a naturalness of expression that runs into idiom: this goes some way, except that a few of the idioms give the impression of having been sought after, towards smoothing over the evidence of painstaking; it is curious however to notice how phrases that might in themselves sound crude are with Palmer ingredients in a method of expression that smoothes and refines them: for example:[16]

> A fascinating world for Lew, one that liberated his mind! He had come out over the bar in a bad mood, chewing the rag, as old Uncle Tony said, because of his feeling that too much weight was being put upon his shoulders. A man shouldn't be forced to carry the heavy end of the log all his days! He shouldn't have to keep his back bent, day in and day out, while the rest of the family got anything good that was going. . . . Pulling continually against a headwind; that was what it was like; and he'd had a bellyful of it!

This passage also illustrates Palmer's faculty of image-making, of which more by and by; and the way in which his conversations are stylized: the upflow from the unconscious is shown, but it is a smoothed, canalized flow. It is also often crystallized into a sentence; here is the conclusion of a passage describing Hughie's delight in carting with his new truck:

> "This is life!" the flickering eyes said. "I've got hold of the wheel of it now."
> And Kunkel, watching him through his glasses from the door of his shop, said with complacency:
> "T'at Hughie all right—by hell, yes. I know all the time he make good when I give him a start. Wort' all the Callaways rolled into one, I tell Mina."

The translation of the expression in Hughie's eyes into words adds life and reality to the preceding description; but the ejaculation by Kunkel that follows, though just as realistic is no more so, with the result that the distinction between the inner and the outer world is dimmed, and the total loss outweighs the gain. And this applies throughout Palmer's novels: he makes the inner world more vivid at the cost of making the outer world less so by comparison; moreover, the literary atmosphere that is unavoidable when a stylist is writing in the first person attaches also to formalizations of this kind: but if Palmer's art here overshoots itself, that is a mistake that could be made only by a considerable artist. One of his most marked gifts, that of description, will have been noticed already; he observes essentials, records them exactly, and gives them clearcut expression; among the most memorable is the account of Lew's long dive in the competition:[17]

> He waited till the two surfers, having lost direction and swum in circles, came up gasping; then he made his plunge, hitting the water with hardly a splash. Down in that world of greenish light he was at home, and he felt the current behind him, giving each stroke of leg and arm twice its proper value, sending him swimming like a startled fish a foot above the white sand.

---

[16] *The Passage*, p. 14. [17] *The Passage*, pp. 85–6.

> He knew every inch of that sea-floor as well as the cropped green where he mended his nets. The dark blur that shot under him was the bottom of one of Uncle Tony's riddled punts; the blob of dancing light away to the right was a new kerosene tin Hughie had dropped overboard when he was baling. Two wavy silver streaks showed up near him: they were the still legs of one of the surf-club men. He consciously clapped on the pace, pictures flitting across his brain. He could see Dot perched breathless on one of the stones of the breakwater, Lena standing on tiptoes with one arm resting on Craig's shoulder, the half-caste's dark head and white teeth appearing above the smooth surface. His own head seemed to have swollen like a bladder and there was a roaring in his ears, but still he drove on. Another twenty yards!
>
> A flood of blinding light poured down on him, dazzling his eyes, as he came to the surface. People were calling out things from the breakwater, rushing down towards him waving their handkerchiefs. A rumble of confused sound; the feeling of a loud surf breaking over him.
>
> "Lew! Good old Lew! You've done it this time, Lew! Home and dry on the pig's back!"

There is plenty of action here. And then, by contrast, in *Cyclone* the lovely little picture of the two half-caste sisters lying asleep on the beach to which they had swum after the wreck:[18]

> The two girls were lying naked a few yards from one another, their arms spread out, their hair matted with sand. Though fully developed they looked like sleeping children. Their breasts rose and fell gently; their breath came evenly from between parted lips. It was plain that in the long fight they had rid themselves of one garment after another and had kept on blindly, driven by something deeper than will. Now they slept the sleep of utter exhaustion, the lids heavy on their closed eyes, life gradually renewing itself in their honey-coloured bodies.

There is also the tragic glimpse of Barbara as old McCurdie saw her just after she had heard of Boyd's death. Few Australian prose writers are so fertile as Palmer in images, and, though his have not the outright and explosive vigour of Kylie Tennant's, they are not conventional and possess an individual life of their own. Each appears natural and also illuminative, a spark that throws light upon what lies about it. A fussy mother "hovering like a white moth about . . . boy's room to see if there was anything he wanted"; a "bright, bird-like mind"; "a mountain of heavy flesh in which a shy spirit flickered uncertainly"; "Poor old boy! If only decent sentiments were enough. . . . How is it they always make you feel as if you'd been filling up with bread-and-milk?"; "She shook out the reins and cantered on, feeling the eyes of other women in her back like the beaks of vultures". The combers "breaking with a soft crash like the splintering of fine glass"; and this, that takes one back to *Essay on Memory*: "So many ghosts could be set walking by the threats of the wind".

Palmer has created a wide range of characters and, in spite of the family resemblance that runs through them, most are, with a qualification to be

---

[18] p. 188.

mentioned, real and individual. Among his principals several of the least characteristic stand out, especially Roger McCurdie; old Sanderson, what we see of him, and Lew: Lew however links these with a more introspective group, of whom the most representative is Hamilton; though these also are individual enough, it is as members of a strongly marked type, whose characteristics are unusual. Some of the most real and striking of Palmer's characters are however among those men and women of whom we catch only glimpses: through them, as through McCurdie, we are brought into close touch with the world we all know. There is Laura, for example, old Sanderson's mistress in the days of his decline, "magnificent in her cerise silk that made a sound of lapping water"; a widow "with a heart of gold and the emotional balance of a rabbit", who yet had a genius for management and for persuading other people to work their fingers to the bone for her;[19] there are Burgoyne and his son in *The Man Hamilton*. And there are the malicious onlookers, practically all of whom are good; there is Ada McCurdie, of whom unfortunately we see very little, another onlooker, but humorous rather than malicious; and perhaps Besanck in *Legend for Sanderson*, and Mahony in *Golconda*. Palmer's vision of life is individual, even if in spite of his centreing upon the ordinary it does not quite accord with ordinary life, and this applies especially to some of his intimate analyses. On account of his strong dislike on the one hand of what might conceivably be taken for granted, and on the other of anything approaching the flamboyant, it has the air of leaving out a good deal that matters, and of being toned down considerably: life insists at times upon detail and flamboyancy. But Palmer's is a self-consistent if highly subjective world, which is conveyed with painstaking care. The chief lack in his style is vitality; as far as he may be called an artist, he is a self-made rather than a born one.

The last one to derive directly from Lawson or Furphy is Frank Dalby Davison (Glenferrie, Vic., 1893-1970), but there is also a dash of Steele Rudd in his literary ancestry: this is not surprising, for he was a farmer for some years and is a farmer now. Davison writes like a countryman, though a countryman who has practised the art of writing. Like Palmer, he writes short stories as well as novels, and it is a question whether he is not at his best in the shorter form: he has learnt something from Palmer, though this is most evident in his short stories, and like Palmer he uses the analytical method; in its application to the minds of animals some of his work represents an attempt that has not been made seriously by any other writer of fiction. Like the rest of his group, he shows his characters as part of a canvas which contains a great deal of background, and sometimes he dwells upon the background for its own sake; but

[19] Compare Lucy Rossingdale, in Kylie Tennant's *Ride on Stranger*.

he does not allow this to lead him away from his story so much as some of the others do. Davison was educated, with intervals of truancy, at a State school up to the age of twelve; then he left, and for three years followed various occupations in the bush. After that, his father took him on a business trip to America, where he wrote of an evening and worked as a compositor in Chicago and New York and as ship's printer on several coastal voyages; on the outbreak of the first World War he worked his passage to England in a ship full of tough men and unbroken horses, and fought with the British cavalry and infantry in France. Followed four years on the land in western Queensland, but drought and shortage of capital beat him; for a while he helped his father with a magazine, for a while he was an estate agent and for a while he had a retainer from the *Bulletin*; during the second World War he was on the staff of the Departments of Aircraft Production, and Labour and National Service, and he then ran a small farm not far from Melbourne. His books include: *Forever Morning* (Sydney, 1931); *Man-Shy* (Sydney, 1931);[20] *The Wells of Beersheba* (Sydney, 1933); *Dusty* (Sydney, 1946); as well as a collection of short stories, a children's fairy-tale, a pleasant little autobiographical chapter and a description of a caravan trip.[21] Davison's novels are tales rather than novels in the ordinary sense; he aims in them to present not so much life itself, in which the most important element is character, as threads of a story which he has discovered in life: these and what they convey are as important to him as the characters concerned; indeed, with the possible exception of *Dusty* and the heifer in *Man-Shy*, none of his characters is seen in the round. His men and women are, except Tom, in *Dusty*, the slightest of sketches, and even of Tom one has no intimate knowledge. As with Katharine Prichard, there is always some general idea at the back of Davison's stories; he never lets this take possession of him but it is illustrated by the succession of incidents that constitutes the story. Except the very short *Wells of Beersheba*, each story seems rather drawn out: Davison is not good at developing a theme, as distinct from stating and enlarging upon it. Nor is he so fertile in incident as are some other members of his group; and though his incidents are lifelike and interesting and such as might naturally have occurred, one does not always feel that a particular incident must have happened exactly when and where it is described as happening. Davison's work is of a simple, unsophisticated, even primitive type, and addressed in the main to readers who are interested primarily in place and occurrence and in the types of men and women who are attached to them: they are all individualized, but it is only

[20] This was awarded the gold medal of the Australian Literature Society for the best novel of the year; it was published in New York as *The Red Heifer*; Davison was also awarded an M.B.E.

[21] For Davison's short stories, see pp. 1241, 1245-7.

in the second place that he, and they, are interested in them as individuals: both Davison and his most appropriate readers belong in fact to the previous generation quite as much as to this; but of its type his work is an excellent example, showing an intimate knowledge of and a genuine sympathy for the beings, human and animal, with which he deals. It is clear that he has lived in intimate contact with what he describes, and he is a minute, exact and painstaking observer, especially, so far as his novels are concerned, of dogs and cattle and horses. He has a genuine and individual talent, and like Palmer he has taken pains to cultivate it; he has neither Palmer's range nor his insight and has not acquired Palmer's literary taste or technical skill; but his stories are, much more than Palmer's, pieces of reality; in reading them one feels that one is watching what might have actually occurred: they are obviously built, but they are built of solid materials.

Davison's work shows a fairly regular development. *Forever Morning* has all the marks of a first novel, romantic in an old-fashioned way, artless, and not well woven together, and more than one of the "properties" of the up-country novel reappears; nevertheless, it is fresh and full of promise, and the most obvious of the "properties" the buckjumping triumph, is among the best of its kind in Australian fiction. *Man-Shy* represents a long step forward, and it is a step in a direction that is new in fiction;[22] for though other novelists have made animals their principal characters and drawn them realistically, Davison was the first to make a serious attempt to get inside their minds; his cow and dog are not only real and individual but an attempt is made to understand and to let us understand them. What is more, the red heifer and the mob of wild cattle to which she belongs are the more significant in that they stand for the spirit of freedom and dogged untameable resistance to its invaders; and their struggle is made extraordinarily real to us: we not only see them, we are among them; here,[23] for instance, after all except the red heifer have been captured:

> Dragged now out of the inaction that had gripped them in the early hours of their captivity, [they] set off in single file along the fence. The beast that had called to the red cow led the way. She would run a short distance, bellowing wildly, and thrashing her sides with her tail; then, stopping, she would push her head between the wires and try vainly to walk through them. When the others had almost reached the spot where she was, she would withdraw her head and run on.
>
> . . . .
>
> In this manner they completed the circuit of the paddock and arrived back at the sliprails.

---

[22] In fiction, it must be noted, for no comparison is or can be made with *Solomon's Ring*. London's dogs are simply dogs as men see them, and he would never have told a story about so unromantic an animal as a cow; and Henry Williamson's stories are simply animated nature studies. [A. J. Dawson's *Finn the Wolfhound* (1908) could have provided a model for *Dusty*.]

[23] pp. 97-100.

> Midday had come. Throughout the bush cattle were camped in the shade of the trees away from the heat, but for the scrubbers there was no rest. . . . The sun beat upon their backs; the bush simmered around them; their shadows were like grey blurs beneath them, and their heads were turned always to the ranges, rising blue-veiled and sun-drenched into the sky.
>
> . . . .
>
> Their ceaseless travelling round and round inside the wire boundaries of their prison had worn away the grass and made a thin dusty track. But now their journeyings had ended. For two days they did not move from their camp near the sliprails. At night, when darkness covered the ranges, they lay down to rest, but at dawn they rose and resumed their watch. All their consciousness of living had passed into a yearning for their hills.
>
> . . . .
>
> Conscious of the resentment which his callousness was arousing among the men, Black was frequent in his assurances that the scrubbers, as hunger pressed upon them, would settle down in the paddock. There was good water and grass, and, after all, a beast was only a stomach on four legs. They would soon forget. He was wrong in that. The scrubbers were dying.

The Wells of Beersheba is in most respects quite different from either of the other two novels. It is true that the centre of interest is again animal rather than human: the horse, as ridden by the Australian Light Horsemen in the famous attack upon Beersheba in the first World War; and again, just as *Man-Shy* has an epical quality, so has *The Wells of Beersheba*. But this time the principal character is not an individual but a type of horse, and the short prose epic of which it is the centre possesses in addition a marked lyrical quality: the epic does sometimes become lyrical at a crisis, and it is with a single crisis with which this story is concerned; also, whereas it is in quality that *Man-Shy* approaches the epic, *The Wells of Beersheba* approaches the lyric, or the epic grown-lyric, in form also: it is something of a prose poem. There is a feeling of both forms in the opening, the description of the horses and their breeding and origins, which is a lesser equivalent of the enumeration of the leaders and ships in the *Iliad*. Only a poet could have achieved the prose poetry that is aimed at here,[24] but this is fine stuff, and certainly in the neighbourhood of prose poetry:

> They all are Australian bred—bone of her bone. They are the troop horses.
>
> The grey with the neat forehand was foaled where Illawarra's hillsides tumble down to the sea. The bay mare with the white off hind ran beside her dam where Jimbour Plains sweep unbroken from sky to sky. She was five-off before she felt a girth around her.
>
> The bay gelding is from the Flinders grass country, out Barcaldine way. The other bay mare—the one with the white fleck on her muzzle—was accustomed to drink from a stream chilled by Kosciusko's snows. Those round, high-walled hoofs and short pasterns were shaped for running on steep and rocky pastures.

---

[24] pp. 13-17.

The brown horse with the balley face was with a drover's outfit, once. He was foaled in the far Kimberleys, beside a lost lagoon, peopled with wildfowl. The bay with a white star on his forehead knows the marches of the painted inland. He was got when a blood stallion covered a brumby mare. His home lies fenceless below the Flinders Range.

. . . .

The bright chestnut was bred on Riverina's tawny plains. He ran with twenty other long-tailed, long-maned colts and fillies in a ten-mile paddock. At sight of a man they would stand with heads thrown up and eyes wide with pretended wonderment, before they wheeled and galloped away.

. . . .

The dark-brown gelding . . . was foaled in emerald pastures, where Yarra Yarra dreams beneath the range at Launching Place. The roan with dark points was first handled by an aboriginal stockman, in the Gulf country. The bony, dark chestnut, standing with his lower lip hanging, comes from Guyra, where the lucerne paddocks lie, all velvety green. The breedy-looking brown—nearly black—is from the Maranoa. In the days before he wore an army head-stall he was thought a master at turning a scrubber in the fringe of the brigalow. The taffy with the game-looking head—he is hardly more than a pony—comes from where the tall trunks of dead trees stand grey-pencilled against the green of Gippsland hills.

These are the veterans.

In *Dusty* a single animal is again the central character, its mental processes are to some extent conveyed to us, and the theme is the conflict, largely unconscious this time, between humanity and civilization and the life that lies beyond them. Dusty is the offspring of a kelpie and a dingo bitch, and he becomes under careful training the best of sheep-dogs; but when away from his master and more particularly by night the kelpie in him fades, the dingo emerges and takes charge, he becomes a sheep-killer and is outlawed. In the attempts at analysis in *Man-Shy*, Davison had tried to avoid overstepping the mental limitations of his wild cattle. After mustering,

> . . . the collective feeling was one of relief—nothing more. There was no looking back to musterings past, and no looking forward to musterings to come.

Davison makes a slip occasionally: more than once he goes close to making a cow think as a man thinks; for example,

> Sustaining her was the idea, dating back to the struggle in the stockyards, that her tormentors were not all-powerful—if one fought them sparing neither hide nor bone, one might win to freedom!;

in *Dusty* however such slips are far fewer. Here Davison visualizes the conflicting consequences of the dog's mixed ancestry, and infers and conveys to us something of his attitude to his problem, even to life itself. Here is the dog as a puppy, growing gradually used to the new world of his captivity:[25]

[25] pp. 61-2.

> Beings, movements and appearances, all bewilderingly strange to him at first, meaningless, alarming and without order, all to become known by their qualities and brought within the realm of infant understanding, without aid from an older creature of his species, or the help of words or names. It was only as the days passed that he perceived relations between one thing and another, only gradually that repeated appearance and reappearance of beings and events produced some sense of order and pattern; only slowly that a sense of imminent danger wore down to a natural shyness and reserve.

Dusty's mind is occupied largely by a series of feelings, scents and images,[26] and the descriptions of what he observes are in general terms that do not imply more humanity than is avoidable: "a small creature of Tom's kind", "the skirted one"; the various meanings of his various scratchings on the ground: a dog's mind may not work like that, but Davison's conception and illustrations of its workings are so persuasive that one is led to accept them; especially since his observations of Dusty's behaviour are so accurate and his reproductions so realistic that one is inclined to assume that the inferences are as true as the observations.

As stories, Davison's are interesting, at times exciting, and they gain very greatly from this: one invariably feels that behind the incident, however adventurous, there is a bedrock of reality. Still it must be added that in *Dusty*, which is a prose tale without any touch of epical quality, the story tends to thin out between incidents, so that the reader is carried along mainly by the interest of the experiment and the realism of the story as a whole; and the subject, apart from its psychological interest, is such that only a high degree of moulding and transfiguring imagination and an art which could in itself attract and draw the reader on would have raised it entirely out of the boy's story class: actually *Dusty* does not belong entirely to any one literary kind, with the result that the standards by which one aspect of it must be measured are in the measurement of another out of place. Davison's style in these stories is simple and natural, with an avoidance of anything like pretentiousness and with an admirable restraint; but it is also boyish and naïve at times, and is by no means without clichés and worn phrases,[27] and there is an occasional sentimental or melodramatic touch.[28] It is even a little clumsy now and then:

> Looking the situation over he came to the conclusion that Dusty had assessed the value of this scrap of shelter more exactly than had he.[29]

---

[26] "The only reassuring things about it were one or two of its smells and the sunlight" (p. 25); "Biddy saw him, her attention caught perhaps by a waft of scent" (p. 183); "living over again, in terms of bright recollective images, his morning's adventures" (p. 69).

[27] "Good steeds" (*Man-Shy*, p. 84); "Mouths were agape" (the same, p. 88); "a monumental bruise" (*Dusty*, p. 205).

[28] ". . . the glory of green and gold that marks the hour of sunset" (*Man-Shy*, p. 90); "just a little band of exiles were they" (the same, p. 92); "a man who rides Red Danger with bit and spur" (the same, p. 87); " 'The battle is ours, sir,' he said" (*The Wells of Beersheba*, p. 75).

[29] *Dusty*, p. 188.

But the principal defect of Davison's style is that it tends to become, especially between incidents, flat and pedestrian; he can write this sort of thing:[30]

> Dusty kept his interest in homesteads, and extended it to any human habitation. A camp would receive his almost undivided attention until he was fully informed of the habits of its occupant;

and even at crises one sometimes feels that Davison is unable to rise to an opportunity of his own creation. Yet one comes occasionally upon an image that in spite of its naturalness startles in its context, as when to Dusty "the days of sheep had dropped down a hole"; and there is the vision of Dusty in the sheep-dog trials, "a dark tan body flying along above a continuous twinkle of light tan paws". And though apart from its novelty it is by its incidents that the book stands, Davison is not far from his best in his description of the mysterious attraction of the bush, especially at dawn and dusk, when in Dusty the dingo awakens, as when from many human beings the constraints of civilization tend to weaken and fade; here Davison abandons his painstaking realities for a world that is changed and quickened by the imagination, and his words and cadences are in accordance with his theme:[31]

> White moonlight on the sleeping homestead would bring him from the shadows of the cart shed to lie in the open, with ears pricked at the silence, *eyes alert to the mystery of moon-made shadow, nose sensitive to the midnight breath of dust and leaf.* He would lie for a long time, turning back an ear toward the chittering of a possum away in the bush paddock, tilting his head to the faint high whisper of migrating wings.[32]

Davison has an undeniable place in the history of the Australian novel, though it is not so near the highest as some of his admirers would have it; his truth, his sympathy and his painstaking sincerity reinforce his very largely successful attempts to present pictures of the animals who are his principal characters from within as well as from without, giving them an individuality that is lacking in those of other writers of the kind. Of these the best known is Henry (George) Lamond (Carl Creek Police Station, Gregory River, Nth Q., 1885-1969), who had a wide pastoral experience, from horse-breaking to station managership, and is an acute and friendly observer of animals: his books, which have been published overseas as well as in Australia, include *Amathea* (Sydney, 1937), which first appeared as a serial in the *Bulletin*; *Brindle Royalist* (New York, 1946), in which the principal characters are a horse and a cow respectively; and *Dingo* (New York, 1945),[33] so that he has covered,

[30] The same, p. 200. [31] p. 103.
[32] p. 82. The italics are not in the original.
[33] The Australian edition was entitled *White Ears the Outlaw*; Lamond has also published other books, including *Big Red*, the story of a kangaroo, and *Horns and Hooves*, since the closing of this History.

on the face of it, the same ground as Davison. But he lacks Davison's gift of characterization and sense of style and his literary craftsmanship; and though his stories are interesting and often exciting, they are stories of animals observed almost entirely from the outside, so that his Amathea, Brindle Royalist and even White Ears the dingo, who is to some extent an exception, do not impress us as individuals and stay in the mind as Dusty and the red heifer do.

Beyond the five who follow the Lawson-Furphy tradition is a miscellaneous collection of novelists who have little in common except that they deal with the countryside generally, or with station life and characters, or with the selection or small farm, or with township or small country town: they share however with the other five a certain breadth and spaciousness which are for various reasons unusual where the setting of a novel is farm or selection, town or township. The station novel of today lacks, as has been said, most of the adventurous material upon which its predecessors were able to draw, and some of the more picturesque incidents that remain are becoming familiar and even rather worn; so that its distinguishing quality is derived not from adventure but from its characteristic atmosphere. There are still exceptions, of course, especially in the far north and the far west, but such novels as specialize in what of adventure still remains about station life will in this History be grouped with novels of adventure generally. Station novelists, even if they had not been affected by the modern tendency towards psychology in both subject and method, are coming to realize that without at least some psychological treatment a story of modern station life as such is apt to run flat,[34] and there are a few novelists who set their stories on stations or an indeterminate countryside, but specialize in the analysis of character and personality. One of the most obvious examples is *Return to Coolami*, but since Eleanor Dark is concerned principally on the one hand with city and suburb and on the other with early Australian history, she is dealt with elsewhere. Another example is *Salute to Freedom* (London, 1938) by Eric (Edward) Lowe (Birriwa station, N.S.W., 1889–1963), which is the third part of a trilogy dealing with station life. The book revolves about the central character, a station-owner of an unusual type: an obstinate and in other ways difficult person who in spite of his sensitivity is fundamentally hard. He yet remains attractive; moreover he is real, which is unusual in a character who obviously reflects an aspect of the author of the novel and carries his sympathies. Nevertheless the countryside and the country life about him are by no means mere background, and their spirit continually reveals itself, through him and otherwise. This is natural, for Lowe belonged to the fourth generation of a station-owning family; the land was in his blood: he was born on his father's

[34] See what has been said in this connection about *Coonardoo*, pp. 1085–6.

station, and educated at The King's School; he served in the Light Horse in the first World War, wandered and worked over much of outback Australia and also resided for a couple of years in Denmark; it is worth noting that Lowe was an experienced rock climber. *Salute to Freedom* is obviously a first novel, though of unusual promise: it is extremely long, it lacks construction, it would be better without the last of its three sections, and the adolescent development of the central character, who has been described as an Australian equivalent of the self-conscious intellectual of the Old World, is by no means new in kind. But it is a novel of some power; almost all the men and one or two of the women are alive, and there are plenty of vivid incidents, some of which are extremely dramatic. Behind the whole stands the mountain, Karluen, which seems to symbolize one aspect of an ideal that is always at the back of the principal character's mind. The first volume of the series, *Beyond the Nineteen Counties* (Melbourne, 1948),[35] tells of the migration of the principal characters in the trilogy to New South Wales, of their settlement in the coastal region, and later, how they cross the Blue Mountains and form a station beyond the area within which the government was attempting to confine the squatters and their flocks and herds. But this first volume, though full of incident and action, is far inferior to the other: the foundations of the trilogy are firmly laid, and in particular the family traits that were to be developed in *Salute to Freedom* are well brought out, but the characterization though strongly marked is comparatively slight, so that this is a story merely, not a reflection of life. Another novel of Lowe's, *Framed in Hardwood* (London, 1940), which stands outside the trilogy, is also better constructed than *Salute to Freedom*, though the end was spoilt by the omission of the last two chapters, which were lost "owing to enemy action" on their way to England in wartime, and it is by no means a mere story, like *Beyond the Nineteen Counties*; it lacks however something of the freshness that attaches more often to first novels, as in this case to *Salute to Freedom*, than to their successors. Again, the principal character is self-centred and difficult, and, if he cannot be called attractive, he is certainly interesting; but, individual as he also is, and entirely different from the principal character in the other novel, there is nothing new about his type either: he is essentially a particular kind of business man, insensitive, efficient, hard throughout, bent upon a single end; it has been asserted that he is crudely drawn, but the fact is that it is his character that is crude. Lowe's style is not distinguished and lacks the vitality of his story and characters, *Salute to Freedom* however shows not only an improvement in structure but also possibilities which, though evident, were not realized. The place of another station novel, by "Esther Roland" (Eena Marie Crowley,

[35] The second part of the trilogy, *O Willing Hearts*, was published in Sydney in 1951.

Mrs G. H. Job, Barraba, N.S.W., 1918-), may be considered debatable, for the station life with which it deals is almost wholly background; but here again the characters are country types and their main importance is in their connection with the countryside. *I Camp Here* (Sydney, 1948) was awarded third prize in the *Sydney Morning Herald's* competition in 1946; it is shorter and more concise than *Salute to Freedom* and less disconnected than *Framed in Hardwood*, but it is still somewhat lacking in construction and much less individualized by the author's personality. Her family has long had the land in its blood,[36] and here also the feeling for the land is evident; it is however partly submerged beneath a triangle of passionate relationships between two men and a woman: all three are clear-cut and alive, but such a triangle might have existed elsewhere. In *Thirsty Earth* (London, 1934), by Francis Rhodes Farmer (Esperance, W.A., 1899-), love of the land is so strong that it cannot be broken either by disastrous drought or steadily worsening relations between the Australian-born wife who owns the station and her weak and defeatist English-born husband. The novel is set on a far-out Western Australian station in which[37]

> The country, as far as the eye could see, was covered with low scrubs; they stood motionless, almost with an air of tension, in the clear, breathless air. The ground below them, parched, dusty and red, was cropped so bare that not even a dry blade of grass remained; and the dust, stirred up by the restless feet of the stock, had coated the spiky foliage of the scrub that seemed to go for ever and ever, in grey-green billows, always with the thirsty red earth unrolling beneath it.

One of the most vivid fictional glimpses, though it is strongly romanticized, of life and work on an outback station, is given in *Sheepmates* (Sydney, 1931), by William (Ernest Chapman) Hatfield[38] (Nottingham, England, 1892-1969); at nineteen he worked his passage to Australia and for ten years turned his hand to various bush jobs. *Sheepmates*, which is in part autobiographical, though a little self-conscious is fresh and entertaining, and contains bright, firm sketches of character and incident; its idealism is however a little sentimental, and at the end it lapses into sheer sentimentality, though it seems to have been founded on fact. Hatfield wrote also, in *Desert Saga* (Sydney, 1933), an excellent story of an Aboriginal boy of the Arunta a generation ago, who becomes after many adventures headman of his tribe and in the end comes into contact with the white men; the tribal life and attitude of mind, the mysterious white invaders and their behaviour, all are shown from an Aboriginal point of view, and the result is a picture that is lifelike and probable. Most of Hatfield's other fiction has taken the shape of romantic

---

[36] A great-grandfather trekked in a dray from the Hawkesbury to the family's present centre, Barraba, N.S.W. [37] p. 1.

[38] His father's name was Chapman, but Hatfield, the name of his mother's family, was legally adopted.

thrillers.[39] *The Emigrant* (London, 1928), by Frederick James Howard (London, 1904-) is, in some respects, a companion but strongly contrasting picture of the Australianizing of a young Englishman of a quite different kind. [Both *Sheepmates* and *The Emigrant* reflect the wave of migration to Australia from Britain during the nineteen-twenties by returned soldiers or their sons, who were disillusioned by the cold welcome accorded to returning heroes; both have a strongly political content, vague and theoretical in *Sheepmates*, detailed and specific in *The Emigrant*. The latter gives an interesting insight into socialist activism, both in Glasgow and Melbourne, revealing a sharp perceptiveness of the different attitudes arising from local conditions. The central figure in each novel finds his "true self" in the bush, indicating perhaps less a capitulation to a myth, than an impulse to put as much distance as possible between the English past and the new Australian future.] Howard is a journalist who has travelled around the United States of America, South America and Russia, and served during the second World War in the second A.I.F. Of his two other published Australian novels, *Return Ticket* (London, 1929) is a simple and rather slight story of a young married couple, again immigrants, who set up as storekeepers in a small Victorian country town; *Leave Us the Glory* (London, 1936) is a much more ambitious attempt, but it wanders and is lost: there are however some lifelike passages about journalism in Australia. Howard's work is never so good as one feels that it might be; well written and in parts excellent, it is weak in organization. The sentimental romances of Dorothy Cottrell, *The Singing Gold* (Boston, 1928; London, 1929) and *Earth Battle* (1930) are enlivened by freshness, whimsical humour and, at times, wit; they certainly had popular appeal in their day. (Ida) Dorothy (Otley) Cottrell (*née* Wilkinson, Picton, N.S.W., 1902-57) lived the last part of her life in the United States. [In spite of the fact that she spent most of her time in a wheelchair, a victim of infantile paralysis, she led an active and courageous life and was an experienced bush-woman.] There is also James Pollard (Otley, Yorkshire, England, 1900-71), who served with the A.I.F. in the first World War; he loves and understands the bush, but handles his subjects in something the manner of the once popular Gene Stratton Porter. Winifred (Gertrude) Birkett (Mrs J. C. Greenwood, Sydney, 1897-1966) published two romantic idylls;[41] but there is plenty of humour in both of them, and the first in particular, *Earth's Quality* (Sydney, 1935), is rather more than an idyll; the book's

[39] *Ginger Murdoch* and *Christmastown* (both, Sydney, 1932) are exceptions, but need not be discussed here. For his boys' story, *Buffalo Jim*, see p. 1229, and for his other work, p. 1388.

[40] Published in the U.S. as *Tharlane*. *The Singing Gold* was republished in Sydney in 1956.

[41] And also a humorous extravaganza, *Three Goats on a Bender* (Sydney, 1934).

principal character, "a sort of dryad in silk stockings, peculiar to almond orchards", is a charming person who leaves her trees to establish a successful business in cosmetics, founded on the products of her father's almond orchard; of the other characters, John Weldon, the half-blind old autocrat who judges sheep before the fire in his sitting-room, helps to give the book a reality that is not possessed by her second novel. *The Shadow Tree* (London, 1936), by Lucy (Amy Beatrice) Heney (Sydney, 1903-), a daughter of the T. W. Heney[42] whose poetry was discussed in dealing with the preceding Period, is a much more complex and distinctly unusual novel, in which the story matters more than with Winifred Birkett, though not so much as the characterization: the author has individuality and a fertile imagination.

A station is a community in itself; so is a country town and so a large farm may be: each of these possesses a life of its own in which a writer of fiction may specialize; but selection and township are so closely connected that one usually involves the other, in both life and fiction.[43] Surprisingly, there has appeared so far no good novel that brings to life an Australian country town: there is of course *Tiburon*,[44] but only one or two aspects of Tiburon's life are dwelt on in that novel; and there are Norrnan Lindsay's best known novels, but these specialize in boyhood and adolescence, though most of them are set in country towns; they will be discussed later.[45] But there are several novels of the kind under discussion which may be dealt with here, though in all of them the life of the town itself is incidental, in one case to an analysis of the reactions of a foreign immigrant and his wife to Australian up-country conditions; in another to an attempt to observe an up-country Australian town from a mainly Joycean point of view and to record the observations in a mainly Joycean manner; and in the third to an analysis of characters by no means all of whom are peculiar to country towns. Nevertheless these novels do reflect certain aspects of Australian country-town life, even if in the second and the third the reflection is distorted and in all it is caught sight of only over the shoulders of figures that almost fill the foreground. Patrick White's *Happy Valley* (London, 1939) suggests a considerable talent, but the book is marred by its modernistic imitations and by a youthful and self-conscious desire to appear sophisticated and to impress, which results sometimes in mere affectation. Patrick (Victor Martindale) White (London, 1912-) has divided his time between Australia, England and the United States: he was born of Australian parents, was sent to England for his schooling and, after some years' work on his family's sheep stations, graduated at the University of Cambridge; he travelled in

[42] See p. 563. Heney also published a couple of novels.

[43] There are of course exceptions, of which the most outstanding are Steele Rudd's selection stories.

[44] See pp. 1097, 1099-1100. [45] See pp. 1143-52.

Europe, served in the second World War and returned to Australia.[46] The New South Wales township that gave its name to *Happy Valley* might have been almost anywhere, but its inhabitants are closely observed, from the borrowed point of view, and clearly recorded, in the borrowed method; and through both of these White's own individuality shows: he has also a real gift for the revelation of character, so that his Vic, who is undoubtedly a relation of Mrs Bloom, and also Hagan, the woman-hater, come alive; so, to at least a partial extent, do almost all the other characters, though Hagan's conqueror, the enigmatic and rather Meredithian Sydney Furlow, deserves a fuller development. Such little affectations as the conscientious unpleasantnesses with which the book is sprinkled and the revelations of Vic's Mrs-Bloom-like stream of consciousness, are sometimes tiresome, but the novel is the work of a genuine writer. Hobbleton, in Blunden's *No More Reality* (London, 1935), is also a small Australian township, observed from a point of view which is disillusioned and sardonic: there is nothing particularly Australian about it; it might almost be American, and indeed now and then the characters talk like Americans. All of them are obsessed by sex, the older people quite as much as the younger, and the author is frank in his treatment of this, but no more. Like *Happy Valley* again, this is a young man's book, a young man of talent who has observed life for himself, but who, unlike White, has recorded what he has seen in his own way: it is rich in both character and incident, and there is a scheme behind it, for Blunden shows the development both of the characters and of the township. Except in subject and in the author's youth, attitude and modernity, the two novels are entirely different; neither in style generally nor in methods of character-analysis is Blunden indebted to Joyce or anyone else, but his attitude is "modern" and he has evidently read some of the American novels of country-town life. The scenes are not static but full of action; the characters are all such as one might have had the misfortune to live among: the lascivious, middle-aged hypocrite Mr Ablet, for instance, and Mr Ablet's confidante, well poised, attractive, ironic, on the one side a hard-headed business woman who was to get the better of Mr Ablet over a deal in land, and who on the other side has had her lovers and may add him to her list. And there are occasional passages of delightful satire, as when the barber, respected for his knowledge of literature, groups as "very good lady writers" Katherine Mansfield and E. M. Hull, and refers to his emotion at his first Communion as ". . . like a kind of pure joy. Such a thing as only

[46] White has published since *Happy Valley*, a couple of novels and also plays, verse and short stories, which do not concern us, and two novels that would have concerned us if they had appeared earlier: *The Tree of Man* (London, 1956) and *Voss* (London, 1957).

Hall Caine or Middleton Murry could describe". But there is a general air of youthful exuberance about the book. Godfrey (Verge) Blunden (Melbourne, 1906–), after practising journalism in several Australian States and then in America, moved to London and became a war correspondent in Portugal, Russia and Sweden; he then returned to the United States, where he was on the staff of *Time* and has published several novels that have nothing to do with Australia. The third novel, Velia Ercole's *No Escape* (London, 1932) is a study of the efforts of an Italian doctor and his wife to assimilate themselves to Australian up-country conditions: the setting is "a little town set in scattered farms", which has grown, like Mann's Mountain Flat, out of a mining settlement, but there is room and fertile ground here, and the township has developed, straggling and untidy, but without the fierce grudging rivalries of Mountain Flat, and friendly in its own way. All this is lifelike, what we see of it; and so are the two principal characters: sensitive, intense, impulsive, trying to assimilate themselves to the new and strange conditions, but hoping to return eventually to their beloved Italy. The doctor, whose professional activities keep him in daily touch with the life about him, comes to find it bearable, and even likeable in the end; but his wife, a singer, who longs to complete her training at the Bologna conservatorium before it is too late, cannot break her own barriers, grows gradually insane and kills herself. The book is written with humanity and an intense sincerity, and its promise is as evident as that of *Happy Valley*; this promise has not been so far fulfilled. Velia Ercole (Mrs Eric Gregory, White Cliffs, N.S.W., *c.*1910–*c.*1975), daughter of an Italian doctor who settled in N.S.W., was a Sydney journalist and later lived in England. The theme of her second novel, *Dark Windows* (London, 1934), is complementary to that of *No Escape*: it is the story of an Australian girl who tries in vain to adapt herself to life with relations in Brittany; well written, it is not distinguished in any way. Still another novel whose background is largely that of a country town is "Brian James's"[47] *The Advancement of Spencer Button* (Sydney, 1950), but its theme is very different. *Spencer Button* has scarcely anything in common with the short stories of the countryside by which James is best known; drawing upon his professional experience, he tells here the story of a State schoolteacher from his boyhood in the bush to his death as head of a great Sydney High School. Spencer himself is, probably by design, flat and colourless, but the book is able to carry him because of its lifelike sketches of various types of teacher, some lively incidents, and a general atmosphere of lightly satiric humour.[48] Also, since Spencer's career is in some ways typical, the story

[47] For James's short stories, see p. 1247.

[48] This novel might conceivably be classed as a satire, but it seems best to treat it as a story of real life, with satiric touches.

gains in solidity from its bearing on the development of State school teaching in New South Wales. "Brian James" is the pen-name adopted by John Lawrence Tierney (Mudgee, N.S.W., 1892–1972), a graduate of the University of Sydney who has also an Oxford Diploma of Education.

Then there are the novelists who deal with selection and township, and first, two writers who are realists in the old-fashioned sense of the term: that is, they show life as it would appear to the ordinary man, if he had eyes to see it. John Keith Ewers (Subiaco, W.A., 1892–1978) was educated in Perth and London, and has been a teacher and a journalist; he began with a couple of sentimental romances which suggest Dickens or one of his modern followers, but the only two of his novels[49] that need be considered here are *Men Against the Earth* (Melbourne, 1946) and *For Heroes to Live In* (Melbourne, 1948). These constitute the first half of a tetralogy which is set in the Western Australian wheatbelt where Ewers lived for three years; they are based on close and accurate observation and recorded simply and naturally, but the record seldom pierces beneath the surface; we know Ewers's men and women only as their neighbours might know them, friendly but not very intimate neighbours, and his style is in keeping: painstaking and smooth but flat and rather commonplace. The second of these two selection novelists, John William Truran (Sheffield, England, 1897–), is a graduate of the University of Sheffield; he fought in the first World War, came out to Australia in 1925 and taught and worked as a farm hand. His only two novels are *Green Mallee* (Sydney, 1932) and *Where the Plain Begins* (Sydney, 1933). Truran is now and then sentimental, even melodramatic, and there is little structure in his stories, but he writes with humour and sympathetic understanding, and has touches of creative imagination; some of his characters, episodes and descriptions make an impression as nothing of Ewers' does. The author of *Karangi* (Sydney, 1934) is realistic in a more modern sense of the word than either of the others: his range is not limited by Victorian conventions, so that he comes to closer grips with life; he has also a more individual talent, creates his atmosphere by means of a sharper selection of detail, and lets us farther into the minds of his characters, some of whom, and their backgrounds, are presented vividly. Frederick Sydney Hibble (Ryde, N.S.W., 1902–56) was office worker, butcher, newspaper editor, postman and dairy farmer, and *Karangi* is set on a dairy-farm in New South Wales; there is an animation and vitality about this novel, in spite of its manufactured ending, which no doubt counted strongly in its award, along with Palmer's *The Swayne Family*, of first place in the Melbourne Centenary Competition in 1934. *The Sow's Ear* (Sydney, 1933), by Bernard Charles Cronin (Ealing, Middlesex, England, 1884–1968) is set in a Tasmanian

[49] Ewers has also written short stories (see p. 1254) and verse.

township, and has in common with *Karangi* a narrowness and drabness of atmosphere, in this case unrelieved, and the compelling of a girl by her parents into a repellent marriage; there is a touch of power about this story, but it lacks *Karangi's* freshness and vitality and the romance that runs through it is sentimental. Cronin migrated to Australia as a boy, farmed for some years and was prominent in Melbourne literary circles; besides the novels mentioned he published several imitation Westerns and thrillers. Cecil (McDonald) Mann (Cudgen, N.S.W., 1896–1967) is not realistic in either of the senses alluded to: that is not to say that his work has not a definite relation to life, but his vision is to some extent a poet's; he was on the staff at the *Bulletin* for thirty-five years and won a Military Medal in the first World War. *Light in the Valley* (Sydney, 1947) was Mann's only novel; he is best remembered for his short stories;[50] and this is in effect a series of short stories related to and flowing into a single theme; more precisely, it is a series of characterizations, with illustrative action, which between them create an image of the little valley township to which Mann's men and women belong. All the characters are highly generalized, and there is about them a certain remoteness, as though they represented reminiscences lightly and humorously touched in; but they are touched in by an artist, for Mann is one of the few prose stylists that Australia has produced. In strong contrast with *Light in the Valley* in both subject and treatment is Don Edwards's *The Woman at Jingera*[51] (Sydney, 1948); Edwards (Sydney, 1905–63) was a teacher at Sydney Boys' High School; he was educated at the Tamworth and Sydney High Schools and at the University of Sydney. Much more realistic but far less highly finished than *Light in the Valley*, this novel is picaresque in tone; its theme is the desire for a strange woman and her capture from her mate by force: she is real so far as she goes, though rather as a type than as an individual, and the little one sees of the township in which the scene is set is lifelike and amusing. It may be noted that, like these two novelists, almost all those who follow are established short-story writers, and all but one have published collections of short stories. Several novels are concerned with townships not far from the rims of the expanding cities; about some of them there is a half suburban air, and some are in process of being overwhelmed, suddenly, not altogether willingly, into a suburb: there may be tragedy here for the small farmer who sees himself becoming isolated as his neighbours sell out to builders of guest-houses and week-end cottages, and his as well as their neighbours' children making for the cities or the far north and west, and this tragedy is made real by a young

---

[50] See p. 1248.

[51] This is practically an expansion of one of Edwards's short stories, "The Woman from the Bend" (*High Hill at Midnight*, p. 119). For Edwards's short stories, see p. 1250.

writer who began with a volume of short stories but has not yet specialized in either form. John (Gordon) Morrison (Sunderland, Durham, England, 1904-) migrated to Australia, after working for a couple of years in Sunderland Public Museum; natural history is a hobby of his; in Australia he has been farm labourer, station hand, wool-presser, gardener, wharf-labourer and process worker in industrial chemicals. *The Creeping City* (Sydney, 1949) deals with Melbourne's infiltration of the Dandenongs; its author understands how to weave his incidents, his various lines of progress, into a pattern without diminishing the life-likeness of his characters. A second novel of Morrison's, *Port of Call* (Melbourne, 1950), is a little disappointing after so good a beginning: it is a picaresque and rather disconnected tale of the varied experiences of a sailor who "swallows the anchor" in Melbourne, and, after some experiences on the waterfront, wanders over the countryside in search of a longshore occupation; what we see of the men and women who bob in and out of the story is however lifelike and entertaining, especially the half-crazy old lady who gives him his first job and wants to marry him. But tragedy need not be involved if the township is a satellite of the city, depending largely upon it from the beginning, and such a satellite is the township in *Now That We're Laughing* (Sydney, 1945),[52] by Margaret Trist (Dalby, Q., 1914-), who is best known by short stories[53] that have a similar setting. This novel is concerned with one of the sleepy little townships dotted along the line of railway that climbs the Sydney side of the Blue Mountains; its little society is observed with humour and sympathy and though Margaret Trist's range is neither wide nor deep, it is a corner of life that she presents to us. In a later novel, *Daddy* (Sydney, 1947), she presents a blustering amatory poet and his second-rate bohemian circle in suburb and city; but the story is not so fresh, the minor characters are not so interesting, and the poet is rather a dull dog.

Farther than these from the atmosphere of the countryside, but still outside the cities, is the work of two writers who deal with the mines, respectively coal and gold. Harold Clyde Wells (Cessnock, N.S.W., 1908-) knows the life of the Northern Coalfields from the inside: at fourteen he had to leave school when his father was blinded in a mine accident; for a while he was a communist; he became National President of the Miners Federation, but resigned and left the party and in 1947 wrote *The Earth Cries Out* (Sydney, 1950). This novel has a social interest and value, especially since it is without the bias and obvious propaganda of Prichard's mining novels; but the characters are little

[52] Published also in New York in 1946, as *Sun on the Hills*. Margaret Trist has since published another novel, *Morning in Queensland* (Philadelphia, 1958).

[53] See pp. 1247-9.

more than types, and not very interesting at that. The two mining novels of the second writer, Gavin Stodart Casey (Kalgoorlie, W.A., 1907-64), are better balanced, the characters coming first and the life they live appearing through what we see of them: but *Downhill is Easier* (Sydney, 1945) is little more than a short story expanded, and the types and attitudes are those of Casey's short stories;[54] and *City of Men* (Sydney, 1950), a historical novel, after a good beginning runs rather flat, in spite of some realistic detail and sketches of character. Another novel of Casey's, *The Wits are Out* (Sydney, 1948), which on the face of it attempts less, is much better than the other two: ostensibly a description of a "keg party" in a Sydney suburb, this is used to present vividly and by no means superficially a number of men and women and their relationships. Casey was educated at State schools and the Kalgoorlie School of Mines; he worked in the mines and at other miscellaneous occupations, became a journalist and later Chief Publicity Officer for the Commonwealth Department of Information, and then Director of the Australian News and Information Bureau, New York; during the last years of his life he lived in Perth.

---

[54] See pp. 1249-50.

CHAPTER VIII

THE NOVEL

Links with the Country Novel: Leonard Mann; Norman Lindsay. City Novels: Cobb; Christina Stead; Eleanor Dark; Dutton; "Jane Laker"; Mackenzie; Cleary; Others

CITY AND country life naturally interpenetrate in fiction as in fact, and some writers set their stories now in the country and now in the city; but as a general rule they incline more to the one type of setting and character than to any other: even with Kylie Tennant it is easy to see where her inclinations lie and where her most characteristic work belongs. But Leonard Mann and Norman Lindsay will not fit into a country-city classification, and, different as are their novels in every respect, they are best considered here, as links between those of the country and of the cities. Only one of Mann's novels is set on the countryside, but it is on the whole his best, the best indeed of all his work, in prose or verse; more than that it is among the best of its kind this country has produced. All Mann's novels are direct reflections of life, but in this life is concentrated, focused at a point: it has a more definite and rounded unity. And both its characters and its actions stand for more than those of the others: it is a small image, not merely of an aspect of life, but of life itself. Here also there is a fierce intensity of passion that is not matched in Mann's other three novels, or in his verse either; it is as fierce in *A Murder in Sydney*, but in one character only, and it has there little representational quality. *Mountain Flat* (London, 1939) deals with a small farming community that is by no means typical, in Australia or elsewhere; perhaps its nearest analogues might be found in the United States. It is a low-toned but striking picture of a group of small farms packed together on a fertile but half worked-out strip of land that is surrounded by the scars of abandoned diggings. The farmers are, as the diggers were, of mixed races, in which the Italian is an important ingredient, owing largely to the personality of the old Garibaldian, Negrelli; and streaks of elemental passion grow out of the bitter and envious struggle for land enough to make a decent livelihood. "If a man had Sutton's," says one of the characters, "he'd have, with his own, almost a farm." Friedel, seeing her youth slipping from her and in love with George; George, held apart from Friedel by lack of land enough to provide for a new family; young Laura, tempting Vanni and Bob, both grandsons of old Negrelli, who is so proud of having killed a man in a private quarrel in his youth; Judith Ainsley, with her remains of beauty and her memories of the past: all these are evoked as though from their creator's actual acquaintance rather than from his imagination and understanding of life in general. So are the actions in which they take part: George's gradual approach, against his will, to Friedel in incident after incident; the scene in which we are shown that Bob has got what Vanni should have had, and Laura's confessions to her mother and to Vanni; the scene in which Negrelli gives Vanni the knife with which he had killed his man long ago; the dialogue between Judith and the old lawyer who had once loved her, and between that old lawyer and the member of parliament: all these are such that they might have been watched and overheard and then reduced to terms of art.

Three other novels had preceded *Mountain Flat*: *Flesh in Armour* (Melbourne, 1932); *Human Drift* (Sydney, 1935); and *A Murder in Sydney* (London, 1937); and one novel, so far, has followed it: *The Go-Getter* (Sydney, 1942).[1] The first is discussed with the other war novels; the second is set in Ballarat in the days of the Eureka Stockade; though it would have been worth mention if it had been Mann's only novel, it does not rise to its opportunities and need not be discussed here. *A Murder in Sydney* is handicapped by its title, which suggests a detective story, but there is no mystery here, except at first to the police, and the story is much more than a detective story and of a different type. It affords a good illustration of Mann's range of character and setting, for not only is the setting quite different in kind from those of his other novels, though like *The Go-Getter* it deals with the latter days of the Depression, but none of the characters can be imagined as occurring in *Mountain Flat* and scarcely any, even incidentally, in *The Go-Getter*. The most important feature of *A Murder in Sydney* is a study of Barbara Hallam, quick-tempered, spoilt and arrogant, who hates her father because of his air of furtive relief and triumph when he finds his invalid wife suddenly dead, and because he proposes to marry and bring home his beautiful mistress, whose character is well known. Barbara hates this woman even more bitterly than she hates her father, and kills her in a fit of fury; but when her father is suspected of the murder she confesses in order to save him. Hallam, a middle-aged but well-preserved business man who has fallen violently in love with this woman, is well drawn, but not in himself interesting; Mat Dyas, a maimed ex-soldier whose first project of seducing Barbara is transformed into love and self-sacrifice, is such a man as one might meet, with luck; the others also are such as one might meet; the artist and the half-crazy journalist are particularly well drawn. But it is a question whether Barbara's

[1] Mann later published another novel, *Andrea Caslin* (London, 1959). For *Flesh in Armour* see pp. 1216–17.

character has been sufficiently realized: her mother was malicious and insignificant, and it is hard to see how the love and pity that Barbara professes for her could have been sufficient, even along with the other circumstances, to arouse such hatred of a woman who had at least tried to be friendly. Sydney's surfers and her surfing beaches; the life savers,

> . . . boys with stiff salty hair and long marmoreal limbs of a dark-brown colour, more beautiful than Phidian statues, their original whiteness darkened by long entombment in the earth but glowing in resurrection with fresh blood;

business men arguing about politics on the beach and in restaurants; artists and idlers; interrogations by police officers and plots to outwit them: behind all these passion glows, and breaks out into tragedy. But *The Go-Getter* is a better book: it centres upon Chris Gibbons and his efforts to get a job somehow, any kind of a job, in the Depression, and upon his relationship with a girl whom he, like Mat in *A Murder in Sydney* falls in love with after at first intending to seduce her. Chris has been a salesman and ends as a truck-driver; his sweetheart is a waitress. There is no attempt at idealization, but the simple honesty of these two, in spite of Chris's first attempt at midwifery to a piece of political corruption, is made evident, and the story has about it an atmosphere of pity and of humanity, as well as of a determination that at last succeeds: such an atmosphere, however, attaches in one form or another to all Mann's prose and verse. Of the minor characters, old Carkeek, the wretched shyster-lawyer, who is drawn in the round, is most memorable; of Chris's mother and his children one sees little, but they are living people; and, as in Mann's other novels, there is plenty of action, in which Chris's fight with the larrikins stands out.

There is about Chris's stubborn resolution not to be kept down an implication, which again runs through all Mann's work, of man's indomitable courage in his struggle with life; a heroic quality which is inherent also in Kylie Tennant's novels,[2] and this indomitability of spirit raises the conception of man to a far higher level than appears in most of the literature of today, much higher than in modern English literature, especially as represented by the poet who is still its leader. In Australia the obvious exemplar of this spirit is, as has been shown, R. D. Fitz-Gerald, but in Australian fiction also there are others besides Mann and Tennant: K. S. Prichard in *Working Bullocks* for instance: and the vitality out of which it ultimately arises is apparent in most novels. As a rule, however, this vitality is exuberant; Mann stands out by himself in that the vigorous life of his work is, speaking generally, overcast as though by the gloom of storm: nevertheless confidence and hope persist: there is darkness in his mind but the stars are the more visible. This perception

---

[2] In *The Battlers* especially, but also in, for instance, *Tiburon* and *Ride on Stranger*.

of brighter possibilities, this grim refusal to be overcome seems to be attained in Mann's work only by means of a concentration whose intensity is felt everywhere, and along with it goes an honesty and single-mindedness that are unusually strong. Seldom has an author cast himself so intensely, so thoroughly into what he observes and describes: Mann thinks each thought, he feels each feeling, he takes part in every action of the men and women he creates. Yet there is nothing subjective about his characterizations: one never feels, as so often with Palmer, that he is translating some aspect of himself; the tone, the atmosphere, the general outlook are inescapably Mann's, but no characters could be more objective. It is not invariably so with his descriptions, however, and on this point it is worth while comparing the description of the suburban drawing-room in *The Go-Getter* with the description of Jamaica's kitchen in *Lost Haven*; Tennant's opinion of the taste with which the kitchen is decorated is obvious, but she is content with implying it; Mann on the contrary tells of "a yellow paper with horrible violet stripes each an inch wide", and he goes on about the effect that sort of thing might be expected to have upon the inhabitants of such a house. Even Henry Handel Richardson is not more earnest than Mann, but there is plenty of humour about his characters, though as with K. S. Prichard it is a quiet humour. Connected with some of his most characteristic and important qualities is a fault that may be illuminated by a comparison with Kylie Tennant again: it has been remarked that her novels are deficient in tension, without which, since the essence of life is struggle, it cannot be represented in depth; Mann's work has exactly the opposite quality; it is too tense: the strain is not sufficiently relieved; in reading Mann one comes to feel as though one were watching so intensely that one had become almost part of the scene watched, which amounts to the gradual bending of a steel bow, further and further until it seems that it must soon snap. It does not snap; the archer lets his arrow fly, and the strain is perhaps not greater than would occur naturally in the circumstances; but it is greater perhaps than is needed for the flight the arrow achieves: in parts of *Richard Mahony* the strain is quite as great, but more is involved there; none of Mann's work achieves that flight.

Mann's style is, even more than with most capable writers, a reflection of his matter. It is constrained, stiff, abrupt, even rough, though it is not true that, as one critic[3] has said, it is never beautiful: it gives at first an impression of lack of art; but one soon realizes, as the same critic has pointed out, that in the best, though not all, of Mann's prose, as in the best of his verse, this is a wrong impression. The constraint, the stiffness, the abruptness, the roughness are in most cases part of the effect at which

[3] M. Barnard Eldershaw, in "Leonard Mann", *Essays in Australian Fiction* (Melbourne, 1938); but this was written when Mann had published only his two early novels.

Mann aims, as though an architect would deliberately leave his beams rough-hewn, or even with the bark on. But this is not to suggest that there is anything archaistic or in any way artificial about Mann's style: it is not assumed, as with Carlyle, like a garment, to attract people to what he has to say. Mann's style reflects his prevailing moods as a writer, that is, or those he wishes his story to reflect: the art lies in the manner in which this is managed, and in which language and rhythm are made to correspond with action and character, and the poet in Mann shows in occasional phrases and epithets; in *Mountain Flat*[4]

> He looked about him at the dark sweep of the sky, the blackness in which the bush and the hills lay, surrounding him and his place, and in those few moments of contemplation in the cold, violent wind he drew within himself the magnificence and turbulence of earth and heaven;

and in *The Go-Getter* he speaks of "the subdued thunder of the city". In his longer descriptive passages Mann's power of projecting himself into a scene or action or persons or personal relationships is very evident, whatever the type of person, scene or action, and there are some remarkable contrasts between these descriptions. Contrast the opening of *Mountain Flat* with the description of the surfers and the beaches in *A Murder in Sydney*; or on the other hand, in *The Go-Getter*, of a Melbourne suburban street on a hot day during the Depression; or, where men and women are concerned, take the dramatic scene in which Laura tempts her two suitors, while their grandfather looks on:[5]

> Instead of senility and apathy the face was full of life and keen, and the eyes shone. It seemed as if behind the wrinkled skin and white hair there was entered a young man whose lips smiled in anticipation of a terrible desire. Westfield sought what vivid interest had summoned this resurrection and saw the old man's grandsons, Vanni Coburn on the left and Bob Galton on the right of Laura Ainsley, saw the big girl with the heavy flushed face from which the expanded eyes looked straight ahead pretending not to notice Vanni and Bob. But what a pretence it was, for she leaned back against the desk so that her breasts stuck out strong and large under the taut blue jumper to provoke them, and over her lying half back like that the two boys eyed each other off. Westfield had some glimmer of perception that the old man, watching the boys and the girl with such strange alert expectancy, was applauding their jealousy. But beyond the capacity of Westfield's understanding, the true cause of his momentary horror, was the feeling the old man conveyed of either what he imagined or what he desired of the future.

Contrast this again with the dialogue between Mrs Ainsley and the old solicitor who had once loved her, or between that solicitor and the member for the district. And, as to brisk action, take the fight with the larrikins in *The Go-Getter*.[6] Chris

---

[4] p. 45.
[5] pp. 54–5.
[6] pp. 212–15.

. . . saw the pale faces above their dark suits, and the paleness of their collarless shirts.

"Thinking of taking his sheila in," said one of them.

"She'd be easy money."

The two were joined by a third, and they almost blocked the foot-path.

Chris took the girl by the arm and slid past them. Four other youths emerged from the shadows in front of him. He looked behind quickly. There were now five behind him. He guessed they were all between sixteen and twenty. They were small, most of them. Two of them were bigger and stronger than the others.

"Come along for a nice quiet bit of love," said one of them in front.

The youth who had spoken lit a cigarette and tossed the match towards Chris.

"What do you want?" Chris demanded suddenly.

"Nobody's asked yer for anything."

"What's yer girl like?"

"Never mind the skirt. Could you let us have a few bob, mate?"

"No, I couldn't."

Chris knew that this mob of youths was dangerous. He could fight three of them, but if he started a fight they would be on him like wild dogs.

. . . .

Suddenly he turned to the right and, propelling Phyllis with his arm, he crossed to the other side of the street where, because of the picket fences, he was no longer completely surrounded.

. . . .

Chris began to move along the fence. It seemed to him that they had drawn closer. He could feel Phyllis's fear in the quivering of her arm.

. . . .

Chris's hand had found what it sought, a loose picket. Quickly he ripped it off the fence. He was armed. He could not leave the fence but, holding the girl between its shelter and his body, he walked forward quickly. . . . Those in front backed away from him. He stopped suddenly.

"If you don't get out I'll smash the heads in of some of you." . . . Their white faces looked towards him and away again.

Now one of them leaned against the fence five yards in front of him. Another was on the edge of the foot-path a yard nearer. . . . He heard the hoarse low words, "Sock him!"

"Hold this and give it to me," he whispered to the girl.

He put the picket into her hands and jumped forward, not towards the fellow on the fence, but the nearer one at the edge of the narrow foot-path. He feinted with his left and punched quickly right into the pallid face. He swung at once towards the youth on the fence and, anticipating the kick, kicked first as the youth's leg came up. At the same time he swung his fist against the falling head.

"Quick!"

He felt for the picket as he swung round. He had it in his hands as the others came in. One was sharper and quicker than the others. Chris lunged into his face, and a cry of pain broke out. He heard for the first time the moans of the fellow who had been leaning against the fence and another sharp cry from him. But he could not turn about. Whirling the picket with both hands he rushed at the others. They turned and fled, but he knew they would not go far.

"Run, Phyl, run!" he cried.

There is a good deal of human nature in this, let alone larrikin nature; where for instance the larrikins try to provoke Chris into starting a fight, in order to work their own feelings up and at the same time give them something that might do for an excuse for attacking him. And it has realism and immediacy enough for the reader to believe that he is taking part in the action. Unfortunately, there is one fault; in such a passage Mann's style is at its simplest and roughest, most dependent upon the rhythms of swift hurried speech; it is a primitive style to fit the primitive action; short sharp sentences are used to accord with Chris's short sharp observations, decisions and acts. So far so good, but the writing is sometimes very careless: there are too many "others", too many clumsy and un-thought-out attempts to avoid repetitions,[7] in ten words there are two "agains", and in a simple eight line paragraph "others" occurs three times, as well as "another".[8] However, such carelessness is an exception, as may be seen by comparing the other passages that have been quoted; the general statement about Mann's style holds. Mann's prose, like his poetry, has been underrated; how often does one hear or see him mentioned in a discussion of the leading writers in Australia today? He is certainly among them; and if he is not more than that, it is not because of a roughness that is usually though not invariably deliberate and artistic, but because of a narrowness in range of mood for which only a talent as considerable as Richardson's can compensate.

Only one aspect of a remarkably versatile talent is represented by Norman Lindsay's literary work, and his art, which stands for many of the qualities of youth, and in particular his talent for book-illustration, has afforded his natural generosity opportunities of helping many young writers of prose or verse.[9] Among those who have thus contributed indirectly to the literature of their country[10] his name stands as high as any except that of A. G. Stephens; and his direct contribution, if it does not reach the highest rank in Australian fiction, has a place that is indisputable and absolutely its own. Norman (Alfred Williams) Lindsay (Creswick, Vic., 1879–1969) belonged, in everything except age, more to the present than to the preceding Period of Australian literature. His birthplace was the original of the little country town that forms the centre of his three best novels; his father was a local doctor, and in view of his outlook generally it is interesting to note that his mother was a daughter of the well-known South Seas missionary, the Reverend Thomas Williams. The Lindsays are an extraordinarily talented family; all Norman's brothers and a sister were artists, several of them notable

---

7 "One of them leaned against the fence", "the one against the fence", "the fellow on the fence", "the youth on the fence", "the fellow who had been leaning against the fence".

8 The last paragraph but one in the above quotation.

9 Including A. H. Adams, Louis Becke, Hugh McCrae, Kenneth Slessor, Leon Gellert, Douglas Stewart, and Kenneth Mackenzie.

10 As Parkes, Woolley, Stenhouse, A. G. Stephens, and J. le Gay Brereton.

as such, and of his sons, one is an artist, and the literary work of two others and of a daughter is mentioned in this History.[11] Norman went to the local school, but most of his education came of his own reading; his physical frailty gave rise to an admiration for bodily strength and vitality, for magnificent physical proportions, for power, which is strongly marked in all his work; but his own vitality is immense: he has been well called an intellectual dynamo. At school he edited and illustrated a magazine in which the characteristics that were to appear in his mature work were visible in cruder form; at seventeen he joined his brother Lionel, who was working for a Melbourne illustrated magazine, and after its death he kept himself going, like Partridge in *A Curate in Bohemia*, by illustrations for various periodicals, including a police gazette, by jam labels, and by Sunday School texts! The character and atmosphere of the miscellaneous group of art and music students and young writers to which Lindsay belonged in those days, admirers of Murger's *Scènes de la vie de bohème*, is reflected in the novel just mentioned, which was his first and written when he was twenty-one: this Australian bohemia is much cruder and less poetic than Murger's, but full of bustle and life. Lindsay's illustrations to the *Decameron*, some of them drawn at night by the light of a kerosene lamp, got him a job on the *Bulletin*; and his association with the *Bulletin* as cartoonist, illustrator and contributor, continued from then on. His exaltation of the physical is accompanied by a passion for liberty and for truth as he sees it, and a hatred of conventions, repressions and pretence, and in particular of the Victorian taboos, which he loves to personify in wowser and curate, caricaturing them with humorous fury; allied with these characteristics is a hatred of romanticism, at least in its decline, though Lindsay himself is something of a romantic. Strong as are his loves and hatreds, they are not stronger than his sense of humour, which is broad and boisterous, sometimes fantastic, sometimes sheer slapstick, crude and adolescent: indeed there is something of the adolescent about Lindsay even at his most mature; one feels that he shares much of the general attitude of youth and some of its most characteristic emotions, though not its bitter despairs, for even his deepest disillusionments are lightened by humour. The life that Lindsay shows us is exaggerated in several directions: naturally therefore he loves oddities and draws them with pen as well as brush; and naturally he admires certain aspects of Dickens, from whom he may derive something here; he is also an admirer of Nietzsche, of whom he is in his own way a follower.[12] Lindsay's enthusiasm is undisciplined: his comedy, though it can be witty as well as extremely funny, is never far from farce;

---

[11] See p. 1206.

[12] Lindsay and Baylebridge were among the followers of selected Nietzschean doctrines in this country, but their Nietzschism is by no means the same.

his satire is so exuberant that it swings away from life towards fantasy. Tragedy lies outside his scope, for real tragedy involves a belief in elements in life which for Lindsay do not exist, and a despair at their loss which is correspondingly deep. Setting aside his representation of boyhood and adolescence, it is as a humorist, a caricaturist, a satirist that Lindsay is to be regarded; there is a distinction here, for though he is emphatically a moralist, some of his caricatures have no motive but love of humorous exaggeration. His outlook is neither wide nor deep, but as an affirmer of life, of the kind of strength and beauty that can be weighed in the scales, of the worthwhileness and enormous humour of things in general, he is particularly important in these days, when so many, disheartened by war and depression and fear of more depression and more war, can do little but whine, in the manner of the earlier Eliot and some of the more disillusioned intelligentsia, about the misery of things. It is not as a conveyor of ideas that Lindsay matters, but as a reassurance and stimulus: his best work indeed is not concerned with ideas; it involves merely a lifelike and humorous, if rather one-sided, record of humanity in embryo, before it has ripened to a stage at which an adult and less limited perspective opens out; when its hates and desires are simple and primitive. Lindsay's outlook on life remained unchanged, but his powers developed and there was little or no decline in his great energy and gusto with the years; his novels are therefore best considered not in their temporal order but according to their kind, with a preliminary reference to *A Curate in Bohemia* (Sydney, 1913) which may be regarded as an introductory experiment. This novel, though written in Lindsay's thirties, is in every way youthful: its characters are said to have been drawn from Norman himself, his brother Lionel, and the artist Max Meldrum; and there is a curate who is never for an instant credible, though he is not the less amusing on that account. But actually none of the characters is an individual: they are all types, and types that have a great deal in common; they do not really live, though a current of life runs strongly through them. First and most important of the groups into which Lindsay's adult novels may be divided are his studies of boyhood and adolescence: *Saturdee* (Sydney, 1933); *Halfway to Anywhere* (Sydney, 1947); and *Redheap* (London, 1930).[13] It is an interesting illustration of both Lindsay's insuperable vitality and the lack of any pronounced rise and fall in his literary development that the second of these three appeared only a few years ago. Saturday is the small boy's day; he has, or rather used to have, to go to church on Sunday, so that this is the only day he has, or had, entirely to himself, at least when he could get away from home. *Saturdee* deals with a pack

[13] This was published in the United States as *Every Mother's Son*; the references here are to the English edition.

of small boys—pack is the word—who dawdle "between the years of ten and eleven; an indeterminate slab of time in which you sometimes stay for years and years"; we get to know their appearance, their general behaviour, their desires and aversions, their language, all as exhibited on that one free day, or rather on a succession of such free days, with occasional overflowings into the next. The book consists therefore of a series of episodes; there is no development and the boys themselves do not develop:[14] what we get is a sharp vivid glimpse of small boyhood on one occasion after another, the occasions being so devised as to bring out their typical characteristics. The revulsion from Victorian romanticism that is shown in all Lindsay's work takes in *Saturdee* the form of a revulsion from the romantic attitude towards small boyhood. Lindsay's little boys are emphatically "hard-boiled", and they are presented in a hard-boiled way; indeed, the pendulum has swung past the centre, for the small boy's wildness, crudity, insensitiveness, destructiveness and impatient antipathy to the ways of the adult world and civilized conventions generally, are, if not much exaggerated, given prominence by Lindsay's lack of reference to different qualities that are as yet not inconsistent with boyhood's grubby vitality. Lindsay's small boys are interesting to read about, though in real life they would not be attractive, as boys often are: but their love of secret hiding-places and plans and documents and even languages, and of nicknames founded on physical peculiarities; their fantastic if limited imagination; their illogicality and power of self-delusion; their boasting and exhibitionism; their self-pity and their melodrama; their desire to lead and be admired: all these typical characteristics are made extraordinarily vivid. Lindsay's small boys are universal, but they belong to the Australian species, just as Tom Sawyer and his friends belong essentially to the American species of small boy; American, that is, of a particular time and place. *Saturdee* is an Australian analogue of *Tom Sawyer*, but there are marked differences as well as likenesses between the two books. To begin with, both are obviously written for adults: that is not to say that they are not attractive to small boys and girls, but considerable parts of *Tom Sawyer* belong to an adult world, and so does the language of the descriptive passages of both books. Of the two, *Saturdee* is much more all of a piece; here, grown-ups appear only incidentally; there is none of the satire upon school and church festivities that is a feature of *Tom Sawyer*, and there is nothing that corresponds to the melodramatic murder episode; nor of course are there the negroes, or the mass of superstitions that arise from them and from a more superstitious age. In both books the boys are seen against a strict and religious background, against which they instinctively and deliberately rebel; but in *Saturdee* the rebellion is inspired at times by

[14] Except for their discovery of the attraction of little girls towards the end of the book.

furious indignation: Tom's attitude to his aunt is one of impatience beneath which there is however affection, as may be seen in the episode in which he tells her how he was sorry for her when she was grieving over his supposed death; but the attitude of Peter and his friends towards parents and their authority appears now and then as actual loathing,[15] and there is not the slightest sign of affection for anybody in any part of *Saturdee*.* And though in each book there is a runaway episode, whereas in *Tom Sawyer* the boys return because they are lonely and homesick, the motive, or at least the motive that is emphasized, in *Saturdee*, is internal quarrelling, lack of provisions and the effects of ham cooked over a smoky candle. The fact is that whereas Tom and his friends are merely temporary rebels from a society to which they realize they belong, and which has after all its pleasures and alleviations, Peter and his friends are outlaws who have no part in civilized society except in so far as they must; like Huck Finn, they belong to a previous stage of the world's development, though in every other way they are quite unlike Huck, at least as he appears in *Huckleberry Finn*. Both books show the small boy's desire to lead and be looked up to, but whereas in *Tom Sawyer* Tom and after him Joe Harper are leaders only in part because they are a little older than most of the other boys, in *Saturdee* the only leadership is that which is conferred and enforced by superior age, and the principal character is not a leader at all: this may perhaps reflect the dislike of leaders and leadership which prevails, with some exceptions, in ultra-democratic Australia. These small boys are all of a common type, or rather the occasional exception, as Bags the scientist, is despised and shown as contemptible, and though the type is strongly individualized, its members are not: often words or actions ascribed to one of them might equally well have been ascribed to another. It is possible, of course, that this may result from a desire to draw the small boy as such, rather than a set of different small boys, or from a theory that individuality is slow to develop: curiously enough, though in both books there is the episode of the new boy, who being a stranger is of course regarded with dislike and suspicion, in *Saturdee* the unusually abusive dialogue does not end, as in *Tom Sawyer*, with an actual fight. The boys' attitude to sex is quite different in the two books: with Tom sex is highly romanticized, but with Peter and Conkey it is simply "bonzer fun"; but it must be noted that Tom was at a later stage of mental development than Peter and Conkey; there is idealism in the courtship of the adolescents in Lindsay's other books in this group. In *Saturdee* the boys' language is much freer than in *Tom Sawyer*, as might be expected

[15] Bill, for instance, of his parents: "They don't want a bloke at home; they hate a bloke, but if a bloke clears out he gets a hiding. So how the hell is a bloke to get even with them?" (p. 91). [There seems to have been dissension in the Lindsay household, according to Robert Lindsay's correspondence in the Latrobe Library, Melbourne.]

* [For all Lindsay's insistence on vitality and passion, one suspects a coldness at the centre.]

from *Saturdee's* comparative modernity, and, probably for the same reason, there is a great contrast between the styles of the two books. Neither is a model for any kind of narration. Both reflect some of the characteristics of the ages to which their authors belong: in both the dialogue is realistic enough, but Mark Twain's connective and descriptive passages are written in the manner of a minor romantic, with touches of journalism;[16] the corresponding parts of *Saturdee* are far fuller of clichés and worn phraseology, and their occasionally heavy and rather clumsy formalism recalls modern journalism of a particular type.[17] This style may have been adopted deliberately, in order to bring out in sharp contrast the vivid realism of the small boys' utterances,[18] but that does not excuse the cliché; they are however offset by such images as "the drab monotony of Sunday richly splashed with colour", Peter's "expression of an outraged woodbug", Conkey's description as "a good bumptious shouter and important in half-mast trousers", "the devil's dance of heated air over the tin roofs of houses". It is not a completely rounded image of small boyhood that *Saturdee* or even *Tom Sawyer* presents, but an image that is more realistic than has been presented elsewhere, and in Australian literature *Saturdee* stands by itself. Both books are full of humour, but in *Saturdee* the humour is much cruder, as indeed are the characters and the story as a whole; still, it is a corner of life that is seen here under the microscope, life near the source, a muddy source, but effervescent with energy.

Halfway to Anywhere is a study of adolescence as *Saturdee* is of boyhood. It takes up Bill and Waldo, the two elder brothers who appear here and there in *Saturdee*, at the stage at which a boy, almost a young man now, becoming aware of girls as embodying a mysterious allurement that is something more than sex at its crudest, abandons[19]

> . . . certain laxities dismissed as trivial in the life crudely masculine: dirty necks and casually washed ears, for example, and shorts worn till the home commanded you to go and put that filthy thing in the clothes basket before daring to come to the dinner table;

Bill, for instance,

> . . . now thought nothing of discarding a shirt after two days' wear, and even sneaked a smart tie from Herbert to replace the grubby length of fabric hitherto tugged into an impatient knot round his collar, or round his neck, as chance willed. Quite often he cleaned his nails.

---

[16] He tells of the sun's "gilding the great river with its splendour", and refers to "Becky's frail limbs".

[17] For example, a gun is "a notable piece of ordnance", which is "to bring down upon itself a blinding glare of notoriety"; Peter is said to have "registered a pardonable exultation"; and Conkey, "having invoked a dangerous subject of speculation, now hoped to minimise its threat of retribution".

[18] There is a suggestion of this in the sentence (p. 43) in which "wisdom attends achievement to prove you never done it".

[19] p. 103.

About this time elements of a hitherto unknown humanity appear, as in the episode in which Bill, after watching a wounded possum dying, declares that he will never shoot possums any more, and in which Jobags Parkin goes so far as to recognize the existence of "a bloke's sense of honour". The story begins with a feud that cuts off Bill and Waldo from all intimacy with refined and sophisticated femininity, so that they have to seek the society of girls of a lower social stratum and even "drabs from the creek flat hovels"; but the feud ends, the two young fellows are admitted to a higher stratum of society, and in the intimacies of the rehearsals for a play into which they are drawn and of the play itself they discover that "your Polly Tanners were the true mistresses of the art of love. Those hoydens who slapped and pummelled you over its possible rewards knew nothing about it." The boys' language, it is true, lags behind their development generally, their slovenly diction being "the effect of inverted class-consciousness; a defence against mob derision at pretensions to social superiority". For example, when Bill discovers Polly Tanner "in all the ultra-femininities of a lady of the eighties", he exclaims:

"Cripes! You look a fair knock-out."
"Do you really think so, Bill?"
"An absolute peach."
"Not re-e-ally, Bill?"
"A peacherino topnotch knock-out. Got all the others knocked cockeyed."

Some of the preliminary episodes, before the boys have been drawn into "Society", and especially those which concern Minnie Triggs and her curious reasoning, are among the best in the book, giving Lindsay the humorist full scope:[20]

"Oh well, no sense hanging about here. What about a bit of a walk down the flat?"
"I ain't going a walk with you down the flat."
"Why ain't you?"
"Because me mother sez I ain't to go walking with boys down the flat."
"But blow it, I'm not asking you to come for a walk. I'm only asking you to come for a bit of a stroll. No harm in coming for a bit of a stroll."
"Oh, I don't mind comin' for a bit of a stroll."

But the last scene, when Bill is taking Polly home after the play, in which humour recedes a little, merely smiling over the shoulder of the passionate lyrist, is delightful in its kind:[21]

Not to waste a moment of Polly's precious company, Bill began kissing her again, under the soft radiance of midsummer night stars, all peering down into the courtyard at Polly's upturned face, murmuring into Bill's kisses, "Oh, Bill, I don't really think we ought to. . . ."

[20] p. 137. [21] p. 227.

Nothing could be more lifelike than the persons, scenes, and actions in this story, and the types are more individualized than in *Saturdee*, but as a reflection of Australian adolescence this is no more complete than *Saturdee's* reflection of small boyhood. Sex is by no means the only preoccupation of country adolescence in Australia, or anywhere else; there are cricket and football, tennis, riding and shooting[22] for instance, none of which play a part here. And other things may override sex even when its appeal is strong.[23]

Redheap tackles problems of adolescence similar to those in *Halfway to Anywhere*, in a somewhat similar manner and with at least an equal insistence upon sex. But this book is not all of a piece like the other two, for there are a couple of interesting oddities,[24] and several other adults and their love affairs, so that *Redheap* links this group of novels with the next. They also illustrate among them the development, according to Lindsay, of the biological urge, from adolescence with its early crudities and later comparative sophistication into manhood and the full assumption of romance. When Arnold is leaving Ethel in the garden,

> "Give me a kiss", he said. "That's what I really came for. I can't stop, anyway. I've ridden fifty miles since ten o'clock and I've got the same fifty to ride back before morning."

But *Redheap* is remembered mostly for the amatory adventure of Robert, who corresponds to Bill in *Halfway to Anywhere*; this adventure is described however in more detail and pursued into its "almost inevitable consequences"; the rest is lifelike, but it has been done so often before, and Lindsay himself has done it in other novels. And good as is *Redheap's* study of adolescence, as compared with *Halfway to Anywhere* it has the drawback of not being all of a piece. In another group of novels boyhood and adolescence are almost abandoned for studies of men and women and their social relationships; but social is here largely understood in the sense of sexual, and the sex is still largely primitive; the attitude is that of the adult parts of *Redheap*. There are four novels in this group: *Miracles by Arrangement*[25] (London, 1932); *Pan in the Parlour* (London, 1934); *The Cousin from Fiji* (Sydney, 1945); and *Dust or Polish* (Sydney, 1950). The first is an ironic study of a family circle in Sydney and a North Shore suburb, mainly of the young men's literary and artistic

---

[22] One shooting episode is described on pp. 153-4 and it is clear from this that the boys must have been out shooting before, but the episode is brought in to illustrate Bill's development in humanity, and shooting trips are no part of the boys' lives as Lindsay represents them.

[23] In the nineties, an Australian country boy of about sixteen, notoriously fond of girls, postponed, with groans but determination, an important feminine appointment for the fortnight immediately preceding the great football match of the year: he was afraid of breaking training. [cf. on this point, Bruce Dawe's poem, "Life Cycle" (1968).]

[24] One of them was drawn from "a roaring North of Ireland uncle of my father's" (Percy Lindsay in *Aussie*, 14th June, 1930, p. 36).

[25] Published in New York in 1932 as *Mr Gresham and Olympus*.

ambitions and the others' love affairs; there is less humour in this than in any other of Lindsay's novels, its place being taken by emotional storms; there is the usual vigorous action, and there are occasional interludes in which Australian conditions are criticized, as in the following dialogue, which contrasts the Australia of the nineties and of today, and both with Britain:[26]

> "I remember those hard drinking old jossers of the eighties and nineties. They may have lived under a repressed social system, but they weren't repressed. . . . In those days Australia was the drunkenest country on earth and every sixth house was a brothel, and on the surface it was a ghastly miasma of Wesleyan Methodism".
>
> "And what is it now?"
>
> "Now! Don't ask me. I see a freed imagery in poetry and art fighting for breath and a vast automatic impulse of mob inertia trying to stifle it. You can see what's happening; the people are rationally sober and prostitutes hardly exist. The wowser's secret ritual of debauch is gone; he's turning the spleen of his repressed lust on an effort to destroy free expression in the arts";

there is nothing particularly astute about all this, but it is expressed vigorously. All but the amusing oddity, Captain Grimble, and we don't see much of him, are Lindsayian types whom yet we never get to know really intimately, perhaps because there isn't very much to know about them. *Pan in the Parlour* is far more interesting; here Lindsay's humour returns, with a liberal salting of wit, and there are also touches of fantasy that link this with the final group of novels. Laurence, that "immaculate juvenile, with his epicene charm and his zany's stare of innocence", is one of Lindsay's most entertaining characters; at first one imagines there is something at least symbolic about him, but it is only by temperament that he is related to Pan: impotent himself, or at least as he says he is, he creates or stirs up latent love affairs among a group of men and women, again in a North Shore suburb. This erotic catalyst is an effeminate and provoking little connoisseur of art and interior decoration; of dress, especially women's dress; and of cookery; who lies on sofas or sits on knees, men's or women's indiscriminately: he is a real creation and the book stands by him and by the epigrams with which his conversations and the story generally are studded. Australia is "a vacuum for sheep to live in"; Laurence calls a couple of his friends a "pair of constipated mugwumps"; and here is a piece of conversation:[27]

> "If the girls of thirty years ago lied about everything and the girls of today blurt everything out, they both *do* exactly the same things."
>
> "Of course, there isn't anything else to do," said Laurence. "I prefer the girls of today because I love indecent conversation. The only difference is that the girls of the nineties lied about the things they did and the girls of today lie about the things they don't do. Why I've known girls who pretended to be accomplished strumpets who didn't know enough to seduce a curate."

---

[26] p. 8. [27] p. 173.

The other two novels in the same group need not be discussed here.

The final group of two, *The Age of Consent* (Sydney, 1938) and *The Cautious Amorist* (London, 1934) are lighthearted and amusing excursions beyond the boundaries of ordinary society, and in them Lindsay is not far from his best. The first tells of a landscape artist who is camped on one of those remote beaches between bush and sea that are sprinkled along the eastern Australian coast; he employs an oyster girl as a model, arousing quite unjust suspicions in her horrible old grandmother, who lives only for gin and money for gin. Too matter-of-fact and realistic to be called an idyll, there is yet something of the idyllic in this story: it shows a handful of simple and amusing characters, with the usual touch of oddity about them, moving through a series of lifelike and amusing incidents, and South Coast scenes that are characteristic and beautiful without being thrust upon one: it cries out to be filmed, not by Hollywood, which would ruin it, but say by the French firm that produced *Marius*. About *The Cautious Amorist* there is an element of extravaganza; it records the experiences of a beautiful and accommodating girl who is shipwrecked on an island with three men: an Irish stoker, a city journalist, and a curate who is quite incredible in the Lindsayian manner; there is nothing unexpected about the consequences, but the story, the incidents, the characters are all fresh and entertaining, and on the whole, given the premises, everything is true to life.

Every literature, every art for that matter, throws up now and then a talent that, however individual in itself, is yet to a greater or lesser degree a type or symbol of some of its prominent attributes; in Australian literature such a type or symbol is Norman Lindsay. Vitality, crudity, a satiric or at least sardonic humour and a disdain for current conventions have all been prominent in Australian literature, and Lindsay's novels possess them all, though the humour is exuberant and the satire amounts sometimes to an undisciplined iconoclasm. Lindsay's point of view is limited and his conception of life is superficial; but through him Australian boyhood and adolescence have manifested themselves if partially yet more strongly and vividly than through any other writer. At his simplest, and that is his best, he is as refreshing as a midsummer dive into a torrent, which if it has not the breadth or depth of the river into which it flows, is yet close to its source.

It is sometimes wondered why Australian novelists do not turn their attention to the cities. To this there are two answers: the first is that they do. They began to set some of their stories in the cities as early as Catherine Spence, and after her Ada Cambridge and "Tasma", whose *Uncle Piper*[28]

[28] See pp. 275, 277–8.

is one of the best novels of its day and well worth reading still; in the nineties, in spite of the country bias of the Australianism of the Period, a number of novels by leading writers[29] were set in the cities, and today the number is increasing. The second reason is that until a couple of generations ago, when Australia began to cultivate her industries, the centre of practical interest was almost inevitably the countryside; this still contained the bulk of the population and remained the centre of business activities, and the cities, great as had been their relative growth, still existed mainly as its organs. And apart from practical interests, two other factors were extremely important: there was the traditional feeling that to settle and develop their back country was the first duty of Australians, and there was also the belief that the essence of Australia, its most characteristic types and scenes and incidents, were connected with the soil and its inhabitants and products and direct influences rather than with the comparatively cosmopolitan cities. This belief, though nowadays by no means universal, still survives because it contains a fundamental truth, although Australian cities are only relatively cosmopolitan and possess individualities of their own which are national in varying degrees. Connected with it on the literary side, and perhaps most influential of all in preserving in Australian literature what may be called the cult of the countryside, is the feeling, conscious or unconscious, that by reason of its suggestions of adventure, the unusual, the unknown, this is the natural sphere to turn to for the setting of a story. Here however an important qualification comes in: among the novelists of today, even in Australia, story is not so much the aim as analysis and development of character; or rather, though story remains extremely important, its action is coming to take place to a much greater extent in the minds of characters than in the outside world; and even if the cities did not nowadays afford a much wider field in every way than they used to do, they constitute a sphere to which the searchers after modern life, modern types, and modern thought, most naturally turn. Still, the tradition, the belief, the feeling that have been alluded to, in their essence romantic, have survived the transmutation of a romantic into a comparatively matter-of-fact age; and they are reinforced by a nostalgic harking back, even among the sophisticated and unillusioned, to days and places which stand in the mind for a simpler life and simpler virtues and vices, and which sometimes stand for them in actual fact, though not so much as may be imagined. So that the novelist is drawn two ways at once, and a great deal must depend upon his individual temperament and point of view; on the whole however, in the complex of motives and attitudes today, there is no doubt about the tendency among writers of

---

[29] Stone, Adams, and Edward Dyson (if in this connection *Fact'ry 'Ands* may be counted as a novel), and there were any number of short stories.

fiction towards a greater use of the cities as backgrounds and of types that are, if not confined to the cities, at least most prevalent in them. No complete idea of the results of such a tendency can however be obtained from this chapter alone: some of the most characteristic of today's city novels are those of Mann, Palmer, Tennant, and others which have been dealt with elsewhere because their authors' work predominantly belongs to other categories than that of the city novel; for example, a number of novels set in the cities have been grouped under the heading of wit, humour, and satire. Discussion of the city novels may begin here with those which are most typical of modern trends, though the first two to be considered are also, rather incongruously, examples of those city novels which are in their essence simple because their author is, except in one important characteristic, comparatively unaffected by modernity. Chester Francis Cobb (Sydney, 1899-1943), is notable as the first to use the stream-of-consciousness method in Australian fiction. Cobb was educated at the Sydney Grammar School; he was for some time a member of the staff of the Sydney *Daily Telegraph*, but in 1921 he left for England, where he married and became assistant editor of the *Countryman*. He wrote only two novels, *Mr Moffatt* (London, 1925) and *Days of Disillusion* (London, 1926), both of which are set in Australia: the first tells the story of a chemist in a Sydney suburb[30] and the other describes a number of episodes in the life of a Sydney business man: the little boy's day, the young man's day, the father's day, and so on; both show by means of a selection of episodes life as it appears to the principal character, and though he does not in either tell the story, in both the present tense is used very largely, and it is as though he were the narrator. Both novels, though full of incident which is fairly realistic, and though there is nothing profound about them, deal fundamentally with the life of the mind: the chemist has an affectionate wife but an extremely selfish and self-centred daughter; the business man's wife, though affectionate enough, is lazy and slovenly and his little daughter is killed in an accident; neither has any close friends; both novels end with a statement of simple philosophy arising out of a lonely life and crystallized by its concluding tragedy. The following illustrates Cobb's use of the modernistic method which gives him his place in the history of Australian fiction; Mr Moffatt is glancing over his newspaper before breakfast:[31]

> . . . Shipping. Burns, Philp, and Co., Ltd. Passages for England by the following routes. Musical instruments. Paling's easy terms. You'd better open the cash-box at once. Fix up the change in the register. Customers will be coming in. Get the change put right, then you can look at the paper. . . .
>
> He shuffled the letters and ran his eye over the envelopes.

---

[30] "Claverley", which is obviously Waverley, where Cobb's father was a chemist.
[31] *Mr Moffatt*, p. 7.

... Invoice, invoice, invoice. Edgington, Angier and Head, Ltd. The quality printers. What will this be? Circular, I suppose. . . .

From this envelope he extracted a card.

. . . Our Mr Head will call on you this morning. Any orders you place with him will have our immediate and careful attention. Dear Moffatt, Will be along between 11 and 12. How are you? Albert Head. Don't leave the cash-box till the last minute. Breakfast will be ready soon. No time then. Old Head. Suppose he'll want me to have a drink with him.

In everything except this modernistic innovation Cobb belongs to the preceding age, but Christina Stead, although with her the stream of consciousness is only occasional and incidental, is entirely modern, and she is among the leading Australian novelists of the day. Only part of her work comes within the scope of this History, for she left Australia in 1928 and afterwards settled in the United States, so that all that can concern us is those of her books which are based upon her Australian life and experience: luckily they include some of her best. She has an extraordinarily acute and detailed and at the same time an extraordinarily imaginative vision, and a corresponding style: she misses nothing, without appearing to deliberately assemble what she describes; and while she observes she imaginatively reflects, not deliberately but along with and as a part of the process of observation, so that what she sees is bathed in her own light, and the world she creates possesses a reality of its own peculiar kind. It is true that everyone's world, and in particular that of every artist, literary or other, depends largely upon the eye of the beholder, but with Christina Stead the individual contribution is much more strongly marked than is usual in novelists; without losing touch with the world as we know it, by a selection which seems to be largely unconscious she so emphasizes certain aspects of it, and in particular certain aspects of human character, that she gives it a strong bias in a particular direction. She cannot help endowing her principal characters and indeed almost all her characters with something of her own imaginative acuteness, waywardness, even of her own general attitude, so that for lack of ordinary elements the world she presents has a certain twist in the direction of a nervous tension that has about it something of the abnormal: all this is accentuated by the unusual quality of her style, of which there will be more to say later. And beyond all this, Stead's visionary imagination is focused rather upon one after another constituent of her subject: characters, incidents, scenes: than upon the subject as a whole, so that her novels lack to some extent the perspective, the wider view, the general grasp which is essential to the unity of a work of art. This is most evident in *Seven Poor Men of Sydney*, which is by far the best not only of that part of her work with which we are here concerned, but of all of it, even including *The House of All Nations*; in *Seven Poor Men* the grasp of the subject as a whole, in so far as it has a single subject, is implied rather than expressed, achieved rather than inherent, by a deliberate knitting together towards the end of the story.

Christina (Ellen) Stead (Mrs William Blake) (Rockdale, N.S.W., 1902–83)[32] was the eldest of the seven children of David Stead, a well-known Sydney authority on Australian fisheries and fishes. The family lived for many years in a rambling old place on a hill at Bexley, where there were paddocks, an orchard, a marine museum and various animals and reptiles, apart from tame pets; when she was fifteen they moved to Watson's Bay, just inside the Heads of Sydney Harbour, the "Fisherman's Bay" of *Seven Poor Men of Sydney*. As a child she lived in a world of her own, reading Hans Anderson, Grimm and the *Arabian Nights*; these were followed later by Poe, Hugo, Maupassant, Balzac, Boccaccio and Rabelais, as well as Shakespeare and the English romantic poets. But she also loved wandering in the bush and by the sea, and, though she did not at all like household duties, looking after the younger children and inventing games for them. She went to the Sydney High School, where she edited the school magazine, and then to the Teachers' Training College at the University, where she became absorbed in philosophy and psychology and an enthusiast for Nietzsche; after teaching for a while she took a business course and worked in an office, and by much self-denial managed, like Teresa in *For Love Alone*, to scrape together enough money to pay her fare to England. Her knowledge of French got her a position in a firm that had branches in Europe, and she worked for a while in business and financial houses in Paris; she married a banker who had however literary interests and settled in New York; at later stages she and her husband lived in Paris and London. None of her books appeared until some years after she had left Australia; but the first, *The Salzburg Tales* (London, 1934), contains a few stories whose settings are Australian;[33] the second, *Seven Poor Men of Sydney* (London, 1934, New York, 1935), is set wholly in Sydney. Of the next three, two are set in Europe, one in the United States. The setting of the last, however, *The Man Who Loved Children*, is a disguise for the childhood background of the author's family: Bexley and Watson's Bay. *House of All Nations*, the finest of this group, does not, unfortunately, come within our scope; the sixth, *For Love Alone*, is set mainly in Sydney, though it ends in London. She was co-editor, with her husband, of an anthology, *Modern Women in Love* (New York, 1945); this contains selections from Richardson's *Maurice Guest*, Mansfield's *Marriage à la Mode*, and her own *For Love Alone*. *Seven Poor Men of Sydney* tells the interpenetrating stories, which are in effect character studies, of a number of men and several women; all are unfortunate, defeated intellectuals, and most of them are unhealthy in mind and body:

[32] For most of the following biographical details I am indebted to *Biblionews*, vol. ii, no. 14.
[33] See pp. 1257–8.

self-centred, perverse, and in various degrees nerve-racked and repressed, they live on nothing much, and are continually arguing about everything in the world and beyond it, reminding one inevitably of the men and women in Chekhov's plays and Dostoevsky's novels. The book has two principal centres: Fisherman's (or Watson's) Bay, where the two principal characters were born and grew up; and a second-rate printery, owned by the shiftless and incompetent Gregory Chamberlain, who has to be bullied into scraping together enough money to pay his workmen's wages, and who is financed by the crooked and greedy and almost as incompetent Montagu. Here many of the characters earn some sort of a living; the two principal are Michael Bagenault, whose "works were all at fault", and his sister Catherine. Restless, tormented, possessed by impracticable ideals and an intense and dreamlike imagination, Michael searches everywhere for peace, but even if he had had the will-power to escape from a world that he found rotten, that would not have helped him, for it was his own nature that was the root of his miseries: it is as though infinity were compressed into his brain, and he found it impossible to bring it into any relationship with the outside world. In the end he kills himself by jumping over the Gap:[34]

> He takes a step nearer the edge, and at the same moment this idea splits him from head to foot: "What if I should fall upon a rock?" He falls into the sea, the wave a moment later cracks his skull against the submerged pediment of the cliff, and his brains flow out among the hungry sea-anemones and mussels. It is done; all through the early morning the strings of the giant mast cry out a melody, in triumph over the spirit lost.

Catherine shares many of her brother's characteristics, but is a stronger character, more alive, though not less tormented:[35]

> . . . dark, furious, thin, poor by choice, a woman of revolution without a barricade, with something of the politician in her, an organiser of Labour Branches, a marcher in strike processions, a person who got excited by caucus decisions, a woman who worked in holiday camps and workers' education theatres, always passionately involved in something, always half-sick.

She is irritable, impatient, and ruled by impulsive emotions with which her intellect struggles continually. But, blown about as she seems to be from one desire to another, she has an underlying and supreme desire, for love, and it is her brother whom she secretly loves. She is also, according to her friend Baruch, the one normal person in the book; he wants her to leave the country, to engage in some heroic undertaking; but, as she says of herself, she cannot really act, "her character is to undergo"; also she will not leave Michael, who would not have gone away with her; at the end of the book she is teaching design in the workshops of an insane asylum. All the characters are lifelike members of

[34] p. 282. [35] pp. 163-4.

their curious world, and they are all individual, though they have so much in common and are indeed so largely emanations from their creator's imaginative brain; but it is Michael and still more Catherine who hold the attention and make the story. It is a sombre book, and though it contains humour, that humour is also sombre; it is ironic, twisted, floating on the surface of a general tragedy. Yet *Seven Poor Men*, incomplete and one-sided, uncharacteristic of any country as is the life that it presents, was yet somehow the first novel to convey an impression of Sydney as a world city, one of the foci of world life: it is full of glimpses of crowds and scenes and places; shabby, bedraggled, gaudy, or simply illustrative of episodes in ordinary everyday life, all of which are characteristic and alive. These glimpses may be compared with corresponding descriptions by Stone or Tennant or even the comparatively superficial Arthur Adams, but they are more imaginative, more individual than even Tennant's, and yet realistic enough; here is part of the view from Baruch's room in Woolloomooloo:[36]

> On the right hand . . . were the wharves of the German, Dutch, Norwegian and Cape lines. In the backyard was a wood-and-coal shed covered with creepers, pumpkins, old tires, kites'-tails, buckets and old scrubbing brushes. There was a clothes-line across the yard, on a clothes-prop, and upon the line the tenants' garments, washed by the woman on the ground-floor, appeared in regular succession throughout the week. . . . The house backing on to theirs was . . . usually very quiet, although lights appeared at the windows at all hours of the night. On Saturdays and Sundays the whole neighbourhood swarmed with children, and everybody was out of doors with sleeves rolled up. Tiny living-rooms with Japanese screens, fans and bead curtains, and reeking of bugs and kerosene, with bric-à-brac, vases, wilting flowers and countless rags and papers sent out their heat and animal odours and old dust at seven in the evening when the hot day had gone down into the violet twilight. . . . Everywhere couples lounged about, the waists encircled, the lips together; henna Titians, peroxide blondes, and uncoloured women faded beneath their hair still rich and young; women blowzy and painted, worn and tired, with crow's-feet and unequal powder, fanned their bursting bosoms or their empty sacks of blouses, as they slumped in rickety easy-chairs at their doors.
>
> The doors opened directly into the sleeping and living-rooms and alone admitted air. Little boys argued outside the windows, shrieking and punching.
>
> "My mother is not a whore."
>
> "She is! Why isn't she?"
>
> "No, Willy's mother isn't; she always has the same blokes, and she has only three."

Here is a glimpse of the workers of an evening returning home:[37]

> Night settled down slowly over the streets and the lamps flicked on. The people were all wilted at the end of the long hot day, but they hurried because they were hungry and they were anxious to get their shoes off. Sometimes they went in pairs and the man carried the girl's shabby paper case; sometimes they did not go straight home but had something first. The ill-lighted greasy chain restaurant opposite was full of people eating ninepennorth of tea, pies and toast.

[36] pp. 156-7. [37] p. 183.

And there are corresponding glimpses of jewellers' shops, of the fishermen and the beach at Watson's Bay, of the overflow of workers from the ferries onto Circular Quay in the morning, of the Island trader held up in the strike, with its native seamen dancing and laughing like parrakeets and calling and gesticulating obscenely to the girls and boys on a passing launch. Or, moving from the world without to the world within, there is Joseph's dream vision of the little bay, as he passed it on the ferry-boat, or, more typical, Michael's dream as a boy:[38]

> . . . I dreamed I was hung by the hair in space and swung over the earth in a sixty-degrees arc. The earth swarmed with people who fought in a claypit and all fled from it when it became, a second later, a battle-field running with blood; a road or river ran by writhing with bodies and blood. But when I swung near, they were only penny china dolls with red cheeks like you put in the pudding. Nothing was real when I came near. And when I swung away, at the end of a pendulum, they came alive again in their blood and dirt. The wind blew upon my body like a knife; they fought faster and faster and yet my body flew ever farther and farther into unimaged space. It came from my heart; my life has been revealed to me in dreams.

If it had been a first novel, *For Love Alone* would have been impressive, but after the other it is disappointing; better organized than *Seven Poor Men*, it lacks the creative exuberance that constitutes the life of that and *The Salzburg Tales*, and at times it is even dull: it is the story of Teresa, who is possessed, like Catherine, or like Steve in *The Pea Pickers*, by the desire for love, but she lacks Steve's curious overriding attraction, she has only a fraction of Catherine's personality, and by comparison with either she is rather drab. She imagines that she loves Jonathan Crow, the leader of a tutorial and admiring discussion group, and when he goes to England on a travelling scholarship from the University, she half-starves herself to save up enough to follow him; but although he has encouraged her to make the voyage, he now tells her abruptly that she is nothing to him and shows her that he has never even opened some of her letters: the story ends in an unmistakeable atmosphere of D. H. Lawrence. The analysis of the mental and emotional states of a woman who is intellectual, however unrestrained, and yet can think of little else but love and sex, is frank and true and has a general bearing, which the study of Catherine has not because she cannot to any extent or from any point of view be regarded as a type. Teresa is at times hysterically melodramatic, as in "You offend my honour! I would kill anyone who offends my honour", or even in the pathetic "Venus, what am I to do? Yes, what am I to do? No one will help me", something of whose theatricality is redeemed by Teresa's character and the context. The unspeakable Crow is an extremely lifelike study, but the egoism of Teresa's father and his attitude and manner generally, though also

[38] p. 249; see also Michael's description of the storm in the desert sand-hills (p. 303).

lifelike, appear ridiculous: yet he is presented seriously; we do not see the author laughing, like Meredith with his Egoist, openly or at least over his shoulder.

In the matter of style we may consider Stead's work as a whole, though *The Salzburg Tales* are discussed elsewhere, among the Period's short stories.[39] In these tales the intellectual and imaginative luxuriance of Stead's style thrusts itself upon one; in *Seven Poor Men*, though still marked it is less obtrusive; and in *For Love Alone* it slackens and fades, and this is one of the reasons why that book falls below the other two. It has been said that in the last resort it is by his style that an author must be judged, and, speaking of literature generally, this comes near the truth, though how far it applies to the novel depends upon one's conception of the novel and its purpose, and in particular of its relationship to life; certainly such a generalization would not apply to, for instance, Dreiser's novels. Other difficult questions present themselves when one is considering Stead's style, as for example the relationship between art and artificiality. Stead's style is as individual as Meredith's, but it does not give the same impression of deliberate construction for a purpose; on the contrary, strange as it undoubtedly is,[40] even far-fetched, the words seem for the most part, though not invariably, to rush from her in the wild exuberance of a luxuriant and individual imagination rather than to have been selected deliberately. This style has a strong bias towards the unusual, the striking, and makes full use of its abundant resources; but in spite of its exuberance, it is compact, sometimes almost to the point of being constipated; it is as though each swift rich moment of vision carried so much that cried out to be expressed that it was necessary to compress and utter it swiftly lest part of it should escape. Seldom has a writer had so much to say, or been in such a hurry to say it; for instance,[41]

> When he looked over the edge of the woven rattan at the garden, everything was more lively than a moment before. The dusty leaves blazed, the grass reared itself with a pugnacious thrust, the plants were marshalled, the snail crawled over the leaf with a rushing voluptuous impulse, and all animal and vegetable creations were aware of the sun, wind, sky, shadow, and of their neighbours and of the footfalls and shadows of men, through prehensile senses. A ladybird on the melon-leaf looked like a tortoise; the melon, scarcely pressing the grass, rolled in space as a green universe, self-creative. He thought of the melon, and immediately saw it bounding towards maturity. The veils of the flesh were torn; he saw the sun pouring in torrents through translucent creatures with millions of cells. Dehiscent seeds burst, pods split, sheaths flew back, grass sprouted, ants scurried, the sun leaped, the sky vibrated, sap hissed, the eucalypt at the foot of the path arched its foolish light head, and the cicadas shouted to turn one's brain.

---

[39] See pp. 1257-8.

[40] Rich and strange, as Barnard Eldershaw has very appropriately called it (*Essays in Australian Fiction*, p. 158).

[41] *Seven Poor Men of Sydney*, p. 12.

There is almost as great a compression in *The Salzburg Tales*, but in *Seven Poor Men* the utterance is generally speaking more flowing than in the *Tales*; there is more interstitial tissue. The most notable and characteristic constituent of Stead's style is its images: all poets, and there is a considerable element of the poet in her, are imagists in the sense that they depend largely on the image and it has been seen that richness in imagery is a characteristic of most of the leading Australian poets; but no Australian prose writer has been so rich in images as Christina Stead. Each image arises naturally in its place and adds something to what is being conveyed, which indeed could not be fully conveyed without it, but Stead's images do not shine out from their context as they might otherwise, because it also shines with a light that is only less focused and condensed than they are.[42] Here are some of the images from *The Salzburg Tales*: of the Festival Director, for whose style the Archbishop "did not give a benedicite",

> his eye grouped the audience this way and that like the parting of thick hair with a comb;

the same Director is described as

> smiling, bowing and turning in the sun like a buoy in the bay.

Of the Viennese Conductor,

> he sometimes took shorter steps and sometimes longer as if to show that in him the passion of rhythm was constant but tidal;

the schoolteacher

> sailed along on her long legs, like a bare pole on a smooth sea;

and the Centenarist

> hummed ever and again to himself like Syrinx when the tide is rising in the reeds.

Here are some images from *Seven Poor Men*:

> [Joseph's] cousins Michael and Catherine bubbled merrily in that soup.

> [Mrs Baguenalt] saw the workaday world through a confessional grille, as a weevil through the hole he has gnawed in a nut. . . . Within, her heart was a stuffed chasuble continually repeating 'Om Om', with censers swinging and the tin cash-box clinking, making a sort of perpetual low mass in her soul—if she had a soul; but it was no soul, it was a dried leaf.

And, from *For Love Alone:*

> There was a glass pane in the breast of each girl through which the other girls could see the rat gnawing at her, the fear of being on the shelf.

---

[42] A somewhat similar remark has been made in this History about McCrae's images.

There is a larger element of poetry in the images from *The Salzburg Tales* than in those from the other books, even *Seven Poor Men*, but those from *Seven Poor Men* go deeper, and *For Love Alone* is relatively poor in images.

If Christina Stead comes naturally under discussion here, because not only most of her settings but also her characters, attitude, method and manner generally are those of modernity and of the cities, it does not follow that she is comparable with any other city novelist; but indeed she is not comparable with any other novelist at all, within or without Australia; apart from anything else, whereas many Australian novelists of the day are talented, and some extremely so, her ability has some of the characteristics of genius. Yet her work does not stand out above theirs so far as might therefore have been expected, for one never feels that she has attained what one is continually expecting of her; not even in *Seven Poor Men*, or, to go for a moment beyond the scope of this History, in *The House of All Nations*: her powers seem to be of a kind that through some excess or some deficiency must inevitably escape complete achievement, however much they may incidentally achieve.

If Christina Stead's ability has at least an affinity with genius, Eleanor Dark's belongs to the category of talent;[43] on the other hand it is a very considerable talent, and has been carefully and systematically developed, so that she is among the leading Australian novelists of the day. This also in two quite different fields, for she has turned from the personal and social to the historical novel; the difference between her work in these two fields is such that although every other writer's novels have been in this History taken together in the category to which they predominantly belong, hers will be divided, her historical novels being discussed in another place.[44] Eleanor Dark (*née* O'Reilly, Mrs E. P. Dark, Sydney, 1901-), is the daughter of Dowell O'Reilly[45] by his first wife, and was educated at private schools in Sydney. She represents a type of novelist that is much rarer in Australia than in older and more cultivated countries: its existence is only now becoming possible with the wider spread of civilization and the growth of a cultivated and intellectual class. It is true that generations earlier there had been a few Australian novelists who wrote, sometimes at least, for and about cultivated people,[46] but they had addressed themselves to English readers and to Australians who were transplanted English, and the life and characters described, so far as they belonged to the type mentioned, appear also like importations from overseas; but Mrs Dark and a few others have proved that

---

[43] Without attempting to define either genius or talent, for present purposes it may be said that whereas genius draws largely upon the resources of the subconscious, talent is more deliberate and depends much more upon the conscious mind.

[44] See pp. 1176-81. [45] For O'Reilly's short stories, see pp. 627-8.

[46] For example, Ada Cambridge and "Tasma", see pp. 267-74 and 275-80.

there are now readers for novels whose atmosphere and characters are at once Australian and those of a wider world: the types represented by her characters and at least a considerable proportion of her readers are in an even smaller minority in Australia than elsewhere, but they do exist and are at the same time rooted in their own country. What is more, they are emotionally as well as intellectually awake; Mrs Dark may be described as an intellectual romantic, for whom the worlds of thought and feeling are equally important: broadly speaking, that is, for while in her earlier novels emotion predominates, in the later novels reflection gains upon it, though neither is ever without elements of the other; as with the typical poet, her emotions are intellectualized, and at the same time her ideas are felt in the blood. And in her principal characters there is the struggle between mind and emotion, so far as these can be regarded separately: a struggle that is often intense, so that in her novels generally, but more especially in the earlier novels, we are conscious of a sometimes almost unbearable strain. The thought in which Mrs Dark's work is bathed is not profound: her men and women think what others of their type are thinking; but with them the thought is made unusually clear and articulate, and their passions and desires are the stronger and more acute because they are thoroughly realized and reinforced by mental activities which yet sometimes hold them in check. Her subject is always love, as complicated and thwarted by unhappy marriage, and since she finds it difficult to leave any of her men and women permanently unhappy, there is always a risk of an inartistic if sentimentally satisfactory ending. Beyond that, the undesired partner in the marriage is usually also undesirable: either abnormal;[47] or incompetent, jealous and nagging;[48] or insensitive and overbearing.[49] As a result there is at the base of her plots something approaching a formula: a man, or woman, with an unsatisfactory and usually extremely unpleasant partner; a third party who is the object of desire; emotional stresses all round; and a final release of stresses by the convenient removal[50] of the undesired partner or partners, so that the lovers may legitimately come together. And, like the plots, the characters though individualized have strong interresemblances, and a number of them follow her husband's profession, medicine.[51]

Eleanor Dark has published eight novels,[52] spaced over a period of

[47] Linda in *Prelude to Christopher*, and Helen in *Sun Across the Sky*.

[48] Phyllis, in *The Little Company*.

[49] Sellman, in *Waterway*.

[50] In *Prelude to Christopher* by suicide; in *Sun Across the Sky* by a divorce which does not seem to have been likely; in *Waterway* by drowning in a harbour collision. And there are other examples of the removal of inconveniences: for example, the death of the inconvenient baby in *Return to Coolami*.

[51] In *Slow Dawning, Prelude to Christopher*, and *Waterway* the principal characters are doctors, and doctors are minor characters in several of the novels.

[52] Besides short stories, verses, and articles in various periodicals. She has also recently published another novel, *Lantana Lane* (Sydney, 1959).

sixteen years: *Slow Dawning* (London, 1932); *Prelude to Christopher*[53] (Sydney, 1934); *Return to Coolami* (London, 1936); *Sun Across the Sky* (London, 1937); *Waterway* (London, 1938); and *The Little Company* (Sydney, 1945); as well as the two historical novels that will be mentioned elsewhere.[54] Her work represents therefore a continuous and unhurried impulse, broken only by the turn from individual and social analysis to history; and even then the two kinds overlap, for the first of the two historical novels precedes the last of the others; and even earlier, the various parts into which *Waterway* are divided are introduced by backward glimpses into Australian history. Mrs Dark's first novel appeared when she was thirty-one, so that there had been time for mental development, but it has faults of immaturity that suggest a younger writer, for which reason, no doubt, its author is inclined to disregard it: nevertheless it is fresh, sincere, interesting and intensely alive. Throughout the novels with which we are now concerned there is a definite though gradual development: beginning with a preoccupation with individual relationships and problems, gradually social relationships and problems assume a greater importance, until in *The Little Company* they matter as much as those of individuals; but the development is not quite uniform, for even in *Slow Dawning* there is a consciousness of social and intellectual background, and in *Prelude to Christopher* social reform plays an important though shadowy part in the plot. All these novels are novels of plot, except to some extent *The Little Company*, in which plot merges in pattern. But though action in the external world is by no means lacking, and indeed it usually constitutes the solid framework of the story, the real substance is in the mental world; emotional states are the final causes of everything that happens, though they objectify themselves and are immediately occasioned by events in the world without. Take for instance *Return to Coolami*, which is perhaps the most characteristic of the early novels and easily the best; indeed it is perhaps the best of all the novels discussed here. In this novel Susan's temperament, her willingness to undertake the "charming and jolly adventure" with Bret's brother without loving him; her growing love for Bret; his initial dislike for her, and the sudden realization that it is really love for her that is tormenting him: these are fundamental. Yet Jim's death and the discovery that she is with child; her marriage of convenience with Bret; the motor trip that compels an association that is close but frequently broken and never involves the strains of their nominal marriage; the rescue of Colin on the mountain: these or a set of equivalent events are needed to provide means for the emotional outlets and developments and discoveries that

---

[53] This was awarded the gold medal of the Australian Literature Society for the best novel of the year.

[54] See pp. 1176-81.

make the story. *Return to Coolami* may legitimately be described as a thriller, but it is a thriller that belongs to the world of literature, not commerce, because it deals with real life and real people, because there is nothing forced about it, and because the emotions it excites have a natural and probable basis. The youthful *Slow Dawning* no more than paves the way for it, and *Prelude to Christopher* is artificial and to some extent unreal, for the eugenist colony in the Pacific upon whose establishment and failure so much is made to depend has no more reality than a recollected dream; even Linda is after all not much more than a penetrating, animated and individualized study in the abnormal: and the wicked uncle, who, insane himself, deliberately cultivates an inherited insanity in her, so that she may become "the final blossoming of all the Hamlins": he belongs definitely to a story-book world. There is in Mrs Dark's work a curious preoccupation with insanity, or the borderline of insanity; but her approach to it is as sane as possible, and another of her characteristics is a frank and open humour. As to her men and women generally, she is not among the few writers whose character drawing is not limited by their sex. Curiously enough, most of her leading characters are men, but one does not feel that they are fundamentally and unmistakeably masculine: one of the most typical, Oliver, in *Sun Across the Sky* and *Waterway*, who is described as "disturbing and dynamic", and of "enormous and abounding vitality", does not quite give that impression, or an impression of the essential masculinity that is implied; of Gilbert, in *The Little Company*, this is not so obvious, perhaps because Gilbert is older and of a milder type, whose masculinity is not stressed; Bret, in *Return to Coolami*, comes perhaps nearest of all, but even here there seems to be a lack of something. With the women it is different: Susan is more real than Bret, though with her one is at least as conscious of the tensions and their causes that have become an increasing torment to her as of the woman whom they are racking. Still, whereas with Oliver, and to a lesser extent with Gilbert, it is the reflective mind and with Bret the emotions of a particular type of person that are laid before us, rather than a fully rounded male individual, with the lesser characters, male or female, it is another matter; setting aside the "lower classes", about whom, generally speaking, there seems to be more literary convention, and that of an earlier age, than actual life,[55] the minor characters are more lifelike than the principals. Here also however there are exceptions: Sir Frederick Gormley, in *Sun Across the Sky*, greedy and conscienceless, is a caricature of a certain type of self-made man, who also does not seem to be based upon experience; and

[55] Consider the names of some of them, and their misplacement of aspirates: Mrs Gillogly in *Slow Dawning*; Maud and Mrs Trugg in *Waterway*; Mrs Sayers in *Sun Across the Sky*; the baker and his wife in *Prelude to Christopher*.

Kavanagh is a mere shadowy suggestion of somebody resembling Brennan, described but not created: however Kavanagh may have been intended to be a mere shadow in the background; if he had been fully drawn he might have stolen the book. On the other hand Drew, in *Return to Coolami*, is an imaginative and yet lifelike study of what seems at first to be a conventional and mentally bounded business man, more common perhaps a generation ago than now, who turns out to be, and still more to become, as his possibilities are awakened, much more than that; and there are his wife Millicent and the delightful Aunt Bee in *The Little Company*; several old doctors; Roger, the "socialist", in *Waterway*; Lorna Sellman, the hard and conscienceless society beauty in the same book; Phyllis, the miserable, nagging and incompetent wife in *The Little Company*; and perhaps Elsa Kay, "that little alley cat", that "little bag of bones and neurosis", in the same book: all these one might meet anywhere: and all the children are real and some of them delightful. Oliver's wife, Helen, in *Sun Across the Sky*, frigid, entirely self-centred and afraid of the mere touch of life, is an interesting study of the abnormal; but though much more credible than Linda it might be argued that she was not entirely real. Among the best drawn of all Mrs Dark's characters, principal or minor, is Lois, in *Sun Across the Sky* and *Waterway*, a fascinating study of a certain variety of the artistic temperament, and yet thoroughly individualized and lifelike: simple, even naïve, and outside her work quite helpless but in her work a master; warm and human and entirely natural; almost as good, so far as it goes, is the glimpse we get of her daughter Chloe.

All these novels are simply, naturally and extremely capably written, never overwritten and without any straining after effect: Mrs Dark's analyses demand a thorough competence in the handling of words and sentences, and this they always possess; what she has to convey is not always particularly illuminating or profound, but we are left in no doubt about it. She can describe scenes and events in the external world at least as well as what goes on in the minds of her characters; there is for instance the vivid description of the beach and the sunbathers in *Sun Across the Sky*, and, best of all perhaps, of the collision and wreck in *Waterway*,[56] with the murder of the old professor by a younger man driven mad with fear.

> The Professor's hands were arrested in mid-movement by the shattering blast of the *Neptune's* siren. Holding aloft the torn fragments of his pages, he sat motionless in a second which seemed like an eternity, conscious of sharply lifted heads, startled faces, a poised moment of uncertainty and apprehension. Then there was a crash. The whole ferry heeled over, and the Professor found himself and Arthur and half

[56] pp. 361–2; it is worth comparing this with the wreck (of the *Quetta*) in Mrs Praed's *Lost Earl of Ellan*.

a dozen other men who had been sitting on the same seat, lying on their backs against the closed windows; and through such windows as were open, and through the door, green water was rushing in upon them.

When the Professor struggled to his feet it was already round his knees, and he was aware of Arthur shouting and struggling just beside him. He gasped out, "Dive for it"! and prepared to launch himself against the rising wall of water which poured through the open doorway. . . . He found it difficult, gripped about the thighs now by the swirling water, to keep his balance, and suddenly he felt Arthur clutch him by the shoulder, dragging him backward. For a second, as he turned, startled, he stared into a face quite insane with fear. He clutched for support at the top of the door, now leaning diagonally above him, and suddenly Arthur's feet drove violently against his stomach, using his body to provide the necessary impetus for a frantic upward dive through the narrowing aperture.

Another aspect of the same shipwreck is shown even more vividly through the mind of a small boy.[57]

A little gleam of enjoyment actually began to creep into the whole affair. Gee, this was a score! He'd have things to tell at school tomorrow! He'd nearly caught the earlier boat too! Gee, what luck! Suddenly he wondered where the ferry was, and turned to look. His enjoyment faded, and a prickle of horror touched him like an electric shock. She was right on her side, what he could see of her, and she was black with madly moving humanity; he realised that the air was loud with the noise of people, grown-up men and women, screaming, yelling, panic-stricken. With a horrified check in his breathing, he remembered that there were people who could not swim.

Eleanor Dark's main contribution to the Australian novel of today consists in her creation of characters who belong to the world of ideas without losing intimate touch with the world of sense, and who belong at the same time to Australia and to a wider world. Her nearest relation in the family of Australian novelists is the much underrated and almost forgotten Ada Cambridge, who also, as has been seen,[58] created characters capable at the same time of reflection and of intense emotion; but Eleanor Dark belongs to a later period in Australian social and literary history and has not found it necessary to earn the money to buy "pretty things for her babies", though on the other hand except in *Return to Coolami* she lacks Ada Cambridge's passionate intensity. Her novels are different essentially from those of the "Australian school", and neither Lawson nor Furphy is among her literary ancestors, but they are no less Australian in their way: they lack the strong and vigorous life of those, for instance, of her contemporary Kylie Tennant, their direct touch with the earth; but they possess constructional qualities that Kylie Tennant's novels lack. And her work is simple and sincere, and, in spite of its preoccupation at times with the abnormal, essentially sane, and these novels fill a place in Australian fiction that needed to be filled. The two historical novels

---

[57] p. 367.

[58] See pp. 267–74.

take, as will be seen,[59] a higher place than any of her other work, except perhaps *Return to Coolami*.

Two single novels, also of educated and professional society, blend cerebration with emotion, though in the second the emotion is less strong, and even at that, as it reaches the reader it is comparatively subdued. *The Mortal and the Marble* (London, 1950) is a first novel of considerable promise and marked defects. Its author, Geoffrey Dutton, a half-Anglicized Australian,[60] harks back to the half-Australianized English novelists of several generations ago: his novel, that is, is addressed largely to oversea readers, to whom it explains the Australian way of life. But whereas Australian novelists before the eighties or nineties typically emphasized Australian vigours and simplicities, scarcely if at all dwelling upon their corresponding defects, Dutton reveals, through the polite comments of four Europeans and the admissions of Australians themselves, Australian crudities and lack of intellectual content even today; indeed he sometimes rather exaggerates these qualities, for example in the hard and pugnacious Col, who seems to be ashamed of anything not purely physical, and rather resembles a caricature of the legendary Australian soldier of the first World War. One of the Europeans remarks, following upon an Australian admission:[61]

> "Yes . . . I have heard the Australians described as a new race of Attic Greeks, but I remember thinking at the time that the Greeks had certain intellectual achievements as well as physical which are perhaps missing from Australian life."

And another says of Australian life[62] that

> ". . . it is too episodic and too scornful to allow any greatness in the people who lead it. You always want to be doing something, your lives consist of short periods of action and your conversation of anecdotes about your actions. Of those who do not think the same as you, of the existence and opinion of the rest of the world, of strangeness, leisure or depth you are scornful. If an angel came to your side you would offer it a drink and ask it where it had left its harp."

There is truth in these criticisms; yet the critics are shown as effeminate and decadent, and it is clear that to Dutton the newer world and its inhabitants are definitely preferable to the old. Along with all this is the story of Mark and his wife, a young couple who are passionately in love, yet not without the usual temporary frictions, which are neither exaggerated nor minimized: Dutton can rise to intensity, but the connective tissue is far inferior. The fundamental defect of the novel goes however much deeper: Dutton is here attempting two entirely different things; to contrast a new and raw with an old and decaying culture, and to tell a story that has no necessary connection with either. For success in such

---

[59] See pp. 1176-81.

[60] See pp. 1073, 1074, where also Dutton's poems are discussed. He has since published a book of travel, *Africa in Black and White* (London, 1956).

[61] p. 76.

[62] p. 108.

an attempt a much larger work would be necessary, and in this the two components are merely patched together. The second novel, *Among the Reeds*[63] (London, 1933), belongs to the period just before the first World War, and is set among the suburbs of Sydney's North Shore Line: it takes the form of an intimate journal, and has no plot, though several stories and one in particular run through it; yet it does not seem disconnected, because it takes a uniform colour and texture from the mind and personality of the diarist, and secondarily from those of a small circle of friends and acquaintances who appear and reappear, becoming gradually better known to us. Here, of course, we are reminded of *Such is Life*, but there can be no comparison between this mouse and that elephant. "Jane Laker" was Alice (Jane) Muskett (Melbourne, *c.*1870–1936), a painter of some ability who specialized in still life; her Jane, having failed as a painter, had taken up bookbinding. Jane Austen is obviously among the literary ancestry of both; but if this Jane lacks the other's genius, she has an unmistakeable talent. She loves to watch and listen and "meditate on the many points of view there are in life". She had the gifts of attracting confidences, but she gave out while she heard, so that they sometimes left her exhausted. And though the confidences are never invited, there is in Jane a very keen curiosity: "Suppose they marry," she says to herself once, "and I never know whether she told him or not—well, upon my soul, I do not think I could stand it!" She has also the gifts of insight and inference; she likes "to get bits of a story" and fill in for herself the gaps in the pattern. Her mind is awake to rhythms, to the perspective of what she observes: "It's the beat backward and forward of things that is so interesting." The journal is very largely a critical commentary on womanhood, from an entirely feminine point of view. Jane's reflections crystallize into a good thing now and then, as when she remarks, speaking of paintings, though her remark has a far wider application, that "producing one thing often means that unconsciously something else is produced as well".

And, from a series of feminine aphorisms,[64]

> Happy is the woman who fears not, and knows she fears not, the backward glance;
>
> . . . .
>
> Dress . . . is based on the shoe and crowned by the hat;
>
> . . . .
>
> While guarding the exquisite perfection of her dress, let a woman be wary lest she defeat it by mere cold precision. Let her temper that precision by a little carefully careless abandon.

Yet the most interesting parts of the journal are the conversations between Jane and her intimate friends about other friends and acquaintances, the piecing out of the real-life stories that absorb her, and her comments

[63] The title refers to the reeds that overheard Midas's secret.

[64] pp. 173–5.

upon them, wise, witty and human. Her style is cool, easy and discursive, frank and yet dignified.

Kenneth Mackenzie's novels[65] are even less what might have been expected from a young country than Eleanor Dark's, but for quite different reasons: they are marked by a rich and subtle eroticism that would seem to belong more naturally to an older world; but it is not intended to imply that elsewhere than in Australia they would merge in the mass of mediocre fiction: they would stand out by reason of the individual quality of Mackenzie's temperament and imagination. Far more than Dutton's single novel they are the work of a poet, and of a poet who is unusually introspective: Mackenzie has the gift of analysis, but this is confined[66] to his own emotions and to the external world in so far as it concerns them; he is unable to look into the mind of another person, or to externalize qualities and aspects of himself sufficiently to create a character that is not, largely at any rate, his own reflection; there is however at least one exception, or partial exception, as will be seen. This defect is seen in Mackenzie's conversations, which are quite unreal; if they had been formalized that would not matter so much, since they might then have at least objectified certain attitudes or states of mind, but they are clearly intended to be realistic: perhaps because Mackenzie was conscious of a defect here, a disproportionately large part of his novels is taken up by descriptions, most of which are however vivid and some of which are beautiful. As in his poetry he is always the complete amorist, and it is still on the sensuous, not to say sensual aspect of love that he concentrates as a rule, so that the atmosphere of his work has often about it something of the oppressiveness of a hot-house. But in his prose he is less self-centred than in his verse; he can be tenderer and more sympathetic towards his not very realistic projections; there are, as in his verse, occasional incursions of freshness and naturalness, and taken all round his conception of love is not quite so limited in his prose. The theme of the first of Mackenzie's two novels, *The Young Desire It*[67] (London, 1937), is by no means new: it is, in the main, the introduction of an extremely sensitive and innocent boy to the roughnesses and cruelties of a large boarding-school. There is not much novelty in the general treatment either, and none of the characters is successful, at least in this part of the book; the vision of the tortured war veteran who is the headmaster does remain in the mind, but it is as a picture rather than as a living person. And the sexual innocence of this boy of fifteen,

[65] Published under Seaforth Mackenzie; for his verse and biographical details, see pp. 1029–34.

[66] In the two novels published before 1950; two more were published before his death: *Dead Men Rising* (London and New York, 1951) and *The Refuge* (London and Sydney, 1954).

[67] The title is said by Mackenzie to have been taken from "Michael Paul's *Anatomy of Failure*", but no such book exists. [Mick Paul was a Sydney cartoonist of the twenties, known as the "Professor of Bohemianism"; there may be some connection.]

who has lived on a farm too, amounts to incredible ignorance when his teacher makes love to him; incidentally, the character of this teacher would have been known, to the headmaster almost certainly, and quite certainly to the other boys and the rest of the teaching staff: the idyllic love episode that runs through the holidays is much better done and comes as a relief after this. In the second novel, *Chosen People* (London, 1938), the erotic atmosphere is heavier and unrelieved; the whole book seems to be steam-heated: it deals almost entirely with the relations of two young men who are not very sharply distinguished from one another,[68] with the mistress of one of them, and with a Jewish family in whom it is not easy to believe. This family consists of mother and daughter and a young man who has been the lover of the mother; he seems to be still infatuated with her, but she has handed him over to the daughter, apparently as an exercise of power, and to increase her power: "These people," says one of the other characters very truly, ". . . are unnatural and unreal": the mother, lascivious, cruel, dangerous; the daughter, unnaturally innocent, again, and yet obsessed by sex; the young man "a perfectly negative Jew-boy with no personality"; a father who is a conventional yet enigmatic shadow in the background. All these belong to a world of their own; as regards the mother at any rate, it is the world of later Elizabethan tragedy; she is real and objective and conveys a striking impression of horror and power.

If this were all that could be said about Mackenzie's novels they would be worth less space here. They depend however neither upon plot or story nor upon the revelation of character, but upon the creation of a particular kind of beauty, which is revealed almost entirely in their style. Rich, subtle, sophisticated, it flows smoothly and easily, lit throughout with an individual imagination: its most noticeable element is its imagery; Mackenzie's prose is, rather surprisingly, much richer in images than his verse. His images are sometimes revealing and often beautiful; from the first book: "There was someone there, walking on the leaves like rain"; "The green sharpness of boys' voices"; a schoolmaster "raped his dim bookshelves with one majestic glance"; and from the second book: "She began to rise from the free depths of sleep"; "In the silence after speech he heard the voice of the water as dispassionate as the afternoon that drowned them in its pale seas of light." Sometimes however the image seems to be there, not because it deepens the impression, crystallizes the atmosphere of what is to be conveyed, but rather for its own sake, and sometimes it is a little strained.[69] In such cases an image

---

[68] One is the principal character of the first book, the other a friend who was not much more than mentioned there, but now plays the principal part.

[69] "A brutal sun stood bronze above the river flats" (*The Young Desire It*, p. 9); "In the lower part of his belly fear kicked and pulsed like a child in the womb, ready to be born" (the same, p. 310); "The fury of the cicadas steamed harshly on the still air" (the same, p. 310).

may give an incident or a person more prominence than is desired or deserved, drawing the reader's attention away from what is more important.[70] A few such images, in the first book, might be defended as illustrating the sharpness with which certain sights impress themselves upon a sensitive imagination at a time of strain, but a few are not so much out of place as definitely bad. There can be no possible defence of this sort of thing:[71] "Her small mouth pouted, weary yet still avid for the many kisses that it had demanded and suffered." And, taken all round, this superabundance of imagery grows in the end tiresome, making one long for a simpler and less ornamented prose. If Mackenzie is unable to create character; if he lacks the self-restraint to prune away everything, however striking or beautiful in itself, that amounts to an excrescence where it is placed; and if his taste is not invariably sure: yet by virtue of his distinctive temperament and imagination he has created something in prose as well as in poetry. Few Australian writers of fiction are able to so focus themselves upon the outer scene, or have so great a command over the verbal means of conveying what they see or imagine.

A picture of an utterly different kind of Jewish family is painted in *Brass and Cymbals* (London, 1933), by Jean Campbell (Melbourne, 1906-), a Melbourne journalist, amateur actress and writer of short stories and plays. Old-established, dignified and honourable, charged with an intense racial and religious pride, with the revolt of the younger generation the family breaks and is scattered; its black-bearded, arrogant and in his way almost magnificent patriarch is strongly drawn, and there are several dramatic situations, though it is sheer melodrama with which the story ends. In a second novel,[72] *Greek Key Pattern* (London, 1935), Miss Campbell tells, realistically and with humour, of the rise to wealth and position of a young Greek immigrant. Unfortunately in both books her style is journalistic and sprinkled with clichés and carelessnesses.

Most of those city novels which, like *Greek Key Pattern*, deal with the wage-earning classes have been considered in other contexts; a list of such novels would of course have to include Stead's *Seven Poor Men of Sydney*, Mann's *Go-Getter*, Kylie Tennant's city novels, and the greater part of Barnard Eldershaw's *Tomorrow and Tomorrow*. Of the few that remain, Ruth Park's *Harp in the South* and Jon Cleary's *You Can't See Round Corners* were awarded respectively first and second prizes in the *Sydney Morning Herald's* first novel competition in 1946 and both were published in Sydney in 1948; they have little in common except that they deal with the lower strata of city life, but they may be taken together

[70] For example, the principal character, about to enter school, is measured for his new clothes by "a powerful Scot, lame and charming" (*The Young Desire It*, p. 10).

[71] *Chosen People*, p. 104.

[72] Miss Campbell has published several other novels, which need not be discussed here.

here because they possess opposite qualities that show out well when contrasted. Ruth Park (Mrs D'Arcy Niland, Auckland, N.Z.) spent her childhood in a small New Zealand bush town; she taught, practised journalism and lived for some time with her husband in a Sydney slum; on her experiences there her prize novel was built. Jon (Stephen) Cleary (Sydney, 1917-) before the war a commercial artist, served in the second A.I.F. as a gunner in the Middle East and as a member of the Military History Section in New Guinea and New Britain. He has published a collection of short stories,[73] has won prizes in drama competitions, and now lives in London. The most obvious influence on Ruth Park is that of Dickens; Cleary says he has been influenced by Conrad, Hemingway and Graham Greene, of the second and third of whom there are traces in his work. Cleary has more talent than any other novelist whom the recent newspaper competitions have discovered, but it was not fully developed when he wrote his first book; Ruth Park's talent also is considerable, but it was fully evident in her first book and has taken a direction that is by no means purely literary. She finds in life plenty of humour and an ultimate excellence and almost all her men and women are good at heart and her story and her style are bright and entertaining; Cleary, especially in his first book, sees life as harsh, and his style is plain, straightforward, laconic, rather hard. He tells a straightforward story, sticking strictly to his theme; she strays continually into incidents which, however entertaining in themselves, have little or no necessary relationship to her plot. Her besetting fault is a sentimentality which discovers an underlying sweetness in the unsavoury, softens what is hard, and makes everything come all right in the end; Cleary's tendency, in this first novel of his, is in the opposite direction: with him nothing is allowed to affect the principal character's inevitable fate; all the accidents are unhappy. The tendency is not however carried anything like so far as Graham Greene carries it; it recalls rather the Greek dramatists' embodiment of the conception of fate. But the fundamental difference between the two writers is that Cleary has an artistic conscience: he looks straight at his object and reproduces it as faithfully as his temperament will permit; Ruth Park has also an eye on the effect her story is likely to produce; for this reason Cleary is convincing, and Ruth Park fails to convince. But she has a sharp eye for the picturesque in incident and character, and since most readers prefer "hearts of gold and a happy ending"[74] her novel is much the more popular of the two; she has since published another novel,[75] which reads as though it has been made up of trifles for which there was not room in the first. Cleary also has published a

[73] See p. 1256.

[74] This phrase is taken from a review by Marjorie Barnard of *The Harp in the South* in *Southerly*, vol. ix (1948), No. 3, pp. 182-4.

[75] *Poor Man's Orange* (Sydney, 1949) and several other novels after this History closed.

second novel, *The Long Shadow* (London, 1949), a psychological thriller, good of its kind but not to be compared with the other; but his third novel, *Just Let Me Be* (London, 1950), fulfils the promise of his first. It deals with very nearly the same stratum of society, but his Hemingway and Greene have been digested, and he is himself and Australian, though his Australianism is of a kind that has only lately come into existence, or at least been recognized in fiction. The closest comparison for *Just Let Me Be* is *The Go-Getter*; it is inhabited by much the same sort of people, the principal character is again a returned soldier, though this time of the second World War, and they live in the same sort of homes, though Chris in *The Go-Getter* was much more straitened owing to the Depression. But Joe also had known what it was to wear out his shoes in the search for a job, his head was not so very far above water, and the housing shortage had prevented him from getting married. And war had left a deeper impression upon him than upon Chris; ambition and the love of adventure that had made him enlist had been worn out of him; all he wanted now, apart from his marriage, was the safe job and the quiet life that he possesses, it can hardly be said that he enjoys, when the story opens. Yet suddenly and without any fault of his own he finds himself struggling with and in the end killing two men: the first to prevent a murder and the second in self-defence. Upon these two killings the plot of the story depends, but its essence is the analysis of Joe's character, of his reactions against the perversity of a fate that drags him out of the calm stagnation to which he has clung, into battle, murder and sudden death; none of the other people in the book can be compared for a moment with Karkeek in *The Go-Getter*. All Cleary's characters are here much more sympathetic than those of *You Can't See Round Corners*: this in itself cannot of course affect the literary quality of the book, but it deepens an impression that its author is following his natural bent more closely here; one feels that left to himself he perceives something ultimately worth while in most people. Not that he ever sweetens the facts like Ruth Park, or that he even goes as far in that direction as Lawson, and the ultimate likeability of his men and women is hardened over with a thin crust of unillusioned modernity; but it is there. In this novel Cleary stretches out a hand to the Australian group of country novelists, as well as to Mann; as before, his style is simple, realistic and direct, and his conversations are much more natural than the conversations of those Australian novelists who are concerned with more cultivated men and women. And Cleary is good again at descriptions of scenes and actions; they find closer parallels with some of Mann's than with those of *You Can't See Round Corners*: his view of Coogee for instance,[76] which may be compared with the description

[76] pp. 8–9.

of the dingy Melbourne suburb in *The Go-Getter*. But even the best of Cleary's scenes of action, Joe's struggle with the two Italians, is not so good as that in which Frankie kills Myra, in *You Can't See Round Corners*, as both are far inferior to the fight with the larrikins in *The Go-Getter*; it seems to lack something, a certain freshness of imagination perhaps. Those of Cleary's novels which have been dealt with here[77] represent the impingement of an aspect of modernity, though this itself is a harking back to the primitive, upon the life and literature of Australia, just as the impingement of aspects which are not primitive is represented by Stead, Dark and Eldershaw; they represent in particular the effects of war upon the lives of working men and women, affected slightly by the neo-barbaric school of fiction in America today. But Cleary does not go so far as for instance Hemingway; he is as outspoken, and shows with little reticence the hard, grim and dingy aspects of the life he describes, but he does not dwell upon these for their own sake, or set them out in such a way as to produce an exaggerated effect; his characters do not build an inhuman stoniness above an abyss of sentimentality.

[77] The others are *The Sundowners* (London, 1952), *The Climate of Courage* (London, 1954), *Justin Bayard* (London, 1955), *The Green Helmet* (London, 1957), and *Back of Sunset* (London, 1959).

CHAPTER IX

THE NOVEL

Historical Novels: Eleanor Dark; "Barnard Eldershaw"; Helen Simpson; Mary Skinner and D. H. Lawrence; Sarah Campion; Others. Wit, Humour and Satire: Dalley; "Martin Mills"; Others

A LARGE territory still awaits the Australian historical novelist. Much of it has been scratched over, but only two of the most promising areas had been worked by real talent until the present Period; both were areas that had an obvious attraction for the romantic spirit that has ruled throughout the greater part of Australian literary history: the Convict System and the Squatting Age. Today the boundaries have been pushed out farther, and it has to be noted that all but one of the leading historical novelists of today are women: Eleanor Dark has elaborated with a creative imagination based upon precise and painstaking scholarship a vast panorama of the founding of Sydney and the early settlement of New South Wales; Barnard Eldershaw has wrapped about a memorable central figure a lively and often amusing sketch of a later period in the colony's early life; and later she has broadened into a vision, founded firmly on the present, of Australia's far-off future. There is also Brian Penton, the exception referred to, who has returned to the rise of the squattocracy, but this time in Queensland, and not romantically, nor with the object of revealing the exact historical truth either, but in a mood of hard and bitter iconoclasm: for this reason his two novels are discussed elsewhere[1] as novels of purpose. After these come three more women, who belong to the fringe of Australian fiction as considered in this History: Helen Simpson, living in England, returned to her own country for a while in her best work; Mary Skinner wrote her one important novel in collaboration with D. H. Lawrence; and Sarah Campion has only visited Australia, but, like Grant Watson in the preceding Period, she is here counted Australian for special reasons. Eleanor Dark's two[2] historical novels are so different from her others that she has been made one of several exceptions to the general rule adopted in this History, of discussing together the whole of the writer's work in the category to which the best or the most characteristic of it belongs. *The Timeless Land* (London, 1941) and *Storm of Time* (Sydney, 1948)

[1] See pp. 1208–11.

[2] But there has since been added a third, too late for consideration here: *No Barrier* (London and Sydney, 1953). Eleanor Dark's non-historical novels are discussed on pp. 1162–8.

raise again the old question whether fiction may not come nearer to the truth than history, if it so illumines some aspect of the past as to make it more real and living than is possible to the historian, whose imagination, creative in its kind, is yet tied down, in theory at any rate, to facts that have been actually ascertained. These two novels also recall the dilemma into which the historical novelist, and to some extent the historian also, must find himself: if he is to make the past, or at least the far past, real to us, he may either infuse into his characters a life that we can recognize by causing them to speak and behave generally more or less as though they belonged to today; or he may reproduce the tone and atmosphere of their time as accurately as possible, and try to make them speak and act in exact accordance with it, thus creating, or re-creating, a world which however strange is self-consistent and alive. If he adopts the first alternative he runs the risk that his very efforts at realism may cause his picture to appear unreal, because of the obvious falsification of the letter, however closely the spirit may be retained; but the second alternative will handicap him from the start, since he must thereby impose upon his readers the need to accommodate themselves to strange facts and a strange attitude and idiom, which it is sometimes a little difficult to accept as natural. This dilemma has not so far seriously affected Australian historical novelists, because most of them have treated their subjects so romantically that for them the question of realism does not arise: with Eleanor Dark, who has adopted the second of the two alternatives, it does arise, though not in an extreme form, because even the beginnings of Australian history are comparatively recent, and they are to some extent familiar to her fellow countrymen. Her fictional reconstruction of the speech, actions, life of the time and place she deals with is built closely and accurately upon contemporary journals, letters, official documents, which however she at the same time illuminates, making the whole mass alive. But though no historical novelist in this country and few of its historians have shown a keener insight than Eleanor Dark into the minds of people and types of another age, and there is no doubt about her realistic power, her style has neither the freshness of the far slighter *A House is Built* nor the fierce individual force of Penton's novels; and she so carefully elaborates the features and atmosphere of her world that, although all her historical characters, as distinct from those who are invented outright, are real to us, so far as they go, all but Phillip and perhaps two or three others show themselves to us as through a thin transparent veil, the veil of the time and atmosphere within which they move. And even Phillip, let alone the other exceptions, sharply defined and living as he is, appears remote, as though observed through a telescope: this may however be a necessary consequence of the method involved. By far the better of Eleanor Dark's two historical novels is the first,

The Timeless Land: the greater part of it might conceivably be regarded as a widely extended life of Phillip; no other book, of fiction or of history either, has brought us so close to the man but for whom the first settlement of Australia might well have failed. The second novel, *Storm of Time*, beginning three years after Phillip's departure from the colony, takes us through the governorships of Hunter, King and Bligh, two of whom were worn out and the third deposed by the military and monopolistic faction that had in effect taken possession of the trade and currency of the colony, and in particular by Macarthur, their directing spirit. By no means the whole of the facts and motives and actions in this historic struggle have yet been brought to light and analysed; but Mrs Dark does not set out to write a standard history of the time, and there is much more in these two books besides the long struggles with which both deal. The "timeless land" is the land as it was in the days before the white man came, the long smoothness of duration experienced by the Aborigines; the "storm of time" represents the rush and struggle that the white man unloosed upon the land. The first book opens with a vision of life as it was in those comparatively happy and quiet days, when "time was only the unvarying cycle of nature"; with the discovery of the wingéd boat, the *Endeavour*; with the fairytale-like canoeing voyage, which takes one back to the Celtic myths; with the appearance of the second wingéd boat and the landing from it of the "mysterious beings with faces pale as bones". This, and the later analyses of Aboriginal mentality, and in particular of the mind of Bennilong, are a triumph of creative insight, and with an exception here and there, in which Mrs Dark romanticizes a little, they are ethnologically correct,[3] in spite of the modest deprecation in her Preface; and only less of a triumph, in that she had more to go on, is the analysis of convict psychology. The story unrolls, like an immense tapestry, one of whose most interesting features is the gradual conveyal to us, through the eyes of the baffled invaders, of the natural characteristics of this difficult and stubborn land, with its strikingly individual patterns, its reversed seasons, its over-stimulating forests, its power, as the sensitive Tench perceived, to convey to the white man that he was an intruder; its threat to impose new characteristics of its own upon him; its continual refusal to give while it was treated as a mere prey: here we see the poetic symbolist in Mrs Dark, and it is true, as she admits, that many of the invaders' difficulties "were not born here. They were brought." From this great tapestry the indomitable personality of Phillip emerges, at once visionary, realist, and stern disciplinarian: sustained, in spite of increasing illness and weariness, by confident dignity and a serene sublimity of ideal, above

[3] My authority for this is Dr A. P. Elkin, late Professor of Anthropology in the University of Sydney.

the intractability of the land itself, the unimaginative inattention of the imperial authorities, the jealous and suspicious perversity of his lieutenant-governor, and the utter inadequacy of the material with which he had to build. Bligh, and also Tench, graceful and witty and light-hearted, literary man and man of the world: these also stand out at times, but even the most prominent of the other historical characters, sharply drawn and alive so far as they go, merge for the most part in their large background. And the non-historical characters do not emerge at all; one would think they were the creations of a novelist whose talent was far inferior to Mrs Dark's: Ellen, Johnny Prentice, the Mannions; it is hard to think of even Bennilong as a living man. Of the comparative inferiority of the second book there are several causes: the division of interest between its three successive centres, Hunter, King, and Bligh; the fact that none of these has anything like the compelling and sympathetic personality of Phillip; and the fact that each has a similar task, which he faces with confidence but which bears him down and in the end overwhelms him. It is true that in a sense this second book has a single centre, the implacable Macarthur, actor and master strategist; but here a chance has been missed, or perhaps passed over deliberately, for to do more with him would have meant four centres, or else the pushing of the three governors into the shade: at any rate, in spite of all we see and hear of Macarthur, in spite of criticisms that ought to show him in the round, he not only remains a mystery—that would have been legitimate enough—but he never comes to life. And the other historical characters matter even less than those of the previous book. Wentworth was only in his boyhood, and Holt and Palmer, both filled with literary possibilities, make only the slightest of impressions; it is true that fully to characterize them would have involved a still further division of interest, but if they were to be introduced at all they should surely have been sharply drawn, even though only in outline: there is some indication that it was intended to do this, but if so it was an unsuccessful attempt. And the invented characters are even less satisfactory than those in the other book; their unreality is the more evident in that more is made of them. Nevertheless, though overshadowed by its predecessor, *Storm of Time* also is a notable achievement.

The style in which these two novels is written is, as was to be expected, individual, competent, and extremely concise and precise: it is the style of a scholar who has not been overweighted by his scholarship, a literary man whom reading has scarcely at all formalized; and this in spite of the extracts from documents, varyingly formal, with which the books are interspersed, in spite of their foundation upon such documents, and in spite of the more formal manners of the time to which they endeavour to hold up the most accurate of mirrors. It is a practical style, in that it comes to the point at once and wastes no words, but at the same time it is sensitive and streaked with poetry: this appears in occasional images, as "the cruel, yellow heat" and "faces pale as bones"; and in occasional sayings, as when the aging and decadent Bennilong says to himself,

> And what shall a man believe who believes no longer in mankind? Shall he look into a still pool and see no image there but the image of a cloud and a tree?

Allied with these is Wunbula's "no tribe could survive without its legends and its songs", in which however the writer's mental attitude cannot be regarded apart from its expression: this is true also of her attribution of an individual personality to the land itself and her conception of its attitude towards its invaders. Mrs Dark's style is so flexible, depends so much upon the matter that it has to handle, that to find characteristic examples is difficult; in the introductory part of *The Timeless Land* there are for instance the legend of the canoe voyage in search of "the place where the sun dwelt", and the description of Bennilong's wooing and subsequent dealings with his wife, and of hers with him. There is no room for quotations from these, but here are some of Phillip's reflections amid the turmoil as the first camp is being pitched, and the momentary vision that follows:[4]

> All day the trees crashed, and the clearing crept back from the shore. Phillip the seaman, who liked everything shipshape, who betrayed in his person and his habits an almost pernickety tidiness, moved in the heart of this chaos, and never by a flicker of expression nor a tone of voice betrayed the almost revolted exasperation with which he surveyed it. Seamen, marines, officers, convicts; pigs, sheep, fowls, cattle; bedding, boxes, ropes, tools, bits of furniture, loads of foodstuffs—this, he thought, wore rather the air of an emergency evacuation than of a planned settlement! [Phillip] knew, long before the day was out, what faced him. He had not enough tools, and those he had were of inferior quality. Not enough clothing for the convicts, many of whom were already in rags. Not enough artisans—carpenters, stonemasons, blacksmiths. Not enough farmers. Only once during the day he paused to think about it. Then, standing on a little rise to the east of the cove he looked down at his community, and realised that he would have to bully it into surviving.

And here is a description of the Reverend Mr Johnson's first convict congregation:[5]

> . . . they had long ago ceased to listen. They did not listen now but stood, a shuffling, ill-smelling crowd, soporific in the moist heat, thinking vaguely of scenes whose squalor stank against the primitive cleanliness of their present surroundings. Thinking of crowded city slums, of thatched hovels in the country, of a land which had repudiated them, but to which, because it was familiar, their thoughts returned with a hopeless longing. Under this torrent of hot, golden light they stood bemused, and dreamed of a gently tinted landscape. The apparent passivity of the country had not prepared them for the fury of the storm which it had loosed on them in the height

---

[4] *The Timeless Land*, 1946 ed., p. 67.

[5] The same, pp. 79–80.

> of their disembarkation. . . . Their nerves still remembered the horrifying sound of a great tree splintering to fragments, their eyes were wearied by the glare of lightning, their ear-drums battered to exhaustion by the crash of thunder. So now, lulled by Mr Johnson's voice, they searched their memories for rain which fell softly, soaking into green fields, splashing on stone pavements, blurring the hard edges of buildings, dimming the distant hills. These images were not thoughts, for all their thoughts were bitter, twisted away from beauty, hardened against hope. They were no more than a shield unconsciously set up between themselves and an alien environment, a respite from the effort of adjustment.

In the second book, Bligh's reflections upon the difficulties that he has to face, in which we may see something of those which had had to be faced by his two immediate predecessors also, contains the illuminating sentence:[6]

> He was a man who liked to stamp his way in a straight line through life, receiving orders and obeying them, giving orders and seeing them obeyed, thrusting obstacles aside, quelling insubordination with a routine punishment, and counting the incident closed. Intrigue and the subtle weapons of slander tormented his pride, frayed his nerves, rubbed agonisingly on that raw spot in his mind where the word "mutiny" stood like a malignant phantom.

And Mrs Dark can show vividly the tension between two opposing characters: there is for instance the famous interview in which Bligh declares that he will take away Macarthur's 5000 acres of sheep land, and the famous sentence, "are you to have such flocks of sheep and such herds of cattle as no man ever heard of before? . . . No, sir". Mrs Dark handles her material excellently, but in this case it was there waiting for her. The first at least of these books is the more impressive the oftener it is read. If the purely invented parts sink farther below the horizon, the re-creation of past life and times, of the characteristics and colouring of the new and almost terrifyingly difficult world as it was then, of the rotten-runged ladder, jagged with barbed wire, up which Phillip and his successors slowly fought their sometimes desperate way, of the character and personality of Phillip; the bold conception and solid base of the book, the breadth and the slow sweep of the creative imagination that constructed it: these combine to make *The Timeless Land* a landmark in Australian historical fiction; and it is not as fiction only that it is important, for it cannot wisely be neglected by students of the first Period in Australian history.

In the breadth of its landscape and the sweep of its design Barnard Eldershaw's *Tomorrow and Tomorrow* comes nearer to Eleanor Dark's historical novels than any other in Australian fiction; it may of course be contended that this is not a historical novel, but for reasons to be given later it will be so treated here. "M. Barnard Eldershaw" no longer disguises the identity of two women, Marjorie (Faith) Barnard

[6] *Storm of Time*, 1948 ed., p. 485.

(Sydney, 1897-) and Flora Eldershaw (Sydney, 1897-1956). Miss Barnard had her schooling at the Sydney Girls' High School, graduated at the University of Sydney and has been in succession a member of the staff of the Public Library of N.S.W. and Librarian of the Sydney Technical College and the National Standards Bureau at the University of Sydney; Miss Eldershaw went to school at Wagga, in the Riverina, N.S.W., where her family lived; the Riverina is the scene of the purely imaginative part of *Tomorrow and Tomorrow*. She was secretary of the Women's Union at the University, senior mistress at the Presbyterian Ladies' College, Croydon, a suburb of Sydney, a member of the Commonwealth Department of Labour and National Services, and an industrial consultant in Melbourne. The collaboration of these two women is among the most successful in literature; either was able to draft a chapter in their combined style which needed scarcely any alteration when it was received by the other in another city.[7] Still there are suggestions that much at least of the humour and broad humanity of the partnership comes from one side of the partnership and much of the imagination and sensitive subtlety from the other. Together, they have written five novels, a volume of essays on Australian novelists, and several historical works, and Marjorie Barnard has written on her own account two historical works and a volume of short stories.[8] Of the five novels, three are historical, if we include *Tomorrow and Tomorrow*; these three are quite different from one another in all respects but two: the theme of each involves, beyond the characters and their story, something more broad and general, in the first two a family and in the third society in its political and economic aspects; and in each there is also involved the idea of planned development. In attitude and method generally the three historical novels, and indeed all the novels, represent different aspects of their authors' personalities; they do not however represent a continuous development, for the first is in almost every way a contrast with the others. *A House is Built* (London, 1929) tied with K. S. Prichard's *Coonardoo* for first prize in the *Bulletin's* first novel competition, and appeared in the *Bulletin* as a serial under the title, *The Quartermaster*: it caught on at once with both the critic and the general reader. The story is of the founding by a naval quartermaster of a family and a great business in the early days of Sydney, and of their rise and fall; it was intended[9] to be the story of the family as a complex unit, not of the personality that dominates it, but in fact the Quartermaster makes the book, and what one perceives is not the natural rhythm

[7] Miss Eldershaw, in conversation.

[8] For the essays, see pp. 1284-5; for the historical works, pp. 1367-9; and for Miss Barnard's historical works, see pp. 1348-50; and for her short stories, pp. 1250-1.

[9] See "The Genetic Novel", Part 2, an article by M. Barnard Eldershaw in the *Sydney Morning Herald*, 28th December 1929, p. 7.

of the rise and fall of a complex unit so much as the rise and fall of an individual and what he has created and gathered about him: that part of the book which follows the weakening of the Quartermaster's powers is not only less interesting, it is not the same kind of book; the nucleus compels our attention, rather than the cell as a whole. Vital, foresighted and therefore lucky, simple and, beyond the requirements of his purpose, limited, but very human and likeable, the Quartermaster is a person whom one remembers, and a surprisingly masculine person to have been created by two young women. The other characters are thinned and weakened by the enforced contrast with him: the wooden and exasperating William, who sometimes compels our sympathy but never our liking, is alive though the stream of his life runs thin; but about the gay, irresponsible and charming Maud, and the more thoughtful and stronger natured Fanny, whose idealistic imagination yet runs clean away with her common sense, there is a suggestion of some old drawer or album and its lavender-scented memories; Adela does not quite come to life, and the handsome and piratical Hildebrand is never more than a dramatic element in the early lives of two romantic "young ladies". The style of the book is bright and graphic but a little abrupt; there is also a scattering of clichés and worn phrases: the authors were not yet masters of their trade. But these little defects are more than compensated by the general interest and the thick scattering of bright images: "Days like bubbles . . . perfect, clear and empty—as if the storm had blown all the life out of the world"; "there was eternity in the room under the lovely shallow candlelight"; "something about a mutiny, you can hear it before it happens, like drums a long way off"; and, when William expressed the opinion that at Christmas time a "cold collation" would best suit the Australian climate,

> "What!" they all cried. "Not keep up Christmas! What are you thinking of?" And they all looked at William as if he had blasphemed his God, repudiated his country, and questioned the honour of his mother.

And the descriptions are full of life: the sounds and smells of the water-front and the store as they float up to Fanny and Maud in their bedroom above; the markets; the dialogue between Maud and her father about the fascinating Captain Hildebrand, a touch of satire on the current romantic novel that recalls *Love and Freindship*; the story of the mutiny on the whaler. More memorable than any, whether the authors like it or no, is the mortifying experience that befell the unhappy William when he was supervising the transport of a great vanful of hurriedly packed furniture to Ryde, when "a thoroughly obscene washstand" upset and wedged itself upon his shoulders just as several members, some of them female, too, of one of the leading Sydney families happened to pass by. The next two novels show an advance in literary craftsmanship, but lack the spontaneity and sparkle of the first, and there is also about them a tendency to the "literary". *Green Memory* (London, 1931) tells how, after the disgrace and suicide of the head of a Government department in the fifties, his eldest daughter refuses her lover and sacrifices herself and her family to a proud determination to restore its prestige and maintain its social standards; the story is well constructed and smoothly written, but it has the monotony of a long passage of music in a minor key, and there are touches of melodrama, particularly in the last lines. *The Glasshouse*[10] (London, 1936) attempts, not quite successfully, a number of interrelated and difficult tasks: it is a novel about a novelist, a romantic novelist, but of a more or less modern type; she is a sophisticated, self-consciously disillusioned, rather "superior" and extremely "literary" young woman; scenes, characters and actions are seen through her eyes and the book takes its tone from her. She makes a string of stories about the men and women she meets on the ship, and thereby encounters another problem, in that they must not seem as real as the main story if they are not to detract from its reality, and yet they must be reasonably lifelike if, as is intended, we are to regard her as a novelist of ability. In the style, which is otherwise extremely competent, literary clichés[11] take the place of the more journalistic clichés of *A House is Built*; and none of the characters stands out like the Quartermaster, or even William: we get to know the novelist herself, but most of the others are little more than re-created memories of a long sea voyage. *Plaque With Laurel* (London, 1937), has something of the better qualities both of *A House is Built* and of its successors: it describes the pilgrimage of members of a Sydney literary society to Canberra, to attend their annual conference and the unveiling of a memorial to a famous Australian novelist, dead, after a tragic life, a few years before. But though he and his story keep recurring in the thoughts and speech of those members of the society who have known him, he never comes to life; nor does the other novelist in whom something of the same tragic motif is repeated, nor the first novelist's young mistress, nor the old friend who has brought her with him to Canberra. But it is quite different with most of the other members of the party: they are so typical that one would know them at once for what they were and so individual that one might have met most of them; yet by a miracle of self-restraint the authors, one of whom was for several years president of the best-known Sydney literary society, have refrained from drawing anyone from life. Best of all is the middle-aged Mrs Helena Josephson, author of a series of second-rate

[10] The title is taken from "the superstructure of glass and white-painted metal that housed the Captain and the passengers" (p. 18). The book was recommended by the London Book Society and the London Book Guild.

[11] "Cribbed, cabined and confined" (p. 11); "lares and penates" (p. 12); "tabula rasa" (p. 39).

best sellers: as she "dipped gently in and out of sleep" in the coach which was carrying her to Canberra,[12]

> . . . her mind seemed half full of tepid water, and in it floated, amid the coronets and raven tresses, the misunderstandings and fidelities of her latest serial, the hale, smooth, and handsome visage of her companion. This was the man to whom she was to be married, for the third time.
>
> . . . .
>
> Something told her[13] that this would be her last wedding . . . so she wanted it to be very beautiful, but, of course, suitable. She must think out some little touch. When Althea had got married in the last chapter of *On the Wings of Love* they had liberated white doves at the church door. . . . But perhaps it wouldn't be suitable.

She was occupied too by her little economies, such as managing, after some persuasion, to engage the bridal suite at the hotel for the difference between what it would have cost and what she and her fiancé were paying for their single rooms, and the using of the society's gala dinner at six o'clock as their wedding breakfast. But the long evening would be rather boring, since because of the recent tragic death of a member of the society ". . . it wouldn't be decent to dance or to go to the pictures. What could they do? They might of course go to bed early. A long night's sleep was always something to the good." And the irony of some of the descriptions also is delightful:

> The Hotel Australasia braced itself to withstand the onslaught of the Australian Writers' Guild. The waiters encased themselves in glacial politeness; the chambermaids screwed themselves up against oppression; and the reception clerk remembered that these people were being taken at a cut rate. The very furniture became more non-committally well-bred, the polished floors more immaculately disinterested, the walls more aristocratically unobservant.[14]

Tomorrow and Tomorrow (Melbourne, 1947) is as different from all these as *The Timeless Land* is from Mrs Dark's other novels. In length it approaches *The Timeless Land* and *Storm of Time*, and is far longer than any other novel by either author; it is as if Barnard Eldershaw, like Eleanor Dark, had gathered herself together for a greater effort. It lacks however the unity of *The Timeless Land* and even of *Storm of Time*, being broken and striated by the interlacing of two quite different components: a record of Australia in the days of the Depression and a vision of the Australia of the future. These two components are however brought together though by no means interwoven under a single theme: the age-long rhythmic struggle between the desire for liberty and the hitherto incompatible desire for efficiency and material wellbeing. In the component dealing with the future, *Tomorrow and Tomorrow* raises the question whether individual liberty is any more compatible with a

---

[12] pp. 21-2. [13] p. 197. [14] p. 24.

society of plenty than with a society of scarcity; and with remarkable prophetic insight the novel considers the dilemmas facing a technologically advanced economy in which automation infiltrates even the inner life.[15] It is not only in breadth and sweep that *Tomorrow and Tomorrow* compares with Eleanor Dark's two historical novels; it has also something in common with her rather more than incidental conception of Australia, the land, the countryside, as individual and compelling, moulding its inhabitants into types that are its proper expression. In this book a professor remarks,[16] "When I look at the American soldiers I'm persuaded that there is an Australian type. It isn't scientifically possible, not in a hundred and fifty years, but it's there." This Australian type is described, and in terms that recall the Australians of the nineties as they are drawn by Paterson, Lawson and Furphy, and Bean's re-creations of the men of the first A.I.F.; but Barnard Eldershaw goes further, and describes the Australians of the days of the Depression not merely as individuals but as a community, their social, economic and political attitude:[17]

> They had been a very strange people, full of contradictions, adaptable and obstinate. With courage and endurance they had pioneered the land, only to ruin it with greed and lack of forethought. They had drawn a hardy independence from the soil and had maintained it with pride and yet they had allowed themselves to be dispossessed by the most fantastic tyranny the world had ever known. . . . They looked always to Government for redress and assistance but they were always scornful of their government and with a persistent lawless streak in them. . . . Tough, sardonic, humorous, they were romantics the like of which the world had never seen. Crusaders without a crusade, they fought for any cause that offered or for the simulacrum of a cause.
>
> . . . .
>
> . . . and yet they weren't a belligerent people. . . . The armies were volunteer, both sections of the community jointed together to refuse conscription. It was one of their gestures of freedom, the curious truncated liberty to which they held.

Barnard Eldershaw's contrast between this "Second People" and the "First People", the Aborigines, recalls that drawn by Eleanor Dark, though only faintly, because Barnard Eldershaw takes into account, and indeed that is the burden of her contrast, developments that occurred only gradually, during the generations that followed after the initial period which is dealt with in *The Timeless Land*:

> The Australians had brought a new sort of death to the continent—not overt violence but the unregarded, unrecorded death of dumb men and beasts, bound luckless upon the machine.

The two components of *Tomorrow and Tomorrow* are related more closely

[15] *Tomorrow and Tomorrow and Tomorrow* (the original title) was re-issued unexpurgated in 1983 by Virago Modern Classics, London.

[16] p. 313. But of course the contrast he observed might mean only that an American type had arisen, as it certainly has.

[17] pp. 9–10.

than the components of *Such is Life*, but no more than these are they welded together: the book opens four hundred years hence, with Knarf, one of the "Third People", brooding over the past history of his country and the novel he is writing about it; he calls this novel "Little World Left Behind", a title he has "lifted . . . from the Ancients". The touchstone and inspiration of Knarf's novel is "the brooding Anzac", the central figure of Rayner Hoff's war memorial, which has just been unearthed among the ruins of Sydney; but there seems to be a confusion of thought hereabouts, for though a four-hundred year interval is not perhaps too long to allow of the realistic and detailed description of life under the Depression, it is obviously the merest fraction of the interval that would be necessary for the development of a new language—the title of Knarf's novel had had to be translated "from the original English"; for the appearance of a set of names that are not related to any in the world today; or for the possibility of a belief that Rayner and Hoff were two separate persons. Through Knarf's references and reflections we hear of vast engineering and agricultural undertakings by means of which the ruined land has been reclaimed, and of some of the characteristics of the Australia of his period, in particular of the Riverina, now the Tenth Commune, in which he lives; we hear also of a Union of Youth, whose leader is Knarf's son, Ren, and whose object is the gradual restoration of individual freedom, for which there is no place in the planned order of that later day. At the end of the book a vote is taken on a motion for the creation of an Auxiliary Council which shall represent the ordinary man, who has no voice in his own government; the motion is declared to have gone by default, since though more have voted for than against it, the majority of the voters have shown themselves indifferent: meanwhile, Knarf has been reading his manuscript to a friend, and we hear the readings with intervals during which we return to the outside world. Knarf's novel is very largely a study of Sydney under the Depression: it begins with a typical scene at Central Railway Station on a Friday evening, and in the train afterwards, in which Ally Munster, exhausted, loaded with parcels and with a seven-months' baby in her arms, struggles for a place in her train, and we see and hear what happened in the carriage, and what happened later when her husband met her at the little station where she had to get out; this part of the book represents the high-water mark not only of *Tomorrow and Tomorrow* but of all its authors' novels. When Ally manages at last to find a compartment that seems a little less full than the others, and squeezes herself into a fraction of a seat, here is what happens;[18] except for the horrible incident with the baby, it is typical of the sort of thing that does happen in real life, but it is artistically focused and no photograph:

[18] pp. 50–1, 53–4.

"I'm that hot," said the fat woman, "I'm just wet."

"I don't wonder," said her sister sympathetically, "open the window a bit. Geoff, your poor mum's suffocating."

"Don't you move, Geoff. If he got up he'd lose his seat, we're that squeezed."

"You do it, Shirl."

The little girl got up self-consciously and began to fiddle ineffectually with the windows.

"Push it up, then down, Shirl."

"Mind your fingers, love."

. . . .

By sheer weight the fat woman settled herself more comfortably and began to discuss with her sister the fortunes of the day.

"The blue at three-eleven-a-half was a bargain. It ought to make up real nice."

"I don't know whether to make it myself or to let Miss Higgins."

"I'm not too pleased with Miss Higgins. She made this and it girt me under the arms something frightful."

"That's her fault. She cuts too skimpy. Thinks we're all bits of girls." The sister laughed richly. The fat woman laughed and her stays creaked. She overlapped her neighbour so that the last comer was forced to sit at an uncomfortable angle and came in contact with the girl's stony shoulder. She tried to elbow back the great soft bulk, but under her softness the woman seemed to be filled with concrete. The baby, awake, tried to crawl round on her lap. She hated the fat woman with an implacable hatred.

. . . .

The baby slackened in her arms. . . . Something had caught his interest. On his troubled, yellowish little face was a look of anxiety increasing to pain. . . . The baby's face fell together, he doubled his body back sharply and yelled with all his might. His mother was taken by surprise and her nerve broke. Darkness rushed at her. With one hand she tried to stifle his screams, with the other she beat furiously at his wildly-threshing legs. Her face was white and distorted with fury. A shock of horror ran through the compartment. The man opposite seized her wrists.

"Now, now, missus. He's only a little fellow."

In a second she relaxed trembling, and he let her go. Everybody was profoundly and sincerely shocked. They stared in silence. Only the child continued to scream as if he were being murdered. . . . Trembling, the woman tried to rock the baby into quiet. . . . Hysteria rose in her. The pack was after her. She wanted madly to explain that what had happened was not her fault. She'd had an awful day, she was trapped, caught, everything was against her, it was her husband's fault. On that her mind reached its dead end, ran into the buffers. She looked from face to face, she must make her defence, but that would be the whole story of her five years' marriage. It was his fault that she had disgraced herself in public, everything was his fault. She groped helplessly for reprisal. Her mouth widened in a sickly propitiatory smile, still trying to soothe the child.

"He has his father's paddy."

The Depression theme is developed, and Munster's long struggle against its tide, he and his being "no more than the dominant in a large pattern": at last after a third World War, a leftist "peace party" arises, with Sydney as its headquarters, and takes charge; the "right" minority appeals to the "International Council", and a strong force of "international police" is landed; the peace party burns Sydney, "a symbol of greed and profit", and that part of the population which will not come to terms with the invaders makes for the back country, where all but a few are starved out. The picture of the Depression and the forces underlying it, and of Munster, the *homo tragicus* struggling against them, make the book; but the other part is by contrast unconvincing, though it provides a suitable background and the necessary machinery: the people of Knarf's world, even Knarf himself, are not much more than abstract figures in a fantastic film, but the Munsters and the other men and women of their society, so far as they appear, are both real and representative, and so are many scenes and conversations besides that quoted. In style also the book makes a distinct advance upon the authors' other novels: dignified, detached, unselfconscious, neither crude nor "literary", varying between marble and rubble without changing its general character, it is flexible enough to handle social and economic analyses and the conversations and actions of the dustiest stratum of society. And again it is lit by illuminating phrases: the "curious truncated liberty" to which we, "the Second Australians", are described as holding; the description of the worn-out Ruth as feeling "as if the flesh were dropping off her bones"; the description of "the Brooding Anzac" as "an immortal ghost in stone"; and of history as "chain smoking in a big way". Like *Such is Life*, this book triumphs over its lack of unity and continuity, and though Barnard Eldershaw has not Furphy's talent or personality, her talent is considerable and she is a literary artist as he is not.

Helen (de Guerry) Simpson (Mrs Denis Browne, Sydney, 1897–1940) was, like Christina Stead, partly lost to Australian literature by her early migration overseas. Her mother's father was a French marquis who had settled at Goulburn, and there is some reflection of this ancestry in *Boomerang*; she was educated at the Rose Bay Convent and at Oxford, migrated to England at sixteen and during the first World War decoded messages for the Admiralty; afterwards she studied music at Oxford. Musician, poet, playwright, historical biographer as well as novelist, she also read four languages besides her own, was an expert on domestic science, a fine horsewoman and fencer and interested in witchcraft and demonology. Her literary work also covers a wide range: some of it is referred to in the section dealing with expatriate writers, and her short novel *The Woman on the Beast* is discussed in the section dealing with fantasies;[19] at present we are concerned only with the two novels, *Boomerang*[20] (London, 1932) and *Under Capricorn* (London, 1937). There is a touch of the extravagant, even of fantasy, in all Helen Simpson's work, and in the first novel it is as evident as in anything outside her fantasies

[19] See pp. 1226–8, and for her "expatriate" novels, pp. 1231–2.

[20] This was awarded the James Tait Black Memorial Prize.

proper; here she sometimes reminds one a little of the prose work of Hugh McCrae. It begins with the governorship of Auguste-Anne de Boissey de Mortemar over a black population in a West Indian island, his incredible marriage to a milliner's apprentice in England, and his settlement in New South Wales. He is killed in a duel with a German officer in France, after he has turned out his son Jack because of his refusal to "put on a pair of red pants and bolster up a set of fool Frenchmen" in the Franco-Prussian War; Jack has some improbable adventures in the West Indies, and then he marries, and the rest of the story is told by his daughter Clotilde. After a tomboy childhood, she becomes secretary, first to a procuress who is impersonating a famous English authoress and afterwards in England to the authoress herself; she marries a viscount who becomes Governor-General of Australia, and the book ends with an escapade of hers, dressed as a soldier, in the trenches of the Somme. There is a fascination about the whole of this scattered extravaganza, and it is presented in such a manner that even the first and last parts become almost credible; Auguste-Anne is as real as most fantastic characters; Gustave-Félicité belongs to real life, though he lives near the borders of fantasy; Clotilde is merely unusual; Jack is rather commonplace and his adventures in the West Indies remind us of the people in Stevenson's *The Wrong Box*: the book as a whole has a faint reminiscence of *Orlando* and *A High Wind in Jamaica*, but it is none the less individual for that. The other novel is only less entertaining and much better constructed: "a highly coloured, improbable and yet simple story", beginning in Sydney with the arrival of Governor Bourke and describing the business and amatory experiences of Bourke's aide-de-camp and sixth cousin. Bourke himself, a character after Helen Simpson's own heart; Mr Flusky, the well-to-do Irish emancipist, with his conscienceless shrewdness, his mild eyes, his smooth voice, when he used it, and his silences; these one might have met, though one does not learn a great deal about most of them; but the rest are more or less conventional. Helen Simpson's imagination is almost as rich as Christina Stead's, but of a much lighter kind; she follows its fanciful audacious course wherever it leads her, as careless of literary or other conventions as she is of the probabilities, and she can make almost anything seem real for the time. As an author she has as much vitality as most, and an all-pervading high spirits which Christina Stead does not possess except in some of the Salzburg tales, but her creative power is more evident in her style and scenes and actions than in all but a few of the best of her characterizations. Humour, wit, a sophistication and penetrating intelligence, audacity and just a touch of a superciliousness that is rarer among Australian than English writers combine to make her work instantly recognizable as quite different from other people's. Her style is concise, short-sentenced and sometimes staccato, clear-cut and lucid, always telling, always entertaining: she has some good things to say, as of the Australians, that they are

> . . . a cold-blooded race under the tropic's burning-glass, self-conscious, distrustful of beauty, gamblers and the world's most unsatisfactory lovers;[21]

and

> None of the people who write novels about love can ever have been married.[22]

Few novelists have so variegated a capacity, so light and witty a touch, so rich and keen an invention as Helen Simpson, but she finds her sphere less in the re-creation of aspects of reality than in a luxuriance of imagination that plays about reality; this marks a definite limit to her talent.

The Australian author of *The Boy in the Bush*[23] (London, 1924), which is set in the Western Australia of a previous but recent generation, was Mary Louisa Skinner (Perth, 1876–1955), who was trained as a nurse and travelled as such in England, South Africa and India. She made the acquaintance of D. H. Lawrence during his visit to Australia and gave him the manuscript of the story, which he took off with him to America; he thought it "a queer bewildered muddle",[24] and told Miss Skinner that "the only thing to do was to write it all out again", but he retained her plot except for the last two chapters, and most of her incidents and characteristics of outback life, and he seems to have left at least the male characters, except that of the hero in his final development, practically unaltered. His aim, he told Miss Skinner,[25] was to give the story "a unity, a rhythm and a little more psychic development than you had done". "The end," he added, however,

> . . . will have to be different. . . . Your hero Jack is not quite so blameless an angel, according to me. You left the character psychologically at a standstill all the way . . . I have tried, taking your inner cue, to make a rather daring development psychologically. You may disapprove";

She did, passionately,[26] but it was too late: Lawrence had made Jack, after marrying one woman, invite another also to live with him; she refused, but it seemed likely that she and a third might yet be added to the *ménage*. When Lawrence had finished his work, style and atmosphere, except for the Australian colouring that Lawrence took over from Miss

---

[21] *Boomerang*, p. 231. This is interesting in view of the opinion expressed by an English reviewer of Katharine Prichard's *Intimate Strangers* that there seemed to be too much love-making in Australia.

[22] *Boomerang*, p. 78.

[23] The title was Lawrence's; Miss Skinner's title had been *The House of Ellis* (*Letters of D. H. Lawrence*, edited by Aldous Huxley, London, 1932, pp. 584–5).

[24] *Letters of D. H. Lawrence*, pp. 585–6.

[25] The same, p. 584. For the account of the collaboration I am indebted to two articles in *Meanjin*, vol. ix, No. 4 (Summer, 1950), by Miss Skinner and by Katharine Prichard, as well as to the *Letters*. There are a few slight differences between the texts of the letters quoted; that of the *Letters* has been followed.

[26] *Meanjin*, vol. ix, No. 4, p. 258.

Skinner, had become markedly Lawrentian. The story tells of Jack Grant, a young Englishman who is sent out to Australia because of his wildness; he goes to live on a farm in the then[27] undeveloped country behind Fremantle and afterwards to a station farther out back, and finally settles down on a farm of his own. Almost the whole of the early part of the book is simple, natural and lifelike: young Lennie in particular; the brutal and overbearing Red Easu, (Esau), whom Jack afterwards kills in self-defence; and, probably most characteristic, the slow and a little stupid but manly and utterly dependable Tom, whom everybody looks up to; the girls however are pure Lawrentian types. Most of the incidents are typical and some are delightful: Jack's reception by the girls at Mr George's home; the baby, the castor oil, the porridge lumps and the scrapings of the pig's bucket; the bride who can't attend her wedding because she has just had a baby. And of the scene in which, after Jack has been all night attending to the injured Herbert, Easu's brother, and Lennie is putting on his best clothes to go for the doctor, part must be quoted:[28]

> Lennie was the centre of excitement for the moment.
>
> "Well, Ma, I has no socks fitta wear. If y'll fix me some, I'll go." For he was determined to go to York in decent raiment, as he said.
>
> "Find me a decent shirt, Ma; *decent*! None o' your creases down th' front for me. 'N a starch collar, real starch."
>
> And so on. He was late. Lennie was always late.
>
> "Ma, weer's my tie—th' blue one wif gold horseshoes? Grace—there's an angel—me boots. Clean 'em up a bit, go on—Monica! Oh, Monica; there y'are! Fix this collar on for me, proper, do! Y're a bloke at it, so y'are, an' I'm no good—Gitt outta th' way, you nips—how k'n I get dressed with you buzzin' round me feet!—Ma! Ma! Come an' brush me 'air with that dinkey nice-smellin' stuff.—There, Ma, don't your Lennie look a dream now?—Ooha, Ma, don't kiss me, Ma, I 'ate it."
>
> "Lennie, love, don't drop your aitches."
>
> " I never, Ma. I said I 'ate it. Y' kissed me, did y' or *didn't* y'? Well, I '*ate* it."
>
> He was gone on Lucy, like a little demon. Jack, sitting stupid on a chair, felt part of his soul go with him.
>
> . . . .
>
> "He saved Herbert's life," said Monica, looking up at Easu with a kind of defiance, when she came back.
>
> "Who asked him?" said Easu.

One incident, however, the young Englishman's taming of the horse that nobody can ride, is evidently a Lawrentian invention, and everywhere there is Lawrence's eternal consciousness of sex, his obsession by dark internal forces, his worship of power.[29] Also, Miss Skinner being

[27] The events of this story are supposed to have taken place forty years before its publication.

[28] p. 90.

[29] "The roar of dark consciousness" (p. 307); "a long, lasting dark desire" (p. 272); "all the mystery of his soul's deadly will" (p. 169); "Jack was learning to keep within himself another sort of power, small and concentrated and fixed like a stone" (pp. 139–40); "that strange, powerful life beneath him and between his thighs" (this was when he was riding the buckjumper) (p. 124).

unavailable for consultation except by letter or cable, there are a number of mistakes in terminology, as for example, "chink" for "clink" (jail), "stosh" for "stoush", the use of the coo-ee as a kind of war-cry, and a curious intrusion of cockneyese into the Australian idiom.[30] This was as queer a collaboration as one can call to mind, but the result was quite worth while. A year later Miss Skinner published a novel of her own, *Black Swans* (London, 1925), which is as different as possible from her share in the first: it is a vague, romantic and almost fairytale-like story of Western Australia in the middle of the last century, a curious mixture of the conventional and the imaginative, interesting but quite unrealistic.[31]

Sarah Campion (*née* Colton, Mrs Antony Alpers, Eastbourne, Sussex, England, 1906-) has spent only two or three years in Australia, and her characters use a cockney dialect much more pronounced than that which Lawrence introduced into *The Boy in the Bush.* On the other hand, she knows the North Queensland which is her principal subject as well as background much better than most of us; and there is something in her mental attitude and in that of her men and women which seems characteristically Australian: there is no sign of that outside point of view, as of a traveller, observing, however appreciatively, a foreign country, which would cause her, according to one of the principles on which this History is written, to be regarded, like Lawrence in *Kangaroo* or Havelock Ellis in *Kanga Creek*, as merely a visiting novelist. Her principal Australian novels[32] are three that form a trilogy: *Mo Burdekin* (London, 1941); *Bonanza* (London, 1942); and *The Pommy Cow* (London, 1944). These are closer to the Norse sagas than most "saga" novels, for not only do they tell the life story of Mo and his friends, but that story is for long stretches lost in a crowd of incidents: they might be regarded as novels of outback life, or as novels of adventure; but they are considered in this place partly because they begin in the Australia of the eighties and partly because they seem to fit in best after *The Boy in the Bush.* The principal character in the trilogy is Mo Burdekin, so named because he was washed up, an orphan baby in an old wooden cradle, by a flood in the Burdekin River; he is adopted by a storekeeper in a little riverside township, and later fossicks for gold and tin over the countryside, part of the time with Lucy, a young woman who is much older than he is, and later with other friends. In the beginning of the second volume he strikes a rich vein of gold, and the rest is occupied by further wanderings and adventures; in the third volume he fights in the South African War,

[30] And an Australian would not be likely to speak of "cutest" little pets (p. 37), or of a "bally" saddle (p. 67), or to exclaim "for the land's sake" (p. 75); and the conversations have often a cockney rather than an Australian flavour.

[31] Miss Skinner also published other novels and some short stories.

[32] Sarah Campion has published two more novels that are connected in one way or another with Australia (*Turn Away No More*, London, 1940, and *Dr Golightly*, London, 1946) that need not be discussed here, and several that have nothing to do with this country.

falls in love with Kate, the "pommy cow", and after a prolonged intermittent argument about marriage, to which she, being a "new woman", objects on principle, they are married. Except for the cockneyisms[33] and a few misuses of terms,[34] one would imagine that Sarah Campion had spent her life wandering about northern Queensland, observing everything and forgetting nothing, except the language. Mo, so irritatingly pigheaded, so tightly enclosed, at least when the fit is on him, in his little prospecting world that he can't be prodded out of it even when his old mate Lucy tells him that she is going to marry and leave him, is real and extremely attractive; and so is Lucy, perverse little creature, from a family of dirty, irresponsible, shiftless cockneys, who is as energetic, as well as being almost as pigheaded, as Mo, as fundamentally feminine as he is masculine, and much less transparent. And for the countryside Sarah Campion has as fresh an eye as for its inhabitants. Like Lawrence,[35] she will draw some aspect of the bush that ordinary Australians have not observed, or not in exactly the same way, but that is easily recognizable once it has been drawn for them; and sometimes she accentuates it by contrast with corresponding aspects of scenery from other lands; here is Mo, on the South African veldt,[36] though it is obviously the author who is speaking:

> Here, in these hills, on that plain and range beyond, light was strong and definite where at home, in Queensland, it would be shifting, opalescent.
>
> . . . .
>
> . . . in his own bush there was no shade, for the gum leaf hangs with its knife-edge to the sun, turning as the sun turns, prudently keeping from that sun's ravages its tiny ration of moisture. So that the earth beneath is not shaded, dark; but only faintly mottled like the coat of a mountain cat. Nor is the pattern of this bush a simple pattern: it is a pattern so subtle that (it is said) the foreigner cannot see the Australian landscape at all, at first. The light is so difficult, the tints so subdued, the tracery of the trees so unlike anything to which the alien eye is accustomed.

And here, on the veldt again, is Captain Daly Hamilton, English-born but become conscious that he is "now above all an Australian":[37]

> The bare russet downs of Northumberland with a grey sky above, and cold purple cloud shadows racing over turf and heather—the rain and sweet rainy smells and rushing rain-filled freshets of his native moors—had faded in the last fifteen years:

---

[33] "Cor" (*passim*), "cor lumme" (*Bonanza*, p. 21), "Nobbut" (*Mo Burdekin*, p. 130), "not 'alf" (the same, p. 186), "abaht" (about, *Bonanza*, p. 50).

[34] "Cockeye-bob", a term, confined to Western Australia, for a particular kind of storm, is applied to a storm in North Queensland (*Mo Burdekin*, p. 1); and "Waler", a term applied originally to horses exported from New South Wales to India for army use and used in modern times (See Baker, *The Australian Language*, Sydney, 1945, p. 71) to mean a light type of army horse, is applied indiscriminately (*Bonanza*, pp. 38, 53).

[35] Not in *The Boy in the Bush*, but in *Kangaroo*, which does not belong to Australian fiction, but is discussed later (pp. 1233-5) as the work of a visiting writer.

[36] *The Pommy Cow*, p. 59.

[37] The same, p. 114.

now when he thought of home he saw fold upon fold of bush, the blue bush-clad ranges rolling away with heavy leaden rhythm to the skyline, and a sky so blue, so heavenly blue, that no words can describe the force and grandeur and sheer beauty of it. He thought of Australian men: ribald, mocking, tough and stringy men following their fancies across desert and bush, scrub and plain; of Australian women dried to the texture of loquats by the greedy Australian sun, women with leather cheeks, scrawny figures, knotted hands; and in their eyes that steady look of search, quite endless search, as if the horizons they watched were so boundless that even hope told them it was vain to go on searching.

Other passages, such as Mo's death at the end of the third volume, illustrate the fatalism, the calm sardonic acceptance of the pain and evil in life as not to be fussed over, being inevitable, the taking of even death in one's stride, that are a prominent feature in this trilogy, and also in the character of the outback Australians of at least the nineties and early nineteen-hundreds: in the picture of the drowning of the children at the beginning of the first book there is plenty of feeling however; it is the more pitiful in that it is quite free from sentimentalism. The children are all worn-out, fugitives from the flood that has destroyed their home and parents, loaded down with remnants of their household possessions; Janey, the eldest, who leads them, carrying a camp oven as well as the baby; they sit down to rest for a few minutes in a soft grassy hollow not far from the encroaching edge of the rising river, just the worst place they could have chosen; and then,[38]

The wave had parted roaring at the junction of the creeks and raced down both, blood-red with the tin-rich soil, foaming, spuming, tossing, thundering, with a wild lacy pattern of uprooted pandanus palms, sword grass, bottle-brushes and all the arboreal jetsam of any Queensland creek over its romping surface. On, on, to the children crouching like young quail in the deep grass, and gaping Janey looking for a way to cross. She saw first a dark casuarina cast sportively ten foot above the grass then dropping like a shot bird back into the flood: she saw the tree, she heard the roar, she saw the red tide of the wave heave up against the rainy sky, she leapt to the children, she caught her foot in the bright grass, she fell with her temple cracking against the cradle's edge, and lay senseless with a punctured skull.

Janey was quickly dead, the children were less lucky . . . leaderless, disorganised, frantic, they fell to crying and screaming, ran hither and yon in the thick grass as the wave went by, tripped in the lush, green, glorious grass, struggled up bemused and made off with one accord, like stampeding sheep, towards the rising tide. Up came the water in the wake of that towering wave: now their dusty little feet were ankle-deep, now their dirty little knees, scored and scratched by a hundred encounters with their mother the Bush, were wet and slimy with the flood: now, wrapping tepid and horrible round the waists, the armpits, the shoulders of these bush babies, the flood surged up. The smallest sister was the first engulfed, tripped among the grasses, gasping her little lungs full of flood-water as she dropped. Fiercely over her the water rose, one by one the cries died, the bobbing heads sank, soon even the grass had gone. Now there was nothing in the whole wide river but tossing water, uprooted trees, a few bandicoots and kangaroo rats feebly struggling still, and an

---

[38] *Mo Burdekin*, pp. 9–10.

> old wooden cradle carved with grapes and acanthus leaves in which a dirty brown baby sat drooling with bubbles at his mouth, snatching at the twigs and floating grass-heads as he floated onwards, southwards, on the broad tossing breast of the Burdekin.

This is among the most poignant episodes in Australian literature at least; but it has the artistic defect that the pain is unredeemed, by desert or beauty or even inevitability. Sarah Campion's trilogy presents a continuous stream of detail, all closely observed with scarcely any express comment, though the whole tone is critical: there is such a lack of indicated development, of observable perspective, that except for such prominences as have been noticed, the general effect, especially in the second volume, is flat, as of a scene observed from an aeroplane; but descend and each scene, each conversation, each piece of action appears, regarded in itself, lively and full of interest. And about it all, along with the sardonic humour, the atmosphere of almost invariably unperturbed common sense, there runs a broad and deep humanity: these qualities together with the author's marked individuality give the flavour of the trilogy, as the psychological penetration and the wealth of detailed observation give it its substance.

Of the other historical novelists, some are honest and painstaking and anxious to inform and some journalistically vivid and anxious to excite; most are rather sentimental, and all are inferior in creative imagination to those already mentioned. Vivian Crockett (Sydney, 1893-1973), a Sydney University graduate and journalist who was when this History closed Director of the Department of Medical Sociology and Research in the Sydney branch of the B.M.A., published two historical novels at the beginning of the Period, which represent a revulsion from the attitude and subjects of the nineties. *Messalina* (London and New York, 1924) presents a number of highly coloured episodes in the life of the cruel and sensual wife of the Emperor Claudius; in *Mezzomorto* (Sydney, 1934) a dissatisfied and imaginative man is hypnotized into believing himself the principal actor in sensuous and adventurous romances of the type of which he has dreamed: both books are written competently and with some individuality. Ernestine Hill, who is better known by her volumes of outback Australian description and travel,[39] published also a historical novel, *My Love Must Wait* (Sydney, 1941), which is built around the romantic love story of Matthew Flinders. Mrs Hill follows Scott's *Life of Matthew Flinders*,[40] but supplements it with researches of her own, and adds to Flinders's tragedy, but she melts romance into sentimentality and heightens drama into melodrama: the story as she tells it is lively, often exciting, and at the end tragic, but the style is

---

[39] See p. 1389.

[40] For a discussion of this, see pp. 846–7.

staccato and her images strained. All but one of the historical novels to be mentioned here deal with early Australian pastoral development. *Southern Saga* (London, 1940), by Roy Connolly (1896–1966), a journalist of British and Australian experience, is set in early Queensland. A Queenslander by descent and birth, Connolly knows what he is talking about, but his attitude is at the furthest extreme from Penton's; though his story is for the most part conventional and his style at times rather heavy, there is humour and some excellent character-sketching, and the passage in which the principal character tells the old lady about his seduction by the notorious Lola Montez, with the old lady's rather surprising comment, would be worth quoting, if there were space enough. *Pastoral Symphony* (Sydney, 1939), a much slighter story, simple and matter-of-fact throughout, is set in the early days of New South Wales: it tells of the breeding of cattle and sheep in what was then outback, by a pair of runaway convicts and their descendants. The author, John Jackson Hardie (Troon, Scotland, 1894–1951), had migrated to this country as a young man and knew his up-country Australia better than most; he had previously published several pleasant but conventional station romances. *The Valley of the Sky* (London, 1937) is a romantic idyll of the pioneering of Gippsland, Victoria, and of the blacks as well as of the whites; it was founded on the life of Angus McMillan, the discoverer of Gippsland, who, like the hero in this story, became a member of a native tribe and a supporter of the rights of the aborigines, and it was awarded first prize in the British section of an All Nations Novel Competition: its author, Tarlton Rayment (1882–1964), was a F.R.Z.S. and published a number of scientific works.

Though humour, wit and satire do not necessarily run in harness together they are so closely connected that they may be taken together here, reasonably as well as for convenience. Australian literature, prose and verse, is fairly rich in all three, from the days of Forster, and, after him, Deniehy, through Furphy and Wilmot, up to the present Period. In verse, Hope and McAuley have been discussed already;[41] there remain the prose satirists of the Period, of whom John Bede Dalley (Sydney, 1876–1935)[42] was the first in point of time; it is an interesting illustration of the youth of Australian literature that he was a son of the Dalley who was Attorney-General under Parkes and a friend of Deniehy and who was satirized in Deniehy's *How I Became Attorney-General of New Barataria*.[43] J. B. Dalley was at once an Australian nationalist and a British imperialist, and he loved both England and his own country; but he hated all forms of snobbery and most of all social and "patriotic"

---

[41] See pp. 975–84 and 985–91 respectively.

[42] The birth date was supplied by Dalley in a letter to me. [Dalley (presumably) drowned while fishing at Avalon Beach.]

[43] See pp. 201–3.

humbugs, and satirized them wherever he found them. He was educated at English schools and at Oxford, spent some time in Paris and Rome, practised at the Bar in London, as well as Sydney, and served three years as a gunner with the first A.I.F.; his oversea experience helped to give him a breadth of view which is reflected in his novels and made them a factor in redeeming Australian literature from the parochialism that had marked the previous Period. Dalley abandoned law for journalism when after a bad fall in a steeplechase he became deaf, and finally settled down on the staff of the *Bulletin*. He had a strong sense of humour, which was rather intellectual than emotional, and he perceived what was amusing and reproduced it faithfully; but he differed from the author of *The Montforts*[44] in that he was not witty, and his serious intent was more obvious; and though his satire can be bitter enough at times, it is never possessed by the cold fury that runs through some of Hope's satiric poems. Dalley is Australia's principal satirist of snobbery, yet it is only in his last novel that satire becomes the main motif. His first, *No Armour* (London, 1928), contains little humour and only a touch of satire, and may almost be called a morality: it tells of a Sydney business man, who, tiring of his wife, falls passionately in love with a chorus girl, with the sort of consequences that may easily be imagined; but, old as is the theme, Dalley works it out in his own way, and the unfortunate little Betty and the more than unpleasant atmosphere of her home, with its dark memories and the twisted natures that are connected with it, are very well done. *Max Flambard* (London, 1928) lacks the continuity of the others, and the English scene reads like something out of a book: the principal character is an English public-school product of an extreme type, able and likeable but whose "philosophy of life was composed almost entirely of prejudices", and who has run through £50,000 in five years; the story tells of his impact upon Sydney and suburban society and suburban journalism just after the first World War, and of its effect upon him. Max is real, at least after he reaches Australia, his wife is rather less so and the minor characters are mere sketches; his reformation is perhaps credible, but the two pieces of luck with which the story ends are not; there are several sharp but incidental satires. *Only the Morning* (Sydney, 1930) is a satire straight-out upon Australian and English society. The development of the principal character, Richard Lorne, is clearly marked: son of an under-gardener, extremely capable within rather narrow limits, he becomes a leading Sydney business man; he takes a trip to England, but society there will not accept him because of his accent and manner, though it does accept his wife and children, and in the end he returns to Sydney. This novel is much better constructed than *Max Flambard*, and contains no improbabilities, except perhaps the slices of

---

[44] See pp. 1199–1204.

luck that started Richard on his career of prosperity; and it is filled with character and incident which are however not crowded and compressed as in *The Montforts*. The sketch of Sydney in the early nineties with which the book opens is true to life, and the representation of the contemptuous attitude of some of the more conservative of the Australian "upper classes" towards the then untried Australian soldier at the beginning of the first World War is by no means overdrawn.[45] The political satires and those at the expense of the Englishman in Australia and the Australian in England; of "country yahoos", of a type afterwards dealt with by Franklin and Cusack; and of up-country drives, shooting "rabbits, hares, foxes, dingoes, wallabies—anything": all these hit deservedly hard. Dalley's style is undistinguished and rather journalistic; but he writes simply and naturally and knows how to convey what he wants to convey, even if he is not a verbal artist; his conversations are much more natural than those of the average Australian novelist, and they are not formalized, as with Martin Boyd. Dalley's place among Australian novelists as such is not high, but in the history of fictional satire and of those novels which contrast the old and the new civilizations his work has its importance.

"Martin Mills" (Martin à Beckett Boyd, Lucerne, Switzerland, 1893-1972) is even more an Anglo-Australian than Dalley, and *The Montforts* is as illustrative, though not quite in the same way, of the double point of view. Boyd comes of an old Victorian family, several members of which were artists;[46] he was taken to Victoria as a baby, and educated in Melbourne, where he studied architecture, but in 1915 left for England and served in the Army and the Royal Flying Corps during the war; after a short time in Australia he returned to England, belonged for a while to a Church of England Franciscan order and then settled down to write; he came back to Australia in the late nineteen-forties but lived the latter part of his life in Rome. Boyd published a number of novels, of which only *The Montforts* (London, 1928) can be regarded as Australian,[47] though part of *Lucinda Brayford* (London, 1946) is set in Victoria. *The Montforts* was Boyd's third novel and so far his best; a revised version was published in Australia in 1963. It is a highly condensed, saga novel which deals with the story up to modern times of a Victorian family whose ancestors migrated from England in the pioneering days; but an important part of the chronicle begins overseas in the early nineteenth century, with the injection into the veins of a conventional and fairly typical English country family of the blood of the gay, witty, beautiful

---

[45] Bean has something to say on this subject in the first volume of his history.

[46] Penleigh Boyd was his brother; Robin, Guy and Arthur Boyd his nephews.

[47] But see note 54. *The Montforts* was published in America as *The Madeleine Heritage*. It was awarded the gold medal of the Australian Literature Society for the best novel of the year. After *The Montforts* Boyd wrote under his own name.

and not-too-virtuous daughter of a French marquis, whose traits emerge disturbingly in each generation. The family migrates to Australia; the eldest son, Simon, for they characteristically claim relationship with Simon de Montfort, founds a squatting family, and a younger son, Henry, practises law and becomes a judge: both intermarry with other pioneering families and through them all, but coloured in by Boyd's satiric temperament, we get to see something of the development of Victorian social life. Each of the men and women who helps to build or branches out from one or other of the connected families is shown in relationship with the other families and with individuals belonging to them as well as being himself, or herself, sharply sketched: but there are so many of them that there is no room in so short a novel for more than their essential characteristics. And though all are interesting, none of them stands out much above the other, except old Sim perhaps, for Henry is after all a conventional type; and none but Sim is memorable except on account of incidents with which he or she is connected, or because of their representative capacity: this is due very largely to the fact that the author has not left himself space to present his characters in the round. As a result, probably, of Boyd's philosophy of life, about which there will be something to say later, some of those who are involved in the most interesting situations are extremely weak, and though we do find doggedness, in no character is there any real strength of will. Though the novel is too small for its content, much of its attraction comes from its compression and succinctness, and if it had been larger its character would have changed; as it is, however, the book is so tightly packed that, especially with the continual appearance of inherited traits, the reader may at first be a little confused, and wish for an index of characters.[48] Through all this may be seen the gradual working out of the two factors of heredity and environment, as the old English stock is affected on the one hand by the French infusion, and on the other by the Australian intermarriages, and in particular the crude but vigorous country intermixtures, and also by the potent infusion from Spain. Actually the human environment is seen as more important than the physical, for the principal characteristics of the city branches of the family alter very little in Australia, and the country branches get their roughening more from the stocks they marry into than from the land on which they spend their lives. The story is told with an amused detachment, whose light irony is never bitter, and the author is never carried away by anything he relates: even the few passionate and tragic situations are presented unemotionally and as a rule in a humorous context, leaving the passion and the tragedy to be conveyed by means of short descriptions and the few words of the characters concerned. All this has the effect of

[48] There is a family tree, and it is needed.

toning down the emotional atmosphere; it would not be right to infer from it that the author does not enter into his characters' feelings, but it does suggest that he regards such crises as without any deep significance. The seduction of the clergyman who was the real founder of the Montforts by the first Madeleine[49] is merely referred to, in an atmosphere of comedy, and even the first love passage between Richard and Aïda, in the Spanish castle,[50] becomes as described merely a pretty little thing:

> The sun had set, but there was a glow over the sky and a half light in the garden. They sank naturally into each others' arms. Now and then he murmured her name.
>
> "Aïda, *Céleste Aïda*, heavenly Aïda."
>
> The warm night enfolded them, the garden gave its scents, and the stars gave light for their mating. Richard, for once, had transcended his code of gentility;

it is true that this is followed by a few lines describing Aïda's wretchedness after Richard's departure, but very soon there arrives a letter from Richard that has "a distinct literary flavour", with indeed a touch of comedy about it, and this shuts the door firmly upon any tragic atmosphere that may have survived. The later scene in which the malicious and scandal-hunting Amy interrupts a second love passage between Richard and Aïda in Australia is again turned resolutely away from tragedy by the description of Amy as she breaks in upon the lovers, ludicrously dishevelled in her passage as she stalks them through the bush; and in the final scene in which Richard confesses to Aïda's husband among his examination papers, Richard's weakness and the husband's feebleness recall the story of the curate's smashing of the umbrella of his wife's seducer, and creates an atmosphere in which tragedy could scarcely survive. Taking into consideration also the all-important part played in the story of the Montforts by heredity[51] and chance, we get the impression that to Boyd there is no such thing in life as freedom, since even when some individual may appear to alter the course of things, he actually does so in virtue merely of inherited traits working upon accident; allied with this is the impression that to Boyd life is a joke, and not a tragic but a comic one.* It is here that the weakness of *The Montforts* lies: not that it is superficial in the sense of running amusedly over the surface of things, but that it is based on the assumption that there is little beneath the surface, and that nothing about life need be taken very seriously; with the truth or untruth of such assumptions we are not here concerned, but it may be pointed out that such acceptance would make real tragedy impossible. *The Montforts* is then a comedy, with a few tragic passages lightly touched upon, toned down, and swiftly passed over; of its kind however there has been nothing approaching it

---

[49] In the book he is said to have seduced her, but the other seems much more likely.

[50] p. 147.

[51] This is emphasized and worked out by Barnard Eldershaw in an acute and interesting analysis of *The Montforts*, in her *Essays in Australian Fiction*; for a discussion of these essays, see p. 1285.

* [This impression is cancelled out by Boyd's later work, though it is true his Christian belief would cause him to see life as a comedy in the Dantesque sense.]

in this country. It is full of witticisms, most of which have a satirically social application, at the expense either of England or of Australia; some of the last are uttered by Australians, or at least by people resident in Australia; for example:

> "But is he a gentleman?" Letitia had cried.
> "Well, in Australia, yes," said Henry.

This reflects a not uncommon attitude of the early settlers who had not yet become acclimatized. The English satires are just as sharp:

> She asked Raoul about New Zealand.
> "The people there are nicer than in Australia, aren't they?" she said. "More like us, I mean?"

And when an Australian soldier is being bear-led round the National Portrait Gallery and the Tower by an English relative, she is a little disconcerted at his pointing out a number of distant connections:

> She felt that a colonial had no business to have all these grandfathers. It was unsuitable, as if one had provided a feast for a charity child, and the charity child said "Oh, we always have this at home."

It was the same lady who presenting Raoul to some fellow war-workers, said: "This is my cousin who has come from Australia to fight for us"; but that reflects an attitude that, apart from the element of truth in it, had a certain amount of currency in Australia as well as in England at the time of the first World War, and the remark is described as having "stirred in Raoul a glow of chivalry". Here are a couple of the satiric remarks at the expense of society in general:

> Mabel looked at her with the cold supercilious stare of the intelligentsia;

and

> "Richard, Jesus loves you," she said. "He wants you always."
> His chin gave a ghastly twitch of embarrassment.
> "I can't discuss religion," he said, after a pause.
> "But it is the only important thing."
> "Yes, I suppose so. I see that Zachary Allman is to be made a bishop."

Apart from this sort of thing, Boyd's style throughout is full of quiet sarcasms, directed against neither society in any particular country nor against any individual, but rather against things in general, against life; there is for instance the apparently casual remark, after telling how Richard scratched the words "Céleste Aïda" on a window-pane:

> Sim locked the door. The house remained empty till his death some years later, when it was sold to a retired wine-merchant from Bristol, who had new glass put in the attic windows.

The longer satirical passages are also excellent: perhaps the best of them is the first part of the Prologue, in which Henry Montfort and his wife are in their cabins during a storm on their way out to Australia;[52] there have been few better satires upon early Victorianism:

> The motion of the ship gave rise not only to physical wretchedness but to mental apprehension . . . Henry . . . wondered how his wife in the bunk below was enduring this discomfort, and raised himself on one elbow to look down at her. She heard him move.
>
> "Are you comfortable, my dear?" she asked.
>
> "I was about to ask you that question," he replied.
>
> "I find it a little difficult to sleep."
>
> "This pitching motion is very disconcerting. I shall be relieved when we are free of 'Biscay's sleepless bay'."
>
> He sank back on to his hard pillow. . . . In former days, watching from the shore the placid surface of the Channel, he had never imagined this vastness of water. Now, churned into great waves, stretching for miles on either side of him, flung in spray above him, and with immeasurable depths below him, the ocean seemed indicative of the majesty of God, and of the insignificance of man, who floated even in these fine ships of seven hundred tons, a mere speck in creation.
>
> And yet man was undoubtedly "the noblest work of God". Compared only with the might of Jehovah himself, was he insignificant. His power to master the elements and unveil the mysteries of science daily increased. This was a remarkable century in which they lived. It was not so long since the Queen had made her first famous journey in a carriage drawn by a self-propelled vehicle, and now trains as a means of transport no longer excited great attention. And did not that Queen rule over increasingly wide dominions, new countries, to one of which he was now migrating with his wife, his children, his servants, his *lares et penates*?

Boyd's crafstmanship is far greater than Dalley's; there is no suggestion of journalism about his style, though he does sometimes think in rather worn phrases, and it would be difficult to find another writer who could preserve through such compression so much life and laughter, or even, though it is strongly formalized, so much realism. Yet the reader does become gradually conscious of a slight feeling of constraint, of fullness after an intellectual meal: a feeling that he must sit back and stretch himself and then get up and go for a walk in the free air; on the other hand, *The Montforts* is, within its limits, extremely natural, not least in the conversations,[53] however "pointed", once one accepts their stylistic formalization. This is not a type of novel to be imitated; an attempt to follow along the same lines would almost certainly be a failure, but in its light most other Australian social novels have a slight air of amateurishness. Of the two other novels of Boyd's that are connected in one way or another with Australia,[54] *Lucinda Brayford* (London, 1946), three-quarters of which is set in England, lacks some of the faults and most

[52] pp. 9–11.

[53] Except where, as in the last extract quoted, it is deliberately made stiff, as part of the satire.

[54] After the two novels mentioned here, Boyd published *The Cardboard Crown* (London, 1952); *A Difficult Young Man* (London, 1955); *Outbreak of Love* (London, 1957); *When Blackbirds Sing* (London, 1962); all these have Australian relevance, as do his two autobiographies *A Single Flame* (London, 1939) and *Day of My Delight* (London, 1965). He wrote a number of novels which are European in setting, some under pseudonyms, a travel book, and anti-war pamphlets and a children's fairy tale.

of the merits of *The Montforts*: it is far less tightly packed, far less witty, [which is not surprising in view of the theme: the wastage of young lives in two world wars. The main character is individual and develops interestingly and the novel is one of the few to dramatize the dilemma of the conscientious objector: Lucinda's son.*] In the other, *The Picnic* (London, 1937), the characters are Australian but the setting is England.

A Warning to Wantons (London, 1934), which appeared a few years later than *The Montforts*, is in its very different way as witty and amusing, though it has no satirical purpose: its central character is again a lovely and seductive lady; she however was by no means careless of her virtue, but wore it like a piece of becoming and seductive jewellery, of which, given sufficient incentive, she was quite prepared to dispose. And, instead of being a legendary figure, barely sketched and revealed mainly in its effects upon her descendants, she is a living and fully developed person, about whom every man and women in the book revolves. As *The Montforts* is a story of real life, set in Victoria, though observed with a humorously satiric eye, so this is a fantastic romance, set in a primitive and somewhat Ruritanian district of south-eastern Europe. The author, Mary Mitchell (Melbourne, 1892-1973) was a third-generation Australian: she was educated in Australia and Europe, where she travelled widely; most of her non-literary work was secretarial. *A Warning to Wantons* was her first novel, and a best seller in three continents, but it does not wear so well as *The Montforts*: its range is comparatively narrow, its charm consists in a comparatively superficial effervescence, and its occasional dips into realism are rather incongruous; nevertheless the book is as light and charming as its heroine. Renée de la Vaillière is a brazen but delicious minx, who conceals beneath an air of starry-eyed innocence an infinitely subtle sophistication, and she is past mistress in the art of flirting, for its own sake and more particularly when there is some practical object to be attained: she might have stepped, with a demure but provocative smile, out of the court of some eighteenth-century French monarch, and her qualities are thrown into vivid relief by the semi-barbarous surroundings in which they are displayed: unfortunately a charming comedy, with an occasional touch of what is almost real enough for real tragedy, tails off into a conclusion that is false to character as well as to the probabilities generally. Renée in her conversations with Count Anton, purring like a satisfied kitten who has never even heard of the saucer of whipped cream; Renée bewitching the Count's clumsy and boring son; Renée insulting his furious fiancée beneath a deliberately transparent veil of ingenuous and respectful admiration: these in their polished and courtly formalism of language, their rich subtleties of suggestion, recall the eighteenth-century French novelists, touched a little with the lighter romances of Anthony Hope

* [See Appendix 1, p. 1485, on Boyd.]

and with *Zuleika Dobson*. Mary Mitchell also published a number of other novels, set some in Australia and some in Europe, of which several recall her first, but none can compare with it.

There have been two short, hard-hitting and extremely entertaining satires on education and on the censorship: both protect themselves against the accusation of attacking individuals; the one ought to be read by all who are interested in education, teachers especially, and the other by all who are interested in literature and especially by everyone who is connected with the censorship or banning of books. The author of *The Fiddlers of Drummond* (Sydney, 1945), Arthur (John Merry) Davies (Balwyn, Vic., 1907–*c.*1964), was a graduate of the University of Melbourne who had experience of stage work and the law, besides ten or twelve years of teaching: he attacks schools, the aims and methods of teaching, teachers, pupils and even parents, in something the manner of Evelyn Waugh: probably most of what he says has some application somewhere, but he stabs so hard and indiscriminately that the point of his satires grows blunted and his little world becomes an extravaganza. The book is so full of good things that it is hard to pick out anything for quotation; here however is what a headmaster says to a new teacher about his programme of work:[55]

> "As you are well aware, timetable is our most serious problem. At present, Mr McInley has to take physics (a subject with which he is unacquainted), while French (Mr McInley's special subject) is in the hands of the senior physics master, who knows none. All a matter of timetable. Still, I shall do what I can."

And here a boy asks his teacher to explain a piece of officialese:[56]

> "Please, sir," said Pritchard, "what exactly does that mean?"
> "It has no actual meaning, Pritchard. It is what is called an ideal."
> A reverent hush fell over the class. Some got a soulful, worthy look; others were just embarrassed.

In the other book, *Harvest of Mischief* (Melbourne, 1947), Dighton W. Burbidge, a lawyer and writer of economics pamphlets, tells how Miss Penthesilia Hewart contrives to protect a banned book from the Customs Department and defeat a prosecution for obscenity; the satire is here much closer to the facts, and the book may provide some ammunition for those who are on the side of Milton. Penthesilia is delightful, and here again there are some good things, but much of the humour lies in the ironical wit of the style generally. The censorship is also attacked in *It Never Fails* (London, 1937), by John Mewton Harcourt (Melbourne, 1902–), who was educated in Melbourne and at the Kalgoorlie School of Mines, had two years' experience with the Broome pearling fleet and was for long on the staffs of several Perth and Melbourne newspapers.

---

[55] p. 47. [56] p. 121.

It describes the improbable experiences of a young Englishman who on the one hand is despised as a "pommy" and on the other obsequiously cultivated by those who believe him to be a member of the English nobility travelling incognito; this provides opportunities for an amusing satire upon Australia's attitude of moral and physical superiority over the countries of decadent Europe:

> "*Mens sana in corpore sano* is our human ideal," explained Colonel Necker the Minister for Public Modesty smiling, "but we translate it, perhaps, a little differently from you English. For us it means, 'The mind of a little child in a sound body'." His eyes bent upwards, responding to an impulse of simple, unselfconscious piety.[57]

Art and science, it is added, are guided, shaped and sterilized, and dangerous influences are carefully controlled, with the result that "a new and vital culture" has been achieved; but the satire becomes so extravagant as to dull some points that might have otherwise struck home, as when the Commissioner for Police remarks that the Arbitration System is used to reduce wages, and the Chief Censor admits[58] that

> ". . . there *are* signs of some of the older peoples following our lead. . . . There is a definite tendency on the part of German leaders to discard old, specious considerations of individual liberty. Their methods are a little crude, but they appear to be effective under German conditions."

An earlier book of Harcourt's, *Upsurge* (London, 1934),[59] though obviously a novel of purpose is not necessarily a satire, and it seems to be the intention here to present the unemphasized truth as the author sees it. *Upsurge* sets out to describe the social injustice and degeneracy of an Australian city, Perth in this instance, during the Depression: it is a much more realistic story than the other; its men and women are much more lifelike, and in particular the principal character, a stipendiary magistrate who does his best to temper law with justice; but the last part of the book reads like a communistic manifesto, though it is much better done than Frank Hardy's *Power Without Glory*. Finally, by Jane Lindsay, Norman Lindsay's daughter (Mrs Bruce Glad, Sydney, 1920-) a novel of pure humour: *Kurrajong* (Sydney, 1945) is in the direct line of descent from Steele Rudd's selection stories; it is slighter, and the talent and personality revealed in it are less remarkable, but it never runs into extravaganza. One might have lived in the little world of the Learys and Miss Wiggins and Mrs Rooney and their gossip and slander and petty pilferings; and Brusher, though only the slightest of pencil sketches, is unique.

---

[57] This may be compared with the criticism of the visiting European in *The Mortal and the Marble*, see p. 1168.

[58] pp. 247-8.

[59] There was a still earlier novel, *The Pearlers* (London, 1933), which was based on Harcourt's experience with the pearling fleet and at Broome.

CHAPTER X

THE NOVEL

Novels of Purpose: Penton; Herbert; Others. War Novels: Leonard Mann; Hetherington; Aldridge; Glassop; Others. Novels of Adventure: Close; Collins; Kaye; Walford; Meller; Others. Fantasies: Helen Simpson; Others. Children's Stories: Norman Lindsay; Others. Detective Stories. Expatriates. Visitors: Lawrence; Grattan

IN A novel of purpose, as in a satire, which is indeed a special instance of purposive writing, an aspect of the life and conditions described is usually emphasized to make some point; but the author is in this dilemma, that if the emphasis is slight his point may be missed, or at least not made strongly enough to be impressive; on the other hand the emphasis if strong may create such distortion as will weaken the effect desired because the picture is too far from reality. The second defect attaches, though in different degrees, to each of the three novels now to be discussed: in the strength of their emphasis, as well as in their subject, Penton's *Landtakers* and *Inheritors* recall *His Natural Life*, which is their nearest analogue, and Herbert's *Capricornia*, which goes still further, recalls *Uncle Tom's Cabin*. On the other hand, belonging as Penton and Herbert do to an unromantic age, Penton, unlike Clarke, never falls into melodrama or deliquesces into sentimentality, and Herbert stops just short of either. Penton is a straight-out iconoclast, determined to explode the romantic conception of pioneering and the pioneers, particularly in the early days of Queensland; Herbert's purpose is to hold up to hatred touched with ridicule the callous treatment of the Aborigines in northern Australia and the clumsy inefficiency of its official persons and institutions. The atmospheres of the work of these two novelists differ widely, for whereas Penton seems to take an almost sadistic pleasure in uncovering and emphasizing hatreds and degrading brutalities that have been hitherto largely ignored, with Herbert the same sort of treatment results from a supersensitiveness that makes him suffer while he describes. Both writers are extremely bitter, but along with Penton's bitterness there is a larger intellectual element, and though by no means without sympathy he has his sympathies well under control and is moved as a rule rather by anger than by pity. With Herbert on the other hand there is at least as much pity as hatred; his sympathies are primarily emotional and sometimes flow like a flood: the result in each case is that the viewpoint is distorted, and the novelist creates, not so much a world in which there is a great deal of inhumanity, as a world in which humanity is the rare exception, so that it approaches, in Herbert's case especially, the borderline of hell. Brian Con Penton (Brisbane, 1904-51), was educated at the Brisbane Grammar School and the University of Queensland. He became a journalist, and was for a while political correspondent at Canberra of the *Sydney Morning Herald*; he paid two visits to England, the second of which was highly successful, and there, incidentally, he was co-editor, with Jack Lindsay, of the Fanfrolico Press;[1] later he became editor of the Sydney *Daily Telegraph*. Besides his two novels Penton published a couple of sociological booklets which are mentioned elsewhere. *Landtakers* (Sydney, 1934) and *Inheritors* (Sydney, 1936, and, as *Giant's Stride*, London, 1936) tell between them the story of Derek Cabell, a young Englishman of good family, sensitive and diffident but defiant and pertinacious, who migrates to Queensland in the early forties to escape the bullying contempt of his father and elder brothers. But in the Queensland of those early days he finds himself in a society of floggers and jailbirds and blackguardly adventurers, cruel, callous and quite conscienceless, whose atmosphere is almost that of a madhouse;[2] here also he is cheated and bullied, but he gradually coarsens and hardens until he can meet his surroundings, human and other, on their own plane. After seventeen years' struggle with every kind of difficulty and misfortune—flood, fire, plagues of all kinds, squalor and drudgery, cheating and loneliness—he emerges a bitter and predatory old hawk, successful but also as coarse and conscienceless as the worst of his neighbours, and on the lookout for even greater wealth. This he attains, and along with it, on account of his philanthropies, a knighthood; finally, after turning out and trying to murder his eldest son, he is subdued and overruled by a younger son whom he had always despised and regarded as harmless, his only relief being the affection of a daughter who had run away from him. Penton refers to the "battered old relic out of the past"[3] who had been Cabell or was the origin of Cabell, to other survivors from the past, and to gossip and memoirs and memories as the sources of his conception of those early days. But his eye was by no means single and he overdoes his case: it is clear that he was as anxious as Furphy to tear up and tread upon what may be called the Kingsley picture of the origins of the squattocracy; but Penton's target is the conception not of the romantic young hero from England but of the "glorious pioneers" in general, men who, according to their descendants, "were gentlemen and lived like gentlemen". And whereas Furphy attacks, at his most outright, in a mood of sarcastic fury, and Herbert

[1] The Fanfrolico Press was founded and managed in London by Australians and published McCrae's poems, Jack Lindsay's version of *Lysistrata*, and several other Australian books.

[2] "Really all these early settlers were just slightly off the hinges" (*Landtakers*, p. 30).

[3] *Landtakers*, p. 28.

throughout in a mood in which fury unsubdued is mixed with sympathy, Penton seems to take a bitter and almost ghoulish pleasure in his iconoclasm; in particular he shows up the pioneers through one of the crudest of their survivors, Old Purvis, at Peppiott's dinner to "the nicest people", some so nice that they "could not stand living in Australia for more than six months at a time"; says Old Purvis:[4]

> "Them were the days, eh Cabell? Nothin' here but blacks, and a durn sight better neighbours than some white folks they were. Pity we shot 'em all off."
>
> "Shot them?" Mrs Peppiott said. "Oh, how dreadful. The poor defenceless creatures. And so interesting. You must come to a meeting of our Aborigines Protection League. You know they prove all about the missing link. So invaluable to science."
>
> "I don't know anything about that," Purvis said. "I know your old man shot 'em the same as we all did." He chuckled. "I mind the time he tied a gin up to a cart-wheel and. . . ."
>
> "Yes, yes," Peppiott said, "Mrs Peppiott merely means that it's a pity the exigencies of the times compelled the white man to take such extreme measures against a people so unique."
>
> "Exigencies of the times, you call it? We called it shortage of wimmin. I mind the day. . . ."
>
> "Do have some more wine, Mr Purvis," Mrs Peppiott put in.
>
> "A drink. Well, I wouldn't spit in it."

As Cabell's outspoken daughter, Harriet, says:[5]

> A horrible, lurking fear of the past was in [the descendants of the pioneers], not only of the brand of convictism but of the spirit of convictism and the wild recklessness of the old hands from which many savage deeds had come. They were afraid of that crude, reckless spirit their fathers had handed on to them and they tried to kill it in themselves as others. And when they couldn't kill it they pretended that it was not there, as when they pretended that she was a little mad, and that Cabell was really a nice man, and that nothing had really happened in the past which was not nice, and that all convicts had been sent out for stealing a loaf of bread.

With all Penton's and Herbert's over-emphasis however, and with Furphy's also for that matter, it is well that the truth underlying what they have to say should be brought to mind. And if the life that Penton describes is coloured by his hatred of hypocrisy and his bitter indignation at the evils that darkened it, we must, in fairness, remember that it is being seen to some extent through the bleared eyes and recorded through the withered lips of the lonely and battered relic upon whom he relies so largely. Some historical errors and anachronisms in the story have been pointed out,[6] but none of these are fundamental, and, allowing for the pervading atmosphere of morbidity that results from the assemblage of so many callous and degrading brutalities, every character and every action is in itself extremely real: Cabell himself and the gradual relentless

---

[4] *Inheritors*, pp. 216–17.
[5] The same, p. 223.
[6] In, for instance, the Brisbane *Courier-Mail*, 7th July 1934.

development of the sensitive youngster into the predatory old hawk; the insolent, bullying, bloody-minded McGovern, of whom the young Cabell lives in fear and hatred, and yet in some subtle way almost admires: these two especially are living men. Their early relationship is illustrated when at the height of his offensive dominance McGovern hands Cabell a loaded fowling-piece, the muzzle against his own stomach: Cabell is so overmastered by McGovern's superior strength of character that he is afraid to pull the trigger.[7] It is interesting to note that, long afterwards, when Cabell has developed a hardness and self-confidence of his own, he produces a somewhat similar effect on weaker men. Cabell is having trouble with his shearers: "See here," says the union organizer,[8]

> "We've got four hundred men with a hundred rifles and revolvers, and soon there'll be a lot of dust. Who'd know where a bullet came from?"
>
> "Ach," Larry said impatiently, "nobody'll shoot him. If you was to put the muzzle up against his heart and pull the trigger you wouldn't hurt him. He's always won. He always will."

And there is the unfortunate Gursey, who lives in fear that he will be caught and returned to the convictism from which Cabell has helped him to escape, and who is yet obsessed by a dread that Cabell himself will betray him to the authorities: Gursey, through whom runs, curiously but as it is made to appear quite naturally, a streak of republican idealism, is, as painfully as McGovern is horribly, real. And the scenes of action are as good as all but the very best of Marcus Clarke's: there is Micky's story of how McGovern got the convicts out of the store shed; there is Cabell's struggle with McGovern, who is finally killed by Cabell's wife with an axe; there is Larry's fight with his father; there is the campaign against innumerable obstacles and misfortunes on Cabell's first trip down to Brisbane with wool. Yet here and there these two novels are relieved by passages that show that Cabell, and Penton, can appreciate beauty; there is for instance the description of the valley in which Cabell finally takes up his run, and there is this, which is a little more typical:[9]

> As he rode north and west he looked anxiously for those stretches of water which made travel a hell at this season of the year but promised good times to come. He saw only the rolling downs of last year's grass, with patches of red earth where the sheep had eaten [it] out. The rains were late, but the sky remained like a dome of bone, and in the last burst of summer the earth pulsed and throbbed, throwing up heat-veils, like swathes of silk stirred by a wind, behind which trees and rocks seemed to be reflected in a distorting mirror. Sometimes it was so hot that the stirrup-irons burnt

---

[7] *Landtakers*, p. 93. There is also, quite as illustrative but too long to quote, the incident in which McGovern, out of casual devilry, crushes Cabell against a doorway, when he is trying to pass through (pp. 44–5).

[8] *Inheritors*, pp. 324–5.

[9] *Landtakers*, p. 380. See also pp. 147 and 337.

> his feet through the soles of his boots. At sundown the stars flashed out of a colorless sky, great, breathing stars. From time to time a steady beat of wings broke the silence as birds passed southwards. A threat hung over the plain, the sheep panting in the shade, the cattle standing belly-deep in the waterholes to cool themselves, and Cabell trailing a cloud of dust along the deserted road.

But indeed the realism of Penton's two novels, limited only by their over-accentuation in a particular direction, is an essentially imaginative realism: Penton sees and records not only what is there, however he may distort his total effects by selection and emphasis, but also what the directly observable facts merely suggest. And his imagination crystallizes the atmosphere of what he observes in occasional images: "A piece of bark flapped like a bird in a trap"; "The darkness was like a jelly"; "The air was heavy—like wadding to the nostrils".

In spite of the gap in time between the events of the two novels, and although, as is almost inevitably the case with a sequel, the second is slightly thinner than the first, there is a definite unity about the story as a whole. But there is little construction: it all fits together neatly and clearly enough, but there are few signs of plot or pattern, and many of the actions and incidents with which it is crowded could be transposed without loss. This crowding, together with the lack of arrangement, produces a slightly confused effect; it is almost as though one were swept through the masses of floating debris carried along by the current of a river in flood: it is not a swift but a powerful current, which there is no escaping, and the sights and the rough contacts create an atmosphere of apprehension; it all partakes of the nature of a nightmare. The two novels are characteristic though exceptional in Australian fiction in their insistence upon individual effort and in their atmosphere of crude power: but they are by no means crudely written; on the contrary Penton is a practised writer, who understands how to say exactly what he wants to say, how to produce exactly the effect he wants to produce. Like Clarke, he understands also how to tell a story; he contrives to draw the reader, fascinated almost in spite of himself, through scenes and actions and disclosures of fact or character that are heavily streaked with what, coming from another writer, would merely disgust.

Capricornia (Sydney, 1938) is much farther from the real world than Penton's novels, because in it there is exaggeration as well as over-emphasis by selection, and, incidentally, because of Herbert's nomenclature, which is so crude and obvious that in some cases it produces the effect of a bad joke; not merely the story as a whole but everything in it is made subject to the general thesis, so that one is almost always conscious of the guiding hand of its creator in the background. Herbert is quite as sincere as Penton, but his purpose is different: he aims at presenting truth, but it is an underlying truth, not actuality, and in drawing his characters and incidents he has always this underlying truth in mind; one feels that, however realistic within their limits, they are always exemplifications: he is concerned, that is to say, not so much with the re-creation of people and things as he has observed them, as with the total impression they have produced upon him, the bitter and sometimes furious emotions they have aroused; he is concerned with them almost wholly as they supply a basis for these emotions and a means of communicating them. Indeed it seems likely that in many cases he has not so much exaggerated what he saw, as seen what in the light of his general impression he has expected to see. He can be much more poignant than Penton, because the callousness and cruelty he exposes are practised at the expense of men and women and children who lack even the possibility of effective resistance to or escape from their oppression and degradation; moreover they have done nothing to deserve their treatment, and they belong not to a past and largely ignored period of history but to the present day, or to a day that may almost be regarded as the present. If the nearest analogue to *Capricornia* is *Uncle Tom's Cabin*, its strongest antithesis is *We of the Never Never*. Herbert and Mrs Gunn deal each with an aspect of the life of the Territory which the other neglects: Mrs Gunn neglects the hard and cruel aspects of that life, either deliberately or because they did not come within her experience; Herbert ignores the pleasanter aspects because they do not suit his purpose, or perhaps it may have blinded him to them. It might have been supposed that the visible guidance of the author's hand in character and incident would detract from the life of the book and cause it to become monotonous; but Herbert's men and women, though types are not mere counters; each possesses a sharply marked and vigorous individuality, even if his sphere is limited and determined, and the abundance of vigorous action makes against monotony. Again, the book is loosely knit and so lacking in construction that on a first reading it is sometimes hard to find one's way about its close-packed pages; yet it is so informed with the author's angry fire, many of the incidents are so dramatic or at least touching, almost all of them are so lively and often so exciting that one is carried forward through the crowded and sometimes confusing improbabilities.

Alfred Francis Xavier Herbert (Port Hedland, W.A., 1901-), was born in the north-west of Western Australia; his father was a railway-locomotive engineer, and as a child he got to know intimately half-wild Aborigines, talking with them in their own language. After attending various schools he studied pharmacy at the Universities of Western Australia and Melbourne; he turned to literature and journalism, travelled over a great part of outback northern Australia, worked as stockman, railway fettler, sleeper-cutter, prospector, and diver for pearls on a

Japanese lugger, and was for a couple of years a Protector of Aborigines at Darwin: on the whole he probably knows as much about outback northern Australia and its inhabitants as most people. He also spent two years in Britain, which impressed him as a country just as foreign as France, and in the second World War was a sergeant in the A.I.F. Besides *Capricornia*, Herbert has published a number of short stories which have not been collected; *Capricornia* was awarded in 1938 the Commonwealth 150th Anniversary Prize for the best novel published or accepted for publication during 1937, and the gold medal of the Australian Literary Society in 1939, and in 1940 Herbert was awarded a Commonwealth Literary Fellowship. Through the crowded scenes and crowding persons of his book runs the story of Norman,[10] the unwanted and at first entirely neglected result of the casual acquaintance of a lubra and Mark Shillingsworth, a young government official who has dropped out of the inflated and snobbish society of "Port Zodiac" into association with disreputable white men and the aborigines; to these and their dogs the baby is abandoned, but he is later adopted, at first very unwillingly, by Mark's brother Oscar, whom he grows to look upon as a father. Norman spends his boyhood on Mark's station and is later trained in Melbourne as a fitter on the Victorian railways; few bother about his dark skin there, and as he grows up he develops character, self-respect and much more ability than the average white man. When he goes north again on a visit to his adopted father he believes himself to be the grandson of a Javanese sultan, and therefore unaffected by the "taint" of aboriginal blood. He easily attains the standards of intelligent white men and makes a number of practical inventions of value to the station; gradually he discovers that the Javanese sultan is a myth, but he refuses to be subdued by the contempt and insults he receives as a half-caste. With Norman's story is closely connected that of Tocky, the poor little mixed-blood whose death, or rather its discovery, is the most poignant episode in the book. In spite of its tragic burden, *Capricornia* is by no means without humour, but the humour is for the most part bitter and ironic. Some of the sarcasms are mordant; good examples are to be found in the account of the first invasion and early settlement of the North: "Primitive people that [the aborigines] were, they regarded their territorial rights as sacred"; and, after telling drily how some of the whites "conceived the idea of making friends with them and giving them several bags of flour spiced with arsenic", Herbert remarks, "Thus civilization was at last planted permanently." There is also the nomenclature, but here the sarcasm is so crude that it falls flat: there is Judge Pondrosass, of the

10 The name Norman was derived from Naw-nim, No-name, the name "usually given by the natives to dogs for which they had no love but had not the heart to kill or lose" (*Capricornia*, p. 40). Another novel of Herbert's, *Seven Emus*, was published in Sydney in 1959.

Capricornian Court; Bleeter and Hollower, missionaries; Brittins Willnot, the discoverer of the site of Port Zodiac, and so on. Official personages had of course to be invented or disguised, but it is hard to say why imaginary names should have been given to places: the identification of Capricornia and Port Zodiac is obvious, and if it were to be argued that Herbert did not want to suggest that the Territory and Darwin were the sort of places he describes, then his thesis would fall down. *Capricornia* is for the most part competently written, but Herbert is no stylist: he is not careful enough and has not sufficient feeling for the sound and associations of words to enable him to give fit expression to some of the actions and situations he conceives; for this reason it is not easy to do him full justice in quotation. The most striking of the tragic scenes are scenes of action, but in the two following[11] there is, in all the circumstances, a deeper tragedy. Norman, insulted and despised when it is made clear that he is a mere "yeller feller", breaks away from friends and enemies into the bush:

> On the third day he became quite cheerful, as the result of discovering for the first time in his life that he was thinking deeply. This he did through solving with a minute's thought a problem in mechanics that had been puzzling him for weeks. Encouraged to ponder other problems with what he thought remarkable success, he began to feel for the first time in his life that he was clever. Soon he forgot his debasement. And he found himself marvelling at the phenomenon of his existence as a creature, of the existence of Mankind, and of nature's contrariety to Man that made Man's ingenuity essential. And for the first time in his life he began consciously to doubt the existence of the conventional Divinity in which he had been trained to believe, and to wonder about the Something he could see in the stars. So he came to marvel at Infinity instead of fearing it. The third night he forgot the phantoms roused by his fire in pondering over the phenomena of combustion.
>
> He retained this pleasant state of mind till he reached Tatlock's Pool. He arrived there at noon on the fifth day, loving all Mankind. He departed two hours later cursing the Universe. For Backhouse and Donniken received him as they might any wandering yeller-feller, questioned him as rudely as they might a nigger, and as though he were a nigger did not ask him in to dinner but sent a portion out to him in a tin plate to eat on the veranda. He was amazed at first. For a while he sat staring at the nigger's dollop, then rose and went away. Backhouse and Donniken were surprised to find him gone, then annoyed to find his food aswarm with ants.

And here is Norman's discovery of how Tocky and her baby, his baby, had died:[12]

> Norman, spluttering with laughter, went across to the stock-tanks to drink. He was drinking from a trough, when he was startled by the sudden appearance of two crows that swept up from out the broken tank. Then he noticed fluttering from the rim of the tank a piece of dusty blue cloth. He stared. The cloth fell limp, fluttered, fell again. Dry grass rattled against the iron. Dry wind moaned through rust-eaten

---

[11] p. 295. All quotations from *Capricornia* are from the (Sydney) 1943 edition.
[12] pp. 509-10.

holes. He stepped up to the tank and peeped through a hole. Nothing to see but the rusty wall beyond. He climbed the ladder, looked inside, saw a skull and a litter of bones. He gasped. A human skull—no—two—a small one and a tiny one. And human hair and rags of clothes and a pair of bone-filled boots. Two skulls, a small one and [a] tiny one. Tocky and her baby!

The crows alighted in a gnarled dead coolibah near by and cried dismally, "Kah!-Kah!-Kaaaaah!"

When a novel has a striking social or historic bearing it is tempting to concentrate upon this to the comparative neglect of everything else: so it has been with many critics in dealing with Penton's and Herbert's novels; and social or historic analysis may indeed affect the literary value of a kind of literature which has to be above all a reflection of life. But even apart from limiting considerations of form, it is as such a reflection that the literary value of such a novel must be considered; the human quality must come before the social or historical: with all their faults, these three novels are emphatically human; their observations are imaginative and not merely scientific, and each in its way is individual and written with considerable force.

In the last year of the Period appeared another large-scale novel of purpose which may be discussed here, though its literary value is small compared with that of *Capricornia* or *Landtakers* and *Inheritors*. It is an exposure of the social and political evils of the capitalist system, as seen mainly in Victoria between 1890 and the present day. Its author, Francis Joseph Hardy[13] (Southern Cross, Vic., 1917-), left school at thirteen and has been at one time or another messenger and news boy, grocer's assistant, fruit and vegetable picker, factory worker and black and white artist; in 1942 he joined the A.I.F.; he has travelled in England, Germany, Poland and Soviet Russia, and now lives in Victoria. *Power Without Glory*[14] (Melbourne, 1950), which is to be "the first of a series of novels, planned to give a picture of the mainstreams of Australian life in the 20th century",[15] was inspired by Balzac, but is actually of the type of Upton Sinclair's novels; it has been translated into a number of foreign languages. It is written to a formula, and its men and women are little more than factors in an equation, so that, though extremely vigorous and by no means without bloodshed, it is a bloodless story; a number of leading politicians and other public men are introduced with little disguise, but none of them is really alive. Crammed with action and incident, the book is almost structureless and quite without perspective and the style is crude and commonplace, so that it is monotonous and dull; nevertheless, it has sincerity and force, and there is no doubt about its author's talent, if he cared to devote it to literature instead of social

---

[13] Hardy has also published a number of short stories, and a novel about the racing industry.

[14] There is an excellent analysis of *Power Without Glory* by Flora Eldershaw in *Meanjin*, vol. ix, No. 3 (Spring, 1950), pp. 222-5.

[15] Author's note.

propaganda.* Another novel of purpose, in this case neither political nor historical but economic, is Marshall's *How Beautiful Are Thy Feet* (Melbourne, 1949). It deals, like Tennant's *The Battlers*,[16] and to some extent her *Foveaux*;[17] like Mann's *Go-Getter*[18] and like a considerable part of Eldershaw's *Tomorrow and Tomorrow*;[19] with the Depression as it affected the Australian worker; in this case as it affected a Melbourne boot factory, the hands, the heads and the business. It is both a story and a study: the story is simple and lifelike and involves some good character-sketches; the study, as embodied in a stream, or rather a succession of small floods, of consciousness, now the author's and now one or other of the factory hands, which introduces many of the chapters,[20] is, in spite of its evident sincerity, dull. Alan Marshall (Noorat, Vic., 1902–84) was educated at a Victorian country school; he had a crippled childhood and had to use crutches throughout his life, but this did not prevent him from travelling in Asia as well as his own country. He is best known as a short-story writer,[21] but also published descriptive works[22] and humorous sketches and won several literary prizes.

The novels that arose out of the first World War did not begin to appear until well on in the present Period, so that two separate sets of war novels are included in this section; but many of those soldiers who left literary records preferred to give straight accounts of their military experiences rather than to wrap them up imaginatively, and these will be discussed later.[23] Of the first set of war novels, only five need be mentioned here, of which two stand out. Leonard Mann's *Flesh in Armour*[24] (Melbourne, 1932) is, as one would expect from Mann, a steady, simple, lifelike story, fundamentally tragic and yet restrained and by no means without humour. It tells, with Mann's characteristic seemingly casual intensity, of a platoon and in particular of three of its members, as they move through the fighting in France and as they fare in England, in hospital and on leave. The impression made on them by official England, cold, formal, condescending, as distinct from private individuals, who are friendly enough, is exemplified in the entertainment of "other ranks" by the duchess in the Lower Servants' Hall; and the widespread distrust of the British generals and staffs, the fortuitous "affairs" of men segregated from almost all womenfolk; all these, with the final quotation from Monash, go far beyond individual and platoon and shadow forth better than any other novel the characteristics and

* [The publication of the novel resulted in Hardy's arraignment on a criminal libel charge, the outcome of which was equivocal; the pros and cons were discussed in Niall Brennan's *John Wren: Gambler* (Melbourne, 1971). The artistic question remains unaffected by the relation of the novel to facts: it gives little pleasure as art, and inspires little confidence as documentary.]

[16] See pp. 1097–8, 1103–4. [17] See p. 1098. [18] See pp. 1139–43. [19] See pp. 1187–9.

[20] Dos Passos used similar introductions in several novels, but on a different plan.

[21] See p. 1247. [22] See pp. 1385–6. [23] See pp. 1406–16.

[24] The armour referred to is the qualities of "duty and military necessity, fortitude, endurance and courage" (p. 63). For Mann's other novels, see pp. 1137–43; for his verse, pp. 994–8.

experiences of the ordinary members of the first A.I.F. A connecting thread that helps to bind the book together is the tragic story of the sensitive and idealistic ex-school-teacher who finds himself increasingly unable to meet the demands of war; and of poor Mary, self-immolated, another war sacrifice *Crucible* (Sydney, 1935) is an even more factual novel. Its author, John Phillip McKinney (Numurkah, Vic., 1891-1966), was educated at Scotch College, Melbourne, served for four years with the A.I.F. Light Horse and Cycle Corps, and was mentioned in dispatches; he was a journalist, and a drover, then a farmer in Queensland, where he married the poet Judith Wright. *Crucible* is narrower in range than *Flesh in Armour*, for it lacks the other's general conclusions, sticking closer to France and direct observation; there is no binding thread of romance, and no "Blighty" episodes are developed: but the novel deals not only with the actual fighting and life in the trenches but with the personal experiences of the narrator as assistant to a Town Major, and with a French "affair" and the problems set by its consequences. It is a more introspective story than the other, if less broadly thoughtful, but there are some amusing episodes, as of the tactful major with a revolver handy, persuading a party of stragglers to return to the front line; and some amusing sketches, as of a typical Australian batman, and the effect of his friendly familiarity upon a couple of "Tommy officers". *Trooper to the Southern Cross*[25] (London, 1934), by "Leslie Parker", pseudonym of Angela Thirkell (*née* Mackail), a popular English novelist who lived for some years in Tasmania, is an entertaining as well as informative account of events which occurred during the first World War; the novel is coloured strongly by the simple, practical, and the consciously and unconsciously amusing personality of the narrator, who was a medical major, of what may well have occurred more than once or twice on a repatriation voyage. Two other Australian novels might alternatively be grouped as fantasies: their subjects are imagined sudden invasions of an entirely unprepared Australia by an Oriental power; they were published during the interval between the two World Wars and intended as warnings. *The Awakening* (Sydney, 1937), by Major G. D. Mitchell,[26] is an adventurous and exciting desciption of the building up in North Queensland by an ex-A.I.F. major, on the basis of a mob of "unemployed cane workers and hoboes from the huts and camps along the seashore", of a bush commando that inflicts huge losses on the invaders until the inevitable tragic end. *Fools' Harvest* (Melbourne, 1939), by Erle Cox, (Melbourne, 1873-1950) a Melbourne journalist and author of a fantasy to be mentioned later,[27] is more detailed and as it were more factual;

---

[25] Reissued in 1939 as *What Happened on the Boat.*

[26] For biographical details, and a discussion of Mitchell's more important "straight" war narrative, see pp. 1406-7.

[27] See pp. 1228-9.

it begins with the smashing of the cities and continues with a bush resistance movement, and with the sabotage that is the only remaining resource after the whole country has been subdued and its inhabitants conscripted to forced labour: in both books the behaviour of the invaders is such as seemed to most people incredible at the time of their publication.

The second World War's crop of novels has ripened earlier than that of the first World War, but several of the best had not appeared by the closing date of this History. Most war novels are novels of adventure, but in those now to be discussed it is more than usually evident, in part no doubt because they are not confined to the deadly monotony of life in the trenches; and perhaps for this reason also, or perhaps because their authors are often journalists, there is a stronger tendency among these later novelists towards romance. This is most evident in three novels set in Greece or Crete, among British and Australian soldiers who were trying to escape after the evacuation; all three are by well-known Australian war correspondents who wrote from personal experience, and who are of the tribe of Hemingway, though in the first and best his influence is confined almost entirely to outlook and atmosphere. John Aikman Hetherington (Sandringham, Vic., 1907-74), was in Greece with the A.I.F. during the war as representative in the Middle East of British and American newspapers and of the Melbourne *Herald*, for which he was a special writer. His only novel, *The Winds Are Still*[28] (Melbourne, 1947), is a simple and moving story, told simply and naturally, sharp in action and characterization; one remembers in particular old Boudaris, who deliberately runs the risk of losing and does in fact lose his own life and the lives of most of his family, for the sake not of the escaping soldiers whom he protects, but of freedom, without which life "is like a song without a tune". There is a touching love episode which recalls but does not imitate a corresponding episode in *For Whom the Bell Tolls*; the author avoids the temptation to a happy ending, and the hard tension set up by the perpetual fear of capture and the continual efforts to discover a way of escape affects the reader as well as the characters: y t the story falls somehow short of what one feels that it might have attained; something is lacking, perhaps in the experience, perhaps in the personality of the author. The other two novels are not strictly Australian; their author, (Harold Edward) James Aldridge (Bendigo, Vic., 1919-), who had some adventurous experiences as a war correspondent and privately, in the Balkans, Greece and Syria, as well as in Finland, Norway and Russia, has not returned from London, where he went in 1938. Still, both novels contain Australian characters, and there is something Australian about them. In *Signed With Their*

[28] This won first prize in the *Sydney Morning Herald*'s war novel competition in 1946. Hetherington also wrote short stories, and other work, for which, see pp. 1413-16.

Honour[29] (Melbourne, 1943) and *The Sea Eagle* (Melbourne, 1944) Hemingway's influence is inescapable everywhere, and in the style this is accompanied by reminiscences of Lawrence and Stein; both stories are bogged down in masses of detail: a succession of short sharp incidents is described in short sharp sentences and short sharp paragraphs, in the early Hemingway manner laconic and restrained. All this makes for artificiality, and there is also an individual artificiality which in the second novel is carried, as in the following,[30] so far that it becomes absurd:

> The one with wild red beard and softening eyes that were benevolent; but the stature was a mountain, and the red hair a forest.
>
> The other a genie, a Greek, black-coated with shiny burnt skin; with square white teeth and a dome, a dome that towered and made the thick eyebrows bush out in wild joy.

There are also out-of-place Americanisms,[31] a profusion of "ands",[32] and occasional clumsinesses: all this makes the style tiresome, reinforcing the forest of detail; nevertheless these books deserve mention because of their piercing vision and sharp realism, and, above all, their vibrant energy. Aldridge was to write at least one far better novel, but it does not fall within our scope. Glassop's *We Were the Rats* (Sydney, 1944) is both factual and romantic; a succession of incidents and episodes, casual, humorous, tragic, illuminating, real and natural but without constructional framework; yet there is about it an atmosphere of romance which is personified in Mick Reynolds, the principal character, and radiates from him, continually escaping through the sardonic crust with which he does his best to cover it, and slipping sometimes into rank sentimentality: nevertheless this is a vital novel; it is concerned with real flesh and blood, and it sets the reader in the midst of the life it describes. (Jack) Lawson Glassop (Lawson, N.S.W., 1913-66), was educated at the Newcastle High School, joined the *Newcastle Morning Herald* and served with the A.I.F. for two years in the Middle East; he was not himself in Tobruk, but used every opportunity to talk to those who had been, and learn all he could about the life of the "rats". He writes sincerely and frankly, and aims at showing the men of Tobruk exactly as they were, without either concealing or parading aspects and in particular sexual aspects of a soldier's life of which everyone is aware, though a few like to pretend that it does not exist; for this reason Glassop was prosecuted and found guilty of obscenity, with the result of course that everybody read his book. But apart from its frankness and vitality, it

[29] For the reference, see opposite the title-page.

[30] p. 119. Also, "He was so without breath it was inadequate" (p. 42); "Nisus was acquiring anger" (p. 71); "Then laughed in quick softening" (p. 107).

[31] "Met up with" (pp. 6, 32); "Like that the two Australians came" (p. 7).

[32] On p. 5, for example.

is individual: with some of the incidents and types of character we are already familiar, but they are natural and so well and sharply realized that the author makes them his own; also the novel is illuminative, not only of an aspect of life, but of an aspect of Australian life. Reynolds's mates represent a large section[33] of modern Australian society, and their remarks and actions, though not of course peculiarly Australian, have an Australian flavour; for example the remark about the Pyramid of Cheops: "I dunno," said Eddie, staring up at the rugged triangle of stones, "it's just a heap of rocks"; and the corporal's explanation to the colonel of the real reason why a patrol went out into no-man's-land, losing two of its members:

> "We didn't go out to get Blue Carter's body. What's the use of bodies anyhow once they're dead? We went out to get thirty-five pounds he won at two-up. We wanted to send it home to his wife."

This novel is however handicapped by the personality of its hero. He is, if we could accept him as a real person, a genuine hero, whom his mates enormously admire, but besides being an Admirable Crichton and ostentatiously modest, he is naïve, self-conscious and extremely snobbish: with an educated companion he talks like a second-rate intellectual and, though with his ordinary mates he is just one of themselves, he not infrequently lets a piece of learning slip out, apologizing for it afterwards; he also refuses a Military Medal for fear that his sweetheart will learn that he is in the fighting line. But if it is hard to imagine Mick as real, and harder still to imagine him as popular, there is no doubt about the reality of the book as a whole. A second novel of Glassop's, *Lucky Palmer* (Sydney, 1949), is concerned with a "sportsman" and his friends who like to bet on races, and will lie and cheat as a matter of course in order to get money to bet with or to win a bet. It is a spirited and realistic study of a particular aspect of life, but this is not given any particular significance. Richard Sydney Porteous ("Standby", Melbourne, 1898–1963) takes his place among the small group of modern English writers about war and the sea who know their job and can tell a story that is exciting and does not overstep the boundary of probable fact. He was a station overseer and a Light Horseman during the first World War and also served on coastal ships; in the second World War he was First Mate on a small vessel carrying troops and army supplies along the coast of New Guinea, and this gave him the material for *Sailing Orders*[34] (Sydney, 1949). The story is conventional, but the conventions are given life; all is shipshape and the style is crisp and succinct.

---

[33] See *We Were the Rats*, p. 84.

[34] This was awarded second prize in the *Sydney Morning Herald*'s competition in 1946 for the best war novel. In 1958 he published *Brigalow*, an outback novel. For Porteous's short stories, see p. 1256.

The spirit of adventure runs across all boundaries, and in this section are included novels in which that spirit on the whole takes charge, no matter whether they deal with land or sea, town or country, farm or station or the Never Never. The general stirring-up of the world, in which wars have been merely the preponderant factor; the revulsion from convention and the everyday and the desire for new scenes and new modes of life; and, in the literary world, the incidental swing away from psychology towards action which is most evident in the neo-barbaric novelists of the United States; these things together have given rise to a crop of adventure novels, as well as to a number of "true" tales of adventure which are dealt with elsewhere.[35] The present Period has produced the first Australian-born novelist to write about the sea and the life of the sailor; others had brought them into their stories, but none had made them his principal subject: this may seem surprising in that Australia has an unbroken sea boundary, but her peculiar situation has caused almost all her writers[36] to be concerned until lately with her own individual life rather than with the comparatively cosmopolitan life of the sea. Robert (Shaw) Close[37] (Camberwell, Vic., 1903-) attended a technical college but at fourteen shipped as apprentice on a sailing ship and afterwards in tramp steamers; he failed for his second mate's certificate owing to colour-blindness, and tuberculosis prevented a possible career as a singer, so that writing was only his third choice. With his two novels Australia's sea fiction has made a good beginning, for Close takes one to sea with him as few writers do. *Love Me Sailor* (Melbourne, 1945) was, like several other good Australian novels, banned for obscenity. Its theme is the shipping of a nymphomaniac on a windjammer in the care of the captain, and the effect upon its rough and simple sex-starved crew; the treatment of the theme is extremely frank, but though Close conceals nothing and slurs nothing, he is never pornographic and the situation acts as a stimulant to bring out the characters of the seamen and their officers more sharply and rapidly than if they had been brought out by ordinary events. The story is full of action and physical movement, out of which the conversations immediately arise; it has something in common with the neo-barbaric novels of the United States, but this does not extend much further than the type to which it belongs, for the main influence here is that of Conrad; there is no suggestion of Hemingway and the author has an individuality of his own. The characters however are only sketched, though sharply

[35] See pp. 1401-6.

[36] Porteous's *Little Known of These Waters* had appeared in the same years; this was a collection of short stories; his first novel, *Sailing Orders*, which is discussed with other war novels on p. 1220, appeared in 1949. There had also been J. A. Barry (see pp. 618, 732) but he was not Australian-born; and in verse there were of course Brady's and others' sea ballads.

[37] Close has also published short stories that have not yet been collected.

and strongly: of the woman herself we do not really know anything that is not obvious. *The Dupe* (Melbourne, 1948) is technically a better book: but though it is vigorous enough, action and conversation are real, and there is plenty of drama, this book has not the zest, the careless abandon of the other, its onrush of quick life. The difference between the two books is exemplified in the style, which in *Love Me Sailor* effervesces more often into images: "She bent against the table to eat, and I knew her breasts would feel like two warm duck eggs"; "Miss Miller was pecking with her eyes around the scrolled saloon like a bird in a new cage"; "I saw her tongue swim swiftly like a red fish after the last drop into the glass. It stretched toward the bottom for a wink, then flipped back"; "the sail was fat with wind". Close's autobiography, *Morn of Youth* (Melbourne, 1948) is both exciting and amusing; it, too, follows in the the wake of Conrad, but even farther astern than the novels.

An earlier talent was much fuller of promise, but it soon wasted itself in mere thrillerism. (Cuthbert) Dale Collins (Sydney, 1897-1956) travelled round the world in a motor-boat for the Melbourne *Herald*, wrote a best seller, and thenceforth made London the centre for a number of sea wanderings. Almost all his stories are concerned with the East or the sea and with the mystery that is traditionally connected with both; only two of them matter: *Ordeal*[38] (Sydney and London, 1924), and *The Sentimentalists* (London, 1927). In the first, a small group of English and American "society" men and women set out on a pleasure trip across the Pacific; the mate, the only officer, is weak and a drug-taker and is incidentally murdered; the seamen are conveniently disposed of; the men passengers are weaklings, and when the vessel becomes derelict, the steward, the one outstanding personality and the only man who knows anything about navigation, takes charge: he is a kind of Admirable Crichton, as in Barrie's play; only this is not Barrie's Crichton, but an acid, arrogant, diabolically clever cockney-Armenian, sick of servitude and greedy for life and power. The gradual unfolding of his personality; the collapse of all but one of the passengers as the armour of society dissolves about their weaknesses—they fear the all-powerful tyrant yet at the same time are fascinated by him: all this is extremely well worked out: in the end, the only other personality, a deaf old lady who has hitherto remained for the most part a close and amused observer in the background, tricks the steward into falling overboard, and a shark gets him. The book has one very serious defect, which is manifest from the first page onward; its style is that of a clever but cheap journalist who is determined to be thrilling at all costs; this is well exemplified in the description of the steward and in the images, with one of which

[38] This was dramatized, by the author, in London, and also filmed.

the story opens: "[he] struck a match which burst a hole in the night as if he had fired a tiny bomb";[39] this sort of thing makes the style jerky and creates an atmosphere of exaggeration and strain. As a matter of fact the desire to thrill is evident in the conception of the book as a whole, and indeed in the conception of each of Collins's books. But the style is by no means all journalese; the story is neatly constructed and dramatic, if sometimes it steps over the edge into melodrama; the characters are sharply sketched; the steward is a real creation, if only in two dimensions; and, best of all, the story is individual and impressive in its own right, though in spite of rather than because of what was intended make it so. *Ordeal* was followed by *The Haven*[40] (London, 1925), a far inferior novel, though superior to the later thrillers; it tells of a matinee idol who maroons himself on an island to escape his feminine admirers, but is pursued by them, one after another; then came *The Sentimentalists*, which is by far Collins's best novel. In this, a gross whale of a sea captain off the Malaysian coast falls in love with and adopts a baby found adrift in a canoe: he persuades a girl who has travelled from England with an "uncle", whom however she has so far disappointed, to come aboard and nurse the baby; romance carries her off, but the mother of the baby turns up, and the captain marries her as the only way of retaining it. The romance, conventional in kind, is individualized and made interesting, and Tina herself is real; but it is Captain Whelan, sweating and swearing in the heat; and after him the mate, bullied, submissive, confident always in the auguries of the astrology he has learnt from a barber in King's Cross, who make the book. It is written much more smoothly and naturally than *The Ordeal* and lacks its cheap journalism and striving after effect, and some of the conversations are both natural and extremely amusing; there is for instance the dialogue between Whelan and Kagoshima, the cook, over the feeding of the baby; there are several dialogues between Whelan and the mate; and, best of all, there is the dialogue between Whelan and Tina in the lounge of the hotel at Macassar:[41]

> "Good evening," she said.
>
> Cap'n Whelan looked up out of his thoughts, startled. His veined eyes goggled. Ladies left him alone. He heaved his body over and considered her, truculently and cautiously.
>
> "What d'y'want?" he grunted, inflating his cheeks.
>
> "I want to talk to you." She gave him a tiny smile, not too bright—just a casual, friendly smile.

---

[39] See also (p. 6): "He flung the cigar stump away. It sailed up as if to join the stars, but, losing momentum and spirit, suddenly plunged down into the oblivion of the sea." Worst of all (p. 13), ". . . it [a cocktail] was novel and exciting with the poppy-breath of the sea".

[40] This has been translated into French.

[41] pp. 61-5.

"Ah," said Cap'n Whelan. He took up his glass and drank, his soft lips meeting upon it and sucking the gin down. "Who are y' anyway?"

"My name's Tina Murray."

. . . .

"Y' a harlot?" he inquired, disinterestedly.

Tina did not smile now; she chuckled. The monster was a collector's piece.

"Yes and no to that, really," she said, with a mock air of weighing a nice question, and then, seriously: "I should rank among the professionals, but I've cheated up to date. Perhaps I'd be a better girl if I were a harlot."

. . . .

"I can't make y' out," complained Cap'n Whelan. "Y' aint like the ordinary run. Why are y' at this business!"

"No excuse [she says, and tells him her story]. . . ."

Cap'n Whelan drained his gin and wiped his mouth on the back of his hand. He considered her, bulging the fat of his chin and neck together.

"I suppose," he remarked, "y'd be one of these modern girls really."

Unfortunately, with the next novel, *Vanity Under the Sun* (London, 1928), a decline set in, and the others are thrillers almost unredeemed.

The vast waste solitudes of Western and Central Australia, all that now remains of the Never Never, have not attracted any Australian novelist of the first rank:[42] this seems strange, since some indefinable fascination about them has probably been a conscious or unconscious motive with many who have invaded them for practical or merely adventurous reasons. One modern Australian novelist of talent has "taken up" this desert or half-desert country, in which the pastoralist invades the waste and wheat farms invade the sheep runs; but though his first novel was full of promise, its many successors have declined gradually into the category of the "Western", importing even American colloquialisms.[43] "Louis Kaye" (Noel Wilson Norman, Claremont, (Tas., 1901-81) worked for many years on stations in the country in which his novels are set; in his first novel, *Tybal Men* (London, 1931), he told in his own manner a story familiar in the eastern States, of the efforts of a far-out station-owner to keep his ancestral run intact in spite of drought, fire, insufficient capital and the encroachment of wheat-growing and modernity generally:

"Once," he would say, "nearly all the money Tybal earned came to Tybal, but now the auctioneers have their cut, and the insurance companies, and the banks, and the railways in freight, and the Government in taxes, and there's not much left to come to Tybal. We're just sweating for the cities. . . ."

This, and a few of the best of Kaye's other novels, is the sort of book one would expect to grow out of the circumstances: rough-grained, crude at times, extremely vigorous, with a feeling of largeness about it,

[42] The nearest to an exception was the Englishman, Grant Watson, who so entered into their spirit, or one aspect of it, that he has been here treated as an Australian (see pp. 630, 702-6).

[43] Hoboes, tough guys, "raising" cattle; "you sayin' any more, Farrel?" (*Trail of Plunder*, p. 42).

and with the freshness of adventure and a brooding intensity that grows at times melodramatic or sentimental. With all their Westernisms there remains something characteristically Australian about Kaye's stories, and they are comparatively credible. All the novels of Frank Walford (Sydney, 1882–?) are thrillers, and most of them deal with the psychologically abnormal, not to say the morbid; but there is one exception, *A Fool's Odyssey* (London, 1942): this is a straight-out story of adventure which deserves mention here because it has a freshness and verisimilitude that are most unusual in a thriller; because it is a thriller of a peculiarly Australian type, uninfluenced by modern Americanism: and, more important, because it is marked by qualities that characterize a particular Australian ideal in its more primitive aspect. Walford has been a shipping clerk, a customs clerk and a bank clerk; a carrier, the operator of a gravel quarry, and a duck farmer; a hunter of buffaloes, kangaroos and crocodiles; a dredger for trochus shell and a fisher for bêche-de-mer; he has also stood twice for parliament in the Labour interest. Most of these occupations and also education at Fort Street High School and a skill in boxing and with the knife and revolver, which are attributed to him in a prefatory note to *A Fool's Odyssey*, are ascribed to its principal character, the teller of the story: it is a story of picaresque and violent adventure, of lucky chances that time and again save the narrator's life, of opium-smuggling and hot-blooded love affairs; yet it is all so simple and unaffected, and, partly perhaps on account of the autobiographic element, so persuasive that it is hard not to take it as a piece of real life. Another of Walford's novels, *Twisted Clay*[44] (London, 1934), is a gruesome study of progressive insanity, but the study is obviously subordinate to a desire to excite and horrify. In a third novel, *And the River Rolls On* (London, 1939), the subject of the study is a small bush township in which isolation and interbreeding have brought about degeneracy of several kinds; again there is a series of murders and again it is clear that the main object is to thrill. Walford's other novels need not be mentioned here, but all his stories are lifelike and told with considerable power. In several novels the adventures were amorous or mainly amorous, but only a couple matter. *Quartette* (London, 1932) and *A Leaf of Laurel*[45] (London, 1933) were written by Leslie (Kirkman) Meller (Adelaide, 1892–1962), who was a land valuer in the South Australian civil service before his enlistment in the first A.I.F.: both books are picaresque romances, and written in a style which though smooth and flowing and rather "literary" is yet simple and unaffected: both contain crayon sketches of character, but none of these amounts to a complete picture,

---

[44] This was banned in Australia, but in 1960 was published in Sydney as a paperback.

[45] " 'The superstitious man . . . takes a leaf of laurel in his mouth, and walks about with it all day.' —*From the Greek*, c.395 B.C.", (title-page).

and the story is, in the first book especially, slight; the essence of each is the atmosphere, which is warm, pleasant, relaxing, and, in the first book especially, sensual. The second book, though comparatively disjointed, is the richer and more varied in incident and the characters, especially the lecherous old innkeeper, are more sharply realized; but except for the glimpses, in the same book, of the woman who had lost her son in the war and the girl with the subdued and drunken but still inquisitive husband, the characters in general are highly generalized or else we learn comparatively little about them. *The Half-Way Sun* (Sydney, 1935) blazes a track that may become a road: it was the first Australian novel[46] to be set in an Eastern country and written from the point of view of its inhabitants. The author is the poet, T. Inglis Moore,[47] who gathered his material by research and personal observation when he was Associate Professor of English at the University of the Philippines; the story is of the Philippine hero Kalatong, beginning with the struggles of tribe against tribe and with the Spaniards, and ending with Kalatong's murder when he is trying to put down head-hunting as an official under the Americans: the everyday life and ways of thinking of two native tribes is presented simply and with sympathy and understanding. In spirit, the novels of Jean Devanny (*née* Crook, Mrs F. H. Devanny, N.Z., 1894-1962) belong to this section rather than to that which deals with novels of country life; she lived in Sydney and North Queensland, and about a dozen of her novels may be counted as Australian. They are highly emotionalized and sometimes over-written, and though of little literary value, some have decided historical importance. *The Butcher Shop* (1926) deals with sexual oppression of women in marriage, and *Sugar Heaven* (1936) details the canefields strikes, and is notable for its feminism and for its picture of tensions between Australian and Italian cane-cutters. Vernon Williams (Maryborough, Q., 1884-1931), aimed to reconstruct romantic episodes from Australia's past, but his novels[48] are so highly coloured that they become sensational adventure stories set on Victoria's coast or on the islands of Bass Strait, packed with mystery, hidden treasure, plots and hand-to-hand fighting, they are full of exciting action and not without individuality.

After adventure, fantasy, into which, indeed, adventure stories are likely to wander; Australian writers are not however inclined to wander far into that realm, and much the best of the fantasies which appeared during this Period was the work of a writer who, though Australian born, lived the greater part of her life in England. Of the three short novels or long short stories contained in Helen Simpson's[49] *The Woman On the*

[46] So far as I know!

[47] For Moore's poems, see pp. 1034–6, 1066–7, and for his critical work, pp. 1286–7.

[48] *The Mahogany Ship* (London, 1920); *The Sea Wolf's Hoard* (London, 1924); *The Straitsmen* (London, 1929).

[49] For her other work, see pp. 1189–90.

Beast (London, 1933), only the last, the title-story, concerns us: all three were written after their author had become permanently resident in England, but this has to do with Australia. It suffers, though not so much as might have been expected, by separation from the fine prologue which binds the three stories together, and from the statement in the foreword: "the book tries to interpret a contradiction, that the most hateful actions are, as often as not, performed for the best of reasons". It appears that a bishop had "pledged the infinite word" to a reprobate king, his convert, that he should win not merely forgiveness but an eternal crown. Heaven refused this, and hell also; it was declared that unless some way out of the tangle could be discovered the world must prepare for the coming of Antichrist. No way out is discovered. In the story that concerns us, in the year 1999 Antichrist is a woman, Emma Jordan Sopwith, who is obviously founded on Mrs Baker Eddy, Carrie Nation and Aimée Semple Macpherson; she calls herself the Eldest Daughter of God. From her residence in Pharoah, California, her gospel has spread, with one exception, over the whole world, the only recalcitrant country, Ireland, having been "evangelised from above" by cloudbursts which liquidated the population; the exception was Australia, which was scarcely worth bothering about, particularly since it might have been hard to handle: its population, now no more than half a million, had abandoned their cities and now

> . . . moved about their vast continent in swarms, like locusts, a thousand or so persons at a time. Whole towns would suddenly quit their dwellings and take to the air, animals and all, making seasonal flights to avoid heat or cold, and to descend upon pastures untouched by drought.

The Australians were divided into two warring factions, which lived separately and had only two enthusiasms in common, horse-racing and sea-bathing; they came together peacefully only at their Annual Festival, at either end of the rusting ruins of the Sydney Harbour Bridge. Mrs Sopwith decides at last to take this heaven-sent opportunity to liquidate everybody, on the excuse that a group of visitors has been unlawfully detained; actually they are waiting for one of their members, who does not want to leave with them, having been seduced by the easy humorous freedom of the life in this strange country, and by something about its atmosphere. The story contains some interesting glimpses of what the author seems to have considered typical of Australia and its people; Jane

> . . . stepped from the air machine . . . on to Australian soil, in cloudless, stupefying weather. The distances were dancing; everything else, trees, waves, and birds, was altogether still with heat. From the pepper-trees came a croaking of locusts, whose carapaces, sloughed and gaping, clung beside the living creatures on the boughs.

> The grass was burnt yellow; there were no visible flowers; but walking as the adventurers soon did into a grove of thin trees, sharp delicious scents came up from plants they trod underfoot.

That is closely observed and individually recorded, but in the next two extracts the author is using her creative imagination:

> The man had the face which they were to come to know as typical; bony, long, with deep eyes, a hooked nose, and a curiously unfinished, slack-looking yet angry mouth;

and the Australians are described as having

> . . . curiously tilted accent and close-mouthed delivery—acquired, said the ill-natured, by much keeping of stable secrets.

Helen Simpson's style has been already characterized;[50] it can be purely beautiful, as in the description of the ringing of the bell for the Angelus at the service in the bush:[51]

> It was a colossal greenish bell, swung for this purpose on the stretched arm of a gum tree, cleared of leaves and minor branches to allow the great bronze hollow room to toss.

The Bishop

> . . . nodded once in the chaplain's direction, and that young man caught the rope with his strength, bracing his feet far apart, and pulled; a note was heard, loud yet mellow, in whose far-reaching sweetness silver sounded. Two other notes followed, then a rest; in that rest the silence of the valley was absolute as though round the bend were only the denizens of the bush, creatures that lie quiet in the heat of the day, snakes and tree-bears and bright furtive birds; but there was a murmur at the back of the silence that sounded like sea on shore.

In the end, when the assemblage at the Bridge Festival has been gassed from the air, Jane persuades the pilot of the plane that was to have dropped her in safety somewhere to ram one of Mrs Sopwith's squadron, so that both planes are destroyed. Follows Mrs Sopwith's final service at Pharoah, California, which is interrupted by the sounding of the Seven Trumpets, the dropping of the blood, the raising of the dead. "Goodness, and warmth, and light had been driven out of existence for ever"; and "the aged and reprobate King of the West, conquerer of God, rules over his ramshackle ill-lit universe". In this book, Helen Simpson's audacious imagination, freed from all realistic ties, not that they ever troubled her much, has achieved something of which it is hard to imagine an equal in its kind. The second fantasy, *Out of the Silence* (Melbourne, 1925), was written by Erle Cox, who has been already referred to among the historical novelists.[52] It is built along the

[50] See pp. 1190–1. [51] p. 409. [52] See p. 1217.

lines of Haggard's *She* and *When the World Shook*, but though boldly imaginative it is stilted in style and weak in characterization; it was published in England and the United States as well as in Australia, and was translated into French and Russian.

Far more children's stories were written during the present Period than the preceding, and they reached a higher level; it would be higher still if we were to take into account the short stories which are here considered separately, and if the category were widened to include not only stories for but stories about children.[53] This time, all the best of the books are set on the countryside. In Norman Lindsay's *The Magic Pudding* (Sydney, 1918) and *The Flyaway Highway* (Sydney, 1936) the spirit of movement and adventure that animates almost all the children's stories is accentuated by the fact that both of these tell of a road, along which the characters travel. *The Magic Pudding* is as much a classic in this kind as *Saturdee* is in another; the acquirement of the pudding that requires nothing but "politeness and constant eatin' ", renewing itself as fast as slices are cut out of it, and the repeated contests between the pudding owners and the pudding thieves is shown with Lindsay's characteristically humorous extravaganzas of fancy and language. In Lindsay's second book it is the road itself that is magic, running through houses and everything and providing its own scenery: a small boy and girl are introduced to it by a bloke with "cows' hooves . . . hairy goats' legs and a fine pair of horns", who is revealed to them when they are foraging in somebody's strawberry beds; they travel along the magic road through various areas of legendary romance, independently of space and time. These two books are for both boys and girls; Hatfield's *Buffalo Jim* (London, 1938) is for boys of any age between ten or so and twenty or more: bright, fresh, humorous and above all adventurous, it is little more a boys' story than *Sheepmates*,[54] with which it may be compared. The standard author of girls' stories till 1950 was still Mary Grant Bruce (Sale, Vic., 1878-1958), though her first book was published in 1910; she lived for many years in England, but her stories, conventional but interesting, are practically all set in Australia. Some of these children's stories deal not merely with the bush but with its original inhabitants: *Allabout* (Sydney, 1935) is factual, not fairy-tale, a direct descendant of Mrs Gunn's *Little Black Princess*;[55] it tells with humour and sympathetic understanding of the life of a little Aboriginal community on Argyle station, Kimberley, Western Australia, where the authors were brought up; they are Mary

---

[53] And in particular, K. S. Prichard's *Wild Oats of Han* (pp. 1082, 1087) and Norman Lindsay's *Saturdee* (pp. 1145-8).

[54] For this and Hatfield's other novels, see pp. 1128-9.

[55] See pp. 699, 732.

Durack[56] (Mrs H. C. Miller, Adelaide, 1913-) and her sister Elizabeth (Mrs Francis Clancy, 1916-). Nubbudah, Polly and her little yellow daughter, Daffodil, whom the Mission claimed; Boxer, old friend of the boss as well as his station-hand, and several others are made very real; and so are corroboree, walkabout, drought and the "breaking of the Wet". *Allabout* was followed by a charming little fairy-tale, *The Way of the Whirlwind* (Sydney, 1941), which tells of Nungaree and Jungaree, dwellers in the legendary country of Dreamtime, and their adventurous search for the Whirlwind, who has stolen away their baby brother. Davison's[57] *Children of the Dark People* (Sydney, 1936) is also a fairy-tale, about Jackadgery and Nimmitybelle, a little Aboriginal boy and girl who are enticed away from their tribe by a wicked witch-doctor, and the flight from him in which they are befriended by Grandfather Gumtree, Old Mr Bunyip and the Spirits of the Billabong, the Caves and the Plains. Except for short passages of conventional sweetness, such as the description of the spirits of the flowers, this also is an excellent children's story. A kind of cross between *Alice in Wonderland* and one of the books of popular science for which the author is well known, is *The Magic Seeds* (Sydney, 1940), by the entomologist, Keith (Collingridge) McKeown (Sydney, 1892-1952); this tells how a little girl, by means of fern seed presented to her by Gilbert the cricket, shrinks until she is able to join a community of termites who adopt her as a spare queen. Finally, by Dymphna Cusack, whose plays are discussed elsewhere,[58] and Florence James, *Four Winds and a Family* (Sydney, 1947), a light, bright and amusing story of three wild little girls and their playmates. There were also a couple of collections of Aboriginal legends: J. K. Ewers's *Tales from the Dead Heart* (Sydney, 1944),[59] and Mary Grant Bruce's *Stone Axe of Burkamukk* (Melbourne, 1922). Ewers's tales are the more realistic and less literary, reading almost as though they had been taken down in shorthand from some Aboriginal narrator; Mary Grant Bruce's tales are the more imaginative, more elaborate: she clothes her skeletons in flesh and blood. Both series are interesting, in their quite different fashions.

As might have been expected, quite a crop of detective stories sprang up during the Period, but no first-rate Australian talent turned to that kind of fiction. This does not apply to "Michael Innes", John Innes Mackintosh Stewart (Corstophine, Scotland, 1906-), but his work in this kind does not fall within our scope. Stewart occupied the chair of English Language and Literature at Adelaide from 1934 to 1946,

[56] Mary Durack has since published a novel, *Keep Him My Country* (London, 1955).
[57] See pp. 1119-25 for Davison's novels; pp. 1245-7 for his short stories.
[58] See pp. 1274-5.
[59] Republished in New York in 1947 as *Written in Sand*.

and during that time he wrote some of the best detective stories that have appeared in English for many years,[60] but none of them is set in Australia; they represent a harking back to his own country. In the case of Dominic Paul McGuire[61] (1903-78), there is perhaps room for argument: a graduate of the University of Adelaide, he served in the Australian navy (Intelligence) during the second World War, and began in England a series of detective stories which was continued after his return to Australia in 1932; he afterwards represented Australia in the U.N. General Assembly. At their best his detective stories are very good, but none of them has anything to do with Australia. The most interesting of the Australian writers of detective stories is Arthur William Upfield (Gosport, Hampshire, England, 1888-1964), largely because of his creation of a new kind of detective. Upfield came to Australia in 1911, practised his trade as an estate agent for some years and in 1927 changed over to the writing of detective stories; his Detective Inspector Napoleon Bonaparte, of the Queensland police, is a half-caste Aborigine, a graduate of the University of Queensland, whose unconventional qualities have more than once brought about his dismissal from the force, and whose exceptional abilities have as often caused his reinstatement. Bony, as he insists on being called, with his humour, his kindly and unpretentiously democratic behaviour, which is yet consistent with a simple vanity, makes a definite impression on the reader; but though the stories in which he appears are capably written there is nothing exceptional about them, as distinct from their principal character, except that almost all are set out back.

There is still a drift of literary talent from Australia to England, and nowadays to America also; but with the increase in population here and in the strength of the local market the impulse to emigrate to the Old World is not quite so strong: nowadays most Australian writers seem content to remain in their own country or to make only visits to the world centres, but during the Period there have been some prominent exceptions, and on the other hand several writers who had left Australia for England have lately returned; in this section writers of verse and prose, of works of pure and applied literature will for convenience be taken together. The best or almost all the best work of Stead and Simpson belongs to Australia and has been already discussed,[62] but Stead's *House of All Nations*, which cannot be considered Australian, shows a combination of qualities possessed by no living Australian writer of fiction. Helen Simpson was among the leading English women novelists; she belonged to a small group of intellectuals which included

---

[60] For example, *Hamlet, Revenge* and *Lament For a Maker.*

[61] For McGuire's other work, see pp. 1388, 1416.

[62] See pp. 1155-62 and 1097-8, 1189-91, 1226-8 respectively.

Clemence Dane, in collaboration with whom she wrote several detective stories. Eric Partridge's works on slang are widely known, but he also published a collection of short stories[63] and collaborated in a war novel. Jack Lindsay,[64] a classical scholar, a translator of Aristophanes, Petronius and others, published also a number of classical and other historical novels, besides verse-plays and critical essays; in the second World War he served in Signals and in the Education Department of the War Office. Philip Lindsay[65] is also a historical novelist, but not classical and much more picaresque; it is worth noting that in *Panama is Burning* he seems to have based the characteristics of Morgan's men on those of the wildest members of the first A.I.F. In spite of the Lindsays' development since their migration to England their literary characteristics have not really altered; they may be said to represent a projection of Lindsayism, of a particular variety of Australianism, overseas, just as early Australian writers represented a projection of the literature of the mother country into Australia. James Aldridge[66] also appears to have settled abroad; he has published several novels in London, of which the most important, *The Diplomat* (1949), tells an exciting story based on the nature and effects of English diplomacy in Iran. Godfrey Blunden[67] published several novels after leaving Australia and then settled in the United States. Marcel Aurousseau (Sydney, 1891-1983), author of *Highway into Spain* (London, 1930), fought with the first A.I.F., lectured in Geology in Western Australia, lived for some years in England and America, and is now in Australia again. By no means the least of the expatriates, but mentioned last because he was taken to England as a small child, was Richard Hillary (Sydney, 1919-1943); his one book, an autobiography, *The Last Enemy*[68] (London, 1943), has according to his biographer,[69] and one is not surprised to hear it, been translated into every European language. Hillary was educated at Shrewsbury and Oxford, after which he became a fighter pilot in the R.A.F.; he was brought down, horribly burned, in the North Sea, and after a series of operations which involved the grafting on of four new eyelids and a new upper lip, he managed to get permission to fight again. He was killed in re-training: "the last of the long-haired boys". This is a most fascinating war book: because of Hillary's literary ability and personality, because of his analyses of his own mental states and because of the sketches, largely psychological, of friends and others whom he met.

---

[63] See pp. 1256-7.

[64] For Jack Lindsay's Australian poems, see p. 943 [*Overland*, no. 83, (Melb., 1981), celebrating Lindsay's birthday, contains much valuable information.]

[65] His autobiography, which deals in the main with his life in Australia, is discussed on p. 1363.

[66] For Aldridge's Australian novel, see pp. 1218-19.

[67] For Blunden's Australian novel, see pp. 1131-2.

[68] "The last enemy that shall be destroyed is death" (I Corinthians 15:26).

[69] Lovat Dickson, in *Richard Hillary* (London, 1950)

In pure literature the only important visitor to Australia during the Period was D. H. Lawrence,[70] and the merits and defects of the novel he wrote as the result, *Kangaroo* (London, 1923), are so marked, and it has had so much influence here, that it may be given more space than would otherwise be devoted to a book which is not a part of Australian literature. Lawrence spent nine months in New South Wales, mostly on the South Coast, and he was extremely interested in what he saw and heard: *Kangaroo* is typically Lawrentian, and its principal character is the author, to as great an extent as any in Lawrence's novels; the "dark powers" barely put in an appearance,[71] but the unconventional point of view, the passionate sincerity, the imaginatively critical approach, the preoccupation with the idea of power, indeed the desire for power and the belief that he might attain it if he liked, the keen insight mingled with misunderstanding, the individuality of expression, the feeling for words and the patches of verbal magic, all reappear. *Kangaroo* is, as Katharine Prichard has remarked,[72] a reflection of Lawrence in Australia; it certainly does not present a true picture of Australia and Australian life, but it contains many truths and half-truths about both. The countryside and in particular the bush fascinated and frightened Lawrence; speaking as his principal character, Somers, he says:[73]

> . . . the vast, uninhabited land. . . . seemed so hoary and lost, so unapproachable. . . . It was so phantom-like, so ghostly, with its tall pale trees and many dead trees, like corpses, partly charred by bush fires: and then the foliage so dark, like grey-green iron. And then it was so deathly still. Even the few birds seemed to be swamped in silence. Waiting, waiting—the bush seemed to be hoarily waiting. And he could not penetrate into its secret. He couldn't get at it. Nobody could get at it. What was it waiting for?
>
> And then one night at the time of the full moon he walked alone into the bush. A huge electric moon, huge, and the tree-trunks like naked pale aborigines among the dark-soaked foliage, in the moonlight. And not a sign of life—not a vestige.
>
> Yet something. Something big and aware and hidden! He walked on, had walked a mile or so into the bush, and had just come to a clump of tall, nude, dead trees, shining almost phosphorescent with the moon, when the terror of the bush overcame him. He had looked so long at the vivid moon, without thinking. And now, there was something among the trees, and his hair began to stir with terror, on his head. There was a presence. He looked at the weird, white, dead trees, and into the hollow distances of the bush. Nothing! Nothing at all. He turned to go home. And then immediately the hair on his scalp went icy cold with terror. What of? He knew quite well it was nothing.

As to the inhabitants of the country also Somers's, or Lawrence's, feelings were mixed and contradictory; almost in spite of himself he appreciated

[70] *The Boy in the Bush*, the novel produced in collaboration with Louisa Skinner, has been already discussed, pp. 1191-3.

[71] See however p. 171.

[72] In *Meanjin*, vol. ix, No. 4 (Summer, 1950), p. 252.

[73] pp. 8-9.

their careless freedom, their loose and easy democracy, but he hated some of the consequences of these:

> There is a great relief in the atmosphere, a relief from tension, from pressure. An absence of control or will or form.
>
> . . . .
>
> But what then? The *vacancy* of this freedom is almost terrifying. In the openness and the freedom this new chaos, this litter of bungalows and tin cans scattered for miles and miles, this Englishness all crumbled out into formlessness and chaos.[74]
>
> . . . .
>
> "Oh, how I detest this treacly democratic Australia," he said. "It swamps one with a sort of common emotion like treacle, and before one knows where one is, one is caught like a fly on a flypaper, in one mess with all the other buzzers."[75]

He felt the need for rule and responsibility:

> "We don't like to have anybody overhead here," said Kangaroo. "We don't even care to go upstairs, because we are then one storey higher than our true ground-floor selves."

But Somers-Lawrence is not always consistent, or rather he has his moods. He

> . . . felt blind to Australia and blind to the uncouth Australians. To him they were barbarians. The most loutish Neapolitan loafer was nearer to him in pulse than these British Australians with their aggressive familiarity.
>
> . . . .
>
> "They just blankly don't care about anything, and they live in defiance, a sort of slovenly defiance of care of any sort, human or inhuman, good or bad."

And when Somers's wife says that Australia feels "as if man had never loved it, and made it a happy country, a bride country—or a mother country", an Australian replies, but we can feel Lawrence in the reply:

> "If you call the land a bride, she's the sort of bride not many of us are willing to tackle. She drinks your sweat and your blood, and then as often as not lets you down, does you in."
>
> . . . .
>
> "They treat the country more like a woman they pick up on the streets than a bride, to my thinking."

All these comments are acute and on the whole quite as much right as wrong, but in several matters that are fundamental Lawrence is led into bad mistakes by personal idiosyncrasy and plain misunderstanding. More or less fascist organizations have not been unknown in Australia, but Lawrence makes far too much of this;* and it is absurd to imagine that Kangaroo, the leader of such an organization, and Jack, an ex-captain in the A.I.F. who is one of his lieutenants, would be likely to

---

[74] p. 23. This is Somers, or Somers and his wife; there are no quotation marks.

[75] This is Somers.

* [The sources of Lawrence's portraits of Kangaroo and his para-military organization are still a mystery, though he seems to have had a glimpse of some kind of emergent fascist activity. See the discussion by Michael Wilding in *Australian Literary Studies* (May 1980).]

admire and try to obtain the support of an English visitor, and in particular such a visitor as Somers-Lawrence:[76] they would be more likely to think less of him than he deserved; and that both Kangaroo and Jack, or indeed any normal Australian, should be represented as embracing this desirable English visitor, and exclaiming, as Kangaroo is made to exclaim, "I love you so. I love you so!":[77] this is ridiculous. *Kangaroo* is neither among the best nor among the worst of Lawrence's novels: like the others, it is stimulating, provocative; and it has a particular interest for Australians because it brings out and illuminates some things that have been ignored or forgotten, and impels the Australian reader to consider and reconsider and discriminate.

A second critic of Australian literature and affairs generally, and who was in his way as important to us as Lawrence, was Hartley Grattan, who may be considered here although his criticisms were not embodied in a work of fiction. If Lawrence helped to open the eyes of our writers to certain characteristics of Australia as a country and as a civilization, as to its inhabitants he made characteristic mistakes, and as to its literature he had practically nothing to say;[78] but (Clinton) Hartley Grattan (Wakefield, Massachusetts, U.S.A., 1902–80), though he did not possess Lawrence's genius, had an acute and all-round critical talent, which he brought systematically to bear upon Australia, Australians and their affairs generally, spending here not six months but altogether about three years. He also made characteristic mistakes, especially in what is nevertheless by no means the least interesting and important part of his criticism, that in which he dealt with our literature; but he appreciated Lawson, helped to discover Furphy, about whom he was enthusiastic, if partly for reasons that have no direct connection with literature, and was on the whole extremely encouraging. His comments are often provocative, but they contain almost always at least an element of truth, and his criticisms are fundamentally friendly; he adopted Australia as his second country, but, as he said, "one can fall out of patience even with those one likes best". Grattan graduated from Massachusetts College, and taught for a while before he became a journalist, or perhaps publicist would be a more appropriate term. He paid three visits to Australia, the second visit as a Carnegie Fellow, and his opinions ripened with experience; he wrote about Australian affairs in both Australian and American periodicals, and also edited the volume *Australia* (Berkeley, California, U.S.A., 1947) in the United Nations Series, to which all the contributors except himself were Australians, besides two books about

[76] p. 82. So does a Labour leader, but this is not quite so unlikely, for Somers has published some articles on democracy that appeal to him.

[77] p. 233.

[78] Except about the *Bulletin*, which he admired. "It was the only periodical in the world that really amused him ... a lively creature, even if it was made up all of bits" (p. 302).

which something must be said here;[79] both these books were written for Australian as well as American audiences. The second, *Introducing Australia* (New York, 1942, Sydney, 1944), is a survey of the country and its people as a whole; its general conclusions are emphatically favourable, much more so than those of some of our economists, though he also has his warning: he sees in Australia[80]

> . . . the opportunity to build a version of European-American civilization which will be unique and perhaps possessed of virtues we are little likely to achieve in our own country. I do not think Australia will ever be one of the Great Powers. I do think that the Australians will one day, if fate favours them, be a great people.

He realizes that American influence is at present small as compared with that of Britain; Australian culture[81]

> . . . is simply a case of a British theme with Australian variations. But it is important to emphasize the Australian variations if you really want to understand the country and the people.

On the political and economic side Grattan falls generally into line with a number of our present-day writers: he remarks that few Labour politicians represent in parliament the leftist attitude of the unions, and that there has been a shift of emphasis since 1914 from the improvement of living conditions to the encouragement and support of private enterprise, and he asserts that if primary industries are deserving of support regardless of cost, so are manufactures; but since, with its far smaller home market, Australia will have in many fields to bear higher costs than the United States, it is our business "to prevent the excessive development of industries which are likely to be expensive". The other book, *Australian Literature* (Seattle, Washington, 1929), is a pamphlet of thirty-nine pages, published only a few years after Grattan's first visit; it is therefore in the nature of a first impression, and though fundamentally that impression remained unchanged, it was, after further investigation, modified and liberalized, so that it will be best to discuss this pamphlet along with the remarks on Australian literature in the chapter on cultural life in the later book. The pamphlet is original, forceful, and stimulating, but it is less careful, less balanced than this later book, and at times it seems to an Australian perverse: Grattan is inclined to confuse political with aesthetic values and personal preferences with literary importance, slashing at whatever does not appeal to him: he provides here therefore a stimulant rather than an impartial estimate. Against his failure to appreciate Brennan and his contempt for McCrae may however be set his appreciation of Lawson and his high estimate of Furphy, and his opinion that[82]

[79] He also wrote introductions to the American edition of *Such Is Life* (Chicago, 1947) and to Evatt's *Rum Rebellion* (Sydney, 1938).

[80] p. 3. [81] pp. 7–8. [82] p. 174.

> . . . the basic Australian literary tradition is a compound of sound learning, rebelliousness, ardent faith in the common man, and an even more ardent faith in the Australian future;

this is certainly the tradition of the nineties and early nineteen-hundreds, except the remark about the "sound learning", which seems in some respects rather flattering. But Grattan was not impressed by the literature of the day in which the pamphlet was written, and went so far as to assert that Australia had not "the proportional literary vitality of South Africa"; it is true that some of what are now Australia's leading writers were then at early stages of their development, but Grattan omits to mention Brennan and Baylebridge as well as others of only less importance: he refers to A. G. Stephens only by name, is contemptuous of McCrae and dismisses Paterson as no more than a popular balladist.[83] Incidentally, he declares that American influence on Australian literature is nil, not apparently having noticed the influence of Bret Harte, Mark Twain, T. S. Eliot, Hemingway and others of the neo-barbarics. In the later book however Grattan's judgment has ripened and is based on a wider or more careful reading; he refers favourably to Baylebridge, Stephens, FitzGerald, Dark, Davison and others, and admits that Brennan's poetry is "unique not only in Australian literature but also . . . of the first interest to all concerned with the art", even if this is only because "he attempted to assimilate French Symbolism to English verse"; Richardson also comes into his field of appreciation, though only as "the greatest of the Australian literary expatriates". Slips and all, Grattan is sometimes penetrating and always sincere; no other oversea visitor has been interested enough to make a special study of the life and literature of this country, of which indeed he knows as much as some of our prominent critics.

[83] He mentions Prichard, Palmer, Esson, Mrs Gunn, Wilmot and Neilson; he omits not only McCrae, but Mary Gilmore, Gellert, Barnard Eldershaw, "Brent of Bin Bin" and "Martin Mills".

CHAPTER XI

THE SHORT STORY

The Lawson-Furphy Tradition: Prichard; Palmer; Davison; "Brian James"; Cecil Mann; Others. Casey; Edwards; Marjorie Barnard. Newer Writers: Stivens; Morrison; Cowan; Others. War Stories: Wheen; Others. Fantasy and Fairy-tale: Christina Stead; Robinson; Skipper. Anthologies: Nettie Palmer; Others

THE SHORT-STORY writer is free to write as he likes, about whatever he likes, bound only by the limitations of his own talent and of a space that varies with circumstances; he is no longer confined within a circle of formal principles that made the earlier short story in effect a miniature novel: accordingly he has abandoned the introduction, the conclusion and the rather too obvious plot; he moves more freely in his larger space, and as a result of this freedom the short story has become a distinct literary kind, which requires of course an art of its own. But the modernization of the short story began well before the beginning of the century, so that it cannot be said that writers who adopt this form are in an entirely different position from those of fifty years ago, or, in Australia, of the *Bulletin* age, with which the century from our point of view began. In the *Bulletin* short story, which was, as has been said,[1] the type and centre of the short story of those days, inessentials had been already cut out, and though the stories were mainly plotted, they were not all plotted; some were, as so many of today's short stories are, "slices of life". A few of the *Bulletin's* requirements, which then, as has been shown, affected the whole field of the short story in Australia, would today constitute a serious handicap;[2] but on the whole they were advantageous at a time when, apart from the requirements of the *Bulletin* as a periodical, the contributors to a young and undeveloped form of literature needed formal discipline and in particular to learn how to condense; one has only to read the novels of that day to realize how these also would have benefited by a similar discipline. Freed from these requirements, the Australian short story today is much longer than its predecessor: the *Bulletin* nowadays by no means insists upon brevity; it would nowadays have room for "The Fall of the House of Usher", which it once admitted[3] would have had regretfully to be refused; and in any case it no longer exercises a despotic rule. Again, sentimentalism is rarer among the short stories of today than it was in

[1] See p. 575. [2] See p. 576. [3] See p. 577, note 17.

those of the nineties and early nineteen-hundreds, or at least it is carefully covered over; whatever might have been the attitude of the early *Bulletin* upon this point, that was a sentimental age as this is not,[4] and it would have been impossible to stamp out sentimentalism altogether, even if the reader would have stood the lack of it; as a matter of fact what we regard as sentimentalism in literature was in those days by no means always regarded as such. Not that sentimentalism is by any means absent from the world's short stories today, least of all from those of the neo-barbarics in America; in Australia it is observable mainly in the work of some of the women writers, though not the best. And the short story today, in Australia and in other countries also, is comparatively seldom melodramatic, as for instance Poe's stories often were, but then it is as a rule less dramatic also, in Britain at any rate, perhaps in America, and in Australia certainly; it is also in Australia less "pointed", there is less observable effort after effect than in the stories of the *Bulletin* age: all these characteristics were a more or less natural consequence of the requirements of Archibald and his "young men". And the freedom of the modern Australian short-story writer in the matter of space tends to assume an easy-going quality; he often takes some time to get into his stride. One consequence of the *Bulletin* restriction as to length was that there could be no fine shades; everything had to be sheer black and white: atmosphere there still might be, and often was, but even this had to be succinctly rendered and sharply defined; nowadays however a short story may be, though it seldom is, almost all atmosphere. And since there is now room for half-tones, there is less of the obvious about the Australian short story than there used to be; even the surprise endings, the catches of some of the *Bulletin* stories, were, after a while at least, not really surprises: one got to expect them. Also there is now room for the psychological analysis which in any case was seldom attempted in those days, when it was customary to allow the characters to reveal themselves by word and action; when indeed, if one got down to bedrock, action mattered much more than character, the story than the people about whom it was told. Moreover next to action came description, though there was of course not much room for that; nowadays the effect desired, human or natural, is obtained as a rule rather by suggestion than by description, and where description there must be it is usually cut down to what is necessary for illustrative purposes, or to provide a basis for the atmosphere. But in spite of all this there is still some point in the old assertion that the Australian short story tends to be anecdotal; it has still very often a "point" upon which the whole depends, and though words are seldom wasted, one does feel sometimes, at least in

[4] By comparison, that is, and in literature and general behaviour, in spite of the radio and the films.

most of the non-analytical short stories, of which there are still many, that full advantage has not been taken of the increased space available, that it is still, after all, the skeleton of the story which has tended to occupy the writer mainly; and also that it is rather obvious where the anecdote has been elaborated and that the flesh on the bones is rather thin.

All that has been said so far has been concerned with form; but in the matter of subject also short-story writers, here as elsewhere, are almost entirely free; in Australia however this freedom has still limitations in the matter of sex, and there are also signs of a growing political limitation, though the average writer is little affected by either of these handicaps. Australian writers have enormous advantages over their fathers and grandfathers taking into account not only their greater freedom but their wider market: the opportunity of selling their stories in England and the United States as well as in the increased number of periodicals in their own country. Unfortunately they have not made the most of these advantages; the fact is that, speaking generally, they have not a corresponding talent. It is certainly not with Australian writers generally that this defect lies: there are Australian poets now living who can stand comparison with any others of their kind; there are Australian novelists now living who, if they do not reach that standard, are still not far from the front rank. But no short-story writer in Australia today can compare with the best in other countries or with Lawson at his best; and a few of the other short-story writers of Lawson's period, however outmoded their methods, are in their own kinds superior to most today: superior in virtue of their individuality and personality, to which no freedom or craftsmanship or labour can in themselves attain. The most likely explanation of this is that in the days when it was hard to get an Australian novel published unless it could be sure of oversea readers, talent turned to the short story; nowadays, when even a mediocre novel stands a good chance of publication as a serial and afterwards in book-form,[5] and also there are prizes to be won,[6] talent turns far oftener to the novel. Still, this explanation is clearly incomplete, for though, as might be expected from it, the best Australian short stories are by established novelists and some of these are excellent by any current standard, as a whole the Australian short story today is disappointing: it is not uninteresting, but with few exceptions it does not quicken the blood or stimulate the mind, and what effect it may produce soon fades. It shows no lack of craftsmanship; its scenes and actions are credible; its men and women are lifelike, and their conversations are more natural than those in some Australian novels that

[5] Or did, until quite lately.

[6] There are prizes for short stories also, but they are comparatively small.

reach otherwise a fairly high standard, but, as a whole again, it lacks vigour and illuminative imagination: these writers understand what they describe, but though they can make it like life, they cannot breathe the breath of life into it. However, this, as has been said, does not apply to some of the stories by established novelists, and one or two of the younger short-story writers are full of promise.

The classification of the short story need not be so elaborate as of the the novel; but here also we may begin with those which follow the Lawson tradition, as constituting the principal part of the larger field of stories of the countryside. For the Lawson tradition is, as was only to be expected, as strong here as among the novelists, though it is not stronger:[7] the leaders are K. S. Prichard, Vance Palmer and Frank Davison, all of whom are better known by their novels; and though there are many other established writers of short stories, some of them specialists, none have reached the all-round standard of these three. None of the new-comers seemed likely, at the date at which this History closed, to displace any of the leaders, but several have pegged out claims upon new ground which add to the short range of the short story in Australia and may help to give its field a new direction. One or two of Prichard's stories are unequalled in Australia today, but Palmer has a greater output and a more uniform level of fairly high achievement. Prichard's stories are of two kinds, which are represented in her two published collections: *Kiss on the Lips* (London, 1932), and *Potch and Colour*[8] (Sydney, 1944). They share the simple directness of style which is common to so many Australian writers, and the lack of psychological analysis in the modern manner, the combination of realistic treatment with poetic feeling, and the descriptional and idiomatic colouring that may have been noted in discussing Prichard's novels: but her short stories seem to have been written more carefully; at least there are fewer worn terms and phrases, and in the first collection there is a conciseness of expression that though usual is not invariable in her novels. In everything else the two collections are unlike one another. There was an interval of eleven years between their dates of publication: the first appeared at the end of its author's best period, the second a couple of years before the first of her propagandist novels; the stories in the second book are not propagandist, but they are founded on yarns of the Western Australian mining and wheatgrowing districts such as those she was soon to use as the basis of propaganda. In the first collection there is nothing of the weakness in illuminative imagination that has been noticed in the contemporary Australian stort story; into these has certainly been breathed the breath

[7] See pp. 1081, 1108, 1119, 1245.

[8] "These stories, I think, are like the chips opal-miners put in a small bottle and call 'potch and colour'—poor and fiery opal, that is" (Foreword). Prichard has since published *N'Goola* (Melbourne, 1959).

of life; nor except perhaps in one or two in this collection is there anything of the merely anecdotal quality that has been mentioned. In "The Cooboo", for instance, which is one of the shortest and which depends upon a single action, it is clear that the author has not seized upon this and built a story about it; that on the contrary she has conceived and rendered the whole story as an illuminative incident, a crisis in the life of a particular person in particular conditions, an illumination of a particular kind of life. But in "The Grey Horse" there is no single centre, no point on which the story depends; it is a rich organic unity which presents a number of closely interrelated aspects: there is the old man, proud of his stallion but jealous of the potency and youthful fire that he himself has lost; the stallion himself, brimming with the life and creative desire that he symbolizes; and there is the earlier parallel and the later contrast between him and the young orchardist who tries to borrow the stallion for his ploughing. Most of these stories are tragedies, and almost all are at least low in tone. "The Cooboo"[9] is the tragedy, horrible if it had been told differently and piercing as it is told, of a gin who, one of the finest of the station's riders after cattle, helping at a muster, finds everything spoilt by the cooboo, her baby, a whimpering bundle squirming against her as she rides: the men yelled at her; her man blackguarded her for her clumsiness; another woman boasted of her own superior performance and the rewards she would get for it;[10]

> She cried out with hurt and impatience. Rage, irritated to madness, rushed through her; rushed like waters coming down the dry creek-beds after heavy rain. Rose wrenched the cooboo from her breast and flung him from her to the ground. There was a crack as of twigs breaking.

Both these stories deserve a place in a world anthology, and perhaps "The Cow" also, though it is marred by a suspicion of subjective fantasizing, in the creation of its heroine, Lucia who, adoring life and jealous of the fecundity all about her, gives herself to the life-giving rain:[11]

> It made you grow, the rain, someone had said to her once. "You need the rain to make you grow, as much as the trees and all other living things."
>
> In the darkness, beside a tree near the veranda, Lucia undid her dress, took off her clothes, not quite sure of herself, a little self-conscious. She stood clinging to the tree; the rain struck her fine and straight, with needle points. . . . She smiled at herself, and at the tree she was clasping as if it were a man; laughed at herself, the tree and the rain. Then free, flung up her arms and stood out giving herself to the rain.
>
> She ran from one tree to another in the quiet garden, among the wattles, over their husks and seeds. The rain was falling through thin moonlight. Trees, hills, all that she could see of them, in light, frail and shining as the rain; sun-dried grass, and trees, broad-backed and heavy-limbed.
>
> Lucia was prostituted to it all;

[9] *Kiss on the Lips*, p. 31.

[10] The same, p. 102.

[11] The same, pp. 139-41.

then she runs back to her husband,

> Cold and fresh, all wet and earth-sweet from the rain and leaves. . . . "I couldn't bear it," Lucia told him, "for the rain not to rain on me too."

About the stories in the second collection there is a comparative looseness, thinness; they seem to show a relaxation of effort; some of the shorter ones are rather anecdotal and the longer seem to need a pulling together, a stronger focusing of powers; they partake of the character not of bush anecdotes but of easy-going bush yarns:[12] the material is there and it is good material, but it is not fused, as for instance Lawson would have fused it. An illustration of the difference in the method employed and the results reached in these two kinds of stories may be obtained by considering what might have been made of "Painted Finches" if it had been handled in the same way as the stories in the first collection. In that collection Katharine Prichard is as a stylist at her best. In the matter of succinctness, for example; it would hardly be possible to give a shorter, clearer, more tightly packed impression than in this short sentence:

> There was a couple of drovers used to come through our place, brothers, six feet both of them, great hairy fellows, strong as their own bullocks, and soft-hearted as children; but demons when they were drunk.

Incidentally, there is something in the above sentence of the tone, the feeling, of a folklore which corresponds to that of the older countries, though it embodies something of the essence of the Australian countryside.[13] Katharine Prichard's short stories contain a great many descriptive passages, but none of them for its own sake; the description is needed either as an inseparable part of the story, as it appears in the mating of Lizzie and the stallion, or as it is used in the extract quoted from "The Cow". And there are the images, small, bright windows upon the stories: of old Gourlay, as the stallion drags him "powerless at the end of his reins, behind the tip-dray as they came down hill", "looking more than ever like some dry, twiggy insect as he jogged there, shrilling fiercely"; of the stallion, "The beauty of him took the breath like a blast of cold wind"; and the image in the passage already quoted, in which Rose throws down her baby, and "there was a crack as of twigs breaking". A writer cannot of course be judged merely by his images, but by means of an image it is possible to indicate momentary heights of power; that is why so much has been made of the image in this History, and in that respect at least it is probable that in "The Grey Horse" and "The Cooboo", as in parts of *Coonardoo*, Katharine Prichard has touched her highest points: indeed, though a short story cannot be

[12] "Yarns that have been told to me" (Foreword).
[13] *Kiss on the Lips*, p. 207.

compared with a novel, she has written nothing better, for their length, than these two, except some parts of *Working Bullocks*.

Palmer's short stories are marked not by high achievement in particular instances, but by an all-round level of attainment, reached, as in his novels, by a systematic and unvarying craftsmanship and a sympathetic comprehension of certain types of character and aspects of life. His general characteristics as a novelist[14] are observable also in his short stories and need not again be discussed; but it is worth noting that his careful construction, without actually involving the old-fashioned method of plot, counterbalances the current tendency towards unorganized impression; and his restraint is a counterbalance to the accompanying tendency, especially among those affected by the new, tough school of writers, towards over-emphasis and the use of every possibility of emotional appeal. The typical Palmer story, and his methods are so little varied that many of his stories are typical, is dependent upon a single point, though it is seldom merely anecdotal, because its essence is always as much as anything a character-sketch, and this sketch is always true to life, so far as it goes. The character is almost invariably, as in the novels, that of an ordinary man; it is not merely that Palmer prefers to avoid extremes, but that, as in the novels again, it is the ordinary man in whom his interest lies. Herein is part of the reason why Palmer's short stories are in one important respect superior to his novels: in these there is less room for psychological analysis of what scarcely needs it, so that there is less danger of boredom. And behind Palmer's sketches of ordinary men and women and incidents lies always something more. Barnard Eldershaw says[15] that some of his stories embody "an aspect of life compressed into an incident so that it has the force of a symbol"; I think one may elaborate this a little, and say that what Palmer has before him as a writer of short stories is life in general, or rather that part of life which has come within his experience and imaginative vision: life like a sea on which float people and incidents and situations, or groups of these bound together; and that upon one or another of these groups he concentrates for his immediate purpose, but concentrates upon it in its context and relationships, of which some implication attaches to what he actually conveys. It is by no means the whole of life that he has before him, and its depths and intensities are usually dimmed, though they are also usually valid so far as they go; but in his work you do get something that is evoked by few short-story writers: the feeling that a vision of life, even if it is a dimmed and truncated vision, lies behind what is definitely set out; and in the best of these short stories, as in "The Sea

[14] See pp. 1108–19. Palmer has published four volumes of short stories: *Separate Lives* (London, 1931), *Sea and Spinifex* (Sydney, 1934), *Let the Birds Fly* (Sydney, 1955), and a collection selected by Allan Edwards, *The Rainbow Bird* (Sydney, 1956).

[15] *Essays in Australian Fiction*, p. 118.

Hawk" or "The Brigadier", the tragedy that takes place in the distance is nevertheless appealing. Palmer's short stories do not quicken the blood, but they are not without stimulus; he is single-minded and sincere, and he upholds a standard of life for its own sake and of the scrupulous art that is necessary for the conveyance of that life; he is never affected by the desire to impress by means of exaggeration or over-emphasis, or by the deliberate cultivation of idiosyncrasy.

The nearest to Lawson of those who follow the Lawson tradition is Frank Davison[16] (*The Woman at the Mill*, Sydney, 1940) and their relationship is most evident, as was to be expected, in the short stories. Fundamentally, it consists in a certain resemblance of scene and outlook: occasionally in Davison's stories there occurs also a literary resemblance; but it is never obvious, except in "The Yarns Men Tell"; and this is acknowledged and in the nature of an affectionate reminiscence, as one might consciously adopt something of his grandfather's manner in telling a story his grandfather might have told. And there is this marked difference between grandfather and grandson: Davison is without the melancholy that in spite of all his humour shadows Lawson's general vision of the outback. Davison spent his boyhood in the countryside and later returned to it, and his attitude as a short-story writer is that of an easy-going countryman, though much more imaginative than most, who, without being himself much in evidence, misses nothing that happens in his neighbourhood, observing it all with a humorous tolerance and talking to himself about what he has observed: Davison is the farmer, Lawson the man with the swag; one thinks of Lawson beside the camp-fire, Davison at work on his farm. And there is another difference, though it by no means thrusts itself forward. The pains that Lawson must have taken to acquire the stylistic perfection of some of his best work are never evident; that is why he has been called so often a "natural stylist": but in Davison's style, easy and natural as it also is, there is observable a certain deliberateness; one can feel that he is being careful. And there is another thing: Davison, small as is his talent beside Lawson's, is a much better educated man; this is apparent in some of his images. Working, then, in the Lawson tradition, and with some resemblance to the attitude and point of view of its founder, Davison is at the same time indebted for his artistic standards generally to Vance and also to Nettie Palmer,[17] and, in addition, to Barnard Eldershaw. To Palmer indeed he owes more than an example of high standards: he has adopted one of Palmer's mannerisms, the habit of imagining conversations or parts of conversations as though they had actually taken place, when in fact they did not exist, except in the

[16] For Davison's novels, see pp. 1119-25.

[17] See the Dedication.

imagination of the speakers themselves;[18] there is an extreme example in "Here Comes the Bride", in which Pa, desperately afraid of not being able to hold out until the drought breaks, resents increasingly the continual piling up of expensive preparations for his daughter's wedding:[19]

> Pa's clenched fist crashed down on the table in a way that made the cups leap in their saucers and the two women turn to him with the arched eyebrows of consternation. "My God, woman," he shouted at his wife, "Have a little mercy on me!";

but, Davison adds,

> This happened only in Pa's imagination. What really took place was that he choked back his feelings and rose, a little white of face, and quietly left the room.

The actual exclamation however is not characteristic of Palmer; in this as in other matters, Davison is much more outright: this may be illustrated by the description of Mrs Gillen's discovery of Hilda and the Dreadnought boy and the ladies' comments upon it later.[20] And there are occasional sentences of Davison's that might have been written by Palmer; for instance,[21]

> At the railhead, neighbours on the platform had been quick to notice the kelpie.
> "Where'd you pick up the kelpie, Cody?"
> "Good looking dog you've got there, Lou!"
> It had been quite gratifying.

Nevertheless Davison's style is individual, a crystallization of the personality that has been noted as informing his stories; it is a marked advance upon the style of his novels, which were written earlier; he has learnt while writing: it is more lively than Palmer's style, more friendly and familiar; it brings one closer to what is described. Like Palmer's style in his novels rather than in his short stories, Davison's is full of images, all of which are natural and most of which are the result of imaginative observation, as

> Conversation with him was an inch-by-inch affair, like shifting a shed with a crowbar;

> His smile, when you worried one out of him, was like a momentary gleam on wintry water; his laugh, at best, was rusty and unwilling;

and

> A singer and her accompanist were taking their places at the piano; Madame Forsster, as she called herself, and that hank of limp seaweed she trailed round with her.

These images are illuminative of what has been observed, but others are not merely illuminative but creative: as in

> For me, de Burgh's block was a place, an escape, and a condition of mind;

> Their eyes met in passing—Jenny's faintly squinny eye, that made you feel that fairy tales might be true.

[18] See p. 1116.
[19] See "Here Comes the Bride", p. 16.
[20] The same, pp. 26, 28.
[21] The same, p. 68.

Davison's characterization is always objective; you never feel, as with many of Palmer's principal characters, that his men and women are, in part at least, emanations of their creator's mind: one rubs shoulders with all of them; they seem to have a three-dimensional existence, and exist outside the book. It has been said that there is a strong likeness between Davison's characters: here it must be remembered that they are almost all country types; also about half the stories in which they appear are told in the first person[22] and all are pervaded by the personality of the narrator, who is also a country type; and, unlike Prichard and Palmer, Davison seldom reaches for the depths or heights of life. Davison's range is perhaps smaller than Prichard's or Palmer's; it is certainly smaller if novels as well as short stories are taken into account: nevertheless, he will bear rereading as much as either of them.

Still in the Australian tradition, but in succession this time from Steele Rudd, is "Brian James"[23] (*Cookabundy Bridge*, Sydney, 1946). James is a chronicler of the commonplace daily incidents of farm and small township life; he has nothing of Steele Rudd's uproarious extravaganza with its grim undercurrent, but stands for humorous and rather hard realism with an occasional satiric touch; lacking also Steele Rudd's force and informing personality, he has his own individuality and is a far better craftsman, and he stands much closer to the actual fact. His range is so narrow that with him monotony is always just round the corner, but he writes so freshly and with such sincerity and intimate understanding of character, incident and situation that it stays there if his stories are not read too many at a time. Alan Marshall,[24] in *Tell Us About the Turkey, Jo* (Sydney, 1946), does not follow any particular branch of the tradition the others represent, but as a whole it is behind him, and most of his stories are set in the countryside; he is more modern than the others, and his work shows the influence of the fiction magazines, though it was only occasionally that he wrote a mere magazine story. He was much further from the soil than James, and made no attempt to record its everyday life; he can be realistic enough, but his essential quality is sensitiveness and a romance that is often dramatic; the danger here is not monotony but sentimentalism and melodrama: these spoil what might otherwise have been some of his best stories; but "Blow Carson, I Say" almost escapes them, and Marshall's stories about little children are delightful. Broadly in the tradition again are three writers who are concerned mainly with the life of small townships: Margaret

---

[22] This, as Davison explains in an author's note, is merely a technical device that suits him; the narrator is not to be identified with the author.

[23] For his novel, see pp. 1132-3. "James" has since published another collection of short stories, *The Bunyip of Barney's Elbow* (Sydney, 1956).

[24] He has also published, since the closing date of this History, a slice of autobiography, *I Can Jump Puddles* (Melbourne, 1955).

Trist[25] (*What Else is There?*, Sydney, 1946); Myra Morris[26] (*The Township*, Sydney, 1947); and Cecil Mann, (*The River and Other Stories*, Sydney, 1945). The work of the two women has some things in common; Mann's stands by itself: he is a literary artist, of a kind uncommon in Australia, and a large part of the attraction of his short stories, as of his novel,[27] consists in the atmosphere in which they are bathed, and through which figures and incidents appear, lifelike, but formalized and a little dim. The centre of most of them is a small coastal township and some of its typical representatives, but there is an undercurrent, which comes to the surface now and then, of memories of the first World War, and of experiences in it shared by old friends: "Stiff Luck for the Colonel" is characteristic; "The Pelican", much less so, is one of the best of the stories. Mann's is a pleasant and friendly style, leisurely, sensitive, quietly humorous, and a tendency to monotony in his work is counterbalanced by its humanity and charm. The stories of both women include country and city suburb as well as township, and, as is natural, some of their characters are similar in type; in both the feminine point of view is apparent and in Margaret Trist's stories it is all-pervasive; and both writers are without illusions: but beyond these things they have little in common. Myra Morris has, as one might expect from her poems, a romantic imagination; there is an undercurrent of sadness in her work, and occasionally with her sentiment approaches sentimentality; the essence of Margaret Trist's stories on the other hand is a bright and humorous common sense; she is not sentimental even when she is sad, and with her the evils of life are accepted with patient or humorous fatalism: hers are not so much stories as sketches; they are largely domestic, and in each of the three parts into which her book is divided they are more or less related, with some repetitions. Myra Morris's are definitely stories and are much more varied: one or two, "Sun" for instance, are exceptionally good, but about almost all of them there is a hint of formula and the magazines; one feels that the idea of making an impression has been on the writer's mind. Margaret Trist's are much nearer to ordinary life; the figure of "grandmother", dominating, impulsive, incalculable, fascinating in youth and attractive in age, in spite of her difficult corsets and voluminous calico undergarments, is hard to match in the local short-story field today. Margaret Trist has also glimpses of life in a cheap boarding house, of adolescent boys and girls and their homes in the cheaper suburbs, and of the easy-going families in which the girls are always having or uneasily expecting babies; all these add up to a view of life which has its chuckles and its pieces of wisdom:

[25] For her novel, see p. 1135. She published earlier another collection of stories, which is far inferior to this.

[26] For Myra Morris's poems, see p. 1057. She has also published several novels.

[27] See p. 1134.

"Keep the kids out of the shop while I serve Emmy," she ordered. "She's a bit touched, but fussy all the same. She don't like the kids licking the biscuits. It puts her off buying them";

. . . .

"It's sin," said Emmy weakly.

"Sin, pooh! You and your sin. A little of that kind of sin wouldn't do you any harm, my girl";

. . . .

"What do you mean? No harm! A girl of eighteen and don't mean no harm! What the devil's the matter with her?" [This, of course, is a man speaking];

and

Grandfather subsided suddenly. "Women will never let bygones be bygones," he grumbled.

"Women have only bygones," affirmed Grandmother.

"Whose fault is that?" demanded Grandfather.

"Their own," returned Grandmother steadily.

With Gavin Casey and to a lesser extent with Don Edwards[28] lack of illusion becomes cold disillusion, a more or less humorously fatalistic acceptance of life with all its faults and shortcomings giving way to a bitter and self-pitying gloom. With both writers however there are qualifications and exceptions; these are much more marked with Edwards than with Casey, and there is in him, as in the title-story of his first book, an element of romantic idealism which brightens the grey atmosphere. With Casey there is no such brightening except as it affects the past, and this by contrast makes the present gloomier still. On the other hand Casey's stories have a greater power, and there is in his principal characters a kind of angry endurance, a clinging to some sort of hope which saves their attitude from being an Eliotean rejection of life. Casey circles about a small radius, Edwards's radius is comparatively large; but in both there are repetitions of names and human types, and Edwards repeats again and again particular themes. Most of the stories in Casey's *It's Harder for Girls* (Sydney, 1942)[29] and *Birds of a Feather* (Perth, 1943) are set on the Western Australian goldfields, on which Casey himself has lived the life of a miner; they are haunted by dread of the future, of "miners' complaint", and of the accidents that mount up gradually in mining life. But these are by no means always the direct cause of the gloom of his stories: comparative poverty; lost boyhood and youth; physical decline; and, bitterest of all, the barriers between man and wife that arise and strengthen inevitably with the drinking that has been the principal character's principal refuge from monotony and disappointment. The attitude of this principal character is always the same; indeed he is actually the same person, whose continually unsuccessful aspiration

---

28 For their novels, see pp. 1136 and 1134.

29 This won the *Bulletin's* S. H. Prior Memorial Prize for 1942.

is accompanied by gradual and inescapable decline. All this is summed up in one of Casey's best and most characteristic stories, "Short Shift Saturday"; in another, the title-story of his first book, which is as good but less characteristic, it is the effects of a "tough" childhood that are mainly to blame for what happens later, and though the boys are able to climb out of the pit whence they were digged, their sister is not. Casey is in fact a moralist; his principal characters or character is an embodied conscience, and his stories might appropriately have been given as an epigraph Ovid's *Video meliora proboque, deteriora sequor*. The gloom of the stories in Edwards's *High Hill at Midnight* (Sydney, 1944) is not grounded in fear of the results of a miner's life; it inheres even more obviously than with Casey in the person rather than in the circumstances; not only however is it less general than with Casey, but the bitterness is more subdued and there is less power in the characters as well as in the stories. The stories are also much more varied, in spite of the repetitions of theme; it is surprising in a capable author to find so many repetitions: three times a wife has left her husband[30] and twice[31] the state of affairs between them seems to be leading up to a final break; two stories deal with the attraction of the strange woman in the bush;[32] in two a small boy's father, himself a boxer, encourages him to fight;[33] and several stories are connected with unemployment during the Depression, by characters that have a good deal in common. But quite often the gloom is wholly or partially broken down, whereas with Casey the only relief occurs in a few minor humorous stories; with Edwards also women play a much more active part and are more individually drawn,[34] and if there are traces of sentimentality there are also, especially in his title-story, glimpses of beauty.

Marjorie Barnard, one of the two collaborators who wrote as "Barnard Eldershaw",[35] has written on her own account a series of tales which however does not fit easily into any of the categories here used. *The Persimmon Tree* (Sydney, 1943) throws a delicate aerial bridge between the old world and the new; it has its root in this new and culturally undeveloped country, but it could not have flowered without an intimate awareness of the attitude and apparatus of a ripe and sophisticated civilization. Miss Barnard, like a few other Australian writers of fiction, mostly women, is concerned rather with mental and emotional moods than with the adventurous experiences that give rise to them; yet such

---

[30] "You Drive Lola Home", "He Walks Home With His Wife" and "Escape for Her".

[31] "A New Job" and "A Move to the City": but these two deal with the same characters.

[32] "The House on the Cliff" and "The Woman from the Bend"; the latter is the story which was later expanded into the novel, *The Woman at Jingera* (see p. 1134).

[33] "Fighting Makes a Man of You" and "A Bit of a Hit is Nothing".

[34] Molly in Casey's "It's Harder for Girls" is the one outstanding exception.

[35] For Barnard's and Barnard and Eldershaw's historical work, see pp. 1348–9, 1367–9 respectively; for their critical work, pp. 1284–6; and for their descriptive work, pp. 1382–5.

moods are shown as arising naturally out of concrete qualities and situations. She is also one of the few who stand for art as contrasted with merely capable and appropriate expression; yet it is by no means art merely, for her men and women are such as one might meet and talk to, though without necessarily being conscious of the shades and implications which their creator perceives and conveys. It is the feminine mind with which she is predominantly concerned, yet one or two of her ironic glimpses of business men are sharp and real; she has also a sympathetic understanding of children, as of the unfortunate little girl whose egotistically common "aunt" insists on helping her to enjoy the ballet, perversely invading her privacies of appreciation with clumsy interpretations. She is concerned almost always with one type or another of feminine frustration, and this and most of her characteristic qualities are focused in the beautiful and symbolic title-story; yet some of her more "ordinary" stories, and in particular "Habit", and also "The Dressmaker" and "The New Dress", though not so charged with emotion, are as revelatory of aspects of life: now and again, however, as in "The New Hat", she handles a theme that without her delicate percipience and power of relating small things to large might appear trivial; and once or twice, as in "The Lottery" and "The Bride Elect", with their trickish endings, she does not quite escape a suggestion of the literary magazine. Her style, sensitive, allusive, a little self-conscious, is permeated with a fanciful imagination, and her frequently satirical comments are often witty and always penetrating: in her stories of the business world, "she had felt everywhere ebbing credit pull like a tide"; and there is the "mild, frail old gentleman, so shrewd that you never suspected it till several months after it was too late to do anything about it"; and in her more characteristic world of the feminine "a fragment of story" is "like a tit-bit among gulls"; and "most of the customers were girls like herself, hunting for a rainbow in the jungle"; and in the curious fantasy, "Dry Spell",

> The trees were black, and their leaves made a little dry sound like ghostly butter pats . . . the torrid lamps were like sores on the night. . . . It was the third waterless summer, and the heat had come down like a steel shutter over the city.

Marjorie Barnard contributes here something that is new in Australian fiction; not that there is anything intrinsically novel about her subjects, her moods, her characters, but because of the delicacy and penetration with which she interprets and illuminates and the novelty with which she invests what in type and general outline are familiar. When Australian fiction is able to combine with her subtlety of percipience and suggestion the freshness, the masculine vigour and the racial individuality which have always characterized its best work, what some of its more ambitious enthusiasts claim of it now will have been achieved.

There remain some younger or at least newer writers. *The Tramp* (London, 1936) by Dal (las George) Stivens (Blayney, N.S.W., 1911-) was at the date of its publication the most promising collection by a young writer since the end of the first World War.[36] His next book, *The Courtship of Uncle Henry* (Melbourne, 1946) was not published until ten years later, and most of its contents were so short as to leave no room for more than the barest skeleton; his later stories have not been collected,[37] and most of them seem to be Munchausenish extravaganzas. Stivens was educated in the country and at Barker College, Hornsby, New South Wales; after three years on the staff of the Sydney *Daily Telegraph* he entered the Army Education Service, and on discharge joined the Commonwealth Department of Information; for some years he was a freelance in London, but he now lives in Sydney. Stivens's work has definite limitations, but they have nothing to do with expression, for in the matter of craftsmanship he emerged full-armed: his manner is his own, except for an occasional faint suggestion of D. H. Lawrence, and, in several stories in the second book, a definite reflection of some of the neo-barbarics and especially Hemingway; and, a good sign in a young writer, he is experimental, trying not so much for new forms as for novelty in expression. Even in the first collection the stories are short: cross-sections of human types and human and animal experiences, revealed directly and in detail, with extreme conciseness and clarity, as though dissected out under a microscope. The theme is usually frustration of one type or another, but it is quite different from anything of the kind in Marjorie Barnard: most of Stivens's are male and comparatively simple types, their frustration arises more out of circumstances than out of their sex as such, and the method of presentation is outright rather than suggestive and not sensitive but blunt. Stivens has been accused of lack of human sympathy, but to this there are qualifications: he does sympathize with men or animals in misfortune, but it is as a rule an intellectual rather than an emotional sympathy; his attitude in general is entirely detached, but he makes it vividly clear at the conclusion on which side his intellectual sympathy lies, and this is especially marked in his animal stories. He may be compared with the surgeon at the dissecting table, whose business is exploratory analysis; or, better, with the scientific investigator of a social or individual evil, who may point out its cause and its injustice, but does so with emotional detachment,

---

[36] There was of course Les Robinson, but *The Giraffe's Uncle* (pp. 1258-9) represented achievement rather than promise: an achievement that might be equalled later, but did not suggest the beginning of something bigger.

[37] Stivens has since published three other collections: *The Gambling Ghost* (Sydney, 1953), *Ironbark Bill* (Sydney, 1955) and *The Scholarly Mouse* (Sydney, 1957), as well as two novels, *Jimmy Brockett* (London, 1951) and *The Wide Arch* (Sydney, 1958). [These were followed by *Three Persons Make a Tiger*, a novel (1968), a volume of *Selected Short Stories* (1969) and a novel, *The Horse of Air* (1970).]

though his conclusion may be emphasized. Herein, however, lies Stivens's fundamental limitation: a lack of the broad humanity that characterizes almost all writers who are really first rate, with the notable exception of Maupassant. Stivens's understanding of widely varied types of character is surprising in so young a man as he was at the publication of his first book; and now and then, when he deals with young and innocent girlhood, especially in "Harvest Time" but also elsewhere, he shows more than merely intellectual sympathy. The stories in John Morrison's *Sailors Belong Ships* (Melbourne, 1947) are of two contrasting kinds: sketches of the work, trials, and sometimes tragedies of labourers on the waterfront; and tales of a more or less fantastic imagination. The first are glimpses of everyday life of a certain type, sympathetic without sentimentality, short, direct, almost structureless and filled with energy; the second are longer, there are definite plots, and the subjects are more or less abnormal: the most impressive, "North Wind", a study of a horrible old witch of a mother-in-law who refuses to stir from the house, even in a blazing bushfire, shows a marked talent for the bizarre. In spite of a touch here and there of artificiality, even melodrama, this collection is most promising.[38] Another writer of promise that has not been properly realized was Percy Reginald Stephensen (Biggenden, Q., 1901-65), who was best known as the author of *The Foundations of Culture in Australia*.[39] Stephensen was educated at the Maryborough Grammar School and at the Universities of Queensland and Oxford, to which he won a Rhodes Scholarship; he was manager of the Fanfrolico Press,[40] and he published a translation of Nietzsche's *Antichrist*. His *The Bush-whackers*[41] (London, 1929) is a short collection of short tales, largely anecdotal, of the countryside on which Stephensen was born and brought up, but they do not bring us into intimate acquaintance with the bush and its men and women, nor are Stephensen's themes new, though his enthusiasm gives them some fresh life; his style is self-conscious and at times crude and touched with a rather facile cynicism, but the tales suggest the makings of something better. More interesting than any of these, from the point of view of future possibilities, is Peter (Walkinshaw) Cowan (Perth, 1914-), whose first published book was *Drift* (Melbourne, 1944); ten years younger than Morrison and three years younger than Stivens, unlike either of these he has not done anything to take the edge off his promise. Cowan had his schooling in Perth and worked as

---

[38] Morrison has since published another collection of short stories, *Black Cargo* (Melbourne, 1955). For his novels, see p. 1135.

[39] See pp. 1438-9 and 1069.

[40] See p. 1208, and note 1.

[41] [Country people lacking in social graces, rough but direct, simple but shrewd. See G. A. Wilkes's *A Dictionary of Australian Colloquialisms* (1978).]

clerk, farm labourer, farmer and casual labourer; he then graduated at the University of Western Australia, and is now Senior Lecturer in English at Scots' College and a tutor at the University. His work belongs to the Australian school and has even some relationship with Lawson's, but it is Lawson on the gloomy side and Cowan quite lacks Lawson's humour; like Lawson, it is women as well as men that he reveals, but with him it is the younger women, and with him also sex plays a part that it never played with Lawson: what Lawson passes over Cowan emphasizes, but not unnaturally; it is simply that in this matter as in others he is much more modern; indeed he is more modern than any other writer of short stories of the Australian countryside. Cowan does not show any individual influence from without, but he has obviously read the modernists and his attitude is akin to theirs; what stands out in his work is its sincerity and its sympathetic insight, as directed to the loneliness, the monotony, and the occasional queernesses of the bush, and to the effects of the Depression upon the young men and women of the cities: here the characters and their language may seem at first sight touched with Americanism, but this is probably due rather to a cosmopolitan modernity to which American life and literature have largely contributed. Atmosphere is important with Cowan, and he achieves it, sometimes by adding detail to detail, or sometimes on the other hand by generalization without specific details that would have made all the difference from a realistic point of view: he writes usually short, almost colourless and rather jerky sentences, approaching life in the manner of the modern American realists; but occasionally, as in "Isolation", the sentences are far longer and the style runs smoothly and connectedly. Cowan is a capable and conscientious craftsman, who has some distance to travel yet;[42] there is no doubt about his powers.

For the rest, so far as stories of the Australian mainland are concerned, J. K. Ewers's short stories of farm and township, in *Harvest* (Sydney, 1949) have the same characteristics as his novels.[43] Ewers observes closely and sympathetically, and sets out the results of his observations clearly and concisely, but a certain lack of imaginative insight makes his stories sometimes insipid. The miscellaneous Australian experiences of George (Mitchell) Farwell (Bath, England, 1911-76), who migrated from England in 1930, are reflected in *Surf Music* (Sydney, 1950). In tone, outlook and even in subject[44] these stories now and then, in spite of their modernity of colloquialism, remind one of Lawson, and in determination to pack

42 He has since published another volume of short stories, *The Unploughed Land* (Sydney, 1958).
43 For these, see p. 1133.
44 See, for instance, "The Darling Cod".

all that is possible into a suggestive sentence, and often in the turn of a phrase, especially in the conversations, there is an obvious debt to Palmer; yet the stories are by no means mere imitations, and they mirror certain outback characters and aspects of life. *Sydney Or the Bush* (Sydney, 1948), by Henrietta (Frances) Drake-Brockman (Perth, 1901–68) should also be mentioned.

The awakened interest in New Guinea and the tendency in Australian writers of verse and prose to look occasionally beyond the Australian continent are exemplified by two collections of tales: in both fresh life is given to people and incidents of the past, and though their subjects are as far apart as civilization and savagery, simplicity and sophistication, both sets of tales are told simply and unpretentiously, with touches of ironic humour. *Indian Tales* (Sydney, 1948) was written to keep in mind "the charm of an ancient civilisation"; *Savage Tales* (Melbourne, 1946) which is set in Papua, to "try to depict primitive people in a stage of development which . . . is being quickly overlaid by at least a superficial layer of civilised habit": the material for *Indian Tales* was gathered by (Mrs) Ethel Anderson[45] during her ten years' residence on the Indian frontier; the material for *Savage Tales* by Lewis Lett[46] (Waddingham, Lincolnshire, England, 1878–1966), from experience of half a lifetime in Papua as planter, trader and engineer. Throughout the first collection: old ladies gossiping in the zenana, a game of living chess in which two fiefs are wagered against a beautiful Burmese slave, love-making, intrigue and murder: there appears something of the essence of India past and present, and "Mrs James Greene" ("spelt with an 'e'") comes in some respects near being a masterpiece. The second collection has a definite sociological importance, but apart from that its two folk-tales: of the creation of the first woman, marred by the first man's insistence upon adding to the other ingredients the tongue of a parrot; and, tragic but beautiful, of the first coconut: and also the stories of the invention of the double canoe, of the outwitting of a repulsive uncle and of the tragic conflicts between native custom and the white man's law, have not only psychological interest but a fairytale-like charm. The greed, brutality and treachery of the Papuan savage are shown as redeemed by his dignity, hardihood and intelligence; and the explanation[47] by the perfect headman of his tribe's attack upon the white men who had done them no harm throws a clear light upon the workings of the Papuan mind.

There were few war stories, and of these by far the most impressive

---

[45] For her poems and essays, see pp. 1010 and 1062–3 respectively. Mrs Anderson published another volume of short stories, *At Parramatta* (Melbourne, 1956); after her death appeared *The Little Ghosts* (Sydney, 1959), another volume of Indian tales.

[46] For Lett's biographical work, see pp. 1374–5.

[47] In "Treachery".

dates back to the beginning of the present Period; though the work of an Australian-born writer and written before he had left Australia, in tone and style it belongs to the old world rather than to the new. *Two Masters* (London, 1929) though published by itself, contains only thirty-two pages; its author is Arthur Leslie Wheen (Bathurst, N.S.W., 1897-1971), best known as the translator of Remarque's *All Quiet on the Western Front.*[48] Wheen was educated at the Sydney High School and the University of Sydney, to whose undergraduate magazine, *Hermes*, the story was contributed in 1923;[49] he fought in the first World War, won a Rhodes Scholarship to Oxford, and became librarian at the Victoria and Albert Museum, London. The story involves a conflict between the claims of one's country and of the moral standard of the individual: these are the "two masters": but it involves also a remarkable analysis of an unusual character through the medium of a friend who quite misunderstands it, though he has clues enough, so that the truth emerges through and in spite of his mistaken conclusions. It is a masterly story, whose only defect is a superabundance of literary allusions and quotations. Of the other collections, R. S. Porteous's *Little Known of These Waters* (Sydney, 1945) deals, like his subsequent novel,[50] with the experiences of some of the miscellaneous collection of vessels that carried military supplies from Australia to New Guinea during the second World War: these sketches are slight but competent; except in "Jellico" there is not much characterization, the story is the thing, but we are placed in close and exciting contact with what is described. Jon Cleary's *These Small Glories* (Sydney, 1946) is sketches of the fighting in the Middle East and of intervals of romantic love-making; less objective than Porteous's sketches, these are more imaginative: naïve and full of Hemingwayisms, they yet show a promise which has been redeemed in Cleary's subsequent novels.[51] *Glimpses* (London, 1928), by "Corrie Dennison", is a series of sketches of service with the A.I.F. at Gallipoli and in France, and also of school life and teaching in Queensland and of study at Oxford, along with some realistic love-making; the author, who has evidently drawn sometimes upon early personal experience, is the well-known authority on English and Australian slang, Eric (Honeywood) Partridge (Waimatu Valley, N.Z., 1894-1979), who was educated in Queensland and at Oxford, and served four years in the A.I.F. before settling down in England. Most of the sketches are scrappy and structureless and there is an amateurish and slightly self-conscious air about them; but except for some superfluous

[48] Wheen has also translated other work by Remarque.

[49] It was reprinted in the *London Mercury*, in O'Brien's *Best Stories*, in *The Mercury Story Book*, and in *Irish Stories of the War*.

[50] See p. 1220. He has since published another volume of short stories, *Close to the Wind* (London, 1955).

[51] See pp. 1172, 1173-5.

details about sport and reading they are interesting, and their style, smooth, self-conscious and a little naïve, is not without a certain charm.

Fantasy in Australia is as rare among short stories as among novels, but in this Period there have been several collections that stand out. Christina Stead's *Salzburg Tales*,[52] which has been referred to in discussing her novels, has no more relation to the Australian short story of today than Richardson's had to the short story of the preceding Period. *The Salzburg Tales* is a much slighter thing than *The End of a Childhood*, but it is fascinating: an extremely miscellaneous collection of tales supposed to have been told at the Mozart Festival at Salzburg in the Austrian Tyrol, as a whole it is outside the scope of this History, for it was not published until some years after Christina Stead had left this country, but something may be said about it here because three of the tales are supposed to be set in Australia and several others may be connected with Australia in one way or another. The collection has been compared with *The Decameron*, Heine's *Florentine Nights*, Hans Andersen's *What the Moon Saw*, *The Arabian Nights* and *The Castle of Otranto*; and flavours of all of these combine in what is however not synthetic but extremely original. If one is looking for resemblances however there is also Anatole France, and, most obvious of all, the Prologue to *The Canterbury Tales*, of which Stead's description of her Personages is however an elaborate and sophisticated modern equivalent rather than an imitation, though the Prologue continually rises to the mind as one reads through it: the acute vision, the sly humour, the satiric touches, the abundant life; there is the Schoolteacher for instance, who "ate delicately of chicken, salad and jelly": think of Chaucer's Prioress. "The Triskelion" is the only one of the "Australian" tales that really matters; it is a story of sexual abnormality and the supernatural, set in Sydney and Terrigal, and told by the Doctress,

> . . . a Scottish woman from Inverness, jolly, fresh-complexioned and round, tall, with a small waist and wide bosom; with ginger hair and russet eyelids and eyes like cats' eyes.

These tales have an extraordinary range of scene, subject, character and manner: comedies, tragedies, fairy-tales, fantasies, extravaganzas; they are idealistic, ludicrous, cynical, adventurous and exciting, pathetic sometimes, but there is something of all these kinds and qualities in almost every one of them. All the tales are fantasies, though most are realistic in their own way, and again they are almost all humorous, though the humour may lie beneath the surface; also, like many collections of their kind, they have a definite bias in the direction of sex, and attitude and manner of telling do not vary so much as the characters

[52] Stead has also written other short stories besides *The Salzburg Tales*; see, for instance, "If I Could But Shiver" in *The Fairies Return* (London, 1934), a collection by several hands.

of the tellers of the tales, though many of these also have a good deal in common. In spite of the resemblances noted, some of which are far-off, there has not been anything quite like this collection before.

A second fantasist, Les (Leslie Frederick) Robinson (Sydney, 1886-1968), is about as like Christina Stead as a grasshopper is like a hippogriff; but this is an extremely unusual grasshopper. As compared with Stead's domain, even as a fantasist merely, Robinson's is a nook, a pigeon-hole, a small cave in the bushy outskirts of some far-off suburb, but within it is something new and individual. *The Salzburg Tales* belongs to an old and cultivated world, full of ancestors and relationships; *The Giraffe's Uncle* (Sydney, 1933) belongs to a minute and almost isolated spheroid, in which grotesque and absurd fancies reveal an impossible but queerly attractive personality, protesting unavailingly but irrepressibly against rationality, common sense and a social scheme which is entirely foreign to its nature. Les Robinson attended, at intervals, various preparatory schools, failed in an examination which would have admitted him to a bank clerkship, and passed rapidly in and out of various occupations, including work in a leather merchant's warehouse and a wool and hides store; what he calls "a deficiency in staying power" was no doubt the result of a certain physical languor, a disinclination to get up early in the morning, and a fondness for fishing and rather desultory nature study, combined with an entire lack of sympathy with civilized routine and processes which made a permanent job impossible. The one thing Robinson will work hard at is writing, and he has contributed fables,[53] fantasies, nature studies, essays and short stories to various newspapers and magazines and in particular the *Bulletin*; he has lived in all sorts of places in which the rent was nominal, including a tumbledown shack in the suburban bush, within which he had to erect a tent in wet weather. Involved in his nonsensical inconsequences and pure fantasies is a quiet irony directed against the extraordinary world in which he is exiled, and whose contemptuous attitude towards his incompetence he professes to accept. "He typifies," according to Kenneth Slessor, in his introduction to *The Giraffe's Uncle*, "the intellectual trapped in a factory, mocking his own impotence for consolation"; this hits the nail on the head, except that Robinson is actually rather the artist than the intellectual, and belongs by rights, if he belongs anywhere, to the bohemia of Murger, whose stories he much admires. He has a remarkable gift for the invention of names and phrases, as in the story[54] in which the Fundamental Podargus, "gwunking" miserably, searches for the duck's beak in the desert, whose sandy surface exclaims in regular rhythm toitoi-toitoi-toitoitoitoi at the impact of Henry's feet. This sort of thing is thrown into high relief

[53] These have been collected, but unfortunately never published.
[54] "The Duck's Beak".

by the grave, precise and rather formal style in which it is embedded; sometimes indeed the effect is a little startling, as when after a short philosophical disquisition upon the indisputable importance, in the arts as in life, of the semitone, Ferdinand suddenly exclaims, "I feel as though excited fish were swimming in my blood!" The story of the giraffe who so bores the other inhabitants of the zoo with his constant chatter of forests and vast plains that an elderly gorilla breaks out of a neighbouring cage and ties the giraffe's tail into a knot that could never afterwards be undone; of the clockwork racehorse, which ends with the narrator's condemnation, because he has forgotten to wind the rajah's watch, to become, first thing next morning, an alligator's breakfast; of the dialogue with the big policeman, who arrests Aubrey for cruelty to animals, on the ground of his "carrying live fish and periwinkles in his pocket, consorting with seagulls and running like mad in the dark": these, varying as they do between inconsequent humour, sometimes just a little journalistically strained, and, in the best though not the most characteristic story, "Ferdinand and Jolinquitus", a kind of more or less conscious mysticism, give some idea of the queer miscellaneous contents of Robinson's small cave. One can understand how some may pass the book by with a smile, and others may acclaim it as revealing some at least of the characteristics of genius.

Mervyn Garnham Skipper (Adelaide, 1886-1959), is a writer of fantastic fairy-tales. *The Meeting Pool* (London, 1929) and *The White Man's Garden*[55] (London, 1930) are the only collections of short stories for children that need be mentioned here, but they are by far the best of their kind[56] that have appeared in this country. Skipper, who was educated in Adelaide and who represented the *Bulletin* in Melbourne, spent several years on the staff of the Eastern Extension Cable Company, and these tales are set and most of them were collected on a little island off the coast of Borneo: they are supposed to be told by the beasts and birds and smaller creatures of the jungle, and by the trees and smaller plants in a garden at its edge. Nobody can tell a fairy-tale better than Skipper: all the speakers are characterized so far as there is room; the dialogue is lively and natural; borrowings are given new and individual life; the conventional repetitions that connect parts of stories and the stories themselves are also individualized, and the stories are suffused with a humorous imagination: the *Just So Stories* could scarcely fail to be among their literary ancestors, but if Skipper has not Kipling's genius, neither has he Kipling's sometimes rather irritating mannerisms. There is plenty of humour and some wit in these fantasies, as indeed there is plenty of

[55] Both books have been translated into more than one European language, and *The Meeting Pool* is included in Penguin's Puffin series.

[56] Norman Lindsay's fairy-tales (see p. 1229) are not short stories.

humour at least in the Australian short story in general, but except in Skipper's fairy-tales it is not an essential feature, as it is in a number of novels. An exception is Ronald McCuaig's[57] *Tales Out of Bed* (Sydney, 1944), a miscellaneous collection of stories, sketches, monologues and conversations, all light, bright and vivacious, and animated by an ironically fanciful and sometimes fantastic humour; these are incongruously accompanied by a number of criticisms, which are often penetrating.

There were quite a number of prose anthologies; the most important from the point of view of the present day is *Coast to Coast*, which, on the same plan as *Australian Poetry*, collects the best short stories of the last year, or, sometimes, of the last two years. As for the novel, to base one's acquaintance with that upon any anthology, however good, would be foolish; of its nature it must consist of snippets, and these from no more than part of the novelists' works: extracts from extracts. Yet, since so many of the best Australian novels are unobtainable outside the larger libraries, some such guidance seems necessary; though too many readers are likely to seize upon an anthology not as a guide-post but as a substitute. Colin Roderick's two volumes, *The Australian Novel* (Sydney, 1945) and *20 Australian Novelists* (Sydney, 1947), are the first of their kind, though in the previous Period there had been a prose anthology that included works of fiction.[58] A third volume by Roderick is to deal with the short story; a fourth, *An Introduction to Australian Fiction* (Sydney, 1950), which has been interposed, is not an anthology but a critical summary. In the two published anthologies the authors are on the whole well chosen, the only important omissions being Catherine Spence[59] and "Tasma",[60] whose apparently quite forgotten *Uncle Piper of Piper's Hill* surely deserves a place; these two novelists are apparently considered less worth reading than Roy Bridges, Dorothy Cottrell, Ion Idriess (*Drums of Mer*) and Jack McLaren (*Sun Man*). The novels and the extracts from them are also on the whole well chosen, though it would be hard to defend the representation of Ada Cambridge by the least Australian of her novels, at the expense of *A Marked Man*, which is the most Australian, with its magnificent death-scene.[61] The critical introductions, parts of which have been repeated in *An Introduction to Australian Fiction*, are poor: Roderick can even say that of Brent of Bin Bin's novels the succeeding volumes are better than *Up the Country*,

---

[57] For McCuaig's poems, see pp. 1040–2.

[58] See p. 632. Since the closing date of this History there have appeared two anthologies, both of which contain verse as well as prose: *Australia Writes* (Melbourne, 1953) and *Australian Signpost* (Melbourne, 1956). The first was edited by T. Inglis Moore, whose poems have been discussed on pp. 1034–6 and his criticism on pp. 1286–7, and the second by T. A. G. Hungerford, whose novels fall outside the scope of this History. Both these anthologies were edited for the Canberra Fellowship of Australian Writers. There was also *Australian Short Stories* (London, 1951), selected by Walter Murdoch and Henrietta Drake-Brockman.

[59] See pp. 219–26. [60] See pp. 275–80. [61] See pp. 274–5.

from which nevertheless his only extract is taken. Another anthology of Roderick's, *Wanderers in Australia* (Sydney, 1949), is good so far as it goes, but would have gained by the inclusion of passages from Lawrence and certain other novelists.[62] Much better than these is C. B. Christesen's[63] *Australian Heritage* (Melbourne, 1949); this attempts in not much more than 70,000 words to show "the slow development of a distinctive utterance" in writers of Australian prose; the gradual growth of an understanding of an Australian way of life, and, incidentally, "the relationship between the imaginative writer and the historian in interpreting life through literature". No fault can be found with the illustrations, given the compiler's point of view, but it is a pity that there are not more of them; as it is, an excellent thesis is scantily substantiated; also, should the cities have been entirely omitted, in a book that has not the excuse of being expressly concerned with wanderers? Of the short-story anthologies, Nettie Palmer's[64] *An Australian Story Book* (Sydney, 1928) is out and away the best: its standard is naturally uneven, but it would be hard to disagree with more than a very few of the inclusions or exclusions, and there are several real finds; for example "Copper Jack's Alibi" by the absurdly neglected Riemann;[65] and, best of all, Skuthorpe's "The Champion Bullock-Driver", a Munchausen story told by a poet, which several writers have lately used as a model, and in particular Dal Stivens,[66] who has built a whole series upon it. Harley Matthews's *Pillar to Post* (Sydney, 1944) may also be mentioned. George Mackaness's[67] *Australian Short Stories* (London, 1928), is rather a medley: there is at least one discovery here also, Roderick Quinn's "A Stripe for Trooper Casey"; in spite of its touch of sentimentality and melodrama this story earns its place, but nothing can excuse the inclusion of that clotted mass of sentimentality, Clarke's once so popular "Pretty Dick", and it would be hard to excuse Myra Morris's "One Little Life", or Gypsy Kelly's "Forbidden"; however this anthology should be useful as a supplement to Nettie Palmer's book. *Coast to Coast* (Sydney, 1941-73) affords readers and writers of the short story even greater opportunities than its companion anthology, *Australian Poetry*, affords to readers and writers of verse, for its field is more scattered, and a good short story is more likely than a good poem to be discovered in some apparently unlikely newspaper or magazine. One thing becomes evident from this series: in spite of variations between volume and volume, story and story, something in the general atmosphere remains the same:

---

[62] Roderick has since published a third anthology, *Australian Round-up* (Sydney, 1953).

[63] For Christesen's poems, see p. 1059, and for his magazine, *Meanjin*, pp. 1328-9.

[64] For Nettie Palmer's poems, see pp. 496-7 and for her biographical work, pp. 1358, 1378-9.

[65] For Riemann's short stories, see pp. 618-20.

[66] For Stivens's short stories, see pp. 1252-3.

[67] For Mackaness's historical work, see p. 1369.

these are obviously Australian stories, for though they include some from New Zealand, which are occasionally among the best, there are not enough of them, even if the New Zealand short story had not certain qualities in common with the Australian, to make any marked difference. The atmosphere of the anthology is of course derived from that of the Australian story as a whole, and if its standard is not comparable with that of the best American or English short stories, or with that of *Australian Poetry*, the fault is in the material available.

CHAPTER XII

THE DRAMA TODAY

General. Stewart; Tomholt; Cusack; Others. Anthologies

THE AUSTRALIAN drama of today had made, at the time when this chapter was written, a considerable advance, though not so much as had been hoped for. Its makers were still heavily handicapped,[1] though it does not follow that the handicap had made all the difference that was sometimes imagined: there was still no professional theatre that would take a risk with their plays,[2] or indeed with any that had not already proved successful on the stage, and they had by no means a monopoly of even the small repertory theatres. It is possible that the playwright's disadvantages may have had something to do with the fact that Australian plays, apart from those which are constructed merely to be effective on the stage, tend to look upon the grimmer side of things. St John Ervine had remarked that "Australians, judged by their playwrights, have found the Greek despondency about death but not the Greek joy in life." At the base of the situation generally is the fact that neither as readers nor as theatregoers were Australians interested in their own drama [at least if by drama is meant serious plays. Australians in the nineteenth century were certainly interested in theatre; they preferred English-style melodrama and extravaganzas, and as long as Australian themes were adapted to these modes, they too were popular. For the lack of interest in serious plays, there were a number of reasons, one of which is simply the absence of the kind of talent which could build on the popular interest in Australian themes.] Another reason may be historical: in the days when the *Bulletin* forced Australian literature upon the attention of its readers there was no local drama to speak of, so that it has had to make its own way. But even with the help of that initial stimulus, it is only during the present generation that Australian poetry, apart from ballads, and even Australian fiction, have found appreciation beyond small groups of enthusiasts; but drama has not done so yet: it has been suggested that the Australian literary genius is descriptive rather than dramatic, and this suggestion

1 "The Australian stage dramatist," says Leslie Rees, in his introduction to *Australian Radio Plays* (Sydney, 1946), "is the most neglected, ill-treated and pitiable of mortals. He has never had a chance."

2 The two managements by which "the professional theatre [in Australia] is exclusively controlled . . . are concerned solely with 'show business', and present with financial success indifferent versions of popular London and New York pieces . . . Nothing Australian is any good is a widely held principle in theatrical affairs—unless of course an Australian artist has been acclaimed overseas": Michael Langham, who visited Australia in 1952-3 on the invitation of the Adult Education Board of the University of Western Australia (*Sydney Morning Herald*, 9th May 1953). See also Ch. 12 of Leslie Rees's *Towards An Australian Drama* (Sydney, 1953) which certainly ought to be read.

finds some support in the character of the Australian novel in general; nevertheless some measure of "protection" may make a very great difference in the early stages of the development of a new art, as of a new industry, and such protection the Australian drama has lacked hitherto. When a local dramatic society thinks of staging a performance it turns as a matter of course to England, or perhaps America, and if some Australian play does happen to be suggested it is usually rejected, either because nobody except perhaps the suggester knows anything about it, or because it has not proved itself: few private societies are prepared, any more than the professional theatre, to take a risk with a play merely because it is Australian, and until this attitude changes, the Australian playwright, unless he specializes in radio drama, must continue to lack the stimulus and the opportunity for criticism, his own not least, to be got by having his work performed in public. Radio cannot take the place of stage performance, for after all broadcasting requirements differ in some respects radically from those of the stage, and by and by the two forms of drama may differ more widely than they do now. Probably because it is harder to get long plays acted no Australian play extends to more than three acts and most have one act only; this state of affairs would be much more noticeable if we were to take into account plays that though staged or broadcast have not appeared in print. In the circumstances it is perhaps curious that Australian one-act plays are, speaking generally, inferior to the others.[3] On the face of it the progress of the Australian drama has nevertheless been considerable, for there are many more good or fairly good plays than during the preceding Period; today's leading Australian playwright is much more talented than any of his predecessors, and there is another some aspects of whose talent are quite exceptional. But it is different if matters are looked into more closely; for the first of these two was born and grew up in New Zealand, and one of his best plays harks back to his native country and is based on a New Zealand legend; and the second has written only one-act plays and published his only collection fourteen years ago. In any case today's dramatic record cannot compare with that of its fiction, still less of its poetry.

No Australian writer, it has been remarked already, has possessed a more varied talent than Douglas Stewart,[4] not only in his use of various literary forms but in his work within each form. Of this fact his plays

[3] Yet St John Ervine, in a review, in the London *Observer*, of *Best Australian One-Act Plays* (quoted in the *Bulletin*, 16th March 1938), was of the opinion that the best of the plays in *Best Australian One-Act Plays* could "bear comparison with the best from anywhere". But the situation since the foundation in 1954 of the Australian Elizabethan Theatre Trust, one of whose objects was to support Australian plays, has entirely changed. With the striking success, not only in Australia but in England and elsewhere, of Ray Lawler's *Summer of the Seventeenth Doll*, which was published in London in 1957, interest in Australian plays has sprung up; they are in the news and in people's minds, and the Australian drama may now have begun to come into its own.

[4] For Stewart's poems, see pp. 1043-6, and for his critical work, pp. 1288-92. His book of short stories, *Girl With Red Hair* (Sydney, 1944), seems on the whole to belong to New Zealand literature.

are as good an illustration as his poems: his first, *Ned Kelly* (Sydney, 1943), is a drama of ordinary flesh and blood and of circumstances that were not extraordinary in the days in which it is set; there is a hero, but he does not rise to a truly heroic plane, though he is as heroic as it is possible to make him in the circumstances. Of Stewart's next two plays, *The Fire on the Snow* and *The Golden Lover*, which were published in one volume in Sydney in 1944, the second will not be discussed here, because properly speaking it belongs to New Zealand, but it must be referred to here for purposes of comparison. These two plays contrast strongly with one another: the second glows with bright colour; the first has the cold clear austerity of a mountain of ice. In the second the poet is uppermost, though the dramatist is by no means merely in the background; in the first they are in indissoluble partnership. Poet as he always is, Stewart never wanders into some fantastic world, and his characters are always real men and women, but the subject of *The Fire on the Snow* transcends the ordinary: Stewart is always a romantic, though a realistic romantic, and the subject of this play is romantic heroism, as of *The Golden Lover* it is romantic love. The subject of the fourth play, *Shipwreck* (Sydney, 1947),[5] is romantic adventure, and of *Ned Kelly* it is a kind of truncated heroism. In *Shipwreck* there is nothing heroic about motive or, except in one instance, about character, least of all about the principal character. It has been remarked more than once that the basic requirement in the dramatic world just now is poetic imagination, the power to convey as only a poet can something fundamental in life, something behind and larger than what is directly shown: this sort of imagination distinguishes Stewart's dramatic work, and gives it a piercing power. Stewart is never merely superficial, as are so many clever writers; almost always one has the feeling, in his plays as in his poems, that what he shows us is there not merely in its own right, but as representing something more. Not that, except in one or two poems, he is definitely a symbolist, except in the sense in which all poets are symbolists, but in his plays the course, and here and there the conversations, and in *The Fire on the Snow* the atmosphere, suggest some of the underlying currents and forces of life. In *Ned Kelly* it is the desire of man the wanderer for liberty, the conflict between man and the surroundings out of which he grew, and the rebellion of the child against its father: these however are on a small and limited scale; in *The Fire on the Snow* the scale greatens, for the characters belong to the world and not to one corner of it; there is displayed an ideal that is no longer merely half heroic. The poet in Stewart does not merely set out this ideal; he creates it, as he does not

[5] There was also a limited de luxe edition with colour plates and pen drawings by Norman Lindsay (Sydney, 1948). The four plays dealt with in the text were published as *Four Plays* in Sydney in 1958.

merely describe but creates the icy world to which it is opposed: the world of cold, hunger, solitude and increasing apprehension, that, as is evident from the diaries and descriptions of other men who were opposed to the same world, could never be re-created without the poetic gift. In *Shipwreck*, which sometimes in richness of language recalls, though at a distance, *The Golden Lover*, but embodies oftenest an echo of the minor Elizabethans, there is a decline: the nearest approach to heroism here is in the obsequious butler, Heynorick, and the characters in general do not fight against fate but take what is coming to them; yet here too there are glimpses beneath the surface, as in Sebastian's "I did not behave Quite as I would have expected", which opens up a world of conscious degradation. Heynorick also was quite a surprise to himself, and Providence too surprised him; and there are other surprises: Lucretia's delight, not long after her rape, in

> Bare feet on the sand; makes you feel free and wild;
> I love the feel of it, Heynorick;

and there are surprises in events as in characters: the play is as full of the unexpected as life itself. And there are the images, by means of which, as well as by the creation of atmosphere and character, the piercing quality of the poetic imagination is displayed. In *Ned Kelly* most of the images are without much content; in the beginning they are splashes thrown off light-heartedly by Mackin or Byrne, sometimes delightful in themselves, but superficial; nothing better reveals the small scale of Ned Kelly's heroism than that it is impossible to put any poetry into it; none of his rhetorical utterances brings forth an image worth recalling. On the other hand about the otherwise prosaic constable Richards there is one thing that is poetic: his continual repetition, always in the same order, so as to give the effect of a recurrent rhythm, of the names of the three men killed by the Kellys—Kennedy, Scanlan, Lonergan; this beats down with the effect of a curse-invoking incantation. And the atmosphere, in the hut in the ranges, of the loosening of bonds with solitude and increasing tension; the atmosphere of terror and increasing apprehension in the scene in which Sherritt awaits what is again inevitable: both of them strike back to something fundamental in human nature; in these two scenes the action is mainly psychological, but it is action and it carries the play forward. In *The Fire on the Snow* the images are not merely more poetic but larger and more striking, though the atmosphere is one in tone throughout:

> The world is spun
> Between two giant hands of ice;

of Evans's death, that he is lost

> In the fog of another man's dream;

and

> . . . the mind holds like a pebble the thought of dying;

each of these is a revealing image. In *Shipwreck* there is Heynorick's Shakespearian

> The appalling things that happen between sky and earth
> Where the beast called man walks upright;

there is Sebastian's

> Each for himself on the slippery deck of the world;

and there is van Mylen's description of the coast of the mainland:

> A desolation of surf and golden sandhills.

There is also the delightful description of Lucretia's cat, "so trusting and innocent"; to this her husband replies:

> If ever I saw a cat that wasn't innocent
> It was that battered old tom. One ear torn off,
> Scars all over his face, bald on the backbone,
> The brute's been eating rats and fighting cats
> And scratching at strumpets in the ports of all the world
> For eight of his nine lives. If he's drowned at last
> It's the sailor's death he deserves; and, I might add,
> It's the first time in his life he was properly washed!

Romantic poet as Stewart always is, whatever else he is besides, he never shows any sign of slipping over the edge of romanticism into sentimentality, or melodrama either: one would expect melodrama if anywhere in *Shipwreck*, with its cold-blooded murders and cruel violences, but the only example is the behaviour of Cornelius when he realizes that he is done for, and there the melodrama is in the character, not the author; the same may be said of Ned Kelly's pieces of boasting rhetoric, which is not to say that from an artistic point of view there are not too many of them. Most of Stewart's minor characters are more than surface presentations; in *Ned Kelly* this is obviously so, with Living in particular: the withered, conventional, humourless, middle-aged bank clerk, of whom Byrne makes such a laughing-stock, but who yet has his self-respect, which he will not abandon; and who stands up for himself, and is human and pathetic about his life-insurance policy; but not all the minor characters are necessary to the action.[6] As to the others, Byrne, "the brains of the gang", who has "jumped the blooming fence", for the sake of "a brumby mare called freedom" and to avoid monotony; who can joke though he is conscious of what lies ahead of him: we are shown several sides of him. Byrne has foresight and a bitter humour and much more imagination than Ned Kelly, in spite of those rhetorical

[6] The schoolmaster, for instance, and a couple of others who were excluded from productions of the play.

flights; Kelly's is after all a rather windy personality, and he has the cheapest of ideals:

> The papers would have it all over Australia,
> All over the world. . . .
>
> . . . .
>
> I'll light a fire in the mountains before I'm finished.[7]

Such ideals, however, are about all that could have been given Kelly in the circumstances; it is true that there is something big about him, but it is big in a small way; he is at least intense and sincere, and human enough; he can be cruel when he is afraid, but he can also be generous, and, except in a passion, he will not descend to unnecessary cruelty: he is all for the underdog, as the legendary outlaw always has been, as indeed he must be, since his existence depends on popularity; the Kellys appealed to certain characteristics in the young Australian in a day that was semi-barbaric, and they appeal to him also in a later day in which similar characteristics have been reawakened by two world wars. In *The Fire on the Snow* even the principal actors though strongly are not deeply individualized: actually, not Scott nor Oates is the hero of that play; the hero is the spirit of adventurous attempt, the heroic quality in the spirit of man. In *Shipwreck* there is more characterization than in *The Fire on the Snow*, and Cornelius and Sebastian are rounded studies: Cornelius is grotesque and terrible, like some minor Roman emperor of the decadence; cunning, humorous out of both policy and temperament, he is cruel but avoids the appearance of cruelty, and indeed dislikes to commit in his own person the murders for which he arranges; he is a piece of life, once we are prepared to admit that such a man can gain the undisputed leadership of a set of bloody-minded mutineers. And Sebastian, on the face of it a bluff and hearty clergyman, who one might have imagined would stand out boldly against evil, breaks at once under strain, and goes on to rationalize even his acceptance of an appointment as brothel-keeper to the mutineers; yet he realizes increasingly what he has become, though it is only in a fit of hysteria after a succession of taunts that he does what he ought to have done at first.

[Two of these three plays can be made into good stage-productions, though each presents problems. *The Fire on the Snow* belongs to narrative epic rather than to drama. The main action required of the characters is endurance over a period of time, a kind which is not easily translatable into theatrical terms. It succeeds best in the form for which it was intended: a dramatic poem for broadcasting. It might also succeed as a

[7] [The thinness of Ned Kelly's characterization is probably due to Stewart's failure to consider him against the socio-economic background of the time and place. His poetic interpretation does not arise from the historical material, but is imposed upon it. His unhappiness with the myth reveals itself in the alternative endings he gave the play. A special edition of *Ned Kelly* was published in Sydney in 1956 on the first professional Australian production at the Elizabethan Theatre. In 1960 the A.B.C. televised the play.]

film, a medium which can handle time better than the stage, and could certainly manage better to present the Antarctic as Antagonist. *Ned Kelly* also has long passages of simply "waiting" and has to be stuffed full of conversation, much of which is undramatic. The broadcast version had to be cut down by half in consequence. Certainly, the opening scene is an excellent representation of the lighter side of bushranging, against which the rest stands out, but it drags towards the end and the substitution of conversational byplay for action, and moralizing and vehement disputation with a set of bushrangers who are nervy and ready to kill on suspicion become harder to accept as the play progresses. *The Fire on the Snow*, which was not written for the stage, is much less verbose; it is stark and severe; nothing is there merely for its own sake; formal in both handling and tone, it deals yet with flesh and blood, but these are dwarfed as they are in the end overwhelmed by the gigantic forces to which they are so hopelessly opposed; as with *Ned Kelly*, this is a study in ever-increasing tension, with an increasing dread of what is gradually seen to be inevitable; the play runs on a single note, but that note is so strong, intense and well sustained, and the poetry is so intimately connected with scene and action that it all comes through, without much variation of incident or depth of character-portrayal.] *Shipwreck* is not only quite different in kind again, but does not reach or attempt to reach such a standard: rich rather than spare like *The Fire on the Snow*, it is yet not stuffed with matter like *Ned Kelly*, and it is better constructed; there is however an obvious fault in the introduction in van Mylen of a character that is too strongly and individually drawn to appear only in the first act. This play does not rise to heroism as in *The Fire on the Snow*, or to the limited and parochial heroism of *Ned Kelly*; on its own plane it succeeds, not least in its avoidance of the melodrama of which that type of play is always in danger; it should act well, and in particular the scenes in which Cornelius takes Lucretia; in which Sebastian stabs Huyssen and is stabbed by Seevanck; and in which Cornelius returns from the island in terror; and the trial scene: on the whole, however, though not constructionally, it is the weakest of the three plays, or of the four if we take into consideration *The Golden Lover*. All Stewart's powers will not be called out until he writes a play with a great action, as in *The Fire on the Snow*, and a great personality who centres that action, not as in *Ned Kelly* a half-hero trying to be great; it will be interesting to see what he can achieve upon that basis.

Sydney Tomholt has scarcely anything in common with Douglas Stewart. A generation older, his only collection of plays, appropriately named *Bleak Dawn* (Sydney, 1936), appeared in the same year as Stewart's first book of verse,[8] though before that he had written plays that have been unfortunately lost; and since *Bleak Dawn* he has published nothing but a single one-act play, "Searchlights", which was included in an anthology in 1937:[9] he was afterwards awarded a Commonwealth literary scholarship to write a full-length play on the subject of Governor Macquarie. Tomholt's work is much more uneven than Stewart's, and his range as a writer is far smaller; he has published no verse and no prose fiction and outside his work as a journalist, no criticisms; yet as a playwright his range is considerable: his eleven short plays include a domestic tragedy in one of the poorer Australian suburbs; a tragedy in the North Queensland bush; a tragedy in a small Australian fishing village; a half-mystical play set on an Italian lake; a more or less Maeterlinckian vision that might be anywhere; a play that introduces Martha and Mary of Magdala; a problem play, or rather a play involving the solution of a problem, which is set in some city; three mystical-supernatural plays arising out of the first World War, one set in France, one in the Sydney War Memorial and one in a hotel facing it; and a single humorous play, set in Sydney. Even in the last the atmosphere is far from lively, and there is scarcely a trace of humour in the rest of Tomholt's work; in this he is in strong contrast with Stewart, who can laugh in the midst of tragedy: Tomholt, in fact, concentrates almost entirely on the grim and tragic aspects of life, which he places before his audiences sometimes directly and sometimes through a veil of mysticism. His strength as a playwright consists in his psychological insight, in his power to draw characters, women as well as men, concisely and forcibly, to bring them out by contrast in action, mental or physical or both, as well as in conversation, and to create dramatic situations which are natural, and which, though by no means always new, appear new under his handling of them; he visualizes them anew and they become new: his weakness consists in a tendency to melodrama, and in a fairly frequent lack of aesthetic sensibility in the matter of words and rhythms.

Sydney John Tomholt (Melbourne, 1884–1974) was educated in Victorian schools, but even for an Australian writer his wanderings have been wide and his occupations varied; curiously enough, many of these occupations have been commercial: before the first World War he was Sydney manager of an electric light company; after some months' service in France with the first A.I.F. he was invalided to England, and would have been sent back to Australia as unfit for further service but that at the instance of Shaw and Drinkwater he was given long leave to study drama in London. On his return to Australia he could not settle down and went off to China and Tibet, where he was one of the very

[8] That was before Stewart migrated to Australia.

[9] *Best Australian One-Act Plays*, edited by William Moore and T. Inglis Moore (Sydney, 1937).

few Englishmen to be allowed a personal interview with the Panchen Lama; he was a partner in a transport undertaking in the Gobi Desert, and financial and commercial editor and feature writer for Chinese newspapers. Business jobs in Manila and Sydney followed, and then several years as musical, dramatic and film critic for the *Sydney Morning Herald*; he resigned to join the Allied Works Council, became a film critic in Sydney and later ran a literary agency.

The two best known and among the best of Tomholt's plays are "Bleak Dawn", the title-piece of his published collection, and "Anoli: the Blind":[10] these two strikingly illustrate his range; they are so different that if come across separately they would scarcely be taken to be the work of the same man; yet they have in common a grimness, an increasing tension, a tragedy which becomes in the end quite hopeless. "Bleak Dawn" is a study of a sensitive and affectionate "working woman" who has divorced her drunken and bullying husband, but still loves him and is lonely without him: they meet again, she invites him to visit her, and would have forgiven and taken him back but for the stiffening of a strong-minded woman friend and the fact that he was drunk and had returned evidently for one purpose only; even then he almost persuades her, and after he is gone she is within a hair's breadth of calling him back. All this appears extremely real, and so natural that one does not at first realize how carefully it has been devised: the contrast between the wife and the husband, and also between both and the hard-headed and rather bitter woman friend, is such as to bring out the characters of all three; yet all appear in their own right, and the spectator or reader understands the woman even better than she understands herself. "Anoli: the Blind" is set in the North Queensland cane belt; three of the four characters are Italian, a blind man, his wife, and her lover; the fourth is a carrier who is barely seen. The play is, as Vance Palmer has remarked,[11] "a well-written piece of Grand Guignol". The woman, beautiful, passionate, and exceedingly lonely in their hut in the bush, has previously blinded the husband in a quarrel; but he seems to be intuitively aware of everything that happens, and is evidently waiting for an opportunity of revenge; the lover plans to kill the husband, with the woman's knowledge but against her will, but the husband outwits and kills him: people and passions are so intense, and so real from the point of view from which the play is written, that they sweep one across the melodrama and make a play that can hold its own. Of the supernatural-mystical plays the most striking is one in which the Unknown Soldier talks to a woman who is mourning her lover and her brother in the Shrine of Remembrance in the Sydney War Memorial; she believes him to be a guard: here the

---

[10] This was included in *The Best One-Act Plays of 1936*.

[11] In *Louis Esson and the Australian Theatre* (Melbourne, 1948), p. 17.

tragedy and the pathos are without sentimentality or melodrama, with a couple of slight exceptions that are merely verbal. Tomholt is a very individual writer, though he has occasional reminiscences of O'Neill and Maeterlinck, and one play, "The Women Wait", seems to be an attempt to Australianize Synge; there is no doubt that Tomholt can, as Shaw remarked of him, make figures live, and no Australian playwright has understood better how to create dramatic tensions. Tomholt's work is however extremely uneven; a few of his plays are among the best of their kind in this country, but some of the others are disfigured by the defects that have been mentioned, and indeed only "Bleak Dawn" is free from them entirely. Of the first of these defects, the tendency to exaggerate tragedy until it becomes melodrama, the outstanding example is "Anoli: the Blind"; but this is melodrama outright and apparently deliberate, which has to be taken as such, and in any case the speech harmonizes with characters, setting and situation; one feels that this way of treating such a subject is legitimate; it is quite different with "The Woman Mary", in which the melodrama and the accompanying sentimentality of the speeches do not suit the subject, are not felt to be deliberate, and are not counterbalanced by the force and realism of "Anoli: the Blind". The melodramatic sentimentalism of "The Women Mary" is everywhere mingled with a corresponding lack of aesthetic sensibility in the matter of words and rhythms; these two defects quite spoil the play. Take first the matter of rhythm: Tomholt does not seem to realize that a blank-verse line in a prose passage is like a spoonful of honey in a plate of roast beef, an incongruity that spoils everything; besides, people simply don't talk like that. There are many such lines; for example, "Dwell well upon the import of my words", "Yes, by the Tiber's flow, he has turned your head", and "The everlasting flame, if such there be"; it is not merely that these are all extremely bad as verse; but that they are verse.[12] Tomholt's lack of verbal sensibility also takes the shape of inversions and other artificialities, and of the use of clichés, which help to produce a cheap and second-rate effect; some of these will have been noticed in the blank-verse lines mentioned, but there are many more, and this sort of thing occurs, though much more rarely, in others of Tomholt's plays; for instance, in "The Last Post" Bill is made to utter this queer mixture of the colloquial and sentimental:

> "That's his sweetheart. We spotted her outside. Blue eyes that hurt a little."

And even in "Searchlights", the woman, who is not represented as affected or sentimental, is made to say, "You guard the dead memory, I crave to enter it"; and the Soldier, whose language generally is that of a

[12] Such lines occur also here and there in other plays: for instance, in "The Coming" "the wind that wafts to her the fragrance of the flower"; and even in "Searchlights" the introductory descriptions refer to the sound of a tram that "pierces like a poignant moan the silence of the night".

representative member of the first A.I.F., is made to say: "Thought—and hope—is like that. *Ever searching*". It would be hard to find, even in a country in which literary ability is not always accompanied by certain ancillary qualities that elsewhere may be taken for granted, a writer of Tomholt's talent whose work is handicapped by defects of this kind. Still in his best plays they are comparatively rare, and in these they are counterbalanced by a passionate sincerity, a power, and an ability to place real men and women on the stage and in situations that are both natural and emotionally tense.

There is performance in a few and promise in many of the works of the remaining playwrights, but none of them can compare in either creative imagination or dramatic craftsmanship with Stewart, and in intensity scarcely any can compare with Tomholt at his best. As with the short stories of today, detailed classification is not needed, but it will be convenient to begin with the writers of full-length plays, including however in each case one-act plays by the same author, whether published separately or included in an anthology. There were three station plays: two set in primitive conditions in the far outback a couple of generations ago, and the third, in conditions that were never quite so primitive, in New South Wales. The authors of two of these three plays were novelists. Katharine Prichard's *Brumby Innes* (Perth, 1940) was written at the beginning of the present Period,[13] and does not reach anything like the standard of her best novels or short stories, but it contains the first serious attempt[14] to stage even part of a corroboree: it is not successful however and the corroboree occupies only a small space. This play is set on "a wild and lonely cattle station of the Nor'-west" a couple of generations ago, and the central figure is a coarse and brutal bully of the same type as Geary in *Coonardoo*, but rougher and not nearly so well or fully drawn; Prichard shows the same sympathy and close acquaintance with aboriginal characters and customs as in *Coonardoo* and elsewhere, but they cannot save the play: much better is Prichard's one-act play, *Pioneers*,[15] which is founded on the first part of her early novel of the same name;[16] it is more realistic than the novel, lacks its sentimentality and gains by conciseness. The second novelist's play, set this time in the far North, where again white women are few, is *Men Without Wives*[17] (Perth, 1938) by Henrietta (Frances York) Drake-

[13] In 1927 it won a prize offered by the *Triad*, and was highly praised by Gregan McMahon.
[14] So far as I know. [A crude attempt had been made by David Burn in *The Bushrangers* (1829).]
[15] *Best Australian One-Act Plays*, edited by William Moore and T. Inglis Moore (Sydney, 1937).
[16] See p. 1083.
[17] This was awarded, in 1938, the prize offered by the 150th Anniversary Committee for the best full-length Australian play. It was republished in Sydney in 1955, along with several other plays.

Brockman (Perth, 1901-68); she also published a number of novels and short stories, but they tend to grow sentimental: conciseness, action and the simple and primitive seem to suit her talent best. There is no central character round whom this play is made deliberately to revolve, but Ma Bates takes possession of it: a fine study of an old lady who, like Mrs Watt in *Coonardoo*, but "as rough as bags", has, along with her husband, pioneered the far outback; the other characters are real only so far as they also belong to the country and the conditions, and the conclusion of the play is artificial. Mrs Drake-Brockman has published also a couple of amusing comedies.[18] The third station play, *There is No Armour* (Sydney, 1945), is the work of Lynn Foster (Rose Bay, N.S.W., 1914-), a writer for the commercial radio; its theme, the domination of the land over its possessors, is by no means new, nor is the device on which it is built: that of a shift, or shifts, in time, by means of which we are shown how a station property dominates the lives of a girl, a middle-aged woman and an old lady, all the same person, and through her equally dominating personality, the lives of her descendants. But both theme and device are given a new and Australian life, and the principal character, especially as the old lady, is most attractive: the play has however this defect, that we are shown practically nothing of the station itself, to which so many lives have been subordinated.

The most interesting of the other playwrights are Dymphna Cusack, Betty Roland and G. L. Dann. (Ellen) Dymphna Cusack (Wyalong, N.S.W. 1904-81), an Arts graduate from the University of Sydney, became a High School teacher, but left the service owing to ill-health; she wrote a number of plays, several of which have won prizes: of these two have been published separately and one is included in an anthology. She also published a youthful novel; other much better novels that have appeared since the closing date of this History, and children's stories that are referred to elsewhere;[19] and she has collaborated with Miles Franklin in a satiric novel.[20] Cusack's full-length play, *Morning Sacrifice* (Sydney, 1943) is a bitter satire upon girls' high schools in New South Wales, though it may also have a wider reference; the title is taken from a hymn the schoolgirls sing: "It conditions them," says one of the teachers; "Prepares them to accept all, question nothing, and grow into nice, well-behaved yes-girls"; and when at the end of the play the hymn is sung again, there is the implication that the sacrifice has been completed, with the life of a girl who has killed herself as a result of conditions at

[18] "The Man From the Bush" (*Eight Plays by Australians*); and "Dampier's Ghost" (*Best Australian One-Act Plays*).

[19] These include *Come In Spinner* (Melbourne, 1951), which was written in collaboration with Florence James, *Say No To Death* (Melbourne, 1951), *Southern Steel* (London, 1953) and *The Sun in Exile* (London, 1955). There has also been a three-act play, *The Golden Girls* (London, 1955).

[20] *Pioneers on Parade* (Sydney, 1929), see pp. 693-4.

the school, and in particular of the behaviour of the Deputy Headmistress. Portia Kingsbury is an extreme example of the nature and characterization of this play: "a middle-aged woman of great beauty and dignity, with an exquisitely modulated voice", she dresses fashionably and with great taste and assumes all the virtues she considers appropriate to her position; but she is shown as a woman without sincerity, conscience or regard for the feelings of others; she is jealous, and one of those apostles of purity to whom all things are impure; and her smaller vices include pettiness, cattishness and a habit of unloading her own work on to other people. Miss Kingsbury is described by one of her staff as utterly evil, and there is little to be said in favour of several of the other characters, or against the remainder; the most unpleasant is Miss Charlotte Bates, but she is also amusing, which Miss Kingsbury is not: a shallow, stupid, utterly selfish and tale-bearing toady, she has all Miss Kingsbury's propensity for discovering evil where it is not, but unlike Miss Kingsbury she gets a sensual satisfaction out of her discoveries. This is a clever play, and, in spite of its tragedy, witty and amusing: "I'm sure," says Miss Bates, "they all suspect that I reported Miss Carwithen for smoking in the wash-room", and to the rejoinder, "You did, didn't you?" she replies, "Yes—but I do hate suspicious people"; and another teacher remarks: "If some of these women ever went wrong, all they'd ever produce would be an illegitimate time-table." The school inspectors are satirized as strongly as the teachers: "Wear a blue frock for Ferdy," a young teacher says of one of them, "and let him pinch your seat and your career was assured". The purpose to which everything is devoted, to show the evil for which such a school as this is responsible, adds force to the play, if it detracts from its realism; but there is no doubt about its effectiveness. "Morning Sacrifice" appeared in Cusack's *Three Australian Three-Act Plays* (Sydney, 1950); of the other two, "Comets Soon Pass" deals with a group of well contrasted but rather conventional types; and "Shoulder the Sky" consists of mixed pickles, the individual pickles being excellent; Cusack has also published separately a couple of other plays: *Red Sky at Morning* (Melbourne, 1942) and "Shallow Cups".[21] "Betty Roland" (Kaniva, Vic., 1903-) is a pen-name taken from the christian name of the playwright's father, Dr Roland Maclean; she was educated in Melbourne, spent fifteen months in Russia, studying the theatre, worked on several Melbourne newspapers, and in the fifties was a freelance radio playwright. Now in her eighties, she produced *Caviar for Breakfast* (1979), a memoir of her experience in Russia. *The Touch of Silk* (1942) is a sensitive study of a Parisian girl whom her husband met while serving in France, and of the difficulties in the way of her Australianization as the wife of a struggling farmer. A somewhat similar study is

[21] This has been included in *Eight Plays by Australians* (Dramatists' Club, Melbourne, 1934).

Velia Ercole's novel, *No Escape*,[22] only Jeanne is a stronger character and makes a heroic attempt to overcome her difficulties. Bright, witty, unconventional and not always tactful, with fastidious tastes, and a lover of beautiful things, she finds the unceasing struggle with rough and crude surroundings a heavy burden; at a financial crisis she buys from a persuasive young salesman a set of satin lingerie; here is the touch of silk from which the play gets its name. And then, quite innocently, she goes off to a dance with the salesman, and when he brings her back in his car the husband quarrels with him and kills him by accident; at this point the play is almost spoilt by Jeanne's unnecessary pretence that the salesman has been her lover, in order to provide her husband with an excuse for killing him: there is some good character-drawing, but the play stands by the delineation of Jeanne. *Fountains Beyond* (Sydney, 1944) also depends on its principal character, a half-caste aborigine: the playwright, George Landen Dann (Sandgate, Q., 1904-77), a draftsman and designer for the Queensland Lands Department and for the Brisbane City Council, wandered over a large part of southern Queensland; Dann wrote quite a number of plays, several of which have won prizes, but only two have been published so far. The theme of *Fountains Beyond* is the expulsion of a settlement of semi-civilized aborigines from what is left of their ancestral camping-ground, because the council wants to build on it and because it spoils the outlook from some modern bungalows: the play is written with deep and sincere feeling, and the aboriginal characters are individual and convincing, in particular the principal character; but the action tends to break down into mere dialogue, the white characters do not come to life, and the conclusion is artificial. Dann's other play, *Caroline Chisholm* (Sydney, 1943), is built even more about a single character, who also is strongly and sympathetically drawn; this is the first time[23] that Mrs Chisholm has been presented in drama or fiction.

Sumner Locke-Elliott's *Interval* (Melbourne, 1942) and Max Afford's *Lady in Danger* (Sydney, 1944), both set in London and designed evidently to appeal to a cosmopolitan audience, make most of the other plays look amateurish, yet their literary value is small, Sumner Locke-Elliott (Sydney, 1917-   ), best known as the author of "Rusty Bugles",* which unfortunately has not been published, is a capable actor as well as dramatist; a number of his plays have been produced but only this has been published so far. *Interval* is an example of the more sophisticated type of "best plays of the year"; it is clever, not to say smart; its characters and incidents are lifelike and individualized, but they are not unfamiliar: its world is the theatre and we never get a breath of freer air. Max Afford (Parkside, S.A., 1906-54) wrote a number of stage and radio plays and

[22] See p. 1132. [23] Again, so far as I know.

* [Published in Eunice Hanger's *Khaki, Bush and Bigotry* (Brisbane, 1969); separately by Currency Press (Sydney, 1980).]

won several prizes; some of his plays have been broadcast overseas and some have been translated into more than one language; he also wrote a number of thrillers: *Lady in Danger* (Sydney, 1944) is less sophisticated than the others, a lively and ingenious mystery play, in which old conventions are brought cleverly to life.

There were a number of full-length historical plays, but though all were sincere and some interesting they had little stage or literary value. The nearest to an exception is *Blood on the Wattle* (Sydney, 1948), by Leslie (Clement) Haylen[24] (Amungla, Canberra, 1902-77), a member of the Federal House of Representatives and a former member of the Commonwealth literary advisory board; this play represents an attempt to dramatize the Eureka affair, but is no more successful than Esson's *Southern Cross*; it is much more alive, but there is no clear structure; it is crowded with characters, and with conversations and confused movement which do not amount to action.

Few one-act plays have been published in book-form, either separately or in collections, though a considerable number have been broadcast. Alexander (Eric) Turner (London, 1907-) came out to Western Australia before he was twenty, founded repertory societies in several country towns, and wrote a number of plays, several of which won prizes; he has published two collections, *Hester Siding* (Perth, 1937) and *Royal Mail* (Perth, 1945), as well as a verse-play, *Australian Stages* (Sydney, 1944). Those of Turner's plays which are set in Australia deal with romanticized aspects of life on the Western Australian countryside; he is in some respects at his best in the three-act play, "Royal Mail", whose theme is that of the chaser of the rainbow's end, the wanderer who cannot settle down, even for love, but the plot fans out into dialogue: Turner's strong points are sincere feeling and the realization of atmosphere, but he lacks strength and depth. Much more competent as a playwright is Lionel (Charles Horace) Shave (Hawthorn, Vic., 1888-1954), an advertising service agent; his *Five Proven One-Act Plays* (Sydney, 1948) are clever and entertaining but everything about them is obviously designed for effect and the life of the characters is stage life: Shave has won several prizes, and some of his radio plays have been broadcast overseas. There were quite a number of anthologies of one-act plays, of which the largest and most representative is *Best Australian One-Act Plays* (Sydney, 1937), edited by William Moore and T. Inglis Moore. William Moore had helped, with his annual Drama Nights, in the foundation of the Australian theatre; his *Story of Australian Art* is mentioned elsewhere;[25] T. Inglis Moore is also mentioned elsewhere, as poet and critic.[26] Their anthology ranges over the whole field up to the date of its

---

[24] Haylen has also published other plays and some romances.

[25] See p. 1364.

[26] See pp. 1034-6, 1066-7 and 1286-7 respectively.

publication, containing plays by Esson and Palmer as well as by playwrights of today: many of its contents have been mentioned already; of the rest, Morris Hay Simpson's "Sending Granny Off" is notable, in spite of its defect of a trick ending, for its lively and entertaining sketch of an old lady. The anthology is uneven, but the largest and most representative of its kind, in spite of the fact that it includes plays which had not at that time been already published; there is an excellent introduction by the second of the two editors, and an equally excellent outline history of the Australian drama, by the first. Two other anthologies had preceded this: *Eight Plays by Australians* (Melbourne, 1934), and *Five Plays by Australians* (Melbourne, 1936), both of which draw only upon plays of today;[27] it was succeeded by *Six Australian One-Act Plays* (Sydney, 1944), which includes Esson's "Drovers"[28] as well as five plays of today. There appeared also an anthology which was the first of its kind in Australia, *Australian Radio Plays* (Sydney, 1946), edited by Leslie (Clarke) Rees (Perth, 1905-). Rees, who has himself published a number of plays,[29] is a graduate of the University of Western Australia, was for some years senior dramatic critic of the London *Era*, and is now Federal Drama Editor of the Australian Broadcasting Commission, and Chairman of the Playwrights' Advisory Board;* his collection includes nothing by Stewart, whose principal radio plays had been published not long before, nor does it include adaptations from stage plays or from short stories: nevertheless its standard is on the whole a high one.[30] In "Portrait of a Gentleman" George Farwell [31] has reproduced to the life the amazing Wainwright,[32] fop, forger and poisoner, with all his witty and rather Wilde-like characteristics, and with his criminal madness as an undertone. E. P. Barclay's "Spoiled Darlings" is also a witty and entertaining playlet set in Governor Darling's days, with more real life about it than is usual in a work of this kind; and Catherine Duncan's "Path of the Eagle" is a fine and dignified poem which yet has been a broadcasting success: in its subject, the Oedipus complex, and also in its treatment it reflects the English poetic tendency of a generation ago. Edmund (Piers) Barclay (Dinapore, India, 1898-1961), a well-known radio script-writer, who won an M.C. with Bar and a Croix de Guerre in the first World War, has published novels and short stories. Catherine Duncan (Mme Roger Copillet, Launceston, Tas., 1915-) is a radio playwright, television script-writer and a maker and director of films.

[27] Both of these anthologies were published by the Dramatists' Club, Melbourne; in neither case is any editor mentioned.

[28] Produced by Mulga Publications; no editor is mentioned.

[29] And some stories about Australian animals and birds, as well as *Towards an Australian Drama* (see pp. 738, note 6 and 747, note 17).

* [Since his retirement Rees has expanded his early short history of Australian drama into an important reference work: *The Making of Australian Drama* (1973).]

[30] See St John Ervine's opinion, quoted on p. 1264, note 3.

[31] For Farwell's short stories, see pp. 1254-5.

[32] This is as good as anything Farwell wrote.

CHAPTER XIII

ESSAYS, CRITICISM, SCHOLARSHIP[1]

Essays: Brown; Crawford; Others. Criticism: Stewart; "Barnard Eldershaw"; Moore; Elliott; Booklets on Brennan; Other Critics. Scholarship, English: Waldock; Hart; Gladys Wade; Greta Hort; Others. Classical: Woodhouse. Miscellaneous: Taylor; Maxwell; Chisholm; Others

MODERN CONDITIONS generally, and in particular their nervous tension and lack of lesisure, do not favour the essayist, and his work is even less popular or likely to be popular than that of the dramatist; but taking into account also the fact that Australia has not yet reached a stage of culture favourable, so far as any culture today can be considered favourable, to the essay, it may be said that it has not done so badly: there has been no successor to Murdoch, but E. T. Brown, traveller and lawyer, though lacking Murdoch's range and appeal, possesses qualities that make it unnecessary to judge him by merely local standards. In the field of criticism, the same may be said of Douglas Stewart, who is a worthy successor to A. G. Stephens, both as a critic and as editor of the *Bulletin's* Red Page; other critics also, taking advantage of the increased opportunities afforded not only by the *Bulletin* but by *Meanjin* and *Southerly* and one or two other literary magazines, have helped in the attainment of a truer perspective upon Australian prose and verse. And in scholarship there has been a definite all-round advance.

If wit and charm, flowering in a characteristic and often taking style, were in themselves enough to make an essayist of the first quality, Ethel Anderson[2] would be that; but Mrs Anderson's style is often artificial and descends at times to a precious prettiness: nevertheless everything she writes, except when she is obviously labouring after some aesthetic effect, is entertaining. Of her two published collections, *Adventures in Appleshire* (Sydney, 1944) and *Timeless Garden* (Sydney, 1945), the first is the simpler and less "literary"; here she reports with a touch of humorous malice choice versions of remarks by inhabitants, not always bucolic, of the English countryside; in her second collection the subjects are miscellaneous and about a third of them Australian, and some of the descriptions, as of old Ike Apricotty and his hut beyond the Burragorang, are most amusing. Another stylist, also elaborate and rather self-conscious

---

[1] See the beginning of the corresponding chapter in the preceding Period.

[2] For Mrs Anderson's verse, see pp. 1010-11, 1062-3, and for her short stories, p. 1255.

in her search after aesthetically effective arrangements of words and rhythms, is (Sibyl) Elyne (Keith) Mitchell (Melbourne, 1913-), who is the daughter of the late Sir Harry Chauvel, and has lived since her marriage on a station on the Upper Murray. Her longer works, on soil conditions and particularly erosion, are dealt with elsewhere,[3] but *Images in Water* (Sydney, 1947) is a collection of short descriptive pieces without ulterior purpose; they deal almost solely with snow and skiing, and the birds and beasts, mountains and lagoons and streams of that southern corner of New South Wales which, though by no means characteristically Australian in its climate and conditions generally, has yet been the birthplace and theme of some of the most typical Australian verse and prose fiction. In spite of the defects mentioned, Mrs Mitchell's sincerity of feeling is everywhere obvious; her essays are however less relieved by humour than Mrs Anderson's. Her descriptions are all real and sometimes beautiful, and though there is not much that is novel about the reflections with which they are mingled, now and then she does convey what has not been said so well before; here for instance is something of the emotional essence of youth and camping out:[4]

> Soon a huge fire was blazing; soon there was soup, and chops, biscuits, and fruit—and much laughter. There was also the hopeless endeavour to dry ourselves, the rain or the sleet soaking whichever side was not to the fire. And still flowing through us was the undercurrent of excitement, almost as if the rhythm to which our lives moved had become charged with a beating vitality which was as yet incomprehensible but which had heightened our perception of every change in the atmosphere, of every sound or movement.

If Ethel Anderson may be considered a far outlying member of the tribe of Lamb, and Elyne Mitchell a type of the poetically descriptive essayist, Edwin Tylor Brown (Melbourne, 1889-1957), belongs definitely to the tribe of Hazlitt, though he lacks Hazlitt's strong literary bias. Brown was educated at a Melbourne State School and at the University of Melbourne, where he graduated in Arts and Law; he has practised law, mostly in New Guinea, as Crown Law Officer, Special Magistrate and Acting Judge, and has travelled in Europe and India. Brown is a philosopher upon things in general, but, though he is not a poet, his many wise sayings are also imaginative and imaginatively expressed: he writes with a wise and humorous irony, and is on the whole nearer than any other to Murdoch among the Australian essayists of today; but he is quieter more restrained, less easy and colloquial than Murdoch, and not given to Murdoch's flights of fancy, the fantastic hoaxes that now and then in Murdoch's essays take one with delighted surprise; he has also a far

[3] See p. 1466.

[4] p. 70.

smaller range, and has published only one collection of essays, *Excursions and Enquiries*[5] (London, 1935). Brown's style is simple, straightforward and without those mannerisms, those small affectations, that are observable in most essayists of talent; he is widely acquainted with men and manners and events, historic and other, and with those natural orders, such as bees, ants, termites, which invite human comparisons, but he knows how to distinguish. He does not address so popular an audience as Murdoch, belonging to the magazine rather than to the newspaper type of essayist; his style is not a light one, but neither is it heavy: he does not disguise the fact that he is reflective, and he makes us reflect also, but he is never dull and always stimulating. He can turn a poetic phrase, such as "wild nights of wind and thunder", but as a rule his phrases are notable for their content rather than their poetic expression; sometimes however the two are combined: "Unhappily we cannot turn time backwards. But space is a different matter. It is, as it were, a scroll which the Fates have somehow forgotten to roll up." He observes that "Inscriptions, like sermons, suffer in quality because they lack the stimulus of interjection and rejoinder"; that "Hardly anything so much eases the heart as to break to pieces what one does not like, to wholly demolish the idolatrous images which the vanquished adversary worshipped"; and that "Man is a passionate being, as well as a reasonable one, and this is perhaps the best that can be said about him." Speaking of English puritanism, he remarks that "With us, more than with other peoples, the serious occupations of life have always enjoyed a prestige totally denied to the frivolous pursuit of pleasure"; and, of the ignoring by the newspapers of political alternatives that may be more important than party projects, he declares[6] that

> It is the control of publicity that counts. For the average man whatever is not shouted about in the Press simply does not exist. It is the daily newspaper, far more than any other agency, which has destroyed democracy even in the very hour of its birth. In these days it is a much simpler matter than it ever was before to keep the people out of their inheritance. Now, you need not oppose their onset with steel and fire and blood. That would be ridiculous. It is enough to keep completely silent about the things urgently and immediately needful, and at the same time to daze and confuse the people's understanding by a bedlam of shouting about something completely indifferent.

Quite as stimulating, and even better perhaps because it will come to many with the force of a discovery, is this:[7]

> . . . until we are something more than human, it is extremely doubtful whether we can afford to pay the price of tolerance. For that price is a great one. It is hardly too much to say that with nine-tenths of mankind toleration implies an almost total loss

---

[5] He has since published another, *Not Without Prejudice* (Melbourne, 1955).

[6] pp. 189-90.

[7] pp. 31-2.

of faith, a fatal disinterestedness in the subject of controversy. The counsels of reason turn out, on closer view, to be something very much like counsels of despair.

. . . .

In these days many of us are beginning to lose that faith. When we lose it altogether, we shall be ripe for political toleration. But in that same hour the times will be ripe for despotism.

Brown has published other books,[8] but it is his essays that matter; it is a pity he is not better known.

R. M. Crawford's *The Renaissance and other Essays*[9] (Melbourne, 1945) is the work of a historian and could not have been anything else, but its contents are, as the title suggests, essays in the larger sense of the term; they are also instinct with a feeling for word and phrase, colour and atmosphere which are unusual beyond the bounds of literature in the narrower sense: these are particularly evident in the description of the first sight of Florence, "simple, austere, even its colour subdued by the torrential rain". Crawford remarks that in the fifteenth century Florence "did not suffer from the indeterminate twilight of suburbs", and that

now, as then, people come out for the breath of air that the river might give, for the city is so ringed with hills that no gusty wind refreshes it after these hot summer days. . . . And through all the stillness, there is a restlessness in that oppressive summer air, a sense of waiting for something to happen.

But as a rule the feeling beyond Crawford's conclusions runs underground; the general atmosphere of the essays is of a cool preciseness, a dislike of loose thinking, a richness of material that are also evident in his historical work generally, though these essays are based on width of reading rather than specialized research. There is also some repetition of idea, perhaps because the material of the essays was first presented in the form of letters. The following passage[10] is more typical than the others; a second reason for quoting it is its modern parallel:

The sixteenth and seventeenth centuries had to be centuries of intolerance in western Europe. It is a mistake to suppose that it is simply that people then were by nature intolerant and have learnt tolerance since. We are no more tolerant today, when it comes to questions of communism and fascism than people were then when it came to questions of Lutheranism, or Calvinism, or, as its enemies called it, of "Popery". They had to be intolerant because their developing insecurity made them fundamentally anxious, frightened of anything which seemed, however vaguely, to threaten their position.

The qualities mentioned are reflected in the general scheme of Crawford's essays: for example, the desire to peel off the vague looseness from the term "Renaissance", whose various characteristics are then brought

---

[8] *This Russian Business* (London, 1932), *Curry and Rice* (London, 1936), *Bread and Power* (Edinburgh, 1940), and *The Sovereign People* (Melbourne, 1954).

[9] For Crawford's philosophy of history, see pp. 1353-4.

[10] p. 140.

out by reference to the life and politics of Florence in the fifteenth century, to the humanist ideal, the Reformation, and so on, and to the lives of certain representative individuals. In particular, there is the sketch of Machiavelli, a plain-spoken analyst of the methods that pay "a political virtuoso in a corrupt community"; and of da Vinci, with whom the

> . . . excitement of investigation, which went hand in hand with the coolest analysis, led him into deeper and deeper inquiry, to that concentration on discovery which always postponed the production of finished works.
>
> . . . .
>
> He could never believe that his investigations had reached the point at which he could call them complete.
>
> . . . .
>
> That is why we must in the end seek the greatness of Leonardo in the manner of man that he was.[11]

More than one scientific man has published a collection of short articles that approach the essay more or less closely, and in particular Thorburn Brailsford Robertson (Edinburgh, 1884–1930). Brought to Australia as a child, Robertson graduated in science at Adelaide but migrated abroad to America where he was for some years a colleague of Loeb at the University of California and occupied chairs of Biochemistry there and in Toronto, and during these years he published standard works on this subject which cannot be considered Australian. But from 1919 to his death he was Professor of Physiology at Adelaide, and his *The Spirit of Research* which appeared in Adelaide a year after his death has a place here. Robertson writes, like T. H. Huxley or his son Julian, not as a scientist merely but also as a man of science looking at the world, and some of his conclusions are stimulating; for instance:[12]

> Society . . . is economically stratified, and it is dying out at the top. Economic ability is being bred out of our race, [the acquisitive instinct is being eliminated,]* society, as at present constituted, is selectively breeding to destroy itself. But that does not mean that human greatness is destined to disappear from the earth, or that an order of society may not be discovered in which other talents may be fitted to succeed and survive.

One of the most interesting of Robertson's essays is that in which it is pointed out how, in spite of the non-inheritance of acquired characteristics, there exists, in the development of areas of the brain which extend far beyond anything that an individual can live long enough to utilize, immense possibilities of human development. In the qualities expected of the typical essayist Robertson is generally lacking; but his honesty, his directness, his deep sincerity bring down the balance. The other essayists, as distinct from those who are essentially critics, are all literary in the sense that they are, and it is evident that they are, practitioners

---

[11] pp. 86–7.
[12] p. 198.
* [Of this clause at least, the opposite seems true in 1980.]

also of some other of the literary arts; they are without the aesthetic extravagances of Ethel Anderson and Elyne Mitchell, or the broad philosophy of life and society of E. T. Brown, and their work takes some of its range and colouring from the nature of their original medium of communication—newspaper, magazine, or lecture hall. With Nettie Palmer,[13] who is of all things a literary intellectual, the main effect of her original medium has been upon the style of the essays in her *Talking It Over* (Sydney, 1932), without whose informal and direct simplicity some of her subjects and her attitude towards them might have seemed scarcely suited to the pages of the newspapers for which they were originally written. Much less general and more literary, and even a little academic, not merely in that they are devoted mainly to books, and to such books as might appeal to a university teacher in his lighter moments, are R. G. Howarth's[14] *Literary Particles* (Sydney, 1946), which read like reviews by a literary scholar, which is just what they are. More obviously learned, general but with a leaning towards literature and to the past, old books, old wine, old homes, old letters, are the subjects of the essays in *In a Shaft of Sunlight* (Sydney, 1948), by F. J. H. Letters, whose work of scholarship will be mentioned later;[15] Letters's is an armchair style, easy, quietly reflective, urbane. The essays of Louis Augustus Triebel (London, 1890-) are more definite, closer to the actual fact: they are indeed a pleasant miscellaneous gossip, mainly about books and writers and aspects of their work; but it is a gossip that implies a wide and scholarly reading and is warmed by a quiet enthusiasm.[16]

There remain those essayists who are predominantly literary critics. Three collections may be taken together: M. Barnard Eldershaw's *Essays in Australian Fiction* (Melbourne, 1938), T. Inglis Moore's *Six Australian Poets* (Melbourne, 1942) and Brian Elliott's *Singing to the Cattle* (Melbourne, 1947). In all these the old crop of Australian writers who formed the subject of critic after critic until they became boring and tended to be under- rather than over-estimated have dropped clean out and most writers discussed here are still alive in 1950. It says something for Barnard Eldershaw's judgment that she was able to perceive the worth of Mann and Dark at a time when their best work had not yet appeared, and it will be agreed that her eight novelists, four men and four women, are well chosen. Palmer seems overrated, and surely no competent critic could agree that Davison writes "great prose"; but Barnard Eldershaw has put into words, perhaps for the first time, the

[13] For Mrs Palmer's poems, see pp. 496-7; for her short-story anthology, p. 1261; for her literary criticism, pp. 1294-5; and for her biographical work, pp. 1358, 1378-9.

[14] Howarth's poems have already been discussed, on p. 1059, his criticism on p. 1303.

[15] See pp. 1309-10.

[16] Triebel is more notable as a scholar, but his principal work of literary scholarship, *Rasser of Alsace*, was not published until 1954.

feeling many must have had, that in Palmer's general handling and construction of a novel he shows a "restraint that at times verges on inhibition", and that he is not "as at home in the major key as in the minor". It was natural that as one woman, Nettie Palmer, was the first to popularize Richardson in Australia, so another, "Barnard Eldershaw", should have provided the first satisfactory analytical estimate of Richardson's work; her analysis brings out many facts that were not so clearly realized fifteen years ago as they are now, as well as several that are not always clearly recognized even yet: for example, that Richardson is neither versatile nor a stylist.[17] There is an illuminating contrast between Richardson and Prichard as creators of character, and between their attitudes to the world:[18] Prichard's

> . . . narratives and her characters are founded on their background and grow out of it as trees from the soil. Richardson's narratives grow out of her characters and her backgrounds are for the most part arranged to display the tragedy in the spirit of the pathetic fallacy, or its converse, the ironic fallacy. Her books draw their light from man's universal heritage, Prichard's from the environment and circumstances in which her group finds itself.

Considering the nature of the problem that Richardson's treatment presents, it is excusable that the essayist should in one place express the opinion that Richardson's outlook (in *Richard Mahony*) is not pessimistic, and in another that she is a pessimist; and, since nobody could have foreseen Prichard's three mining and propaganda novels, that "she is too great an artist to grind axes in the sight of her readers": but it is surprising that a stylist like Barnard Eldershaw should not, apparently, have noted the careless craftsmanship of which Prichard is so often guilty and Richardson also, particularly in her first novel. Barnard Eldershaw's critical judgments crystallize here and there into a striking phrase: of Madeleine in *The Montforts*, and her influence upon her descendants, "She stands behind their lives plucking at their destiny"; and of some of Palmer's short stories, that they are "an aspect of life compressed into an incident so that it has the force of a symbol"; nothing could come closer to the essence of Christina Stead's novels than that they are "rich and strange"; and, of Katharine Prichard it is well remarked that "Her books display a sort of artistic preference to unionists." Barnard Eldershaw has the great advantage of a thorough experience and understanding of the art whose practice she is criticizing, the more so as the fact of collaboration may well have led to the deliberate formulation of principles. She takes her critical work extremely seriously, being careful to rationalize all her emotional impressions: her seriousness is sharpened by the clarity and definiteness of her style and relieved by

[17] Except in her short stories; see this History, p. 599.
[18] p. 25.

her images: this collection is among the landmarks in Australian criticism. The second collection differs in almost every way from the first: whereas Barnard Eldershaw aims to present the facts, as she sees them, in such a way that they may appeal to the reason, Moore appeals, in the first place anyhow, to the sympathy and the imagination; and whereas in Barnard Eldershaw's essays everything is put as succinctly as possible, and in its proper place with regard to everything else, Moore does not sufficiently condense or organize his thought, with the result that there are here and there repetitions, not so much of words or phrases as of ideas, or of the atmosphere of an idea. Moore's expression is often, especially in the introductory survey to the collection, scrappy, so that one steps from paragraph to paragraph, looking for some final expression of the critic's opinion upon a particular point: the whole book reads as though it had been poured out hot with the writer's enthusiasm, and left without a final moulding and compression into form. These remarks are not intended as merely fault-finding; there are various kinds of criticism, of which Barnard Eldershaw's is one and Moore's another: still, Moore's has faults even in its kind. But he is a man of ideas, and more and more of them appear, floating in the enthusiasm, as one reads on: he attempts more than Eldershaw, and it was time that such an attempt as his should have been made. Barnard Eldershaw is concerned merely to set certain individual writers before us, analysing their work, though underlying her individual analysis there lies the implication of a standard; but with Moore the standard is both overt and deliberate: his aim is to set up, in the words of Hartley Grattan in his foreword, "a canon which will include only those writers with whom one must make one's peace before considering minor figures"; at the same time Moore is far from contending that his canon is more than provisional and an enlarged edition of his book is under way: except in the case of Slessor[19] and FitzGerald,[20] Moore's subjects had, by the time he was considering them, done their best work, but, he feels, on reconsideration and in the light of criticisms, that his canon ought to be extended. As with the novelists, so with the poets and, partly no doubt owing to the influence of these two books, Australian literature is now beginning to appear in a truer perspective; it may have been Moore that dealt the final kick to the Gordon legend.[21] Moore also alludes caustically to a perversion of the Australian democratic ideal which results in "a characteristic dislike of criticism, standards, and values", and he goes on to speak of the effects of this upon "the divorce between poet and

[19] Slessor had not yet published "Five Bells".

[20] FitzGerald's last two books had not yet been published, and his "Heemskerck Shoals" and "Fifth Day" had not yet appeared in the *Bulletin*.

[21] But it does not, of course, follow that because Gordon and Kendall have been overrated they have not their places in the history of Australian poetry; the tendency now is to underrate them.

public", though here the question arises whether they were ever married. The introduction, in which all these points arise, is perhaps the best part of the book; Moore has nothing basically new to say about any of his poets, though he has some apposite remarks to make about them: of Neilson, for instance,[22] that with him love is

> . . . the romantic sentiment of dreaming youth. . . . The stronger emotions associated with love are . . . not attempted. . . . His gentle intuitions are feminine rather than masculine; his quality is sweetness, not strength;

he points out Baylebridge's naïvete and the religious passion with which he upholds his faith; he defends McCrae against the accusation of escapism; and there is his remark about FitzGerald,[23] that he is

> . . . a poet of power, of intellectual and imaginative energy, exerting, like Browning, an almost muscular force upon thought and language. Not that there is any direct influencing by the Victorian master, but there is the same fondness for the dynamic verb, the rugged image, and the half-colloquial idiom and rhythm. . . .

All these ideas were more novel when Moore's book appeared than they are now, and if Moore's critical judgments were fundamentally emotional rather than intellectual, as with his poetry there is intellect dissolved in the emotion. The third is a more miscellaneous collection. Brian (Robinson) Elliott (Adelaide, 1910-), was educated at the University of Adelaide, where he became Senior Lecturer in English and Lecturer in Australian Literature. In *Singing to the Cattle* (Melbourne, 1947) Elliott[24] expresses his point of view clearly and concisely in a careful-casual manner that is a little self-conscious, and he brings out about Hay and Baylebridge facts that are often passed over by their admirers: he is at his best in a penetrating study of Hay, which emphasizes the narrowness of Hay's world, "a jungle of evil which reflects the terrors of the soul"; his melodrama, which yet conveys "an impression of a deep, even an agonised sympathy with suffering"; and the "rambling, fabulous and extraordinary" nature of his plots; he describes Hay as a muddled genius, though to call his talent genius seems to be rating it rather high; all these points have to be taken into account in estimating novels which are "works of genuine art", and yet "grand and fascinating failures". As to Baylebridge again, Elliott has some acute remarks, as for instance that "as poetry, his work is too philosophical, as philosophy it is too poetical"; and that with him "style is a kind of high horse which he rides to the reader's very great discomfort sometimes, and also to his own frustration as an artist"; and he brings out[25] one important fact about Baylebridge and his generation, that

---

[22] pp. 166-7.

[23] p. 191.

[24] Elliott has also published a novel and several short critical biographies, for the latest of which, *Marcus Clarke* (Oxford, 1958), his university awarded him a Doctorate of Letters.

[25] p. 141.

> . . . they did do one thing what was well worth doing: they enlarged by their own conceptions and by their attempts if not their attainments, the field and scope of Australian poetic expression.

But the leading Australian critic today is unquestionably Douglas Stewart;[26] with him as with FitzGerald in the field of poetry there is a possibly bigger man in the historical background, with whom it is too soon to attempt a final comparison, but their qualities may be contrasted or compared; and Stewart has some qualities that A. G. Stephens did not possess, of which the most obvious is an unselfconscious simplicity. With Stephens, that eccentric near-genius, one almost always feels, even in those piercing judgments that illuminate his subject like a glow of sheet lightning, that he is glancing over his shoulder at the reader, whom he obviously desires to impress;[27] not that Stewart also has not to consider his readers, but with Stewart one does not feel that this consideration is deliberate. And though Stephens was by nature unconventional to the point of eccentricity, one does feel that his eccentricities are often deliberate: it was not merely that it was his nature to be eccentric, but that he cultivated eccentricity because it helped to attract notice to him. Yet he was invariably dignified; Stewart, on the other hand, becomes excited at times, and, regardless of dignity or anything else, lets himself go: here he also is deliberate, but one feels that he is following his nature rather than aiming at the public eye; not that in such cases he appears undignified, it is simply that he stands aside from dignity as he stands aside from self-control; there is about him then a sort of don't-give-a-damnativeness, if such an expression may be allowed, which finds vent in a satirically humorous extravagance, a flamboyant and almost schoolboyish fling at some object of attack: this sort of thing in Stewart has been criticized, but actually it gives a freshness and sparkle to an expression of outright opinion. Stewart's judgments, like Stephens's, light up here and there with intuitional flarings that cast new light upon his subject and open out new points of view; they are not quite so striking or so frequent as with Stephens, and they have not the same weight of personality behind them, but they are similar in kind. Stewart has plenty of personality, but it is not overwhelming, like Stephens's: on the other hand he never pontificates as Stephens so often did; anything of this sort is quite foreign to Stewart's nature and to his style, which is far lighter than Stephens's throughout; it is not more entertaining, but its entertainment is of a different kind, simpler and more natural, never deviously planned. Stewart again, is spite of his humorous extravagances, does not follow his fantasy beyond the world of common sense: he is never

[26] For Stewart's poems, see pp. 1043–6, and for his plays, pp. 1264–9.

[27] Low has caught this other-consciousness of Stephens admirably in the caricature which shows "A.G." strutting along the pavement with his chest stuck out and the corner of his eye on the artist, who is sketching him as he runs along the gutter to one side.

guilty of those strange lapses which make one wonder whether A.G.'s extraordinary wideawakeness of judgment was not offset by periods during which it was asleep. Stewart has of course, like other critics, his personal preferences and prepossessions, with which are allied those of his forum, the *Bulletin*, and one or other of these undoubtedly affects his judgment now and then: few would agree with his estimate of Norma Davis, or Brian James, or *The Pea Pickers*, or with his contention that Paterson ought to have been included in Moore's *Six Australian Poets*. But he never lapses, as Stephens does sometimes,[28] into sheer critical blindness, or veers off into such a fantasy as that of the "nousometer",[29] which seems to suggest that Stephens, an admirer of Lombroso's theory of the alliance between genius and madness, liked to feel, and perhaps to make it quite evident, that his own mind was upon the borderline. Allowing for legitimate differences of opinion, Stewart seems on the whole about as unbiased as could reasonably be expected of a critic, and his fits of humorous extravagance, his apparently careless, offhand colloquialities, never extend beyond the method of expression: what is expressed in this way represents always a serious and deliberate conviction; this may be seen in the extravagantly satirical dialogues between his two imaginary characters, Mr Gallagher and Mr Shean, and the delightful little beast Willie, with whom he too seldom varies and relieves what is more obviously serious. These dialogues contain some of Stewart's most illuminative comments; there is for instance "How to Read Tom Collins": recent panegyrical analyses of *Such is Life*, and even of the far inferior quarryings from its original mass, have been all to the good; it was time that the critics busied themselves from every angle with that neglected and misunderstood classic, and it was natural that the balance so long unreasonably depressed against Furphy should swing up again, even rather too high; but it is time now for it to steady a little, for a discrimination between literary and other aspects of Furphy's value. Stewart by no means underestimates the book that has become an indisseverable part of Australia's literary inheritance, but he perceives its faults; in reply to a remark by Mr Shean, that since *Such is Life* is now generally available Mr Gallagher will of course read it at once, Mr Gallagher replies:[30]

> Are you suggesting, Mr Shean, that it is my duty to read Tom Collins?
>
> SHEAN. I would as soon suggest to a bullock that is its duty to eat grass. Professors, critics and others of the depressed classes may have to read books from a sense of duty; but you and the bullock, you graze where you will for the pleasure of it.
>
> GALLAGHER. Nobody ever invited me before to read Tom Collins for the fun of him.

28 See this History, p. 772.
29 In "The Genealogy of Genius" (*The Red Pagan*).
30 *The Flesh and the Spirit* (Sydney, 1947), pp. 133-4.

SHEAN. Come, Mr Gallagher, literary gentlemen have been talking about him for years.

GALLAGHER. Literary gentlemen have been talking about his politics.[31]

. . . .

I will let you into a great secret: Tom Collins wrote about bullockies because they amused him.

But he goes on to talk about Furphy's circumlocution and the advisability of skipping,[32] and declares that Furphy is not quite amusing enough to fully merit all the space he allows to himself; Mr Shean adds that one of Furphy's faults is oversubtlety: "A novel," he says, "is not a crossword-puzzle, and whimsical fellows have no right to lead their readers up a gum-tree." And then we have Mr Shean's, and Stewart's final judgment,[33] of which the last sentence may not entirely satisfy the Furphy-worshippers:

As a novel based on the humour of character, essentially not a political tract but an image of the great tragi-comedy of man upon the earth, a wandering, sprawling, richly earthy tale [*Such is Life*] is to be placed in the company of the great picaresques, *Don Quixote*, *Tom Jones*, *The Pickwick Papers*. In Australian writing it stood alone until Eve Langley wrote *The Pea Pickers*.

GALLAGHER. And you seriously maintain that Tom Collins is in the class of those giants?

SHEAN. A. G. Stephens said that *Such is Life* was "fit to become an Australian classic or semi classic". It is still difficult to be more precise. Collins is a lance-corporal in the company of which Cervantes is the captain.

One of Stewart's attractions is his vituperative power, but he reserves this for his oversea subjects; at its extreme it is seen in Mr Gallagher's remark about a silly and sentimental play of Clifford Odets, *Golden Boy*;[34] Mr Gallagher's comment is self-explanatory:

"This revolting old man", said Mr Gallagher, "this monster of a parent who tries to keep his son at home playing the violin when he is thirsting for life and adventure; this ancient dimwit who cannot perceive that the young man instinctively and rightly prefers to be a good boxer rather than a second-rate violinist; this elderly prude who thinks that blondes and money—the delights and rewards of combat—are a corruption; this timorous old goat who has himself retired beaten from the struggle of life and tries to make a failure of his son before he has even started to fight and who obstructs him at every step of his career; this vulture gloating over the slain body of his son—he is, of course, the villain of the play?"

"The poor old vulture", said Mr Shean, "is the hero."

It is interesting to compare this, in its context of course, with Stephens's attack on Kipling as a plagiarist: that however was an appeal primarily

---

[31] The reference is in particular to an article by Hartley Grattan, in the *Australian Quarterly*, September, 1937; Grattan admires Furphy's "dangerous thoughts".

[32] On p. 260 of *The Flesh and the Spirit* Stewart refers to "Furphy's intolerable discursiveness".

[33] *The Flesh and the Spirit*, p. 139.

[34] p. 3.

to the reason rather than to the emotions; quite as devastating and much weightier, if far less entertaining, in that it was backed by a formidable display of scholarship and the target was an eagle rather than a sparrow. But Stewart's utter disregard for emotional restraint in a matter on which he feels strongly makes no exception even of Shakespeare, or of Shakespeare as represented by Laurence Olivier's film version of *Henry V*, presented under the conditions of Australian censorship: he refers to those "ruthless, Machiavellian clerics", the Archbishop of Canterbury and the Bishop of Ely, as "two dismal old goats";[35] and a page or two later he says that Mistress Quickly, "the gabbling old hen whom Falstaff has so merrily wronged in *Henry the Fourth*", "has a mouth about as soft as an old boot"; and finally, he sums up against the censorship of this play:[36]

> . . . because the healthy lewdness has been cut, the film is not as funny as it should be; because of the political censorship, it is not as fierce and dramatic as it should be; because scenes of pathos have been over-emphasized and scenes of comedy omitted, the film is sadder than it should be. And that is the first result of the censorship: comparatively speaking, the film is dull, tame and glum.

It will be noted that the subjects of some of Stewart's best critical work are oversea subjects; here again he differs from Stephens, who did, with one or two notable exceptions, all his best work upon Australian writers. Stephens had little interest in oversea authors, except as a background and measuring-rod for Australians, or as affording material which might in form or otherwise benefit Australians, or when, as in the article on Kipling which has been referred to, he found good material for attack; Stewart's interests on the other hand fan out, from his more immediate concern, Australian writers and their work, to writers all over the world, whether they have an Australian bearing or not: it is partly for this reason that he is one of the few Australian critics who are always worth reading on non-Australian subjects. Stephens belonged to what was in Australia a parochial age, and though he did much to broaden the views of young Australian writers, and to introduce them to new ideas and new literary methods, there was after all a parochial element in even himself; in this respect Stewart has an advantage over Stephens, as belonging to an age that is characteristically cosmopolitan, though even today, with few exceptions[37] the Australian literary intelligentsia confines itself fairly closely to the Australian scene, or else it is unable to present a foreign subject satisfactorily. Some of Stewart's best illuminative crystallizations have a foreign setting; for instance:

> Trying to analyse William Blake . . . is like trying to define the sunset;
>
> [Yeats's plays] never got down to life, and consequently never quite reached hell and heaven.

[35] p. 252.
[36] p. 254.
[37] Hope and FitzGerald for instance, and one or two other writers in the *Bulletin* or *Meanjin*.

And, perhaps the most penetrating of all, of *Samson Agonistes* Stewart says:

> Samson is an image of hate; but a hate so gigantic that it becomes a kind of black affirmation of life.

It is curious how Stewart's easy-going and natural freedom of expression is accompanied by a careful precision and a general attitude of moderation that almost approaches conservatism in the literary field. Equally curious is his combination of the intuitive and the rational faculties: it is not unusual for a critic to be able to point out the good or the bad in a writer or a book, but he is much less often able to say in what the goodness or badness lies; Stewart can do this, and so of course could Stephens. Stewart's style, like his thought, is clear, direct and logical; so was Stephens's, but Stewart's is also natural, which Stephens's was not; and Stewart can also be, as might have been expected from a critic who is also a playwright, extremely dramatic: Stephens had every art of expression except that, and the art that conceals art and will have nothing to do with artifice. And finally, it is probable that Stewart has a better grasp of critical principles than Stephens, who preferred to be a law unto himself; this may account for some of his absurdities. Stewart's is a lighter, trimmer craft than Stephens's, and less fond of voyages into strange seas; it has not the tonnage or heavy guns of the other, or its captain's demonic fire, but its armament is first rate of its kind, and it is perhaps as comparable with the other as could be expected of two vessels of so different a class.

There have been four booklets on Brennan and his poetry, and, since what biographical matter they contain is only incidental to their criticism, they may be considered here;[38] none of them attempts anything like a full commentary, but all their writers knew Brennan and have studied his poetry, and between them they go some little way towards filling the gap that must exist until the appearance of a critical biography.★ The first of these booklets, *Australian Writers: Chris. Brennan* (Sydney, 1933) appeared within six months of Brennan's death; it is on the face of it surprising that this, which is the least illuminative of the three, should be the work of A. G. Stephens: that Australia's most notable critic should be so little appreciative of Australia's most notable poet. As has been shown already,[39] Stephens's fine discernment did not prevent him from committing a surprising number of errors of judgment; this booklet exemplifies one of the worst of them, and it happens to be com-

[38] All these booklets have been alluded to in the chapter in this History that deals with Brennan and his poetry.

[39] See p. 772.

★ [See the biography by Axel Clark (Melbourne, 1980).]

paratively easy to account for. The fact is that Brennan's work was quite outside Stephens's range. Not that this was by any means confined to the Australian sphere; as has been said here,[40] Stephens had read enough to relate Australian literature to that of the outside world. and he was in his own way a genuine scholar; but the Greek and Latin classics and English poetry that has its roots in them had little interest for him: as to Milton, for instance, after making the qualified admission[41] that "a considerable body of opinion still holds that only very bad taste can refuse to recognize *Paradise Lost* and *Paradise Regained* as two of the highest poetical achievements of the human mind", he added, "In reality, according to the standards set by present fashion, there is little more poetry in the 'Paradises' than there was in Queen Victoria". And, as to another side of Brennan, though Stephens was interested in French poetry he considered that Mallarmé counted for little in it, and that his art was "a game of artifice"; the sort of poetry Stephens preferred, and in regard to which his mind moved most freely, was Australian in outlook and atmosphere, and, as has been said already, he was always inclined to over-estimate it:[42] so that he was badly equipped for an appreciation of Brennan. He considered that Brennan's "learning, for final value, was too much influenced by schools and academies, by precedent and authority, by tradition and doctrine", and that his form was stiff and sometimes heavy or turbid: there is some truth in this, and even the further assertion that Brennan's poetry is "an apparatus of patient craft that seldom becomes an artistic engine" contains a substratum of fact upon which to build an exaggeration. But when Stephens declares that "the effect [of Brennan's *Poems*] is that of a book of artifice, encumbered with intellectual paraphernalia", and that "Brennan wanted heat to set his words in motion . . . and sense of melody to make their motion musical" he went badly astray; he could not perceive the feeling, sometimes the passion, behind the often laborious form that was repellent to him. Worst of all is the air of superiority, the patronage that colours Stephens's little book on Brennan throughout: "Our lad," he calls Brennan, "a good lad, a kind lad. With all merits, (and they were not low) he was a modest lad, a striving lad. . . . But he never understood Mallarmé"; nevertheless, Stephens did perceive that Brennan's *Poems* were "a performance honourable and rare in the Australian field", and that they "make much hasty local verse trivial and insignificant in comparison". The second booklet, *C. J. Brennan: An Essay in Values* (Sydney, 1934), by Randolph Hughes (Sydney 1890–1956), contains an analysis of the often tortuous workings of Brennan's mind and a study of his poetical relationship to Mallarmé

---

[40] See p. 765.
[41] In "Malevolent Mummy", *The Red Pagan*, pp. 93–4.
[42] He could even assert that "O'Dowd shows a keener intellect [than Brennan]".

which has not been bettered so far: here also, however, the manner of presentation is a handicap: if Stephens patronizes his subject, Hughes patronizes everybody else, and some of his literary judgments are perverse;[43] also, Hughes approaches Stephens's error when he says that Brennan's poetry lacks lyrical music.[44] Admitting Brennan's laboriousness, his occasional failure of inspiration, he points out however that "the virtue of Brennan's poetry lies in an expanding progression of effect, in a slowly gathering amplitude of power"; and declares that "he wrote some very great poetry, in which he transcends [his] weaknesses". Hughes was educated at the Sydney Boys' High School and the universities of Sydney and Oxford, where he had a distinguished record in medieval and modern French; for a while he was English tutor at the École Normale Supérieure in Paris, and for several years he lectured in French at King's College, the University of London. The third booklet, *Christopher Brennan* (Sydney, 1939), is by the present writer, but it may be permissible to say that it points out Brennan's debt not only to Mallarmé but to a number of English poets, and in particular Milton, Tennyson, Keats and Yeats; and that it also discusses "The Wanderer", its rhythms and its general application. The fourth booklet, *Christopher Brennan: The Man and His Poetry* (Sydney, 1946) is by A. R. Chisholm, whose critical work is discussed elsewhere:[45] it contains some additional personal and biographical information, has something more to say about Brennan's relation to the French symbolists, and mentions a debt to Schopenhauer; Chisholm emphasizes also a fact that has no doubt influenced all those of Brennan's critics who knew him personally, that though the man is inseparable from the poet, Brennan was greater than his work.

The lack of demand for connected and systematic works of literary criticism did not prevent the appearance of several, quite early in the Period. The first and from a historical point of view not the least important was Nettie Palmer's[46] *Modern Australian Literature* (Melbourne, 1924), which won a prize offered by a Melbourne publishing firm for an essay on Australian writers since 1900: in about 18,000 words it contrives to present, along with an excellent summary description of the emergence of Australian literature from the Colonial Period, a generally clear and just outline of the Australian literature of the first quarter of the century, as seen through the eyes of a woman of literary judgment whose wide reading enabled her to regard her subject in perspective. It is not quite the perspective that has developed since: nowadays most critics would

[43] Joyce and Eliot are "fumbling *pasticheurs* and purloiners", Burns is "a minor poet", and Martin Tupper and Marie Corelli are grouped with Matthew Arnold.

[44] p. 140. On this point, see before, p. 1293.

[45] See pp. 1310–13.

[46] For Nettie Palmer's poems, see pp. 496–7; for her short-story anthology, see p. 1261; for her essays, p. 1284, and for her biographical work, pp. 1358, 1378–9.

give a little more space to Brennan, and also to Paterson, even at the expense of McCrae and O'Dowd; Baylebridge, whose *Selected Poems* had been published a few years earlier, is not mentioned; nor is Dyson's *Fact'ry 'Ands*; but it showed the way to later and more elaborate works of this kind. Next, perhaps, may come *An Outline of Australian Literature* (Sydney, 1930), which attempted, in less than 290 octavo pages, to cover the whole ground from the beginning; this was the work of the present writer. In the same year appeared *Queensland Poets* (London, 1930), by Henry Arthur Kellow (St Andrews, Scotland, 1881-1935), who went to Queensland in 1912 to become headmaster of the Boys' Grammar School, Rockhampton: Kellow devoted well over 90,000 words to an account of Queensland verse from the establishment of the colony; he indexes fifty-eight subjects, but scarcely a dozen of them can be called poets, most are minor, and the bulk of the space is devoted to versifiers whose talent is microscopic. As a researcher Kellow was indefatigable, within the limits he had set himself,[47] and as to matters of fact and sheer analysis he is often excellent; but as a critic, even apart from a pervading over-generosity of estimate, he is not always to be relied upon; in speaking of Baylebridge for example he says that

> One may search through the work of other poets—in spite of a haunting recollection of the elder brethren in Baylebridge's work—without finding more than the most fleeting resemblances;

he adds that "it is a sign of incipient greatness when a poet has a recognizable message", and is capable of the banality, "It is because Baylebridge combines good matter with good form that he is above the commonplace." *Queensland Poets* has however a sociological value, as indicating the amount and kinds of verse that are likely to be produced in a newly colonized country, the sort of people likely to produce them, and the probable effect upon them of their new surroundings; and it is useful for biographical and bibliographical reference, This seems the best place to mention also the miscellaneous work of William Albert Amiet (Geelong, Vic., 1890-1959) who, after a distinguished record at the University of Melbourne and a post-graduate course at the University of London, served in France with the first A.I.F. and settled down at Mackay, Queensland. Amiet was a popularizer of information and ideas mainly literary and linguistic, but ranging as far as astronomy; he published a series of collections of short articles, of which the most interesting is *Literature by Languages* (Sydney, 1932). This is too individual to be considered a mere compilation, but it suffers from a compression that makes one feel occasionally as though one were wading through sawdust, though it is

---

[47] But he refers to A. G. Stephens as "author of *The Pearl and the Octopus*" without mentioning the far superior *Red Pagan*; and in his introduction he says that Serle "is said to have" done what in the preface to *A Bibliography of Australasian Poetry and Verse* he says definitely that he *has* done.

fresh sawdust with a tang of its own; and from an apparent lack of perspective that springs from the author's desire to pay attention to even the smallest and least significant literatures. There are also lapses of judgment;[48] but with all his faults Amiet provides information which it would be hard to find elsewhere.

It is natural that there should be some reminiscence of thesis and lecture-room about scholarship generally, because the writer is so often a lecturer or a professor who hopes to use it as a means of obtaining a Chair or a better Chair, or at least as material for lectures; and this reminiscence has been most evident in scholarship whose subject is a work of pure literature, probably because historians, economists and so on are more concerned with the world of practical affairs as well as with that of books; but it is much less evident nowadays, partly because of the age's revolt from convention in general and in particular from the critical conventions of a previous generation. The difference between the tone of the Australian literary scholarship of this Period and the last is no doubt traceable in the main to this mood; but there is also the fact that Australian scholarship has become more adult: and, though there is of course no such thing as nationality in scholarship, it is possible that the greater proportion of native-born upon Australian university staffs may have made for a willingness to depart from traditional conventions.

Several of the writers in this section have won reputation overseas, and one of the most notable is Arthur John Alfred Waldock (Hinton, N.S.W., 1898-1950); a graduate of the University of Sydney, where he studied under MacCallum, he lectured first at the Royal Australian Naval College, Jervis Bay, and then at his own university, in which he afterwards succeeded Professor Brereton in the Chair of English Literature: by the time this History closed he had published three books,[49] which showed a gradually ripening scholarship. The first, *Hamlet: A Study in Critical Method* (Cambridge, 1931), is of mainly though not entirely historical importance. Its attitude and general conclusions are not new to the Shakespearian critics of today, but at the date of the book's publication some English and most Australian critics of Shakespeare were strongly influenced by nineteenth century hero-worship, to which Shakespeare's creations represented life itself and the art of his best plays was in most respects almost beyond question. Waldock however led the way here in insisting that the plays had their faults, that in each of them it was the direct effect upon the audience that Shakespeare had in mind, not what might be got out of it in an armchair afterwards, and

[48] Few critics would agree to the representation of George Moore by *A Mummer's Wife*, or of Joyce by *Haveth Childers Everywhere*; and even the shortest summaries ought surely not to omit Mann and Rilke from German literature or Furphy and McCrae from Australian.

[49] Another, *Sophocles the Dramatist* (Cambridge, 1951), was published after his death.

that *Hamlet*, for instance, must be regarded as a play, not a philosophical treatise; and he reminded us that it was an Elizabethan audience for which the play was designed, an audience that was familiar with its structure and drift from its predecessors and took them for granted; not a modern audience, influenced, mostly no doubt at second-hand, by a mass of critical interpretations. Waldock followed J. M. Robertson in emphasizing that Shakespeare was "not deeply concerned to secure perfect artistic consistency", and the American critic, E. E. Stoll, in emphasizing that even Shakespearian characters should not be considered as real persons, with a life beyond what is shown us on the stage; this last is of course disputable: we know more of Hamlet, for instance, than of a neighbour whom we see only in his backyard or front garden. The problem with which Waldock is principally concerned however is that of Hamlet's irresolution and delay: he argues that if we take into account only what is shown to us on the stage this delay is much less evident; it does not disappear,[50] but most of what suggests delay to us is simply a result of Shakespeare's imperfect adaptation of materials that were incompatible. Waldock frankly admits that the ghost's injunction to Hamlet not to forget his "almost blunted purpose" remains a difficulty, and that there are other difficulties; but he argues that their importance diminishes when we regard the play as a whole: at the end of Waldock's analysis the play represents to us, if we follow him, not, as it used to be, a mystery, a standing invitation to the imagination, but "a tremendous *tour de force*", in which "an old plot is wrenched to new significances", and which "shows signs, in fissures and strain, of all this forceful bending". An amiable weakness of Waldock's was a tendency to puns, and his second book, *James, Joyce and Others* (London, 1937), is a collection of essays upon Henry James, James Joyce, Thomas Hardy and one or two more: it says something for the critic's thoroughness, penetration, and individual approach that there are still new things to be found in these essays, particularly in the one on Henry James, who was perhaps his favourite author. Waldock reminds us how after James had technically reached his goal, and gone indeed too far for some of his readers, he relentlessly revised all his previous work, even that little masterpiece, *Daisy Miller*, in the effort "to impose the later technique upon the earlier material";[51] he "does what he can," says Waldock, "to re-write *The American* in the manner of *The Ambassadors*:" there are none of the relaxations of the earlier books, and the "suave and genial loveliness" of *The Portrait of a Lady* is replaced by a "more difficult beauty". It is not merely the style that has altered, though that has now become "almost

[50] Waldock here refers to a suggestion by C. S. Lewis, that there might be *no* psychological cause for the delay.

[51] Just as Yeats did.

a dialect", but the whole method of representation; "its main principle is the consistent employment of consciousness as the medium of exposition": all traces of the intrusion of the author are removed; everything that happens is shown as mirrored in the minds of one or other of the characters; these are " 'burnished reflectors' and the beams they cast make the novel". Waldock has a discriminating comment upon two outright and characteristic criticisms by H. G. Wells: as to his "irresistible picture" of Henry James "clambering over huge metaphors", he remarks that although this "possesses at least the truth of caricature . . . the metaphors rarely . . . fail to justify themselves"; and though he agrees with Wells that James narrows his material by ruling out "blood and dust and heat", he seems to agree with James's reply, that what is left is more than a mere "residuum", that it consists of the "finer vibrations of experience", the ultimate 'worth-while' of life: this essay is so closely packed that it seems a pity that Waldock did not write a whole book on Henry James. In his third book, *Paradise Lost and its Critics* (Cambridge, 1947), as in his first, Waldock introduces to Australia a critical attitude which had already in Britain and the United States succeeded that of the previous generation; but the critical mind that now reveals itself is riper and more assured than in the handling of the first book, and it is now focused, as in the second book it was not, upon a single subject, for which the critic is thus able to allow himself more room. The old question, Who is the hero of *Paradise Lost*?, having been by this time thrashed out until there was mainly dust upon the threshing floor, Waldock begins with its successor: What really happens in the poem? What does Milton really mean in it? E. M. Tillyard had declared that poets don't tell stories at all, that their meaning, and the meaning of the poem is simply what was in their minds when they wrote. But, Waldock remarks,[52]

> If that is true we can only feel that chaos is come again, for it almost removes the possibility of our ever coming to grips with a work of literature. How much, after all, do we know or *can* we know about the true state of Shakespeare's mind when he was writing *King Lear*? How much does it concern us to know about it?;

it is true that in *Paradise Lost* we are conscious here and there of what Milton's state of mind was when he wrote, but, and this is one of Waldock's most important points, "the effect of such passages, in general, is rather to distort the meaning than to reinforce it". Milton's plan was to date the story in Genesis "and project it on an enormous canvas", but the canvas "was like a stretch of film minutely flawed", and the enlargement showed up every imperfection; Milton did not foresee such a result, partly because to him the fable was God's own truth, and partly because he lacked the literary experience, the technique for assessing the practicability of certain themes for literary treatment, which we

[52] p. 14.

possess today mainly as a result of the development of the novel. Actually, says Waldock,[53]

> . . . the poem asks from us . . . two incompatible responses. It requires us . . . with the full weight of our minds to believe that Adam did right, and simultaneously . . . that he did wrong;

the fact is that in a number of cases Milton is carried away, his material gets out of hand, and he adds a short comment to drag it back: but, says Waldock, it is quite wrong to allow the comment, the afterthought, to overrule the demonstration. Take for instance Adam's reaction to Eve's announcement that she has eaten the fruit: from the passages beginning

> How can I live without thee, how foregoe,

and

> However I with thee have fixt my lot,

it is clear that Adam's reason for deciding not to abandon Eve, is neither "comradeship" (Tillyard) nor "uxoriousness" (C. S. Lewis) but simply that he is in love with Eve and cannot bear to be parted from her. Yet, a few lines later, Milton tells us that it was merely that Adam was "fondly overcome with Femal charm"; this, Waldock says,[54]

> . . . is merely Milton's way of inciting us to take a certain view of a matter that he has already presented with a quite different emphasis and to a quite different effect.

The same sort of thing occurs also in other connections; Milton

> . . . will put some glorious thing in Satan's mouth, then, anxious about the effect of it, will pull us gently by the sleeve, saying . . . "Do not be carried away by this fellow: he *sounds* splendid, but take my word for it. . . .";

And there is actual "literary cheating" when Gabriel accuses Satan of having

> Once fawn'd, and cring'd, and servilly ador'd
> Heav'ns awful Monarch,

an assertion that does not in the least agree with the character of Satan as it has been already shown to us. Waldock also points out that a passage cited by Lewis as helping to prove that Satan's mind is in process of decay, the passage from his "speech from the throne" that begins,

> Powers and Dominions, Deities of Heav'n,
> For since no deep within her gulf can hold
> Immortal vigor, though opprest and fall'n
> I give not Heav'n for lost,

---

[53] p. 56.
[54] p. 49.

proves nothing of the kind: certainly this speech contains contradictions and illogicalities; nevertheless it is exactly what was needed in the circumstances, "the kind of speech that able commanders, one supposes, have been making at such critical junctures since the dawn of history", and is by no means to be put to the test of logic and hard fact. On another occasion Milton is caught in a dilemma which lands him in sheer contradiction: on the one hand he declares hell to be "A Dungeon horrible", a place of unceasing torment in which there can never be rest or peace or hope; yet on the other hand we are allowed to see by the behaviour of the fallen host that they are by no means without hope, that they are scarcely inconvenienced and are even able to engage in field sports; in the one place Milton is describing a real hell, and in another a rallying ground, a base for reorganization and the planning of future military operations. The fact is, Waldock concludes,[55] that

> For narrative the material of *Paradise Lost* was intractable. Milton did his best with it, but there are things that he tried to do with it that simply could not be done.

It is impossible to do more than give a general idea of the argument of a book that is so tightly packed; but one thing must be noticed: the attractiveness and as it were the innate suitability of the style; its slightly Jamesian subtleties and qualifications provide exactly the machinery needed for critical work of this particular kind. But if Waldock has learnt something from Henry James, his style is still his own, and indeed it exactly mirrors the man himself: smooth, precise, gentle but resolute; it would be impossible to imagine Waldock either discourteous in his disagreements or stepping an inch aside from a carefully considered opinion; and though definitely a calculated, indoors style, it is by no means artificial, moving easily and naturally and expressing itself freely in realistic and always illuminating idioms and images which contribute towards its quiet but vigorous life: of one of the inconsistencies in *Hamlet*, Waldock remarks that

> . . . what we have here is a slight bump in the highway of the plot. Shakespeare has left a little gap between two surfaces. Travelling at speed, we scarcely notice it; when, in our leisurely surveys, we slow down, we feel it;

of Henry James's work,

> The later novels move forward insensibly, with a quality almost sidereal in their motion;

of Dr Tillyard's theory that the meaning of a poem is the state of mind of its maker:

> Can we properly think of a work of literature as if it were connected by a kind of umbilical cord with its maker?;

[55] p. 146.

of C. S. Lewis, when he

> . . . suggests that we ought to wish that Adam had acted "correctly" he is asking us to wish that Adam had been, not Adam, but Sir Charles Grandison;

and there is his own remark that every critic should take to heart:

> Of all the bad judges of literature, no judge, perhaps, is quite so bad as a good critic in the grip of a preconceived theory.

Waldock was one of the very few masters of prose style in the applied literature of Australia, and one of the not very many in Australian literature as a whole.

Another writer whose work is known overseas is Alfred Hart (Iowa, U.S.A., 1870–1950), who was born of British parents during a visit to America; his work is discussed here because it was not published until well on into the present Period. Hart came to Australia as a boy, had his schooling in Melbourne, and was a Master of Science and a Doctor of Literature of the University of Melbourne; he also taught science and mathematics, but his principal interest was in Shakespeare, and particularly in the text of the plays, and his two major books, *Shakespeare and the Homilies* (Melbourne, 1934) and *Stolne and Surreptitious Copies* (Melbourne, 1942), represent the most notable textual emendation of Shakespeare that Australia has produced. Hart's first book is based on lectures delivered to the Melbourne Shakespeare Society, of which he was president; its preparation was assisted by a grant from the University of Melbourne and that of the second by a grant by the Commonwealth Literary Fund, and both books were published by Melbourne University Press. In the first essay in his first book, Hart argues that Shakespeare took his views on the divine right of kings and the proper relationship between them and their subjects from the official book of "Sermons or Homilies", which he would have heard read at church. He reminds us that Shakespeare never obtruded his own personality or beliefs;[56] yet says that he not only

> . . . outdoes every other important dramatist of his time in the number and variety of the allusions made to the divine right of the reigning monarch, the duty of passive obedience, enjoined on subjects by God, and the misery and chaos resulting from civil war and rebellion,

but treats these doctrines as "the accepted and immutable law of almost every land in every age"; he did not get this attitude from his source books, or from current political literature, or from preceding dramatists; nor did John or Richard II or any of their successors up to the time of Henry VII consider that their power was immediately derived from God: Shakespeare seems to have "accepted, in a semi-philosophic spirit,

[56] p. 27.

the divine right of kings as a fundamental principle of the system of government that he knew best". In a couple of essays on the abridgment of plays and the time allotted for their performance on the stage, Hart attacks the opinion that the normal length of an Elizabethan play intended for the stage was about 3000 lines: he points out that plays of this length and upwards were very rarely written, except by Jonson or Shakespeare; that there was no certainty of more than two and a quarter hours of daylight on winter afternoons, which, would not allow of the acting of more than 2400 or even 2300 lines;[57] Shakespeare and Jonson were idealists and wrote as much as they felt inclined to write, but they did not complain against abridgement for stage purposes. The second book is more than three times the size of the first; its title refers to the introduction to the First Folio, in which its editors speak of the "diuerse stolne and surreptitious copies" of certain plays with which readers were abused before. Heminge and Condell were hitting at what are nowadays commonly known as the "bad quartos": it is Hart's thesis that each of these is "a garbled abridgment of an acting version made officially by the play adapter of the company from Shakespeare's manuscript"; he has no difficulty in disposing of the theory that they represented Shakespeare's rewriting of older plays by other men; as to this, he declares that there is no evidence that Shakespeare was ever a cobbler of other men's plays,[58] and that to a man of his temperament and imagination such rewriting would have been "infinitely more tedious than the retelling of a hundred thrice-told tales"; what is more, the vocabularies of the "bad quartos" and of the received texts are almost the same, whereas when one man rewrites another's play there is bound to be a considerable difference in, among other things, vocabulary. Hart also quotes blunders and omissions which are explainable only after consultation with the accepted texts: in explanation of the fact that it has sometimes been possible to amend an accepted text from a "bad quarto", he points out that, since according to his theory its immediate source was the official acting version, which may have been prepared from Shakespeare's manuscript for the use of the prompter, and as to difficulties in which it was possible that he himself might have been consulted, it would not be surprising if among thousands of omissions and blunders there might be a few useful readings. As to an alternative theory, that the "bad quartos" represented shorthand reports of acting versions made in the theatre, Hart points out that a shorthand writer would hardly add to his notes of one scene an extract from another;[59]

[57] Hart says that there is not the slightest evidence that there was artificial lighting in theatres, at least before 1616, except by "smoking torches and guttering candles" (p. 114), and that there was no reservation of shorter plays for the winter season (pp. 115-17).
[58] *Stolne and Surreptitious Copies*, pp. 159-60, 442.
[59] Chambers also made this point (*William Shakespeare*, 1930 edition, p. 157).

and he adds the interesting piece of information that Professor Scott, who had been for many years a member of the staff of Commonwealth Hansard, told him that he had taken the trouble to learn one of the Elizabethan systems, Bright's *Characterie*, and that it would have been useless for reporting a play.[60] Hart's elaborate and painstaking researches, with their detailed textual analyses, might easily have been dryasdust; on the contrary they are often extremely entertaining to a reader who has any interest in the subjects: he has the virtue of the best of modern Shakespearian commentators, in that he is precise without being in the least academic in the narrower sense of the term; he knows how to systematize his material and marshal an argument, his style is easy and informal without incorrectness, and it is direct and often outright. While freely acknowledging his indebtedness to Greg, Pollard, Chambers and others, Hart has no hesitation in emphasizing his disagreement with any of them[61] where it exists, and he damns bluntly groups of critics whom he does not name: he speaks of "the froth and bubble generated during the turbid workings of the iconoclastic mind", and declares that

> . . . certain literary critics have for thirty years been employing methods practised in the dark ages, and, to use an expressive Americanism, have been "getting away with it";

and, in his first book,

> . . . had [his own] or similar methods been used with honesty and judgment by the self-styled "scientific" literary critics and disintegrators of Shakespeare's plays, most of their books would never have been written.

The only other Shakespearian commentator of the Period who need be mentioned here is R. G. Howarth, whose essays and poems have been already discussed,[62] and he is represented only by *Shakespeare's Tempest* (Sydney, 1936) which in its original form was delivered as a lecture to the Australian English Association. A considerable part of this little book is devoted to a discussion of Caliban, whom Howarth believes to be neither an amphibian nor a creature of fantasy, but an unusually deformed human being; he believes that the structure of the play is best understood by appreciating "not only its preternatural but its 'historical' basis", and he does not consider Prospero to be Shakespeare's ideal of himself, or the famous speech beginning "Our revels now are ended" to represent Shakespeare's farewell to his art: "It is [merely] the sense of transience in our apparent stability that informs these marvellous lines."

---

[60] But, according to Chambers (p. 161), German students of stenography believe that "the thing could be done and was done".
[61] For example, Pollard and Wilson, in *Stolne and Surreptitious Copies*, pp. 56–66.
[62] For these, see pp. 1284 and 1059 and n.18 respectively.

There were two women scholars of importance. Thomas Traherne is now among the principal English seventeenth-century mystics, though it is only just over the half-century since he was discovered, and just under that since the first publication of some of his poems; nevertheless it is only during the present generation that the man has been made real to us and his verse generally available, and both these things have been done by an Australian. Gladys Irene Wade (Guildford, W.A., 1895-1982) was Headmistress of the Methodist Ladies' College, Burwood, New South Wales, from 1941 to 1959; she was awarded a scholarship from the University of Western Australia to the University of London: she took as her Ph.D. thesis Traherne, and this was the basis of her book: it involved elaborate researches in Traherne's native county, Hereford, in Oxford, where he took a degree, and in the great London libraries. Dr Wade published first *The Poetical Works of Thomas Traherne* (London, 1932), which brought together much that had not been published before; and later, *Thomas Traherne* (Princeton, U.S.A., 1944). This is both a biography and a criticism; though a number of the facts of Traherne's life had to be deduced from his writings, and there is still a great deal that we do not know, Dr Wade discovered much about him, and now for the first time the man is brought before us: spiritual, and yet by no means contemptuous of wordly success; a cultivated man, a thinker and a scholar; essentially a poet, and yet at his best in his best prose; a man of great personality and charm. "He comes to us," says Dr Wade, quoting from Masefield, "in these latter days like the first of the larks in spring": yet he is not a poet of the first order, because "he trusted reason too much and imagination too little"; not content with a vision of inaccessible beauty, he insisted upon interpreting and commenting upon it, and he thought that for poetic purposes "one plain word was as good as another". But with his prose it is another matter: here he combines the old with the new, standing between Jeremy Taylor and Addison; his style[63]

> . . . could still be stately and sonorous when occasion demanded; but it need no longer be pompous when the occasion for dignity had passed.
>
> . . . .
>
> He, and those of his temper, refrained from the far-fetched and erudite; they drew their comparisons from the simple and ordinary; but they were not afraid, as those of Addison's day were afraid, of that high truth of poetry which is not the truth of fact.

But Dr Wade points out that Traherne's prose has in general this defect: its unit is the sentence, or little group of sentences; there is no organic unity between his paragraphs, still less between his chapters; yet at his best he is free from this defect, and Dr Wade quotes that glorious passage from the *Centuries of Meditations*, which begins:

---

[63] p. 200.

> The corn was orient and immortal wheat, which never should be reaped, nor was ever sown. I thought it had stood from everlasting to everlasting.

Until, or unless, a good deal more is discovered, and there is still a volume of Traherne's poems which has not yet come to light, Dr Wade's critical biography seems likely to remain the standard. The second woman scholar, Dr Greta Hort (Denmark, 1903-67), went back to *Piers Plowman*,[64] which she considers to be essentially a theological poem and not least important among the forerunners of the Reformation in England. Dr Hort is a distinguished graduate of the Universities of Copenhagen and Cambridge; she emigrated first to England and thence to Australia, was for twelve years Principal of the Women's College at the University of Melbourne, and now lives abroad. In her *Piers Plowman and Contemporary Religious Thought* (London, 1938) she does not distinguish between the successive texts of the poem, or consider the question of diversity of authorship, but she has some interesting things to say, not all new but all individualized, about the poem considered as a whole and as the work of a single individual: she comments upon the ease with which the concrete characters become allegorical and the originally allegorical characters become human; and she emphasizes the fact that whereas in the ordinary epic, assuming the poem to be an epic, what generally matters is what the characters do, here the actions are merely "a part of the machinery for making them talk". In her opinion *Piers Plowman* originated in a clerical circle, appealed first to the clergy, and spread to the laity, so that it may be "the best introduction we have to the spread of learning"; and, along with the work of Richard Rolle of Hampole and of John Wycliffe, it helped in

> the awakening of the "lewed" to intellectual pursuits [and] the filling up of the gap that separated priest from people;

it is in this respect that it prepared the way for the English Reformation.

In an age in which Donne's reputation "stands higher and is more widespread than it has been for 250 years" it seems strange that only one book, and that a very little one, has been written about him in Australia. This book is *Donne's Influence in English Literature* (Morpeth, N.S.W., 1932), by Robert Cecil Bald (Melbourne, 1901-65), a graduate of Melbourne and Cambridge, and later Professor of English at Chicago, who wrote the book as a young man when lecturing at Adelaide. Donne "gave to his successors new attitudes, new themes, a new style, and, above all, a new conception of the aims and methods of poetry"; yet after his own century, in which his enormous influence was "by no means wholly for good", he was not really appreciated until the Romantic

[64] Dr Hort's other publications include *Sense and Thought: A Study in Mysticism* (London, 1936) and *Two Poems* (Melbourne, 1945).

Revival; today however, his spirit is in accord with our restlessness and disillusion, and the verse of the most significant poet of this revival, T. S. Eliot, "reveals from the first the complete absorption of many of the things for which Donne stands in poetry". It seems a pity that this short study has not been followed by others of the same type but on a larger scale.

There was only one eminent classical scholar during the Period, and he was Australian only by adoption. William John Woodhouse (Clifton, Westmorland, England, 1866-1937) is considered to belong to this Period because all but one of his books were published in 1930 or later. After a brilliant career at Oxford and distinctions involving important excavations and explorations in Greece, he held several university lectureships in Classics and in Ancient History and was in 1901 appointed to the Chair of Greek in the University of Sydney. His books published after that date include, besides a *Tutorial History of Greece* and translations and annotated editions of Greek authors, *The Composition of Homer's Odyssey* (Oxford, 1930), *King Agis of Sparta* (Oxford 1933), and *Solon the Liberator* (London, 1938). Of these by far the most notable is the *Odyssey*. Woodhouse was technically a "unitarian", in that to him the author of the *Odyssey* was an individual, whatever the sources upon which he drew; but he was also among the "analysts", in that he explored and examined these sources. He illustrates the complexity of the *Odyssey* as compared with the *Iliad* by saying that it "shows something more nearly resembling the involution of plot with which we are all familiar in modern fiction"; it is a highly composite work of art, a romance whose strand is twisted of three main threads: the "saga of Odysseus", the poetical tradition of his life, to which Woodhouse has added elements derived from folk-tales and "Deep-sea Yarns"; and the fortunes of Penelopeia and of Telemachos,[65] without which, according to Woodhouse, there would have been no *Odyssey*, for the whole story was delayed and for this purpose the whole Kalypso episode invented because the poet wanted Odysseus to have a son of an age to be able to stand by him at the end. There is also[66] what Woodhouse calls "The Poet's Cement", by which he means the "episodes or pieces of narrative and description made or inserted for purposes of juncture or for embellishment": in these, including Agamemnon's eulogy of Penelopeia and the whole Kalypso episode, in which the poet was "free to invent after his own heart, we find an extraordinary poetic beauty and depth of quality, which make each such passage stand out in a quite special way". Woodhouse's high opinion of Homer's constructive genius does not hide from him the complications, the inconsistencies, the unmotived actions, the

[65] Woodhouse preferred the Greek spellings.
[66] Though this involves an element of cross-classification.

motiveless changes of plan that result from the incomplete twisting together of the diverse threads in the strand; yet the *Odyssey* remains for him "the first and greatest of [the world's] romances . . . one of the most wonderful and precious things in the world". If, as has been said,[67] Woodhouse's main originality lies in his recognition of the numerous folklore themes which are among the ingredients of the *Odyssey*," the book has nevertheless a flavour of its own, an individual method of presentation, which, with its lovingly painstaking study, its acute analysis, and its effortless and in a queer way both formal and informal style, make it hard to surpass as an introduction to the *Odyssey* and even to the Homeric question as a whole. In *Agis of Sparta* it is the critical element in Woodhouse that is most apparent. This is a detailed and elaborate analysis of Thucydides' account of the Mantinean campaign of 418 B.C., in which Agis smashed the far-reaching designs of Alkibiades and restored the damaged prestige of Sparta. Thucydides had made out that this victory was merely a piece of lucky blundering; according to Woodhouse it was the result of brilliance in strategy and tactics, and he declares that Thucydides' account of it is "simply a tissue of incoherencies, irrelevancies, and even downright absurdities". Woodhouse's criticisms have not had the effect that might have been expected, perhaps because they reflect so much discredit upon Thucydides; but there is no doubt that he at least set up a case to be answered, and established the fact of a bias here which Thucydides had also shown elsewhere. The third book, *Solon the Liberator*, deals with Solon's land reforms, and in particular his "disburdening ordinance", the wiping out of debtors' liabilities, in the light of a study of the agrarian problem in Attica in the seventh century B.C. Woodhouse makes the interesting suggestion that Solon had visited Egypt in his travels, and got there some inspiration for the legal and economic reforms that helped to lay the foundation of Athenian democracy. Woodhouse's style is not concise; he takes his time in making his points; and the principal criticism to be made of this third book is that it represents a fairly large structure built upon a comparatively slight foundation: there is really not very much to go upon, or indeed very much to be said. But his work as a whole gives Woodhouse a definite place among the humanists of classical scholarship.

The work of two scholars shifts from English to French literature. A. B. Taylor's *Introduction to Mediaeval Romance*[68] (London, 1930) sets out merely to provide a systematic survey of its chief themes and features

[67] By E. R. Dodds, in *Fifty Years of Classical Scholarship*, edited by Maurice Platnauer (Oxford, 1954), p. 7.

[68] Taylor's other publications include editions of the thirteenth-century English romance, *Floris and Blanchefleur*, and of several of Shakespeare's plays.

for readers who have made no deep study of the subject; it is however not a mere summary but a thoughtful study of the manner in which the romance arose, its characteristics, and the differences between British and French romances: indeed it is a work of imaginative scholarship. Albert Booth Taylor (Manchester, England, 1896–1971) was a graduate of Auckland University College and Oxford; he lectured in English at the University of Durham, served in the first World War, and was Professor of English Language and Literature in Tasmania from 1926 to 1957. The basis of his study is French romance, not only because most British romances are more or less close translations from the French originals, but because with these originated the form and spirit of medieval romance in general. Taylor shows how though at first romance meant merely history written in the vernacular instead of Latin, its authors, whose object was not to record facts but to entertain, added so many other ingredients that any element of truth became unrecognizable. In France of the twelfth and thirteenth centuries, with the Eastern influences that were brought back by the Crusaders and with the incorporation of Celtic folklore and classical legends, there came about a temporary renascence in scholarship and a desire for luxury and refinement, and the *chanson de geste* gave way to the romance; the *Chanson de Roland*, heroic in type, romantic in detail, links the old and the new type of fiction. Taylor shows how women, with more leisure and more education than men, became the principal patrons of romance, and demanded a gentleness, courtesy and refinement which the poets had to introduce; the result was that in the development of the Arthurian theme heroes represented not so much what the knights actually were, as what women would have liked them to be. As for the English romances, not only were they mostly adaptations by men who had small literary skill, but they were written, at least until the fourteenth century, for the uneducated. For these reasons they emphasized the adventures but cut down the love sentiment of their originals. Taylor concludes that "there is more genuine romantic glamour in even the clumsiest English versions of French love romance, simply because this stifling philosophy of courtly love is absent and the spirit of adventure has more play". The second of these two scholars is Ian (Ramsay) Maxwell (Melbourne, 1901–79). A graduate of Melbourne and Oxford, he practised law in Melbourne and lectured in English at Copenhagen and Sydney before becoming Professor of English Language and Literature at Melbourne; in *French Farce & John Heywood* (Melbourne, 1946) he tackles the problem why the work of John Heywood, a "so comfortably John Bullish author", should stand so apart from the English drama of his day. It was clear that he must have been affected by some foreign influence, and several of his plays were admittedly free adaptations from the French, but in spite of a short article on the subject[69] which Maxwell uses as a scholastic springboard, its conclusions were not established and only in part accepted, and the whole subject remained indefinite. Maxwell's book proves, not only that Heywood was the adapter of several French farces, but that his knowledge of French farce went far beyond these: that he borrowed from it not merely a few characters and situations, but a type, or types, of play; that "his whole conception of drama . . . leans towards that of the French playwrights"; that he was in fact "a regular pupil of the French stage". Maxwell knows how to make detailed scholastic analyses entertaining; he has a light touch, an eye for the picturesque and an instinct for the revealing image. "In England," he remarks, "as elsewhere in Europe, the serious drama, cradled in ritual and nourished on holy writ, gradually forsook the cathedral for the market-place." And, speaking of Heywood's dramatic isolation: "His work, despite its merit, remained strangely barren; and he is rather the great uncle than the grandfather of our comedy."

The scholastic work of Francis Joseph Henry Letters (Gympie, Q., 1897–1964) touches upon aspects of German, as well as French and Latin, literature. Letters was a graduate of the University of Sydney and Associate Professor of Classics at the University of New England; his *Introduction to Thomas Mann* (Armidale, 1945) is a compact and thoughtful study which reads like the generalized summary of what ought to have been a much larger and more elaborate work: In less than thirty thousand words Letters analyses Mann's attitude to life and to tragedy, and his first three novels, *Buddenbrooks*, *Royal Highness*, and *The Magic Mountain*.[70] The theme of tragedy, or at least of great tragedy, has always been a struggle with destiny, and it has been often said that whereas with the Greek tragedians the destiny is imposed from without, with Shakespeare it consists in something in the character of the hero, thus involving some approach to the Buddhistic doctrine of karma; but with Mann tragedy results from "a form of mental or physical illness or abnormality". His works, says Letters, "are an unadjudicated debate between Nietzsche and Schopenhauer"; they represent the alternate affirmation and denial of the value of life. Letters remarks upon that "'sympathy with death' so characteristic of the heroes of the new tragedy"; they are romantic intellectuals better equipped for thinking than for living, and Mann is of their number: there is something decadent about them; but their preoccupation with death is not the cause but rather the consequence of decadence. So far as this is true, it may well be, though Letters makes no

---

69 "The Influence of French Farce Upon the Plays of John Heywood", by Karl Young, in *Modern Philology*, vol. ii (1904), pp. 109 *et seq.*

70 *Joseph and His Brethren* and *Lotte in Weimar* are omitted because "these have received sufficient attention from English and American reviewers". But in any case surely Letters's bowl would have flowed over if these had been included.

such suggestion, that at the root of it lies, as at the root of Spengler's *Decline of the West*, a disappointment at Germany's failure in her immense and straining effort at world supremacy. "Tragedy," says Letters in conclusion, "asks a question of life and itself finds an answer. It is Mann's weakness that his readers are uncertain of his answer, and whether he really has one to give." But does tragedy inevitably find its answer, and is not Letters asking too much of a novelist, however talented and philosophical? In *Joris Karl Huysmans* (Armidale, 1945) Letters moves from an author whose chief concern is the abnormal to one who specializes in decadence, and who was himself a classic example of development from the naturalism of Zola and his followers, through decadence, to reception into the Roman Catholic Church. It is interesting to note that Letters compares, and contrasts, Hans Castorp with Des Esseintes: he deals, in this short book, with *En Ménage*, whose "chief concern is the trials and miseries of a bachelor existence for the average man", that is, the average man as Huysmans sees him; with *A Rebours*, "one of the most original books" as well as one of the most perverse; and with subsequent volumes, including *La Cathédrale*, "the terminus of a spiritual journey". He analyses their heroes, and especially Des Esseintes, that connoisseur and devotee of "the novel mental states resultant from artificially heightened sensation", with their inevitable result in satiety, dreariness and the despair, which leads to his conversion. In this latter book Letters's style is formal and rather cumbrous, though with occasional flashes: he speaks of "that culmination of the ignoble, an unmade bed", and remarks that "the ordinary sensualist is a glutton, where the decadent is an epicure", and that "the despair of philosophy may be the beginning of religion". Letters also wrote an excellent little guide to Virgil.[71]

A couple of scholars specialized in French literature. Alan Rowland Chisholm (Bathurst, N.S.W., 1885-1981) was educated at the universities of Sydney and Paris and at the Tilley Institute, Berlin; he lectured in modern languages at the Sydney Teachers' College and at the University of Melbourne, served with the A.I.F. in the first World War, and was from 1921 to 1957 Professor of French at Melbourne; he also edited the short-lived *Modern Language Review*,[72] a periodical which its time was unfortunately unable to sustain, and which incidentally found a place for some of Brennan's critical work. Chisholm's principal publications are *The Art of Arthur Rimbaud* (Melbourne, 1930) and *Towards Hérodiade* (Melbourne, 1934). The first is a short but interesting and individual study not only of Rimbaud's art but of his place in modern French poetry; Chisholm emphasizes the importance of the part Rimbaud

[71] And also, after the closing date of this History, *The Life and Work of Sophocles* (London, 1953).
[72] See pp. 781, 799-800.

played in bringing about the change of outlook that separates the Symbolists from the Romantics, the replacement of the old plastic basis of the French poetic point of view and poetic activities by the conception of a universal flux, a conception which was expressed in musical values. This change Chisholm regards as an example of what Spengler considered the characteristic tendency of the modern Western mind, which is exemplified in its art, science and philosophy:

> . . . a tendency to dissolve the solid, to push beyond the frontiers of that finite world which was the very basis of classic . . . art.

Rimbaud imparts the movement and fluidity of water not only to the sky but to solid objects, to civilization, to life, to the whole universe; he speaks of a ploughed field as though it were the sea, and describes a statue in terms of movement and music, and his literary "musicalism" makes him a forerunner of the symbolists. Chisholm goes on to examine the extremely varied sources of "Bateau Ivre", which include Lucretius and Jules Verne's *Twenty Thousand Leagues Under the Sea* as well as Edgar Allan Poe and such French poets as Leconte de Lisle and Hérédia; and he discusses Rimbaud's imagery, comparing it with that of other writers. "Bateau Ivre" represents an attempt to escape from the intellectual limitations of Europe, to be absorbed in the universal ocean, but the attempt is unsuccessful; Rimbaud is held back by the "*anciens parapets*" of Europe; he is absorbed in the ocean, with which he identifies himself, and yet he also identifies himself with the boat, which survives, a symbol of his personality. *Towards Hérodiade* represents a far larger project; it is a study, not of a single poet, but of French poetry of the nineteenth century, in order to show how

> . . . the most representative French poets from Leconte de Lisle to Mallarmé attempted to break down the plastic structure of the universe and found behind phenomena, first, an immense and incessant flux, and then a sheer void;

this book therefore includes incidentally the ground covered in the *Rimbaud*, which indeed, though written first, might be regarded as an amplification of part of the second book. *Towards Hérodiade* is by no means a mere chronological study; it examines the attitudes of the poets concerned and their aesthetic relationships and those of the movements for which they stand, including their relationships to German romanticism, to the philosophy of Europe, especially that of Schopenhauer, and of India, and to the whole culture of their time; it is not a history but rather an examination of the organic development of a particular aspect of French poetry and French poetic thought. Chisholm begins with an account of Dionysism, the desire to break the bonds of the individuality by identifying it with the world-spirit, enlarging it or dissolving it in Schopenhauer's cosmic will or in the ultimate void;

this, as Chisholm points out, is sheer decadence: the culture of Western Europe is rooted in the idea of being, stability and the value of the individual. "The first victim of Dionysos in the nineteenth century", whom the Cosmic Will pursued as the Hound of Heaven[73] pursued Francis Thompson, was Leconte de Lisle, with whom it takes the form of a vast energy; but it is also an eternal flux, an increasing music. As the principle of life, it manifests itself as Eros, but also as hunger and cruelty. In his analysis of Leconte de Lisle's symbols, and of those of other poets also, Chisholm is sometimes drawn away from the direct course of his survey; symbols have a special fascination for him and his analyses of them are extremely interesting. He goes on to deal with Baudelaire and his doctrine of correspondences, with occultism and its association with that doctrine, and with the "musicalisation" to which he had already alluded in the *Rimbaud*: to him, Hérédia represents a halt on the way in the course of this historical decadence; he is "the last priest of Apollo resisting the onslaught of Dionysos . . . the most uncompromising plastic poet of modern times". His characteristic symbol is that of the mirror, which, in its combination of object and image, is an expression of his desire for symmetry; earth and sea correspond to each other almost as a physical reality and its reflection; the "Angélus du Soir" reflects the "*vaste rumeur*" of the sea; Cleopatra, standing on the deck of her trireme, is imaged in the poet's mind by the hawk that adorns its prow; and in "Après Cannes", when Rome is fearfully awaiting the conquering Hannibal, one-eyed, riding on an elephant, his image

> . . . is projected on to the mirror of its terror-haunted brain in the form of the red eye of the sun riding on the back of the Sabine Hills.

Just as classicism had followed upon the exuberance of the renascence, so, to Chisholm, Mallarmé disciplines and rationalizes the romantic data into a pseudo-classicism of his own; Parnassianism had attempted something of the sort, but it had not gone far enough. In handling his materials however Mallarmé alters them, proceeds beyond them, proceeding beyond music for instance into a silent harmony, as in the sonnet, "Sainte", in which the saint, with her faded viol and old music book in the church window, as it shines in the setting sun, is "*musicienne du silence*". When he comes to "*Hérodiade*", "a dramatic poem conceived according to the traditions of classical tragedy", Chisholm discusses Mallarmé's constant use of negative forms, as for instance in the muse's description of the tapestry sybil whose head alone is visible, her dress and the background of the sky and birds having been cut away, so that she is clothed in "a dress of departed flights". But the most beautiful of Mallarmé's symbols, of his stylizations of the void of life, is that of

[73] This comparison is not Chisholm's.

Hérodiade herself, whose cold, severe, hermetic beauty sums it up, a beauty that exists, like that of Salammbô, only for and in itself, a symbol[74] of the desire for escape from the eternal Becoming, even at the cost of death. To Chisholm

> . . . it would seem that Hérodiade is the last word of French poetry, the perilous point at which literature passes over into the unexpressed, and European intellect faces suicide. . . .

Another piece of Mallarméian scholarship lies near the borderline of this History, since it was written not only in French but in France and published in Paris; nevertheless there are reasons for regarding it as Australian. (William) Gardner Davies (Melbourne, 1921-), who is Cultural Attaché at the Australian Embassy in Paris and Australia's permanent delegate to UNESCO, has not abandoned his Australian domicile. He and another Australian[75] who has hitherto published only one book have been grouped together[76] as constituting "the Australian school of Mallarmé". Davies has published several books, of which only the first, *Les tombeaux de Mallarmé* (Paris, 1950), appeared before the closing date of this History; together with the second[77] it was awarded the Prix Rivarol for the best book by a foreigner during the year. Davies here sets out to interpret Mallarmé's commemorative poems by comparing their images with parallels from more easily decipherable passages in his other work; or, failing a parallel image, by comparing the sense in which Mallarmé generally uses the individual words. This book throws light upon Mallarmé's poetic methods; it also tells how various poems came into existence, and it has something interesting to say about the element of obscurity that Mallarmé introduced deliberately, "d'un désir passioné . . . de protéger le sanctuaire de son rêve".

One piece of scholarship may be mentioned though it does not profess to be an original contribution to knowledge. *Off the Beaten Track in the Classics* (Melbourne, 1936) is a collection of recapitulatory but at the same time critical essays on the records of ancient geographical exploits and scarcely more wonderful legends and travellers' tales. There is the famous voyage of Hanno of Carthage, away down the north-west coast of Africa in the fifth century before Christ, when he came across hairy creatures that he called gorillas; there is a study of Aristarchus of

---

[74] p. 160.

[75] L. J. Austin, who was also one of Chisholm's graduates, and who is now Professor of Modern French at the University of Manchester. The book is *Paul Bourget* (Paris, 1940). But he has since published a couple of others: *Paul Valéry* (Grenoble, 1954) and *L'Univers poetique de Baudelaire* (Paris, 1956).

[76] In the *Times Literary Supplement.*

[77] This was *Vers une explication rationnelle du "Coup de dés"* (Paris, 1953), which at the time of the award was still in manuscript.

Samos, who anticipated Copernicus by 2000 years, and there is an account of such legendary "poison damsels" as the one of which Hawthorne made a story. These essays grew out of genuine affection and a wide reading of the original texts, and they are so presented as to feed and stimulate the imagination; the author, Carl (Henry) Kaeppel (Mittagong, N.S.W., 1887-1946), was a Sydney graduate and travelling scholar and a schoolmaster by profession; he won an M.C. in the first World War. Kaeppel published also *A Short History of Latin Literature*.

CHAPTER XIV

PHILOSOPHY, PSYCHOLOGY, EDUCATION, RELIGION

Philosophy: Gunn; Gibson; Merrylees. Education: Anderson; Ashby; Burgmann; Portus; Others. Religion: Angus

IN ALMOST all of the subjects considered in this chapter the work produced was on the whole disappointing. In philosophy, though several new chairs were founded, there were only three writers who need be discussed here, only one of them was Australian by birth and all three were critical rather than creative; in psychology, in spite of the development of the subject and the creation of chairs accordingly, there was nothing in book-form worth considering;[1] and the educational works of the Period were either critical again or little more than collections of historical and other facts.

In philosophy and psychology however the actual situation was much better than all this would indicate, for a good deal of work in these subjects, some of it of a high order, appeared not only in the *Australasian Journal of Psychology and Philosophy*,[2] but also in oversea periodicals, and was never published in book-form. This applies in particular to the philosophical work of John Anderson, Professor of Philosophy in the University of Sydney; he has been referred to abroad as[3] the leader of the only indigenous philosphical school in the Southern Hemisphere. Anderson's range is wide, but beyond the periodical world he has produced no more than a single booklet,[4] a collection of essays; which is referred to in the section of this chapter that deals with education. Conditions in Australia are not very favourable to the production of philosophical work, except in the shape of short articles: it has been said that Australians are intelligent without being intellectual, and it is true that comparatively few in this country are inclined towards abstract studies; but this would not necessarily affect the psychologists, whose ends, and methods, are sometimes practical enough:[5] the explanation of the appearance of so few works of philosophy or psychology may be partly due to the conditions in the Philosophy and Psychology depart-

[1] The eminent philosopher, Samuel Alexander (1859-1938), though born in Sydney, left Australia in 1878, before he had written anything of importance, and did not return.

[2] Now the *Australasian Journal of Philosophy*.

[3] By A. N. Prior in *Landfall*, March 1952; Professor Anderson retired in 1958.

[4] And another, on aesthetics.

[5] As, for instance, in the work of Muscio in the preceding Period; for a discussion of this, see pp. 885.

ments at the universities: they are usually undermanned, so that their staffs have little time or energy for constructive work except on a small scale. John Alexander Gunn (Liverpool, England, 1896–*c.*1945) is in some respects typical of the writers considered in this section. Of Scottish descent, he was educated at the Universities of Liverpool, London and Paris, where he was a Research Scholar at the Sorbonne, and he was awarded medals for his work on French philosophy and on Spinoza; he is a lecturer in psychology at the University of Melbourne, and has published since his arrival in Australia two philosophical works, of which however the first was partly written and the second was planned before he left England,[6] so that he barely comes within our range. *Benedict Spinoza* (Melbourne, 1925) is a biographical sketch with a critical summary of Spinoza's thought; Gunn shows the influences that affected Spinoza, and makes the point that he "began the revolt, which was accelerated by Goethe, against the orthodox dogma of a fallen human nature and the deist conception of an absentee God". *The Problem of Time* (London, 1939), which is much longer and more elaborate, traces, with critical comments, the successive conceptions of Time from the days of the Greeks to the present: there are interesting chapters on the theories of Kant, whose merit lay, so Gunn considers, not in his attempt to solve the Time problems but in his statement of them; and on the attempts of modern physicists at the measurement of Time. Gunn is not an original thinker, but a conscientious expositor and critic of the views of others; even his final chapter on "The Nature of Time" is very largely a commentary, and though Gunn's own views are made apparent there is nothing particularly novel about them. Alexander Boyce Gibson (London, 1900–72), son of the W. A. Boyce Gibson who has been referred to in dealing with the philosophers of the preceding Period,[7] was brought to Australia as a small boy and, after graduating at the University of Melbourne, proceeded to Oxford, lectured at Glasgow and Birmingham and in 1935 succeeded his father in the Chair of Philosophy in Melbourne. While in Australia he published a forty-five-page pamphlet, *Should Philosophers be Kings*? (Melbourne, 1939), which investigates the question in the light of the problems of democracy today. Plato saw in the rule of philosophers a means of salvation for Greek culture in the days of its decline; but Gibson points out that such rule would in fact be bad for both the philosopher and the people: the philosopher would cease to be a philosopher and the people would be deprived of freedom. Still, the modern philosopher-king should by no means stand apart from public affairs, and in particular it will be his duty to defend democratic institu-

---

[6] He also has published a play, *Spinoza, the Maker of Lenses* (London, 1932), and, before he came to Australia, works on Bergson, modern French philosophy, and social progress.

[7] See p. 882.

tions: this duty is particularly important today, when "reason . . . is distrusted and condemned. . . . Intransigence is claimed as a virtue, and open-mindedness spurned as feeble and unreal"; yet,

> . . . the ordinary man is capable always within the limits of his own experience of behaving philosophically . . . Much of the unreasonableness which is democracy's greatest danger is due not to stupidity but to the manipulation of untrained minds by men with a lust for power. It is in fact induced stupidity.

Gibson's style is much more lively than that of most philosophers; he has a feeling for words and phrases, and his short study, though not exactly profound in itself, is sprinkled with acute remarks that are not without humour: he speaks of "unfounded and passionate certainties"; he remarks that "no one who really thinks is so wrong that one cannot learn from him"; and he declares that

> . . . no philosopher can properly be said to "have" a philosophy. It will not stay put, square and solid, like a pound of butter in the larder. The man who 'has' a philosophy is no longer philosophising. Instead of continuing his effort, he is merely parading his product. He has begun to substitute the congealed past for the living present.

In collaboration with A. A. Phillips, senior English master at Wesley College, Melbourne, Gibson wrote also an excellent little textbook, as readable as it is efficient, on the art of clear thinking: *Thinkers at Work* (London, 1946). *Descartes* (Melbourne, 1934),[8] by William Andrew Merrylees (Charlton, Vic., 1900–69) is a critical exposition of certain fundamental questions raised by Descartes, together with the answers he gives to them, or alternative answers which are put forward as more satisfactory. Merrylees was a Victorian grazier, but was also a Rhodes Scholar and a graduate of Melbourne and Oxford, from which he proceeded to Heidelberg, and he was for nine years Senior Lecturer in Philosophy at the University of Melbourne; he was an experimenter in irrigation, and it is not surprising, after reading his book, to find that one of his pastimes was "devising things". Descartes was not always self-consistent, and in Merrylees's restatement his arguments gain in clarity; it is this perhaps that helps to bring out the mediaeval quality of some of them: of for instance the proofs of the existence of God. The most interesting part of the book is however Merrylees's contribution to the never-ending discussion of the famous "*Cogito ergo sum*", which depends on the assumption that clear and distinct perception must be true: Merrylees makes the point that sometimes such a perception is mistaken, but he says that in this case "we have [practically] conclusive evidence that it is not." There still remain, here for instance, and no doubt there always will remain, points for the critics to seize upon; but Merrylees

[8] The substance of this book was originally intended to be included in a review of Professor A. B. Gibson's *The Philosophy of Descartes* (London, 1931) (Preface).

brought to his task a clear and ingenious mind and an analytical logic that has about it sometimes a flavour almost of mathematics.

In the sphere of education most of the works published during this Period were conventional and dull; it might be possible to find a connection between this and the principal defects of which the Australian educational system or systems has been accused: traditionalism, lack of imagination, worship of the syllabus and fear of examinations. Far more vital and interesting were several books by writers who stand outside the world of schools: the most notable, by a professor of philosophy, is broadly critical from a humanist point of view; the most striking, by a professor of botany, attacks the whole educational system, root and branch; in the others, by a bishop and a professor of political science and history, the criticism is less outright, more general again. John Anderson (Stonehouse, Lanarkshire, Scotland, 1893-1962) graduated at Glasgow with first-class honours in Mathematics and "Natural Philosophy" as well as in Philosophy, and, after lecturing at several British universities, was from 1927 to 1958 Professor of Philosophy at Sydney. His influence upon his students and as an upholder of the spirit of free inquiry at the University as a whole have been exceptional, and he has contributed numerous articles on philosophical, ethical and social questions to *Mind* and the *Proceedings of the Aristotelian Society* as well as to the *Australasian Journal of Psychology and Philosophy*,[9] which he edited for a number of years. The contents of *Education and Politics* are thoroughly characteristic of its author, as a writer, as a lecturer, and in conversation with his students in the cloisters: they are an expression of certain principles for which he stands, all of them manifestations and outgrowths of the spirit of freedom, which is in greater need of expression and support in this period of post-war timidities and regimentations than it has been for many years. It has been said that Anderson is nothing if not critical, but all his criticisms are essentially positive, in that their object is not to destroy but to build: of universities he remarks that they do not exist to keep up the supply of qualified professional men, that their business is the criticism of preconceived ideas and arbitrary standards, as the only means by which public spirit can be fostered; of censorship, that life that is guarded by an extensive system of precautions is a mean and base existence, tending away from carefree and forceful activity and towards a neurotic sense of guilt and defeat; and of education, that it is *the finding of a way of life*,[10] as contrasted with the mere acquisition of a number of arts or accomplishments; that it should lead us to "dispense

[9] Now the *Australasian Journal of Philosophy*; for a further reference to Anderson and his work, see p. 1315.

[10] The italics are in the original.

with symbols and deal directly with things themselves", and that "it is a more intensive treatment of existing subjects, and not the addition of odds and ends to the curriculum, that will enliven education". It is surprising to find how freshly these essays read; no one would imagine that they were twenty or thirty years old: the secret of their freshness lies in an intensity of conviction that has its roots not only in intellect but in temperament, and in a directness of vision that is not led astray by convention or the inessential, and that is reinforced by a temperamental inclination to take the other side. These qualities are accompanied by a corresponding directness of expression, by a dislike for surplusage, by a logic in argument that is yet never dryasdust; and, not least, by an instinct for the effective word and phrase. Eric Ashby (London, 1904-),* has a markedly clear mind; in *Challenge to Education*[11] (Sydney, 1946) he brings a scientific approach to his criticisms, and his attitude, while too enthusiastic to be called disinterested, is quite free from bias, scientific or other. He was educated at the City of London School and the Universities of London, Geneva and Chicago; for eight years he occupied the Chair of Botany at the University of Sydney, which he then resigned for a similar appointment at Manchester. It would be hard to find criticism more vigorous, outspoken and direct than Ashby's: he believes that the youth of Australia is as intelligent as the youth of any other country in the world, but he also believes that it is being given a third-rate education; there is no clear vision of its purpose, it is incredibly formal, and[12]

> Except in certain private schools, which defy the system rather than exemplify it, the teacher is in constant anxiety about examination passes, and the child becomes convinced that the seven deadly sins at school are: originality, resource, scepticism, critical judgment, non-conformity, lack of deference to those in authority, and wanting to know more than is in the syllabus.

So far as concerns the collection and memorizing of facts Ashby considers that our school system succeeds; but in the cultivation of what he calls "intellectual health",[13]

> . . . the ability to think clearly, to balance evidence, to reach conclusions uncoloured by personal likes and dislikes, to state both sides fairly; integrity in the use of words and sincerity in the expression of opinion:

in all this it fails. On the proper purpose of public examinations, on the teaching of science, on the qualities to be expected, or at least to be hoped for, in the ideal pass graduate, and on many other matters this little book is well worth quoting: it is rich in ideas that are stimulating,

* [Still lives in England, where he is now Baron Ashby of Brandon.]

[11] This collects, with some pruning and the addition of some introductory matter, a number of pamphlets published and wireless talks broadcast during Ashby's residence in Australia.

[12] p. 5.

[13] p. 23.

and most educationalists would agree with Ashby in his general conclusions, though not invariably in matters of detail. He expresses himself with a smooth urbanity that is yet consistent with incisive vigour and the use of familiar and vivid comparisons, as when he refers to "the magpie-picking of useless knowledge which goes under the name of science" in school examination papers, and "the intellectual Woolworths of the general science curriculum". *The Education of an Australian* (Sydney, 1944) is somewhat less tightly packed; it is more discursive, and not so purely intellectual; it is also more personal, though its critical conclusions are more generalized, and it is quite lacking in clerical rhetoric. Its author, Ernest Henry Burgmann (Lansdown, Manning River, N.S.W., 1885-1967), was a graduate of the University of Sydney and of the Australian College of Theology; he was made Bishop of Canberra and Goulburn, was Warden of St John's College, Armidale and of St John's College, Morpeth, and editor of the *Morpeth Review*.[14] History, he remarks, "is the story of man's education", and he tells how he was influenced by his parents, his little bush school, a larger school in the city, and, not least, by the bush itself; he was brought up the hard way, became an expert axeman, and is probably the only bishop of whom bullockies have said, "That b— parson knows more about bullock-driving than we know ourselves." The book expands into a discussion of the education of the young Australian generally, and of the society in which he is to live, and which he is to help to form: crude as we still are, by comparison with older civilizations, we should seek, Bishop Burgmann says, not to imitate them but to come to terms with our own environment. We must cease to worship property and help our old men to remain young in spirit, so that youth may not be swamped by age; but youth must be taught to distinguish between Hitler and Heracles, and that it does not always do so is the fault of the adults: we need leaders, and if we cannot create them we can sow the seeds of leadership and provide conditions in which natural leaders may find their opportunities. *Free, Compulsory, and Secular*[15] (London, 1937), by Garnet Vere Portus (Morpeth, N.S.W., 1883-1954) has a large historical scope; it explains the growth of the Australian educational system as a reflection of political and social forces, themselves determined by their economic and material backgrounds and by tradition. Essentially critical, it yet regards the Australian educational system as "a serious effort to tackle a big job", and, as against its bureaucracy, rigidity and traditionalism he balances its uniform training of teachers and its provision of equality of educational opportunity

[14] For a discussion of this magazine, see p. 1333.

[15] This consists of three Joseph Payne Lectures delivered in the University of London Institute of Education, and published for the Institute by the Oxford University Press. Other books by Portus include an excellent little textbook, *Marx and Modern Thought* (Sydney, 1921); a history for children, *Australia Since 1606* (Melbourne, 1932); and *Australia, an Economic Interpretation* (Sydney, 1933).

and educational facilities in the poorest and remotest areas. Portus, a Sydney University Rhodes Scholar, had sixteen years' experience at that University as Director of Tutorial Classes and lecturer in Economic History, after which he became Professor of Political Science and History at Adelaide; his style is slightly formal, leisured, logical and systematic, but it is enlivened by an occasional natural simplicity, as that "we are tattooed in our cradles with the beliefs of our life-times".

Setting aside several historical reviews of education or of some of its aspects in one or other Australian State or in the Commonwealth as a whole, as well as textbooks, technical works, and descriptions of educational experiments that do not come within the sphere of this History, the most notable of the professional works is the most recent: *The Educational Thought of Matthew Arnold* (London, 1950), by William Fraser Connell (Lockhart, N.S.W., 1916-), who became in 1955 Professor of Education at Sydney. Arnold's attitude and conclusions have still some bearing upon educational problems, Australian and other, and here, though there is no direct Australian reference, they are examined, critically and in historical detail. The book is so tightly packed that its generalizations and illustrations only just redeem it from dryness, but it is a work of painstaking scholarship, which should be useful to anyone who is interested in the development of English educational thought or of Arnold's ideas upon education and the part it should play in the humanization of man in society.

In the religious sphere, though there was only one work of importance, it was quite out of the common. Samuel Angus (Ballymena, Ulster, Ireland, 1881-1943) was born of poor parents, but he won a scholarship to Queen's College, Galway, and carried on his education at Princeton, Marburg, Berlin and Edinburgh; several other universities awarded him honorary degrees and he was otherwise recognized abroad; for example, Bertrand Russell quotes from him in his *History of Western Philosophy*.[16] From 1914 until his death he was Professor of New Testament and Historical Theology at St Andrews (Presbyterian) College, the University of Sydney, and he also lectured at Princeton, Yale, Columbia, Chicago and elsewhere in North America. The freedom of Angus's views, his disregard for orthodoxy and his dislike of dogma caused him to be three times charged with heresy, but after long and vehement arguments his Church failed to find him guilty. He published a large number of works,[17] of which two must be discussed here: these two, *The Mystery-*

[16] See Fourth Impression, 1954, pp. 251 and 350 note 2.

[17] Including *Christianity and Dogma* (1933), *Jesus in the Lives of Men* (1933), *Essential Christianity* (1939) and a novel, *The Auld Sinner* (1938). He was also a contributor to the *Encyclopaedia of Religion and Ethics*, *The Temple Dictionary of the Bible* (London) and the *Standard Bible Dictionary* (Chicago).

Religions and Christianity (London, 1925) and *The Religious Quests of the Graeco-Roman World* (London, 1929), are best taken together, for they draw upon the same material and cover practically the same ground, though with a difference of emphasis, the second, curiously enough, giving the more space to Christianity, its early development and its problems; this book also contains some repetitions and many recurrences to subjects dealt with already in the other, though they are presented with different, or mainly different, and supplementary information: indeed, absorbed in some interesting passage, and there are very many interesting passages, one may look up and wonder for a moment which book he is reading.[18] The second book is very largely a supplement to the first; yet it is not only considerably larger but the better of the two: speaking generally, it contains less summary and more generalization and comment; it is riper and moves more freely, as though the writer, having put behind him the great bulk of his material, felt himself able to pause and supplement, and, regarding his subject as from a little distance, to formulate some personal conclusions. In *The Mystery-Religions and Christianity*, Angus begins by emphasizing the fact that Christianity cannot be understood if studied in isolation from its background, the mystery-religions among which it came to birth and the world they grew out of and represented; he tells how the Greek religion of beauty and joy, weakened by scepticism as to the nature and certainty of knowledge, was invaded by Orientalism, with its mystical pantheism, its appeal to the emotions rather than to the intellect, its asceticism and its love of fantasy and sacramental symbolism. A mystery-religion was[19]

> . . . a Sacramental Drama which appealed primarily to the emotions and aimed at providing psychic and mystic effects by which the neophyte might experience the exaltation of a new life. [it] responded to the prevalent *appétit d'un monde meilleur.*

According to Angus, the great majority of the commentators agree as to the ethical and religious value of the mystery-religions, and there is no doubt that they served to educate men in the doctrine of a future life; but, he adds, they inherited a primitive barbarism; they were linked with magic and astrology, which, however these helped them to become popular, undermined them spiritually, and they were unbalanced. A number of reasons are quoted for the emergence and survival of Christianity: its historic and personal centre and its ancient Holy Book, its noble ideal and its promise of immortality, the efficiency of its organization and the reasonableness of its dogma. *The Religious Quests of the Graeco-Roman World* begins in much the same way as the other,[20] but its introductory sentiment is enlightened with images, as for example:

[18] The sub-titles of the two books are practically the same: "A Study in the Religious Background of Early Christianity", and "A Study in the Historical Background of Early Christianity".
[19] pp. 58 and 64. [20] Foreword, p. ix.

> The Graeco-Roman world was the soil on which the Sower went forth to sow the Christian seed; the growth depended not only on the vital forces inherent in the seed but on the preparation and fertility of the soil;

and Angus laments the fact that[21]

> Much New Testament study is of the same order as if Shakespeare were studied in the background of Victorian Britain . . . instead of in that of "the spacious times of great Elizabeth".

Angus goes farther in this than in the other book into the material crises which marked the blending of East and West, in those "harassed Roman provinces which had served as battlefields for the Roman armies"; he examines the grounds of the attraction to Judaism, Greek morality and mystical philosophy, the mystical religions and Christianity, and he discusses[22]

> . . . the progress of Christianity from a sect of Judaism to a catholic religion . . . by various stages and conflicts in the advance from the religion of Jesus to the religion about Jesus, and from the religion about Jesus to a highly contentious metaphysical Christology concerning a pre-existent descending and ascending Lord.

Angus says that soon after Paul's death Christianity became a mystery-religion, and that, indirectly, "sacramentarianism traced its ancestry to Paul"; referring to the dangers of the revival of the crudities of bygone superstition, he remarks that[23]

> . . . it is easier to concentrate on the visible than to penetrate with the inward eye into its background in the invisible. . . . Sacraments may themselves become surrogates for the Reality or become objects of devotion in themselves;

and finally he discusses "the third and perhaps the greatest crisis in the history of early Christianity", the attempt, through agnosticism, to Hellenize, almost to Orientalize it; to sweep it away as a historic religion: the Church won, but to do so she[24]

> . . . surrounded herself with the threefold wall of apostolic authority in the Episcopate, thus ending democratic freedom, the Apostles' Creed . . . fluid theology, and the New Testament canon.

Angus's principal defect, apart from the fact that later investigations have affected some of his conclusions, is in the organization of his material. The most obvious example has been mentioned already: the distribution between two separate books, with frequent reworkings, supplements and overlappings, of what should properly have formed a single book; some condensation mainly by omission would not have involved a loss. But the same tendency is observable in each individual volume. It is

---

[21] p. 1.
[22] p. 103.
[23] p. 234.
[24] p. 400.

not that Angus does not realize the need for organization of the mass and detail of his material, and indeed he is over-fond of the apparatus of organization, expecially of series of numbered categories; but some of his categories do not read on with the general statement that precedes them, producing an effect of incoherence; sometimes the numbers do not really refer to categories but merely to sections of the argument, and would be better omitted; and, beyond this, Angus writes often carelessly and he has a rather extraordinary fondness for theological jargon.[25] But together with a far-reaching scholarship he possesses a sympathetic insight that enables him to build an extremely vivid picture of the Graeco-Roman and partly Orientalized society in which Christianity came to birth, and especially of its inner world, of what was going on within men's minds and hearts. He writes with charity and sincerity and quite without intellectual, religious or emotional bias, so that we are able to look as through a temporal telescope upon that restless and uncertain age with its intellectual perplexities, its consciousness of sin and nervous dread of demons and sorceries, and its recourse to spells and ceremonies and the protection of the gods represented by the various cults in its fervent desire for material and spiritual salvation.

[25] In the first book, "aniconic" (p. ix), "apotropaic" (p. 82), "tauroctonous" (p. 120), "chthonic" (p. 174); and in the second book, in which however such terms are more thinly scattered, "chiliasm" (p. 279), "soteriology" (p. 297) and so on.

CHAPTER XV

MAGAZINES

The Bulletin; Meanjin; Southerly; *the* Economic Record; Oceania; *Others*

THE ACCELERATION in Australian literature in general is noticeable in this department also: it is not only that there are far more magazines in existence than there were at the end of the preceding Period, though an even greater proportion of them are commercial and industrial, but again every type has lived longer. What is much more important, the Period has produced seven magazines, two literary, one philosophic, one economic and two scientific, which taken together have not been equalled in Australia. *Meanjin* has been in existence since 1940 and *Southerly* since 1939; the *Australasian Journal of Psychology and Philosophy*[1] since 1923; the *Economic Record* since 1925; the *Journal of Experimental Biology* since 1924; *Oceania* since 1930, and the *Australian Quarterly* since 1929: all may therefore be regarded as well established, particularly since each has backing that does not seem likely to fail it. If we take into consideration also the *Bulletin* and its Red Page, which flourished until 1960, this represents a remarkable achievement. On the other hand, Australian civilization and the beginnings of its culture have suffered a serious loss by the death in 1942 of *Art in Australia*, which had increased its size, become, like the *Studio*, more modern in tone, extended its range to cover the art of other countries, and increased the number of its literary articles; and the *Morpeth Review*, which might conceivably have developed into something like an Australian equivalent of the *Hibbert Magazine*, lived only seven years. The principal extremist magazine, *Angry Penguins*, which in spite of characteristic and blatant absurdities filled a place in the literature of youth, died at the age of ten; an excellent little review, *All About Books*, lived only ten years, and several purely literary magazines of the twenties died quite young. And, in spite of its achievement, there were in 1950 several gaps in the Australian magazine world. Except in the Red Page it fell short on the critical side, for though *Meanjin* and *Southerly* were giving critical talent an additional opportunity, only occasional articles, notably A. D. Hope's explosion of a fictional absurdity by Max Harris, stood up to the best of Stephens's criticisms; the rest were, generally speaking, intelligent

[1] Now the *Australasian Journal of Philosophy*.

but not remarkable. There is no good literary and popular magazine, such as the *Lone Hand*; and there is still a need for at least one weekly or fortnightly of the type of the *New Statesman* or the *New Republic* on the one hand and of the *Spectator* on the other. And, though being without a "Third Programme" or the range of ability that can be drawn upon to fill it, we could scarcely expect anything comparable with the *Listener*, Australian broadcasting has been unable so far to produce even one wireless magazine worth mention here. But on the side of literary criticism the situation has much improved since 1950, as will be seen later on.

There is no such "Australian" group among the purely or mainly literary magazines as there was during the preceding Period, but it will be convenient to collect them together, beginning with several that have obvious links with their immediate predecessors. The two principal editors of *Vision* (Sydney, 1923-4) were Jack Lindsay and Kenneth Slessor; it was followed, after Jack Lindsay had settled in England, by the *London Aphrodite* (London, 1928-9), which he again edited, along with P. R. Stephensen, who was then in England on a university scholarship. Each of these magazines was illustrated by Norman Lindsay; the Lindsay influence, coming through father and son, was strong in both; and they were so similar in other ways that it seems permissible to accept the second also as Australian. *Vision* was a quarterly, which harks back to the nineties and reminds one of the *Triad*. In strident opposition to so-called "bush-radical-nationalist-realist" writers, its object was

> . . . primarily to provide an outlet for good poetry, or for any prose that liberates the imagination by gaiety or fantasy. . . . We [say its editors], would vindicate the youthfulness of Australia, not by being modern, but by being alive . . . *Vision* is the form of mental sight that defines the concrete image. It is the sense of Vision that is lacking in all moderns. . . . The old world is dead. Literature is dead. . . . We stand for the younger generation;

the essence of *Vision* was in fact a flamboyant and youthful extravagance, in living and loving and also in thinking. The *London Aphrodite* was a little, but not much, more adult: "We stand," its editors declared, "for a point of view which equally outrages the modernist and the reactionary. . . . We affirm life and for definition quote Nietzsche. . . . We affirm Beauty" and so on; its contributors included, besides several of the Australian contributors to *Vision*, Liam O'Flaherty, Sacheverell Sitwell, W. J. Turner, Karel Capek, and Richard Church: both magazines, *Vision* in particular, were adolescent and for adolescents, yet both are full of vigour and at times brilliant. At a far extreme from these two, thinner and less vital, lacking their fine youthful enthusiasm and also their youthful absurdities, were several small verse magazines, and in particular the *Spinner* (Melbourne, 1924-7), and *Verse* (Melbourne, 1929-33): both were "little magazines" of the same type as *Birth* of the previous period;

besides verse, the *Spinner* published notes on contributors, portraits of some of them, and short reviews; and *Verse* contained short articles on such subjects as Philosophy in Poetry, The Refrain in Verse, Rhythm and Rhyme, and The Translation of Anglo-Saxon verse.

Next, the three leading literary magazines of today: the *Bulletin*,[2] *Meanjin* and *Southerly*. The *Bulletin* still comes easily first; indeed it is only the recent remarkable development of the other two that has made it legitimate to speak of them all in the same breath. If the literature of the present Period is not the creation of the *Bulletin*, the *Bulletin* remained until lately its principal centre: many of the best Australian writers still turn to it automatically; publication in it is still a hallmark, though there are now also other hallmarks; and it still does more for Australian literature than any other periodical, though *Meanjin* and *Southerly* nowadays support it, and several newspapers, and in particular the *Sydney Morning Herald*, have offered considerable prizes for literary works. The Red Page has not quite the range or anything like the miscellaneous variety that it had under Stephens, but its critical reviews are still, speaking generally, by far the best in Australia, though those of *Meanjin*, *Southerly*, and the *Australian Quarterly*, which however reviews books only occasionally, have to be taken into account, and have trained critics who are badly needed in the Australian literary world today. It was at the instance of the *Bulletin* that the two principal annual anthologies, prose and verse, were instituted, though here a debt is due also to Angus & Robertson Ltd, of Sydney, the book-publishing firm that took the risk of issuing them at a time when it was almost certain that they would not pay. The *Bulletin* established in 1928 an annual literary prize that has been won by several writers who have since become established, or more firmly established; it published several of its prize-winning novels as serials—a great departure for the short-story-loving *Bulletin*; and it still publishes serials by Australian writers; it tried, but failed, to resuscitate the ballad; it still cultivates the short story and has helped to bring forward several notable short-story writers. This nearly eighty-year-old newspaper-magazine, the same and yet markedly different, has reorganised itself, in various ways; it has exchanged a few old features for new ones, and it has worked round the circle from red-rag republicanism to an imperialism and a conservatism so marked that, with its still unaltered headings, "Business, Robbery", etc. and the "Wild Cat Column" and with its dread of a communist under every bed, it resembles a conventionally respectable old lady attired in the rather startling garments of her flighty youth.

Meanjin (Melbourne, originally Brisbane, 1940-) is the first Aus-

---

[2] Taking, this time, the *Bulletin* and its Red Page together, since there are no longer the same reasons for considering them separately. [The Red Page moved from the inside covers with the 15th March 1961 issue. A column of that name (only a book review column) was retained until the November 1964 issue. With the 21st November issue, the column became "Books" and consisted entirely of book reviews. In 1980 a nostalgic attempt to revive the Red Page was made in the form of a literary quarterly supplement under the editorship of the poet Geoffrey Dutton, which it is to be hoped will continue.]

tralian literary magazine that can be regarded from a broader than a merely local point of view.[3] An American professor[4] declared in 1946, "I found nothing in Australia and few magazines indeed in the United States to compare with *Meanjin* for genuinely good editorial taste and liveliness of content." *Meanjin* began as an eight-page leaflet of verse of which only 250 copies were printed; previous Australian "little magazines" have been as promising, though few as individual as this was from the first, but few of them have ceased to be "little", and none has shown so amazing an all-round development. "Meanjin" is an aboriginal word for spike, a name that was given to the point of land upon which a considerable part of Brisbane stands, and the original title was *Meanjin Papers*.* The magazine's achievement has been due to the faith and indomitable ambition of its founder and editor, Clement Byrne Christesen (Townsville, Q., 1912-); he was educated at the University of Queensland, has practised journalism in Britain as well as Australia, and was at the time of *Meanjin's* foundation a publicist for the Queensland Government; he has lectured for the Workers' Educational Association, and has published travel books and books of verse and anthologies which are already referred to elsewhere.[5] Christesen had a long struggle with printers and publishers and to obtain the contributors he wanted, and whom it has only lately been possible to pay, but the position has become at least less difficult now that *Meanjin* is backed by Melbourne University and the Commonwealth Literary Fund (later the Australia Council Literature Board). It was, as this History closed, a large octavo quarterly of about seventy pages, which aimed to be

> . . . a magazine of ideas, built around literature and art, to encourage discussion and to determine thoroughly sound canons of literary criticism, to present advance-guard writing as well as the more traditionally-based creative work, to develop cultural contacts with other countries . . . in short, to work for a healthy climate of opinion and literary activity;

it aims to "mark out a meeting-ground for progressive cultural thought and values", and its "political tendency is 'democratic left of centre' ". There is nothing very novel about such aspirations, but they had not hitherto come so near to realization, and no other Australian magazine has concerned itself so broadly with the world in general. During the last few years *Meanjin* has published articles on Rilke, Valéry, Pushkin, Goethe, German Poetry Since the War, Henry James, The English Theatre, Koestler on the Intelligentsia[6] and a poem by a member of the circle that surrounded Stefan George; and, beyond the purely literary, there

[3] Except the *Bookfellow*; but this, or that part of it which is first rate, was too sharply specialized for a comparison; it represented, like Stephens's Red Page, an extension of his critical powers and his personality.

[4] F. J. Hoffman, Professor of English at the University of Wisconsin.

* [*Papers* was deleted at Vol. 6, no. 1; *Quarterly* was added to *Meanjin* at Vol. 20, no. 1, 1961.]

[5] See pp. 1059, 1261.

[6] Reprinted, by permission, from *Horizon*.

have been articles on The Renaissance Movement in China, Dutch Civilization in Indonesia, and The Future of the Documentary Film. But this does not mean that Australia has been neglected, for there have also been articles on Henry Lawson as Craftsman, The "Cultural Cringe," Lawrence in Australia, The Poetry of Peter Hopegood, and Bernard O'Dowd's Last Writings; and, outside the literary world again, on The Eureka Stockade, The Felton Bequest, Aboriginal Art, and The Little Magazine. Australian art and drama are not neglected; there have been oversea letters from England and even Japan; and there are reviews, by no means merely of Australian books, and short stories by Australian writers. *Meanjin* has a definite individuality, which reflects not so much, as with the *Triad* or the *Bookfellow*, its editor's personality as his judgment, which is represented by his choice of contributions. The essence of *Meanjin* is its stimulative quality; its awareness that Australia has a place in modern life with its problems and perplexities, and its literature a corresponding place in modern literature; and it attempts to define that place, raising questions that are important to the world in general and to Australia as part of that world. The trouble is that *Meanjin* is not always able to come to grips with these questions: it invites all sorts of controversy, but its invitation is insufficiently accepted; it cannot always draw upon contributors who possess adequate analytical imagination and the will to exercise it: either they lack the spare time and energy to get to the bottom of their subjects; or else, in this convention-ridden, timorous, and by no means free community, they prefer to pull their punches rather than to take an intellectual or social risk. *Meanjin's* hope lies in the chance that more of its contributors may be persuaded to think hard and to take the risk of saying what they think; a risk that may very well dissolve in that case into mist. *Meanjin's* strength lies in its editor's determination to persevere, not to be satisfied until he has obtained the contribution he desires and needs; that there is no sign that he is yet satisfied is an excellent augury for the future. What is more, *Meanjin* has developed considerably since the above was written. *Southerly* (Sydney, 1939-) is as different as possible. This is due in part to the different characters of the editors of the two publications and what stands behind them *Meanjin* has had to work out its own tradition; at first rather incalculable, its aims have gradually settled and crystallized; but behind *Southerly* stand not only a person but an institution, and, in broad outline, a given tradition. The editor, and founder, Robert Guy Howarth[7] (Tenterfield, N.S.W., 1906-73), whose verse and prose have been already mentioned, was a Sydney graduate who won a scholarship to Oxford, and became Reader

7 Howarth became Professor of English Literature at the University of Cape Town; his place as editor of *Southerly* was taken by Kenneth Slessor, for a discussion of whose poems, see pp. 942-54. Professor A. G. Mitchell was co-editor of *Southerly* for the first few years.

in English at the University of Sydney. The institution is the Sydney branch of the English Association, whose centre is in London and whose objects are the study and teaching of English; *Southerly* is the organ of this branch, and publishes its annual reports and summaries of papers that are read at its monthly meetings. This association is one of the principal Australian literary and cultural institutions; its attitude is conservative, but it is not hidebound, and the association protested, though only after long argument, at the banning of *Ulysses*. Its tradition is that of academicism, for a large proportion of its members and almost the whole of its committee are Sydney University graduates and a number of them are members of the University staff: it will be obvious that there are limits to what the editor of *Southerly* can do; but as a matter of fact the three factors in its production have worked smoothly together, and Howarth also has worked out an individual editorial attitude and policy. *Southerly*, as well as *Meanjin*, has had a long struggle to keep going; but it also has now financial backing, that of a Sydney publishing firm, Angus & Robertson Ltd, and also that of the Commonwealth Literary Fund again. *Southerly* combines something of the solidity of the academic magazines of the end of the second Period, though in a more modern dress, with a point of view that is a descendant of the nationalism of the nineties; conscientious and comparatively conservative, it proceeds steadily along a well-charted road, specializing in Australian literary developments, past and present, devoting a good deal of space to elaborate analyses of the works and methods of Australian writers, and issuing special numbers devoted to biographical and critical accounts of Australian classics: a Brennan number, a Furphy number, and so on; it has also published a series, "Writing Poetry: The Why and The How", analyses by poets themselves of their methods of composition. There have been articles on The Blank Verse of "The Wanderer", A Harpur Discovery, Kenneth Slessor, The Poetry of Peter Hopegood, The Function of Vance Palmer's Novels, Mary Gilmore and Henry Handel Richardson: but *Southerly* concerns itself also with oversea comparisons and oversea influence upon Australian writers, as in such matters as Surrealism and Poetry, The Symbolism of Brennan and Mallarmé, Gerard Manley Hopkins and Marcus Clarke; and occasionally, though not nearly so often as *Meanjin*, it discusses European writers and their work. These two magazines have therefore quite distinct functions, though of course here and there they overlap; the one considering Australian culture as a part of world culture and its literature as a part of world-literature, and the other devoting itself largely to the literature of its own country. The characteristic of *Southerly* is its informative quality; it does not stimulate or provoke discussion so much as record and recall and analyse: its interest is not so much in the broad general problems, literary and other, of the day, as in Australian literary performance and techniques. It is sometimes dull, particularly after the implicit promise of its title, which suggests a fresh and life-giving wind from the south; but *Meanjin* also is not without a corresponding defect: there is a dullness of the *avant-garde* as well as of the conservative in the world of literature and thought, and in reading either of these magazines one is seldom surprised; what we are about to receive is sometimes a little too evident. But, after all, these criticisms apply, more or less, to most magazines; each of these two has in its own way made the utmost of the material available to it, and each performs a valuable service: Australian literature could not spare either of them.

Next, the "advanced" magazines, which, since they vary considerably in their outlook and degree of advancement, may be considered chronologically. The earliest and mildest was a magazine of a type which is commoner in the Old World than in this. *Manuscripts* (Melbourne and Geelong, 1931-5) was an illustrated "miscellany of art and letters", edited by Henry Tatlock Miller, a Melbourne bookseller who became interested in art and the ballet; this magazine ran from sixty to about 120 pages, had been planned with some imagination, and covered a wide range of subjects many of which were attractive; but the articles themselves were, with a few marked exceptions, much less so. Its contributors included several leading Australian authorities on the subjects on which they wrote, and a number of leading Australian writers; but they were not often anywhere near their best, a few of the subjects were rather faded, and the general effect of at least the earlier numbers of *Manuscripts* was rather superficial, rather arty and crafty. This criticism certainly does not apply to the *Australian Mercury* (Sydney, 1935), almost half and by far the better half of which consisted of the first instalment of an essay by the editor, P. R. Stephensen, which was later enlarged and published as a book, *The Foundations of Culture in Australia*:[8] the *Australian Mercury* failed, Stephensen asserted, "because no philanthropist could be found to nurse it financially", but it had not the look of a long liver; later he found his philanthropist and brought out the *Publicist* (Sydney, 1936-42), which preached a sort of Australian fascism, and was vigorous but dull. Next, some magazines which were not merely advanced but extremist; these by no means confined themselves to literature, but literature predominated in them. The first and not the least interesting was *Stream* (Melbourne, 1931), "a medium of international art expression", seeking "only what is vital and genuine in contemporary art, literature and thought". It presented "contributions by artists, writers and critics, many of whom [had] hitherto remained unrecognized", but its contributors included also Nettie Palmer, A. R. Chisholm and Bertram

---

[8] See p. 1069, and for Stephensen's other work, p. 1253.

Higgins. Clever, arrogant, sometimes silly, this highbrow and rather humourless magazine was at least individual and stimulating. *Comment* (Melbourne, 1940–7) made *Stream* appear ordinary and conventional: its paper and type were of assorted colours; scattered about it were modernist designs, and the language of some of its contributors was obviously derived from Joyce and Stein. Beneath all this youthful exhibitionism there was however vigour and a certain amount of celebration. The most notable, however, and not the least exhibitionist of the extremist magazines was *Angry Penguins*[9] (Adelaide and Melbourne, 1940–6); it was originally the organ of the Arts Association of the University of Adelaide, but became independent and transferred to Melbourne: it still retained something of an undergraduate flavour, but this was in part an emanation of the personality of its editor. *Angry Penguins* specialized in poetry, but contained also short stories, articles and reviews, and extended into the spheres of art, music, the theatre and politics. Its principal contributors were, besides some modernist poets most of whom are mentioned elsewhere in this History, C. R. Jury,[10] an old-fashioned romantic who somehow or other found his way into this galley; and Brian Vrepont,[11] who, since his own work contains an element of the bizarre, does not look quite so out of place as Jury. Most of the prose is very poor stuff; just as the poets tend to rely on imagery so the prose writers tend to rely on turgid and pretentious jargon to suggest profundity, and this sort of thing does not go so well in prose: nevertheless of three of the essentials of literature, vigour, confidence and sincerity, the Penguins possessed the first and second in a remarkable degree, and they also possessed something of the third, though it is here, after all, that their fundamental weakness lies. And they thought it advisable to blow great blasts on their collective trumpet, which suggests an underlying element of doubt. But perhaps more illuminative than anything else was the manner in which *Angry Penguins* hailed as authentic poetry a parody of its own kind of verse which was sent in, more as a test than as a hoax, by two leading Australian poets.[12] The Penguins refused to accept the truth when it was disclosed, and converted an exposure into an advertisement. There were several small but useful critical reviews. The alleged object of *All About Books* (Melbourne, 1928–38) was to provide information rather than criticism; "recommendations of the best new books, without having to read long critical reviews". If it had done only this, it would not, of course, have been worth mention here; but its principal reviewers, Nettie Palmer and afterwards F. T. Macartney,

---

[9] The title was a quotation from a poem by its principal editor, Max Harris ("as drunks, the angry penguins of the night"), whose verses have been already referred to (pp. 1072–3).

[10] For Jury's verse, see p. 1058.

[11] For Vrepont's poems, see pp. 1019–20.

[12] James McAuley (see pp. 985–91) and Harold Stewart (see pp. 1050–5); for the Ern Malley hoax, see pp. 1072–3.

were not satisfied to save its subscribers the trouble of thinking: their articles contained critical work that would have been hard to better in the small amount of space provided, and they helped to raise the magazine to a higher plane. Another publication of something the same sort, although, lacking the regular contributions of the two who made *All About Books*, it could not reach the same standard, was the *Australasian Book News and Library Journal* (Sydney, 1946–8).

In sociology and in the humane studies generally there was a marked increase in the number and what is more in the quality of the Period's magazines. Of these, first several that contain an element of literature in the narrower sense of the term. The *Australian Quarterly* (Sydney, 1929–), a large octavo of about 120 pages, is the first Australian magazine of the general type of the *Nineteenth Century and After* and the *Contemporary Review*, and though it cannot stand comparison with these, its standard is high, considering the difference in the quality of the material available; it is published by the Australian Institute of Political Science, and was at first a review of Australian politics, but now covers Australian affairs generally and reaches out occasionally into the purely literary sphere. The *Australian Quarterly* has published articles on The Inflation Drift in Australia, A Defence of the Arbitration Court System, The Squatter and Australian Labour; spreading its net wider, The Decline of the Intellectual, The Church as a Planned Society, and The Corruption of Public Taste; and, in the purely literary sphere, on *Such is Life*, *For the Term of His Natural Life*, Goethe, Swinburne's "Lucretia Borgia", Chinese Poetry, and Arthur Koestler. One of the most interesting might-have-beens was the *Morpeth Review* (Morpeth, N.S.W., 1927–34), which, though primarily theological, covered a wide range of social subjects; it was the organ of St John's College, Morpeth, an institution for the training of Anglican clergy, and founded by its Warden, the Reverend E. H. Burgmann;[13] when he left to become Bishop of Goulburn it expired. From a badly printed amateurish-looking affair of about sixty pages it developed into a well appointed magazine of over a hundred; its contributors included A. P. Elkin, later Professor of Anthropology at the University of Sydney, T. G. Taylor, the well-known geographer, F. A. Bland, afterwards Professor of Public Administration at Sydney,[14] and several professorial and other authorities on economics. Besides such articles as might have been expected, and articles on such borderline subjects as Science and Religion and The Church and Art in the Middle Ages, there were others on The Future of the Hunter River Valley, The Practical Value of Anthropology, Our National Flora, Population and Disease, The Vitamins of Inflation and

[13] For Bishop Burgmann's educational booklet, see p. 1320.

[14] For other work by these writers, see pp. 1447–50, 895–7, 1437–8 respectively.

Deflation, and Bacteria and their Value to Man; some of these articles were rather thin, and the *Morpeth Review* could not stand comparison with oversea magazines of the same type, but there should have been room for it and with the support of the Anglican Church as a whole it might well have survived. Several other specialized magazines exemplify the marked progress that has been made lately in the subjects they represent. It may be contended that *Historical Studies: Australia and New Zealand* (Melbourne, 1940-) is merely a collection of articles, but the fact that it publishes reviews may perhaps be regarded as settling the matter: it is conducted by a board that consists of several leading historical authorities of varying views; Miss Ida Leeson, former Mitchell Librarian, was also a member; it is intended for the general reader and the teacher as well as the specializing student, and has dealt with such subjects as The New State Movement in Queensland, The Historian's Craft, and Private or Company Ownership of New South Wales Pastoral Stations; its reviews vary in quality, but one looks here first for an estimate of the latest Australian historical work. *Historical Studies* was needed, but the foundation of the *Economic Record* (Melbourne, 1925-) was an event of first importance for Australia: a quarterly of about 150 pages, it is the organ of the Economic Society of Australia and New Zealand, and is edited by a Melbourne professor, with the assistance of economics specialists in the various Australian States; it contains articles, notes which are in effect shorter articles, and reviews, and its contributors include practically all the Australian experts in economics and political science; this magazine, like almost all the books in its line that have been discussed in this History, is concerned not so much with economics as a subject, as with economic and political facts and conditions in this country and in so far as they affect this country. Another review that was equally valuable within its widely different sphere was the *Australasian Journal of Psychology and Philosophy* (Sydney, 1923-47).[15] This also was a quarterly, the organ of the Australian Association of Psychology and Philosophy; each branch provided an assistant editor, but its editor was a member of the Philosophy Department at the University of Sydney. The original magazine covered an extremely wide sphere: theoretical and applied psychology, psychoanalysis, mental tests, the philosophy of religion, ethics, metaphysics, education and sociology generally; most of its articles were addressed to students of the subjects dealt with, but some were of general interest; the magazine was not the organ of any particular school of thought and was not used for propaganda, and it did not, to quote one of its editorials, either "scorn the old fogey . . . or disdain the new faddist, although it may criticise both". It compares well with the rank and file of British and American magazines of its type, though not with, for instance,

[15] After this date it became the *Australasian Journal of Philosophy*.

Mind; most of the principal universities of the world subscribed to it, and it was used regularly by abstracting institutions abroad. In 1947 the "Psychology" was dropped from its title and sphere of operations in view of the approaching publication of an *Australian Journal of Psychology*; the first number of this, the organ of the Australian Branch of the British Psychological Society, appeared in 1949.

There is still, in 1950, no magazine, popular or otherwise, of general science that can find a place in this History, but in the area of applied sciences two have, in their own lines, as high a standing as any that have been mentioned here. One is the *Medical Journal of Australia*, whose long descent has been mentioned in dealing with the scientific magazines of a previous Period;[16] the other is *Oceania* (Sydney, 1930-), which is the more important in that its subject-matter is peculiar to Australia and its Pacific environs. It is an anthropological quarterly of about 130 pages, edited at the time of writing by the Professor of Anthropology at the University of Sydney, and maintained by an Australian National Research Council grant; it is devoted to the study of the native peoples of Australia, New Guinea and the islands of the Pacific, and represents the modern attitude, that the culture of a people can be satisfactorily studied only by men and women who have been scientifically trained for that particular purpose. The articles in *Oceania*, which are the results of field work by experts, range from The Social Origin of the Australian Tribes to Local Divisions and Movements in Fiji, from Aranda Phonetics to Language Study for New Guinea Students, from A Dart Match in Tikopia to The Nature and Functions of Secret Societies. It is illustrated, and contains Reports and Proceedings, Notes and News, Reviews of Books and Bibliographical Notes; and it comes the nearer to the main purpose of this History in that its articles, apart from their technical value, are particularly well written. The *Medical Journal of Australia* is a survivor from the preceding Period; engineering and others of the applied sciences are also represented by periodicals of high standard, but none whose discussion is appropriate here. Besides a number of scientific publications which do not concern us because they are of primarily technical interest, there are several periodical publications addressed by scientific bodies to the ordinary intelligent reader, and, in particular, the *Australian Museum Magazine* (Sydney, 1921-) which became *Australian Natural History* in 1962, and *Walkabout* (Melbourne, 1935-74), a geographical, descriptive monthly that resembles a light sketch for something corresponding to the American *National Geographic Magazine*.

The second World War produced a number of military magazines, but one stood out as *Aussie* had done in the first World War, though it was

[16] See p. 328 and note 33. There is also the *Australian Journal of Experimental Biology*, but that is too technical for discussion here.

fundamentally different in kind. *Salt* (Melbourne, 1941-6), a sixty- or seventy-page monthly, began as the purely official magazine of the Army Education Service, but it came to include fiction, verses, and humour of a kind that reflected the taste and ability of the average man who had become a soldier, until quite half of its contents represented contributions from the forces. Carried by troop train to Townsville, by ship to the Islands, and by plane to the fighting fronts, it was in demand by British and Americans as well as Australians, and had a circulation of over 100,000; more professional and far less crude than *Aussie*, it yet lacked something of *Aussie's* individuality. As the universities received larger grants and broadened their bases by more and more scholarships and exhibitions, the number of undergraduate magazines again increased, and their standard rose accordingly: some were solid and capable; others resembled the more professional extremist publications, and were not far behind the best of them; it has been already noted that *Angry Penguins* was originally an undergraduate publication. There were also a number of youth magazines, prominent among which was *Barjai* (Brisbane, 1943–7), whose editors were eighteen and seventeen respectively when what had previously been typescript emerged into print. Finally, the domestic magazines, which have improved mechanically as well as increased in number: slick, smart, stereotyped, the influence of one aspect of American civilization is marked among them; they have large circulations and are read by men as well as by women. But this sort of thing is common in every country of the modern world; what is not so common is the immense development of the Australian magazine generally, so that a few of its best, literary and not purely literary, are now able to take their place in a broader sphere.

CHAPTER XVI

HISTORY, BIOGRAPHY, DESCRIPTION

History. The Convict Days: O'Brien; Forsyth. Colonization and Settlement: Mills; Madgwick; Roberts. Bligh and Macquarie: Evatt; Barnard. The Pacific: Roberts; Ward; Dakin. Europe: Hentze. Philosophy of History: Crawford. Other Histories. Biography. General. Biographies of Writers: Richardson and Palmer; Neilson; Moran; Others. Histories of Art

NEW IDEAS have invaded the province of the historian, as they have invaded other provinces of Australian literature: new conceptions of history as such, and of the proper relationship to be sought between past and present; new conceptions of the historian's business generally, and new methods of historical treatment; but no more in this province than in any other have Australian writers made any radical innovations. This does not mean that they have merely followed the tracks of their predecessors; on the contrary, not only have aspects and figures of the past been re-examined, more carefully, with increased data, and in a new and sometimes revolutionary light, but other figures and aspects have been investigated for the first time. Perhaps the most outstanding characteristic of the Australian historian of today is his thoroughness in scholarship: not that this was by any means lacking during the preceding Period, but today precise and painstaking research is taken as a matter of course, and historians of lesser than first-rate talent will spend years upon the establishment of as sure as possible a basis for their conclusions, and their investigations cover a far wider area than those of their predecessors. In this thoroughness may be traced the influence of Oxford and other oversea universities as well as those of their own country, from which many have proceeded abroad on travelling scholarships. Of course new sources, documentary and manuscript, have become available and new points of view have opened up; but apart from these there seems nowadays a more conscientious insistence upon the basing or in some cases the propping up of every assertion upon first-hand evidence, so far as it can be obtained. There are many more writers of history than there were a couple of generations ago, and their average standard is higher than it was; still, by the date at which this History closed, few[1] new talents had presented themselves that could be considered to rank with those of Scott or Wood, whose influence is evident and acknowledged in the work of several who have been their pupils. On the whole, the primary characteristic of Australian history today may be said to be thoroughness. Next

[1] Hancock is one of these few, and Crawford, but he had published little at the date mentioned.

to this comes a common sense which is, with one or two marked exceptions, rather unimaginative; indeed the literary element, using the word "literary" in its narrower sense, is small: the most obvious exception is Barnard Eldershaw, and that member of the partnership who writes also as a separate individual, Marjorie Barnard; these two apply to history the methods of fiction, just as another novelist, Eleanor Dark, has recently applied to the novel something of the method of history, as well as taking her subject from history. In both cases there has been a real gain, though it must be remembered that this particular novelist has historical ability and that this particular historian happens to be also a novelist. Another obvious exception, but this time primarily on the intellectual rather than the aesthetic side, is R. M. Crawford, who, surprisingly in an Australian historian, has gone so far as to philosophize on history: yet neither Crawford nor Barnard, nor Barnard Eldershaw, stands out in other respects; the historian of literature would therefore lose much, including an interesting comparison, by interpreting strictly Elton's statement[2] that applied literature "is only literature at all just in so far as it possesses form". Australian historians are, like those of other countries, sometimes biased; where bias exists it is very seldom due to hero-worship, which indeed is not, outside sport of course, an Australian characteristic; but apart from the fact that all historians have their likes and dislikes, there seems in this country, perhaps because few fields have been so worked as to leave no room for conjecture, a desire to discover possibilities and to treat them as practical certainties; hence there has been at times a stretching of some of the facts and an ignoring of others. Australian histories are however usually straightforward accounts; it would be going much too far to call them chronicles, but there is not infrequently an element of the chronicle about them and sometimes one has the feeling that the basic facts have not been entirely digested; but our writers are so often concerned with the earliest period of Australian history, as to which the basic facts are available mainly in chronicle or at least in disconnected form and are particularly difficult to generalize: it may perhaps be said that a tendency towards the chronicle is one of the two most prominent faults in Australian historical work today. The other prominent fault is the lack of "literary" quality that has been already mentioned; it extends in a few of even our leading historians to weakness in literary taste: these and some of the other general conclusions apply, as will be seen later, to our biographies as well as to our general histories.

In accurate and detailed scholarship, whose conclusions are arranged logically and expressed with clarity and precision, Eris O'Brien's *The*

---

[2] *A Survey of English Literature, 1830–1880*, vol. i, p. 5.

Foundation of Australia[3] (London, 1937) sets a high standard: it belongs to that kind of historical work which states and describes rather than imaginatively re-creates; it is a document rather than a piece of life; yet in spite of the use of a number of conventional expressions it is written too simply and directly and is too outspoken to be dull. Dr (Edrisford Michael) O'Brien (Condobolin, N.S.W., 1895–1974) lectured in modern history at St John's College, the University of Sydney, and in Australian history at the University; he was Roman Catholic Archbishop of Canberra and Goulburn, a graduate of the National University of Ireland and of the University of Sydney, and also a Doctor of Social and Political Science of Louvain. Yet, though it is clear that he did not love England, all but one of his books are remarkably free from racial or religious bias. *The Foundation of Australia* is a result of several years' research in Britain and Ireland as well as in Australia, and though it covers ground some of which has been covered before, that ground has never been covered with such detailed thoroughness; and O'Brien goes farther than any other Australian historian in elaborating the background of "the System", and relating the foundation of the penal colony to the political, social, and economic conditions in the England of the later half of the eighteenth century. Discussing several contentions that have been put forward with regard to the convict strain, O'Brien remarks that "Probably the more reasonable way to look at the subject is to accept it as an unpleasant fact, from which, fortunately, all evil effects have long been obliterated in Australia." The troubles of the colony arose largely because its problems were not understood, and O'Brien refers not only to the carelessness of the preparations for the voyage, but to the "gross delay and negligence" in leaving the settlement without inquiry or assistance for more than a year and a half.[4] Indeed[5]

> The British Government, once it had paid the costs, did not much care what happened to the prisoners either in transit or at the settlement. . . . The task of founding a penal colony . . . was left almost absolutely to a handful of officials. . . . None of those on whom this great responsibility had been thrust were men of outstanding ability. . . .

This is unfair, and not even quite consistent; elsewhere O'Brien says of Phillip[6] that

> Endowed with common sense, kindliness, breadth of vision, firmness and sincerity, he was an ideal founder for any new colony;

[3] References here are to the second edition, Sydney, 1950.

[4] But the British Government was probably, as indeed O'Brien points out, relying on Banks's assertion that Botany Bay was a place in which 200 or 300 convicts would be able to maintain themselves after the first year. It (and apparently Banks also) had forgotten his previous remark about the barrenness of New Holland.

[5] pp. 193–4.

[6] p. 134.

moreover, the thoroughness, integrity and impartiality of Collins in particular were probably worth more, in the circumstances, than outstanding ability. And O'Brien says later[7] that

> . . . the true strength of British imperialism, which is the disinterested efforts of private patriots, was strongly exemplified in the work of Banks, Phillip, Hunter, King and others, who strove for the welfare of the colony, while the military settlers, pursuing their own private gain, were at the same time laying the foundations of a new economic empire of the south.

It is interesting to note, however, that O'Brien devotes less space to any of these men, except Phillip, than to Macarthur, whom he considers[8]

> . . . the supremely commanding figure of the Settlement up to 1809, and . . . a personality of vast importance, both political and pastoral, after his return to Sydney at the end of 1817, following eight years of enforced exile. . . .

Nevertheless he admits that Macarthur was an "extraordinary but unscrupulous man" who "so contrived it that all [his] activities were co-related, and all together served the main end of increasing the Macarthur stature". From the purely penal point of view, O'Brien concludes, the transportation system was a failure: "Free men, whether immigrants or the offspring of the transportees, were the real founders of Australia." *The Foundation of Australia* was preceded by two other books by O'Brien: one, *The Life and Letters of Archpriest Therry*,[9] has been treated here as biography;[10] the other, *The Dawn of Catholicism in Australia* (2 vols, Sydney, 1928), deals with the period immediately preceding Therry's work of organization; this book is neither so concise nor so well arranged as the others, and is marred by several examples of anti-British feeling which one would have scarcely expected in a scholar.[11] In *Governor Arthur's Convict System* (London, 1935) penal colonization is studied from a narrower angle and without the same wealth of background; this book is nevertheless important in that it shows the failure of "the most determined attempt that has ever been made to render Transportation on a large scale an efficient system of colonisation". Its author, William Douglass Forsyth (Casterton, Vic., 1909-), is a graduate of the Universities of Melbourne and Oxford, has worked in the Federal Departments of Information and External Affairs, has represented Australia on several United Nations conferences, and in 1950 was Secretary-General of the South Pacific Commission at Noumea. Forsyth shows Arthur's creation of an official class upon whom he could depend, his systematic

---

[7] p. 252.
[8] p. 228.
[9] In a later edition the sub-title, "The Foundation of Catholicism in Australia", became the title.
[10] See p. 1380.
[11] O'Brien goes so far as to allude to Britain as "the old beldame eternally brandishing her rod of authority in the hope that it would make the awakening proletariat learn obedience and develop love" (vol. i, p. 3).

policy of terrorism, of incessant watchfulness, and of keeping the convicts "on their proper level"; and how the system had yet to be abandoned: because it did not prevent crime, and because of the evil of its effects upon masters as well as slaves; and also, though Forsyth does not say this in so many words, because the tide of time and the process of enlightenment were heavily against it. There is an excellent picture of Arthur, the tyrant of an ideal, a fountain of energy, just according to his lights, but cold, formal and self-righteous and deficient in the more human qualities. Forsyth's is an excellent analysis, well arranged and clearly written.*

The peopling of Australia, as distinct from its colonization in the full sense of the word; the lack of theory and the conflicting theories that underlay the establishment of the Australian colonies, were analysed in Mills's *Colonization of Australia (1829-42)* (London, 1915) and Madgwick's *Immigration Into Eastern Australia: 1788-1851* (London, 1937). Although there is necessarily some overlapping between these two books, neither subject nor point of view is the same, for the first is a study of the Wakefield experiment in empire-building, and the second, which has a wider range in time and a narrower in space, mentions Wakefield's theory only incidentally and gives a far fuller account of the development of the machinery by which emigration from England was ultimately controlled, and of its defects. Richard Charles Mills (Ardmona, Vic., 1886-1952), was a graduate of the University of Melbourne, of the London School of Economics and of the University of London; after serving in a British siege battery in the first World War, in which he was wounded and mentioned in dispatches, he occupied the Chair of Economics at the University of Sydney for twenty-three years, and was afterwards Chairman of the Commonwealth Grants Commission and of the Universities Commission. With E. R. Walker, whose work in Economics is mentioned elsewhere,[12] he published also a textbook on *Money*, which was adopted as such by the University of Cambridge, a most unusual thing to happen to a work by an Australian author. *The Colonization of Australia* was the first adequate account of the Wakefield system of colonization in theory and practice; it describes the situation, not so much social and economic as political and administrative, which underlay the foundation of the British colonies, particularly in Australia,[13] and the conflicts between officials of the Colonial Office who had no personal experience of Australian conditions and Sir George Gipps who had learnt from local experience what was practicable and what was impracticable in the Australia of his day. Mills explains how at the beginning of the period

* [His book was reprinted with a new preface and an annotated bibliography in Sydney in 1970.]

[12] See pp. 1427-8.

[13] New Zealand is also discussed, and a chapter covers Wakefield and the Durham Report.

with which he deals the colonies were regarded as a costly nuisance, and bound sooner or later to separate from the mother country anyhow; he quotes the assertion that in parliament " 'any party would sooner lose a colony than a division' ", and says that in 1830 the public attitude towards colonies "may be described as one of indifference tempered with uneasiness". Mills has an interesting portrait of Wakefield, energetic, persevering and courageous, overwhelmingly persuasive and extremely unscrupulous, yet by no means self-seeking. His "matured proposals" are summarized: the sale of waste lands at a uniform "sufficient price", the settler being quite free in his selection; the use of the whole or at least a fixed proportion of the purchase money in aid of immigration; the judicious selection of immigrants; and colonial self-government. The Wakefield system as a whole was never enforced, and indeed the "sufficient price" was quite unascertainable; but some of its principles, modified as a result of experience on the spot, "had a remarkably full realization in practice". In New South Wales by 1842 transportation had been abolished; waste land was sold instead of being granted away for nothing; some of the proceeds were devoted to immigration and a central Board had been established to control both immigration and the sale of land to immigrants; and the first step had been taken towards the grant of responsible government. If it had not been, says Mills,[14] for the work of the "systematic colonisers"

> Australian history would have been very different. Swamped by convicts, lacking free settlers, the penal colonies would have grown slowly as large overseas gaols, where the population was divided into an oligarchy of free landowners and a servile class of convict labourers. In time, no doubt, the feeling for separation, which existed to some extent before responsible government was granted, would have triumphed, and an independent republic, an Alsatia of the Southern Seas, would have been established. Only gradually and painfully could the penal colonies have escaped from their past.

With the very important qualification that Mills does not allow for the effect of the gold-rushes, this seems to be true enough. Even apart from the analysis of the Wakefield system as applied to the Australian colonies, which seems likely to stand for a long while, this book provides[15] "an admirable example of the part which may be played in the development of human institutions by conscious political thought". The author of *Immigration Into Eastern Australia*, Robert Bowden Madgwick (Sydney, 1905-79), was a graduate of the Universities of Sydney and Oxford, was Senior Lecturer in Economic History at Sydney and afterwards Director of the Australian Army Education Service, and later Vice-Chancellor of the University of New England. Madgwick makes three points that

[14] p. 340.
[15] Graham Wallas, in an introduction to *The Colonization of Australia*, p. xiii.

are important as having a general bearing on colonization and colonies: that Australia was the scene of the first great attempt at assisted immigration, that is, of course, in modern times; that Australian immigration during the period with which he deals is important in imperial history as providing the experience for later schemes of assisted immigration; and that it taught the lesson that "countries which desire a large immigration must be prepared to receive, not the highest types from the population of other countries, but only the best of those who are prepared to emigrate". Madgwick outlines the causes, political and economic, of Britain's attitude towards colonization and colonies, showing how the War of American Independence and the Napoleonic War caused the English ruling classes to regard democratic and liberal ideas with disfavour: New South Wales was therefore founded "in an atmosphere of distrust and suspicion", and having discovered an outlet for her convicts Britain was inclined to put the Australian colonies as far as possible out of mind; it was different when it began to be realized that they might provide valuable markets. Madgwick analyses in some detail the government and bounty systems of immigration upon which Mills had touched; and he quotes a letter from Sir James Stephen to the Treasury in which he says that "in the conduct of the emigration to Australia every opportunity has been taken . . . to render it as far as possible subservient to the relief of distressed districts at Home". Apart from the wish of the mother country to get rid of its undesirables, there was the fact that the kind of men and women the colonies wanted were the least willing to emigrate; yet according to Madgwick, who supports his assertion with figures, between 1832 and 1835 "very few of the arrivals were unsuited to colonial needs", and "the number of country workers was still large in proportion to the total arrivals". He declares[16] that

> . . . the paupers, the drunkards, the prostitutes and the convicts who formed perhaps too great a section of the arrivals before 1851, were not inferior to the later arrivals in their willingness and ability to work. . . .
>
> . . . .
>
> Despite their lack of moral and political ideals they laid the foundation of future Australian prosperity by the work they did on the farms and stations throughout the colony. . . .
>
> It is therefore a grave mistake to acclaim the gold miners as the true founders of Australia, or to condemn out of hand the less spectacular immigration of the previous years.

This also, if there is visible in the paragraph quoted a tendency to be carried away by enthusiasm, is a clear and fair-minded study, and its analysis of emigration methods and types of emigrant and of the reasons for Britain's initial lack of interest in the Australian colonies and her varying policies regarding them is the best that has yet appeared.

[16] p. 251.

The settlement of the Australian countryside has been studied in great detail and upon a basis of wide and elaborate research by Stephen Henry Roberts (Maldon, Vic., 1901–71), who was educated at the Universities of Melbourne, London and Paris, was for some time Professor of History at the University of Sydney, and later its Vice-Chancellor. His first book, the *History of Australian Land Settlement (1788–1920)*, (Melbourne, 1924), investigates what Professor Scott called in his introduction to it "the fundamental subject in Australian history"; it is perhaps also the most difficult, for it would be hard to imagine anything more unsystematic, tangled and complicated than the land laws of the Australian States. Roberts had at first intended to limit himself to the conquest of an unknown countryside by the squatters, "a body of adventurers who spread over hundreds of miles, and who occupied principalities in the face of the Government, the natives and all manner of natural difficulties"; as his material opened out, his plan broadened into a survey of the whole field of land settlement, but eleven years later, in *The Squatting Age in Australia: 1835–1847* (Melbourne, 1935), he returned to his first project. It says much for the mass of material Roberts unearthed that the second book, though in fact it discusses in greater detail what was outlined in one section of the first, reads like an entirely new work, and includes scarcely any repetition. It is strange that neither the larger nor the smaller subject should have been tackled before[17] except incidentally and incompletely; but in addition to the difficulty of the land legislation, it is probable that few were aware of the mass of unpublished letters and diaries of squatters until Roberts had hunted them out. These two books, and also two others upon entirely different subjects which will shortly be discussed,[18] are remarkable for their author's energy and systematic determination to cover every corner of a wide field. The results, in all four books, of Roberts's researches, are elaborately organized, but on a plan which involves treating separately the various overlapping phases of a subject, so that material which is in part the same is often handled first from one and then from another point of view: as a consequence there is in each book a good deal of repetition, and sometimes processes of selection and digestion are left to the reader, which the author might have handled himself: when a historian is working over difficult and practically unexplored country he has to map his journeyings, but here they form too detailed a chart. The effect of all this is accentuated by a style that is in general far from succinct; it is also, though easy and by no means academic, rather loose and given to clichés. Yet Roberts can at times express himself concisely enough, and his too infrequent general-

---

[17] There was of course Collier's *Pastoral Age in Australasia* (see p. 836), but that was far slighter and far less solidly based.

[18] See pp. 1350–1, 1351.

izations are not only much to the point but have sometimes an epigrammatic touch. He says that in New South Wales free selection meant "mixed settlement in the coastal belt, a squatting triumph in the best part of the colony and a premium on blackmail in the West"; and that, because of the density of population in the smaller State and because both squatters and goldminers were more insistent on their rights, "the campaign in New South Wales was merely an agitation, in Victoria, a conflict"; and he quotes the definition of "a typical run boundary, as sanctioned by the Commissioner", which is more amusing to the reader than it could have been to the parties concerned:

> It followed Mr White's *ploughed line* as far as a *rock* described by Mr Grant as situated about 350 yards from a *tea-tree spring* (should it not touch the rock to be drawn from the nearest point to it), then a straight *plough-furrow* to be drawn to the Intersection of Mr Henty's plough-furrow with a *Creek or Marsh*. . . .

Roberts divides land settlement into five periods: the Period of Experiments, in which land was disposed of quite unsystematically by means of grants; the Period of Wakefield, with the influence of his theories upon sale and immigration, and the wrecking of his policy of concentration upon the squatting movement; the Period of Squatting, whose increasing flood overwhelmed the embankments of the "nineteen counties"; the Period of the Emergence of Agriculture, with the struggle between squatter and selector; and the Period of Closer Settlement, which began in the nineties. Even in the second book Roberts was led into a wider sphere than he had at first intended, into providing an economic, social and political survey of the life of the period, and "an account of the clash between such colourful personalities as Wentworth, Lowe and Gipps"; but its subject is simpler and more straightforward than that of the other book, and the result is a greater clarity and unity. It was in 1835, says Roberts, "when the infant colony began to assume its distinguishing characteristics," that the real story of Australia's progress began. He tells how "the Government [had] erected a huge non-trespass sign over the interior", and how this was of no avail whatever against the irresistible urge to find new lands for the cattle and sheep; he tells, using an expression which he finds so attractive that he repeats it five or six times, of the rush to "put everything on four feet",[19] how "the life of the colony was on the frontier" though "its Governors and its successful men were striving to keep it back in the puerile quarrels of a convict age that was going"; and he tells of the wild rush out back, when[20]

> . . . shop-boys and teachers, soldiers and merchants all joined the rush, which was every bit as pronounced as the later exodus in search of gold. . . . Men changed their

[19] Or "on four legs".

[20] p. 11; there is some repetition on p. 83.

> black-drab beavers for cabbage-tree hats, their coffee-coloured *tails* for dungaree shirts, and set off for the inland. . . .
>
> . . . .
>
> . . . every able-bodied man thirsted for the bush and pined to ride in the dust behind masses of smelling sheep and live on an unchanging diet of mutton-chops, unleavened damper, and *post-and-rail tea.*

Roberts tells how from 1836 onwards the types of squatter changed, "army officers, the young sprigs of the Macarthur and Riley trees, immigrants of means (and often of good family), ex-officials" all joining the movement.[21] But in analysing the composition of the community he surely goes too far when he says that now "practically for the first time, strata in society could be discerned". Lifelike sketches of Bourke and his policy and of Lowe are followed by another of Wentworth, whose powers of oratory are however much underestimated.[22] We see the would-be squatter searching for land, how he takes up a run and how he settles down upon it. We also hear of the "sordid, filthy existence" of even a prosperous squatter, though here Roberts must be thinking of the unmarried and undercapitalized squatter of the early days; indeed this description of his is by no means borne out by the glimpses of highly civilized station existence in a novel that Roberts considers "typical of ordinary bush life . . . a history of this early period rather than fiction": *Robbery Under Arms.* And we hear of the difficulties the squatter had to face, and of radical changes in methods, until finally squatting became a capitalized profession, and most of its romance and opportunity were gone. In the matter of form the second book has the merits and defects of the first but it tells a brighter and more human story, and is inspired throughout by a spirit of adventure and discovery. As in his preface to the first book Roberts had said that he "confined [his] efforts to explaining trends and providing a basis from which research on particular points might be made", so of the second book he says that it is merely "a preliminary monograph on a neglected period in Australian history". But both are much more than he claims for them, and it will be long before the second is superseded.

So much for settlement in general; *Cattle Chosen* (London, 1926) is an individual example; it is by no means the least interesting book in this section, and is indeed a classic in its kind: it tells the story of the first group settlement in Western Australia; how the Bussells, a Hampshire clergyman's widow and seven of her children, came out in the twenties

[21] The first book had contained (p. 172) examples of squatters "of a fine type", and here (pp. 273-5) there is a much longer list, which includes some repetitions.

[22] According to Roberts, Wentworth's "speeches were bad" (p. 273), and he quotes Wentworth's rough clumsiness as described in "a contemporary news-sheet". This was *Heads of the People*, in an article on "the orator". But Roberts omits the article's concluding remark, that "a growl from Wentworth has ofttimes more weight than an exquisitely polished sentence from Mr Lowe". And there are other tributes to Wentworth's oratory; for the secret of this, see pp. 53-4 of this History.

and in the south-western corner of the colony built up a home in the bush. The story is constructed out of letters and diaries, and edited by E. O. G. Shann,[23] who wisely allows the Bussells to speak for themselves. John, the eldest of the sons, who was to have been a clergyman, was only twenty-six; yet they battled successfully with the immense and stubborn timber that had to be felled and with hardships that must have seemed even worse in those days than now; they had so little capital that they lived for some time on kangaroo, and once only a fishing-net from England saved them from starvation. There are several curious intrusions of modernity: it seems natural that Fanny should "agonize" about a letter entrusted to one who turns out to bear a "character of the doubtful order"; but it is a little surprising to find that Patrick, who had married into the family, thought that his baby daughter "looked like a brandy-faced fishwife that had had too much grog tea".[24] The book tells an almost ideal story, until, like the intrusion of an evil fairy, a heated discussion about the division of the common income arose out of a series of marriages, and after a while the family broke up.

In *Rum Rebellion* (Sydney, 1938), H. V. Evatt,[25] then a Justice of the High Court, brought his expert knowledge and powers of analysis to bear upon a number of legal questions connected with the deposition of Governor Bligh; he pointed out that "the Courts were the true forum of the little colony. They had no competitors[26] as a means of expressing individual or public grievances", and therefore they were the centres of the conflict between the officers of the New South Wales Corps who made money out of the rum traffic and the Governor who was determined to put it down. Evatt however goes beyond the courts and examines the whole circumstances of the conflict; it was time, he says, for a re-examination of the facts underlying what he calls "the copybook tradition". According to this tradition "the progress of the colony" was to Bligh "not so important as its discipline",[27] and the rebellion was caused by his tyranny, while Macarthur stood for liberty. The founders and followers of the tradition no doubt remembered that Bligh had been deposed under somewhat similar circumstances before, and that Macarthur was the father of Australia's most important industry; but Evatt goes farther in the opposite direction: his attitude and method are those not of a judge but of a Crown Prosecutor determined on a verdict on every count; Bligh can do no wrong and his opponents are wrong everywhere. There was no doubt about Macarthur's cold obstinacy and overbearing

---

[23] For Shann's other work, see pp. 1418-21. [*Cattle Chosen* was reprinted in Perth, 1978.]

[24] Another instance is the giving of the homestead its name because a truant cow had independently discovered it; an alternative name had been "The Pleasaunce".

[25] For Evatt's other work, see pp. 1440-1 and 1371-3.

[26] There was the pamphlet, of course (see this History, pp. 49-50).

[27] See Jose, *History of Australia*, 12th edition (Sydney, 1926), p. 41.

egoism, his identification of the public interests with his personal concerns, his hatred of Bligh and his employment against him of every device his ingenious mind could invent: Evatt quotes King as saying that Macarthur had "taken the offensive against all the Governors of the colony"; and there is no doubt, again, that the smaller settlers were for Bligh as their supporter and against Macarthur as standing for the monopoly that was ruining them.[28] Evatt's analyses of the legal situations that arose, or were contrived, between Bligh and Macarthur or their representatives must of course be accepted, and he has no difficulty in uncovering Macarthur's hand in the proceedings that led immediately to Bligh's deposition. But from all this it does not follow that Bligh's own behaviour was not a contributing cause to the feeling that led to his deposition: he was quite as obstinate and could be quite as infuriating as Macarthur, the fundamental difference between them being that his temper was hot and undisciplined whereas Macarthur's was cold and controlled. And Mr Justice Evatt would certainly have pointed out flaws in parts of the case presented by Mr Evatt in his role of Crown Prosecutor: in the matter of the famous sheep story for instance: it is contended that Bligh would never have used abusive language about the imperial authorities; but it is admitted that a court martial had reprehended Bligh for using intemperate language,[29] and some of the examples of such language given by Mackaness, whom Evatt quotes with approval in other connections, suggest that there were scarcely any limits to which Bligh would not go when his temper was aroused. Again, with all respect to Evatt's powers of legal analysis, his "probable inference" that Macarthur was never actually promised more than 5000 acres out of the 10,000 he insisted upon is not well supported. It seems unlikely that when some future historian shall once more examine the circumstances of the rebellion and the characters and previous records of the two principal figures he will agree with Evatt that "the two mutinies will turn out to have both immortalized Bligh and vindicated his character"; nevertheless it was well that pending a final judgment every piece of evidence in Bligh's favour should be brought forward.

The subjective element is naturally stronger in the humanist than in the documentary school of historians, in those whose object is not so much to describe as to re-create some aspect of past life, and it is likely to be particularly strong in the work of a writer whose principal concern has been with fiction: consequently one is not surprised to find this element marked in the historical work of Marjorie Barnard.[30] What she presents in *Macquarie's World* (Sydney, 1941) is a series of bright impressionistic

[28] See pp. 106–7, 110–11, 178.
[29] p. 92.
[20] For her other work, see pp. 1250–1; see also Eldershaw, Barnard.

pictures in which the artist offers as truth whatever presents itself to her mind's eye, after brooding upon the facts. Of Macquarie she says that "the Highland melancholy, latent in his blood . . . invaded him", and[31]

> For hours Macquarie sat on deck, the fine military carriage of his shoulders sagged a little, his chin on his breast and his dark grey eyes under their stiff brows staring out to sea . . . From the sea and the distance he could see his world, that he had shaped out of chaos, more clearly than ever. It was as if it hung there on the blank sky like a finely drawn chart complete in every detail.

But Macquarie, or Miss Barnard's Macquarie, is remarkably well analysed:[32]

> Here, clear to see, are the permanent strands of his character: the delight, sometimes beneficial, sometimes merely fussy, in reorganisation; the impulse to tidy and docket; the will to favour but the inability to cooperate; the precipitancy, the patent honesty, good intention and energy;

and again,[33]

> He was a man who always would make enemies, because though he went through the motions of tact he had none. His vanity was hypersensitive and he defended it at the expense of far worthier objects.

On one point however Miss Barnard's judgment may be questioned: she calls Macquarie "a commonplace man";[34] could such a man have achieved what he achieved? An undoubted sympathy with her principal character seems to have conflicted with a "subconscious antagonism"[35] that blinds her to a strength of personality, a vitality, an enthusiasm and an organizing power beside which Macquarie's defects seem little things. The artist, seeking individual expression, is evident in the scheme of Miss Barnard's book: it opens with a picture of Macquarie leaving the world he had made, "so nearly in disgrace that you could not tell the difference"; it continues with a series of sections characterizing The Town, The Bush, The Convicts, The Officers and so on, in which Macquarie merges in the world about him; and it ends with two sections in which he and his rule are at their happiest, and a final section which deals with his decline and fall. What strikes one most about these presentations of the various aspects of life in the Australia of these early days is that they are presentations rather than descriptions, illuminative presentations, and that permeating all of them is a marked individuality in the point of view and in the manner of expression: "Sydney society, though

---

[31] pp. 6, 7. I have taken the liberty of transposing the two extracts here quoted.
[32] p. 167.
[33] p. 171.
[34] Marion Phillips had described him as "a man of very ordinary ability" (*A Colonial Autocracy*; Preface, p. vii).
[35] See a review by Sydney Tomholt of *Macquarie's World* in *Southerly*, vol. viii (1947), no. 4, pp. 238-42.

small, had as many circles as Dante's Inferno"; "the Colonial Secretary . . . evidently looked on the Colony as something like a septic tank. 'If,' he wrote, 'you continually send thieves to one place, it must in time be super-saturated. We must let it rest and purify for a few years and it will again be in a condition to receive.'" Miss Barnard has the art of weaving historic facts into a pattern of life; she weaves with intuitive imagination, and if the pattern now and then runs a little beyond those facts which are definitely ascertainable, and may even once in a way conflict with them, this is as small a matter as are Macquarie's faults in comparison with his virtues.

Of those historians whose subjects are not Australian, first the two who have found them in this or largely in this part of the world. Before Roberts's *History of French Colonial Policy*[36] (2 vols, London, 1929) there was no attempt in English to unravel its recurrent rhythms, to distinguish between its theory and its practice, to bring out the principles and repossessions that underlie what are often little more than merely nominal changes. Roberts's book is based, not on actual colonial experience but on researches in Australia, France and Britain: it is divided into two main parts, in the first of which the theory is analysed, and in the second the actual practice in the individual French colonies; but the chapters on theory involve analyses of the same thing from a number of different points of view, and one or more of the four French theories of colonial relationships, subjugation, autonomy, assimilation and association, continually recur. This, of course, is to some extent unavoidable, but Roberts's tendency to elaborateness of scheme and repetition of subject-matter and argument are even more noticeable here than in his Australian books. As with them, again, his investigations have been painstaking and thorough, his exposition is clear and logical, and his points are well made, even if some of them are made more than once; and again, though he is generally speaking rather verbose, some of his statements are neat and concise to the point of epigram: "the French colonist was not the peasant but the franc"; and, in connection with the French policy of destroying Islamic institutions in Algeria, "if these reforms were obtained, there would remain no Arab organization, but only a mass of unorganised individuals, floating between a shattered past and a hopeless future". Roberts traces the various and sometimes conflicting strands in the French colonial tradition, and shows how behind them all is a consciousness of the need for a colonial empire as providing both men and material wealth; he also shows how there is "Always a tendency to direct rule, always centralization within the colony and from Paris, and always executive control,—these remain the pillars of the colonial structure." Roberts draws an interesting contrast between

[36] For Roberts's other work, see pp. 1344-6.

English and French colonization with its "lack of any innate sense of racial superiority . . . combined with a certain naïve egoism regarding French civilization and strengthened by faith in a logical principle"; "England," he remarks, "deals with a number of young organisms, France with outflung limbs of the central organism." A second book of Roberts's, *Population Problems of the Pacific* (London, 1927), involves a historical study of both the social and the racial problems of the Pacific islanders, as complicated by the European and later the Asiatic invasions, and to some extent as illuminated by similar problems in other parts of the world. Roberts's task is here particularly difficult in that everything is at present in a state of flux, and he claims no more for his book than that it is a preliminary statement of the situation as it presented itself at the time when it was written; he makes it clear, however, that the arrival of the white man only accentuated a decline that, after the age of early invasions and long canoe voyages, had already reached a serious stage: a decline that took the form of a general lassitude, of a physical and psychological inertia. He finds that the results of the racial fusion that has taken place within the last few generations have been favourable so far as concerns the mingling of native groups with Asiatics, but with Europeans only in special circumstances, as in New Zealand. The general position, as Roberts saw it in 1925, was that the decline generally had been checked, but that the situation remained full of problems, not one of which was within sight of settlement. Both books are important and interesting attempts at analyses, which must, as their author realizes, be ultimately superseded; the second, however, will need, he suggests, some "ideal being . . . who is at once the anthropologist and the administrator and the historian." Ward's *British Policy in the South Pacific (1786–1893)* (Sydney, 1948) has affinities with one or other of Roberts's books, in the area in which it is set, in that it deals with the expansion into that area of the influence of a European power, and in the general handling of its subject: it also is at times rather loosely written, and it lacks Roberts's occasional sharp and enlightening phrases and paragraphs; nevertheless it is a pioneering work of importance. John Manning Ward (Sydney, 1919–) was one of Roberts's students, and, after a distinguished career, which included a law degree, he lectured under Roberts and finally succeeded to his Chair: his book is based on a close and detailed investigation of printed and manuscript sources studied mainly at the Mitchell and National libraries. Like Roberts again, Ward attempts no more than to blaze a trail across a wide field: individual parts of this field have been, as he says, thoroughly examined, but "the detailed surveys of particular aspects of British policy have suffered from the lack of adequate research into broad trends". He makes it clear, though he does not definitely say so, that there has been no more unity in British policy in this field than in the colonial policy of France: in its vicissitudes it amounts actually not so much to a definitely planned policy with its necessary developments and changes, as to a series of different kinds of behaviour forced upon Britain by the pressure of events. In its recital and an analysis of changing situations and of the facts on which they were based, and of the accompanying changes in Britain's attitude lies the value of his book: there is room, as Ward points out, for a further examination when further facts become available. A third writer deals, not with general problems connected with the Pacific, but with a particular aspect of activities in that region: they are adventurous activities, and *Whalemen Adventurers* (Sydney, 1934),[37] by William John Dakin (Liverpool, England, 1883-1950), might, so far as its atmosphere is concerned, be included among tales of adventure; nevertheless it is in its contribution to the history of the Pacific that the book matters. Dakin filled in succession chairs of Biology in Western Australia, Zoology in Liverpool, and Zoology in Sydney; in 1930 he was asked by the Commonwealth Government to report on whaling in connection with a committee of the League of Nations. His book is based on information obtained from old whalers' log-books, lent him or consulted in the Mitchell and other libraries; on visits to old whaling ports in Norway and the United States; and on his own experience when he lived for a time with Norwegian whalers whose base was on the Western Australian coast, and went out with their chasers. He tells of the life and work of the southern whalers from the earliest days, when they sailed in blunt-nosed wooden barques of 250 to 300 tons that had the appearance of being "built by the mile and cut off in lengths as you want 'em"; some of these early whalers were first cousins to pirates, fighting as mercenaries in the Maoris' tribal wars, helping convicts to escape, or sometimes carrying them off to help work their ships; but Tasmanian whalers of about the middle of the century had a much higher standing: whaling was a favourite pursuit with young Tasmanians. Dakin tells also of the many connections between whaling and early Australian history, some of them hitherto almost unknown; how for instance many of the vessels that carried the convicts to Sydney were whalers, and some of them, after they had unloaded what was left of their human cargoes, set out on whaling voyages. His intimate knowledge of the subject and his enthusiasm rather than any strictly literary quality carry Dakin's story through, but his book seems likely to remain for some time the standard authority upon whaling in southern seas.

It is as uncharacteristic for an Australian historian to turn to a European country as to the philosophy of history; but *Pre-Fascist Italy* (London,

[37] A second edition, published in 1938, contains many additions; it is to this edition that the references here are made.

1939), by Margot Hentze (Melbourne, 1909-47), not only fills a gap that needed to be filled, but fills it so well that her book seems likely to remain the standard; Miss Hentze's turn to Europe may be partly accounted for by the fact that her father was Belgian. After a brilliant career at the University of Sydney and two years at the London School of Economics, she lectured in History at Sydney, worked in Europe and the Pacific for the U.N.R.R.A. and, in Europe again for the U.N.R.R.A., obtained personal as well as documentary material for her book. This is, as its sub-title, "The Rise and Fall of the Parliamentary Regime", makes clear from the first, a political history; indeed it had to be, since the unification and guidance of an Italy which had been no more than formally assembled was in the first place a political problem; but it depended upon underlying conditions, social, regional and economic, and these and the background generally are broadly drawn. There is an excellent survey of the situation on the achievement of formal unity: the Risorgimento had not been "a popular movement, but a rebellion on the part of an elite", inspired rather by an instinct of revolt against the domination of the foreigner than by a real awakening of national consciousness; and "united Italy" consisted of a medley of peoples who belonged to a number of States and spoke a number of dialects and among whom there were different standards of education, different forms of government, different methods of taxation, and different systems of law. Three-quarters of the population were illiterate; their rulers, besides being politically inexperienced, were largely exiles, "derelicts from many shipwrecks", or else they were bounded by the limits of their provinces; and worst of all, as a result of centuries of oppression and misgovernment, there prevailed an indifference, a scepticism, a social and psychological malaise which was the worst possible preparation for the creation of a new and living entity: this country, this collection of peoples had to assume "the responsibilities of a nineteenth-century power when its economics and resources were still fundamentally those of a seventeenth-century land". Follows a long chronicle of efforts, idealisms, mistakes, pettinesses, corruptions, ineptitudes of government after government; by and large, nevertheless, there resulted, says Miss Hentze, a solid material achievement, though it was accompanied by no general spiritual impulse: and then the first World War, disappointment with its results for Italy, and the breaking down of government into "a nightmare of confusion"; the driving of the people into the arms of a movement which no one in parliament had taken seriously, and Mussolini's march on Rome.

Crawford's *The Study of History: A Synoptic View* (Melbourne, 1939) is of more importance than its size would indicate; while its analyses and conclusions are not exactly novel in themselves, they are the outcome of a thoughtful, precise and richly furnished mind, which is that of an expert on the subject, and which has so concentrated upon them that they appear as its objective manifestations: but as important as the conclusions themselves, indeed scarcely to be distinguished from them, is the atmosphere out of which they are crystallized, an atmosphere of respect for the truth as a whole and of impartiality in the search for it and in its presentation. The author, Raymond Maxwell Crawford[38] (Grenfell, N.S.W., 1906–), was educated at the Sydney High School and the Universities of Sydney and Oxford; since 1937 he has been Professor of History at the University of Melbourne, but in 1942–4 he was given leave of absence, during which he was First Secretary to the Commonwealth Legation at Moscow. Crawford begins with an analysis of the assumptions of the political historians, "repeatedly challenged, but not finally dethroned",[39] of which the most extreme amounts to saying that "History is what . . . persons [in prominent positions] choose to make it"; incidentally, this involves, as Crawford points out, the assumption that man is able to decide irrespective of "the medley of legacies from the past" amid which he finds himself. Examining various forms of revolt against the political historians, Crawford rejects the materialist conception of history, largely because of its over-emphasis upon the role of the economic structure of society, which however he makes clear is not the only factor that Marx and Engels recognized. Crawford's own "synoptic view" is based upon an attempt to discover all the factors in historical change, and to analyse their complex interaction; he sees human activity as

> . . . a confused and complex groping towards ends which vary, conflict, and to a large degree remain undefined;

and history is to him

> . . . *the study of human societies agitated from within the universe of themselves and their setting to work out their nature, a nature never defined until achieved.*[40]

This definition goes, as he says, so far as to hint at a philosophy of history; but then all definitions worth the name are the results of philosophies, from which they are precipitated as crystals in solution.[41] Finally, Crawford believes that even though it may be the historian's duty to pass judgment, it will be his voice that is heard, not that of history, and that

> . . . there is all the difference in the world between a confident assertion that he has achieved finality, which no historian can make, and that courageous declaration of his considered conclusions and their grounds, which is his duty.

[38] For Crawford's other work, see pp. 1282–3. Since the closing date of this History he has also published *Australia* (London, 1952).

[39] He even gives an example from Trevelyan.

[40] The italics are Crawford's.

[41] Crawford is not to be blamed for this image.

There were several regional histories, including a couple of the Northern Territory. Of these, the latest, *Australia's Frontier Province* (Sydney, 1950), includes some account of the bombing of Darwin, and a summary of the Payne Report, which was invaluable, and pigeonholed. The author, Charles Lydiard Aubrey Abbott (Sydney, 1886–1975), served in the first World War, was Federal Minister for Home Affairs, and was also for nine years Administrator of the Territory. The only general history that need be mentioned is *A Concise History of Australia* (Sydney, 1936), by Frederick Lloyd Whitfield Wood[42] (Sydney, 1903–); he is a son of G. A. Wood,[43] from whom he probably derives his interest in history and his instinct for style: it is partly on this account that though a textbook his short history is mentioned here. Wood is a graduate of the Universities of Sydney and Oxford and Professor of History at Victoria University College, Wellington, New Zealand. This book is built on much the same general lines and has much the same general outlook as those of Scott and Jose, of the preceding Period; it is by no means an imitation, but does not differ from either much more than they differ from one another. Remains another short textbook, A. L. Sadler's *Short History of Japan* (Sydney, 1946); this is mentioned here because of its subject, and because it illustrates, though its author is English-born, the tendency among some Australian writers to look beyond their native borders: it is based largely on the work of Japanese and English historians, and was compiled "owing to the lack of any convenient book of the kind in English".[44]

The Period was rich in biographies, so far as number is concerned, and, though in a lesser degree, it was rich in quality also. There were far more subjects than in the preceding Period, when the leaders and opponents of Federation and also many leading writers were too near at hand; this however holds of some of the writers even now: for various reasons definitive biographies of Lawson, Furphy and Richardson will have to wait a while. Biography again, like history, though not to the same extent as the essay or the drama, belongs to a comparatively late stage in national development; for effective practice it must wait, like history, until a country's past stretches out behind its present like a long wake, and becomes interesting not merely in itself but as a revealer of first causes, as throwing light upon the present, and as containing figures with which those of the day may be compared: the developing universities have provided biographers with opportunities, but biography cannot flourish except where communities contain a large element that

[42] For other work by Wood, see pp. 1445–6.

[43] See pp. 842–4.

[44] For Sadler's best work, a biography of a Japanese statesman, see pp. 1375–7.

is in the best sense literate, a state of affairs that has only been approached in Australia so far. As for subjects, in Australia today leadership, and in particular political leadership, is neither encouraged nor much respected, and, partly for this reason perhaps, notable leaders are comparatively rare: still that is more likely to concern tomorrow's biographers than today's. On the whole, taking into consideration the occasional help afforded by competitions and by the Commonwealth Literary Fund, Australian biographers have a wider field and greater opportunities than in the past; but it is worth noting that, as with the recent literary competitions, the best work has not been dependent upon such assistance; it has not brought out much new talent. With biography as with general history the standard attained has been especially high in basic research, but there has been sometimes a striking contrast between the excellence of the material and the mediocrity of its presentation; here, as in other departments of Australian literature, may be seen the influence of the journalistic method that is evident in all but the best of it. Partly because our biographers are paying so much attention to background, and partly because the general historian has often chosen a period that centres upon some individual figure, the boundary between the two kinds of history is sometimes largely a matter of opinion: this particularly when the same period, with its central figure, has been dealt with by two writers, one from the point of view of the general historian and the other from that of the biographer. Among the biographies Evatt's *Australian Labour Leader* stands out; but Barnard Eldershaw's *Phillip of Australia*, and also her *Captain Piper*, though this is a minor work, combine the virtues of pure and applied literature to an extent that is quite unusual in this country; these and perhaps Nettie Palmer's *Henry Bournes Higgins* are among the leading Australian biographies of today. The biographies of writers are on the whole disappointing, partly no doubt because the most attractive subjects are still unavailable, or at least not fully available, and partly because of the journalistic influence that has been mentioned. In the circumstances the order in which they have been taken here has depended as a rule upon the importance of the subject. The most notable were the unfinished autobiography of Henry Handel Richardson and the study by Nettie Palmer; the second followed so closely upon the first that there was not much biographical information that could be added, at present anyhow. *Myself When Young* (London, 1948), ends with Richardson's marriage; it had been intended to carry it on through the early years of her married life in Germany, up to the departure for England on Robertson's appointment in 1903 to the Chair of German Language and Literature at the University of London. To this point it was continued by Olga Roncoroni, an old friend who had lived with Richardson for many years as her companion and secretary, and who became her executrix: the continuation was based on Professor Robertson's notes and diaries, as well as on Miss Roncoroni's personal knowledge. *Myself When Young* contains also a supplementary essay on "The Art of Henry Handel Richardson", by her husband: this had been written in 1928–9, before the publication of *The End of a Childhood* and others of the short stories, *The Young Cosima* and the complete *Richard Mahony*; but several of the short stories had appeared in magazines during Robertson's lifetime, and in spite of Richardson's dislike of showing even her husband anything that was unfinished, he may have seen some of her later work in draft. The autobiography makes clear a number of points about which there was more or less doubt before: the date of Richardson's birth for instance, and, more important, the extent to which her work was indebted for incident as well as character to members of her own family, to friends and acquaintances, and to herself. More important is the light thrown on the passionate intensity of *Maurice Guest* by Richardson's comment upon her husband's remark that she was "emotionally very experienced"; by her account of her infatuation as a young girl for a very unusual clergyman; and by what she has to say about her infatuation for the girl who is called Evelyn in *The Getting of Wisdom*:[45] these confirm and elaborate what might have been in substance inferred before. The autobiography, perhaps because it is unfinished, reads a little like a first draft; it looks as though it had been just jotted down and left at that, as perhaps it was. Professor Robertson's appreciation is informative but not particularly penetrating: he emphasizes that the complete objectivity in the presentation of the theme of *Maurice Guest* is in the European as contrasted with the English tradition; he points out the influence upon this book of *Crime and Punishment* and *The Brothers Karamazov*, and suggests that its passionate intensity has something of the quality of d'Annunzio's *Il Fuoco;* Marion Crawford's Italian novels might perhaps have been added. Professor Robertson also remarks that there is in *Richard Mahony* a note of personal sympathy that is quite absent from *Maurice Guest*; there may be some reason for this however, in that in *Richard Mahony* it is the author's father who is being analysed, whereas *Maurice Guest* consists largely of emanations from Richardson's own experience and feeling. One or two points strike one as rather strange: the remarks about Richardson's style,[46] and the statement that "from first page to last [*Richard Mahony*] is a book about money";[47] that the book is without "such adventitious

---

[45] These points have been already referred to, in discussing Richardson's novels (see pp. 645, 646, 647, 655, 658).

[46] On this matter, see pp. 652–6 of this History, on which Richardson's style is discussed.

[47] p. 177. The need of money is certainly at the root of the story, but the assertion gives an entirely wrong impression nevertheless.

aids" as that of plot;[48] and that Richard "takes part in . . . the affair of the Eureka Stockade", when all he does is to make an unsuccessful speech at a miners' meeting. In Nettie Palmer's book, *Henry Handel Richardson: A Study* (Sydney, 1950), the strictly biographical part occupies only twenty-seven pages out of 207, but a good deal of biographical material is at least implicit throughout. This book is illuminative as to the circumstances and method of composition of the novels, as to the novels themselves and their principal characters, and as to the relation of these to real men and women, places and incidents. Few of the facts or ideas conveyed will be new to the student of Henry Handel Richardson and of what has been published about her and her work, but it is only fair to say that almost all the best of this was written by Nettie Palmer herself: it is here for the first time gathered together and systematized, with what there is of corrective or supplementary material from the autobiography. Mrs Palmer was probably better acquainted with her subject than anyone else except Professor Robertson and Richardson's sister and her two intimate woman friends; she had visited Richardson in England and corresponded with her over a period of twenty-five years; she was also, as has been already said here, the principal agent in introducing the novels to their own country. She makes some good points about *Maurice Guest*: for instance that Maurice "is raised from an amiable mediocrity to something like a tragic figure" by Louise and his passion for her; this however raises the question whether it is possible for a great passion to be experienced by a mediocre person. Mrs Palmer points out also that it is Maurice's "lack of any real absorption in music" that "leaves him open to this consuming passion for Louise"; but as to the most difficult part of the book, the "strange thing that happened to" Louise, the temporary transfer of her feeling for Schilsky to Maurice, there is no real attempt at explanation: one feels that there must be more in this episode than that "for the time being [Maurice] satisfied [Louise's] craving for emotion", and that this also may be connected in some way with the author's own experience. There is an interesting comparison of Louise and Madame Bovary, but as to the assertion that "Louise . . . depends for her charm largely on the author's sympathetic treatment of her", we can feel it strongly enough, quite apart from the descriptions and analyses, through its effect on Maurice, just as Helen's beauty in the *Iliad* is felt through its effect upon the old men. Mrs Palmer touches only lightly and in passing upon Richardson's infatuation as a schoolgirl with the original of the Evelyn of *The Getting of Wisdom*, and also for the young clergyman; she does not go into the effect of these upon the passionate feelings analysed in *Maurice Guest*. She also makes one or two surprising assertions: for instance as to the "gaiety" of *The Getting of Wisdom*, which

[48] On this matter, see pp. 653-4, for a discussion of the plot in Richardson's work.

she compares with *Huckleberry Finn*; she adds, it is true, that the two books have in common "just this, that they were written with no holding back, no recognition of the conventions of the day or the attitudes decreed for young people", and she admits that "oceans divide [them] and the width of seas", but the mere mention of the two books together is apt to be misleading. A large part of Mrs Palmer's book is taken up with acute analyses of *Richard Mahony* and his wife and of their development: of his slow but gradual capture of the sympathy of the reader at the beginning of the book, and of his gradual decline, without losing that sympathy, towards the end; and of Mary's development from the "ingenuous little person of the period" to the not very sympathetic or even understanding wife in the days of Richard's success and his decline, who yet when Richard descends to the depths, rises magnificently to the occasion. Mrs Palmer's study is more enlightening than Professor Robertson's, and not merely because she has more room to elaborate: but Henry Handel Richardson remains, after all that has been written, the enigma that she was before, and it is quite clear that there is still a good deal about her that can only be surmised.[49]

Not exactly autobiographical but still in place here is the same author's *Fourteen Years* (Melbourne, 1948). This consists of connected extracts from a private journal, glimpses of notable writers, scores of them, whom Mrs Palmer has met in Australia and England: glimpses clear and distinct, observed through the lightly tinted glass of Mrs Palmer's personality and point of view; sympathetic, urbane, intellectual, by no means offensively, but yet inescapably Australian. Here is Havelock Ellis:[50]

> His profile was fine and balanced, his white mane, his white beard not hiding the firm lips, large, clear-blue eyes almost untroubled-looking, almost childish, with a slight unstrained cast seeming to give a personal quality to them, as in Louis Esson's eyes. He was dressed as if he had ordered his suit perhaps forty years ago, and—his figure and habits not altering—had had it copied in some very uncrushable tweed, soft and silky-surfaced. Like a grand Whistler portrait he sat there, but not silhouetted against the wall; more florid and ample, with the October light coming through remote bay windows behind him.

There are many good things: Wilmot's retort when Esson asked him, at a performance by the Pioneer Players, if he had come to act as chucker-out: "Looks as if it isn't a chucker-out you want, but a chucker-in"; A. H. Adams's frightful lapse about *The Way Home*, that it read like "a dull chronicle written by a 'retired grocer'"; Will Dyson's acute remark that "The trouble about this country is its mental timidity . . . put it face to face with a new idea and it goes all of a tremble. . . . In things of the

[49] In 1957 there appeared in Sydney *Henry Handel Richardson: Some Personal Impressions*, by Edna Purdie and Olga M. Roncoroni, but this neither solves nor attempts to solve any problems.
[50] p. 183.

mind we show as much spirit as a suburban old maid"; Conrad's observations upon the writing of fiction, which ought to be taken to heart by more than one Australian journalist of today. And this, quite as illuminating, seems almost too good to be true: Sir Macpherson Robertson's reply[51] to an innocent remark about his air-race prizes being so much larger than those given for literature. With a curious stare,

> "Literature? What do you mean by that?"
> "Well, original writing. Prizes were offered for novels, stories, poems, you know."
> "Oh, books. I never read them."

In one instance however where Mrs Palmer speaks of "Rigby's brilliant talk", her Australianism runs away with her. Incidentally, she once remarks, "With a swallow, the flight is the bird":[52] is this a deliberate recalling of FitzGerald, or a mere coincidence? *Fourteen Years* is a rich book, that can be read more than once.

Of the other biographies, James Devaney's *Shaw Neilson* (Sydney, 1944) is exactly what the author says in his Introductory that he would like to write: "a simple intimate book that lovers of Shaw Neilson would like to have—a somewhat rambling record of his ways, his sayings, the personality of the man himself"; Devaney also says that "no thought is given here to style, but only to presenting facts": actually the manner of presentation so blends with what is presented that the question of style scarcely arises. Neilson appears as Devaney saw him, especially when he was convalescing with the Devaneys in his later years: simple, yet not so simple after all; quite unselfconscious; gentle and kind, but by no means weak in character; faddy and now and then extremely difficult; a despiser of men in general,[53] but a lover of children and an idealizer of girlhood; and, rather surprisingly, considering the nature of his poems, without any feeling for the beauty of landscape.[54] Neilson's methods of composition, which, though strange on the face of them, may throw some light on poetic composition generally; his relations with A. G. Stephens; his carelessness about his work: these are revealed largely in conversations with Devaney. Roderick's *In Mortal Bondage: The Strange Life of Rosa Praed* (Sydney, 1948) contains a good deal of new and often interesting material about this very "Australian" woman novelist of the nineties and early nineteen-hundreds; unfortunately the style in which the book is written, the whole atmosphere that has

---

[51] As recorded by Brian Penton in a newspaper interview.

[52]
all is become sheer action which perceives
bright leaves themselves as rustling of the leaves,
the bird's flight as the bird.
("Essay on Memory", *Moonlight Acre*, 1938, p. 65).

[53] "Men are the vilest things on earth, except monkeys" (p. 7).

[54] See this History, pp. 487-8.

been imposed upon it, is that of a popular thriller.[55] Colin Roderick (Mount Morgan, Q., 1911-) is a graduate of the University of Queensland, which awarded him a doctorate for the original typescript of this book, which however was not written in the same style. *The Making of a Sentimental Bloke: A Sketch of the Remarkable Career of C. J. Dennis* (Melbourne, 1946) is easy and natural and entertaining, if its subject is not of first importance from a literary as distinct from a popular point of view. Its author, Alexander (Alec) Hugh Chisholm (Maryborough, Vic., 1890-1977), naturalist, journalist and editor-in-chief of the second *Australian Encyclopaedia*, was an old friend of Dennis's and does him full justice brimming over, bearing lightly on his indebtedness to others and bringing out his wit, ingenuity and technical skill; he even considers "The Glugs of Gosh" to be "one of the brightest products of the author's nimble mind".

First among the autobiographies of writers is that of Herbert Michael Moran (Darlington, Sydney, 1885-1945), a distinguished cancer specialist, a pioneer in the use of radium therapy in Australia, and in his youth a prominent international footballer, who possessed a marked literary talent and an extremely individual style; he was educated at the Universities of Sydney and Edinburgh, read Dante as well as Shakespeare, spoke as well as read Italian, and read also French and German. Of his three books, all more or less autobiographical, the first, best and most characteristic is *Viewless Winds* (London, 1939): this sometimes recalls on the one hand Gogarty and on the other Axel Munthe, who may have contributed to Moran's original impulse to write. But though Moran also has a strong sense of humour and a number of amusing anecdotes, the undercurrent of his humour in general is stern, sardonic, even grim; with him also the facts and their practical bearings are of primary importance, and he lacks entirely the touches of half-mystical half-fairytale imagination that contribute to Munthe's charm. Moran was essentially a critic, a destructive critic, particularly in the medical, social and religious spheres; he considers it his business, and one cannot help thinking it was also a somewhat bitter pleasure, to point out bluntly and unsparingly the evils that his keen eye observes; and though he can bestow full credit where credit is due, his exposures and his sometimes devastating comments give its tone to at least the second half of the book: the result was that *Viewless Winds* had an unusual success but caused also a good deal of indignation. Moran's professional colleagues were indignant at the indiscreet and public prominence given to what was not characteristic of their profession as a whole; they objected to such assertions as that

[55] It is a rather old-fashioned thriller however as may be seen by the following example, from p. 53: "As the darkness thins and the stars begin to turn to silver, the weary red-eyed young woman sinks into a be-rugged cane chair at the foot of the bed. Her nights of watching have led to the last scene of Matilda's earthly pilgrimage."

medical men "have the mob impulses of sheep", and to such comments as that upon the young quack doctor who had lost the confidence of his patients: "So, in the end, he went to Sydney and became a proper specialist in Macquarie Street". And the co-religionists of a man who was yet as sincere a Roman Catholic as he was a medical idealist were annoyed at the exposures of the commercial spirit and breaches of the vow of chastity among some of the clergy; at the assertions that ecclesiastical authorities "usually display more energy in covering up scandals than in correcting them", and that "the figure of Christ on the walls [of some luxuriously furnished Catholic hospitals] seems always a little shabby and out of place". Moran's general emphasis on the darker aspect of things is sometimes quite misleading: it may be arguable that he is right when he asserts that "only in distant spaces, far from the indecent scurry after wealth, is the Australian race still breeding true"; but he goes too far when he speaks of Lawson as though he were temperamentally allied with Boake; and he is quite wrong when he speaks of Professor Wood as though the attempt to remove him from his Chair on account of his attitude during the Boer War was not strongly resisted by MacCallum and others who vigorously opposed any invasion of the right to freedom of speech. Yet Moran was not only sincere, but unselfish and public-spirited, and he was beloved by his patients and never looked for payment from a poor person. Also, he is by no means always gloomy; many of his good stories are without a hint even of irony, and he does not in the least mind if a story goes against himself, as in that of the old lady whom he used to visit regularly and without any question of payment to try to relieve the pain of her incurable osteo-arthritis:

> . . . when I dropped in, as usual, one afternoon late she told me in broad Scots: "Doctor dear, since you were last here I took a guinea from my savings and went over to Macquarie Street and saw *a really good doctor.*" She paused, a little surprised to hear me chuckle involuntarily, then she went on—now in a surprised tone: "and he says *just the same as you.*" The dear old thing was so sure that this was a great compliment!

The book is full of sharp sketches, one or two of which amount to portraits, of leading medical men and a few other notables[56] of the day. And Moran has an instinct for epithet and phrase which is surpassed only by that of our best novelists: speaking of Maud Gonne in her later years, he recalls Homer when he says, "to see her aged now made all the world grow old". Moran's force and individuality and the sincerity of his idealism, however twisted, lift *Viewless Winds* far out of the category of merely interesting and stimulating reminiscences. He published two other books: a kind of novel, which resembles the case-book of a young doctor, *Beyond the Hill Lies China* (London, 1945), and *In My Fashion*

[56] MacCormick, for instance, the famous surgeon, Scot Skirving, Henry Chapman, and Mannix and O'Reilly.

(Sydney, 1946): this last is again a case history, but of the "defeated tenth", of those who came before the British Medical Boards of which Moran was a member, for examination as to fitness for service in the army in the second World War; it is a disheartening record, but the last of it was written while Moran was gradually dying of the disease in which he was a specialist, recording and analysing his symptoms for the benefit of future sufferers and of his profession. A piece of autobiography by Philip Lindsay[57] (Sydney, 1906–58), a son of Norman Lindsay, which goes back to his life in Sydney before he migrated to London, *I'd Live the Same Life Over* (London, 1941), recaptures the atmosphere of the last fading days of bohemianism in Sydney in the early nineteen-hundreds. Simple, natural, quite unreserved and sometimes, deliberately perhaps, a little naïve, it describes Philip's childhood in a semi-bohemian home in Brisbane, and his boyhood and early manhood: hawking revolting little statuettes from shop to shop; in Julian Ashton's studio, trying to be an artist; and on the fringes of daily journalism; always hard-up and boyishly happy even in misfortune, and always hoping to write novels. Casual, temperamental, and, as one would expect of a Lindsay, full of exuberant delight in life, the book skims along the surface of things and people. There are glimpses of the larrikins just before they were superseded by the razor-gangsters; of a New Year's festival at Darlinghurst; and of the founding of *Vision* magazine and the Fanfrolico Press;[58] there are also glimpses of writers, Slessor, Stephensen and FitzGerald, as well as a sketch of his hero-worshipped brother Jack, and others of Philip's friends and acquaintances; but the only real portrait is of himself. Not the least among the autobiographies of writers is *Peter Lecky: By Himself* (London, 1935), though it is almost over the borderline of this History. It is as much a work of art as the poems of its author, Peter Hopegood:[59] an extremely interesting chronicle of the adventures that are to the adventurous, and through it all appears a friendly and engaging personality.

There were a number of biographies and autobiographies of artists, of which one must be mentioned, and so must three histories of art in Australia. Ashton's *Now Came Still Evening On* (Sydney, 1941), was written when he was ninety. Julian (Rossi) Ashton (Surrey, England, 1851–1942), born of an American father and an Italian mother, began as a railway clerk, studying after a while at the West London School of Art and afterwards in Paris; in 1878 he came to Australia, engaged by Syme

[57] Philip Lindsay is discussed among the other expatriate writers on p. 1232.

[58] See pp. 1208, 1253, 1326 of this History.

[59] For Hopegood's poems, see pp. 1046–9.

as a draughtsman for the *Illustrated Australian News*, and afterwards became an illustrator for the *Picturesque Atlas of Australia*. As a painter, of portraits and landscape, Ashton has a definite place in Australian art, but he sacrificed much of his own talent to the work of establishing, in the words of Norman Lindsay,[60] "a sound tradition of the dignity of art and its importance to a country's future stability". Something, but by no means all, of Ashton's lovable nature and strength of personality comes out in this work of his old age: there are light sketches of the prominent Australian painters of his day, and of course there is the story of the breakaway of the Society of Artists from the Art Society; but the colours of everything are slightly faded. There are a number of good things nevertheless: the account of how the Society of Artists managed to obtain its government subsidy; the story of the young lady who got out of bed in such a hurry to look for a lost raincoat in the thick wet grass that to the delight of the passengers in a passing train she forgot to put on her clothes; and, something that ought to be taken to heart by all young writers and a few older ones too, what Stevenson said to Ashton about the contents of his waste-paper basket:

> "Look at that, Ashton. There's stuff in that basket that my publishers would give me golden guineas for."
>
> I asked him why it was in the basket, and he answered: "Because it doesn't help my story."

And there is the fantastic interlude, about Ashton's short visit to the Valley of Heart's Content, in which the old artist gets away, entirely justifiably, with something that would certainly have been seized upon by the police if they had noticed it, at any rate if it had been written by anybody else. The standard history of art in Australia has still to be written but the Period produced three forerunners. *The Story of Australian Art* (2 vols, Sydney, 1934) is indeed not a history but a story, but it is also a reference book for facts, and covers so wide a range and is so impartial that the future historian cannot afford to neglect it. Its author, William Moore (Bendigo, Vic., 1868–1937), was a dramatic as well as an art critic, and among the small group by whom the Australian drama was founded; he wrote several one-act plays, and with T. Inglis Moore he edited *Best Australian One-Act Plays*.[61] The book is pleasant and human, and, dipping into it for some fact or other, one may easily be led on to read about the artists as human figures, their schools and their lives and the life of their time; and Moore is not without occasional gentle comments, some of which are enlightening, as when he speaks of Streeton's landscapes conveying "the sense of space as seen from a hill top". Badham's *Study of Australian Art* (Sydney, 1949) owes a good deal to Moore's book, which however, after fifteen years, it is able to supplement. Herbert

---

[60] In "Homage to Julian Ashton".

[61] See p. 1277.

Edward Badham (Sydney, 1899–1961) was a pupil of Ashton and Lambert and was a teacher of art at the National Art School, Sydney; his is a history, not a story, and he is much more critical than Moore, but his criticisms are not particularly illuminating; his book suffers from an attempt to mention everybody, so that in places it is little more than a catalogue and some worthwhile artists tend to be missed in the crowd. The third book, Bernard Smith's *Place, Taste and Tradition* (Sydney, 1945) is much the most notable of the three, though it is influenced by a bias which is political as well as artistic. Bernard Smith (Sydney, 1916–), a graduate of the University of Sydney, was seconded from the New South Wales Education Department to inaugurate Travelling Art Exhibitions to country centres, and, as a result, was awarded a British Council scholarship, on which he studied art in England; there at the request of the Hakluyt Society, he prepared a catalogue of the drawings and paintings by the artists who travelled with Cook, which recently appeared in a new edition of Cook's journals. He was a lecturer in Fine Arts at the University of Melbourne.* Smith attempts to provide not so much a history as the foundation of a historical perspective, presenting the course of Australian art against a background of oversea fashions and tendencies, and showing how these were altered as they were absorbed. He emphasizes the fact that Australian art based itself upon English art of the eighteenth century, from which it took over "only those art-forms . . . that could be practised in a society struggling for existence for many years in a harsh and uncongenial environment". Our landscape painting began therefore with a search for the picturesque, the romantic, the sublime, and a lament for the absence of autumnal tints and historic ruins. And when impressionism reached Australia, though, as a product of France, it undermined local traditions derived from England, it was via England that it arrived, and had an English colouring. Smith goes on to tell of Roberts and Streeton and the landscape painting in which they became the dominant influence, creating "the first authentic vision of the country", but also, in his opinion, "thwarting the natural development of original artists". One example of Smith's width of reference is that he makes comparisons between the growth of Australian art and the parallel growth of Australian literature; he has an interesting comparison between Lambert and Brennan, pointing out that the reputation of both men depends as much upon their overpowering personalities as upon their actual works. This is true, but Brennan was not so fine a craftsman as Lambert, nor is it by his craftsmanship that he must finally stand; and he has not left anything like the same amount of work. On the other hand Lambert's personality, though as striking perhaps, was not so overpowering as Brennan's, and though both were egoists, they

* [Smith was later Foundation Professor of Contemporary Art and Director of the Power Institute, University of Sydney, from 1967 to 1977.]

were egoists of different kinds: Brennan wrote, quite simply, about Brennan, but that is almost always his avowed subject; his is a monologue about what happens in his own mind; Lambert on the other hand dips his brushes in his own personality even when his subject has nothing to do with it. Smith does rather less than justice to some of his subjects, Lindsay, Hilder and even Streeton, for instance, and conversely, sets Dobell upon a pinnacle. *Place, Taste and Tradition* is always interesting, and stimulating even when one disagrees: it looks beneath the surface, seeking the reasons and explanations of things; its criticisms are downright and unconventional, but based upon observation, reading and thought; and in spite of the bias mentioned it is always sincere. Not least interesting are some of Smith's incidental observations, which, if not always novel, sometimes make definite for us ideas that may have hitherto merely flickered along the surface of the mind, though they have sometimes carried a question with them; for example:

> English eighteenth century art was based on complacency and power, and those who found themselves in Australia were neither complacent nor powerful;

and, speaking of the romanticism of early Australian art,

> One of the uses of art resides in its value as a soporific . . . and the homesick artist, who painted for homesick patrons, probably neither desired, nor was asked to provide, a landscape depicting the brutal realities of the new environment.

CHAPTER XVII

HISTORY, BIOGRAPHY, DESCRIPTION

Early Governors: Barnard Eldershaw; Mackaness; Ellis; Kathleen Fitzpatrick. Statesmen and Politicians: Evatt; Melbourne; Lett; Sadler; Palmer; Ross. Other Biographies. Description: Barnard Eldershaw; Others. Central Australia: Madigan; Finlayson; Myrtle Rose White

THERE WERE several biographies of early governors, which may be taken in their subjects' historical order. Barnard Eldershaw's *Phillip of Australia* (London, 1938) is a work of imaginative re-creation as contrasted with a record of facts; yet it does not constitute the standard biography of the founder of Australia for which we have waited so long. It is of course impossible to re-create a historical character *in vacuo*; there must be also a reconstruction of his social and political world, a reconstruction whose extent will depend upon the distance of that world from the present and upon the part he has played in creating it; but, as will be seen, the historical biographers here discussed have paid, on the whole, at least as much attention to the world as to the man, to the background as to the portrait: it is much easier to build up backgrounds than personalities from the documents on which the historian depends. In this matter *Phillip of Australia* is both an example and an exception. One must not, of course, forget the sub-title, "An Account of the Settlement at Sydney Cove 1788-92"; and though Phillip remains the centre, this book contains a good deal that is foreign to a biography: much of the chapters on The Voyage, Justice and the Courts, The Church, Parties of Pleasure, The Natives, and Norfolk Island is only very indirectly connected with Phillip; and the arrangement of the chapter on The Struggle for Existence as an annual chronicle, as with Collins, suggests what is the actual fact, that it is not so much Phillip as the life of the settlement that is being here recorded; all this involves a lack of unity in the book. On the other hand, as will be seen, the character and personality of Phillip are here re-created more vividly than by any other historian; the only such re-creation that can be compared with it occurs in a novel, Eleanor Dark's *The Timeless Land*. It is true that more actual facts about Phillip have been accumulated by Mackaness than by Barnard Eldershaw; but apart from her novelist's gift of characterization, by temperament as well as by deliberate purpose she is concerned not with facts merely as such, but with facts as representing the general principles and human qualities that lie behind them: the result is that her description of the preparations for the voyage of the First Fleet, and of Phillip's attempts to improve and organize them; of the voyage itself; of the settlement, the struggle for existence and the rest: however much they may extend beyond any biographical purpose, are refreshing, after so many other accounts, full or in outline. They are refreshing, not so much because of any new material they introduce, but largely because they take us away from a world of documents and summaries to the human world of which these are only one expression; from a world of more or less isolated facts to what the facts represent, the currents and colouring of human life: in all this one may perhaps infer something of the influence of that most human of historians, the late Professor Wood, of whom both collaborators are admirers, and to whom their book is dedicated. They make clear the absurdity of the assertion that Phillip was no more than a man of ordinary quality, who contrived by perseverance to make something of a great opportunity; that his choice was in fact one of the luckiest that a British minister ever made. He was[1]

> . . . a man of outstanding ability, an unusual man in his own or any day. He had that steadiness of mind that can embrace the most trivial detail without losing sight of the main issues; he had imaginative grasp allied with the most uncompromising commonsense; he was completely honest. Lord Sydney met a granite wall of competence under his Captain General's quiet exterior. In the months that followed his appointment he forged not only the practical details but the theory of the undertaking. He conceived a "Colony of Disgracefuls" as an empire. . . . He took a criminal folly and made of it a reputable and enduring settlement.

This may go a little beyond what is definitely ascertainable, but a bold creation that seems probable is better than a figure of dry sawdust[2] built wholly upon ascertained fact. Barnard Eldershaw makes us realize how but for Phillip's foresight, his organizing and administrative powers, his self-control, his impartial justice, his power of keeping his head in a crisis, the First Settlement might well have failed: Phillip, the whole man, is never focused for us however; his character is scattered through the text: it may be that Barnard Eldershaw considered that this was as it should be. Most of the principal figures in the story are sketched, lightly but realistically so far as they go, or so far as the facts will allow them to go, and always illuminatively: Ross, that "man of aggravating rather than strong character"; the "cultivated and charming" Tench, an ingrained optimist who saw no more than he wanted to see; Collins, with "the ability, shared with Phillip, of seeing even the most controversial events in a dry light and of judging them on their merits"; Johnson, "a typical young parson of his day": Barnard Eldershaw could make even a dull story interesting by her manner of telling it, and this story is at the farthest extreme from dullness, though elsewhere it has often

[1] p. 26.

[2] This is not intended to suggest that, for instance, Mackaness's Phillip is a figure of dry sawdust, but he is not a living creation like the Phillip of Barnard Eldershaw.

been told dully. It flashes into something approaching epigram at times: "A rash of discontents broke out in the first fortnight"; "Tench's anecdotes are like dew-ponds in an arid waste"; Ross was "a natural focus for storms"; "there is a touch of the Swiss Family Robinson about the whole affair" of the First Settlement. In this book again, as in quite a number of the Australian novels of the day and in particular in *The Timeless Land* and Eldershaw's own *Tomorrow and Tomorrow*, Australia appears, in her relations with her invaders:[3]

> . . . the most mysterious country in the world, the most elusive, the most difficult for Europeans to comprehend and utilize . . . a land that resisted them inch by inch, not unfruitful, but with the secret of its fertility locked away from them because it was not the kind of fertility they were used to—a great amorphous resistance against which, till they learned its ways, they were helpless. . . . To the newcomers it was "the woods", and it was the bush that was the true possessor and holder of the country against them. . . . One square mile of bush was like another square mile, clueless, a sea of green, with here and there the contorted silvery limbs of a tree standing out in a sort of petrified agony. . . . The eucalypts have beauty, but Phillip's men could not see it. They have a proud grace, a delicate, fugitive outline, pencilled on space, so that when the full light strikes them they seem to tremble into air. . . . It was a quarter of a century before [the conqueror's] eyes could see the deathless beauty of the landscape that is like no other in the world, find the infinite variety in its monotony, the colour in its monotone.

Mackaness's *Admiral Arthur Phillip: Founder of New South Wales, 1738–1814* (Sydney, 1937) and his *The Life of Vice-Admiral William Bligh, R.N., F.R.S.* (Sydney, 1931) are as different as possible from Barnard Eldershaw's work; they do not re-create the man or his time, but they present a great bulk of material, much of it new and some of it not easy of access. George Mackaness[4] (Sydney, 1882–1968), a Doctor of Letters of the Universities of Melbourne and Sydney, was for many years Lecturer in Charge of the Department of English at the Sydney Teachers' College and a member of the Advisory Board of the Commonwealth Literary Fund: his *Phillip* is by far the better of the two books; it tells a comparatively simple story clearly, and the "Final Estimate" is excellent; the *Bligh*, though it amasses an immense amount of information, is verbose and repetitive and full of journalistic clichés[5] which are comparatively rare in the other. But both books are valuable to the student of the times and their principal characters, and in particular as guides to the literature on their subjects.

---

[3] pp. 93–7.

[4] For Mackaness's anthologies, see pp. 506, 1076, 1261.

[5] They are most plentiful in connection with the mutiny and its causes. The sailors form "tender connexions with the dusky damsels" (p. 179) of "this fair island set in southern seas" (p. 17), and are "anxious to drain Otaheitan pleasure to the lees" (p. 163).

Lachlan Macquarie, His Life, Adventures and Times[6] (Sydney, 1947) was a labour of love and enthusiasm that filled the spare time of twenty years, and in it Malcolm Henry Ellis (Narine, Q., 1890–1969), better known as "Ek Dum" of the *Bulletin*, does Macquarie full justice, sometimes perhaps a little more. Macquarie's enthusiastic energy and devotion to duty; his dignity, increasingly self-conscious; his pride, increasingly irascible under the strain of the task that wore him down as it had worn down his predecessors; his sensitiveness, which was wounded by the slightest opposition; and above all his fundamental kindness and humanity: all these appear, in a full-length picture painted in extremely bright colours, against the large, varied, effervescent and extremely difficult background of the unformed, untamed colony, full of vehement incompatible desires and punctuated by rebellious oppositions, not all of which were wholly selfish, though to the biographer they usually appear so. Amidst all this Macquarie is shown directing his difficult course, by no means without fault, but on the whole with statesmanlike devotion; and other figures, Macarthur, the Bents, Marsden, stand out also, though not strongly: vigorous personalities, as to whom there will have to be further analyses of fact and motive before the standard life and times of Macquarie can appear. On the side of expression this book has however serious faults: there is no doubt about its scholarship, but there are occasional doubtful assertions[7] and the scholar is in unfortunate partnership with a journalist who sometimes uses meretricious artificialities, melodrama, clichés and cheap humour; still, the book's merits remain. The question whether biography and history should be written with any object except the revelation of fact and the re-creation of times, persons and institutions is raised by *Sir John Franklin in Tasmania* (Melbourne, 1949). The author, Kathleen (Elizabeth) Fitzpatrick (Omeo, Vic., 1905–), was educated at the Universities of Melbourne and Oxford and is Associate Professor of History at Melbourne. Franklin has generally been thought of as the romantic hero of the attempt at the "North-West Passage", and his six years' governorship of Tasmania has been ignored or regarded with sympathy but as a failure due to a sensitiveness and refinement which made him unfit for such an undertaking; in this book, based on research into material some of which had been hitherto unavailable, Professor Fitzpatrick shows that Franklin was the victim of conscienceless self-seeking with which he was constitutionally unable to cope, and that his treatment

[6] This was awarded the Harbison-Higinbotham Award. In an earlier form it was delivered as a John Murtagh Macrossan Memorial Lecture in the University of Queensland, and awarded the *Bulletin's* Prior Memorial Prize. Ellis has been elected a Fellow of the Royal Historical Society and the Royal Australian Historical Society and has been awarded the C.M.G., for his contribution to Australian literature. His other publications include biographies of Greenway and Macarthur.

[7] As for instance the assertion that Macarthur was "purely . . . by nature an expositor of other people's notions".

generally and his final dismissal from the colonial service "like an office-boy without a character" were grossly unjust. This is the work of a counsel for the defence; but if it is occasionally obvious that no effort has been neglected to make the most of Franklin's case, it is also obvious that the counsel is just and equitable within the limits of her brief.

In *Australian Labour Leader: The Story of W. A. Holman and the Labour Movement* (Sydney, 1940) the sub-title comes nearest to describing the book: actually, it tells the story of Labour from its entry into politics until the death of Holman, and of Holman almost solely as a political leader and the centre of the Labour movement in New South Wales. As such, the book, in spite of certain defects, seems likely to remain the standard authority on its subject for many years: it gives the best account so far of political Australia during one of the most interesting and vital periods of Australian history and the only account, so far, of Holman's life. Its author, Herbert Vere Evatt (Maitland, N.S.W., 1894-1965), was a Justice of the High Court, Leader of the Opposition in the Federal Parliament, and then became Chief Justice of New South Wales; he had a career as brilliant as that of any writer mentioned here: his course at Fort Street High School and the University of Sydney was studded with medals and, apart from his legal and political achievements, he represented Australia in many capacities abroad, and also published other, though lesser, political and historical works which are mentioned elsewhere, and a legal work of importance.[8] This book is based on private letters and old newspaper files, and on memories of friends and associates and parliamentary officials as well as on Holman's unpublished memoirs and on documents deposited by him with the Mitchell Library. After a short introductory outline of the circumstances in which Labour decided to abandon direct for political action and of the part played by Holman in bringing about that decision, the institution of the Labour pledge and the need for it, and the introduction of "gradualism", which thrust the party's social objectives into the background and laid emphasis upon the fighting platform which had a far wider appeal, the main business of the book begins. We see Labour in the New South Wales Parliament, at first as a third party, giving its support in return for concessions, and then in opposition; its gradual increase in parliamentary membership, its attainment of office, to which it clung for some time only by its fingertips and by means of the astute generalship of Holman, its *de facto* leader; at the same time we see the gradual growth of the federal movement, the part played in this also by Holman, and by Hughes: their co-operation and then their rivalry. Holman's many-sided genius is well brought out: his immense and fundamentally unselfish labours, his extraordinarily attractive personality,

---

[8] See pp. 1348 and 1440-1.

his persuasive and oratorical power, his idealism and generosity, along with a strategic and tactical ability that amounted at times to an artfulness in which he delighted for its own sake. Evatt brings out also that intellectual, aristocratic and even remote quality in Holman which sometimes aroused suspicion and even enmity; and along with these qualities a loyal but not invariably merited trust in his colleagues that caused him to be associated with actions that were not his own and got him into serious trouble now and then; and his difficulty in realizing that others, except a few of his bitterest opponents, could be without his honesty and sincerity of purpose. All these characteristics are used to build up an image of Holman which makes one feel, as for a hero of romance, the tragedy of his decline; indeed Holman may easily be regarded as a romantic hero, and actually he was at bottom romantic, though in politics he was also, with lapses, a realist; Evatt however is a thoroughgoing realist and records without bias, in spite of his sympathy with Holman, all his faults as well as his merits, and he is quite as much interested in the party that Holman led and finally abandoned as in the man himself. As to this abandonment:[9]

> The departure of Holman and Hughes from the Labour organizations which they have so largely created and moulded raises a general problem affecting many social democratic organizations. Can there ever be real justification for the Labour leader leaving his party? What is the cause of such a disaster?
>
> . . . .
>
> . . . black treachery is most rare, and the disastrous results of division and split may be caused as much by lack of loyalty to a chosen leader as by the leader's failure to appreciate that his primary duty is to the working classes whose sacrifices have enabled the political organization to succeed. In the particular case, whatever the cause, the leader is lost. He rarely, if ever, returns to the party. Even then, the tragedy is incomplete. For the leader's social or radical background is seldom shifted and, for a time at least, he may succeed in repelling the attacks his new conservative allies desire to make upon working-class legislation or standards. He may even appear to have "converted" such allies to Labour or radical ideas. But the pressure from the Right gradually increases and the leader must surrender to its demands or go out of politics. If he remains, he may surrender with indecent readiness or perhaps with undying resentment. If he abandons politics, his fate is denunciation by his new allies of the Right, unsoftened by forgiveness from his old comrades of the Left. Finally comes the annihilating realization that he should never have abandoned the cause which he first espoused. In that is the element of great tragedy.

Evatt thinks that Holman's most important contribution to Australian life was perhaps "his bold establishment of State industrial enterprises in competition with private concerns",[10] and he shows that they were in the main successful. The most interesting and perhaps the most valuable parts of the book are the short introduction with its important generaliza-

---

[9] pp. 3-4; all quotations here are from the 1942 edition of Evatt's book.
[10] See, for detail, Chapter LXVII of the biography.

tions, and the final chapter, Judgment, with its analysis of Holman's character and the comparison with Hughes. But the other characters in the story, to whatever party they belonged, are also brought alive: Hughes of course, though no mere sketch could do him justice; and such others as Reid, Wise, Wade and McGowen, though it may be questioned whether Evatt is fair to Reid. The account of the underlying motives of the supporters of the federal movement may also be questioned, at least so far as concerns the most outstanding of its leaders and the great majority of the rank and file: it was a young man's movement, in that it appealed largely to youth and idealistic enthusiasm. The assertion that Holman was "probably the greatest orator to whom Australia ever listened", and that Deakin lacked "capacity for enthusiasm or indignation", the coupling of Deakin with Lyne as having a "hunger for office" and the allusion to Deakin as having "aways posed as Labour's friend": these are quite indefensible. On the side of literary form also *Australian Labour Leader* stands out above most of the biographies of the Period: the extract quoted does not do justice to the illuminative phrases with which the story occasionally sparkles; few of these are Evatt's own, but he had a fine ear for a good phrase. There was his account of Holman's attempt to "rationalize political tendencies from the point of view of a Leftist turned half-Right"; and Holman's assertion that "the attractiveness of a public career varies with the reverse of the square of the distance at which it has to be carried on"; there was the phrase so often quoted against Holman, which he was once careless enough to apply to a Labour supporter who has purported to witness a signature without verifying it, that he was "a well-meaning enthusiast"; and there was the really brilliant remark, which Evatt ascribes to "the political roundsman", at a time when Holman was leader of the government in all but name: that "McGowen led the parliamentary Labour Party as the headlight leads the Melbourne Express". One or two other biographies are at least as notable for their scholarship, and, though none can compete with Barnard Eldershaw's from a purely literary point of view, behind this book there is a weight of personality that is not possessed by any of them.

A good deal has been written about statesmen and politicians, from Wentworth to Hughes and from Australia to Papua and even Japan; but only the Japanese biography can be regarded as full-dress and perhaps, at least as regards Australia, final. *William Charles Wentworth*[11] (Brisbane, 1934), by Alexander Clifford Vernon Melbourne (Adelaide, 1888-1943), is an excellent short summary of the part played by Wentworth in the constitutional development of New South Wales and Australia; but it

[11] This book represents an expansion of the John Murtagh Macrossan Memorial Lecture for 1932. For Melbourne's other work, see pp. 1441, 1442-3.

sketches also his early life, and the circumstances, so long avoided, of his father's emigration to Australia and of his own birth, and it examines the manner in which his father's association with the emancipist faction influenced the first part of his political career; it shows also the fallacy in the charge of political inconsistency that has been so often made against Wentworth: "I will not admit," Melbourne quotes him as saying, in defence against such a charge, made in his lifetime,

> . . . that I commenced my life . . . a Republican, that I became in middle age a Whig, and that I shall die a Conservative. . . . I shall die with Conservative principles; but . . . I deny emphatically that I was ever a democrat or a republican.

Melbourne grants, of course, Wentworth's love of power, but, he adds

> . . . he consistently associated power with service. . . . He wished to establish the influence of his own class because he thought democracy would destroy the colony; and he was not dissimulating when he claimed that the love of country had been the master passion of his life.

Melbourne was educated at the University of Adelaide, served with the A.I.F. in the first World War, and became Associate Professor of History in the University of Queensland.

Papua has been lucky in her administrators, and in particular Sir William MacGregor, who brought the country into something like law and order, and Sir Hubert Murray, who carried the process a stage farther and systematized its administration; Lett's *Sir Hubert Murray of Papua* (Sydney, 1949) will probably remain the standard life for some time.* Lewis Lett[12] (Waddingham, Lincolnshire, England, 1878-1966) had lived in Papua for thirty years; he had been Superintendent Engineer of the British New Guinea Development Company, a prospector for petroleum, a manager of a couple of local companies. His biography, which is based on Murray's diaries and on information supplied by his brother Sir Gilbert Murray and by other relatives and friends, is detailed and scholarly, and at the same time enlivened by incidents and descriptions which illustrate the difficulties Murray had to face: internal, in the more savage of the natives themselves and in those of his own officers who were offended by his strictness; and external, as the result of variations in Australian political policy and support. Like MacGregor, Murray was a man of physique as exceptional as his strength of character;[13] he was reserved and aloof, unyielding on a matter of principle or on which he had made up his mind; and yet, like some other strong men, sensitive, and in his later years apt to be distrustful of people who were actually his supporters: Lett tells of his immense labours, and how he

* [But see Francis West: *Hubert Murray: Australian Pro-consul* (Melb., 1968), and *Selected Letters* (Melb., 1970).]

[12] Lett's *Savage Tales* is discussed on p. 1255; he has written a number of other works on Papua.

[13] As a young man he had been amateur champion heavyweight boxer of England.

yet found time for wide reading. He was determined that justice should be done to the natives, and that they should learn to trust and respect white men; he carried the policy of indirect rule which MacGregor had introduced to Papua a stage farther, appointing in addition to MacGregor's village constables, counsellors with whom the magistrates must consult. He realized the need for native labour, but

> . . . the conditions of employment must be such that natives would engage willingly, and would learn to find in labour, for themselves or for others, an outlet for their energy and a reason for living to replace the warlike occupations of which the Government had deprived them;

this did not at all suit some of the planters, yet there was no doubt about Murray's popularity among white as well as black.[14] Murray's attitude to the relationship of the two races was thoroughly realistic. Lett says: "While he refuses to regard black and white as necessarily antagonistic, he also refuses to claim for the native Papuans social equality with their white overlords."

> A black man is not a white man, and there is no use pretending that he is, or in trying to believe that both must be treated in exactly the same way. The facts of race and colour are as stubborn as any other facts, but it would be fatal to regard the recognition of those facts as irreconcilable with unity of administration.

Incidentally, Lett tells some excellent stories: particularly that of the disreputable character who was furious when Murray refused him a recruiting licence, but perfectly satisfied when Murray informed him that it was because he was "a drunkard, a thief and a libertine":

> "Oh, is that the reason?" he said. "Of course that is all right. I thought it was because I am a Greek. And I came to tell you that it was the Greeks who civilised Europe."

The Japanese biography was written by an Englishman during his twenty-six years' occupation of the Chair of Oriental Studies at the University of Sydney; he afterwards returned to England; Arthur Lindsay Sadler (London, 1882–*c.*1966) had been educated at Oxford and lived for some time in Japan; he wrote on Japanese art, architecture and history, and translated some Japanese plays and texts; but *The Maker of Modern Japan: The Life of Tokugawa Ieyasu* (London, 1937) seems the most likely to be remembered. Here again, an important factor in the interest of the book is its subject, for although the author's enthusiasm carries him rather far when he describes Ieyasu as "unquestionably one of the greatest men the world has yet seen", he was no doubt among the foremost examples of his type: the dictator, in the political, military or business world, whose success is based upon subtle and astute diplomacy, a thorough understanding of human nature, so far as it affects himself or his plans, and a general observance of the practical

[14] See, facing pp. 288 and 289, facsimiles of addresses presented, one by the blacks and one by the whites, on Murray's completion of thirty years of office.

principles that animated the princes of Renaissance Italy and still animate some of the leaders in the modern business world. These principles are illustrated by the maxims in the "Legacy" which Ieyasu left for the benefit of his successors in the shogunate; in these, says Sadler,

> Sometimes he is purely didactic and rather conservative, while at others he exhibits his very shrewd insight into human nature and his rational plans for taking advantage of it. Again, he will strike the note of benevolence, and even go so far as to stand up in the pulpit and proclaim himself a model of single-minded altruism and loving-kindness that merit the admiration and imitation of posterity. And since he can hardly have been lacking in a sense of proportion, he may well have stepped down again with a grin.

But it must be remembered that the benevolence which bulks so large in these maxims is quite frankly a means to an end; Ieyasu says:

> If the golden rule that what one does not like oneself is not to be done to others be not forgotten, the inferior will be influenced by this good example, and not only vassals but the whole Empire will become docile as water.

Another of his maxims, which has a wider than its obvious reference:

> The right use of a sword is that it shall subdue the barbarians while lying gleaming in its scabbard. If it leaves its sheath it cannot be said to be used rightly.

Sadler shows that Ieyasu was an organizer rather than a creator, but that "taking all in all, it is he who made the system under which Japan as we know it was forged into shape". Like certain other makers of world history he had to start if not at the bottom at least near it; but he succeeded by means of a combination of diplomatic subtlety and military genius, an utter fearlessness of anything seen or unseen, extreme cruelty and unscrupulousness,[15] an inflexibility that did not prevent him from yielding when it seemed desirable, a complete self-control, and a cautiousness and sleepless vigilance that made it almost impossible to catch him off his guard. Sadler's is a hurried and rather careless style; the sentences are long and involved and so crowded with detail that it is not always easy to keep pace with the author; it is as far as possible from the dramatic, getting its effects by means of implication and a quiet but all-pervasive humour. In his preface, Sadler seizes the opportunity handed to him on a plate with parsley round it by some particularly simple reviewer, who had observed of another Japanese work that it was a pity it contained so many Japanese names; to this Sadler drily rejoins that "this is now a world in which it may be advisable to get used to them, for unquestionably people of the land of Nippon will always have Japanese names". As drily, when a lady complains that her husband has "cut off the nose and ears of her foster-mother because she opposed him in some trifling

[15] "He . . . put his eldest son to death to keep political faith with Nobunaga" (p. 18); yet "while shaking hands with Hideyoshi he was meditating a closer alliance with Hojo" (p. 24).

matter", Sadler remarks that "he must have been a trying companion"; and, speaking of Japan's treatment of Western missionaries and conquistadores, "None have ever shown themselves more skilful than the Japanese in licking off the bait of knowledge and leaving the hook of fanaticism standing naked." In its strict chronological arrangement and in its masses of names that are without associations for most readers this book has some resemblance to a Norse saga, but there the resemblance ends: the sentences in a saga are for the most part short and sharp, leaving detail to the imagination; also, the sagas, like their makers and their subjects, were comparatively simple, and though the Norsemen could be cruel enough they were nothing like so cruel as the comparatively "civilized" Japanese.[16] The book has a particular interest for Australians in that in Ieyasu we are made intimately acquainted with "a very perfect example of a type that Japanese nationality and training tend to produce".

To return to Australian politics: *Crusts and Crusades* (Sydney, 1947) and *Policies and Potentates* (Sydney, 1950) are strings of reminiscences, bright and amusing however hard the facts, from the long life of "Billy" (William Morris) Hughes (London, 1864-1952), afterwards Prime Minister of Australia and her representative at the Versailles Peace Conference. Whatever his birthplace, irrepressibly Australian, we see Hughes here as swagman, shearer, stone-breaker and stage soldier, living in a cave in the Domain and being cook's assistant in a restaurant. He tells of the days when Labour was a religious movement, and yet knew how to arrange an election as well as any other political party, and how when Kitchener objected to having an Australian nominee in the War Office (partly) on the ground of his low military rank Hughes immediately made his nominee a general. There are some lively personal sketches, though not so sharp as Deakin's,[17] and a number of good things: the Italian fruiterer's political suggestion, "Parliament no good; one little bomb very good"; and John Haynes's description of the coat of arms of a political opponent, a squatter in private life, as "a branding iron and a moonless night". Best of all perhaps is the story of the Irish cane-cutters on the Northern Rivers, old friends of Billy's, who, hearing that he was standing for parliament, threw up their jobs and rushed to Sydney to give him the whole of their savings, £150, to help him in his election campaign. *George Swinburne* (Sydney, 1931), by (the Reverend) Edward Holdsworth Sugden (Sheffield, Yorkshire, England, 1854-1935), late Master of Queen's College, Melbourne, and (Sir) Frederick William Eggleston (Melbourne, 1875-1954), a former Victorian cabinet minister and diplomatic representative of the Commonwealth, involves a detailed

[16] See for example the previous note, and the incident described on p. 99.

[17] See pp. 831-5.

history of Victorian public affairs in the beginning of the century, with many of which the subject of the biography was involved. It is redeemed from parochiality by the bearing of its principal episodes upon political problems generally, and by Eggleston's[18] practical knowledge of his subject and his occasional succinct analyses in precisely the right words.[19]

The subjects of two other biographies were not politicians in the ordinary sense of the word, but their work was inseparable from the political life of their times, and indeed from Australia's political and social history. Nettie Palmer's[20] *Henry Bournes Higgins: A Memoir* (London, 1931) shows the development of its subject not only personally but as belonging to a community that itself was rapidly developing, though from his boyhood in Ireland Higgins is revealed as essentially the same character and animated by the same principles that distinguished him later as the President and largely the maker of the Federal Arbitration Court, and, in effect, the establisher of the basic wage. Mrs Palmer sketches the Melbourne of the day and beyond that the State of which it was the capital, and even the continent: the gradual supersession of colonialism by nationalism, the opening up of the great estates, the social experiments, the entry of Labour into politics, its early behaviour in the political sphere, and the long struggle for Federation. She tells—and this, though she does not say so, is an example of the breadth of feeling of the day, as well as of the incomplete development of the caucus system—how a Labour Prime Minister[21] invited Higgins to become a member of his cabinet, though he was not a member of the party, and how as a result of Higgins's interpretation of the phrase "fair and reasonable" in the famous Harvester Case the principle of the living wage was established and its amount for that day laid down; Higgins's scrupulous integrity, his democratic and nationalist sympathies, and the wide range of his abilities, his interests and his reading are also shown. Part of an address on "The Muses in Australia" which he delivered to the University Society in 1885 is pertinent here; Higgins said,

> The powerful feelings which are the only birthplace of true poetry are confined to no class or kind of society, and are as plentiful in places which have not any historical associations as in those which have.

But the kind of Australian poetry which would have importance in the future

---

[18] Sugden was responsible only for that part of the book which deals with Swinburne's private life.

[19] For example, "What was most impressive was the spring of his [Swinburne's] mind on to an idea" (p. 65), and "The laws of responsible government are like the laws of war; everybody knows them but few carry them out, mainly because they lack courage" (p. 88).

[20] For Nettie Palmer's other biographical work, see pp. 1358–60; for her short-story anthology, p. 1261; for her essays, p. 1284; for her literary criticism, pp. 1294–5; for her poems, pp. 496–7.

[21] Watson.

> . . . must be distinctively Australian in tone. . . . [At the same time] Let us not praise a thing merely because it is Australian; but let us not sneer at anything Australian as "colonial".

Here may be noted the curious assumption, common enough until quite lately, that "historical" must mean historical along old-world lines; and the contention, necessary in a day in which old-world models were still widely considered the only models worth following, that Australian literature must be distinctively Australian in tone; we are only emerging from that necessity today. In arrangement this book is smooth and straightforward, so that one thing seems to flow naturally out of another; in style it is clear and logical, quiet rather than dramatic, sometimes even a little flat. As important, perhaps, from the point of view of its subject and his influence, though not in other respects, is *William Lane and the Australian Labor Movement* (Sydney, 1937). Its author, Lloyd (Maxwell) Ross[22] (Brisbane, 1901-), is a graduate of the University of Melbourne, which awarded him a Doctorate of Literature for his work on the Labour movement. He has been Secretary of the New South Wales branch of the Australian Railways Union and was Director of Public Relations in the Federal Department of Post-War Reconstruction, Australian delegate to the Pacific Relations Conference in Canada in 1942, and Australian representative in the Ministry of Information in Britain in 1943. The book contains a great deal of useful information about the New Australia experiment in Paraguay, its social causes and the character and personality of Lane himself; but it is not well arranged and is at times inconsistent and even careless;[23] some assertions are hard to check because they are not documented,[24] and there are a few obvious errors.[25] The book as a whole is enlightening however, and from it emerge what seem to be the fundamental reasons for the failure of the experiment: Lane's idealization of the Queensland workers, which made him expect too much of them; the difficult conditions, especially in the second colony; and Lane's growing tendency towards a rather tactless despotism. But his selfless enthusiasm and compelling fascination are felt, and it is made clear that he and his followers were not deserters

---

[22] He is also represented in *Best Australian One-Act Plays*.

[23] On p. 3, for instance, Ross speaks of the eagerness of spirit and zest for life of Australians in "the nineties", but on p. 12 he refers to the pessimism of this period, to the need for social change, and to the despair of those who could see no way of escape. This is followed by a number of literary illustrations, at the head of which is Favenc's *The Last of Six*, which is asserted to contain "no gleam of cheerfulness;" this will surprise readers of "The Parson's Blackboy", "Tranter's Shot" and "The Rumford Plains Tragedy".

[24] Such as the extremely improbable assertion that Deakin was willing to shoot down strikers (p. 147) and that Lawson, who is represented as being thoroughly in sympathy with the New Australia movement, "wanted to stow away on the 'Royal Tar' ".

[25] Such as the reference to Professor "Guy le Brereton" of the university of which Ross was Assistant Director of Tutorial Classes.

from the Labour movement, but aimed at teaching Australia and the world a lesson by showing what could actually be done.

The subjects of the remaining biographies include a priest, a man of science, a pioneer pastoralist, and one of Australia's most eminent women. In *The Life and Letters of Archpriest John Joseph Therry: Founder of The Catholic Church in Australia* (Sydney, 1922), which was reprinted in the same year as *The Foundation of Catholicism in Australia*,[26] the life-work of the principal character is again inseparable from at least a large part of the life of the community in which it was carried on. The author, Dr Eris O'Brien, whose purely historical work is discussed elsewhere,[27] has written a human and sympathetic but unbiased study, based on a thorough and painstaking examination of letters and diaries by Therry and others, early newspapers and official and private documents, of the man who in spite of much injustice and innumerable obstacles, some of them largely of his own creation, founded the Roman Catholic Church in Australia. It is pleasant to find that Therry's supporters included a number of leading Protestants. Another Irish-Australian work, which covers lightly a wider sphere, was *Australia's Debt to Irish Nation-Builders* (Sydney, 1933), by Patrick Scott Cleary (Bendigo, Vic., 1861-1941), editor for nineteen years of the Sydney *Catholic Press*. Protestants as well as Roman Catholics are included, and the book is interesting and often amusing, apart from its value as a contribution to Australian history; Cleary's net is stretched rather wide, however, and some of his estimates are rather highly coloured. *Professor David* (London, 1937), by his daughter, Mary Edgeworth David (Mrs W. K. McIntyre, Maitland, N.S.W.), commemorates one of the most distinguished figures in the Australian scientific world of his day; as a man he was equally distinguished, and apart from the record of his achievements, geological and other, here he lives again, particularly to those who knew him. His magnetic and inspiring personality and ringing voice, the untiring energy that enabled him at nearly fifty to lead the expedition to the southern Magnetic Pole, and at fifty-eight to act as Geologist with the Australian Mining Battalion in the first World War; his courage and humour and unfailing kindness and courtesy; the romantic idealism that was accompanied by a very thorough and practical efficiency; and also the incurable absentmindedness that was yet consistent with keen powers of observation: all these characteristics are illustrated by anecdotes. The spirit of this simple and straightforward biography is one of hero-worship, but it would be difficult for anyone who had known David to write of him in any other spirit. *Christison of Lammermoor* (London, 1927), by his daughter, Marie Montgomerie (Mrs C. D.) Bennett, tells of a man who is remembered as a defender of the

[26] With the sub-title, "Being the Life and Letters of John Joseph Therry".

[27] See pp. 1339-40.

Aborigines, whom he trusted, and who deserved the trust: not that Christison took any risk however; building his homestead on the land he had taken up,

> As he made a clearing against ambush and fire, so he made loop-holes in the walls for rifles,—"not that they will be wanted," he told [the man who was helping him], "but we ought to be ready."

And then, like Governor Phillip, he captured an Aborigine, made friends with him, and used him as an intermediary with his tribe; the friendship lasted throughout both their lives. But all this represents only one aspect of Christison's life and character: his daughter tells, basing her story on his letters and diaries, how, without capital, struggling through drought and floods and working often fourteen hours in the saddle, he "eventually worked up Lammermoor and Cameron Downs into two of the finest stations in Australia"; she tells how he was one of the early bore sinkers and supporters of the frozen meat industry. Christison's life was full of striking episodes, one of which recalls the forestalling episode in Boldrewood's *The Squatter's Dream* except that Christison anticipated and got the better of the forestaller. *Caroline Chisholm* (Melbourne, 1950), by Margaret (Loch) Kiddle (Melbourne, 1914-58) was the first full-length biography of the woman who played a greater part than any other in Australian social history. Mrs Kiddle was a graduate of the University of Melbourne, in which she was a tutor in Australian History; her researches uncovered much new material, though unfortunately Mrs Chisholm's private papers could not be traced. Her own accounts of some of her most picturesque experiences are drawn upon: her first night in the rat-riddled old barracks that was the origin of her Female Emigrants' Home, and her trips up country with drayloads of girls for whom she was seeking situations; but not her equally picturesque character-sketches of some of these girls. There are full descriptions of the series of obstacles she had to overcome: governmental and general apathy; the inveterate prejudice against the intervention of women in public affairs; the opposition of the squatters, who wanted cheap labour, not people who might in a few years be able to take up holdings of their own; and the opposition of the churches, the Protestants being afraid lest she might proselytize in favour of her own faith, and the Roman Catholics lest she might not. But we are shown how her persevering determination and persuasive power, her indefatigable and entirely selfless labours, her businesslike common sense and organizing ability were such that she overcame all of these obstacles, and succeeded in practically all her schemes. The book is well organized and clearly written; but, although an excellent record of facts, it seldom goes beyond the fact and is particularly weak in characterization.

Two biographical collections may be grouped together as such, though they were quite different in kind. *Founders and Pioneers of South Australia* (Adelaide, 1929) by Archibald Grenfell Price (Adelaide, 1892–1977), Master of St Mark's College, the University of Adelaide, geographer, historian and educationalist, consists of lives upon which fresh information had become available. Wakefield, Light, Sturt, Angas and others are presented from a more or less fresh point of view, with an enthusiasm that is yet by no means uncritical; Price's previous book, *The Foundation and Settlement of South Australia* (Adelaide, 1924), had covered a wider range. Light was also the subject of a biography by Mary Penelope Mayo (Adelaide, 1889–1969), a graduate of the University of Adelaide. *Life and Letters of Colonel William Light* (Adelaide, 1937) is a sympathetic recital of the facts of Light's life, some of them hitherto unknown, but his story is not told realistically and neither he nor Hindmarsh nor any of the other characters comes to life. Vance Palmer's *National Portraits* (Sydney, 1940) sketches the character and life-work of men who have played a leading part in the historical, social or economic development of the continent: this is a work of popularization rather than scholarship, depending almost entirely on secondary sources; it is journalism, but literary journalism of the best kind. In some cases, of which Lawson is the most obvious, all that can be said in so short a compass has been said elsewhere; but in others, and particularly that of Batman, large, naive and exuberant, overflowing with life and schemes, the man comes freshly alive. And Palmer quotes a number of good things, as of Macarthur's "cold but turbulent spirit"; of Marsden, who "prays for our souls on Sundays and takes it out of our bodies during the rest of the week"; and of the painter, Buvelot, who "wore the clothes of a peasant and had the look of a king".

The descriptive or mainly descriptive works of the Period fall into several well-marked groups. There are the stories of adventure, true, however imaginatively recorded; there are a number of accounts of patrols, largely explorative, by government administrative officers of Papua and New Guinea;[28] these are fascinating, and but for their importance as records they might well be included among the stories of adventure; and there are descriptions of parts of outback Australia in various aspects: some of these are written from an aesthetic or mainly aesthetic point of view; others, dealing with the country as a whole, or with large parts of the lesser known outback, deal with the land itself and the human types it produces. Most of the books of this last type merely run over the human and natural landscape, so to speak, seldom digging beneath the surface; but one, Barnard Eldershaw's *My Australia* (London,

---

[28] It should be noted that what was formerly British New Guinea is now called Papua, and that what was formerly German New Guinea is now called New Guinea. But either term is sometimes applied to the island as a whole!

1939), whose various aspects look in upon various classifications, goes farther. The land is too big, and its marked individuality too many-sided and largely yet unrealized, and the effects that this individuality has had upon its inhabitants are at present too inchoate to be more than in part reflected in any picture; but *My Australia* is a sketch for such a picture, and it is natural therefore that it should lack organic unity. Sharp and often piercing observations, poetic descriptions, reflections, speculations, lie thickly scattered about a structure that is not one but several, though connected and on the same ground-plan. First a "Mask for Inaudible Voices", mystic and futuristic; then, under the heading "New World", "a shape of history, a review of the raw material from which we shall mould our future". Barnard Eldershaw discovers "two eras of experimentation", from the beginnings to the gold discoveries and from these to the first World War; after them there is beginning a third, "an era of experiment along national reconstructive lines" which "is still a matter of faith rather than works": "within these two arcs there have been three cycles of power, each of which has produced [its] oligarchy"; military, pastoral, and that of capital and finance. Then comes the question whether there will be a democratic recoil against the third oligarchy, for

> It is clear that democracy is threatened in Australia, that we are letting slip the past without laying strong hands on the future;

and next, under the heading "Old World", comes the land itself, with its influences: we have a series of glimpses of their foci in the great and hugely varying scenic panorama. We go on to hear of man's struggle with the land; there is a chapter upon the aborigines and their culture; and a final chapter on the precursors of a white Australian culture, its traditional overshadowings, the stereotypes of oversea fashions, its beginnings in painting and literature and so on, "the exposed peaks of a submerged continent", its attempts at a revelation of the still nascent Australian spirit:

> Like everything else here, culture had to begin from scratch. The combination of the Anglo-Saxon race and the Australian soil was something new in the world's history. Certain forms of expression have been arbitrarily labelled cultural: art, music, literature. . . . But it goes deeper than that. The first stage, the seed-bed of culture, is an attitude to life, a partaking of life. . . .
>
> . . . .
>
> Culture is deeper and broader than any of its manifestations. Its ultimate expression and, indeed, the final creation of any people is the national character. In the last resort we must stand or fall by what we are.

Among the series of glimpses of the Australian countryside there is this, of the Riverina:

> Largely deforested, the contours of the land are revealed, pure smooth lines of little hills, brown or green as the seasons change, with here and there a timbered or rocky ridge. There is a beautiful sequence in it like that which binds the notes in music. The earth folds and flows as if it had been modelled in the hands of peace. It is shape that matters rather than colour, but the colour is there.
>
> . . .
>
> The roads are coloured threads through the landscape. They all go a long way, even the telegraph posts march valiantly towards the horizon. This is a country to steal the imagination away. It has shape, colour, incidence and a deep sky.

But the poetic imagination, notable everywhere in Barnard Eldershaw's work, often congeals, here as elsewhere, into images which are always revealing and have sometimes a very practical bearing: "Australia has a short history and a long legend. The last continent to be discovered, it had long hung, insubstantial as a wreath of cloud, on the horizon of man's imagination"; "Cobb & Co was big business come to the bush"; and[29]

> Circumstance and history have fostered independence in the Australian character—but independence of action rather than thought.

And again,

> The Australian genius is in the middle register. It is at home in practical things, and it builds not so much with principles and ideals as with policies directed towards the standard of living. The unusual, even if it be the creative artist, is all too likely to be thrown like a speck of dust off the revolving disc.

It has been asserted that *My Australia* was written for an oversea audience: judging by its authors' work as a whole this is very improbable; they write to discover Australia to the Australians, including themselves. The value of the book is in its attempt to get to the roots of things; it should be read by all who are interested in Australia and in particular by all our social historians. In the same authors' *Life and Times of Captain John Piper* (Sydney, 1939) pure and applied literature are so inseparably married that it would be hard to say whether we read for the story itself or for the manner of telling it; the biographical element is here again closely entwined with the historical, but it is social rather than political history, and there is about it a quality almost of fairy-tale: the authors' remark about the life of the Piper family at Alloway Bank, a gentleman's residence near Bathurst, applies only to a lesser extent to the whole story:

> It is a curiously unreal world looked at from the perspective of almost a century. It floats like a transparency over the eternal plains.

Piper himself was absurdly generous, quite unpractical, amiably extravagant, a "genial man who loved all the world", "a man born to be

[29] pp. 113 and 283-4.

happy". After what J. D. Lang quite rightly termed "expensive and ruinous courses", dismissal from his far too well-paid office and a luckily thwarted attempt at suicide, he retired from what would for anyone else have been irretrievable ruin to an Eden at Alloway Bank, and, after a second disaster, to the twilight of a smaller estate beside the Macquarie, where he lived to be seventy-eight. All this is pictured against a background which is realistic and sometimes grim enough, as in the description of the building of the settlement at Sydney, "raised under the most agonizing difficulties", by "the most extortionate labour" of men who were "reduced to feebleness and apathy by hunger and sickness" and who were without proper material or tools; yet even here aesthetic aspects appear in watercolour:[30]

> To the eye the settlement was light coloured. The few stone cottages were of pale sandstone, the huts built of bricks baked at the brickfields a mile inland and roofed with tiles from the same source, *café-au-lait*, "quite romantic", as a sailor on the *Royal Admiral* saw them. The wooden buildings, such as the soldiers' barracks, each 68 feet long by 25 feet wide, to house a company, were pipe-clayed a brilliant white, thatches of reeds or cabbage palm bleached under the sun, shingle roofs of ironbark chips quickly turned to silvery grey. The sun, which warped wood used too green till large cracks appeared in the walls, and crumbled away the makeshift cement of the brick buildings, blended and softened all the colours to pastel tints.
>
> . . . .
>
> Because of the danger from fire, the thatched huts had no chimneys and the fireplaces were built in the open air, so in the dusk of summer and the darkness of winter, when the evening meal was prepared, Sydney glowed with five hundred points of light, the dark land starred like the sky above it.

And there is the bush; Lawrence did not awaken, but he did stimulate the vision of its fascination that has possessed some of the leading Australian prose writers of today:

> The first settlers were met by a wall of trees, trees such as they had never seen before. Individual trees they knew well, but this was a vast community of trees as numerous as the stars and almost as aloof. The woods pressed in upon them like a cloud of witnesses, endless repetition of form and colour; they might go on like that without a break to the west coast of the continent for all men knew, an insupportable burden upon the imagination.

Often the style in which the book is written flowers naturally into images: "the great curve of the continent hung, an anonymous entity on the port bow, like the shoulder of a dead leviathan thrust out of the sea"; "Entering Port Jackson was like passing through the grey rind of the continent into another world"; and "the days turned softly, slowly on the axis of the year". In Alan Marshall's *These Are My People*[31] (Melbourne, 1944), the interest is almost purely human. In spite of being

---

[30] pp. 8–10.

[31] For Marshall's short stories, see p. 1247

crippled, during the last war Marshall travelled with his wife in a caravan through western and north-western Victoria, collecting messages for relations and friends of Australian soldiers for publication in the *A.I.F. News* in Cairo; his quiet, simple and engaging personality, though like many who are physically handicapped, he loved to tell of fighting, his gentle and whimsical humour, are reflected in all he wrote: he had a wide and understanding sympathy and a keen eye for personal idiosyncrasies, so that the people he met in his journeyings are both living and Australian. He had pieces of wisdom, also, which, if not novel in substance, appear so as he uttered them; this is from the elderly man with the club-foot, who has a face like a gum-nut and drives a covered wagon:

> "If a bloke don't mind being hit, he's jake. Nothin' can touch him."
>
> . . . .
>
> "It's only your body you're worried over, and our bodies ain't worth worryin' over. I don't worry over mine. And for why? Because I was in a paddock with a bull and when he came at me I was scared stiff on account of me being crippled. Then it came over me all of a sudden, what's it matter?—and I stopped being frightened and the bull stopped a yard from me."

But fond as Marshall was of his country and his people, he was not blind to their faults; he quoted this, from a Scottish Australian:

> ". . . Australians use newspapers for brains and their newspapers are English before they're Australian."

Among those who concentrate upon the land itself or some aspect of it, which has for them, as well as for our poets and some of our writers of fiction, a beauty that they try to convey in appropriate language, is Elyne Mitchell: this perception and attitude characterize all she writes. One of her books takes the form of essays,[32] and in another the subject is such that it is here discussed along with works of science;[33] but there remain two, *Australia's Alps*[34] (Sydney, 1942), and *Speak to the Earth* (Sydney, 1945), whose place is here. In addition to what has been said about Mrs Mitchell personally in discussing her essays, it may be added here that her favourite spare-time occupation is skiing and that she has won championships in Canada as well as in Australia, and has represented both Victoria and Australia. Her home, Towong station, looks straight up the Murray at the Alps; her first book is a record of skiing and climbing expeditions among them with her husband, and is full of exuberant enthusiasm, of the delight that comes with the expenditure of youthful energy, with the strain of a healthy body to an extreme of weariness that is yet almost forgotten in the long return trek down hill, "heads still high up in the mountain peaks"; such weariness becomes almost a

[32] See p. 1280.
[33] On p. 1466.
[34] References here are to the second edition, Sydney, 1946.

pleasure, sitting over the fire in the evening when it is combined with a hunger so sharp that one could not have moved without having something to eat. But it is not necessary to be filled with youth and energy, or to be a skier and a mountain climber, to appreciate this book, for the suggestion of isolation, timelessness, mystery that hangs about high peaks and vast snowy slopes and rocky chasms informs it everywhere. The second is however a better book, for here the poet in Mrs Mitchell finds, with experience in writing perhaps, fitter utterance: it is set in her station home, and tells how she helped in the running of it, tussock-burning, gassing rabbit-burrows, drenching sheep, in the lambing-paddock, helping to draft sheep and cut out steers, and even trying to learn to shear, while her husband was overseas with the A.I.F., at Singapore and then as a prisoner of war in Malaya; but actually the book amounts to a kind of chronicle of the life of a Murray River station through the seasons, and underlying all that is again the theme of the land itself, its compelling beauty and the love it engenders in those whose life is bound up with it. Mrs Mitchell's style is by no means verbose, but it is easy-going: "Endless time," she says, "and the slow accomplishment of appointed labours, with heavy, perhaps unthinking, effort, has become a traditional picture of the land life"; and this feeling of endlessness comes through, in a seasonal rhythm punctuated by lines and phrases and clear-cut little paragraphs in which the essence of physical and mental experiences is crystallized out. As she was riding after sheep in autumn, dropping once below the steep bank of a creek so that she was "enclosed for a moment, with only the sun and slow-moving water as my companions . . . a sudden light-wave of memories came down the motes of a sunbeam—Tom's voice still hanging in the air"; and "the warmth of the sun made another world of the bitter, steel-grey morning"; "A flood of fatigue seemed to rise up in a wave and roll over my head as I jogged home, with the smell of sheep like a cloud around me"; "the tar made a faint gulp as it started to pour out of the tin into a little jar that I had ready for it". Or there is this, of action:

> The flat below the Cathedral an orderless mass of cows and calves—reds, ballies, blacks, dark roans, light roans, blue roans—continually herded into a mob by shouting horsemen. Then comes the ascent of the bank, when the fun really starts, when the calves invariably break, and there is a galloping and a shouting and cracking of whips mixed with frantic bellowing.

There is no attempt at character-sketching and what humour there is is scarce and by-the-way, but through it all the miscellaneous life of the station flows by, real enough, though largely subjective in that it is strongly coloured with the writer's personality, and instinct with a charm that is visible through the roughest and most ordinary scenes and activities.

And then there are the journalists. Paul McGuire's *Australian Journey* (London, 1939) is superficial compared with *My Australia*, but more likely to be widely read: it is, for the most part, a literary guide-book for oversea readers, whom it provides with a good deal of useful information in an entertaining manner, but sometimes it becomes much more than this. Along with easy and overdrawn generalizations, the more misleading for the fraction of truth in them, there are others in which McGuire seems to forget that he is explaining and commending Australia for the benefit of those who know little about it, and gives individual expression to critical comments that Australians ought to take to heart. Sentimental nonsense such as that about the "heavy shouldered and lean-legged" young men in Sydney and its girls that are "browner than an autumn vineleaf", and about outback Queensland, where men are "made of steel and whipcord with narrow screwed eyes that watch the distances" would have been better left to American "westerns"; but now and again, curiously enough only when McGuire is in a critical mood, we get this sort of thing:

> The Australians have some repute abroad as a violent sort of people. . . . Actually the general tone of life is the tone of a solid bourgeoisie;
>
> . . . .
>
> As the machinery of the State is elaborated to protect working conditions and to secure wages and to provide pensions, the concern of the masses with politics declines. Mr Belloc said long ago that a well-fed secured democracy would easily be robbed of its liberties, and this process appears in Australia.

Sharpest of all, and truest:

> Industrialism, mass-education, mass-production, mass-consumption, mass-entertainment, mass-propaganda; these are the environment in which Sydney is shaped. It takes its evening pleasure at the movies, for the Australian theatre is almost dead, or in very dull dance-halls. It takes its opinions from an odd collection of newspapers and perhaps, sometimes, from the new race of dons who frequent the national airwaves. . . . It belongs to the great new civilisation of canned-goods and contraceptives.[35]

William Hatfield's *I Find Australia* (London, 1937) has the same fresh and rather schoolboyishly adventurous charm, the same effortless realism as his novel *Sheepmates*:[36] the first part of it is simply a recital of the personal experiences which it is clear that the novel followed almost exactly; they are not, as in the novel, deliberately romanticized, but in themselves they are romantic, and they are coloured by a romantic atmosphere that emanates from the author himself. The two most popular of the journalist descriptive writers are Ion Idriess and Ernestine Hill (*née* Hemmings, Brisbane, 1899–1972), and unfortunately in them many characteristics of first-rate journalism are accompanied by attitudes

[35] p. 138.

[36] Hatfield has also published other descriptive work. For a discussion of *Sheepmates*, see p. 1128.

and methods that are a long way from first rate. Both possess an enthusiastic and untiring curiosity, keenness of observation, the story-telling faculty, an instinct for drama and the power of putting their readers in close contact with the surface of all they describe; but they possess also an only too obvious determination to impress and a crudeness of taste that cares nothing for, probably does not even notice, the shabbiness of the verbal bricks with which they build, so that pathos becomes bathos and drama melodrama; an atmosphere of strain and exaggeration is created even though the facts are true and simple. Idriess is rather more than a journalist, with all his faults; he knows the wildest parts of outback Australia as no mere visitor could know them, and it is largely owing to him that these places have become to us more than mere spaces on the map. He is simple and sincere and unsophisticated and he has small literary skill, but all he writes is full of action and colour, and appears real and exciting even through his theatricalism: he loves excitement, adventure and outlaws; in fact he is in essence a romantic. The earlier of his long list of books, which includes novels, short stories and biographies, are the best, and in particular the more autobiographic, though there is an autobiographic element in almost all of them: after *The Desert Column*, which will be discussed later,[37] *Madman's Island* (Sydney, 1938)[38] and *Men of the Jungle* (Sydney, 1932). Ernestine Hill's most representative book is *The Great Australian Loneliness* (London, 1937),[39] which describes her five years' wanderings over a considerable part of outback Australia, with swag and typewriter, by camel, pack-horse, motor truck and coastal lugger. Unlike Idriess, she writes as a visitor, but a visitor who is sympathetic and keenly observant; she was quite fearless and went cheerfully where no other white woman has gone, and her stories and sketches of outback types are so good that even worn phraseology and occasional streaks of crude prose-poetry cannot spoil them. Mrs Hill shared with Idriess a characteristic that is rare in all but the best of modern journalism: it is their subject that interests them, not themselves.

Of those descriptive writers who have found their subjects in Central Australia, three deserve mention here: they do not cover the same area, one is concerned mainly with the physical features of the country, another mainly with its animal life, and the third with pioneering; but all three know intimately what they are talking about. Cecil Thomas Madigan (Renmark, S.A., 1889-1947), was a graduate of Adelaide and Oxford, to

---

[37] See pp. 1410–11.

[38] This is the revised edition, printed as it was originally planned, without the romantic element that had been imposed upon it.

[39] Her other books include *Flying Doctor Calling* (Sydney, 1947), *Water Into Gold* (the story of the Murray River irrigation settlement) (Melbourne, 1937), and a novel based on the life of Flinders. After the closing date of this History, she wrote *The Territory* (Sydney, 1952).

which he won a Rhodes Scholarship; he was a member of the Australian Antarctic expedition of 1911-14, fought throughout the first World War and lectured in Geology at the University of Adelaide. Madigan took part in several expeditions into Central Australia, including an aerial reconnaissance of Lake Eyre, which he afterwards visited by car, and of the Simpson Desert, and these expeditions, together with a preliminary outline of the history of the Territory as well as of the Centre, are described in *Central Australia* (London, 1936). Like all who know the Never Never, Madigan was fascinated by "this vast lonely inland region", and particularly by the Lake Eyre basin,[40] of which he says:

> There is a thrill and fascination in all the deserts of the world, but there is something more in the Lake Eyre basin, an element of depression and fear. There is a lifelessness in all deserts, but not the vast deadness of this great extinct lake . . . [a] haunting sense of something more than the loneliness of the desert; it has been a tradition among the aboriginals from the most remote times.

In a second book, *Crossing the Dead Heart* (Melbourne, 1946), in which Madigan again visits Lake Eyre, he speaks of its "haunting sense of desolation and death". But the principal part of this second book consists of an account of the crossing of the Simpson Desert, a "pink and gigantic circular gridiron, ribbed with close straight sandridges from horizon to horizon", which lies in the south-eastern corner of the Territory: this is the "stony desert" that held up Sturt,[41] and it is here suggested that it may have been the death of Leichhardt; Madigan had however the advantages of camels, wireless, his preliminary aerial reconnaissance, a good season and knowing what he had to face; he was the first white man to travel right through this desert, and he had to cross an ordinarily waterless stage of 250 miles, though curiously enough he was held up in the middle of it by rain! Except for a few short passages such as those which have been quoted, Madigan's style is matter of fact and rather flat; but this is forgotten in the interest of the subject-matter. The other writer about Central Australia is Hedley Herbert Finlayson (Adelaide, 1895-), who was educated at the University of Adelaide and is Honorary Curator of Mammals at the South Australian Museum; in his book, *The Red Centre* (Sydney, 1935)[42] he is concerned mainly with the great aboriginal reserve which lies at the intersection of the boundaries of Western, South and Central Australia, and also to the south-east. This is "the environment which moulded the most remarkable fauna in the world", and Finlayson pleads for its preservation as a National Park; he calls it the "Red Centre", because "sand, soil and most

[40] p. 166.
[41] But of course the conditions were very different.
[42] Reprinted in the Australian Pocket Library in 1945; this edition is used here for purposes of reference.

of the rocks are a fiery cinnabar, and the grey mulga is liberally splashed with the clear green of ironwood and sterculia". There are the ranges, bare rocky chains, which yet contain nooks and gorges, small green plains and broad valleys, with their herbs and grasses; and beyond the ranges there are salt lakes, parklands in which the vegetation is dense, sand-hills, stony tablelands, and isolated rock outcrops, from little granite "jump-ups" to great tors like Ayers Rock and Mount Olga; these, says Finlayson, "may well stand as symbols of the land itself: huge; red; bizarre". Finlayson feels the fascination of this country even more deeply, or at least expresses it more aptly, than Madigan. "Even when the heat is at its worst," he says,

> . . . one cannot escape a realization of the magnificence of the flood of radiant energy that beats upon the land. In retrospect, it is not the passing discomfort of the temperature that comes to mind, but rather a vision of great red landscapes, wide open to the splendour of the sun.

The animal life, plentiful in places, is unobtrusive, except at night: insects of course, and birds about the waterholes in the early morning; snakes and kangaroos and emus and euros and rock-wallabies; rabbit-bandicoots; the rat-kangaroo that had been long thought to be extinct; hare-wallabies, marsupial moles, lizards in great variety are described so simply and sympathetically as to make them interesting to readers who are not naturalists: all this in a quiet and friendly style, which is ordinarily undistinguished, but now and again, under the pressure of an enthusiasm which is aesthetic as well as scientific, it strikes fire in a phrase or a paragraph which is more illuminating than pages of ordinary description. *No Roads Go By* (Sydney, 1932)[43] by Myrtle Rose White (*née* Kennewell, near Broken Hill, N.S.W., 1888-1961), is the best account of pioneering life in the Never Never that has yet appeared. Mrs White, a city-bred woman, with her four-year-old daughter joined her husband when he had just become manager of a cattle station of a million acres in the sand-hill country between Lake Frome in South Australia and the Queensland border. As compared with *We of the Never Never*, *No Roads Go By* is a story of real life, unromanticized, let alone sentimentalized, no aspect being omitted or toned down; on the other hand Mrs White, though she writes capably, has not Mrs Gunn's literary gift: it is probably for both of these reasons that although the book has gone through six Australian editions, besides one in England, and has been translated into German, it is not nearly so well known as *We of the Never Never*. Loneliness, for her husband had to be away for two or three weeks at a time, and married couples as help were hard to get, hard to keep, and with

[43] Mrs White also wrote a novel of life in the Never Never, but it is not nearly so good as the true account. She has since however published in *Beyond the Western Rivers* (Sydney, 1955), a continuation of the story told in *No Roads Go By*.

manners that often made their departure a relief; no doctor within 150 miles, and in those days there was no Flying Doctor; stores delivered twice a year; mails once a fortnight and then delivered at another homestead thirty-five miles away; ants, flies, snakes and dingoes; dust-storms and drought, in which the birds died in the heat, and the sun slid down so slowly that Mrs White wanted to hit it with a sledge-hammer as it hung like a ball of brass over the horizon; and the only water was bore-water, so hot that it was not drinkable until evening, and laden with salts that would not allow garden plants to grow, so that they had to eat dried vegetables with the beef (mostly salt) and goat: these were the trials that Mrs White had to face, and she faced them with resource and indomitable courage, but with the arrival of her babies conditions became too difficult. There is an affecting description of how her baby boy fell into convulsions at midsummer, only a few months before another baby was due to arrive; of the struggle to keep him alive until it was cool enough to carry him away to the doctor; of the terrible journey through the heat-waves over the baking sand, in a car that had to be dragged by horses over "the big sand-hill" and gave out at last in the dry bed of a sandy creek. Yet Mrs White has plenty of humour and a number of good stories. There is the story of the five-year-old boy who wandered thirty miles from home, and whose first remark when he was found was "I'd like a gwilled chop";[44] later, this young outback Australian

> . . . told his mother how he had walked all day, and then, when night came some cattle frightened him. "I getted under a bush and went to bed," he said. "First I took off my boots, and then I took off my socks; I put my socks in my boots, and I put my boots under my head, and I went to sleep";

there is the story of the cockatoo who drilled the ducks, and rode on their backs until they dived into the creek and left him wet and swearing on the bank; and there was the rabbit plague, during which the cats used to bring in up to three dozen a night. And the life had its compensations: the eldest little girl so took to it from the first that before she was nine she used to be called upon to settle questions as to a horse's age or breeding; and a little later, knowing that a mob of five or six hundred cattle had to be brought up from the swamps, she saddled her pony, and, with the help of a cattle pup she was breaking in, drove them up by herself. The station homestead is now half buried by drifting sand; the little girl who drove the cattle is married and she and her husband own and manage a station near Broken Hill; of the two boys, one became a bomber pilot in the second World War and is now a station-owner in far-out Western Australia, the other was a gunner on a plane that went out to attack a Japanese convoy and did not return.

---

[44] pp. 35-6.

CHAPTER XVIII

HISTORY, BIOGRAPHY, DESCRIPTION

Records of the Papuan Patrols: Humphries; Champion; Hides. Stories of Adventure: McLaren; Muspratt; Attiwill; Blakely; Others. War Books: Mitchell; Williams; Black; Idriess; Wilmot; Hetherington; Others

THE RECORDS of the Papuan patrol officers deal with journeys across parts, usually unexplored, of a country in which travel "is as difficult as anywhere in the world, and the explorer D'Albertis has left on record his opinion that it is easier to cross the Alps than to ascend an ordinary hill in Papua";[1] between them they convey a moving picture of the patient, painstaking and sometimes really heroic work of the white patrol officers, of the courage and loyalty of the half-civilized native police who accompany them, and, by no means incidentally, of the life and characteristics of the tribes with which they come in contact. None of the authors of these books has the literary ability of Monckton,[2] who belongs to the preceding Period, but all have literary ability, and their directness and sincerity, as well as the fascination of their experiences, make their published work well worth record from the point of view of this History. The first book in point of time was *Patrolling in Papua* (London, 1923), by Walter Richard Humphries (Surrey, England, 1890-1951), who, after a number of years as an apprentice on seagoing vessels, joined the Papuan government service and became eventually Resident Magistrate. He was the first Papuan officer to make his way through almost impenetrable swamp and over almost inaccessible mountains across Papua and German New Guinea; he made other exploratory patrols, but it is this, in the main, with which his book deals. Nevertheless the most interesting part of it is its picture of the work of the patrol officers generally, of the native police, and of the carriers, some of whom had on this expedition to carry fifty-pound swags through a swamp when they were suffering from influenza: more than one of them, and indeed more than one of the constables also, were actually convicted murderers, but then, as Sir Hubert Murray says in his introduction:

> ...[to] the ordinary Papuan murder is not a crime as we consider it—it is . . . "sometimes a duty, sometimes a necessary part of social etiquette, sometimes a relaxation, and always a passion".

[1] Sir Hubert Murray, then Lieutenant-Governor of Papua, in his preface to J. G. Hides's *Papuan Wonderland*.

[2] See pp. 839-40.

Humphries has the keen eye and practical curiosity of a scientist in the field, a human interest in everything with which he comes in contact, and an easy and unassuming manner of writing that should assure him of the interest of the ordinary reader, for whom the book was written. The backbreaking toil that was inseparable from his journey; the leech and insect plagues; the danger to life from which only courage and judgment saved the expedition, as when Humphries successfully called the bluff of hundreds of naked and threatening savages: all were met with even-tempered patience and are described with a good deal of humour, and Humphries's unfailing interest in all about him gives life to his story. He has a real interest in human nature, here of course principally Papuan human nature, which appears in the episode of Mary Bundoni, the captured Kukuku girl; in her frantic desire for the wallaby, not, as it turned out, for a pet, but to make a meal of; and in her plot to escape to her native village. More humorous is the chase by the Filipino-Australian aborigine Rose of her naked pupils to worship; and there is the misunderstanding of the carriers who came suddenly upon a white doctor who was conducting a post-mortem: they dropped their loads and with yells of terror ran off into the bush, telling their masters:

> "We come up along road. We see old fella doctor he been cut em up one boy. He look close up inside belly belong him. He look for something good to eat, all the same bad New Guinea boy who savee kai-kai [eat] man. We fright too much. We lose 'em swag and run away. This old fellow doctor he no good. Maybe by and by he want to kai-kai us."

A later book, *Across New Guinea* (London, 1932) is a classic of New Guinea exploration, and has been called much more than that. It describes a now famous expedition in 1927-8 up the Fly River, which flows down to the south coast, and thence across the main range to the sources of the Sepik River, and down the Sepik to the north coast; again the island had to be crossed, but this time at its widest part, by two white men, a few native police, and some carriers. The white men were Charles H. Karius, Assistant Resident Magistrate of Papua, and the author of the book, Ivan Francis Champion (Port Moresby, Papua, 1904-). Champion joined the Papuan administration as a patrol officer in 1924, and became Resident Magistrate; he served as lieutenant in the Royal Australian Naval Volunteer Reserve in the second World War, acting as pilot and hydrographic surveyor in New Guinea, and was awarded the Gill Memorial medal of the Royal Geographical Society for explorations and surveys in Papua and other distinctions after the date at which this History closed. Champion does not set out to tell the full story of the expedition, but only of his personal experiences; nevertheless it records the greater part of what Sir Hubert Murray calls, in an introduction, "a really fine achievement", which won for Karius the Medal of the Royal Geograph ical Society. Champion's account is quite selfless and his style concise, matter of fact, restrained; but it is always realistic and at times it becomes lively enough, as when his raft strikes a submerged snag in a swift current and turns over, pinning him underneath it, until he is dragged out by a native lance-corporal just in time. There are graphic incidental descriptions of the natives, their appearance, customs and weapons, their burning desire for steel implements, their generosity, once they have made friends, and their gratitude for small gifts:[3]

> . . . the Chief, bearing a string bag, came and sat beside me on my bed. He took from this bag a very large taro, and holding it up for my inspection, slowly turned it round and round to show its good points, at the same time explaining that it was grown by him and that it was for me. He put it down and produced another, and talked of it; then another, and so the performance went on until there were at my feet six of the finest taro I had yet seen. He put down his bag and gazed into my eyes; slowly his glance stole towards my pile of tomahawks, rested a moment on them, and then he looked at me again, without a move or a word, but his eyes were the appealing eyes of a dog. I took the hint, got up and brought one of the tomahawks and gave it to him. Nine savages out of ten that I have known would have snatched it immediately and have run outside to show it to their friends; but not he, he did not even look at it, but continued to gaze at me, without saying a word, and without changing his expression, but he could not disguise his eyes—they thanked me more eloquently than words.

Among the patrol officers however one man stands out. In daring and in patient fortitude, in initiative and in the power to make an instantaneous and life-and-death decision and also in modesty and disregard of self generally, Hides was not alone, for these qualities seem to have been shared by most of Murray's officers; and Hides was by no means the only one whose work was extremely important, though it may be noted that Sir Hubert Murray, who was rightly proud of his men and loved to do full justice to them, was particularly enthusiastic about him; in a preface to one of Hides's books[4] Murray calls the expedition it describes

> . . . a really remarkable piece of work; work which demanded an unusual amount of pluck and endurance on the part of all concerned, and, on the part of the leaders, a rare power of inspiring courage and enthusiasm in men who, like the leaders themselves, were half dead from hunger and fatigue. And perhaps as remarkable as anything else [was their] skill in bushcraft. . . .

But though all the patrol officers seem to have possessed a certain fellow-feeling and even friendliness for the brave, cruel, in many ways attractive and sometimes lovable savages whom it was their business to keep in order and set in the first steps towards civilization, none seem to have had a more deep and sympathetic understanding of them, to have been able to get so far under their skins; moreover, on top of all this, Hides

[3] p. 95.

[4] *Papuan Wonderland*, p. xii; Murray is here referring to the assistant patrol officer, O'Malley, as well as to Hides who led the expedition.

had a real literary gift. Earlier in this History it has been remarked on the curious and fortunate fact that Australia's greatest explorers have all possessed some literary, or at least journalistic, ability, and this is true, if not quite to the same extent, of the Papuan patrol officers. Jack Gordon Hides (Port Moresby, Papua, 1906-38), loved as a child to talk to the prisoners in the Port Moresby jail, headhunters and cannibals, who "told me of their homes in far-away and mysterious places, on mountain slopes and river plains"; he learnt from them Koiari and Motu, and also "to differentiate the lying romantics from the more serious-minded". Once when as a child of eight or nine he was whipped for disobediently talking with "murderers" and eating "the rice of prison warders", he ran away into the bush and spent a night with a party of Koiari killers and sorcerers; at nineteen he entered the Papuan government service as a cadet, served under Champion[5] when he was a patrol officer, and, after a number of expeditions, became Assistant Resident Magistrate; he resigned to join a gold-prospecting expedition, which left him broken in health, and he died soon after, when only thirty-two:[6] his principal books are *Through Wildest Papua* (London, 1935), *Papuan Wonderland* (London, 1936), and *Savages in Serge* (Sydney, 1938). Murray, in his introduction to the first of these books, speaks of the Loloipa patrol, one of the two with which it deals, as "in many ways typical of the police work that is being done in the Papuan mountains"; he considered it typical because the expedition was understaffed,[7] because the arrests that were its principal business were made without bloodshed, because the prisoners were brought more than 200 miles across mountains and through rivers to Port Moresby without mishap, and because they were tried by a judge who "took [a] sensible and merciful view of their case", setting the principal murderer free on his solemn promise to stop killing and to induce his people to stop also. Hides said that his greatest fear was of having to shoot to kill; this would show that his plans had not been well thought out: yet, if he had not been always ready to shoot on the instant, the patrol might sometimes have failed utterly, and every member of it might have been killed. The country through which Hides had to pass, in the patrol described in his first book, was such that W. R. Humphries,[8] then Resident Magistrate, who knew what he was talking about, said that it might well have been introduced with Dante's line, "All hope abandon, ye who enter here"; and of the country covered in the second book Hides himself said, "It is a frightful stretch of country—

[5] For Champion's work, see pp. 1394, 1395.

[6] The tragic story of this expedition, of his own illness, and of the death of his white companion is told in his last book, *Beyond the Kubea* (Sydney, 1939).

[7] The service had been cut during the Depression, with the incidental result that risks had to be taken with the natives.

[8] For Humphries's work, see pp. 1393-4.

a desolate, silent land, where only bandicoots and pythons can find a home": "This," said Murray,[9] "is the most difficult and most dangerous patrol ever carried out in the whole island of New Guinea." The third book, which is not introduced by Murray, contains a notable tribute to him and to his predecessor, McGregor:[10] "but," says Hides, "it is Murray's Papua"; to this may be added the last words of the dying constable, Emesi, in *Papuan Wonderland*: his lamp, he said, was going out, but no matter; he was wearing "Judge Murray's clothes". At times the accounts of these patrols approach the ethnological studies that are discussed elsewhere, among works of science;[11] this relationship is observable, not only in the accounts of native institutions, habits and customs, but in the incidental revelations of native attitudes of mind, and some of the most interesting of them occur incidentally to character-sketches; Gopa-Gelu in *Through Wildest Papua*, when he was asked why he had killed, replied:

> "You know our fashion. We look at these people; we look at them for a long time. We say: They are there: good we kill them. We think of this all the time; when our bellies get too hot, we go and kill them. No more."

Gopa, says Hides, was a murderer but no criminal; they became quite friendly; "What would you?" he said once, "I am good man. I have never stolen another's something"; it was Gopa again who, when asked whether a piece of bread and jam that Hides had given him was not better than human flesh, replied, "You don't seem to understand. Man is like cassowary, only much better"! When the patrol was nearing Port Moresby, Gopa asked whether his throat was to be cut; Hides explained that he would be tried by a judge, who would decide whether he was really a bad man or no; this did not satisfy Gopa:

> "Taubada," he said, "I am a man of the big mountains; I do not know the ways of this judge, and of the white men you speak of; therefore do you speak for me. Tell them that Gopa-Gelu has finished with fighting. Tell them that if they will let Gopa-Gelu go back to his people, he will look only for the gardens, for the pigs and women, chew betel nut and dance; tell them he will never kill again."

It was extraordinary, says Hides, how within an hour or so of an attack with bloodshed he and his men would be sitting among the cooking-fires, in the midst of hundreds of natives, all genuinely friendly: "They seem to treat a fight like a football match." Hides's attitude is that of a scholar in the best sense of the word: "The more I see of Papuans," he says, "and the more I learn about them, the more I realize the little that I really know." A natural leader of men, Hides would have made a

[9] Quoted in a foreword by W. M. Hughes, from a communication by Sir Hubert Murray to the Commonwealth Government.

[10] Author's note.

[11] See pp. 1458–62.

fine soldier; he would also have made a capable anthropologist; and probably, with a little training, a good novelist. His literary ability appears, not as a rule in the sometimes unfortunate pseudo-poetic passages that are quoted with approval by Sir Hubert Murray, but in his descriptions of actions and the men who take part in them: he misses nothing that matters, he knows just what to tell, and he knows how to tell it; his style is simple, unaffected, and extremely vivid without being in any way forced, and his sympathy is quite without sentimentality.

The records of the Papuan patrol officers, and Hides's in particular, are, as has been seen, filled with hairbreadth escapes and exciting experiences, but with them adventure is incidental to a particular purpose, whereas in the "tales of adventure" now to be discussed the theme is the adventure itself, wrapped up in the personality of the adventurer, and he is not bound by the requirements of an official report: essentially these tales are all true, and they are quite as interesting as the adventure novels that have been already dealt with.[12] None of the tales discussed here[13] is a bare recital; each is personal and imaginative: the mind of the writer is always observable at work upon the fact, and it may be noted that his outlook is not so romantic as might have been expected: on the contrary it is in some respects extremely practical. Almost all the tales are well written, though it is true that some of their authors are established novelists; several may indeed be called stylists, but there is an individual quality in the writing of all of them, even in one, and that not the least, whose book had to be "prepared" for publication: most of these adventurers fought in one or other of the World Wars, and all but one were born in Australia, though two have made England their home. By far the best known of the tellers of true adventure tales, Jack McLaren (Melbourne, 1887-1954), was the son of a Presbyterian minister and had been intended for medical work in the missionary field; he was educated at Scotch College, Melbourne, but at seventeen he ran away to become ship's boy on a deep-sea sailing vessel with a sour-tempered master and a bullying mate; it was not that he felt any romantic "call of the sea", but simply that he hated school and wanted some way of earning a living. Nevertheless, practical as he shows himself in every situation, that he is romantic essentially[14] appears in everything he wrote; in his novels the romanticism is emphasized, but that may be for practical reasons, and the novels are of little or no literary importance. Apart from the experiences described in the books to be discussed here, McLaren has had

[12] See pp. 1221-6.

[13] There were also several other such tales: these have been treated in this History as appendages of their author's output of fiction.

[14] In spite of Burke's preface to *My Odyssey* (Australian Pocket Library edition), McLaren himself says: "To my particular kind of youth adventuring was life" (*My Crowded Solitude*, p. 9). This and all the references here are to the 1930 edition of *My Crowded Solitude*, and the references in *My Odyssey* are to the Australian Pocket Library edition.

about as variegated a life as any Australian-born writer, and that is saying a good deal; but through all his adventures he always wanted to write stories, and he finally settled down to write them in London, where life was not easy for him until he had made his way. The book by which he is best known, *My Crowded Solitude* (London, 1926), has become an Australian classic: it is the story of eight years spent in establishing a coconut plantation in what was at first unbroken jungle on the western coast of the Cape York Peninsula. Here McLaren lived an almost Crusoe-like life, except that there was a whole tribe of Man Fridays, and that they were quite unable to work systematically or continuously and might all go walkabout for months at a time; he had his adventures here, and all his experiences were interesting: the Crusoe-like building of his house; the struggle with the six-foot carpet snake in the darkness; the elaborate smoke-signals; but perhaps the best part of this book is McLaren's accounts of the nature, beliefs and habits of his irregular assistants in the attempt at the "making of the black man's jungle a white man's garden"; of their knowledge and intimate understanding of the bush, its ways and its life, and of their failure to appreciate the white man's civilization and point of view. One of them said to him wistfully, "S'pose I all-time got them things you give me, then I all-time walkabout." And there is their habit of staying up, singing, half the night and then sleeping far into the morning when they were supposed to be working in the plantation; their distress at the heat, since they had been accustomed to sleep in the shade during the middle of the day; their ceasing work at any time to eat anything handy or to sneak off to spy on their wives, just in case; their affectionate nature, their physical endurance, their courage and care for the sick and aged; their profound awareness "that blame should be attached to intention rather than to effect", their songs and plays and dances:[15]

> In the cool of the dusk . . . suddenly, as though something had stung him, a man would begin singing in a high falsetto which had in it a curiously challenging note; and for a space of maybe half a minute he would sing; then he would rise slowly, dreamily with in his eyes an empty stare, and alternately beat his hands against his sides and raise them wide apart above his head, and in a slow succession of rounded notes the falsetto would go down, down, down, down, half an octave at a time, to a living, throbbing drone. Then another would vent the curiously challenging note, then another and another, each making the play with his hands as he rose; and soon the women would abandon their cooking and join in, and the children come running from the beach; and presently the men would whiten their faces and their bodies with clay and adorn their heads with feathers of coloured birds, and the women hang about their breasts strings of orchid-flowers and with white ashes make phallic markings on their groins; and then, to the accompaniment of the Old Men beating one piece of flat wood against another, the dancing would begin—a mad glad dancing, highly sexual and sensual, full of rhythmic leaps and swayings, with all the while a roaring

[15] pp. 61–2.

> four-note song which brought echoes from the jungle and went out across the sea like sound of devils screaming.[16]

McLaren's life in this little cleared patch in the jungle would have been almost impossible without Mary Brown, the ugly little old black woman who landed from a Thursday Island lugger and became his exceedingly competent cook and housekeeper; she had been trained by a "missionary missus" and served as a waitress at a sly-grog hotel; she cured McLaren of fever and saw that he was properly fed:

> "You all-time eat from tin three times one day," she said once; "that's 'leven times a week, about twenty times a year—my word! that make your belly come angry feller and you come sick. Belly not like have one-kind food all-time."

Almost as well known is *My Odyssey* (London, 1923), which tells of previous experiences as a trader, recruiter and pearler in the islands, which did definitely have a romantic call for McLaren. Here the experiences described are more varied but not more interesting; some however are exciting enough: for instance the struggle between Treacle, the "swim-diver", and the shark who had got his head and left shoulder in his mouth; and here again there are some interesting savage comments on the white man's civilization:[17]

> Was it not true [a puri-puri man] demanded, that in big villages like Sydney, 'Merica, Townsville, and Beretani [Britain] . . . many went hungry in the midst of plenty? Did not the people quarrel and steal so much that strong men called policemen continually walked the villages' streets to keep the peace? Did they revere and faithfully tend their Aged? Their non-related Aged? Did they help one another as members of a village should? Of course they didn't. . . . Such things couldn't happen at Mailala;

there was however another side to all this: the women had no rights; "A woman was a possession to be bought or sold, just as a pig was bought or sold." Not much inferior to at least the second of these two books, and easily the best account of a boy's initiation to the sailor's life that has appeared in this country, is *My First Voyage* (London, 1947).[18] Hauling in the main sheet, "a straggle of almost completely invisible men"; broaching tinned foodstuffs in the lazarette, where young McLaren had been imprisoned for striking the captain when he threw a dish of curry at him; fighting with a Russian friend for nothing in particular in the shadowy darkness, one of the many fights that broke out in an "emptiness of sea" in a desolate part of the Indian Ocean; yarning with "Sails", the gigantic but gentle Finn who afterwards half-killed the mate for hitting a man when he was not looking; listening to the queer little sailor's story of how the sea was made: these together constitute a fitting prologue to McLaren's adventurous life.

---

[16] This a little recalls Conrad's "Heart of Darkness", but the whole atmosphere is different.
[17] p. 28.
[18] This is a revised edition of an earlier version, *Blood on the Deck*, which was published in 1933.

Eric Muspratt (Essex, England, 1899-1949) was an adventurer of an entirely different kind: a good deal has been said in this History about Australians, exemplified here by their writers, as wandering adventurers; it is interesting therefore to find that perhaps the widest and most adventurous wanderer of them all is by birth an Englishman, though he came out here at eighteen, adopted Australia as his home, and returned to it at intervals ever after. "Few Australians, I think," he said, "have ever cherished their country as I have cherished it", and there is probably some truth in this exaggeration. Muspratt's father, one of those amazing eccentrics whom England seems to produce more than any other country, had, beginning as a clergyman, shifted through a long series of miscellaneous occupations, quarrelling and fighting as he went. Muspratt himself, before he was thirteen, had been newspaper boy, baker's boy and dentist's apprentice; at sixteen he went to sea and wandered as a hobo and filler of odd jobs in the United States, Canada, Mexico and Hawaii; then, after a few months' sundowning in Australia, at eighteen he enlisted in the A.I.F. just before the Armistice. Repatriated to Australia, he left a pineapple farm to become temporary manager of a coconut plantation in the Solomons; he tells about this in *My South Sea Island* (London, 1931);[19] afterwards he carried his swag over a great part of Australia, returned to England and vagabonded his way about Europe, living anyhow amidst the most squalid conditions, begging, smoking cigarette butts, and spending intervals in various prisons; all this is described in *Wild Oats* (London, 1932), which is on the whole his best and most representative book. The same sort of life continues in *My Journey Home* (London, 1933): in both these books there are roundabout attempts to get back to Australia by such means as "jumping the rattler", stowing away on tramp and other steamers, and tramping the roads; the latter book extends Muspratt's wanderings to Egypt and India; other books[20] record experiences among the Greek islands and the West Indies. In the second World War Muspratt served in the A.I.F. and in the navy, and was a war-correspondent in New Guinea and elsewhere; he tells about this in *And See the World*, to write which he was given a Commonwealth literary grant. Muspratt was a big young man—it is difficult to think of him as anything but young—powerfully and beautifully built, and religiously idealistic of physical beauty, strength and fitness. What he wanted from life, he said, was experience, in order to be able to help the world by writing about it: he draws conclusions from every aspect of life that he touches, and together they amount to a philosophy, but it is a superficial philosophy, because for want of depth

[19] The references here are to the 1932 edition.

[20] *In Greek Seas* (London, 1933) and *Going Native* (London, 1936), and there have been other books also, which involve some repetition, and a novel by no means as good as his best true stories.

in his own nature he never goes far beneath the surface of things, or thinks of anything very new. Nevertheless, he has something important to convey, though it is not conveyed deliberately: a cheerful zest for life, at least in its physical aspects, that is not blunted by any hardship or the most sordid experiences, and a matter-of-course courage that pays no attention whatever to risks and dangers; Muspratt takes these things in his stride, getting out of everything what suits him best, and moralizing continually in a manner that is naive but thoroughly sincere. Of the innumerable character-sketches of the men and women with whom he comes in contact all are slight; the nearest to a portrait is that of Mumford, the unpleasant but rather pitiful coconut planter in *My South Sea Island*; but behind and over all these is the self-portrait, frank and quite unself-conscious, of the writer; it is a portrait of youth, proud of its physical qualities, highly intelligent and within limitations thoughtful, and carrying an inescapable charm: it is the portrait and the charm that remain with us after reading Muspratt's books, rather than any of their scenes and people. Muspratt's descriptions are generalized and scattered as compared with McLaren's; one sees them all not directly but through the author's consciousness: good examples are the feasting, dancing and wrestling on his South Sea island; the "*warme Brüder*" in Venice; and the food-gathering and "snipe shooting", or collecting cigarette butts, in Marseilles. One description may however be quoted, for though different from any of the others, it is yet characteristic of the man and his books; it deals with a bathe in a mountain stream in an out of the way part of the Riviera:[21]

> [The road] . . . led through undulating vineyard country with blue-ridged mountains in the distance on the one side and glimpses of the Mediterranean a couple of miles away on the other. . . . The clear warm air was scented with pine and flowering heather. . . . In this warm, dry climate there is no better bed than a lonely patch of earth under a starry sky. Habituated to it, it is perfect rest. And there is no better bath-place than a mountain stream sparkling in the sunshine. In hot places, sweaty, dusty and tired with travel, I have plunged into pools, clothes and all, in the eagerness for the wonderful refreshment of such washing. Generally I've washed myself and my clothes together, sitting in the shallows of a pool, then smoked peacefully in the shade, while the clothes dried out in the sun.

Muspratt's stories flow smoothly, easily, colloquially; he takes his time and is far from being concise, but he knows how to write, and to infuse what he writes with his own personality: his books amount to an autobiography in a series of instalments, but the adventure motif is so strong that they are dealt with here. Another adventurer, who in the intervals between journalism, mostly in London; war service, which brought him an M.C. and imprisonment by the Japanese; and travel widely over

[21] *Wild Oats*, pp. 110–11.

sea and land, wrote plays and films and accounts of his own experiences, was Kenneth Andrew Attiwill (Adelaide, 1906–). His *Horizon* (London, 1930) tells vigorously, extremely frankly, and without a sign of sentiment, the story of his experiences on a Finnish windjammer, on which he worked his passage, at a shilling a month, from Australia to England: he shows us the crew of young men, almost all Swedes and Finns, who took her round the Horn, the cold, the wet, the filthy conditions, the hard labour. Most prominent is the food, which they somehow survived, but which left them always hungry: five-year-old salt junk that gave them boils; musty fish preserved inadequately in ammonia; fermenting fruit and vegetables; very dead sides of pig. We breathe with Attiwill the atmosphere of the filthy fo'c's'le, inhabited by men who had not enough water to wash properly, and by more than men; the filthy cookhouse, and the filthy language; yet all this, which to older, softer, more civilized men would have been unendurable, is lifted and enlivened by the fresh unsubduable vitality of youth. We get light sketches, if no more, of many of these young men: of Gösta, the sixteen-year-old apprentice, Attiwill's fo'c's'le mate, a youngster with a "brain like a choked sewer"; of Frog, the cockeyed and conceited French vagabond, with his useful hands, his unprintable language, and his "lewd tattoo markings from bum to breakfast table"; the bullying mate, who had to be conciliated by the loan of a typewriter; and the captain, who, like most of his crew essentially simple, would talk to Attiwill about the stars, the sea and its ships, but could be hard enough and was the last man to be taken in; beyond these there is the mass of the crew, large, rough, powerful, melancholy. This book is full of interest, without, except in one case, the importation of any of the conventional incidents that are usually thought necessary to enliven a sea-story. The most Australian of all these books of adventure is Fred Blakeley's *Hard Liberty*[22] (London, 1938). [Blakeley, whose young brother Arthur had a distinguished career in politics and public life, was born at Gilberton, South Australia, in 1882 and died in Sydney in 1962.] His book tells of wandering in Central, Northern and South Australia, prospecting, opal-mining, driving camels and working in the mines at Broken Hill: the book is constructed around a journey by bicycle across Australia from White Cliffs in New South Wales to Darwin. The drovers, when they heard of the proposed treacherous journey, thought Blakeley and his two mates must be mad; in

[22] The title is taken from *Paradise Lost*, Book II:

> . . . Let us . . . rather seek
> Our own food from ourselves, and from our own
> Live to ourselves, though in this vast recess,
> Free, and to none accountable, preferring
> Hard liberty before the easy yoke
> Of servile pomp.

that country a gallon water-bag will dry up in seven hours, and from a previous expedition Blakeley had taken a month to recover:

> There are still marks on my tongue where the teeth pierced it when swollen; for eight days I had to use warm wet bandages over my eyes because they had no moisture left; my hair came out and the skin scaled as from frost-bite in New Zealand. . . .

Farther north, they passed through the Parakeelia country, in which horses and cattle need no water and on their first introduction to it have to learn to drink; they caught fish in a waterhole in one of the many river valleys that run through Australia's "Dead Heart", though Blakeley declares that the Dead Heart does not exist; and when they finished their journey, their bicycle-wheels were built up of fencing-wire, and their inner tubes stuffed with grass. The book was organized by Miss Muriel Morley, a High School teacher to whom Blakeley had brought a written account of his crossing of the continent; he lacks education in the conventional sense of the word, but he is a man who thinks for himself, and knows perhaps more of the secret of happiness than those of us who spend our lives in cities which "have no power of rest; they only make one weary"; Sydney, for instance, is to Blakeley "a huge ant-hill where people scurry endlessly, only to find their way home as the ants do when night comes". He has a style that is quite his own, which Miss Morley has wonderfully preserved, taking down his conversation, suggesting topics, linking and arranging. One of the most interesting things in the book, particularly as coming from a man like Blakeley, is his account of the "big-run squatters" in the Far West, who, in the bad years "saved the country by sticking to [their] fellow-man:" Blakeley illustrates from his own experience, hitting at "The Yabber-men who follow politics as a trade", who "broke up the big runs" so that the next drought ruined "every man who got the parings" of them. There are many things here that are still new to some of us who live in the "ant-hills" of which Blakeley speaks with scorn: there is the "swelling soil", soft grey sand, silky-smooth to touch; it does not drift, tracks disappear in it after a day or two, and as one passes through, not over it, it makes no sound; there are the meat-ants, which will eat a disabled man to the bone; and there are the aboriginal note-runners, one of whom would cover in three days the three hundred miles between Powell's Creek and Darwin, on the return journey carrying a two-gallon demi-john of rum: through a large part of the story we are accompanied by Jethro, a three-quarter bred dingo, who is as much of an individual as Davison's Dusty, though his mental processes are not analysed. But much of the attraction of the book is in the personality of the narrator, whose simplicity and lack of journalistic effort make even the strangest experiences natural and credible.

Two writers deal with adventure at sea; both write in the first person, and the second might reasonably have been included among the biographers, but its general interest has placed it here. Alan John Villiers Melbourne, 1903–82), took to the sea as a boy of fifteen, and, except for a spell, after several voyages, on the staff of the Hobart *Mercury*, he never returned to Australia except upon short visits; he lived in England, after he retired from the sea, and in the second World War he commanded a squadron of small vessels in the Mediterranean, so that it is hard to say how much of his work can be reckoned Australian. Villiers sailed, mostly before the mast, over a great part of the world, in Danish and Finnish as well as British ships, and even in Arab dhows; twice he won the grain race from England to Australia, and he made the original films for the famous *Windjammer*, though he declared that as a record of facts it was ruined by director, script-writer and actors. Villiers stands for the romance, the realistic romance, of the final period of the Age of Sail: he knows the ships of that period, the firms that built and sent them out, the men who sailed them, and in particular the great whaling captains; he writes like a sailor who knows how to write; his style is fresh, simple and straightforward and he makes one feel on board. Almost all his books are autobiographical, more or less, and some of the best tell of his experiences when he first went to sea: among these are *The Set of the Sails* (London, 1949), and *Whalers of the Midnight Sun* (London, 1934); the first tells Villiers's own story; the second is built largely upon his experiences as a recruit under the famous whaling captain Carl Anton Larsen in the Antarctic. Both are schoolboy stories, as real as they are exciting, and the account of the steel ship caught in the pack, her plates starting, so that the ice had to be sawn in strips from round her and farther off blown up; of the flensing of a dead whale; and of the harpooned whale that, diving, dragged a small vessel down with her: these help to make the book a classic of its kind.

In *Journal of a Voyage: North-west by North*[23] (London and Toronto, 1935) the adventures are almost wholly psychological, though it is a record, based on diaries, of a voyage in a thirty-four foot cutter from Sydney to Singapore; the author, Dora (Eileen) Birtles (*née* Toll, Newcastle, N.S.W., 1904–), is a graduate of the University of Sydney and has been a schoolteacher; she spent five years in Europe, with a visit to the East. There were three women and two men[24] on the cutter; the women and at least one of the men were sensitive and self-conscious and two at least of the women neurotic; there was a frustrated and rather "teasing" flirtation and constant disagreements with an element of jealousy in them which sometimes hardened into quarrels, and two of the women were seasick most of the time. The atmosphere is tense

[23] Dora Birtles has published also other works of description and fiction.
[24] Three for part of the time, but the third man makes no impression.

throughout, with dramatic intervals, but the situation and the characters are, from the point of view of the author, extremely well handled and made interesting and uncomfortably real.

Finally, a record that links up with the accounts of the South Polar adventures of the previous Period. Charles Francis Laseron, F.R.Z.S. (Manitowoc, Wisconsin, U.S.A., 1887-1959), who was brought from the United States as a child and became Assistant Biologist to Mawson's 1911 expedition, published in Sydney in 1947, *South With Mawson*, which is one of the most human of these accounts. Since the closing date of this History, Laseron has published also *The Face of Australia* (Sydney, 1953) and *Ancient Australia* (Sydney, 1954). He served with the first A.I.F. and was wounded on Gallipoli.

Most of the books in the following section deal with personal experiences during the first World War, three of them with life in the trenches in France; but there are two excellent records of the Light Horse campaign in Sinai and Palestine, and one of experiences in captivity in Turkey, whose author met there one of the writers of the famous *Road to En-Dor* and is referred to in that book. Up to the end of 1950 the only published records of the second World War on land were the work of two war correspondents: no part of the official history had yet appeared, but one of these correspondents, Chester Wilmot, who was to contribute its Tobruk-El Alamein section, had published in *Tobruk* a book that gives an excellent picture of the campaign. Mitchell's *Backs to the Wall* (Sydney, 1937) stands, along with Williams's *Gallant Company*, among the true narratives of the first World War where Mann's *Flesh in Armour* stands among its works of fiction. It lacks many things that Mann's novel possesses, but it is as close as any other book to the everyday life of the Australian soldier in France and in particular to "the long endurance of the A.I.F. in 1918". The author, (Major) George Deane Mitchell[25] (Caltowie, S.A., 1894-1961), fought with the A.I.F. from the Landing to the finish, won a commission in the field, a Military Cross and a D.C.M., and escaped without a wound; in the second World War he was for two years a major in charge of a Guerrilla Warfare Group in the Kimberleys and elsewhere in the north of Western Australia, and also in charge of landing-craft in New Guinea; in civil life he was in turn a potato farmer, garage owner, motor salesman and member of parliament: Bean has declared him to be "the most powerful and impressive Australian soldier-writer that I know of". This book is a piece of biography, realistic, detailed, dramatic and pictorial, of Mitchell's fellow-soldiers as well as of himself; there are no psychological problems,

[25] For other work of Mitchell's, see p. 1217.

we hear little of leave in England, and there is no love-making: this is a straightforward story without contrast or background. But the interest does not slacken; it is all too sincere, too vividly outspoken; five-point-nines scream down from the skies at regular intervals, and "at the first faint sound of approach, one's guts would gather up in a ball, and nerves tauten 'till it seemed they would twang like violin strings"; the nights are so cold that when a man tries to write home the ink freezes on his nib; the men feel that they are "in an interminable night of hell"; yet amid all this, worn-out as they all are, the spirit of mateship still holds:[26]

> I walked to a corner and dropped in a heap, tin hat clanging against the wall. Finish, absolute dead finish. I had lain unmoving for perhaps ten minutes, when I heard Sergeant Foster say, "Mitchell—you are to go back straight away to Flers for dixies." Rot, I thought, I can't, and what's more, I blasted well won't even try.
>
> But I went. Someone else would have to go if I didn't;

and through it all there are frequent sprinklings of humour and an unself-conscious and, except at intervals, even cheerful high-heartedness that is indomitable. Mitchell wrote also a small military handbook, *Soldier in Battle* (Sydney, 1940), which must be mentioned, in spite of the general practice of this History to exclude books of the kind, because it would be hard to devise a better handbook for the purpose: written for the citizen soldier, "the man who is not afraid to think . . . reason and act for himself", it contains the most important of the lessons that were learnt by the A.I.F. in the first World War; it tells how acceptance of fate is not sufficient; how the soldier must become complete master of his weapons, himself and those about him; it tells how "[the] greatest battle is not with the enemy—it is with yourself"; how ability to think and act in the last stage of exhaustion is the supreme test, and how no army that will continue to use its weapons is ever beaten. *The Gallant Company* (Sydney, 1933) by Harold Roy Williams (Cooma, N.S.W., 1889-1955) was hailed by an English critic as "one of the best half-dozen soldiers' stories of the War to be found in any country". Quite as realistic as *Backs to the Wall*, but neither dramatic nor pictorial, it conveys precise and detailed observations of men and events, gravely, thoughtfully, and as a rule with detachment; there is plenty of feeling and human sympathy, but the story is balanced, restrained, and the style is quiet and little relieved by the dialogue which takes up a considerable part of the other book. Williams breaks out occasionally into a pictorial phrase, telling how when he first put on a gas helmet he "felt like a cat with its head stuck in a salmon tin", and speaking of "having such an appetite that we could have eaten a dead man's boot"; several times he refers to the rigorous training in the desert in 1915, which "hardened those who survived it to the toughness of working bullocks.

[26] p. 31.

It was the mainstay of many of us . . . in the mud of the Somme winter"; and he has a graphic description of the notorious desert training march, after which only thirty-eight N.C.Os and men could be mustered out of a battalion over nine hundred strong; we get a glimpse also of the break-through at Amiens, on Ludendorff's "Black Day". Finally, there is an excellent analysis of the foundations of the fighting spirit of the A.I.F.; the mateship that is recognized as among them is not mentioned in this place, but elsewhere, when a mere acquaintance, who happened to be the battalion two-up king, forces ten pounds upon Williams as he is going off on leave,[27]

> There was no certainty that Bill would ever see me again, but this was the spirit among the men of the Australian battalions—what's mine is yours, what's yours is mine, and it applied to everything from ready money to boot-polish. It is one of the things that the Tommies could not understand about us, but it helped to found the fighting qualities of the Australian infantry.

A second war book of Williams's, *Comrades of the Great Adventure* (Sydney, 1935), is a kind of pendant of the other, lighter and more disconnected and comparatively lacking in substance; it consists of a series of experiences and anecdotes, mainly amusing, and of snapshots of character, in which one or two from the other book reappear. Williams served four years with the A.I.F., after which he was discharged as medically unfit; he then became a softgoods agent. *Jacka's Mob* (Sydney, 1933) gives, according to Bean, "a vivid and completely true picture of the life of the Australian infantry", and, unlike the other two books, it includes something of the life on Gallipoli and in France; its author, Edgar John Rule (Cobar, N.S.W., 1886-1958), was a farmer who had other adventures before he enlisted, working also on the construction of the Panama Canal. He won a Military Medal, and, after being commissioned on the field, a Military Cross, and then became an orchardist at Shepparton, Victoria; his book is based on notes made during the war, to keep his memories alive; it was Bean who urged that a book should be made out of them. The book has a hero, not the author but Jacka, the first Australian V.C.; he was sergeant-major of Rule's company on Gallipoli and they became friends; he crops up frequently in the book, and with Rule he lives again: we hear also of Jacka's methods, which, as Rule says, would not suit every officer, as when he gives one of his men who is drunk and rowdy the choice of coming before him officially in the morning or standing up to him for a few rounds; among the other figures who show their faces in the story is Birdwood, about whom Rule is franker than most:

> He had a lovable personality, sincere and earnest, but he ruined much of the effect of it by ladling out what we called "bulsh" by the cartload.

[27] p. 131.

This is a simple, commonsensible and colloquial story, neither intense nor particularly imaginative, but very real nevertheless, and one phrase sticks in the memory, in which Rule recalls how during a bombardment "the swishes of the shells followed one another so rapidly that they sounded like a flock of geese going overhead"; such a comparison would come natural to a farmer, and one can see the careful farmer in Rule's comments on the wicked waste of equipment and unused ammunition; now and then a description also, like that of the men of the First Division coming back from Pozières, stays in the mind:[28]

> Although we knew it was stiff fighting, we had our eyes opened when we saw these men march by. Those who watched them will never forget it as long as they live. They looked like men who had been in hell. Almost without exception each man looked drawn and haggard, and so dazed that they appeared to be walking in a dream, and their eyes looked glassy and starey. Quite a few were silly, and these were the only noisy ones in the crowd. Their appearance before they had a night's sleep and clean-up must have been twice as ill as when we saw them.

Of the two writers who deal with the campaign in Sinai and Palestine, both were young, one only a boy; both were members of the Fifth Light Horse, and the periods of their service overlap; both took part in the great advance under Allenby, and they may well have fought in more than one of the same engagements. But the books are almost as different as possible; not that their records disagree, but the one writer is reflective, sardonic, and rather self-consciously literary; the other simple and straightforward, crudely journalistic, and concerned almost wholly with observation and action, which he makes as dramatic as possible: the two accounts are complementary and produce between them a stereoscopic effect. "Donald Black", whose real name is John Lyons Gray, the author of *Red Dust* (London, 1931), would prefer to remain anonymous; he appears to belong to a station-owning family, went straight from school into the army at seventeen, and is much more sensitive and better educated than any of the authors of the other true war stories that have been mentioned. If they are without illusions, he has been disillusioned by what he has seen and experienced, and his youth is obvious in his reflections, most of which are truisms though sound enough; with him the life within is quite as important as the life without, and the facts are always related to general considerations; his experiences are clearly recorded, but in a manner that is slightly remote: there is no attempt at characterization, or even to sketch his closest friends. We hear of the hardships of the advance through the desert, of the continual thirst and frequent semi-starvation, so that the men rush to drink without waiting to find whether the water is contaminated, and eat greedily of dried apricots found on the Turkish

[28] p. 61.

dead, merely tearing off a corner of a packet that is stained with blood; we hear of the snakes and scorpions and the rats that scamper over the men at night; and of the "mental twist, that Jordan Valley madness which so distorts all our ideas". But we hear also of the fascination of the desert, "which, to those who have dwelt upon it, will never quite dim"; and of close friendships in the ranks, which, however apparently incongruous, are fast and sincere. Nevertheless the most moving and sympathetic passage is not of the death or wounding of a friend, but of the writer's parting from his horse, Blackboy, whom he had hoped to turn out for the rest of his days in a paddock for himself:[29]

> Taking him off the line in the early morning I walk with him away from the camp. I cannot saddle or ride him on this his last day of life, we are friends, not man and beast. I do not even bridle him; as I walk away he follows alongside with his head near my shoulder. I talk to him and tell him how I feel, stroke his muzzle and feed him with a little sugar I have stolen for him. He nuzzles my hand; it isn't only the sugar, he likes the feel of my flesh; it is his way of showing affection.
>
> . . . .
>
> It is mid-afternoon when we return, the time set down for the condemned horses to go; I have had these last few hours with him.

The author of the second book, *The Desert Column* (Sydney, 1932), is Ion (Llewellyn) Idriess (Sydney, 1890–1979); he was better known for his stories, true and fictional, of travel and adventure in Australia and New Guinea,[30] but this is his best book. He was educated mainly at Broken Hill Central Public School and School of Mines, and knew as well as most men a great part of inland Australia and in particular North Queensland, the Cape York Peninsula and Torres Strait. *The Desert Column* is probably Idriess's earliest work, in its original form a collection of little diaries, to make room for which in his haversack he had to throw out his iron rations; the story begins on Gallipoli and ends in France in January 1918, when Idriess was returned to Australia as unfit for further service: it is a series of strikingly realistic pictures that Idriess draws so that we forget the journalese, the clichés, the attempt to heighten what does not need heightening and is indeed sometimes half spoilt by this attempt. We fight with the horses struggling for water at the troughs among the palms; we hear the "*choick, choick, choick* of their squelching hooves in the sand", for Idriess has an inventive imagination when he forgets his models; we take part in the bayonet fighting, though this is made not more but less realistic by the method of description; we "nearly howl with rage when the flies swarm all over the jam and cannot be kept out of one's hungry mouth"; and we shiver with the

[29] p. 294; the horses could not be taken back to Australia for fear of infectious disease; they had therefore to be destroyed.

[30] Idriess also wrote, like Mitchell, an excellent small military handbook, *The Australian Guerrilla* (Sydney, 1943).

young reinforcement when maggots drop on him from the side of the trench. We hear also, and remember Idriess's Welsh descent, of the phantom armies that seem to stand by watching the advance of the Light Horse; of "weird looking soldiers riding beside them" without sound; of the "tall stone temples with marble pillars and swinging oil lamps—our fellows could smell the incense"; and, more realistically, we hear also of the Turkish Divisional Commander with his "body-guard of mostly Arab cavalry all done up like wedding cakes", who complained to the Australian brigadier of his men's "disgusting coarseness" and demanded that Chauvel himself should escort him back to headquarters. A third book, *Guests of the Unspeakable* (London, 1928), reads like one of Buchan's adventure novels; in 1915 the author (Sir) Thomas Walter White (Melbourne, 1888-1957), then a Captain in the R.F.C., was sent with the first oversea flying unit to Mesopotamia; he tells of his capture by the Turks, of his experiences in captivity, and of his escape, via Russia, in 1918. His story is the more fascinating in that it is told quietly and with restraint; it is also told with an unfailing cheerfulness and even humour that must have done much to make his hardships endurable; but they were little compared to those of others, particularly of the unfortunate rank and file; the Turk had nothing to learn from the Japanese in brutal inhumanity.[31] In hospital at Constantinople White met Hill, Jones's companion on *The Road to En-Dor*, and was able to help him with food and drugs; his help is acknowledged in that book.[32] In the second World War White commanded an infantry battalion; he had meantime entered the Federal parliament, become Minister for Air and Civil Aviation, and then Australian High Commissioner in London.

Of the accounts of phases of the second World War that are discussed here, Wilmot's *Tobruk 1944: Capture—Siege—Relief* (Sydney, 1944), differs from the accounts of phases of the first in being a history rather than a personal narrative; and it differs from the two accounts of the second World War that follow it in being in tone as well as matter the work of a historian rather than a journalist, though Wilmot also was a journalist by profession. "Chester" (Reginald William Winchester) Wilmot (Brighton, Vic., 1911-54), a graduate in Arts and Law of the University of Melbourne, was war-correspondent first for the A.B.C. in Greece, Syria, Tobruk and New Guinea, and then for the B.B.C. in Western Europe. He was Assistant Editor as well as a contributor to the collection of dispatches broadcast in the B.B.C. programme, "War

[31] "Hill's life was saved by the fact that he was not a melancholic and by the care taken of him by Captain T. W. White, a prisoner-patient in the ward. Hill confided in White, who smuggled medicine and milk to him, and helped him in many ways" (*The Road to En-Dor*, London, 1933, p. 302).

[32] See, for instance, White's account (pp. 77-89, Australian edition, 1932) of the treatment of Indian and British prisoners on and after a march of some hundreds of miles, half-fed, half-clothed and in the depths of winter, during which those who dropped from exhaustion were flogged to their feet, and a guard broke the butt of his rifle on a sepoy's shoulder.

Report"; at the time of his death he had been living in England, and it is a question whether he ought not to be regarded as an expatriate; if he had lived he was to have written the volume of the Australian official war history that deals with the Tobruk campaign. The material for *Tobruk* was collected when Wilmot was working for the A.B.C. in the Middle East; it is based on official A.I.F. and enemy documents, upon Wilmot's own observations, and upon accounts, written and oral, by officers and men who were engaged in the fighting at Tobruk: but because complete information was not at the time available, this did not claim to be a full history, and it does not extend to Rommel's capture of Tobruk in 1942, by forces far larger than he had used in 1941, and which had proved strong enough to defeat the Eighth British Army. In point of view and method generally Wilmot had learnt from Bean: his style is clear, concise, restrained, with complete avoidance of any attempt to excite by rhetoric or deliberate emphasis; as with Bean however, this is by no means to suggest an absence of excitement, but only that events are allowed to produce their own effect in their own way; and, as with Bean again, the story is lit by anecdotes and comments illustrative of the nature of the fighting and the preparations for it, and the life and characteristics of the Australian soldiers engaged. Wilmot makes clear the importance of the capture and holding of Tobruk: without it Rommel could not have been checked on the frontier of Egypt and Wavell could not have advanced to Bengazi; it helped to block the attempt to envelop Turkey and to postpone the attack on Russia, which would then have been open to attack from the south as well as from the west; and but for the absorption by Tobruk of so many planes and pilots[33] and so much petrol, British bases, airfields and supply lines in Egypt would have been far more heavily bombed. Moreover Tobruk represented the first defeat of Germany's crack troops after their long series of successes in Europe and North Africa; it put an end to the current theory that ground troops could not hold against a complete command of the air; it gave Britain time to recover from the disasters of Greece and Crete and to reorganize the defence of Egypt, and also for American aid to become effective; and the effect on British and, in the reverse, on German morale was considerable. Wilmot shows in detail the elaborateness of the preparations that resulted in the taking of Tobruk before an effective counter attack could be organized: twenty-nine hours after the first Australian troops broke through the Italian perimeter, a Digger hat was hoisted to the head of the flagpole outside the Italian Admiral's headquarters; yet it is clear that the Italians' had not been a mere token resistance; "they were out-generalled and out-fought";

[33] According to Wilmot, Rommel must have lost 150 planes shot down and twice as many damaged and the pick of his pilots were killed over Tobruk (p. 275).

> . . . basically . . . Tobruk was a victory for planning and perfect co-ordination of land, naval and air forces and of British and Australian troops.

And, once taken, Tobruk was held because of the complete understanding between British and Australians, because of the generalship of their commanders, and because of the spirit of the men, which was such that in spite of hardship, sickness and boredom, dust, flies, and fleas, as a result of which the infantry battalions lost nearly two stone per man in five or six months; when a set of N.C.Os were offered a commission and a trip on a destroyer to Alexandria and thence to Australia by the first available ship, there were no volunteers. Among a number of tributes from the enemy, that of a bewildered German doctor is particularly enlightening; he had served through the European campaigns:

> "I cannot understand you Australians," he said. "In Poland, France and Belgium once the tanks got through the soldiers took it for granted that they were beaten. But you are like demons. The tanks break through and your infantry still keep fighting."

There is an almost equally interesting explanation of the failure of the Italians, of which many instances are given: Mussolini, says Wilmot, had glamourized war for them; he had told them that "the young, virile Fascist legions had only to march and the jaded, effete British would collapse"; they could not face the facts, and the hardships and dangers of desert warfare. There are some excellent sketches of Morshead, "a citizen-soldier in the Monash tradition", and of some of his officers. Among the anecdotes is that of a sergeant who jumped onto the running-board of Wilmot's car; he was herding a column of Italian prisoners: "Would you drive us along a bit?" he said; "I want to head these bloody weaners off down the road to Bardia"; and there was the reinforcement who had been in some hard fighting before he joined the battalion. "After two days' almost unopposed foot-slogging at Tobruk [he said], 'Fightin'? Call this fightin'? Gawd. . . . The police in Tel-Aviv give us a better fight than this.' " Most amusing of all is the story about Brigadier-General Vasey, widely known, because of his language, as "Bloody George". The operational order he gave to his brigade when it took up what was thought to be a "do-or-die" position in Greece was: "Here we bloody-well are, and here we bloody-well stay"; this order his Brigade-Major redrafted to read: "The 19th Aust. Inf. Bde. will hold its present positions, come what may." A second war correspondent was John Hetherington, whose war novel has been already discussed;[34] he published two books both of which are in manner essentially journalistic, but it is first-class journalism, and at times something more. The first, *Airborne Invasion* (New York, 1943), describes the Battle of Crete, one of the most desperate

[34] See p. 1218.

episodes of the war; here Hetherington tells of the 50,000 members of the British Expeditionary Force, English, New Zealand and Australian, who, driven back by overwhelmingly superior numbers of men and planes, fought their way across the Greek mountains to the port from which they were somehow got over to Crete. There was not nearly enough arms, ammunition and food, it was only at Suda Bay that supplies could be landed, and there the German bombing from the air was such that unloading could not be done in daylight; there were no inland aerodromes, though there were suitable places and there had been time enough to prepare them, from which the British planes, few as they were in numbers, could at least have attacked the Luftwaffe when the coastal aerodromes were so exposed that they could not be used. Yet the R.A.F. delayed the invasion for a week, during which trenches and gun emplacements were dug and thousands of untrained men were trained as far as possible; then, when the last of the defending planes were gone, the Germans attacked with high-level bombers, dive-bombers and machine-gun fighters, to clear the way for their troop-carriers.[35] They were

> . . . easy targets, as easy as fat pheasants to a crack gun-shot. . . . Here and there, one of the lumbering aircraft lurched and nosedived into the ground. Some burst into flame and the Germans they were carrying burned alive if they did not break their necks first. But for every aircraft hit twenty flew on through the ruddy brown fog of dust stirred up by the bombs. . . . They were like circus horses trained to a routine.

This was "the first full-scale paratroop invasion in . . . history", and Hetherington intends his book as "a serious study of a revolutionary branch of military science"; but he says also that he has "endeavoured to neglect none of the aspects which made of the Battle of Crete a great human drama": it was actually made up of a series of small dramas, all of which are described as though by an eye-witness. Hetherington tells of men fighting for six days without rest and with only a few hours' sleep; of a New Zealand brigade band throwing away their instruments and attacking with the bayonet, shoulder to shoulder with the Maoris; of soldiers who had had stevedoring experience unloading supply-ships in the dark with the bombs dropping round them; of men who, hiding on the beach near Maleme, as a German plane touched down would dash to close quarters and fling their gasolene-filled bottles, "Molotov cocktails", at them: "the fabric of the aircraft flared up like dry leaves and the Germans inside burned alive." We hear of Germans who advanced, pretending to yield, and when at close quarters threw bombs that had been hidden in the hands they had held up; and of the torture of villagers to persuade them to tell where they had hidden their arms; yet the Germans respected the Red Cross and their combatant prisoners were

[35] p. 55.

treated well enough until arrival of the Hitler Youth squads; at last, when there was no hope of further defence, we hear of the escapes of worn-out, half-starved and sometimes badly wounded men to the coast and to the ships; but thousands had to be left behind. Crete was lost because there were neither the men nor the material to defend it; it was lost, says Hetherington, using much stronger words, by those who had misdirected British foreign policy for so many years: yet, he adds, the campaign was indispensable, militarily as well as politically; Britain at least had kept her promises, and Germany's

> . . . casualties in trained men and aircraft compelled the Nazi generals to realise that such a campaign as that in Crete could not profitably be repeated even by a nation as prodigal of lives and material as the Third Reich.[36]

Hetherington's second book, *The Australian Soldier* (Sydney, 1943), describes incidents from four Middle East campaigns, because he believes this to be "the simplest means of portraying the character of that many-sided, contradictory, elusive figure—the Australian Soldier": he chose these particular campaigns because he was familiar with them; he alludes mostly to the men of the 6th Division because it played here a bigger part than other Australian formations; and he refers to Australians alone because he wanted to paint a single portrait, not a gallery. But, he adds, the Australian soldier is not one man but tens of thousands, each with a character of his own; he is not a swashbuckler who talks big and drinks hard, though he is tough enough; he is often a quiet fellow: in this war he had his traditions, too: in Bardia more than one man said to Hetherington, "Correspondent, eh? Well, when you write to the papers tell them we're as good as the First A.I.F." One of Hetherington's illustrative anecdotes is of the dying man who, when an enemy post had to be taken and there was no cover to enable a Bren gun to be brought to bear on it, pulled free from his mates, and crawled to the top of a ridge, so that the gun might be laid over his body; but many of the stories and almost the whole of the first part of the book are by no means tragic: an Italian divisional commander sent a message to an Australian brigadier offering to capitulate with 7000 men. "I'm too busy now," said the brigadier. . . . "Tell 'em to come back in the morning." Best of all, perhaps, and characteristic enough, provided one realizes that the speakers, a couple of Australian privates, had been celebrating in captured chianti, and that their pride rested on the achievements of their mates rather than on their own:

> "You know, Bill," said Australian Number One, "these 'Pommies' a man meets out here are good blokes."
>
> "My oath!" said Australian Number Two.

---

[36] p. 176.

"As a matter of fact, Bill, after what I've seen of 'Pommies' out here, I'm never going to sling off at a 'Pommy' again."

"No, Harry, neither will I."

"In fact, Bill," said Number One, warming to his subject, "I'll go so far as to say this: They're as good as us."

"Cripes, Harry," said Australian Number Two, "you can't say that. But they're bloody wonderful fellers just the same."

Among the few accounts of one aspect or another of the war at sea, *The Price of Admiralty* (Melbourne, 1944), by Paul McGuire[37] and his wife, Frances Margaret McGuire, tells the story of H.M.A.S. *Parramatta* and of Jefferson Walker, who commanded and went down with her when she was torpedoed off Bardia in 1941 while engaged in the Tobruk ferry service. Both man and ship however are handled not as individuals but as representing the smaller vessels of the Australian navy and those who commanded them in the second World War; we hear of the "tough" training at Jervis Bay, of the cadet midshipmen on whom depended the reputation of the first officers of the R.A.N., and of Walker's experiences as he rose in the ranks, in peace and war; the tale is given perspective and made the more lifelike by extracts from Walker's letters to his wife and by other letters: the book is rich in miscellaneous and rather discursive detail, and abounds, especially at crises, in short paragraphs and short abrupt sentences that are dramatic but sometimes a little overloaded; but it gives an excellent idea of the life and scenes it describes.

[37] For McGuire's other work, see p. 1388. Mrs McGuire wrote also, in *Twelve Tales of the Life and Adventures of Saint Imaginus* (London, 1946), a delightful little series which contrives to combine light and amusing satire with a spirit of genuine piety. Her other works include *The Royal Australian Navy* (Melbourne, 1948), though this was revised and partly written by Paul McGuire. The McGuires also wrote, with Betty Arnott, *The Australian Theatre* (London, 1948).

CHAPTER XIX

ECONOMICS, POLITICS AND ADMINISTRATION, SOCIAL CRITICISM, LAW

Economics: Shann; Fitzpatrick; Hancock; La Nauze; Walker; Copland. Industrial Surveys: Mauldon; Alan Walker. Politics: Eggleston; Fitzpatrick; Childe. Administration: Bland. Social Criticism: Stephensen. Law: Stone; Evatt. Constitutional Histories: Melbourne; Sweetman; Wood

NO SINGLE heading will cover the material included in this chapter without covering also much that might as suitably be discussed elsewhere; yet all this material is in one way or another related and the terms used above cannot be taken as representing exact categories because their contents continually overlap. Some of it is also related to material that belongs to categories outside this chapter, works on economic history to works on history for example: the economic histories are largely political, and indeed almost every book here dealt with, even if its subject is a legal one, contains a considerable political element, the only notable exception being a work on jurisprudence; and at the same time there are economic elements in most of the books here grouped under the heading of Politics. Again, everything in this chapter, and particularly the economic histories, is in at least some respects a work of social criticism; yet only one book deals with social criticism alone, and it is comparatively slight and its range comparatively small, being confined almost wholly to the literary sphere. In Economics the Period has seen the rise of what may be called an Australian School, whose members, and they include almost every Australian economist of any note, are concerned almost wholly with questions which, if not peculiar to this country, arise out of its political policy and industrial problems; their work makes a considerable use of statistics. Up to the date at which this History closes there had appeared scarcely any notable works on pure economics; the best-known exception, Mills and Walker's *Money*, is not discussed here because it is a textbook. As for the economic histories, they extend not merely to history in general but to such broadly Australian considerations as enter into books like Barnard Eldershaw's *My Australia*, which has been in this History included with works of description. It may be noted that all the economists and political writers who touch upon the subject, and most are drawn to it by a magnetic compulsion, are, though in varying degrees, strongly critical of the Australian protective policy, and in particular of the increasing subsidy of industries which could not stand on their own feet and are becoming a financial burden to the community. With scarcely any exception the economists here dealt with are concerned not so much with theory as with its practical application, and with that only so far as it affects problems that are either primarily local or have at least a strong local bearing; yet some of these problems have a wider bearing also, so that there have been some not unimportant contributions to at least practical aspects of the science of economics. Finally, it may be noted that some works of importance are not mentioned here, either because, being highly specialized or narrow in purpose or largely statistical in method, they do not come within the scope of a history of literature; or because they are not Australian in the sense in which the term is here used.

There were three economic histories of Australia, if the word economic be taken in a very wide sense, but they differ almost as widely in attitude, emphasis, and even in material as books on such a subject could do. Only one of the three can be described as objective; the other two were written to a thesis and are, the one almost and the other quite, bitterly critical of everything that does not fit in with it; indeed each of them is actually a polemic. Shann's *Economic History of Australia* (Cambridge, 1930),[1] is concerned with Australia alone, and may be described as a disquisition upon Australian economic policy from the point of view of a chronicler and commentator who entirely disagrees with it. Fitzpatrick's two volumes, *British Imperialism and Australia, 1783-1833* (London, 1939) and *The British Empire in Australia . . . 1834-1939* (Melbourne, 1941), cover a far wider range,[2] being concerned, as the titles show, with Australia largely, but by no means entirely, in its British relationships: the first volume disparages Britain and her methods of colonization; the second attacks the capitalistic system in Australia, as reflected in its governments, their instruments, and the organization of society generally, and Britain, as the centre of that system, so far as Australia is concerned. The third book, Hancock's *Australia*[3] (London, 1930) is also critical throughout, but it is a much less disappointed criticism, nor is Hancock a polemist, like Shann, much less a bitter polemist writing to a hard-and-fast thesis, like Fitzpatrick; he manages indeed to combine emotional detachment with an underlying fondness both for his own country and for its parent, but there is nothing romantic about this fondness. Edward Owen Giblin Shann[4] (Hobart, 1884-1935) was a graduate and Scholar in

---

[1] References here are to the reprint of 1938.

[2] The sub-title of the first volume is "An Economic History of Australasia", but it contains only a few incidental references to New Zealand. The sub-title of the second is "An Economic History"; it deals with New Zealand rather more than incidentally.

[3] It was reprinted in the Australian Pocket Library in 1945.

[4] His other books include *Cattle Chosen* (see pp. 1346-7) and *Quotas or Stable Money?* (1933).

Constitutional History and Economics of the University of Melbourne and a Research Student at the London School of Economics; he became in turn Acting Professor of Philosophy at Adelaide, Lecturer in Charge of History and Economics in Queensland and Professor of History and Economics in Western Australia, and just before his death he had been appointed to the Chair of Economics at Adelaide; he had also been Economic Adviser to the Bank of New South Wales and among the advisers of the Premiers' Conference on Depression problems. This book's thesis, for that is what it amounts to, is that in the access of wealth after the first World War

> Clever men stampeded the democracy into measures seemingly designed to make our economy a hermit one.
>
> . . . .
>
> . . . Australia has allowed her "national policies" to eat up the gains of a period of unusual plenty and to exceed the effort towards self-sufficiency which she can afford without over-capitalization.

But actually Shann traces the beginnings of the tendency to which he is so vehemently opposed as far back as the paternalism of the earliest days of the colony, when the need for rationing "confirmed in economic childishness that first company of marines and convicts":

> More than the crooked ways of Sydney streets may thus be traced to the period of military rule. Wage earners under the wing of a benevolent government, traders meeting every increase of wages by exacting higher prices for their wares, a country population between the upper and nether millstones of regulated wages and prices seeking state assistance but ready to pursue its own interest by the most direct means —all may be descried in the first dawn of exchange in New South Wales.[5]

Shann loses no opportunity of enforcing his point of view: he tells how the attempt to grow food supplies by public agriculture brought the colony to the very brink of collapse, and how Ruse emphasized the painstaking cultivation of his own land by comparison with the government farm, which was "just scratched over"; and coming to the "Rum Puncheon Rebellion" Shann says that Macarthur stands "head and shoulders above his fellow colonists in economic foresight as well as in money-making"; but if Bligh is not, as he was with earlier historians, the villain of the piece, neither is he, as with Evatt, the hero who can do no wrong; to Shann the rebellion involved

> On one side a Governor blinded by prejudice to the ability of the little community's only first-class brain; on the other a group of officer-traders whom McArthur himself despised. . . . The "Rebellion" . . . was a boil in an unhealthy body in which certain useless elements came into a conflict of mutual destruction which could be ended only by the surgeon's knife;

Shann's is in fact the least one-sided account of the rebellion that we have

[5] p. 27.

had so far. Coming to the unlocking of the land, after the acute remark that the pastoralists have been handicapped by the fact that they have "used the forms of law to overreach public policy", Shann's thesis appears again in the further remark that their small representation in parliament "goes far to explain the persistence with which the politics of 'development' ignore the economic facts of environment and oversea marketing. Perhaps this is Australia's 'tragic flaw'". But it is when Shann reaches modern times that he is most characteristic, and this is also the most notable part of the book: the description of the land boom of the late eighties, with its over-borrowing, free-and-easy bank advances and extravagant living generally, and then the withdrawal of oversea supplies of money, together with the fall in wool and wheat prices and the all-embracing crash that followed, are made very vivid.[6] Discussing the fixation of wages, Shann points out that "fluctuating wages have a social function to perform in minimising unemployment", and urges that the increased costs laid upon industry by protection are deadlier than those of drought; he emphasizes that in a protectionist country "the voice of the special pleader is never stilled", and ends with the warning that a Government "deranges and weakens its whole economy if it forces [its citizens and producers] to work with costs that the outer world is under no obligation to meet". The *Economic History* was preceded, earlier in the same year, by a small book, *Bond or Free?: Occasional Economic Essays* (Sydney, 1930), which was a by-product of it, and may be regarded as supplementary to its last part; too specialized to be grouped with essays in the narrower sense of the word, it will best be discussed here. Its burden is an attack upon what Shann calls "the cult of manipulation", upon "the attempts by Australian Governments to control economic forces during a period of rapid changes in international markets"; but it is clear, from this as from the larger book, that Shann would object to the attempt to control such forces in any circumstances. He regards what Mr Justice Higgins called "the higgling of the market" as "a sanction of economic wisdom", and draws striking parallels between the period in which he was writing and the 1888-90 boom; he points out that falling prices and the refusal of further oversea credits, both of which were of course about to occur, were bound to create a crisis similar to that of the early nineties, as in fact they did; and he urges the reduction of costs in the exporting industries by "scrapping all freak legislation" and by the cessation of "wage-dictation by financially irresponsible bodies". Shann stands in both books for a reversal of Australian policy generally, and he pays no attention to what that policy has achieved outside the field of finance: but whatever may be urged against the

[6] But in Shann's account of the labour upheaval he quite wrongly describes Lane as "an immigrant journalist breathing 'socialism in our time'" (p. 320).

practicability of some of his proposals, it is impossible to deny the justice of much that he says; the warning he utters was badly needed, and it deserves far more attention than it has received. Shann's style is clear and vigorous; he is among the most lively of the writers whose works are included in this Chapter, or in those dealing with history or description either.

Brian (Charles) Fitzpatrick (Warrnambool, Vic., 1905-65) was a graduate of the University of Melbourne, which helped by grants from several of its foundations in the researches leading to the publication of the two books to be mentioned, and for which he was for some time a Research Fellow in the Department of History. Fitzpatrick was General Secretary of the Australian Council for Civil Liberties, and also a teacher and journalist in Sydney, Melbourne and London; he was Assistant Editor of the Sydney *World*, and then became Editor of the *Australian News Review* (Sydney, 1953-4), but for many years his principal occupation in life was that of historical scholarship and research. These two books took four years to write, which seems little enough, seeing the amount of reading involved, and they are a valuable contribution to Australian economic history; they are valuable because they represent an outlook which differs widely from that which was for a long time accepted as a matter of course, though it is approached by more than one historian of today. Two prepossessions run through *British Imperialism and Australia*. The first is that Britain's attitude towards her Australian colonies has been from the beginning entirely self-regarding; that they were to the imperial authorities no more than a dumping ground for her criminals and "redundant poor", and later for surplus capital that was seeking investment after the Napoleonic wars: there is no doubt a good deal of truth in this, though Britain's attitude was probably natural enough in the circumstances of the time; the importance of the statement is in its refutation of the once popular doctrine that the formation of the Australian colonies formed part of a "grand Imperial design". It is true that there remained actually little of this doctrine to refute, though Dr Evatt, in his introduction, goes so far as to refer to the blurring and distortion of the picture by "a romanticism which curiously enough seems to infect most economic historians"; he seems to suggest that among them was Shann, whose faults lay actually in another direction. Fitzpatrick's second prepossession has much less truth in it and lacks in any case the necessary documentation: he has an excellent summary of Britain's attitude to early New South Wales:[7]

> Whatever changes the wars had wrought in English society, the demand from England remained insistent that the colony should not cost much; should absorb shiploads of convicts sent as opportunity offered; be the scene of perfect adminis-

[7] p. 16.

> trative harmony, though the Governor had no executive assistants save those whose vested interest was opposed to Government's; create a public agriculture, though Whitehall omitted to send ploughs or trained farm managers; settle effectively time-expired and pardoned convicts, though an officers' ring closed to them the only colonial market, the store of the Commissary;

but he goes beyond this when he declares that from the beginnings until 1821[8]

> . . . every Governor was required to maintain a prison and plant a peasantry, [although] this could not be done because of the development of a special local interest during the period of uncontrolled military rule. . . . Such an awful consistency, on the part of the British policy for New South Wales, during thirty-three years, is the lamp by which the economic as well as the political history of the times must be read.

This does not fit in very well with the statement on the preceding page that "a spasmodic irritability was almost all the Imperial Government vouchsafed in respect of the insignificant colony"; and no real evidence is brought forward in support of the contention that for thirty-three years Britain aimed consistently at the establishment in Australia of "a country of peasant proprietors". In another instance what appears to be a straining of the facts in support of the thesis would appear to have been altered on second thoughts: Fitzpatrick says[9] that "transportation to New South Wales was at length abandoned when, and only when, it had become clear that capital export and pauper emigration to Australia would be the most profitable form which English interest could take"; but in *The British Empire in Australia*, speaking of the turning back of the *Hashemy* with its cargo of convicts, he says[10] that "the public protest which was made in Sydney was so angry that the Imperial authorities abandoned the attempt to send convicts or disguised convicts to New South Wales". *The British Empire in Australia*, which carries on the story from 1834, is much larger[11] and more detailed, but it is not well organized and the detail is not well digested; the argument is clear enough, but it is overloaded and therefore slowed down, and the reader has to do a good deal of selection and summarizing that ought to have been done by the author: Fitzpatrick says, in his Preface, that "in the wilderness about us it is not easy to see the wood for the trees", and the reader feels a little like this in making his way through the book. The mass of material includes however some that is new, some that is little known and much that was well worth bringing together, and Fitzpatrick's general attitude is valuable as a corrective. It seems a pity that Australian historians should find it necessary to go over the same ground so often, and sometimes

---

[8] p. 17. I have transposed the two parts of this quotation.

[9] p. 19; see also p. 375.

[10] p. 133. But see p. 108. On this point see also Trevelyan's *British History in the Nineteenth Century*, 1931 edition, p. 259.

[11] 504 pages as against 376.

from closely comparable points of view;[12] but such repetitions have been to some extent inevitable, and most of them, including Fitzpatrick's, involve something new and different. In this book the thesis is the growth of the empire of capitalism in Australia and its close relation to its imperial parent, in support of whom it makes continual contributions:[13]

> The reservoir of Australian labour and industry has never failed to provide a stream tributary to the broad river of English wealth. The State did much towards building the reservoir, it maintains it, and it allows no blockage of the stream that flows to Imperial England.

The trouble about Fitzpatrick's argument is that in it facts and their no doubt unconscious manipulation for the purpose of his thesis are so mingled that they are sometimes hard to dissociate: in support of the thesis in general the evidence is to say the least of it insufficient, and Fitzpatrick is inclined as usual to ascribe to deliberate governmental policy much that seems to have resulted in fact from lack of foresight, inefficient planning, accident, and an over-strict adherence by the courts to the letter of a law that is slow to change with the changing needs of the society about it, or to the seizing of opportunities by conservative or capitalistic minorities. There is little doubt that, as Fitzpatrick says, in the defeat of the "workers" in the great strikes of the early nineties "the decisive factor was the participation of governments"; but it does not follow that this participation was a compulsion "to assume a special responsibility to the overseas bondholder"; and again, where he says[14] that Queensland's attempt to induce the Imperial Government to annex the unclaimed part of New Guinea was due to imperialistic motives, at least the general feeling in those days was simply fear of attack from without. However Fitzpatrick makes many points which had not been made or had not been made so well before: for example, his remark that "the prosperity of every new country" originated in Britain's "ever greater dependence on supplies from overseas"; his account of the large part played by great companies in the colonization and development of Australia and New Zealand, and of the effect on the wool industry of the cutting off of supplies of cotton during the American Civil War; his emphasis upon the retreat in State intervention in the economic field, which he considers the peculiar characteristic of Australian development in the twentieth century so far; and his outspoken comment, by reference to named judges, upon the conventional assumption that "the passage of a party politician to a judgeship involves rebirth": he adds, quoting from an American lawyer, that "Courts have often struck down laws designed

[12] The English background to the foundation and early development of the colonies; the Wakefield system, its necessary modifications in practice, and its effects; the attempts in the various colonies to "unlock the land", the failures of the attempts at closer settlement and their reasons, and so on.

[13] p. 504.

[14] Following Hancock (*Australia*, pp. 65–6).

to aid labour, by conservative construction of the constitution, and have emasculated them by interpretation". *The Australian People, 1788–1945* (Melbourne, 1946), which was intended for a wider and more popular audience, has the virtues and defects of Fitzpatrick's other books: like them, it is individual, stimulating, and one-sided, conferring novelty upon facts that are familiar by presenting them in a new colouring, which is often heightened, and with such conviction that the reader may be inclined to accept what he has to say as the whole truth, until some epithet or phrase or marked exaggeration lets the bias out of the bag. It was time that someone emphasized, as Fitzpatrick does, the "drastic modifying", against the background of wars and the expectation of wars, of democratic institutions, and there is some though by no means the whole truth in his description of the "economic separation of Australians, as producers, and British or Anglo-Australians, as shareholders"; but to speak of Macarthur, with all his faults, as "the boss of the Sydney community of sneak thieves, sheep-stealers, procurers and prostitutes" would be outrageous if it were not absurd. As in the other books, Fitzpatrick makes some sharp points that have not been made before, as when he accounts for Labour's failure, in spite of its declared policy, to propose any socialistic measure by the fact that it "gets most of its Ministers of the Crown from the ranks of the only Church which is openly and habitually 'political', and in particular anti-socialist". He says that Labour, as politically organized, "was as set on nation-building within a capitalist economic structure as was Conservatism", but adds that even "the working Australians" have never had "a programme for radical change".[15]

(Sir) William Keith Hancock (Melbourne, 1898–) is a graduate of Melbourne and Oxford, to which he won a Rhodes Scholarship. He has occupied in succession chairs of Modern History at Adelaide and Birmingham and of Economic History at Oxford, and was for several years Director of the Institute of Commonwealth Studies at the University of London; he was also Editor of the United Kingdom War Histories (Civil Series) and then Director of Research, School of Social Science, and Professor of History at the National University, Canberra. His *Australia*[16] makes use for the most part of secondary sources, and, apart from that, little that is said is new in substance; nevertheless the book is by no means unoriginal, for everything Hancock says is the result of individual opinion thoroughly thought out and expressed in an individual manner, so that it is often presented in a new light. In the matter of politics and economics he relies largely upon Shann and Eggleston, and it is probably for this

[15] He mentions, however, as a possible exception, Lane's new Australians (p. 43).

[16] His other works include *Ricasoli and the Risorgimento* (London, 1926), as well as several books written after he had left Australia. Those of his later works which concern us here include *Country and Calling* (London, 1954).

reason that he has been called a *laissez faire* liberal, but this needs qualification: his criticisms, however friendly at bottom, are forthright enough, especially of the increasing cost of our tariff-fed industries and of the policy that has produced them; it is possible, he says,[17]

> . . . to argue strongly for Protection as a policy of power, whereby the nation decides that certain industries are essential and that it must protect them at any cost. . . . But it may be doubted whether it is possible in a democracy, where the State attempts a weak impartiality in distributing its favours, and concessions are wrung from it by partnerships of covetousness. . . . There tends to be a drift towards a position in which nearly all industries enjoy protection; but obviously, before this position has been reached, Protection will have ceased to protect.

What is commonly called in Australia "State Socialism" is actually, Hancock contends, paternalism; it originated in the fact that in Australia, as distinct from the far more richly endowed United States, settlement involved a heavy expenditure which only the government could meet; but he emphasizes the two principal defects of this policy, as practised here. The first has been exposed in detail by Bland: governments do not use the best talents available;

> Democratic sentiment applauds the sound argument that every office boy should have a chance to become a manager, and perverts it into a practical rule that no one shall become a manager who has not been an office boy;[18]

the second weakness has been emphasized by Eggleston: it consists in the pressures put upon the administrators by the politicians, as upon the politicians by their constituents. As remedies, Hancock quotes Bland on public control by means of representative boards with financial autonomy, and Eggleston's reliance upon a realistic individualism; but he urges that "a State should give up running businesses if it will not run them on business principles". As to wages and political Labour, Hancock emphasizes the evils of an equalization that tends to ignore unusual ability, and he points out that Labour, having long ago realized its initial aims, has no longer a policy that will attract the floating vote, so that it has to rely upon the mistakes of its opponents. But Hancock is by no means least interesting outside the political and economic fields, when he has to consider Australians in general, and their origins; as to these, "If there could be such a person as a typical convict," he remarks, it would be "not the countryman who snared rabbits, but the Londoner who stole spoons." And although it was true that ninety-eight per cent of Australians were born either in Australasia or in Britain,

> "Non-Britishers" have played a far from negligible part in developing Australia, and they and their children number more than 10 per cent of the population.

[17] p. 95.
[18] p. 142.

As to characteristics, he accuses Australians of "easy-going good-nature and intellectual laziness", and he sums up their "prevailing ideology" as

> . . . the sentiment of justice, the claim of right, the conception of equality, and the appeal to Government as the instrument of self-realisation.

But Hancock's faculty for pointed and sometimes epigrammatic criticism extends over a wide area: Canberra, he remarks, "is less a national capital than the monument of a compromise between jealous provincialisms"; and, in a chapter on literature and art, "Norman Lindsay's religion is a sort of topsy-turvy Puritanism. It is as if a seventeenth-century Antinomian from Massachusetts had won miraculous access to the works of Nietzsche and Freud." Taken all round, this is the least biased and not the least informative and interesting of the three books here grouped together [and it is certainly the most stylish].

The Period has produced, in La Nauze's *Political Economy in Australia*[19] (Melbourne, 1949) the first connected and by far the most enlightening account of Australia's few economic thinkers of any importance: it amounts to an outline of economic thought in Australia up to the rise of the Australian School which has been already referred to, together with a short summary of the principal characteristics of that school. It is a valuable study, and not from an Australian point of view only; for, since each of the economists it discusses has a greater or lesser place in the history of economics generally, and since new light is thrown on some of them, it represents a real contribution to the general history of economics. John Andrew La Nauze (Boulder, W.A., 1911-) is a graduate of Western Australia and Oxford, to which he won a Rhodes Scholarship; he has lectured in his subject in Adelaide and Sydney, was for several years Professor of Economic History in Melbourne and is now Ernest Scott Professor of History there. The individual studies in his book are of Jevons, Hearn and Syme:[20] Jevons spent five years in early Sydney, where he was an assayer to the Mint, and these years are said to have been extremely important for his mental development; La Nauze lists Jevons's miscellaneous writings in this country, paying special attention to an interesting fragment which he calls a "Social Survey of Sydney".[21] Of the work of Hearn, the first Australian economist to attract attention outside Australia, there is an elaborate critical analysis; La Nauze points out however that Hearn received some of his highest praise for parts of his work that were derivative; indeed he convicts him of plagiarism; nevertheless he admits that "Hearn's book has an enduring, if minor,

---

[19] Professor La Nauze was kind enough to lend me the MS of this book some years ago, when I was writing that part of this History which deals with the early Australian economists. The very considerable debt I owe to it is acknowledged there.

[20] All three have been already discussed in this History (see pp. 355-66).

[21] See this History, p. 356.

place in the history of economic thought." Syme is discussed not merely as an economist but as the converter of Victoria to protection; but La Nauze shows that he was not the "father of protection" in the sense in which the phrase is usually applied to him, and convicts Pratt, his biographer, of important inaccuracies. Neither Hearn nor Syme founded a school; it was not until after the first World War that an Australian school of economists came into existence, largely as a result of the founding of departments of Economics in the Australian universities, and of the Economic Society of Australia and New Zealand and its periodical, the *Economic Record.* La Nauze's critical perceptions are acute; he has the eye of a hawk for a defect, and particularly for anything in the nature of an imposition. His reading is wide and systematic, and his style is clear and logical, with a faint flavour of cynicism and self-consciousness; it is at the same time sharp and imaginative, lighting at times in a revealing phrase or sentence: quoting a remark that Hearn had been "picking holes" in the accepted doctrines of political economy, La Nauze says, "Actually Hearn picked few holes himself; but he did as it were build with holes." "Syme," he says, "did not always create waves, but sometimes [he] rode on their crests"; and he refers to "the usual sign of creative pride, a new terminology".

The formulation and implementation of political policy and the problems arising out of them during the Depression, the second World War, and the reorganization that followed it have greatly increased the number of economists appointed as governmental advisers;[22] E. R. Walker has held several such positions, and his *From Economic Theory to Policy* (Chicago, 1943) is an analytical study of the extent to which the economist may be able to afford such help as is asked of him, and of the methods to be adopted. Edward Ronald Walker (Cobar, N.S.W., 1907-) is a graduate of Sydney and of Oxford, of which he is a Doctor of Philosophy and of Literature; he was formerly Professor of Economics at the University of Tasmania, was Economic Adviser to the N.S.W. Treasury and to the Tasmanian Government and represented the United Nations on a number of international conferences; he was also appointed Australian Ambassador to France. Though *From Economic Theory to Policy* is not an essay in economic theory, a discussion of various types of economic theory is involved, and revisions are suggested in the light of attempts at its practical application. Walker sets out the position clearly and succinctly, and with a general avoidance of technical terms: it is necessary, he points out, to bridge the gulf self-imposed by old-fashioned economists between their theories and the actual world; yet, that being so, the information required may be anywhere, and some of it will be

[22] But Walker quotes a recent count, according to which "there may be as many as five thousand 'economists' in the federal service of the United States" (p. 17).

unrecorded and some hidden from the inquirer by "the obstacle of privacy". The economist must take into account motives and influences that have nothing to do with the markets, with which the conventional economist was alone concerned: pressure groups, sit-down strikes, illegal acts, and a number of problems concerned with human behaviour, in which he may have to call in the psychologist or the sociologist. Since what is asked for is almost always "definite conclusions rather than a nice balancing of all the relevant considerations", he must keep in touch with the political situation as it changes, and must have made his researches in advance, anticipating the direction in which he thinks the political wind will blow; he must be ready to pronounce even if his data are incomplete; and, what is more, since political and other situations do not remain static, he must be something of a prophet; he must formulate a satisfactory theory of economic development, taking into consideration the predictions of other sciences when they are available; he must apply this to the particular circumstances, and hope that it will work. Again, he is often asked to advise upon methods of attaining an objective quite apart from whether he may consider it economically sound, so Walker considers a number of "Objectives of Policy": increase of production, increase of the national real income, economic freedom, security as against progress, increase of population, and so on. There is a final chapter on the reconsideration of the doctrine of Economic Welfare; this Walker considers so vague and subjective that as a guide to policy it has only a limited value; but he suggests that the objectives of the immediate future may well include a minimum standard of consumption and the improvement of working conditions. The essential characteristic of this book is its practical common sense: there is for instance Walker's opposition to the sacrifice of facts to tidiness of theory, since "if the theories are untidy, so is the real world"; and there is his dislike of what he calls "theoretic blight", "the development of economics under the impulse of theoretic construction, for its own sake, along paths which become ever more remote from the real world". The style in which the book is written is in keeping with what is conveyed: simple, logical, and quite unacademic.

Two writers have dealt with the Depression as it affected this country: E. R. Walker again, in an earlier work, *Australia in the World Depression* (London, 1933), and (Sir) Douglas (Berry) Copland (Timaru, N.Z., 1894-1971) in *Australia in the World Crisis: 1929-1933* (Cambridge, 1934); this book had the advantage of appearing a year later than the other. Copland was educated at Canterbury College, New Zealand, and was awarded doctorates by New Zealand, Melbourne, Queensland, Harvard and McGill. He held chairs of Economics in Tasmania and of Commerce in Melbourne, and held positions as Commonwealth Prices Commissioner and Economic Consultant to the Prime Minister, Vice Chancellor of the National University, Canberra, and Australian High Commissioner to Canada. Both books are on the borderline of this History, the second especially, since it has a considerable technical element and is often concerned with tables and figures; but both books must be mentioned here. Walker's is again an essay in applied economics, being, generally speaking, concerned with theory only in order to demonstrate its relevance to the subject, but on some points that are not yet settled and that are essential to his exposition he has made a contribution to pure theory: one of the most important of these concerns the effect of wage reductions upon the Business Cycle; Walker comes to the conclusion that everything depends upon the use to which the entrepreneur puts the resulting gain:[23]

> . . . for a wage-cut which merely increases profits to lead to a decline in unemployment, it must be assumed that entrepreneurs are eager to invest and expand output immediately their profits improve, that the prices of other factors of production are low, and that the banking system is not endeavouring hard to improve the liquidity of its assets. These characteristics are more likely to appear after the Depression has continued for some time. It is when the stage is already set for recovery that the process . . . is most likely to occur. But in the earlier stages of the slump a general wage-reduction will . . . exercise no beneficial effect; on the contrary.

Walker draws parallels between the economic crisis of 1930–32 and those of 1893,[24] of the early forties, and even of 1826–8, and points out the connection in all these cases with economic disturbances in other countries: "Australia is but a corner of the world, and . . . her economic depression has neither its beginning nor its end within her boundaries"; if, as he says, we gain nothing else from knowing this, at least we are able to watch how their doctors treat other countries, and what follows from their prescriptions. He outlines the factors that contributed to the Depression, so far as we are concerned, and in particular the fall in wool and wheat prices and the suspicion that Australia was being extravagant in her use of loan money. He also outlines the defensive measures that were taken and other circumstances that helped Australia through the crisis: Britain's suspending of interest on war debts and, later, of gold payments; the attempts to meet governmental deficits; the mild degree of inflation that resulted from the growth in short-term indebtedness of the governments to the banks; and certain political changes that encouraged the confidence of entrepreneurs. But he pointed out, writing just before the Depression was over, that a substantial and rapid recovery must depend on a rise in the prices of wool and wheat, and on a resumption of oversea borrowing, "of course under proper safeguards". Copland's book is based on a series of lectures delivered at the University of Cam-

---

[23] p. 174.
[24] Here he quotes from Shann's *Bond or Free?*

bridge, and is obviously addressed largely to British readers. He claims that Australia's was "a bold and unorthodox policy at a time when most other countries either refused to take strict measures or sought to conceal from their people the facts of the depression", but he points out that Australia's economic position was affected by certain structural weaknesses: an undue dependence of industry upon the tariff, wasteful capital expenditure, the attempt to maintain an uneconomic standard of living, and governmental deficits. He discusses the recommendations of the Copland committee and the Premiers' Plan, and suggests the adoption of a future policy which would include the selling of certain State undertakings; the confining of public borrowing to the domestic market; the right of debtors to convert loans after a certain date, or, alternatively, a variation of the rate of interest according to price changes over certain periods; and the elimination of the more costly of the protected industries. Unfortunately Copland, writing, it must be remembered, in 1933, advances from chronicle and comment to prophecy: he asserts that Australia's population "*will increase at a much lower rate than formerly*",[25] and that "a slackening of pace with a much reduced inflow of both capital and people appears inevitable in the new world economic forces that are now emerging from the depression".

Surveys of the staple industries of the community and of the life and conditions associated with them are comparatively rare in this country; but there have been several of late years, two of which deal with one of the most important of Australian industries, coal-mining: the first book is an analysis of the conditions, difficulties, and prospects of the industry generally; the second is a study of mining life and conditions in a community of 15,000 people which is almost wholly dependent on mining. Both books are of real importance: the first as providing a broad survey from a general and economic point of view; the second as a study of the men and women concerned, their attitudes, their states of mind; and both are extremely disquieting. The author of the first book, Frank Richard Edward Mauldon (Sydney, 1891-1961), was a graduate of Sydney and Melbourne and of the London School of Economics; he was a Y.M.C.A. officer in the first A.I.F. and Professor of Economics in the University of Western Australia 1941-58; his *The Economics of Australian Coal* (Melbourne, 1929) is one of several of his books on the coal-mining industry.[26] Mauldon describes the extent of Australia's coal resources and the failure to recover more than three-tenths of the material contained in one of the richest and most accessible of our coal deposits, our relative backwardness in mechanization, and our declining export

[25] p. 179. The italics are in the original.

[26] Mauldon has published also works on Australian industry in general or some particular aspect of it, and on other economics subjects.

trade: the causes of this last he puts down to the development of coal mining in some of the countries to which we used to export, the increased exports from South Africa, the increasing use of substitutes for coal, and, not least, our high prices and irregular deliveries. In 1913, he says, the coal of New South Wales was among the cheapest in the world; it is now among the dearest; there are too many mines and a large number of men are employed during only about two-thirds of their time, so that the industry is "burdened with a heavy excess of under-employed capital":

> The situation is essentially that the Australian coal industry and all concerned in it are to-day being squeezed between the upper millstone of a relative decline in demand and the nether millstone of over capacity.[27]

And then there are the troubles due to the nature of the industry itself: "Wherever there is a coal industry there is a field ready for the seeds of dissidence or already ripe with a harvest of troubles." Mauldon finds possibilities of improvement, though they are obviously difficult possibilities, in the adoption of improved technique, in the amalgamation of those collieries whose costs per ton are lowest, and in the closing down of the rest: this would result in the squeezing out of some 5000 mine-workers, who must be absorbed somehow in other industries; they should be compensated at the cost of those who gain by their loss; that is, of the remaining coal-owners and mine-workers, and of the community at large. In the second book, *Coaltown: A Social Survey of Cessnock* (Melbourne, 1945), we descend from Mauldon's aeroplane view and are brought into contact with the miners themselves, their families, and their daily lives, though here also it is necessary of course to generalize. (The Reverend) Alan (Edgar) Walker (Sydney, 1911-) is a graduate of the University of Sydney, has travelled in England and Europe, has represented the Methodist Church of Australasia at the Assembly of the World Council of Churches at Amsterdam, was a Vice President of the Australian Institute of Sociology [and in 1978 became Director of World Evangelism for the World Methodist Council]. Cessnock is "built upon the richest and most extensive coal deposits in Australia", earnings are generally good, and many miners are home-owners; yet their lives are monotonous and dull, short strikes are frequent, there is little community life except that of the unions, and little civic consciousness. Many of the miners dislike their occupation; so do most of their wives, and few of their boys look forward to work in the pits; they take to it however because of the comparatively high wages paid to youth: there is a "fear-psychology", which is related not merely to the work itself but to future prospects, and which plays a part in some of the strikes and stoppages.

[27] p. 263.

The causes of this state of affairs, as Walker sets them out, are in large part historical: they trace back to the Bellbird disaster, in which twenty-one men lost their lives; to the industrial upheaval a few years later, which included a clash with the police, the firing of a number of shots, the wounding of many men, and the killing of one miner; and to the Depression, which swallowed up most of what remained of the miners' savings and half-bought houses, and in which the refusal of the dole to those who had any private resources had the effect of discouraging thrift. The result of all this, coming upon the ordinary discomforts and dangers of a miner's life, has been a continuing bitterness, an intensification of class antagonism, a lack of confidence which destroys public and private ambitions, and a generally pathological state of mind. Among the remedies Walker suggests are the establishment of secondary industries in order that the community may not be dependent upon mining alone, and to help reduce the isolation which constitutes a large part of the trouble; the adoption of some means by which the men shall share in the control and profit of the mines; and the abolition or at least modification of the contract system, which is, he says, a cause of hostility, friction and strikes. This is at once a scientific and a very human study, painstaking and detached, and set out simply and straightforwardly.

State Socialism in Victoria (London, 1932) has a relevance that extends beyond the particular State with which it is immediately concerned; indeed it extends beyond the boundaries of the Commonwealth; its author, (Sir) Frederick William Eggleston (Melbourne, 1875-1954), served in the first A.I.F. Eggleston's political experience has been wide and varied, within and without Australia: he was on the staff of the Australian Delegation to the Paris Conference and has been Chairman of the Australian Delegation to the Institute of Pacific Relations in several conferences and Australian Minister to China and the United States; in Australia, he was a member of the Victorian parliament for seven years, during which he was Minister in charge of several of the great government departments. This experience converted him "from a strong advocate of public ownership and operation of all common services to the view that under present circumstances the conditions for the successful operation of many of these services do not exist in Victoria." Eggleston stands therefore with such economists as Shann and Copland in opposition to Australian economic policy in general, but with some important qualifications; he does not condemn State Socialism wholly or in itself, but considers that it has been carried much too fast and too far; he thinks that it is justifiable within a certain area, and that that area might be gradually ana experimentally extended; on the whole, however, it has been a failure: it has achieved no striking success; from a financial point of view it has been disastrous; it has demoralized politics and is impeding social progress.[28] Yet Eggleston considers that its record is by no means discreditable: the internal management of the State departments has been almost entirely free from incompetence, patronage and corruption; some of the managers have shown great administrative capacity and some of the political leaders have shown "no little statesmanship"; and success has been achieved in certain undertakings in which political interference has been avoided. Like Shann, Eggleston traces back the origins of State interference to the abnormal circumstances of the penal settlement. Criticizing the government departments individually, he considers that the worst of the failures has been the attempt to settle the land: here, he says, "the planner has always been wrong; the most successful methods resemble the process of throwing the puppy into the water and letting him find out how to swim". The most interesting part of the book however is the estimates of the causes of the general failure of State socialism in Victoria: Eggleston sets these down as political interference, vested interests, and the incapacity of parliament for business management[29] and for enlightened and consistent policy; he blames, first, the politician, and ultimately the average citizen, who "does not elect sufficiently enlightened leaders, and is not a sufficiently magnanimous follower". In fact, "the ideals behind socialism are humane and Christian; if socialism fails it is because we are not good enough for it". The dominant type among Australian citizens is what Eggleston calls "the Self-contained Man"; indifferent to tradition and resistant to influence, he wants leaders like himself, who will do as they are told; we must not build, as in the past, upon his weakness, but take advantage of his strength:[30]

> His strength is his self-reliance and independent thought; his weakness is his incapacity for co-operation; he cannot be swayed like the mob, nor can he be moved as part of a machine like a proletarian: he must be persuaded to join in. . . . There is, indeed, a more profound weakness, and that is his selfishness and willingness to devolve his responsibility.

As Eggleston himself admits, his book contains defects in the way of arrangement and repetition; also, it is not quite consistent, but it does contain some careful and individual thought; like most of the leading Australian economists, Eggleston is clear, logical and succinct, and his style is exceptionally alive; not infrequently it sparkles: "Democracy," he says, "is an aspiration, not an achievement"; "Canberra . . . is a glorious place, but people refuse to live there unless necessity compels;

[28] He even goes so far as to say that "political operation of business concerns brings about a diseased condition of the whole body politic" (p. 257).

[29] A realization of this brought about the creation of autonomous corporations to which certain State services were handed over.

[30] p. 342.

it is occupied by public servants living in the various suburbs planned for them according to salary";[31] "The mind, unless it is reinforced by character, is a sycophant; distrustful of itself, it longs for authority and power, and therefore worships force"; "workers' organisations give one the impression of immense power completely uniformed by intelligent direction"; "When Mr Micawber signed the promissory note he said, 'Thank God that's settled.' This is not an unfair picture of the modern community." But Eggleston differs from some of the other critics of the Australian economic system in that though he can be cynical he is not bitter; on the contrary his book as a whole contains a core of sympathy and even of qualified hope. Another book of Eggleston's, *Search for a Social Philosophy* (Melbourne, 1941), is based in the main on his academic training and international experience, as the first book grew out of his political experience in Victoria: it embodies a search for a unity underlying the social sciences, whose interrelationship he describes as having been obscured by their specialization in separate compartments; Eggleston finds this relationship in patterns of life and conduct which are the results of corresponding mental patterns, and whose practical realization has involved the creation of specialized institutions. His theories and analyses are seldom basically novel, though there is novelty in some of the ideas incidentally expressed: the most interesting part of his book is in the final chapters, which deal with international affairs, the clash of State interests and the concept of power in a changing world order; and most interesting of all is his conclusion, which amounts to a repetition of that of the other book, enlarged to a world scale. In that book the failure of certain methods and institutions adopted by an Australian community with the purpose of bringing about a preferable state of society was traced back to the selfish and short-sighted attitude of the ordinary citizen; here the failure to resolve the differences between world communities by other means than force is traced to the same cause: "Progress," says Eggleston,[32]

> ... cannot be regarded as an automatic process; it depends ... at the present juncture ... on the conscious choice of sufficient numbers of leaders and people to install the higher standards that are necessary and to refuse to accept crude forms of power-organization.... Men tend to surrender to them because they are afraid of their share of responsibility.... These vast mechanisms not being fully animated by the human spirit are only responsible for their own maintenance and expansion and are therefore non-ethical.... [They] cannot provide a feasible way of life; they will succeed, if they do succeed, only at the expense of converting the world into a desert.... We refuse to believe that human values will be so crushed, but we cannot say that it is impossible, because the decision that it shall not happen ... must be made by the free man.

Eggleston's style has not here the sparkle that helps to give its life to the first book, but it is full of pithy summaries that make clear and often

[31] This, of course, was written back in 1932.
[32] pp. 351–2.

striking pictures in the mind: "Armaments will destroy the objective in order to secure a victory which will be useless because of that destruction"; the Austinian theory "is a theory for the lawyer and not for the student of social institutions"; "The human mind cannot think out the position on each occasion on which decision is demanded. . . . Man, therefore, . . . builds up a system or pattern of ideas which becomes for him a routine method of solving his day to day problems."[33]

Brian Fitzpatrick's *Short History of the Australian Labor Movement* (Melbourne, 1940) is based on a wide reading, though it is sometimes dependent upon secondary sources; it should be extremely useful, if its admitted bias is borne in mind. It is a highly compressed digest of fact and opinion: the facts, some of which are by no means widely known, and those conclusions which are based strictly upon the facts, are reliable, and some of them throw new light upon the development of unionism in Australia; the opinions, and those generalizations which proceed beyond the fact, are sometimes extremely unjust. Fitzpatrick makes the interesting and important point that 1890 does not mark nearly so distinct a line of cleavage in the history of the Australian Labour movement as is commonly supposed; that "what was done after 1890 was to elaborate and extend what had been done before, and especially in the five years from 1885"; and the reason why it was in 1890 that class warfare broke out was "because this was the time at which, a long period of prosperity having unmistakably closed, capitalists decided that the time for making concessions to the unions had closed also." Again, Labour's entry into the political field did not amount to an abandonment of industrial action, except for the time being; it involved merely a realization that industrial action could not hope to succeed until the unions had recovered after their defeat in the great strikes. On the other hand, the assertion that "the possessing classes that have opposed Labor have not . . . attempted to . . . redistribute wealth in the interests of social justice" is true perhaps if construed quite literally, but it is certainly misleading; income tax, land tax, arbitration laws, the breaking up of large estates, are obvious instances of efforts, even if they have by no means always been successful, to redistribute wealth in the interests of social justice, which would have come to nothing without the assent of a majority of the possessing classes:* and few economists would agree that "real" wages were lower when Fitzpatrick's little book was published than at the beginning of the century. His bias is evident again in his discussion of conscription, and in his references to the "perfidy" of those who left the Labour movement on that issue: that Holman was a "'Labor' careerist" could not have been alleged by any unbiased person who knew him, and is certainly not made

[33] After the closing date of this History Eggleston published *Reflections of an Australian Liberal* (Melbourne, 1952).

* [But assent to taxation means little if the possessing classes find means of circumventing payment; tax evasion is now a major industry in Australia.]

by Evatt, in *Australian Labour Leader*, which Fitzpatrick regards as "the obvious approach to the study" of these matters; also, Evatt is just to Holman's "socialistic" achievements, which Fitzpatrick belittles. Still, it is hard to imagine a history of Labour written without bias, and there is no difficulty in allowing for it here.

Although written nearly twenty years earlier,[34] Childe's *How Labour Governs* (London, 1923) may be regarded as complementary to Fitzpatrick's book. Vere Gordon Childe (Sydney, 1892-1957) left Australia in the early twenties, and beneath his world reputation as an archaeologist this first book of his had been overshadowed and almost forgotten.* Childe is a graduate of Sydney and Oxford, and was for several years private secretary to John Storey when he was Labour Premier of New South Wales; after travelling in Central Europe he became Librarian to the Royal Anthropological Institute and then Professor of Prehistoric European Archaeology at Edinburgh; he was later Professor of Prehistoric European Archaeology and Director of the Institute of Archaeology in the University of London. The chapters that have been added to the history of political and industrial Labour during the last twenty years contain little that is radically new, and though after some of the recent historical work Childe's book is in some respects out of date, it contains several analyses that are new if not profound, and that are worth reading today. Labour sympathies are always evident;[35] but the facts, as distinct from the terms used sometimes in describing them, are presented fairly, except that full justice is not done to those who have for one reason or other left the Labour Party, and in particular to Holman. Perhaps Childe's most interesting chapter is that in which he discusses the heterogeneous elements of which the party is composed; after distinguishing between its two main sections, the industrialists, and the socialists who are in a small minority, he discusses Labour's principal allies outside the "working class": the democrats and the nationalists, who are attracted for what Childe calls sentimental reasons; the small farmers and shopkeepers, prospectors and small mining proprietors, whose motives are economic; the Roman Catholics, who hope, perhaps, for educational concessions, or perhaps, though Childe does not suggest this, they side with Labour because the Church desires power, and believes it stands a better chance with this party than with the other; also, it may hope to break down socialistic

---

[34] It ends with 1921 (Preface).

[35] Childe says in his preface that though he has assumed "the hypothesis that the present organisation of society involves some sort of exploitation and enslavement of the workers", this must not be taken to imply his "personal acceptance of the theory in question", and that "on the other hand" he hopes to publish a sequel on the work of Labour governments which "may be regarded as the most serious criticism of the whole position". But he speaks of "ratting" (p. xiv), "apostasy" (p. 10), "a yellow union", "a tame union", and "a bosses' organisation" (p. 97), all without quotation marks, and of "the selfish and cowardly opportunism which has distinguished the workers' parliamentary representatives" (pp. 52-3). The sequel has not appeared.

* [It was reprinted, edited by F. B. Smith, with an excellent Introduction, in Melbourne, 1964.]

aspirations from within; and there is the liquor trade, whose object may be to prevent no-licence or nationalization, and perhaps to extend the hours during which public-houses are allowed to remain open. Childe has also an interesting analysis of the reasons why the I.W.W., which was once powerful in Australia, and which, according to Childe "can claim the credit for the defeat of Conscription", has now quite faded out. This book is compressed and sometimes a little clogged with detail, but it contains some shrewd observations; for example:

> In general Caucus likes an able man as leader, but in filling other posts inclines to pay more attention to personal qualities . . . than to fitness for Ministerial responsibility;

and

> The aggressive radicalism of Labour has . . . forced their opponents into the *role* of guardians of the constitution . . . and defenders of the rights of property.

Probably no one person in his day in Australia had a more thorough acquaintance with the administrative functions of its governments than Francis Armand Bland (Macdonaldtown, Sydney, 1882–1967). From a suburban State school he entered the civil service, and, working at night, graduated in Arts and Law; he spent a couple of years at the London School of Economics, became Assistant Director of Tutorial Classes and finally was appointed Professor of Administration, the first in Australia, at the University of Sydney. Bland published a number of books[36] on aspects of government and its activities, through all of which run a critical point of view and certain principles that are set out and illustrated in his first book, *Shadows and Realities of Government* (Sydney, 1923): its object is to "get behind the shadows and fictions which darken our thoughts, and to reveal the agents in whose hands rests the actual administration of affairs". Bland points out[37] that "it is not the business of a Cabinet Minister to work his department. His business is to see that it is properly worked", and he urges that it should be possible to "discriminate between matters of fact in administration and matters which are primarily questions of party politics". On the other hand, though "competitive examinations and the elimination of patronage have got rid of most of the artful and indolent" in the civil service, even Ministers, let alone other members of parliament and the general public, are at the disadvantage that they know little of the methods of procedure of specialized officials and their departments: the remedies suggested are "the comprehensive education of the citizens in public affairs"; the encouragement of public officials to publish

---

[36] These include *Budget Control* (Sydney, 1931), and *Planning the Modern State* (Sydney, 1934).

[37] p. 72. This is a quotation; see Bagehot's *English Constitution* and compare Lowell's *Public Opinion and Popular Government*, p. 296.

their views on important administrative questions; and even their admission to the floor of the House, to explain the underlying principles of and reasons for particular measures, from the administrative point of view.

But Bland realizes that there is plenty of room for improvement in the civil service itself; he would admit university graduates to the higher ranks, establish grade tests, transfer officers from one department to another, second selected officers to the universities for whole-time study, and in special cases send them abroad while they are still young: none of these proposals is new, except in Australia, but they needed emphasis. Bland also urges that in recruiting to the civil service a sharp line should be drawn between the higher and lower grades of work, and, of course, that departmental heads should be appointed on merit alone, with entire disregard of seniority. Bland has been called an old-fashioned Liberal, and his political leanings are fairly evident; also, in spite of what he has to say about the need for better training of officials he is almost always on the side of the official as against the politician. In spite of his outright and unqualified criticisms, his style is dry and uninspiring, and yet, as with certain other Australian writers upon practical subjects, it brightens now and then to something approaching epigram.[38] *Shadows and Realities of Government* was planned as a textbook, but it is also an original investigation of a kind of which there have been many in Britain but few in Australia: some of the reforms here urged have since been adopted or partially adopted, but there is still much to be done; in the meantime Bland's work is known to every intelligent civil servant, and ought to be known to every politician and to anyone else who is interested in governmental administration and its problems.

The general attitude of P. R. Stephensen's[39] *The Foundations of Culture in Australia* (Sydney, 1936), which had begun in his short-lived *Australian Mercury* in the previous year, is curiously reminiscent of the nineties; but it emphasizes, and sometimes over-stresses, truths that still hold, or partly hold, today: "a gumtree is not a branch of an oak", Australia must develop a culture of her own in which what she takes from Britain or any other country can be no more than an element; at present our culture is "stultified, smug and puerile", largely because second-rate minds have crawled to the top, and our lazy intellectuals "lurk in their castles of isolation", re-echoing the ideas of English books and magazines and making no effective protest against our monstrous censorship of books, or against the Fascism that is a greater menace than Bolshevism could ever be. In at least

---

[38] For instance: "Political expediency plays havoc with public principles" (*Shadows and Realities of Government*, p. 48); and "We might have described this story [of the conflict between political theory and administrative necessities] as a pilgrimage from patronage to proficiency."

[39] For biographical details see the discussion of Stephensen's short stories, p. 1253.

the literary sphere there have been some advances since this book was written: Australian publishers, or some of them, are nowadays willing to take a risk with a worthwhile book; the Dad and Dave tradition has worn itself out; the Arts faculties of the Universities are no longer "colonial" strongholds; and if an Australian professor were to talk such nonsense as Cowling did about the impossibility of there being an Australian literature he would be received with amusement rather than with indignation. There are a few errors of judgment: it is absurd to say that "Archibald's *Bulletin* . . . did little more for the real development of Australian culture than to substitute larrikinism for convictism"; and to assert that there were "more than a dozen men and women of real literary genius in Sydney" when Stephensen wrote, or now either for that matter, is to confuse genius with talent. Still, the book has some historical importance and remains worth while because of its vigorous and sincere enthusiasm, even if its tone is sometimes rather shrill, and because of its warning against an increasingly serious fundamental weakness in Australian society: [fear of independence, blandness, cultural passivity].

Of the few legal works of the present Period that may be discussed here, most are historical. Only one, Stone's *The Province and Function of Law* (Sydney, 1946), deals with the theory of law as distinct from its practice, though it has a thorough and elaborate basis in the Common Law, and it comes by no means wholly within the sphere of this History, since its author is English by birth and the greater part of it was written before he became resident in Australia; nevertheless it cannot be ignored here. Julius Stone (Leeds, England, 1907-), became Professor of International Law and Jurisprudence at Sydney in 1942; he is a graduate of Oxford, Leeds and Harvard, has occupied Chairs of Law at Harvard, Leeds and Auckland, and has held a Rockefeller Fellowship in Social Sciences. It is not surprising that this book should have taken fourteen years to write, for it is a work of extremely wide reading and fills nearly 800 large octavo pages. In the days of Austin and his school attention was focused upon law as a logically self-consistent system, a system of closely related precedents; modern inquiries have been occupied, not with law in isolation, but with law as reflecting justice, with its effects upon man's attitudes and behaviour, and, in reverse, with the effects of these upon the law: from this point of view Stone examines the English, American, Dominion and also foreign systems of law, and he analyses the Austinian tradition in the light of the conclusions of the social sciences of today. He discusses the interaction in judicial decisions between precedent and the facts of the case, and the gradual processes of change that are due to the creative power which remains in the hands of the judge: he quotes the dictum of Lord Wright, that "A good judge is one who is the master, not the slave, of the cases", and of Mr Justice O. W. Holmes, that "the whole outline of the law is the resultant of a conflict at every point between logic and good sense", and that "the actual life of the law has not been logic; it has been experience". He discusses the various theories of legal justice, and points out that the search for it involves a constant criticism of the existing law, a constant unwillingness to accept it as more than a means to other ends, and that justice involves at least the organization of society in such a way that man's varying wants may be freely expressed and provided with the means of attempting to satisfy them from society. This book is the product of an individual mind and a wide learning working upon an immense mass of material, whose multiplicity of detail tends at times to blur the edges of its conclusions and to crowd upon the paths by which they are reached; another result is a general effect of diffusiveness, though there is no individual passage that is not succinct. The style is logical and as a general rule clear and precise, yet there is also a tendency to generalizations that are not invariably perspicuous; the book is elaborately organized, indeed rather too elaborately, for it is divided into a series of compartments, often quite small, with the result that the argument tends to become discontinuous: nevertheless it is a real achievement, in that, apart from its thesis, it represents a systematic survey of common-law theory, bringing together for this purpose "an otherwise hopelessly dispersed literature".

A particular aspect of the Law of the Constitution that concerns Britain as well as Australia, and that concerns also the other British Dominions and involves precedents from them generally is H. V. Evatt's[40] *The King and His Dominion Governors* (London, 1936). This is a study of the Reserve (or Emergency or Crisis) Powers of the Crown, of the legal conventions or unwritten laws that govern the relations between the monarchy or its representatives in the Dominions and their ministers in parliament. At some kinds of political crisis, when for instance the leader of a government asks for a dissolution, or in Britain for additional appointments to the House of Lords or in a Dominion to the Upper House, the question may arise whether his request should be refused, or perhaps, in the case of a Dominion, reserved for the decision of the imperial authorities. Evatt points out that a clear understanding of the law on the subject may then be of great importance to the political parties concerned, to the electorate, and also to the Crown or its Dominion representative, whose neutrality must remain beyond suspicion; yet these powers are nowhere adequately detailed, precedents sometimes conflict, and constitutional authorities may differ widely.[41] Evatt quotes Lowell[42] to the effect that

---

[40] For Evatt's historical work, see pp. 1347–8, and for his biographical work, pp. 1371–3.

[41] For example, Jenks and Keith, on the question whether the Crown may act directly on the advice of Dominion Ministers (p. 4).

[42] p. 8.

> "The forces to be studied do not lie upon the surface, and some of them are not described in any document or found in any treatise. They can be learned only from men connected with the machinery of public life. A student must, therefore, rely largely upon conversations which he can use but cannot cite as authorities, and the soundness of his conclusions must be measured less by his references in footnotes than by the judgment of the small portion of the public that knows at first hand the things whereof he speaks."[43]

This book analyses in detail a series of instances, mostly but by no means invariably Australian, in which the exercise of such Reserve Powers has given rise to disputes, in order to try to discover the principles that underlie them; Evatt urges that "however 'un-English' precise definition may be"[44] it will be dangerous "to allow uncontrolled discretion, and the anarchy resulting from the absence of any binding rule, to prevail in the future"; as he points out, in similar circumstances two Governors or a Governor and the imperial authorities may proceed upon entirely different principles, and he compares in particular Sir Philip Game's dismissal of the Lang administration in 1932[45] and the Imperial Government's recall of Sir Gerald Strickland when he proposed to dismiss the Holman administration in 1916.[46] What is required, it is contended, is the regulation and control of the exercise of great prerogative powers "by general principles openly stated and applied with complete indifference to the welfare or detriment of particular parties or interests". It is true that a considerable proportion of the decisions Evatt considers unsatisfactory were unfavourable to Labour, but they were made by Governors who may occasionally, as a result of their early training, have had some unconscious bias; and there is no doubt about the bias of Professor A. B. Keith, who is usually accepted as a constitutional authority but with whom Evatt is continually at variance: Keith could go so far as to refer to "the extremist views" and the "wild promises of prosperity" of a Labour leader.[47] Evatt's authority as a constitutional lawyer, his thorough investigation of precedents and his logical reasoning make his book a valuable reference for politics students, as well as this area of unwritten constitutional law. [His apprehension was vindicated by the Governor-General's 1975 dismissal of the Prime Minister.]

There were three constitutional histories, only one of which, however, extends beyond the attainment of self-government by New South Wales; by far the best is A. C. V. Melbourne's *Early Constitutional Development in Australia* (London, 1934), which is extremely full and detailed and is

---

[43] Lowell's is a general reference, but "he intends," says Evatt, "to include in his comment the rules governing the relationship between the Crown on the one hand, and the other elements of British policy on the other".

[44] He is here quoting King Magnus in Shaw's *The Apple Cart*.

[45] Chapter 19.

[46] Chapter 17.

[47] *The Constitutional Law of the British Dominions*, 1933 edition, pp. 155, 159 (quoted by Evatt, p. 6, footnote 2).

based on researches in Australian and British libraries which were made possible by a Rockefeller Fellowship. This was preceded by Edward Sweetman's *Australian Constitutional Development* (Melbourne, 1925), which is even fuller at some points and extends to the attainment of self-government in the other Australian colonies; the third, F. L. W. Wood's much smaller *Constitutional Development of Australia* (London, 1933), deals with events up to the date of its publication, but it is much less detailed and slighter throughout than either of the others though in it scholarship is combined with a more general appeal: in all three books the subject is treated fully, in the sense that not merely the various constitutions are discussed, but also their working out and the circumstances, local and British that led up to them. Although Melbourne's book[48] ends with the attainment of self-government in New South Wales, it includes, up to that point, the whole of the territory within that colony's original boundaries; there were to have been two more volumes dealing with the other colonies. It begins like a general history of Australia, with an outline of the circumstances in which the settlement of the colony was decided upon; here Melbourne differs from most Australian historians in remarking[49] that

> It is difficult to believe that ministers in the United Kingdom were thinking of a convict colony, for Phillip was given authority over an area infinitely larger than was required for that particular purpose. Possibly they hoped that they were laying the foundations of a second empire, possibly they were anxious merely to forestall the French;

but he does not go further into this question, and seems to have come to no definite conclusion upon it. In describing the original machinery of government Melbourne raises the question as to the invalidity of Macquarie's proclamations, including his pardons, and of the constitution of the Criminal Court. He notes that before the end of 1822 there was no popular demand for representative institutions, the Exclusives were afraid these would give power to the Emancipists; the Emancipists thought only of their legal status. Wentworth had to create his party; he "was not the mouthpiece, he was the inspiration", and his object was to win power and influence.[50] Melbourne shows how the British authorities regarded each of the various Constitution Bills as a merely temporary measure, and were prepared to advance further towards meeting local demands as the colony developed. But they were faced with this difficulty, that such demands were for long contradictory, coming as they did on the one hand from the Emancipists and on the other from the Exclusives; but in any case the changes made in the Act of 1823, and in particular the creation of a Legislative Council and the alterations in the judicial system,

[48] For biographical details and for Melbourne's *Wentworth*, see pp. 1373-4.
[49] p. 6.
[50] On this point see Melbourne's *Wentworth*, which is discussed on pp. 1373-4 of this History.

were necessary to remedy the legal defects caused by the Governors' taking, and indeed being compelled to take, too much upon themselves. The struggles between the opposing parties and between their representatives in England, their petitions and counter-petitions, all of which drew more attention to the colony and its needs and led to the first instalments of self-government in 1828, are made very real; and it is shown how antagonisms weakened with the combination of the two parties against the discontinuance of transportation, and faded out as the free element in the population increased, as the popular feeling against transportation grew, and as it became clear that it was to be, and indeed would have to be, discontinued and that free institutions would follow. Melbourne goes on to show how

> The Act of 1842 gave to New South Wales the form of government known as representative government, that is, it admitted certain elected members to the legislature, but withheld from it that power to control the administration which is the essential characteristic of responsible government.

Melbourne also makes clear, as most historians do not, how eight years after the cessation of transportation in 1840, so far as New South Wales was concerned, the British authorities proposed to renew it, in order to relieve Van Diemen's Land, and under the excusable impression that it would be acceptable; it was the general public, as distinct from its old leaders, who protested vehemently and turned back the *Hashemy*. This book is so tightly packed that there is a risk of being lost in detail, particularly since the early constitutional history of New South Wales proceeds in a spiral, of which each curve almost parallels its immediate predecessor. The style is correspondingly condensed; though clear and logical, it may be described as constipated; but given close attention, the landscape opens out with only occasional passages of density. This is the standard work on the subject,[51] and seems likely to remain so for as long as it is possible to look ahead.

Edward Sweetman (Lancashire, England, 1875-1966) migrated to Australia as a young man, and then became a lecturer in History and Education at the Melbourne Teachers' College, and afterwards in British History at the University: he had a Melbourne Doctorate of Letters and a London Doctorate of Philosophy, the first of which was awarded for the thesis on which was based his *Australian Constitutional Development*; and Melbourne also twice awarded him a Harbison-Higinbotham scholarship. Sweetman published a number of other books, whose subjects include the early constitutional history of Victoria and the history of Victorian State education. He divides the constitutional history of New South Wales into

---

[51] Scott, though he had written an appreciative introduction to Sweetman's book, considered that Melbourne's would not be superseded (*Economic Record*, June 1935, p. 133).

four periods, from the foundation to the Jurisdiction Acts of 1823 and 1828; thence until 1842; thence to the Act of 1850; and finally to the attainment of full representative government and responsible government in 1856: Melbourne follows the same scheme, except that he divides the first period into two; this however is a natural, perhaps the only natural, plan of division. The two books have the same story to tell, and they depend, broadly speaking, upon the same material, though their emphases may and do differ and different phases of the story are elaborated: Melbourne's book is more neatly constructed, in that some of Sweetman's descriptions are in the nature of excursions; nevertheless, if Sweetman's, though earlier, is taken as supplementary to the other, this adds to its value. Sweetman's chapters on the Australian Patriotic Association, the foundation, its aims and its opponents, the Exclusives, are in themselves well worth reading: he gives a clear indication of the respective backing of the two parties in a quotation from a dispatch of Bourke's in 1836, which says that a petition transmitted through him by the Exclusives contained less than 400 signatures,[52] as against 6000 in a counter-petition by the Association. Sweetman also describes the influences that combined to postpone the grant of further instalments of self-government before 1842, in particular the books of Macarthur, Mudie and Lang, whose authors also were in England in 1837-38; and the Canadian rebellions in 1837. He mentions as among the events that helped to bring the Exclusives and Emancipists together, their mutual opposition to the British Government's proposals to subdivide New South Wales; and as one of the indications of approaching unity he mentions James Macarthur's expression of regret for "the erroneous opinions" contained in his book. There is also a detailed account of the colonists' dissatisfaction after the 1842 Act, and their reasons:[53]

> . . . the great increase in the free population, the period of financial depression through which the colony was then passing, the influence of Canadian constitutional affairs upon the people and politicians of New South Wales, and . . . the publication in the press of the stirring speeches of Wentworth and other members of the Legislative Council upon the land question and other grievances.

This book is not so tightly packed as the other, and its style is now and then rather verbose, as well as being comparatively formal and just a little old-fashioned; it is however easier to read, more lifelike and less like a logical summary, though it does not produce quite the same effect of unity. Melbourne's book does not entirely supersede Sweetman's, in

[52] "As I am informed" (pp. 118-19). The second petition was adopted at a public meeting, the first "at a private house of one of the members of the Executive Council"; this would no doubt account for the large number of signatures to the counter-petition, but of course the Exclusives also could have called a public meeting if they had thought it advisable.

[53] p. 180. The financial depression would be one cause of the Council's opposition to the Governor's estimates.

virtue not only of Sweetman's fuller and more realistic description of certain phases of Australian constitutional history, but of the dispatches, official letters and statutes of importance to the subject which it reprints in appendices.

Wood's[54] much smaller *Constitutional Development of Australia* contains comparatively little that is new in the way of actual fact, and he does not invariably go back to first sources; but this is not to suggest that he neglects them, and all he says has taken the impress of a mind that is remarkably clear and is able to generalize without neglecting anything that is really essential, so that his narrative is never clogged by detail; his arrangement is logical and consistent, and yet never merely "documentary", and he makes no excursions. There is something curiously attractive about the simplicity of Wood's language, which is remarkably unsophisticated for a writer of today; yet he is able to cope adequately with whatever comes within his range; his style, like his father's, by which, as in his history, it has evidently been influenced, is a model in its kind. He often conveys more lucidly what others have said before him, but he has also some shrewd points of his own: speaking of the illegality of the early system of government of the colony, he says [55] that

> . . . since the Revolution of 1688, Parliament had claimed the right to make laws for the colonies as well as for England; and when in 1774 a constitution had to be given to the new possession of Canada, this was done by Act of Parliament. In fact, it was reasonably clear that the King alone had no longer the right to give a constitution to a colony, and that the politicians were legally wrong in following the precedents of the seventeenth century instead of the precedent of the Quebec Act of 1774.

And he gets to the root of the matter when he says, first, speaking of the need for a Council to advise the early governors,[56] that

> . . . a despotic Government was finding it necessary to secure the help of representative men, and despotism was working its own cure;

and yet, speaking of the resistance of the Victorian Council to Latrobe at a later stage of colonial development,

> Everything seemed to show that Governors and Councils could not share power. Unless the Governor were to be a despot, there must be set up full Parliamentary Government.

Wood's remarks about the period of political confusion after 1856, that lasted until organized parties had arisen and politicians had been trained in parliamentary procedure, are interesting not only in themselves, but as suggesting a comparison with what Margot Hentze has to say about

---

[54] For Wood's historical work, see p. 1355.

[55] p. 15.

[56] p. 28.

similar difficulties in Italy after the attainment of independence.[57] And finally, at the end of a fairly full though generalized account of the gradual attainment of Federation and of the development of the Caucus system, referring to the claims that Caucus itself should be subservient to a non-Parliamentary party organization, Wood remarks shrewdly[58] "It is possible that Parliament may become just a convenient device for expressing decisions reached by the rank and file."

[57] See this History, pp. 1352-3.
[58] p. 234.

CHAPTER XX

THE SCIENCES

Anthropology. The Australian Aborigine: Elkin; Basedow; Hasluck. Special Studies: Strehlow; Phyllis Kaberry. American Contributions: Porteus; Warner. Papua and the Pacific: Williams; Hogbin. Other Sciences: Agar; Others

As in the preceding Period, science means here largely anthropology, for there has been plenty of that and little else that can be recorded in this History. The anthropologists have found a threefold opportunity in the establishment in 1925 of a Department of Anthropology at the University of Sydney, which has trained most of them; in the Australian National Research Council, which has subsidized many of their researches;[1] and in the periodical *Oceania*,[2] which has provided them with a forum; indeed, as with the philosophical output of the Period though to nothing like the same extent, the anthropological output must not be judged by books alone, for many valuable articles have appeared in *Oceania* only. For the first time since Baldwin Spencer the life of Australian Aboriginal communities has been investigated in what remains of the tribes on or beyond the fringe of civilization, and to this investigation two American visitors have contributed; native communities in Papua and New Guinea have also been investigated on the spot, and so have others in the Pacific.

Until the appearance of Professor Elkin's *The Australian Aborigines* (Sydney, 1938) there had been no thoroughly satisfactory account of the Australian natives generally, their social life and organization, their customs and beliefs, all within one cover.[3] Information on these subjects had been of course obtainable, but it was scattered and much of it could be found only in the larger libraries; what was needed was a single volume which would serve as an introduction for scientists, administrative officers, missionaries and universities, and which should also if possible meet the needs of members of the general public who would like to know something about the first Australians. The attainment of such a twofold purpose must naturally be difficult; the scientific worker and the expert in training are well provided for in Elkin's book, but parts of it are rather too detailed and technical for the general reader. This is, however, more than the

[1] They have also received substantial grants from the Rockefeller Foundation and the Carnegie Corporation.

[2] See p. 1335.

[3] See, however, what is said on pp. 1450–1 about Basedow's book.

ordinary reference book and summary; it is based not only on reading but on field-work among the tribes: indeed without a basis of field-work it could not have been written, for an account of such a kind requires an intimate understanding of the Aborigine as a human being, especially since one of its objects is to suggest lines of treatment that should be followed if this misunderstood, ill-treated and in many ways attractive race is not to be left to die out in squalor; the book is written with sympathetic understanding, but without any tendency to idealize, sticking to observed fact and practical suggestion. Adolphus Peter Elkin (Maitland, N.S.W., 1891-1979) was for over twenty years Professor of Anthropology at the University of Sydney, and became the leading authority regarding the Australian Aborigine in general. A graduate of Sydney and London, he was a Church of England clergyman and Examiner for the Australian College of Theology, Past President of the Royal Society of New South Wales, Chairman of the Australian National Research Council[4] and of its Committee of Anthropology and President of the Association for the Protection of Native Races and of the Anthropological section of A.N.Z.A.A.S. The National Research Council some time ago awarded him a Fellowship in aid of his field-work in North-west and South Australia. Professor Elkin was also a Fellow of the Australian and New Zealand Association for the Advancement of Science and editor of the anthropological periodical *Oceania*,[5] which is dealt with elsewhere.

Discussing the origin of the Australian Aborigine, as to which the available evidence points to Indonesia, Elkin remarks that, judging by his exploits along the northern Australian coasts, there is no reason to doubt his ability to have crossed the sea; he probably spread along the northern and down the eastern and western coasts, and gradually southward across the central deserts. As to when he came to Australia there is no evidence at present, but it may have been one or two thousand years ago;* this would afford plenty of time for the development of the various languages and dialects: according to Elkin's estimate, at the time of the white man's arrival there may have been about 300,000 Aborigines, divided into some 500 tribes. In material culture, being compelled by circumstances to be nomadic hunters and food gatherers, the Aborigines rank, he says, lower than most horticultural and village people; but they are capable of a high standard of craftsmanship and of "quite praiseworthy" artistic expression, and[6]

> . . . their social organization, marriage rules, taboos, philosophy and ceremonial life are, in some respects, no lower nor less complicated than our own. True, some

[4] He has also been president of the Australian Institute of Sociology, and Australian member of the Council of the Pacific Ocean Science Association.

[5] See p. 1335.

[6] p. 20; on this point see Porteus and Warner.

* [There is now evidence of Aboriginal presence in Australia at least 41,000 years ago.]

> of the Aborigines' customs and beliefs are crude, but the same is true of some of ours, or was true in many white communities not so long ago;

moreover the systematic and elaborate organization of their social groupings shows that their intellectual capacity is by no means small. The basis of their social behaviour is relationship: "indeed it is the anatomy and physiology of Aboriginal society and must be understood if the behaviour of the Aborigines as social beings is to be understood". Elkin describes in detail how the family is enlarged until it includes the whole tribe, classifying the members of the various groups as mothers, fathers, uncles, and so on, marriage between close relations being forbidden even if they are not related by blood; but the system extends beyond the tribe, thus forming a connecting link between one tribe and another. He also describes various social groupings on the basis of age, sex, relationship and locality, which together constitute an extremely complex and elaborate organization regulating the Aborigine's whole life. Connected with these groups is the system of totemism, which, sometimes regarded as merely a device for regulating marriage, is actually[7]

> . . . a view of nature and life, of the universe and man, which colours and influences the Aborigines' social groupings and mythologies, inspires their rituals and links them to the past;

it involves[8] "a relationship between an individual or group . . . and a natural object or species . . . a relationship which is denoted by the bearing of the name of the latter, the totem, by the individual or group". So that every man has several totems, some concerned with social relationships, others with mythology, cult and ritual: the social totem not only symbolizes the common relationship of members of the group it represents, but is supposed to act as its friend and helper; the cult totem symbolizes not merely the group it represents, but also the heroic ancestor whom the cult commemorates. By their ceremonial re-enactment the myths are kept alive, and in this way the Aborigines remain in touch with the creative "dream-time" to which the myths belong, drawing from them tribal and racial life and confidence; the myths are usually associated with certain features of the landscape, whose origin is explained by reference to the actions of the ancestral heroes: after the tests and ceremonies of initiation, the young men become the custodians of these myths and their ritual, at the same time that they are accepted as adult and disciplined members of the society. The objectiveness of Elkin's approach and his lack of racial or religious bias are exemplified in his comparison of the Aboriginal marriage system with that which was until lately in force in Europe; in his comment on a missionary's loathing of the blood-drinking

---

[7] p. 126.
[8] p. 127.

rite that forms part of the initiation ceremonies in most tribes—"surely this is unreasonable for a Christian, especially one with strongly developed sacramental views"; and in his remark that among the Aborigines the sight of the sacred and symbolical bull-roarers "stirs the deepest feeling of reverence, akin to those experienced by the faithful when contemplating the Blessed Sacrament in some Christian churches". In a smaller book, *Aboriginal Men of High Degree* (Sydney, 1946)[9], Elkin deals with the Aboriginal medicine men in their capacities as doctors, magicians, and sometimes sorcerers. He disagrees entirely with the common belief that they are mere charlatans: in their chantings and their pretence of extracting a stone or magic bone from a patient's body, they are following traditional methods, which also they have found effective; their object is to give the patient an assurance of his cure, to restore his will to live. In this respect the medicine man is a faith-healer; but he believes in his own powers and will call in a fellow practitioner if he is ill himself: if he fails in his attempt at a cure, that is because he was called in too late, or because superior magic has been brought to bear, or because the patient has broken some important taboo. The medicine men are outstanding personalities; they have gained insight into men's minds, and seem to be able to influence them hypnotically, and also to be clairvoyant. Their occult practices are of the same order as those of the Tibetan yogis, though they are not so highly developed, and Elkin suggests that they may have "degenerated from a common source"; "I have long thought," he says,[10]

> ... that the silence and solitude of the Australian "bush" ... were conditions favourable to meditation and receptivity, to "tuning in" with the world, and to conjuring up pictures of persons and events not present. Sometimes the old white bushman or the Aborigine "just sits", but sometimes he "just sits *and thinks*", and to the latter at least, the thinking may include receiving, and for the man of high degree it may include "sending messages on the wind", to use a Tibetan term.

Elkin's book had been preceded at the opening of the Period by Basedow's *The Australian Aboriginal*[11] (Adelaide, 1925). Herbert Basedow (Kent Town, S.A., 1881-1933), was a Ph.D. of Breslau, an M.D. of Göttingen and a B.Sc. of Adelaide; he led a number of governmental and private exploring expeditions in Central and Northern Australia, and became Chief Medical Officer and Chief Protector of Aborigines in the Northern Territory and Special Aborigines Commissioner for the Northern Territory and South Australia, and also, incidentally, a member of the South Australian Parliament. His book covers a wide range, dealing with the physical characteristics of the Aborigine, his daily life from birth on-

[9] Originally delivered as John Murtagh Macrossan Memorial Lectures for the University of Queensland. Elkin has since published *Social Anthropology in Melanesia* (London, 1954).

[10] p. 74.

[11] A more popular book, *Knights of the Boomerang* (Sydney, 1935), was published after Basedow's death.

ward, his habits and customs, his tribal organization and administration, his art and religious ideas and his language; it suffers from the fact that many of its descriptions are so highly generalized as to produce a superficial effect, but Basedow had seen what he described and the book is still useful as a general account of the Aborigine's daily life and hunting and other occupations.

For practical as well as historical reasons there is badly needed a history of the Australian Aborigine since he came in contact with the white man, of his behaviour and of his treatment by individuals and governments; in the meantime we have Hasluck's *Black Australians* (Melbourne, 1942): the sub-title is "A Survey of Native Policy in Western Australia, 1829-1897", that is, from the foundation of the colony until about the end of its pioneering period and the handing over of the control of native affairs by the Colonial Office to a local and responsible government. Paul (Meernaa Caedwalla) Hasluck[12] (Fremantle, W.A., 1905-) has always been interested in Aboriginal affairs and was Commonwealth Minister for Territories; he is a graduate of the University of Western Australia, where he was Reader in History, and for several years he was engaged in writing the political volume of the history of Australia in the second World War.[13] Hasluck's book is an honest and straightforward outline. It shows how in the early days of the colony three main principles were adopted: the Aborigines were to be civilized and Christianized; they were to have the full status and rights of British subjects; and their physical well-being was to be fully protected: unfortunately, neither the Colonial Office nor the settler had the least understanding of the Aborigine; only the settler realized the difficulty of applying these principles, and in his struggle to establish himself and his flocks and herds, however liberal-minded at first, he came inevitably to regard the native as at the best a nuisance and at the worst a danger. Hasluck records[14] the case of a young Irish ex-barrister who took up land in the thirties on the Swan: he was sympathetically interested in the Aborigines, passed over with an adventurous tolerance a couple of attempts to spear him, and recognized that

> " . . . after all these uninformed creatures think they have as good a right to our swine as we have to their kangaroos";

yet finally, when more of his stock and also a settler had been killed, he lost patience, and regarded as "a painful but urgent necessity" the killing of nearly thirty Aborigines by a body of soldiers and settlers led by the Governor. What few attempts there had been to "civilize" the Aborigine were gradually abandoned, his status as a British subject steadily declined, and at least until lately the protection of his physical welfare amounted to

[12] For Hasluck's poems, see p. 1072.
[13] This has since been published as *The Government and the People 1939–1941* (Canberra, 1951).
[14] pp. 173-7.

no more than "a blanket a year and a ration of flour, tea and sugar". A Canberra conference in 1937,[15] which was attended by administrative officials, declared that half-castes should be educated and ultimately absorbed; that the semi-civilized should be better educated and employed, but excluded from contact with the rest of the community; and that the uncivilized should be maintained in Reserves: Hasluck attacks this division into classes, and urges a return to the old conception of the native as a British subject, to whom special conditions can be applied only temporarily.

One of the most intimate and sympathetic accounts of certain aspects of the beliefs and ceremonies of the Arunta[16] tribes is contained in Strehlow's *Aranda Traditions*[17] (Melbourne, 1947); Strehlow is a specialist in linguistics rather than in anthropology, and as to the social bearing of these beliefs and ceremonies he has little to say that is new in principle; but his records of the myths themselves and in particular of the ceremonial chants connected with them and his appreciation of their aesthetic importance have never been approached. Theodor George Henry Strehlow (Hermannsburg, N.T., 1908–78), was a son of the Reverend Carl Strehlow, who was formerly in charge of the Hermannsburg Mission in Central Australia, and whose anthropological work was referred to in dealing with the previous Period;[18] he spent his childhood among the Western Arunta, and not only learnt their dialect but was able to think in it as well as in English: Strehlow was a graduate of the University of Adelaide, a research worker in native languages in Central Australia for the Australian National Research Council, and also Deputy Director of Native Affairs in the Northern Territory; he visited oversea universities on a Research Fellowship from the Australian National University, then became Reader in Australian Linguistics in the University of Adelaide. Strehlow attacks the work of past investigators, not always justifiably, and emphasizes the misleading results that may be obtained by conducting inquiries in pidgin; but as a matter of fact few reputable Australian anthropologists have relied on pidgin alone. He says that the Arunta used by the skilful native storyteller is "an instrument of great strength and beauty", though owing to the abundance of archaic words and expressions and the complications of language and diction the chants at any rate are extremely difficult to translate: the few short examples of Strehlow's own renderings show that, apart from his intimate understanding of the material, he has a real appreciation of these chants and a feeling for words and rhythm; one wishes his renderings had been longer and more frequent.★ The

---

[15] pp. 205–6.

[16] Spencer's spelling of this word, which has been adopted by Australian anthropologists generally, is used here, except of course in quotations from a writer who spells it differently.

[17] Strehlow has also published, in mimeograph, a booklet, *Aranda Phonetics and Grammar* (Melbourne, 1947), and some pamphlets.

[18] See pp. 892–3.

★ [This wish has since been met by Strehlow's magnificent *Songs of Central Australia* (Sydney, 1971).]

Aborigines are, in his opinion, not a primitive but a decadent race; in this few Australian anthropologists would agree with him, and whereas he says that "The tradition and the tyranny of the old men in the religious and cultural sphere have effectually stifled all creative impulse", actually Spencer and Gillen showed that changes had been brought about through the councils of these old men. Strehlow also considers that the ancestral heroes of the Aborigines were morally inferior to their descendants of today; yet he says although the Arunta men are contemptuous of their women, their mythical female ancestors "are usually dignified and sometimes awe-inspiring figures, who enjoyed unlimited freedom of decision and action". And the old men of today, lamenting their lack of power, are proud, greedy and overbearing; they declare that young men nowadays are no longer hardy enough to endure such pain as used to be inflicted during initiation ceremonies, so that concessions have to be made to them.[19] Strehlow well conveys[20] the tragic lament of one of these old men whose authority has faded: sitting round a winter camp-fire at Alice Springs, the men were complaining about Makarinja's greed and haughtiness; suddenly there was a hush, and

> Makarinja himself approached, his white hair and white beard streaming in the cold wind. His steps were slow and stately; his bearing was proud and erect. In the days of his prime, his height had exceeded six feet and his figure still stood out above the heads of the younger men present. He beckoned me to approach. He spoke with passion.
>
> "Do you see these young men who are always murmuring against me? . . . They profess to be 'old' men. They have grown grey beards and white hairs for a pretence: they are just a pack of liars. Look at me, at my white beard, at my white hair. I am older by far than any of them. I have, it is true, become a little hard of hearing. But I remember all the stories that I ever heard; I know all the chants given to me by my elders and by their fathers. . . . I can still walk and hunt all day long. When you and I travelled to Ljaba, did I not keep pace with you from morning till night?[21] When I was a young man, no one equalled me in prowess with the spear. My skill in hunting was known from Ntarea to Ilbma; men were afraid to arouse my anger. . . . You see, they are all silent now. They know that I am speaking the truth."

As tragic is the lament of the other old man for the desecration by the white men of his country, every part of whose landscape, its creeks and springs, its rocks and hills and waterholes, had been moulded by the all-powerful hands of his ancestral heroes. The lament concludes:[22]

> "There is little here for strangers to see; there is no mountain cave here, only a storehouse in a mulga tree. But though the soak has been forsaken by almost all our people,

---

[19] p. 114. "We no longer tear off their finger-nails . . . we give the tjuringa [tjurunga] to them at a much lower cost" (The tjurungas are sacred objects, but the word has many meanings. See pp. 85–6).

[20] p. 171.

[21] Strehlow comments: "On some days we walked more than twenty miles in the fierce heat of the summer's sun; and I was occasionally more weary than my old companion when evening set in."

[22] p. 31.

a few of us old men still care for it. It still holds me fast; and I shall tend it while I can: while I live, I shall love to gaze on this ancient soil."

Without formulating any new theory, by discovering fresh facts and reinterpreting facts already known, Phyllis Kaberry's *Aboriginal Woman: Sacred and Profane* (London, 1939) presents her subject in a new light; what is more, it suggests reconsideration over a wider sphere. It is only lately that the life of the Aboriginal woman has been investigated at all, largely because the inquirers into Aboriginal life in general have been mostly men, and handicapped by their sex: Professor Elkin, who has himself felt this handicap, remarks,[23] in his introduction to Dr Kaberry's book, that when an Aboriginal man is asked some question about women's affairs, he will say, "That woman's business; you ask along woman", but the white inquirer does not care to break the women's taboos. As a result, Aboriginal women, and indeed this may be said largely of primitive women in general, have been until lately regarded as downtrodden drudges, compelled to perform the most exacting and monotonous tasks;[24] badly treated by their husbands, and "profane" in the sense that they are excluded from the sacred ceremonies of their tribe. Dr Kaberry's is the first full and detailed description of the life of an Aboriginal woman;[25] it is based on eighteen months' field-work in the Kimberleys in 1934 and 1935-6, and was financed by a grant and a Fellowship from the Australian National Research Council. Phyllis Mary Kaberry (San Francisco, U.S.A., 1910-77) was born of English parents; she was a graduate of Sydney[26] and of London, of which she was a Ph.D.; besides her Australian researches she carried out field-work in New Guinea and West Africa; she held research Fellowships at Yale, was also a Research Associate at the Royal Institute of International Affairs and later Reader in Anthropology at the University College of London. The Kimberleys contain a native population of about 6000, divided into tribes: most of the natives work on the stations, but once a year they "go walkabout" fifty or a hundred miles in the bush; there they hold their tribal meetings, their corroborees and other ceremonies; Dr Kaberry spent six months with the largest of the tribes, went out foraging with the women and shared their work. From her experience and inquiries[27] the Aboriginal woman emerges as an active social personality, whose work is of fundamental importance to her tribe

---

[23] Introduction, p. xx.

[24] See the quotation from Malinowski, *The Family Among the Australian Aborigines*, in *Aboriginal Woman*, p. 15.

[25] There were, of course, the incidental references in Mrs Langloh Parker's *The Euahlayi Tribe* (see this History, p. 894); as well as an article by Roheim in the *Journal of the Royal Anthropological Institute*, vol. lxiii (1933), pp. 207-65; and by Miss U. McConnel in *Oceania*.

[26] Where she took an M.A. in Anthropology.

[27] She used, as a rule, pidgin English, but "learnt phrases, acquired large vocabularies, and used native terms whenever possible. I was also able to keep some check on native conversations and the answers of informants" (p. x).

and her husband; it is no more compulsory than his, except that both are necessary to the tribal life; it is leisurely, but by no means merely monotonous and has its intervals of excitement, and Dr Kaberry, who speaks from experience, says that it is not nearly so hard as the men's.[28] It is true that on an expedition together the woman carries everything except spear and tomahawk; but a hunter must have his hands free, and her burden

> . . . does not tax the strength unduly, and is less tiring probably than the load the European housewife often carries home from the market;

the woman is by no means a drudge, but does the work for which she is best suited: man and wife co-operate, and their rights and duties are reciprocal. It is the same in marriage: the young woman has little freedom of choice, but neither has the young man, and in courtship the woman may make the first move; wife, as well as husband, demands fidelity, a wife may leave her husband for another man if she thinks she has good cause, and though the husband may beat, or try to beat, his wife if she is lazy, she sometimes does the same by him. It is true that she is excluded from his religious ceremonial, except that an old woman may sometimes take part in the increase ceremonies; but she has her own secret rites, which are concerned with birth, menstruation and puberty, and her own secret corroborees; and though she has nothing to do with the politics of the tribe, that is because they attach to the territory in which she lives, which is her husband's. Dr Kaberry's constant and perhaps natural attitude of defence gives the book a feministic undercurrent, but she makes no attempt to avoid facts: she admits that the women's rites are "less spectacular[29] and fewer in number" than the men's, and that in the performance of these

> . . . the women, on the whole, have not the vigour and fire of the men. Their steps alternate between a kind of shuffle and a half-skip.

Dr Kaberry's account is much more than merely descriptive: "The anthropologist," she remarks, "needs the eye of a novelist", and this she has: she presents a realistic and very human picture of the life she describes; in her account of her day's foraging with the women for instance. Incidentally, she has something to say on a subject about which there is still a great deal of argument; she insists that[30]

> . . . these natives in spite of over thirty years contact with the whites had still no idea of the true relation between sexual intercourse and conception;

conception occurs only when a man, usually the husband, finds a spirit

---

[28] "Merely to follow [the men] in their hunting over rugged hills and [in] the blazing sun left me so exhausted that after two attempts, I was content henceforth to amble with the women over the plains and along the dry river beds" (p. 15).

[29] This is obvious in her two comparative photographs (facing p. 264), but here the women performers, unlike the men, are half-dressed in European clothes, producing a ludicrous effect.

[30] p. 43.

child, which enters the woman by the foot. It is, however, admitted that sexual intercourse prepares the way for the entry of the spirit child; and as to a half-caste, either the white father must have found the spirit child, or else "Might be him whitefellow tucker—tomato, pumpkin, lolly: him no bin tell me."

Two important contributions to Australian ethnology have come from the United States, and since each has involved field-work in this country, covering in one case a period of three years, they may be discussed here: each disputes with convincing arguments certain commonly accepted conclusions by older writers. The first book in point of time was Porteus's *Psychology of a Primitive People* (London, 1931). Stanley David Porteus (Box Hill, Vic., 1883-1972) was educated at the University of Melbourne, where he was co-Director of the Laboratory of Educational Anthropology and lectured on Experimental Education; but he then emigrated to the United States and for nearly thirty years was Director of the Psychological Clinic and Professor of Clinical Psychology at the University of Hawaii. In 1928 he was invited by the Australian National Research Council to investigate the mental status of the Australian Aborigine; nothing of the sort had been attempted hitherto except in a couple of studies of small populations. Realizing that mental tests merely would be quite inadequate, and that he must consider the Aborigines' adaptability to their natural environment and the psychological bases of their life and social organization, Porteus spent some time among the tribes in the Kimberleys and Central Australia, and in several respects he quite disagrees with Frazer and even with Spencer and Gillen: whereas they had considered the tribesmen of Central Australia to be comparatively backward, in Porteus's tests they came out definitely better than those of the Kimberleys; and he disagrees quite as strongly with the opinion that because the Aborigine uses stone tools and goes naked he represents an "unchanged remnant of primitive mankind". Porteus remarks that the Aborigine uses the skins of animals for so many purposes that it would be absurd to suppose that he could not conceive of their use as clothing; but because of his frequent need to travel long distances in search of food and water the less he has to carry the better, and it is not cold that troubles him, but wet; in the circumstances to build permanent habitations would also be foolish, but he does build huts in wet seasons, or when he lives near permanent food supplies. When it came to the application of intelligence tests, Porteus was however faced by the difficulty that there were scarcely any that tested innate capacity as distinct from capacities developed by environment and upbringing, so it was only to be expected that the Aborigines' scores should be lower than those of other races; still they were "not markedly inferior to some of the other racial groups". Moreover, there were some marked exceptions to the general average, an

Arunta native making in one test a perfect score; and a test specially devised to suit the Aboriginal cultural background and acquirements[31] showed that

> . . . with test material with which they are familiar the aborigines' ability to discriminate form and spatial relationships is at least equal to that of whites of high-school standards and of better than average social standing.

The second book was *A Black Civilization* (New York, 1937) by William Lloyd Warner (California, U.S.A., 1898–1970), Professor of Anthropology and Sociology at the University of Chicago. Warner graduated at the University of California and made a number of field researches in the United States; this book, which was written under the auspices of the Australian National Research Council, records the results of a study of eight tribes, of which the principal was the Murngin, in north-east Arnhem Land: there was at the time of Warner's investigations a total population of about 3000[32] and European influence was negligible. The eight tribes had practically the same organization, myths, ceremonies and culture generally, and the whole of their social system was based upon a complex system of kinship. Warner aimed not merely to present a detailed picture of their social life, but to attempt to discover some of the general principles that underlay it, and also the social meanings of the symbols used in the community rituals. Wherever possible a statement is illustrated by a recital of actual occurrences, a story or legend as told to the author: for example, the chapter on warfare contains, among other illustrations, a long history of a clan feud, and the chapter on magic and medicine contains a number of case histories. Two incidental discussions, on "soul stealing" and the reasons for the effectiveness of black magic, and on the commonly accepted belief that the Aborigine does not understand the physical facts of conception, are particularly interesting. As to the first,[33] the explanation suggested is purely psychological:

> When the supposed theft of a man's soul becomes general knowledge, the sustaining social fabric pulls away from the victim . . . the collaboration of the victim and his society . . . ceases. The group now acts with all the ramifications of its organization and with countless stimuli positively to suggest death to a suggestible individual.
>
> The society itself creates a situation which, if unchanged, makes it impossible for the individual to adjust himself to it even though he tried; and in addition he not only makes no effort to live and to remain part of his group but actually, through the multiple suggestions from it, co-operates in his withdrawal therefrom. He becomes what his society's attitudes make him, committing a kind of *suicide*;[34]

on the second question, Warner thinks that in spite of Spencer and Gillen's opinion, even among the Central Australian tribes

---

[31] This was a test involving the recognition of footprints, which had been photographed (pp. 399–401).

[32] pp. 157–8. This was in 1926–9.

[33] p. 240.

[34] The italics are in the original.

> . . . possibly this knowledge [of physiological conception] does exist but is not considered important, the spiritual conception of the child looming so large in native thinking that the field worker obtains nothing but facts concerning the latter.

And he has no doubt at all that the knowledge exists among the Murngin; when he asked some of the old men what the semen did when it entered the uterus of a woman

> They all looked at me with much contempt for my ignorance, and informed me that "that was what made babies";

on this point Warner makes a comparison[35] which is as amusing as it is illuminating:

> The relationship between the primitive men of northeastern Arnhem Land and me as a field worker would be the same as that between the colonial Puritans of Massachusetts and the traditional visitor from Mars. Had the latter asked Cotton Mather or any other member of the community "where babies came from", he would have discovered that they came from heaven, that God sent them, and that it was the special duty of the church to look out for them. He might have been told that the stork brought them, and discovered totemic "spiritual conception".

Like Porteus, Warner points out the absurdity of inferring a low state of intelligence from the fact that the Aborigine does not wear clothes, and there are other incidental points of particular interest: for example the account of what Malay influences the tribes have felt. According to Robert H. Lowie, Professor of Anthropology at the University of California, in his introduction to the book, Warner was "the first to deal with amplitude of the structure and supernaturalism of a *tropical*[36] Australian people", Baldwin Spencer's trips to the North having been relatively short, and their results less authoritative than his work on the central tribes.

Francis Edgar Williams (Malvern, S.A., 1893-1943), at his death Government Anthropologist of Papua, has published four important and also very interesting books on various aspects of more or less out-of-the-way Papuan communities; but some were also presented as theses for university degrees. Most of these books were originally written as government reports. Williams was a graduate of Adelaide and Oxford, where he took a Diploma in Anthropology; he has been awarded the Wellcome Medal of the Royal Anthropological Institute and the Cilento Medal for work on tropical hygiene and native welfare. His first book, *Orokaiva Magic* (London, 1928), consists of three studies almost entirely of the magical and religious beliefs and customs of a group of tribes that occupy the greater part of the northern division of Papua; but these studies have a much wider bearing, for they further undermine the old assumption of the conservatism of primitive beliefs and the static nature of primitive

---

[35] p. 24.
[36] The italics are in the original.

culture, and show how it may evolve either gradually or by means of sudden and violent change. An example of the last is a new religious movement, the Taro cult; this is only one of a number of new cults but it is the latest and most widespread: Williams shows how it came into existence as the result of a series of visions, and how it has spread by reason of its adaptability to existing beliefs, its provision of a social and emotional outlet, feasting, singing and dancing, acting upon the native's emotional instability and his craving for excitement; he even sees in the observance of its ritual an influence making for law-abidingness, and in the inter-tribal friendliness which it creates and the recognition of its leaders in widely separated tribes a tendency towards cohesion which might conceivably "give the initial impetus to some more or less spontaneous political organization". In the same book another study shows how magical practices in general may arise spontaneously with an individual, out of a desire and hope which find outlet in symbolic representation of the result desired, according to the "universal primitive belief that 'like produces like'". Williams's next book, *Orokaiva Society* (London, 1930), is an outline, detailed and matter-of-fact, of the life, customs and beliefs of the same group of tribes; it was based upon two visits which lasted together about fourteen months, and presents a realistic picture of a rather likeable people, formerly quarrelsome, bloodthirsty and treacherous towards strangers even within the same ethnic group, but good-tempered and orderly, honest, courteous and dignified within their own village or clan; nowadays among these tribes the old warlike spirit survives mainly in sham fights, particularly when strangers enter a village, and in fearless hunting expeditions.[37] The description of the daily habit of the Orokaiva provides further evidence against two once widely accepted beliefs that "the native is nothing but a grown-up child", and that the woman does all the work while the man loafs in the shade. As to the first, "he is in all essentials of character a grown man" and probably "in all fundamentals he resembles us as closely in mind as he does in body"; and as to the second, though the woman works longer hours,[38] the descriptions of the villagers' daily life make it clear that the man does the heavier as well as the more skilled work: the women play little part in the public life of the community, and they are at least nominally under the complete control of their husbands,[39] who quite overshadow them, but "by virtue of his restraint on the one hand, and her powers of personal expression on the other", husbands and wives

---

[37] A bush boar may be a very formidable opponent to a man who is armed with nothing but a palm-wood spear.

[38] A fairly systematic investigation in two villages showed that of a total potential working time, men were idle 50 per cent and women 33 per cent.

[39] Though Williams notes some striking exceptions (p. 92).

usually get on very well together.[40] There seems to be something distinctly new in what may be called the spiritual beliefs of the Orokaiva: not only a man but every other creature or object has an *assisi*, a spiritual counterpart or substitute, not a "soul" or animative essence, but a shadow or reflection; also, every human being becomes after death a *sovai*, which is quite different from the *assisi*, though the two are sometimes confused. The *sovai* remains, for a while at least, about the village, a kind of ghost, which may take human or animal form, so that it is not always immaterial; it may appear as a fiend or hobgoblin; it is usually though not invariably malevolent, and even a man's friends and relatives go in fear of it, so that it has to be placated: for instance, the Orokaiva are fond of the dance, or ballet, and simple drama, usually comedy or farce and almost entirely in dumb show, but this also represents a ceremonial placation of the dead, and afterwards the paraphernalia of the players are put on rafts and floated down the river, in the hope that the *sovai* of the dead who have been celebrated will go away with them. The ballet, says Williams, is "a beautiful and valuable creation", and the play is "a thing of charm", in spite of a good deal of incidental obscenity. In a third book, *Papuans of the Trans-Fly* (Oxford, 1936), it is again the life, customs and beliefs of a native community that are recorded, but this time it is a poor and scattered community, the Keraki, in the south-west corner of Papua, who are somewhat lacking in spirit and energy, partly because of the unattractive nature of their territory and partly because until comparatively lately they were continually harried by more warlike tribes across the border. This book was the result of ten months' field-work spread over a number of visits, but owing to the sparsity of the population and the confusion of cultures and dialects, much of the information had to be gathered through interpreters. Generally speaking, the attempt is made to explain the customs and beliefs recorded, not historically, in terms of their origins, but psychologically: "it is one of the first aims of this book to discover the Kerakis' *motives*[41] for doing things as they do them"; examples are the exchange of wives, and also of food. Marriage by abduction or capture is very rare: usually when a man wants a wife he offers a sister in exchange; if he has no sister one is provided for him by his relatives, and failing that he buys a girl of his own matrimonial group for use as a sister for this purpose; there are also reciprocal exchanges of food, in which quantities and qualities are carefully noted, and there is the not uncommon custom of temporarily exchanging wives at feasts and dances. The interesting thing about all this is the reason suggested: that these exchanges "serve to bring the groups concerned into closer connection with one another; they

[40] On these points, compare what Dr Kaberry has to say about Australian Aboriginal women in this History (pp. 1454-5).

[41] p. ix. The italics are in the original.

establish relations and confirm them"; Williams compares the exchange of Christmas presents in civilized communities. The status of a wife is "as low as any I have yet encountered"; nevertheless

> She has a great deal of leisure and a good deal of amusement; she is devoted to her husband and children; a loyal servant to her community; and on the whole remarkably well satisfied with her life as she knows it.

Before actual marriage the girls are chaste; they are closely watched by their husbands' people: the young men also are chaste, so far as women are concerned, but they all practise sodomy, which is considered necessary to a boy's growth. Some of the Keraki myths, for instance of the "*gainjan* time", the beginning, when men and women "were greater than they are today", suggest the mythology of the Australian aborigine; and there is an interesting parallel with the Orokaiva, in the beliefs connected with survival after death; as among the Orokaiva again, though there is a more or less nominal headman, whose position is hereditary, his status is vague, and actual leadership depends upon character and personality. Finally, *Drama of Orokolo* (Oxford, 1940), which is an elaborate and detailed study of a single institution, the *Hevehe*, a great cycle of religious ceremonial which until lately dominated the cultural, artistic and social life of the western Elema, a people living along the coast of Orokolo Bay, at the head of the Gulf of Papua, only three days by coastal boat from Port Moresby; Williams spent much more time upon this than upon any of his other studies, and apart from what he was able to observe for himself his information was obtained not through interpreters but by conversation in Motuan. Orokolo is only one of a number of villages in the district to which it belongs; it was chosen because it is only in this and one other village that the *Hevehe* survives in an almost complete form: the coastal territory is rich, the people are prosperous and energetic, and their two villages have not suffered from the feeling of confusion and inferiority that so often follows upon the impact of the white man and his new ideas;[42] otherwise it would have been impossible to maintain a cycle whose performance has sometimes lasted fifteen years, and whose ceremonial demands a great deal of enthusiastic labour and the provision of a great deal of material. Like the other villages in the district, Orokolo is divided into smaller communities, each of which has or is supposed to have its *eravo*, or men's house: this is the centre of all its religious and ceremonial life, the habitation of spirits and their symbols, totemic masks, plaques and bull-roarers; when an *eravo* falls into ruin another has to be or ought to be built, and another ceremonial cycle must begin, in order to fill it with its *Hevehe*. The preparations for the cycle are described, including

[42] Williams suggests that it was this and the continued interest in the old ceremonial that saved these two villages from the wave of hysteria that swept over that part of Papua and was called "the Vailala Madness"(Foreword, p. viii; see also the index of this book for other page references).

the making of the *Hevehe* masks and their decorative designs, formalized representations in colour of birds, beasts, plants, rocks, winds and so on, which are often striking and sometimes beautiful. And we proceed through the series of ceremonies: the descents of the *Hevehe*, young men already initiated, dressed and masked to represent the spirits, from the now almost completed *eravo*; the visit of the sea spirits; the interspersed initiations of the novices; the feasting and the dancing, each *Hevehe* surrounded by his admiring group of girls; and finally the passing of the *Hevehe*, with their pretended slaying and the burning of the masks and last remains. Some of the scenes and situations, as Williams describes them, are exceedingly dramatic,[43]

> . . . but none can compare with this supreme moment when the *hevehe*, after wellnigh twenty years of confinement, issue forth to commence the brief fulfilment of their existence. In the grey light of early morning the first of them, "Koraia", stood framed against the blackness of the open door—a tall fantastic figure, silvery white, its coloured patterns in the atmosphere of dawn appearing pale and very delicate. The garishness, the grotesquerie, that full daylight and a new view might discover were now blurred; they faded into something fairy-like. One of the spirits—of forest, sea or air—one of the Magic People, one of the Immortal Story Folk, was about to lead its companions out of their long immurement to dance and make merry in the village. A strange, other-worldly figure, and a heathenish one, no doubt; but none who saw it poised on that dark threshold could have failed to call it beautiful.
>
> For a brief moment "Koraia" stood there, the great crowd of spectators gazing in silence. Then, with a thump of the drum and a prodigious rattling of *harau*,[44] it started down the gangway.

Williams urges that apart from its aesthetic achievement, the Hevehe Cycle provides the people who practise it with an objective and an opportunity for organization, constructiveness and leadership, and a recreation; and that it encourages a group spirit, a social initiative and a cultural pride all of which are extremely important to the vitality of a primitive people that has been denied some of its characteristic outlets: this is by far the best of Williams's studies and incidentally it presents a rich and living pageantry.

A number of Australian anthropologists have found their spheres in the islands of the Pacific, but only one had, up to the time at which this History closed, published his researches in book-form. Herbert (Ian Priestly) Hogbin (Yorkshire, England, 1904-), is Reader in Anthropology at the University of Sydney; he came to Australia as a boy, was educated at the Universities of Sydney and London, and was a member of several anthropological expeditions to the Pacific and New Guinea; with the rank of Lieutenant-Colonel in the A.I.F. he was adviser to the army on native rehabilitation in 1944-46, and afterwards Instructor in the

---

[43] pp. 356-7.
[44] Rattles of dried seeds.

Commonwealth School of Pacific Administration. Hogbin has been awarded the Wellcome and Rivers Memorial Medals by the Royal Anthropological Institute of Great Britain, and his researches have been assisted by Rockefeller and Australian National Research Fellowships; he has published a number of books.[45] The first, *Law and Order in Polynesia* (London, 1934), was in its original form a thesis for the London Ph.D.; it was the result of nine months' field-work in Ontong Java, an atoll north-east of the Solomons, supplemented by such documentary material as was available on Tonga, Samoa and Hawaii; but the actual writing was done while Hogbin was working in London under Malinowski, whose theories it largely supports. The book follows a rather unusual plan, in that the theory precedes the research: it has a definite bearing upon jurisprudence, for Hogbin affirms[46] that

> The system of clearly recognised obligations that has been discovered wherever a primitive tribe has been carefully investigated, does not trace its origin to a series of express commands issued by some superior authority, nor is it the outcome of a purposive effort;

he finds that in Ontong Java obedience to social standards of conduct is the result of the moulding force of training, as a member, first, of the family unit, and later of larger economic groups, reinforced by tradition, which is kept alive by tribal and religious ceremonies. Hogbin's survey concludes that primitive societies have their civil and criminal law, though without the institutions to which civilization is accustomed, and though it is not based on any single force; the book is highly generalized, and even in the illustrative descriptions we are not brought into any real contact with the people and the facts. Hogbin's next book, *Experiments in Civilization* (London, 1939), is less in the nature of an academic thesis, more independent, closer to life; though there are some repetitions, it has also a greater unity, the whole of it depending on the writer's own researches. Its centre is a native community in the north-west of Malaita, in the Solomons, where Hogbin spent six months. The book is divided into three parts: in the first he describes the community as it was before the white men came; in the second the changes that have come about as a result of contact with them; and in the third he makes some suggestions which he hopes may be useful to the Administration and the Missions. Hogbin made his inquiries at first in pidgin English, but later he acquired a working knowledge of the native language, and took part in the life about him: that he was a close and sympathetic observer is clear from the remark of a native friend: "At last we have found a European who is a

---

[45] Besides the two referred to here there were *Development and Welfare in the West Pacific* (Sydney, 1943; this was written in collaboration with C. H. Wedgwood), *Peoples of the Southwest Pacific* (New York, 1945) and, after the closing date of this History, *Transformation Scene* (London, 1951).

[46] p. 78.

black man, even if his skin is white." In Malaita, as in Melanesia generally, the principal social unit is the district group of families, which is derived from a common ancestor but regards male and female relationships as of equal importance, and whose members may marry anyone except their immediate family and first cousins; leadership of a group depends on social standing and generosity, so that there is keen rivalry and a considerable expenditure of energy in accumulating the wealth without which generosity is impossible. The man who wishes to be a leader accumulates pigs and enlarges his gardens, with as much help as he can get from friends and relatives, and he holds feasts, at which the guests gorge until they cannot move; at the dances that follow there are orchestras of pan-pipes,[47] and nothing else is talked about for a week beforehand: "'Our bellies are full, our bodies are light, and we think only of laughter' . . . Music and dancing throw anger out." There is little crime; the headman is seldom called on to settle disputes and he can usually handle them; small offences are revenged by magic, which also serves as a safety-valve for jealousy and anger; and there are curative spells for illnesses: if an offence is serious there may be a fight, in which a man's relatives sometimes help him, and in the case of certain sexual offences the spirit of the dead may interfere. There is no doubt, says Hogbin, that the population is declining, but he emphatically disagrees with Roberts[48] that this is due to a decadence that had showed itself before the arrival of the white man and to a weakening of the will to live as a result of the interference with old customs and of the white man's overwhelming superiority: the decline in population is simply a result of the diseases that Europeans have introduced; "*Joie de vivre* is . . . conspicuously present in Malaita." When the native has accepted Christianity, it has been "squeezed into the old mould", he prays against a man who has injured him, instead of casting a spell upon him; but the missions' disallowance of feasts and dances has brought about the collapse of the headman system, since it has deprived the would-be headman of the principal means of acquiring social standing, and this disallowance has also weakened the incentive to hard work. Far less deference is paid to parents and elders generally, partly because the young men have all the money, earned by working on the plantations, and partly because the children are deprived of home influences: they are free from school in the afternoon, but instead of going home they play games and pay visits to relatives who do not like to refuse them food and a night's lodging. Hogbin suggests that missionaries might be more tolerant of customs that play a considerable part in native life, and that more missionaries should be trained in anthropology;[49] that the Administration might recognize the

[47] Hogbin makes here the interesting observation that whereas he found the native music beautiful but melancholy, it made the natives happy (p. 69).

[48] pp. 125–6. See Roberts's *Population Problems of the Pacific*. See also *Experiments in Civilization*, pp. 132–6.

headmen and adopt the principle of "indirect rule",[50] and that education should be given a direct bearing on native life and needs.[51] He has no doubt of the disastrous effect of indentured labour upon social life, though he realizes that any attempt to encourage the native to work for himself instead of on a white man's plantation would be vigorously opposed; nevertheless he points out that[52]

> The question is, will the Administration of the Solomons follow the line of least resistance and pay heed to the requirements of the local planters, or is it going to give consideration to the consequences of wage labour on native society . . .?

Of the other sciences, only biology produced a notable work of a kind that comes within the scope of this History. Agar's *Contribution to the Theory of the Living Organism* (Melbourne, 1943)[53] is unusual among Australian works of science in that it is purely theoretical, though each stage of the theories is supported by the results of experiments: it is an individual contribution to the study of life, particularly in its lower forms, and most particularly in the cell; and its contentions are such and so supported as to be stimulating even to those who may disagree with them. Wilfred Eade Agar (London, 1882-1951) was a graduate of Cambridge and Glasgow, where he lectured in Zoology; in the first World War a captain in a Highland Light Infantry battalion in Egypt, he was Professor of Zoology at the University of Melbourne for more than twenty years. Agar approached the old problems neither as a mechanist nor as an upholder of direction from without, or from within either: instead of reducing the "higher" forms of life to a complex of mechanically and chemically determined cells, whose responses are also mechanical or chemical, he regarded the activities of the cell, and even of its component parts, as of a kind usually considered to pertain only to a developed many-cellular organism as a whole. His thesis is that all living organisms are what he calls "subjects", by which he means that they are capable of perception, or they are organizations of such subjects: they feel and perceive; their responses to stimuli are purposive; that is, they are directed towards immediate ends. They are not purposeful; Agar reserves that term for actions directed towards some biological goal: the animal's response to a sexual urge would be purposive; if such an action were concerned with the perpetuation of the species it would be purposeful. Not only is the cell a subject in Agar's sense, but so are its constituent parts, and finally there may be a central subject, the Central Agent, as Agar prefers to call it,

[49] But Hogbin remarks that the position is much better than it was: "the Department of Anthropology in the University of Sydney during the last few years has trained over seventy candidates for the mission field in New Guinea, Papua, Fiji, and Australia".

[50] He quotes 26 examples from Africa, and might have added New Guinea.

[51] In an author's note he says that a beginning has been made in this matter.

[52] p. 242.

[53] A second and revised edition of Agar's book was completed in 1951, just before his death.

which is concerned with the behaviour of the animal as a whole: this is the brain, but whereas ordinarily[54]

> . . . a pain in [for instance] the finger is conceived as due to a purely physical stimulus travelling from the finger to the brain, where it somehow, in a manner which it is not the business of physiology to explain, gives rise to the subjective feeling of pain . . . the feeling itself originates in the finger and is transmitted to, and re-felt by, the Central Agent.

Agar supports this contention, which is the centrepoint of his theory, by showing how unicellular free-living creatures, such as the amoeba, and also cells that are parts of a higher organism, and even fragments of cells, develop and adjust their behaviour to circumstances without the presence of a Central Agent. Some of his incidental remarks are such as one would not at first sight expect from a man whose theories are the reverse of mechanistic: for example that "nothing but technical difficulties stands in the way of our synthesizing a human being by putting together separate cells", or, for that matter, from synthesizing cells out of non-living materials. He does not claim originality for any of the propositions he puts forward, and his theorizing relies largely, as he himself says, on Whitehead's theory of the living organism; but his thesis retains an individuality of its own: it is an example of the creation of a unity which is more than the sum of its constituent parts.

Elyne Mitchell's[55] *Soil and Civilization* (Sydney, 1946) is treated here as a work of science, because its subject is soil erosion, in the ancient world as well as in Australia; but that is only the skeleton of the theme, which is developed in the manner of a poetic essayist. The book becomes a discussion of man's need to achieve a unity with his environment; of the consequences of his forgetting that he is made from earth, of his cultivation of "the false values of city life", which "dims all intuitive vision". In this there are important truths, if their expression is sometimes a little high-flown; and, like Dark and Barnard Eldershaw, Mrs Mitchell perceives beneath the surface of the landscapes we all know something that belongs to Australia and to no other country:

> That which seems the essence of Australia is the sense of endless space—horizons dipping in the sky—and, where it is held by blue mountains or a barrier of snow, the space merges with infinity and will not be enclosed. . . . In the abstract space of Australia there seems a stronger affinity with planetary space than is to be found in many younger countries.

---

[54] p. 75.

[55] For Mrs Mitchell's essays, see p. 1280.

CHAPTER XXI

NEWSPAPERS

Ultra Modernity: The Country Newspaper; the Sun News-Pictorial; *the* Sydney Morning Herald; *Other Newspapers*

THE AUSTRALIAN newspaper may now be considered to have grown up and to have taken its place, technically, among the newspapers of the world, though it does not rank so high from a literary point of view. An Australian newspaper is easily distinguishable from an English, let alone an American newspaper of the same type. Speaking generally, the new ideas and methods have been adapted rather than merely adopted in Australia: certain journalistic conventions and features that differ little from those of oversea newspapers are actually, given the adoption of certain basic ideas, the product of conditions that happen to be much the same here as overseas; but different conditions have sometimes given rise to different features, as for example the Australian Cable Page, as it was at its full development a generation ago. Still, no strikingly novel and fundamentally important journalistic principle or practice has yet originated in Australia, any more than Australian writers have yet originated any new and important literary idea or form. It is clear that the immense proliferation that has been one of the principal characteristics of the Australian newspaper throughout the greater part of its history has now come to an end; indeed a contrary tendency, towards diminution in numbers, appears to have set in. There had been signs of such a tendency earlier among the metropolitan dailies, but it had been far from consistent and during the preceding Period their numbers had actually increased. Today there are fewer such dailies than there were a generation ago; this time the country newspaper has been affected also, and therefore, since it constitutes by far the largest element in the total, the newspaper as a whole. In neither case, of course, does this imply a diminution in the strength of the journalistic demand and impulse that have been so marked an Australian characteristic. It represents rather, in both city and country, a consolidation of resources that has resulted in larger and more efficient newspapers, with much greater circulations, though, as will be seen, this has been accompanied by certain definite disadvantages from the point of view of their readers, and also of the community as a whole. To the general diminution in numbers there have been two exceptions: the number of bi-weekly, weekly and fortnightly newspapers has increased, but most of these do not come within our scope; and the increase in the number of suburban newspapers had been marked. Most suburban newspapers are free, depending for their income entirely upon advertisements, and some of the country newspapers are now also free. By the end of 1950 the number of metropolitan dailies had dropped from twenty-three to sixteen, and the number of country newspapers from 620 to 496. Of suburban newspapers there were 124 in 1950, but an exact comparison with the numbers at the beginning of the Period cannot be made because in this case the record is not exact.[1]

Strange as it may seem, in a Period that has seen a second World War quite as terrible as the first, the newspaper has been comparatively little affected by events outside the journalistic world. Both wars brought about, of course, a shortage of newsprint, but in the first World War this difficulty was to some extent got over by making pooling compulsory and in the second World War newsprint was rationed. There remained however a shortage whose results were seen in the smaller size of papers generally, in the dropping of certain established features, and in a decrease in the number of newcomers. But with the coming of peace and additional supplies of newsprint sizes gradually increased, dropped features were gradually reintroduced, and the decrease in numbers merged with the general decrease that has been already mentioned. Methods of collecting and handling news had been systematized during the first World War; it was necessary only to apply them to the new conditions and to use the latest scientific means and devices, for example, beam wireless, as they became available. Some however were not available in wartime; for example, aeroplanes were used to deliver newspapers in the early part of the Period, at least in special cases, but this became impossible once war had broken out. And with the second World War there was even less division of feeling in the Australian community and therefore between Australian newspapers than in the first, during which both the Irish question and conscription had created fundamental issues. Even the Depression, though it was fatal to a number of papers, did not affect the newspaper world as much as might have been expected. The principal changes within that world were however extremely important, though they represented largely the further development of the principles of the New Journalism, whose adoption had made so great a difference in the development of the newspapers of the preceding Period. But they depended also upon the development of the Australian community generally, and the resulting drive for circulation and advertisements. The increase in population, especially in the capital cities, and more especially in the two largest capitals, combined with the decrease in the number of

[1] These figures are based on a comparison of the records of the *Press Directory of Australia and New Zealand* for 1951 and 1925. No *Directory* was issued for 1924, but the comparison will be near enough.

newspapers, meant of course that individual papers were confronted with new and greater problems and opportunities. What is, at least from the point of view of this History, one of the most important events in the journalistic world of the period was produced by the reactions of the leading metropolitan dailies to these problems. By the beginning of the present Period the Sydney *Daily Telegraph* had fallen far below the leading rank, but it gradually picked itself up again, until so far as circulation is concerned it caught up and passed the *Sydney Morning Herald*. But changes that were more important and far more surprising occurred in Melbourne. Here the supremacy of the *Argus* and the *Age*, which had been as it were clamped down for generations, was uprooted by a newcomer, the *Sun News-Pictorial*, which had been founded in the last year of the preceding Period. This paper, a pictorial tabloid of the type of the London *Daily Mail*, has still the largest daily circulation in Australia, and the difference in comparative circulations has carried with it a considerable volume of advertisements, mostly of the pictorial kind. The ultimate cause of the success of the *Sun News-Pictorial* was Melbourne's need of a modernized morning daily. Both the *Argus* and the *Age*, when they realized that their supremacy was seriously threatened, moved with the times, but they had been too sure of themselves and their readers; they put off the changes over long. There seemed at first a chance that what had happened to the *Argus* and the *Age* in Melbourne might happen in Sydney to the *Herald*, but the *Herald's* administration awoke earlier to the course of events, and the *Herald* managed to modernize itself without changing its nature. It is true that all these newspapers had in a sense modernized themselves during the preceding Period, but they moved still in the shadow of the London *Times*, which had always loomed large over Australian journalism, had helped it towards the attainment of high standards, and had at the same time tended to hold it back, for good and evil, from the influences of modernity. It might have been hoped that if the *Age* and the *Argus* remained as they were, or almost as they were, at least a majority of their readers and therefore of their advertisers would still follow them; that the average Melbournian might glance over the *Sun News-Pictorial* now and then and yet continue his subscription to the more conservative and older-established papers to which he had been brought up; or it might have been hoped that without lowering their standards, the *Age* and the *Argus* might perhaps issue some ultra-modern publication as a bread-winning sideline. *The Times*, convinced that it could not compete with the popular Press and yet remain *The Times*, had deliberately chosen to remain, except for a certain brightening and liberalization, what it had been: a paper of record rather than entertainment, admired and honoured but usually from a distance, the Britannia of the world's Press. The *Manchester Guardian*, and also the Edinburgh *Scotsman*, had adopted the second alternative; they had published also modernized evening papers, which helped largely to keep them going. In a similar manner the Sydney *Daily Telegraph* had been assisted during the preceding Period by the *World's News*,[2] and during the present Period it is assisted by the *Australian Women's Weekly*. The *Argus* attempted to obtain this sort of support, but failed; it then rushed to an extreme and turned itself, in form at least, into a tabloid; the *Age* also modernized itself, though not to the same extent, but the circulation of both papers continued to shrink. Yet the situation is not quite what it might appear at first glance. The number of readers of a newspaper is not necessarily the same as the number of copies sold: such papers as the *Argus*, the *Age* and the *Sydney Morning Herald* are essentially family papers; as a rule they are read over the breakfast table by the husband and left at home for the wife; but the husband and any other member of the family who goes out to work may buy another morning paper to glance over on the way back, and yet one or all of the family may return of an evening to the paper for which they subscribe;[3] and something of the sort may happen even in the case of a bachelor household. The modern newspaper reader wants entertainment, it is true, but sometimes he wants information that is given as such and not whipped up into a short story in which factual perspective may be endangered; to this end he, or she, may be willing to put up with a less stimulating presentation, and for this purpose a comparatively old-fashioned paper may suit him best. On the whole, then, the *Age* and the *Sydney Morning Herald* at least are likely to have many more readers than their circulation figures show, and this must make an important difference to some types of advertiser. Circulation is however becoming more and more important, and in the pursuit of it city newspapers have pushed out into the country, even where the cost of delivery by plane has amounted to several times the price of the paper.

Running over the files of Australian newspapers today, and considering appearances only, the fact that first emerges is not so much the high technical standard that has been reached by certain individual papers or types of paper, as the range of application of that standard. Hitherto the few leading dailies of the two largest capital cities had stood out far beyond the rest; next came the leading dailies of the other capital cities, and then the leaders of the country dailies, though a few of the best of these took occasionally a higher place. But the present state of affairs

---

[2] Somewhere near the middle of the preceding Period a *Daily Telegraph* reporter was asked what paper he represented. When he had replied, "Oh, yes," said the questioner, "that's the paper that is printed in the *World's News* office!" There was just a little more than a joke about this.

[3] This point, which seems to me distinctly important, was suggested by Mr Leigh Scott, lately Librarian of the Melbourne University Library; on the other hand, as Mr Scott also pointed out, several copies of evening papers may be bought by members of a family on their way back from work in the city.

is different. Today, broadly speaking, and with certain important exceptions, every Australian newspaper, of no matter what State and whether it is published in a city or in some country town, provided that district is of some importance, is in appearance bright and up to date; indeed some of the leading country papers are in general appearance, though not in content, quite equal to the leading dailies of at any rate one or two of the lesser States. Speaking generally, today's newspapers, country or city, give less space to everything. The length of the leading article has not altered much since the end of the preceding Period: it runs from a column or less in the tabloids, and even this space may be occupied by more leaders than one, to as much as a column and a half in the *Sydney Morning Herald*, or a couple of columns in the *Age* if the "News of the Day" paragraphs are included. The average article is far shorter than during the preceding Period; it is more brightly written and invariably it begins with the gist of the news; but there is no column line around the "special" writer, and quite often a "special article" may run into a column and a half or even more. Articles of any length are invariably well broken and cross-headed, and even in the more conservative papers the page is brightened by the use of a far greater number of photographs. Also, the morning dailies print only the most important of the news that has already appeared in evening or Sunday papers, and they write it up differently and give it comparatively little space. The same applies to the evening papers: stale matter is no longer published; the "holdover" has been dropped. But the most striking difference is in the headlines. The present position seems to be that there are no longer any conventions about headlines; they may be of any size and may be used in any number; anything is permissible, provided a striking effect is produced, and provided, at least in the conservative papers, that an eighteen-inch gun is not used to shoot a mosquito. But the headlines are used with more discrimination: the long series that conveyed merely a blur have been finally abandoned. It would seem that the size of the headline has at last reached its effective limit. In the second World War, when Doenitz capitulated, the *Sydney Morning Herald*[4] came out with the following headlines:

> Germans Proclaim Surrender. Totally Crushed. Fighting Ceases After Nearly Six Years.

The letters in the first of these headlines were more than an inch high: it stretched right across the face of the paper, and though it contained only three words, there had to be a turnover. The letters in the second headline were nine-tenths of an inch in height. The second and third headlines were flanked on the right by a large photograph of Winston Churchill; beneath all this a five-line, large black lower-case paragraph ran right

---

[4] 8th May 1945.

across the page, and the remainder was black and bold enough. On the same occasion the Sydney *Sun* went farther still, with a headline, "It's All Over in Europe", printed in two-inch lettering over a background of fainter headlines taken from issues earlier in the war; this device, though not new, was very effectively carried out.

Though make-up and display are the most obvious factors in the greater attractiveness of the newspaper of today, certain other factors are also important; in discussing them it will be best to deal mainly with the great metropolitan dailies, which, now as ever, set the pace. The first of these factors concerns the arrangement of the paper. When the Period opened, the whole of the front page of every metropolitan daily was given over to advertisements, except, in some cases, for a column of short summaries of the day's news, and, in Melbourne, for the Births, Deaths and Marriages. In this matter there has been a practically universal revolution. Except for an occasional advertisement, which never occupies more than a small proportion of the space, the metropolitan dailies have now come to fill their front pages with news, though it was not until the Period was almost over that it became universally recognized that a newspaper front page was its shop window. Next come certain popular constituents of a paper which though not new are used more generally than they were: cartoons for instance. When the Period opened, among the leading morning dailies only the *Daily Telegraph* used such "wordless editorials"; now however most of the leading papers have followed. The serial has run an extraordinarily varied course: for a long while all the leading morning dailies published serials, but by the opening of the present Period they had shrunk in length from as much as three columns or more to about a column; during the second World War, owing to pressure on space, they were discontinued; with peace they were reintroduced for a while, and given as much space as ever, but sometimes dropped again. Sometimes also short stories are printed, but this is not so common, except in the evening papers. Many of the serials and some of the short stories are syndicated importations; it is complained that Australian novels seldom make good serials.[5] Book-reviews are now almost universal, forming part of a special or magazine supplement, but they vary in quality; some are mere summaries, and newspaper reviews seldom reach the standard of those in the *Bulletin* or the best of the literary magazines. So much for features that were in existence already, even though they were by no means universal and were not given the space they receive now; but

[5] A good novel may make a bad serial; for example, *Coonardoo* (see p. 1086). Some of the best Australian novels are too long for serialization; *The Fortunes of Richard Mahony* for instance. Others are unsuitable in their very nature; apart from its length, it is impossible to imagine *Such is Life* in serial form. The serial is a particular type of novel, and demands qualities which are not necessary to the novel as such and may even amount to faults in it. For example, every instalment of a serial should contain action and interest, should possess its own individual appeal.

certain quite new features have been introduced. The "Stop Press" was one of those devices that seem obvious and necessary as soon as they have been invented; it had been heralded by the heading "Late News", or "Late Edition", in the previous Period. There could be no more striking indication of the way in which the world was speeding up; the Stop Press represents the ultimate offering to the tyranny of time: its use is not however universal. Two other new features would have been considered by our grandparents to be gross vulgarities: one is the publication of comic and adventure strips, sometimes in colour, and the other is coloured supplements. The first is almost universal in leading Australian papers; the second is fairly rare outside the Sunday papers. Changes in the evening dailies have been fewer; they had not so far to go. The very nature of the evening paper is such as to bring it nearer than the family morning daily to the extreme left of the New Journalism, whose aim is to appeal to readers disinclined for anything but a series of short informative snippets of up-to-date entertainment. The Australian evening paper filled or almost filled its front page with news even at the opening of the present Period; and it used the Stop Press long before any morning paper used it. Its preference of short stories to serials is explainable on the ground of lack of continuity; the average reader of a morning paper usually has it delivered to him every day, reads it regularly and does not care to miss a number; but the reader of the evening paper buys it on the way home from work and does not mind much if he misses a number now and then, at least if he can get another evening paper instead. Many of the short stories published in the evening papers are Australian, but they are poor stuff, superficial and sensational; they are in fact crude examples of the types of story published in the cheaper "domestic" magazines; anything better would not suit the average evening paper reader, according to present-day journalistic ideas. Evening papers were also quicker to adopt the cartoon and the comic strip, and in conciseness, choice of the most striking parts of the news, modern use of headlines and sub-editing generally they led the way in introducing the methods of the New Journalism. The Sunday papers are few in number though their circulations have enormously increased; three States out of six still do without them.[6] An already noted characteristic of the New Journalism, that it aims rather to entertain than to influence, applies more to the evening than to the morning daily, and it applies most of all to the Sunday papers, whose idea of entertainment is far narrower than that of the leading dailies: as a

---

[6] [The Victorian Police Summary Offences Act, prohibiting publishing, selling or distributing Sunday newspapers, was not repealed until 1969. All the main capital cities, except Hobart, now have one or two Sunday papers. It was alleged in the nineteen-fifties that proprietors and staffs themselves were reluctant to provide Sunday papers.]

rule it excludes almost everything whose appreciation would involve even the mildest interest in the world of art, literature or thought, and most of its comic and adventure strips are mass-produced and imported syndications. Still, no Australian Sunday paper is anything like so large as the typical American Sunday paper, the "department store" in which everyone is supposed to find something to suit him, and which would, one imagines, prevent brain-fag during the whole of a long Sunday.

The modernization of the country paper is one of the most striking facts in the present phase of the history of Australian journalism; it has been attained not by the introduction of new features but by the manipulation of existing material in a skilled and up-to-date manner, and also, unfortunately, by the abandonment of any attempts at literary or cultural entertainment. But there is no doubt about the technical advance. Broadly speaking, even at the beginning of the present Period the country paper printed its news on the front page; it seldom felt the need of summaries, serials, short stories, book reviews or cartoons, and there were then, of course, no comic strips or coloured supplements. Broadly speaking again, the situation remains in these respects unchanged, but the difference in appearance is most marked: in almost every leading country paper type is well chosen, matter is well arranged, headlines are suitable and properly displayed, and there is due recognition of the value of white spaces, of balance and of contrast. Of the nearly 500 country newspapers about two-thirds are weeklies and most of the others appear two or three times a week; there are only thirty-two dailies. The diminution of numbers that has already been referred to is probably due, as Sommerlad suggests,[7] to consolidation; the amalgamation of several newspapers has often enabled a pooling of resources without which the high technical standards that have been reached would have been impossible. And, without actual consolidation, country newspapers that have common interests have sometimes grouped themselves together to maintain central offices in the capital cities, and State and Commonwealth Press Associations have also been formed. As to news-content, the country paper no longer depends for city and oversea news upon city papers and letters from city correspondents, but has its own collecting agencies and its own telegraphic service, and many country as well as city newspapers have interests in radio stations. Some two-thirds of the country papers are published in New South Wales or Victoria, about half in each; no country paper has established such a clear-cut and continuous leadership as that of the *Argus*, the *Age* or the *Sydney Morning Herald* during the greater part of Australian journalistic history, but among the leaders today are the Launceston *Examiner* (1842-) and the *Newcastle Morning Herald & Miners' Advocate* (1858-), which are however country papers only in the sense

[7] See p. 1467.

that they are not issued in the capital cities; and also the *Geelong Advertiser* (1840-), the *Ballarat Courier* (1867-), the *Northern Daily Leader* (Tamworth, 1871-), the *Toowoomba Chronicle* (1861-), and the *Border Morning Mail* (Albury, 1903-).[8] The best of the country dailies are by no means provincial, but they appear even more superficial than the dailies of the capital cities; except for occasional political excursions and weekly articles in the interests of women and children they seem to have no notion that there is anything in daily journalism beyond supplying summaries of current news. As for the country weeklies of the old type, they have practically disappeared, unless we take into account the *Bulletin*, which as has been said, is here treated as a magazine. The *Queenslander*, once one of the best and (for its time) most characteristically Australian of country weeklies, died in 1939, and most of the survivors are merely technical publications, containing, like *Country Life*, the present title of what used to be the *Stock and Station Journal*, practically nothing but general news and information of practical value to the countryman; or else, like the *Australasian Post*, once the *Australasian*, they have become magazines of the cheap domestic sort. The *Weekly Times* and one or two others retain some vestiges of the old-fashioned type, but they are only vestiges. Most of these country weeklies seem, like the country dailies, to proceed on the assumption that for anything but current news and matters of fact their readers will naturally depend on city publications, upon the potted extracts of the Sunday papers and upon the magazines whose type some of them approach; besides, the modern city dailies, the much-improved country dailies, and also the broadcasting stations, have absorbed most of the advertisement pool. Of the city weeklies, bi-weeklies and fortnightlies almost all are either highly specialized publications or of the general magazine type; of these a large number are addressed to women, though men also read them, and their circulations are extremely large: they are slick and Americanized and have scarcely any literary value.

No one can fail to notice the immense technical improvements that have been made by the New Journalism in the newspapers, Australian among others, of today; but there are also corresponding defects, some general, some along the debatable boundary of journalism and its left wing, the Yellow Press. The New Journalism, which is in a sense, of course, a reflection of the New Democracy,* has become in the newspaper world a reflection largely of the less cultivated sections of the population, who, in the opinion of the more popular magazines, desire entertainment quite as much as mere news, and entertainment of a kind that shall involve little or no exercise of the mental faculties. Popular entertainment of this kind, unlimited by questions of taste, runs the danger of slipping into

[8] Northcliffe declared the Burnie *Advocate* (Tas., 1890-) to be the best provincial newspaper he had seen in all his travels; but it is hard to find good reason for such an assertion.

* [Or perhaps, more accurately, an expression of the attempt to keep the New Democracy under control.]

vulgarity, as for example in the personalism that has invaded the Australian as well as the oversea newspaper world. A generation or two ago almost the only writers who signed newspaper articles were famous war correspondents, though here and there an exception might be made of some notable political commentator or even essayist; and reports and articles generally were written as impersonally as possible: even a star special-writer or reporter would take great pains to avoid the use of the first-person singular; for example, in *On the Wool Track* when a first-personal pronoun seemed necessary Bean used "one" or "we". During that period for political reasons an endeavour was made to compel the signature of leading articles; but the newspapers got round their obligation by stating formally that legal responsibility for all utterances to which a signature was required would be accepted by certain persons who were named: each newspaper thus preserved its collective and anonymous voice, since for all the public knew, one or all of those who signed might have been merely whipping-boys. The anonymity of the leading article has been maintained up to the present, but the rest of the paper is anything but impersonal; critical and other articles, even in the more conventional of the metropolitan dailies, are usually signed, even if with initials only, and where they are not, the writer's individual point of view is not hidden. This applies in particular to special daily or weekly columns, which have multiplied, under American influence, from the few that existed in the previous Period until scarcely any city newspaper is without at least one of them; but in Australia all these columns take the form of "newsy" and humorous, usually satirical comments on current events; the American practice, by which such a column often invades the province of the editorial, had not up to 1950 been adopted here, though there were signs of such an invasion. But personalism, as it has been here called, goes beyond the revelation of a writer's personality, to that of his human subjects; its underlying principles are that people are as much interested in personalities as in events, and that journalism should satisfy that "human interest". The first is of course true and the second legitimate, within certain limits; but the practice is sometimes carried so far as to involve an assumption that "bright" journalism has a right to invade privacy to almost any extent: ideally, every interview, every quotation of opinion, must bring the personality of the human subject before the reader, and the easiest way to do this is of course to sketch his physical characteristics. The following example[9] exemplifies the method sometimes employed by a "smart" reporter, not of the first grade:

> The usually smiling, moustached, round face of the Right Hon. James Chuter Ede, Britain's 62-year-old Home Secretary, carried a brow-wrinkled look.

[9] "Today News Magazine", supplement to the *Sunday Telegraph*, 23rd December 1945.

Below the always incorrectly tied bow tie, his comfortably bulky body moved uneasily while he talked to legal experts in his ministry.*

Allied with this defect is sensationalism, which represents another aspect of vulgarity. It is too often assumed, at least in practice, that because the average reader wishes to be entertained as well as informed, to be made to feel as well as to know, an effort must be made not merely to entertain him better than any rival newspaper can, but to give him something more striking, to excite him at all costs. The cost often is that the sensibilities of the journalist become so blunted that he overdoes the excitement without realizing it; and that he thus blunts the sensibilities of the reader also, causing him to want stronger and continually stronger stimulant. This sort of thing is due to defective taste and short-sighted enthusiasm, and to a kind of over-specialized thinking which concentrates upon the principal object, in this case the attraction of the reader, to the neglect of everything else. Hence also, occasionally, misleading headlines; for example, an evening paper prints in large type, "Great City Fire", and the man in the street hurries to buy a paper, only to find that the fire is in some far-off part of the world.[10] Mere carelessness, of course, may be an important factor in such cases, and there seems to be more carelessness today than hitherto in the journalistic world. In the obtaining of news, in its preparation for the press, in its sub-editing, newspaper men are not nearly so careful as they were a generation ago; mistakes of fact are commoner, style is oftener slipshod, there are more doublets,[11] and paragraphs that ought obviously to be grouped together are often separated: all this though the newspaper staffs are larger and better paid than in the preceding Period, even allowing for the reduced value of money. Even the conservative morning dailies are by no means guiltless in these respects, and, for the matter of that, English newspapers as well as Australian. In part, such defects are probably a reflection of the modern revolt against care and convention generally, but that by no means absolves the Australian journalist from blame; a better excuse would be the speed of modern journalism, but that would really shift the responsibility from staffs to managers and proprietors. From the point of view of this History one of the worst faults of the newspapers is the misuse of English;[12] this is extremely important, seeing that the average man or woman derives his ideas as to the use of words and the correctness of style mainly from the newspapers. And there are other faults. The average man and woman of today are far better informed and educated generally than were their grandparents, and they want from the newspapers more than was wanted in the early days of

* [This obsession with personalism has moved further into the political sphere. Voters are now asked to vote for manufactured "images": Mr A looks better on television than Mr B, so will make a better Prime Minister.]

10 See also Sommerlad, *Mightier Than the Sword* (Sydney, 1950), pp. 83-5, on misleading headlines.

11 Paragraphs unintentionally duplicated.

12 In Australia there is one outstanding exception, however; the English of the *Bulletin* remains almost perfect, for its use of slang is neither here nor there.

the New Journalism; it is a question whether newspaper managers and proprietors recognize this fact, and whether insufficient recognition of it does not act as a brake upon the intellectual development of the community. It is also a question whether the newspapers do not confuse the tenets and desires of democracy with those of what has been called "mobocracy", the least intelligent and cultivated element in the community, an element not confined to the less affluent section of it. On the other hand newspaper ethics in Australia are on the whole high; most of the faults that have been mentioned have been due largely, as has been seen, to shortsightedness and lack of care. It is sometimes asserted by political or other opponents of a particular newspaper or type of newspaper that it deliberately distorts the news, and this has even been asserted of the modern newspaper as such: of the Australian newspaper of today in general, and, setting aside some sectional organs, such an accusation is certainly not justifiable.* The political and social outlook of every paper is naturally reflected in the kind of news it presents to its readers, in the amount of space it gives that news, and in the method of its presentation; and it is a fact that matters of great importance have often to compete with others that in themselves matter very little, but are capable of being so expressed as to produce a sensational effect; this applies not merely to local news but to news from abroad, so that a fact of world-importance may receive little attention, or may even be ignored. Then there is the accusation that the newspaper is the servant of its advertisers, which ought to be less true of the Australian newspaper of today than of a generation ago, owing to its increased wealth. On the other hand, the newspaper is even more than it was a generation ago an inseparable part of the business world; nevertheless it has other affiliations also, and one can imagine circumstances in which it might be willing to support some section of its public whose interests ran for a while counter to those of the business world.[13] These changes in the Australian newspapers have been accompanied by changes in their form and constitution and in their interrelationship. In the matter of size there is nowadays a tendency in the newspaper to turn back in its tracks and return to almost the size of the *Sydney Gazette*: in this however it is of course form that is referred to, not number of pages; there has also been a change in the legal constitution of the newspaper: practically every paper of importance is nowadays a limited company, even those that are owned by families. And there have been changes in administration. In the early days editor and manager, or even editor, manager and proprietor were sometimes one; but apart from that, editors sometimes possessed great power, though the balance between editor and manager might sway this way or that with the character and personality of the men concerned. But nowadays the direction of a paper

* [This statement ceased to be true during the Vietnam War and could not be made now. See McQueen, *Media Monopolies* (1977).]

[13] See before, note on p. 906, note 7.

is coming more and more to lie in the hands of the management: perhaps the manager, perhaps the managing director.[14] As to interrelationships between newspapers, in spite of business and journalistic rivalries and disputes, which are conducted with much more dignity than in previous Periods, the existence of a common bond, at least between newspapers of a similar general point of view, has always been recognized, and there is now an Australian Newspaper Proprietors' Association, as well as Country Press Associations, to protect mutual interests. Also, during the present Period the chain system, under which groups of newspapers are linked by a common ownership, has been introduced into Australia, and outside such groups there is some interlocking of share holdings.

The leading Australian newspaper in the present Period is the *Sydney Morning Herald*. In point of circulation[15] it ranks only third among the morning dailies, and fourth if evening dailies are taken into account: in this respect the *Sun News-Pictorial* leads, the Melbourne *Herald* comes next and then the Sydney *Daily Telegraph*, but the *Sunday Sun*[16] has a larger circulation than any of these. Still, though these three leading papers are bought by more people than buy the *Sydney Morning Herald*, none of them has attained anything like a similar position in the estimation either of the public or of the business world. At the beginning of the present Period the *Sydney Morning Herald* was not far from its most conservative in policy, and also, allowing for certain modern developments that could hardly have been avoided, it remained conservative in make-up and journalistic methods generally. It was still a paper of record, aiming to report as fully as possible every event of importance, whether it had been published before or not. Its front page carried a column of three-line summaries of the news of the day, and the whole of the rest of that page was occupied by advertisements. It published a serial to which it devoted a column or more, and it had its regular book-reviews, but not cartoon or short story or Stop Press, and it would have been hard to imagine that it would ever publish a "Sporting Supplement". All this has now changed. In the early twenties, when it was still printing news summaries on its front page, it began to use the term "Home News" to refer to news that was Australian; this was a bold step for those days. It faced the problems that arose after the second World War with some daring and some imagination; its management decided that it should become as modern as was possible without ceasing to be the *Sydney Morning Herald*. It did not throw its bonnet over the windmill, but it put on a rather attractive looking modern hat; its "Granny" column is easily the most interesting of the kind among Australian newspapers. It turned its adver-

[14] On the other hand, managers are sometimes drawn from the editorial staffs, as for instance recently with the *Sydney Morning Herald* and the Melbourne *Herald*.

[15] These figures are for 1950.

[16] It has since become the *Sun-Herald*.

tisers out of its front page; it cut down its summaries, altered their form, and published a revised version of them upon an inner page. It introduced a Stop Press and comic and adventure strips. It expanded its book-reviews into a literary supplement that remained part of its regular Saturday issue; it reintroduced a serial, and gave it much more space, together with line illustrations and ornaments that relieved the monotony of the columns of type. It published some short stories, brightened its Saturday articles, got up its literary pages more attractively, and even issued a Sporting Supplement, including a "Turf Guide". Gradually it became again a paper of record, with however the qualification that it no longer published, or at least it gave much less space to, news that had been already recorded in an evening or a Sunday paper. And politically and socially it introduced a strong liberal colouring: the *Herald* could never be anything but conservative in attitude and atmosphere, but it is at present a liberal conservative, even liberal outright for a little while now and then. The *Argus*, as has been shown, was late in accepting the new situation: it seems to have assumed that its supremacy was unshakeable; the result was that the *Sun News-Pictorial* obtained a flying start. And when it became obvious that modernization was inevitable the problem seems to have presented itself to the *Argus* proprietary in an extreme form: *Times* or tabloid. It became a tabloid and even rushed to the extreme of issuing a coloured supplement; in fact it indulged in orgies of colour. It reintroduced and expanded its serial and added short stories, some of them Australian; and it not only introduced the cartoon and the comic strip, but, alone among Australian dailies, it "broke" its leading articles with cross-headings; its front page became brighter, but its other pages, printed in smaller type than the *Sydney Morning Herald's*, and less relieved by illustrations than those of the *Sun News-Pictorial*, were less attractive than either. Actually, its changes displeased its old subscribers and gained few new ones, and it was visibly failing when it was taken over by the proprietary of the London *Daily Mirror*, under whose influence it adopted at first something approaching a Labour or at least advanced liberal point of view, though its politics did not seem to have firm edges.[17] The *Age* had not quite so far to go as the *Argus* in the process of modernization, and it did not go to such an extreme: it began the Period with neither summary nor serial, cartoon or comic and adventure strip or Stop Press; but without altering its broadsheet size, it has made changes gradually, adopting Stop Press and strip but not cartoon, and retaining the usual Saturday articles and reviews. But, though the literary pages of the *Sydney Morning Herald* and the *Age* are of the same general type, those of the *Herald* are the more attractive, owing largely to the *Herald's* greater use of white spaces and light line illustrations. The *Daily Telegraph* had a comparatively short distance to travel to modernity. It published a cartoon when the Period

[17] The *Argus* expired in 1957.

opened and it became a tabloid before the *Argus*; since it had already lost the solid conservative tradition of Ward's day, this did not come as a shock. The *Telegraph* also ceased to publish summaries and removed the advertisements from its front page; so far as was possible it developed those features which the *Sydney Morning Herald* had dropped or cut down during the second World War, in the attempt to do to its rival what the *Sun News-Pictorial* was doing to the *Argus* and *Age*; it succeeded at least in building up its circulation beyond that of the *Sydney Morning Herald*, and even in capturing some of the *Herald's* advertisements. It has something of the brightness of the typical tabloid, for example of the *Daily Mail* or the *News Chronicle*, obtained not merely by display, but, in the modern manner, by a dramatization, sometimes a melodramatization of the facts. As regards expression, the difference between the broadsheet and the tabloid, which generally speaking fairly represent the ultra-modern and the comparatively conservative newspapers today, is not a matter of degree; it is the outcome of a difference in aim and ideal: whereas the broadsheet gives the fact all the emphasis it will bear without putting it out of perspective, the tabloid gives it all the emphasis that can be given it. It is a paper to which a jaded man or woman is likely to turn on the way home from work, but he is not so likely to turn to it when he feels fresher or wants to find what has actually occurred; not that the Australian tabloid is likely to falsify the facts, but it may very likely exaggerate them, by headlines for instance, falsifying their atmosphere. In make-up, in general arrangement, and in factual dramatization the *Daily Telegraph* belongs more or less to this type of newspaper, but differs from it in several respects. It can be thoughtful, as, for example, in its leading articles, which are read more than those of most tabloids, and it has attained some political influence; also not only its leaders but its articles generally are much longer than those of the typical tabloid. But no Australian newspaper has ever had so large a circulation as the *Sun News-Pictorial*. Compared with the million circulation of several English newspapers of a similar kind, let alone the five millions of the *News of the World*, the 426,000 of the *Sun News-Pictorial** is tiny; but it is surprisingly large if we consider not merely the smallness of the population of Australia but its division into States whose capital cities are so far apart and their interests so distinct that they limit the circulation of a metropolitan daily; even the *Age* and the *Sydney Morning Herald*, papers which have still a record value, have little sale beyond the borders of their own States. From an Australian point of view the general appearance of the *Sun News-Pictorial* is not unlike that of an evening paper, but that is largely because it is the first thoroughgoing pictorial tabloid to be published in Australia as a morning daily: even the *Daily Telegraph* is less fully illustrated, and lacks the purely

* [Circulation in 1980 was 649,000, the largest for a daily, though surpassed by the *Sun-Herald* (Sydney), a Sunday paper, with 670,500.]

pictorial double page in the centre which is an important feature of the *Sun News-Pictorial*; but as a matter of fact the Australian evening papers also lack purely pictorial centre pages, so that the *Sun News-Pictorial* in this matter actually goes beyond them in what might be considered to be their own line. Incidentally it is worth noting that the original idea had been to establish an evening paper, but since for business reasons this proved to be impracticable at the time, the new paper was launched as a morning daily. It was a success from the first. In its early days its circulation was "boosted" by a free insurance scheme, but circulation continued to improve after the boosting had been dropped. The Melbourne *Herald* had accustomed Melbourne readers to ultra-modern journalism, and the slowness of the two old-established morning papers to realize the need for development in that direction gave the intruder its chance, as has been explained already; since then its progress has continued, both in circulation and the attraction of advertisements. It is a curious fact that in the *Sun News-Pictorial* ultra-modern characteristics have been pushed farther than in the evening paper whose proprietors publish it. The *Sun News-Pictorial* has the usual evening tabloid characteristics, but publishes on Saturdays "feature articles", book-reviews, serials, mainly imported, and short stories, mainly Australian. Its general attitude, social and political, is much what one would expect to find in an Australian evening daily: it is a paper not of record but of entertainment, and of entertainment in the narrow sense. Its articles are short, its headlines striking, its general get-up bright and attractive, its display excellent: it is just the sort of paper that even those who had already run through the *Age* at breakfast would be likely to glance over on the way to work. But as a matter of fact the *Sun News-Pictorial* is read also in many homes, subscriptions gained by the early boosting device mentioned having been continued by a generation that had become used to subscribing to it, and a free insurance scheme has been added. The leading evening paper in Australia is now undoubtedly the Melbourne *Herald*, which was brightened and modernized by (Sir) Keith Murdoch; unlike most evening papers, it has, or had during the early thirties, a good deal of political influence, and it has been declared to be the best evening paper in the British Empire. Like the Sydney *Sun*,[18] it is a small broadsheet, whereas the Sydney *Daily Mirror* (1941-) is a tabloid; and whereas the two Sydney papers publish short stories daily, the Melbourne *Herald* publishes a short story only now and then. Of the city weeklies, by far the most interesting was *Smith's Weekly* (Sydney, 1919-50) during its comparatively short life. Incorporated in its planning were the last stirrings of the genius of J. F. Archibald, who, after his resignation from the *Bulletin* and after regaining his mental health for a while, devoted the remainder of his powers to help in forming what was to be

[18] But the Sydney *Sun* has since become a tabloid.

during its comparatively short existence the *Bulletin's* most serious rival. There can be no more marked indication of the versatility of Archibald's genius, in so far as it was that to which *Smith's* was indebted, for *Smith's* was far less literary and far more a paper of news; it did not review books at all; it published short stories, but their standard was not to be compared with that of the *Bulletin*; and though its tone was markedly Australian, it never set out to become a focus for Australian literature. Its popularity depended upon its quite individual humour, and particularly upon its humorous illustrations: these included comic strips that were definitely Australian in type, and other illustrations that mingled humour with sex-appeal: *Smith's Weekly* contained also clever and amusing reviews of and inquiries into current affairs, and it paid special attention to the affairs of the "diggers" of both World Wars.

The decline in numbers that has accompanied the increase in circulation and wealth of the Australian newspaper is not only significant of the drift of things, but may have important consequences. So far as country newspapers are concerned it is obvious that if the process were pushed very far the individual needs of many districts would be neglected; nevertheless so far the result has been good, in that the concentration of wealth and power has involved a definite improvement in news services and in organization generally. But it does not follow that the decline in the number of metropolitan dailies has involved corresponding gains: it would be absurd to suggest that Sydney, with its population of over two million, has sufficient journalistic representation with two morning and two evening dailies; or that Melbourne, with little less, is sufficiently represented by two morning dailies and one evening daily. It is the business of a newspaper to provide the news and the opportunity of expression that its readers require, and this the present-day city newspaper, however large and open minded, cannot do: there are many sections among its readers, and some of these have therefore to be content with a paper that is far from representing them, and to which it subscribes simply because the others are farther still. It is only majorities that are able to get the sort of paper they want, and not all majorities at that, otherwise in Brisbane the most important newspapers would have been Labour for many years[19] and every Australian capital city would have a large and important Labour daily. In this matter journalistic and political conditions have combined to create a problem that is of the greatest importance in the Australian democracy. For reasons that cannot be gone into here, only a very large and highly organized political party can exist without a newspaper, and the men and women who form an at least potential majority in the Commonwealth, men and women whose political and other views may be described as liberal in the proper sense of the word, are without political

[19] This was written in 1950.

representation, largely, it may be argued, because no great newspaper is devoted to their interests; it is true that several of the great dailies are sometimes liberal in attitude, but what is needed is a journalistic organ that is liberal all the time. The need extends far beyond the political sphere, and it is a need whose importance is fundamental. A modern democracy cannot function effectively or without danger, indeed it is a question whether it can permanently exist, without journalistic representation for every important section of the population; lack of such representation is apt to lead to suppressions, to more or less stifled discontents, to a mass-produced pseudo-uniformity that are ideal from the point of view of the extremist in every sphere. The ultimate cause of such a situation is the enormous cost of creating a large daily newspaper,[20] and of keeping it going without the revenue derived from advertisements: or without most of it, for commerce and industry would certainly, for a long while at any rate, prefer newspapers of the existing type. And, since revenue from advertisements covers at least half the cost of a newspaper's production,[21] readers of such newspapers would have to pay at least twice as much for them as for a newspaper of the existing type, even leaving out of account interest on capital expenditure. There seems to be only one conceivable way out of this impasse: the discovery of a multi-millionaire who is more concerned with practical politics and the survival of democracy than with the establishment of libraries or the endowment of universities.*

[20] And, ideally, there should be more than one in most of the States.

[21] See Sommerlad, *Mightier Than the Sword*, pp. 145–6.

* [The views expressed in the foregoing paragraphs have increased in cogency, first because the manipulative power of newspapers has increased with the concentration of ownership in a few powerful hands; second, because this power has lately been reinforced by the appearance in Australia of deliberate social engineering organizations, such as *Enterprise Australia*. The appearance of the much-needed millionaire who funded *Nation Review* during the seventies altered the situation briefly, but only marginally.]

APPENDIX I

CHAPTERS III AND IV

Green's division of poets into groups such as intellectuals, lyrical, and lyrically descriptive poets is less acceptable now than at the time at which he wrote. Until the early nineteen-twenties, the lyric, or the descriptive lyric, was the dominant mode in Australian verse. By the time his History was published in 1961, reflective, narrative and dramatic modes were gaining ground. In spite of the careful qualifications attached to his categories at the beginning of Chapter II, problems of classification were already occurring. Green left a note, for instance, indicating that he wished to group Judith Wright with Hope and McAuley, though whether this grouping is more satisfactory is debatable. What is clear in Wright's verse is that behind its lyricism is a carefully thought-out view of life and of the proper relationship between mankind and his environment, views which were to become clearer after the closing date of Green's History.

APPENDIX 2

CHAPTER IX

One of the few instances in which the writer feels compelled to dissent strongly from Green's general evaluation of a novel is that of Martin Boyd's *Lucinda Brayford.* The point has some importance in view of the fact that Boyd himself was convinced that this was his best book: "*Lucinda Brayford* c'est moi", he remarked of it, implying that he had given the best and deepest of himself to its making. Certainly the novel is an example of a recurrent theme in his work, founded on personal experience: Boyd, like Lucinda, had expected a bright future, and a bright future was expected of him. Neither realized their expectations. There are other parallels, which there is no room to discuss here. The chief point, however, is that Lucinda gradually grows through suffering from being an unreflecting, innocent extrovert, into a woman who is the image of her time and, indeed, of the history of women: the Eternal Mother with the Slain Son. Two world wars cheat her of husband, lover and son; and the son himself dies as a conscientious objector, so that the line of which he is the heir has no prospect of continuity. Behind the novel as a whole is the symbol of Good Friday and the Cross; the Cross is made up of the divine moral law, and the law of man on which the Body of Christ, which is man himself, is crucified. Behind the pity for Stephen, who is an ordinary young man, Boyd makes us feel pity for a whole generation of young men, as well as for the moral and cultural collapse initiated by the first World War and ratified by the second. What has survived since, as Theodor Adorno pointed out, is hardly even a semblance of civilization, a result which Boyd foresaw.

Opinions on Boyd as a novelist are sharply divided, though the swing of the pendulum at the moment is in his favour. It is only fair to point out, however, that the critic A. L. French, for example, makes a formidable case against Boyd as a novelist, on the grounds of both style and content, in his attack on *Outbreak of Love* (in *Southerly* No. 4, 1966), which has not been satisfactorily answered. His essay raises important questions about the possible ways of reading novels, but the proper place to discuss them is Volume III, in reference to Boyd's later work.

A second novel of the Period which deserves reconsideration is Robert

Desmond Tate's *The Doughman* (Sydney, 1933). The novel was known to Green, since there are notes on it in his files. It appears that it was finally excluded on stylistic grounds, that the crudities referred to by nearly all contemporary reviewers must have seemed to outweigh its originality. Nevertheless, it deserves to be remembered as possibly the first serious attempt by an Australian writer to present a detailed exploration of a particular industrial scene, anticipating Alan Marshall's *How Beautiful are Thy Feet* by sixteen years. There is much to be said for Douglas Stewart's reading of *The Doughman* in his Boyer Lectures of 1977, in which he rescued the novel from oblivion. He sees it as a precursor (though there is no direct influence) of David Ireland's *The Unknown Industrial Prisoner* (Sydney, 1971), considers that it moves on the two planes of realism and symbolism and believes its force, vitality and bizarre originality outweigh its faults.

Tate was born in Melbourne, in 1888, of English parents, and educated in Australia. Among his later occupations he was a mineworker in Scotland, a freelance journalist and a commercial traveller in London, and then a baker in his own country.

A SELECT LIST OF REPRINTS AND NEW EDITIONS

A select list of reprints and new editions of works discussed in H. M. Green's *History of Australian Literature* (1961)

ALDRIDGE, James, *The Sea Eagle*, Melbourne, 1944. (Sydney, Horwitz, 1960.)

The Diplomat, London, 1949. (London, White Lion, 1972.)

ASTLEY, William, "Price Warung", *Tales of the Convict System*, Sydney, 1892. (Brisbane, University of Queensland Press, 1975. Edited by B. G. Andrews.)

BACKHOUSE, James, *A Narrative of a Visit to the Australian Colonies*, London, 1843. F.3558. (New York, Johnson Reprint Corporation, 1967. Landmarks in Anthropology series, facsimile.)

BANFIELD, Edmund James, *The Confessions of a Beachcomber: Scenes and Incidents in the Career of an Unprofessional Beachcomber in Tropical Queensland*, London, 1908. (Sydney, Angus and Robertson, 1980. A & R Non-fiction Classics.)

Last Leaves from Dunk Island, Sydney, 1925. (Melbourne, Lloyd O'Neil, 1982.)

BARNARD, Marjorie, *Macquarie's World*, Sydney, 1941. (Sydney, Angus and Robertson, 1971.)

BARRINGTON, George, *A Voyage to Botany Bay, with a Description of the Country, Manners, Customs, Religion & c. of the Natives*, London, 1795. F.206. (London, Brummell Press, 1969. Bound in a case with a sequel to Barrington's voyage to New South Wales.)

BARTON, G. B., *History of New South Wales from the Records*. Vol.1—*Governor Phillip 1783-1789*, Sydney, 1889. (Sydney, Hale and Iremonger, 1980, facsimile.)

BATTYE, J. S., *Western Australia: a History from its Discovery to the Inauguration of the Commonwealth*, Oxford, 1924. (Perth, University of Western Australia Press, 1978. Historical Reprint series, facsimile.)

BAXTER, Annie, *Memories of the Past by a Lady in Australia*, Melbourne, 1873. (Adelaide, Sullivan's Cove, 1980. Under title *Annie Baxter's Memories*.)

BAYNTON, Barbara, *Bush Studies*, London, 1902. (Sydney, Angus and Robertson, 1980. Foreword by A. A. Phillips.)

Human Toll, London, 1907. (Brisbane, University

of Queensland Press, 1980. With other work under title *Barbara Baynton*. Edited by Sally Krimmer and Alan Lawson.)

BEAN, C. E. W., *On the Wool Track*, London, 1910. (Sydney, Angus and Robertson, 1969.)

The Official History of Australia in the War of 1914–18, Vols I–VI, Sydney, 1921–1942. (Brisbane, University of Queensland Press, 1981–1983.)

BECKE, Louis, *By Reef and Palm*, London, 1894. (New York, Books for Libraries Press, 1970.)

Under Tropic Skies, London, 1904. (New York, Books for Libraries Press, 1970.)

BONWICK, James, *Western Victoria, its Geography, Geology and Social Condition*, Geelong, 1858. (Melbourne, Heinemann, 1970. Introduction by C. E. Sayers.)

The Last of the Tasmanians, London, 1870. (New York, Johnson Reprint Corporation, 1978. Landmarks in Anthropology series.)

BOXALL, George E., *The Story of the Australian Bushrangers*, 2v. London, 1890. (Melbourne, Penguin, 1974. Penguin Colonial Facsimiles.)

BOYD, M. à B., *The Montforts*, London, 1928. (Melbourne, Lansdowne, 1975.)

Lucinda Brayford, London, 1946. (Melbourne, Lansdowne, 1969.)

BRENNAN, Christopher, *Poems*, Sydney, 1913. (Sydney, Sydney University Press, 1972. Introduction by G. A. Wilkes, Australian Literary Reprints, facsimile.)

BRENT OF BIN BIN, *Up the Country*, Edinburgh, 1928. (Sydney, Angus and Robertson, 1984.)

BROWNE, T. A., "Rolf Boldrewood", *Old Melbourne Memories*, Melbourne, 1884. (Melbourne, Heinemann, 1969, Heinemann Pioneer series.)

Robbery Under Arms, London, 1888. (Sydney, Angus and Robertson, 1982, Australian Classics.)

The Miner's Right, London, 1890. (Sydney, Sydney University Press, 1973. Introduced by R. G. Geering, Australian Literary Reprints, facsimile.)

The Bulletin Reciter, Sydney, 1901. (Melbourne, Lansdowne, 1975. Under title *The Old Bulletin Book of Verse*.)

The Bulletin Story Book, Sydney, 1901. (Melbourne, Lansdowne, 1973. Under title *The Old Bulletin Reader*.)

BUSBY, James, *Treatise on the Culture of the Vine, and the Art of Making Wine*. Sydney, 1825. F.1004. (Sydney, David Ell Press, 1979, facsimile.)

——— *A Manual of Plain Directions for Planting and Cultivating Vineyards and for Making Wine in New South Wales*, Sydney 1830. (Sydney, David Ell Press, 1979, facsimile.)

CARBONI, Raffaello, *The Eureka Stockade*, Melbourne, 1855. (Melbourne, Currey O'Neil, 1980.)

CARNEGIE, David Wynford, *Spinifex and Sand: a Narrative of Five Years Pioneering and Exploration in Western Australia*, London, 1898. (Victoria Park, W. A., Hesperian Press, 1982.)

CASEY, Gavin, *It's Harder for Girls*, Sydney, 1942. (Sydney, Angus and Robertson, 1973. Under title *Short Shift Saturday*.)

CHAMPION, I. F., *Across New Guinea from the Fly to the Sepik*, London 1932. (Melbourne, Lansdowne, 1966.)

CHISHOLM, A. H., *The Making of a Sentimental Bloke*, Melbourne 1946. (Sydney, Angus and Robertson, 1982. Under title *The Life and Times of C. J. Dennis*.)

CLARKE, Marcus, *For the Term of His Natural Life*, Melbourne, 1870–72. (New edition, 1929. Introduction by Hilary Lofting. Reprinted, Sydney, Angus and Robertson, 1982. Australian Classics.)

——— *Old Tales of a Young Country*, Melbourne, 1871. (Sydney, Sydney University Press, 1972. Australian Literary Reprints, facsimile.)

CLEARY, Jon, *You Can't See Round Corners*, New York, 1947. (Sydney, Horwitz, 1967.)

——— *The Long Shadow*, London, 1949. (London, Severn House, 1976.)

CLOSE, Robert, *Love Me Sailor*, Melbourne, 1945. (London, White Lion, 1972.)

——— *The Dupe*, Melbourne, 1948. (Sydney, Horwitz, 1963.)

COGHLAN, Timothy Augustine, *Labour and Industry in Australia from the First Settlement in 1788 to the Establishment of the Commonwealth in 1901*, London, 1918. (Melbourne, Macmillan, 1969.)

COLLINS, David, *An Account of the English Colony in New South Wales*, 2v. London, 1798–1802. F.263. (Adelaide, Libraries Board of South Australia, 1971. Australiana Facsimile Editions no. 76.)

COTTRELL, Dorothy, *The Singing Gold*, Boston, 1928. (Sydney, Angus and Robertson, 1956.)

——— *Wilderness Orphan*, Sydney, 1936. (Sydney, Ian Novak, 1961.)

COUVREUR, Jessie C., "Tasma", *Uncle Piper of Piper's Hill*, London, 1889. (Melbourne, Nelson, 1969. Edited by Cecil Hadgraft and Ray Beilby.)

CUNNINGHAM, P. M., *Two Years in New South Wales*, London, 1827.

(Sydney, Angus and Robertson in association with the Royal Australian Historical Society, 1966. Edited by David Macmillan.)

CURR, E. M., *Recollections of Squatting in Victoria*, Melbourne, 1883. (Melbourne, Melbourne University Press, 1965. Abridged, with a foreword and notes by Harley W. Forster.)

DAKIN, W. J., *Whalemen Adventurers,* Sydney, 1934. (Rev. edn, 1938, Sydney, Angus and Robertson, 1977.)

DARK, Eleanor, *Prelude to Christopher*, Sydney, 1933. (Adelaide, Rigby, 1961.)

Return to Coolami, London, 1935. (Sydney, Angus and Robertson, 1981.)

Sun Across the Sky, London, 1937. (London, Collins, 1962.)

Waterway, London, 1938. (Sydney, Angus and Robertson, 1979.)

The Timeless Land, Sydney, 1941. (Sydney, Angus and Robertson, 1980.)

DAVIS, A. H., "Steele Rudd", *On Our Selection*, Sydney, 1899.
Our New Selection, Sydney 1903.
Sandy's Selection, Sydney, 1904.
Back at Our Selection, Brisbane, 1906.

These four titles reprinted in one volume, Melbourne, Lloyd O'Neil, 1973. Australian Classics.)

DAVISON, F. D., *Man-shy*, Sydney, 1931. (Sydney, Angus and Robertson, 1981.)

Dusty, Sydney, 1946. (Sydney, Angus and Robertson, 1983. Australian Classics.)

DEAKIN, Alfred, *The Federal Story: the Inner History of the Federal Cause, 1880-1900*, Melbourne, 1944. (Melbourne, Melbourne University Press, 1964. Edited and introduced by J. A. La Nauze.)

DENNIS, C. J., *Songs of a Sentimental Bloke*, Sydney, 1915. (Sydney, Angus and Robertson, 1981.)

The Sentimental Bloke and Other Selected Verse, Sydney, 1915. (London, Angus and Robertson, 1981.)

The Moods of Ginger Mick, Sydney, 1916. (London, Angus and Robertson, 1982.)

Backblock Ballads, Sydney, 1918. (Sydney, Angus and Robertson, 1983.)

Digger Smith, Sydney, 1918. (Sydney, Angus and Robertson, 1982.)

Doreen, Sydney, 1917. (Sydney, Angus and Robertson, 1981.)

The Glugs of Gosh, Sydney, 1917. (Sydney, Angus and Robertson, 1980.)

Jim of the Hills, Sydney, 1919. (Sydney, Angus and Robertson, 1983.)

Rose of Spadgers, Sydney, 1924. (Sydney, Angus and Robertson, 1982.)

DRAKE-BROCKMAN, Henrietta, *Men Without Wives*, Perth, 1938. (Sydney, Angus and Robertson, 1955.)

DURACK, Mary and Elizabeth, *The Way of the Whirlwind*, Sydney, 1941. (Sydney, Angus and Robertson, 1979.)

DYSON, E. G., *Rhymes from the Mines and Other Lines*, Sydney, 1896. (Sydney, Pollard, 1973. Famous Australian Poetry Classics.)

"ELDERSHAW, BARNARD", *A House is Built*, London, 1929. (Adelaide, Rigby, 1978.)

Phillip of Australia, London, 1938. (Sydney, Angus and Robertson, 1977.)

The Life and Times of Captain John Piper, Sydney, 1939. (Sydney, Ure Smith, 1973.)

Tomorrow and Tomorrow, Melbourne, 1947. (London, Virago, 1983. Under title *Tomorrow and Tomorrow and Tomorrow*.)

ELKIN, A. P., *The Australian Aborigines*, Sydney, 1938. (7th edn, Sydney, Angus and Robertson, 1981.)

Aboriginal Men of High Degree, Sydney, 1946 (2nd edn, Brisbane, University of Queensland Press, 1977.)

ELLIS, Havelock, *Kanga Creek*, London, 1922. (Melbourne, Nelson, 1970. Introduced by John Heuzenroeder.)

ELLIS, M. H., *Lachlan Macquarie*, Sydney, 1947. (5th edn, Sydney, 1973. Reprinted, Sydney, Angus and Robertson, 1978. Famous Australian Lives.)

ESSON, Louis, *The Time is Not Yet Ripe*, Melbourne, 1912. (Sydney, Currency Methuen, 1973. Edited by Phillip Parsons.)

EVATT, H. V., *The King and His Dominion Governors*, London, 1936. (Melbourne, Cheshire, 1967. Introduced by Zelman Cowen.)

Rum Rebellion, Sydney, 1938. (Sydney, Angus and Robertson, 1978. Australian Classics.)

Australian Labour Leader: the Story of William Holman, Sydney, 1940. (Sydney, Angus and Robertson, 1979. Under title *William Holman*.)

EYRE, Edward John, *Journals of Expeditions of Discovery into Central Australia and Overland . . . in the Years 1840–1*, 2v. London, 1845. F.4031. (Adelaide, Libraries Board of South Australia, 1964.

Australiana Facsimile Editions no. 7.)

FAVENC, Ernest, *The History of Australian Exploration, 1788-1888*, Sydney, 1888. (Sydney, Golden Press, 1983, facsimile.)

FIELD, Barron, *First Fruits of Australian Poetry*, Sydney, 1819. F.738. (Sydney, Barn-on-the-hill, 1941. Preamble and notes by Richard Edwards.)

FINLAYSON, H. H., *The Red Centre*, Sydney, 1935. (Adelaide, Libraries Board of South Australia, 1979. Australiana Facsimile Editions no. 206.)

FINN, Edmund, "Garryowen", *The Chronicles of Early Melbourne*, 2v. Melbourne, 1888. (Melbourne, Heritage Publications, 1976. 3v. Vols 1 and 2 facsimile; Vol 3 biographical notes by Michael Cannon and index.)

FISON, Lorimer and HOWITT, A. W., *Kamilaroi and Kurnai: Group Marriage and Relationship, and Marriage by Elopement, Drawn Chiefly from the Usage of the Australian Aborigines*, Melbourne, 1880. (Oosterhout Netherlands, Anthropological Publications, 1967.)

FITZPATRICK, Brian, *British Imperialism and Australia, 1783-1833*, London, 1939. (Sydney, Sydney University Press, 1971.)

Short History of the Australian Labor Movement, Melbourne, 1940. (2nd edn, Melbourne, 1944. Reprinted, Melbourne, Macmillan, 1968. Introduction by Ian Turner.)

The British Empire in Australia, Melbourne, 1941. (2nd edn, Melbourne, 1949. Reprinted, Melbourne, Macmillan, 1969. Foreword by Geoffrey Blainey.)

FLINDERS, Matthew, *A Voyage to Terra Australis*, 2v. and atlas. London, 1814. F.576. (Adelaide, Libraries Board of South Australia, 1966. Australiana Facsimile Editions no. 37.)

FORSYTH, W. D., *Governor Arthur's Convict System*, London, 1935. (Sydney, Sydney University Press, 1970.)

FOWLER, Frank, *Southern Lights and Shadows*, London, 1859. F.9709. (Sydney, Sydney University Press, 1975. Introduced by R. G. Geering, Australian Literary Reprints, facsimile.)

FRANKLIN, Miles, *My Brilliant Career*, Edinburgh, 1901. (Sydney, Angus and Robertson, 1982. Australian Classics.)

All That Swagger, Sydney, 1936. (Sydney, Angus and Robertson, 1982. A & R Classics.)

My Career Goes Bung, Melbourne, 1946. (Sydney, Angus and Robertson, 1983, Australian Classics.)

FULLERTON, Mary, *Bark House Days*, Melbourne, 1921. (Melbourne, Melbourne University Press, 1964.)

FURPHY, Joseph, "Tom Collins", *Such is Life*, Sydney, 1903. (Melbourne, Lloyd O'Neil, 1981.)

Rigby's Romance, Sydney, 1905-6. (Adelaide, Rigby, 1971.)

The Buln-Buln and the Brolga, Sydney, 1948. (Adelaide, Rigby, 1971.)

GILES, W. E. P., *Australia Twice Traversed*, London, 1889. (Sydney, Doubleday, 1979.)

The Journal of a Forgotten Expedition, Adelaide, 1880. (Adelaide, Sullivan's Cove, 1979.)

GILMORE, Mary, *Old Days, Old Ways: a Book of Recollections*, Sydney, 1934. (Sydney, Angus and Robertson, 1963.)

GLASSOP, J. L., *We Were the Rats*, Sydney, 1944. (Melbourne, Lloyd O'Neil, 1982.)

GOODGE, W. T., *Hits! Skits! and Jingles!*, Sydney, 1899. (Sydney, Pollard Publishing Co., 1972. Famous Australian Poetry Classics.)

GORDON, Adam Lindsay, *Bush Ballads and Galloping Rhymes*, Melbourne, 1870. (Adelaide, Rigby in association with Golden Press and Lloyd O'Neil, 1975.)

GREY, George, *Journals of Two Expeditions of Discovery in North-west and Western Australia During the Years 1837, 38 and 39*, 2v. London, 1841. F.3228. (London, Borges, 1969, facsimile.)

GUNN, Jeannie, *The Little Black Princess*, London, 1905. (Sydney, Angus and Robertson, 1982.)

We of the Never-Never, London, 1908. (Sydney, Angus and Robertson, 1982.)

HAMILTON, George, *Experiences of a Colonist Forty Years Ago*, 2nd edn, Adelaide, 1880. F.10184. (Adelaide, Libraries Board of South Australia, 1974. Australiana Facsimile Editions no. 196.)

HANCOCK, William, *Australia*, London, 1930. (Brisbane, Jacaranda, 1961.)

HARDY, Frank, *Power Without Glory*, Melbourne, 1950. (Sydney, Angus and Robertson, 1982.)

HARRIS, Alexander, *Settlers and Convicts*, London, 1847. F.4529. (Melbourne, Melbourne University Press, 1969. Foreword by C. M. H. Clark.)

The Emigrant Family, London, 1849. F.5061. (Canberra, A.N.U. Press, 1967. Edited with an introduction by W. S. Ramson.)

HARTIGAN, P. J., "John O'Brien", *Around the Boree Log*, Sydney, 1921. (London, Angus and Robertson, 1976.)

HASLUCK, Paul, *Black Australians*, Melbourne, 1942. (Melbourne,

Melbourne University Press, 1970. New foreword by the author.)

HAY, William Gosse, *The Escape of the Notorious Sir William Heans*, London, 1919. (Adelaide, Rigby, 1975.)

HERBERT, Xavier, *Capricornia*, Sydney, 1938. (Sydney, Angus and Robertson, 1981.)

HETHERINGTON, J. A., *The Winds are Still*, London, 1948. (London, Sphere Books, 1971.)

HIDES, J. G., *Papuan Wonderland*, Glasgow, 1936. (Sydney, Angus and Robertson, 1973.)

HILL, Ernestine, *The Great Australian Loneliness*, London, 1937. (Sydney, Angus and Robertson, 1974.)

Water into Gold, Melbourne, 1937. (Sydney, Angus and Robertson, 1981.)

My Love Must Wait, Sydney, 1941. (Sydney, Angus and Robertson, 1981.)

The Territory, Sydney, 1951. (Sydney, Angus and Robertson, 1981.)

Hobart Town Gazette and Southern Reporter, Hobart 1816–1825. (Vols 1–2, Hobart, Platypus, 1965; Vols 3–4, Hobart, Platypus, 1967. William Dixon Foundation Publication no. 9.)

HOGBIN, H. Ian, *Law and Order in Polynesia,* London, 1934. (Hamden, Connecticut, Shoe String Press, 1961.)

HOWITT, William, *Land, Labour and Gold*, 2v. London, 1855. F.10618. (Sydney, Sydney University Press, 1972. Introduced by S. J. Butlin, Australian Historical Reprints, facsimile.)

HUNTER, John, *An Historical Journal of the Transactions at Port Jackson and Norfolk Island*, London, 1793. F.152. (Adelaide, Libraries Board of South Australia, 1968. Australiana Facsimile Editions no. 148.)

IDRIESS, Ion L., *Men of the Jungle*, Sydney, 1932. (Sydney, Angus and Robertson, 1953.)

Madman's Islands, 2nd edn, Sydney, 1938. (Sydney, Angus and Robertson, 1954.)

The Desert Column, Sydney, 1932. (Sydney, Angus and Robertson, 1981.)

"JAMES, Brian", *The Advancement of Spencer Button*, Sydney, 1950. (Sydney, Angus and Robertson, 1974.)

JORGENSEN, Jorgen, "A Shred of Autobiography", London, 1891 in *James Hogan, The Convict King*. (Hobart, J. Walch and Sons, 1967.)

JOSE, A. W., *Builders and Pioneers of Australia*, London, 1928. (New York, Books for Libraries Press, 1970.)

KENDALL, Henry, *Leaves from Australian Forests*, Melbourne, 1869. (Adelaide, Rigby in association with Golden Press and Lloyd O'Neil, 1975.)

KIDDLE, Margaret, *Caroline Chisholm*, Melbourne, 1950. (2nd edn, Melbourne, Melbourne University Press, 1957.)

KINGSLEY, Henry, *The Recollections of Geoffry Hamlyn,* London, 1859. (Melbourne, Lloyd O'Neil, 1981.)

—— *The Hillyars and the Burtons*, London, 1865. (Sydney, Sydney University Press, 1973. Introduction by Leonie Kramer, Australian Literary Reprints.)

LAMOND, H. G., *Dingo*, New York, 1945. (Melbourne, Sun, 1978.)

LANE, William, *The Workingman's Paradise*, Brisbane, 1892. (Sydney, Sydney University Press, 1980. Introduction by Michael Wilding, Australian Literary Reprints.)

LANG, John, *The Forger's Wife*, London, 1855. (Sydney, Ferguson, 1979, in *John Lang and the Forger's Wife*, by N. Keesing.)

LANGLEY, Eve, *The Pea Pickers*, Sydney, 1942. (Sydney, Angus and Robertson, 1976. A & R Classics.)

LASERON, C. F., *South With Mawson*, Sydney, 1947. (Sydney, Angus and Robertson, 1957.)

LAWRENCE, D. H., *Kangaroo*, London, 1923. (Melbourne, Lloyd O'Neil, 1982.)

LAWRENCE, D. H. and SKINNER, M. L., *The Boy in the Bush*, London, 1924. (Melbourne, Macmillan, 1980.)

LAWSON, William, *When Cobb and Co. Was King*, Sydney, 1936. (Sydney, Pacific, 1970.)

LINDSAY, Norman, *A Curate in Bohemia*, Sydney, 1913. (Sydney, Angus and Robertson, 1981.)

—— *The Magic Pudding*, Sydney, 1918. (Sydney, Angus and Robertson, 1978.)

—— *Redheap*, London, 1930. (Sydney, Angus and Robertson, 1979.)

—— *The Cautious Amorist*, New York, 1932. (Sydney, Horwitz, 1969.)

—— *Saturdee*, Sydney, 1933. (Sydney, Angus and Robertson, 1981.)

—— *Age of Consent*, London, 1938. (Sydney, Ure Smith, 1968.)

—— *The Cousin from Fiji*, Sydney, 1945. (Sydney, Angus and Robertson, 1979.)

LOVELESS, George, *The Victims of Whiggery*, London, 1837. F.2300.

(London, Communist Party of Great Britain, 1969, facsimile.)

MACCALLUM, Mungo, *Shakespeare's Roman Plays and Their Background,* London, 1910. (London, Macmillan, 1967.)

MACKANESS, George, *The Life of Vice-Admiral William Bligh, RN, FRS*, Sydney, 1931. (2nd edn, Sydney, Angus and Robertson, 1951.)

MACKENZIE, Kenneth, *The Young Desire It*, London, 1937. (Sydney, Angus and Robertson, 1972. A & R Classics.)

Dead Men Rising, London, 1951. (Sydney, Angus and Robertson, 1973. A & R Classics.)

MCLAREN, Jack, *My Crowded Solitude,* London, 1926. (Melbourne, Sun Books, 1966.)

MADGWICK, R. B., *Immigration into Eastern Australia 1788–1851*, London, 1937. (Sydney, Sydney University Press, 1969.)

MADIGAN, C. T., *Crossing the Dead Heart*, Melbourne, 1946. (Adelaide, Rigby, 1974.)

Central Australia, London, 1936. (Melbourne, Melbourne University Press, 1964.)

MANN, D. D., *The Present Picture of New South Wales*, London, 1811. F.518. (Sydney, Ferguson in association with the Royal Australian Historical Society, 1979, facsimile.)

MANN, Leonard, *Flesh in Armour,* Melbourne, 1932. (Sydney, Angus and Robertson, 1973. Introduced by Marjorie Barnard.)

The Go-getter, Sydney, 1942. (Sydney, Angus and Robertson, 1972. Introduced by Marjorie Barnard.)

MARSHALL, Alan, *How Beautiful Are Thy Feet*, Melbourne, 1949. (Melbourne, Penguin, 1980.)

These are my people, Melbourne, 1944. (Melbourne, Currey O'Neil, 1984.)

MAWSON, Douglas, *The Home of the Blizzard, Being the Story of the Australasian Antarctic Expedition, 1911–1914*, London, 1915. (Adelaide, Rigby, 1969.)

MELBOURNE, A. C. V., *Early Constitutional Development in Australia*, London, 1934. (Brisbane, University of Queensland Press, 1963. Edited and introduced by R. B. Joyce.)

MELVILLE, Henry, *The History of the Island of Van Diemen's Land from the Year 1824 to 1835 Inclusive*, London, 1835. F.1986. (Adelaide, Libraries Board of South Australia, 1967. Australiana Facsimile Editions no. 104.)

MILLS, R. C., *The Colonization of Australia, (1829–42)*, London, 1915. (Sydney, Sydney University Press, 1974. Australian Historical Reprints, facsimile.)

MITCHELL, Elyne, *Australia's Alps*, Sydney, 1942. (2nd edn, Sydney, Angus and Robertson, 1962.)

MITCHELL, Thomas, *Three Expeditions into the Interior of Eastern Australia*, London, 1839. F.2811. (2nd edn, Adelaide, Libraries Board of South Australia, 1965. Australiana Facsimile Editions no. 18.)

MOORE, William, *The Story of Australian Art*, 2v. Sydney, 1934. (Sydney, Angus and Robertson, 1980, facsimile.)

MORRIS, E. E., *A Dictionary of Austral English*, London, 1898. (Melbourne, Currey O'Neil, 1982. Under title *Morris's Dictionary of Australian Words*.)

MORRIS, Myra, *The Wind on the Water*, London, 1938. (Adelaide, Rigby, 1960.)

MORRISON, John, *The Creeping City*, Sydney, 1949. (Melbourne, Gold Star, 1972.)

Port of Call, Melbourne, 1950. (Melbourne, Gold Star, 1972.)

MUDIE, James, *The Felonry of New South Wales*, London, 1837. F.2312. (Melbourne, Lansdowne, 1964. Edited by Walter Stone.)

O'BRIEN, Eris, *The Foundation of Australia, 1786–1800*, Sydney, 1950. (2nd edn, reprinted, Westport, Connecticut, Greenwood, 1970.)

OGILVIE, W. H., *Fair Girls and Grey Horses*, Sydney, 1898. (Sydney, Angus and Robertson, 1958.)

O'REILLY, John Boyle, *Moondyne*, Boston, 1879. (Adelaide, Rigby, 1975. Introduction by Brian Elliott, facsimile.)

PALMER, Vance, *The World of Men*, London, 1915. (Melbourne, Cheshire, 1962.)

The Man Hamilton, London, 1928. (Adelaide, Rigby, 1960.)

The Passage, London, 1930. (Melbourne, Cheshire, 1970.)

National Portraits, Sydney, 1940. (Melbourne, Melbourne University Press, 1968.)

PARK, Ruth, *The Harp in the South*, Sydney, 1940. (Sydney, Angus and Robertson, 1980.)

Poor Man's Orange, Sydney, 1949. (Sydney, Angus and Robertson, 1980.)

PARKER, Langloh, *Australian Legendary Tales*, Melbourne, 1896.

More Australian Legendary Tales, Melbourne, 1898. (Both titles reprinted, London, Bodley Head, 1978 in one volume under title *Australian Legendary Tales.*)

PARKES, Henry, *Fifty Years in the Making of Australian History*, 2v. London, 1892. (New York, Books for Libraries Press, 1971.)

PATERSON, Andrew Barton, *The Man from Snowy River*, Sydney, 1895. (Sydney, Angus and Robertson, 1982. A & R Classics.)

Collected Verse, Sydney, 1921. (Sydney, Angus and Robertson, 1982. Introduced by Frederick T. Macartney.)

Happy Dispatches, Sydney, 1934. (Sydney, Lansdowne, 1980. Preface by Walter Stone.)

PEDLEY, Ethel, *Dot and the Kangaroo*, London, 1899. (Sydney, Angus and Robertson, 1982.)

PENTON, Brian, *Landtakers*, Sydney, 1934. (Sydney, Angus and Robertson, 1972.)

PETRIE, Thomas, *Tom Petrie's Reminiscences of Early Queensland, Recorded by His Daughter, Constance Campbell*, Brisbane, 1904. (Sydney, Angus and Robertson, 1983. A Queensland Classic.)

PHILLIP, Arthur, *The Voyage of Governor Phillip to Botany Bay; With an Account of the Establishment of the Colonies of Port Jackson and Norfolk Island*, London, 1789. F.47. (Melbourne, Hutchinson, 1982. Australiana Facsimile Editions.)

PHILLIPS, Marion, *A Colonial Autocracy: New South Wales Under Governor Macquarie, 1810–1821*, London, 1909. (Sydney, Sydney University Press, 1971.)

PRICE, A.G., *The Foundation and Settlement of South Australia*, Adelaide, 1924. (Adelaide, Libraries Board of South Australia, 1973. Australiana Facsimile Editions no. 57.)

Founders and Pioneers of South Australia, Adelaide, 1929. (Adelaide, Mary Martin, 1978.)

PRICHARD, Katharine, *Brumby Innes*, Perth, 1940. (Sydney, Currency Methuen, 1974; with *Bid Me to Love.*)

Working Bullocks, London, 1926. (Sydney, Angus and Robertson, 1980.)

Coonardoo, London, 1929. (Sydney, Angus and Robertson, 1982. A & R Classics.)

Haxby's Circus, London, 1930. (Sydney, Angus and Robertson, 1979.)

PRIESTLEY, Raymond Edward, *Antarctic Adventure: Scott's Northern Party*, London, 1914. (Melbourne, Melbourne University Press, 1974. Introduced by Sir Vivian Fuchs.)

QUICK, John and GARRAN, Robert, *The Annotated Constitution of the*

Australian Commonwealth, Sydney, 1901. (Sydney, Legal Books, 1976.)

RICHARDSON, Henry Handel, *Maurice Guest*, London, 1908. (London, Virago, 1981.)

The Getting of Wisdom, London, 1910. (London, Virago, 1981. Introduced by Germaine Greer.)

The Fortunes of Richard Mahony: Australia Felix I, London, 1917. *The Way Home: Second Part of the Chronicle of the Fortunes of Richard Mahony*, London, 1925. *Ultima Thule: Third Part of the Chronicle of the Fortunes of Richard Mahony*, London, 1929. (Sydney, Angus and Robertson, 1983. In one volume. Australian Classics.) (Melbourne, Penguin, 1982. In one volume. Afterword by D. Green.)

ROBERTS, S. H., *History of Australian Land Settlement 1788-1920*, Melbourne, 1924. (New York, Johnson Reprint Co., 1968.)

The Squatting Age in Australia 1835-1847, Melbourne, 1935. (Melbourne, Melbourne University Press, 1970.)

The History of French Colonial Policy 1870-1925, London, 1929. (London, Frank Cass, 1963.)

ROBINSON, M. M., *Odes of Michael Massey Robinson*, Sydney, 1946. (Dubbo, Review Publications, 1976.)

ROLAND, Betty, *The Touch of Silk*, Melbourne, 1942. (Sydney, Currency Methuen, 1974. Edited by Jonathon Shaw, preface by A. D. Hope.)

SADLER, Arthur, *A Short History of Japan*, Sydney, 1946. (2nd edn, Sydney, Angus and Robertson, 1962.)

SAVERY, Henry, *Quintus Servinton*, Hobart Town, 1830-1. F.1391. (Sydney, New South Wales University Press, 1984. Under title *The Bitter Bread of Banishment*. Edited by Cecil Hadgraft.)

The Hermit in Van Diemen's Land, Hobart Town, 1829. F.1290. (Brisbane, University of Queensland Press, 1964. Edited with an introduction by Cecil Hadgraft; notes by Margaret Roe.)

SHANN, E. O. G., *Cattle Chosen*, London, 1926. (Perth, University of Western Australia Press, 1978. Introduced by Marion Aveling, Historical Reprint series, facsimile.)

SMITH, Bernard, *Place, Taste and Tradition*, Sydney, 1945. (Melbourne, Oxford University Press, 1979.)

SPENCE, Catherine, *Clara Morison*, London, 1854. (Adelaide, Rigby, 1971. Introduced by Susan Eade.)

Gathered In, Adelaide, 1881-2. (Sydney, Sydney

University Press, 1977. Introduced by R. L. Waters and G. A. Wilkes, Australian Literary Reprints.)

An Autobiography, Adelaide, 1910. (Adelaide, Libraries Board of South Australia, 1975. Australiana Facsimile Editions no. 199. Edited and introduced by Jeanne F. Young.)

Handfasted. (Melbourne, Penguin, 1984. Edited by Helen Thomson.)

SPENCE, William Guthrie, *Australia's Awakening: Thirty Years in the Life of an Australian Agitator*, Sydney, 1909. (Sydney, Workers' Trustees, 1961.)

History of the A.W.U., Sydney, 1911, (Sydney, Workers' Trustees, 1961.)

SPENCER, T. E., *How McDougall Topped the Score*, Sydney, 1906. (Melbourne, Lloyd O'Neil, 1980.)

SPENCER, Walter Baldwin, *Native Tribes of the Northern Territory of Australia*, London, 1914. (Oosterhout, Netherlands, Anthropological Publications, 1966.)

Wanderings in Wild Australia, London, 1928. (New York, Johnson Reprint Co., 1967, facsimile.)

SPENCER, Walter Baldwin and GILLEN, F. J., *The Native Tribes of Central Australia*, London, 1899. (New York, Dover Publications, 1968.)

The Arunta: a Study of a Stone Age People, London, 1927. (Oosterhout, Netherlands, Anthropological Publications, 1966.)

STEAD, Christina, *The Salzburg Tales*, London, 1934. (Sydney, Angus and Robertson, 1983.)

Seven Poor Men of Sydney, London, 1934. (Sydney, Angus and Robertson, 1980.)

For Love Alone, New York, 1944. (Sydney, Angus and Robertson, 1982.)

STEWART, Douglas, *Ned Kelly*, Sydney, 1943.

Shipwreck, Sydney, 1947. (Both reprinted in *Four Plays*, Sydney, Angus and Robertson, 1970.)

The Fire on the Snow, Sydney, 1944. (Sydney, Angus and Robertson, 1976.)

STONE, Louis, *Jonah*, Sydney, 1911. (Sydney, Angus and Robertson, 1981. Introduced by Ronald McCuaig, A & R Classics.)

STURT, Charles, *Two Expeditions into the Interior of Southern Australia During the Years 1828, 1829, 1830, and 1831*, London, 1833. F.1704. (Sydney, Doubleday, 1982, facsimile.)

Narrative of an Expedition into Central Australia During

the Years 1844-46, London, 1849. F.5205. (New York, Greenwood Press, 1969.)

Sydney Gazette and New South Wales Advertiser, Sydney, 1803-42. (Vols 1-8. Sydney, Trustees of the Public Library of New South Wales in association with Angus and Robertson, 1963-70. William Dixon Foundation Publication nos. 2, 3, 6, 8, 10, 13, facsimile.)

TAYLOR, T. G., *Australia: a Study of Warm Environments and Their Effect on British Settlement*, London, 1940. (7th edn, London, Methuen, 1959.)

TENCH, Watkin, *A Narrative of the Expedition to Botany Bay*, London, 1789. F.48.

A Complete Account of the Settlement at Port Jackson, London, 1793. F.171. (Both titles reprinted, Sydney, Library of Australian History in association with the Royal Australian Historical Society, 1979. Under title *Sydney's First Four Years*. Introduced and annotated by L. F. Fitzhardinge.)

TENNANT, Kylie, *Tiburon*, Sydney, 1935. (Sydney, Angus and Robertson, 1981.)

Foveaux, London, 1939. (Sydney, Angus and Robertson, 1981.)

Ride on Stranger, London, 1943. (Sydney, Angus and Robertson, 1980.)

Lost Haven, Sydney, 1946. (Sydney, Macmillan, 1968.)

The Battlers. London, 1941. (Sydney, Angus and Robertson, 1983.)

THERRY, Roger, *Reminiscences . . . of Thirty Years' Residence in New South Wales and Victoria*, London, 1863. (Sydney, Sydney University Press for the Royal Australian Historical Society, 1974. Introduced by J. M. Bennett, foreword by Mr Justice Else-Mitchell, Australian Historical Reprints, facsimile.)

TOMPSON, Charles, *Wild Notes from the Lyre of a Native Minstrel*, Sydney, 1826. F.1092. (Sydney, Sydney University Press, 1973. Australian Literary Reprints, facsimile. Edited by G. A. Wilkes and G. A. Turnbull.)

TROLLOPE, Anthony, *Australia and New Zealand*, London, 1873. F.17333. (London, Dawson, 1968.)

TUCKER, James, *Adventures of Ralph Rashleigh*, London, 1929. (New edition, Sydney, 1952 under title *Ralph Rashleigh*. Reprinted, Sydney, Angus and Robertson, 1975.)

TUCKEY, J. H., *Account of a Voyage to Establish a Colony at Port Phillip in Bass's Strait*, London, 1805. F.418. (Melbourne, Taylor and Walsh, 1974, facsimile.)

TURNER, Ethel, *Seven Little Australians*, London, 1894. (Sydney, Lansdowne, 1983.)

The Little Larrikin, London, 1896. (Sydney, Ure Smith, 1978.)

Miss Bobbie, London, 1897. (Sydney, Ure Smith, 1978.)

TURNER, H. G., *A History of the Colony of Victoria from its Discovery to its Absorption into the Commonwealth of Australia*, London, 1904. (Melbourne, Heritage Publications, 1973.)

The First Decade of the Australian Commonwealth, Melbourne, 1911. (Melbourne, Heritage Publications, 1975, facsimile.)

ULLATHORNE, W. B., *The Catholic Mission in Australasia*, Liverpool, 1837. F.2391. (Adelaide, Libraries Board of South Australia, 1963. Australiana Facsimile Editions no. 24.)

VAUX, J. H., *Memoirs of James Hardy Vaux*, London, 1819, F.770. (London, Heinemann, 1964. Edited with an introduction by Noel McLachlan.)

VILLIERS, A. J., *Vanished Fleets*, Cambridge, 1931. (Hobart, Cat and Fiddle Press, 1974.)

Whalers of the Midnight Sun, Sydney, 1949. (Sydney, Angus and Robertson, 1982.)

WALDOCK, A. J. A., *Hamlet: a Study in Critical Method*, London 1931. (Sydney, Sydney University Press, 1975, facsimile.)

WALFORD, Frank, *Twisted Clay*, London, 1933. (Sydney, Horwitz, 1966.)

WARNER, W. L., *A Black Civilization*, New York, 1937. (New edition, New York, 1958. Reprinted, New York, Harper Torchbooks, 1964.)

WELLS, Thomas, *Michael Howe, the Last and Worst of the Bushrangers of Van Diemen's Land*, Hobart, 1819. F.716. (Hobart, Platypus Publications, 1966, facsimile.)

WENTWORTH, W. C., *A Statistical, Historical and Political Description of the Colony of New South Wales and its Dependent Settlements in Van Diemen's Land*, London, 1819. F.771. (Sydney, Doubleday, 1978, facsimile.)

Australasia, London, 1823. (Sydney, Department of English, University of Sydney, 1982. Introduced by A. Wilkes.)

WEST, John, *The History of Tasmania*, Launceston, 1852. (Sydney, Angus and Robertson, 1981. Australian Classics. Edited by A. G. L. Shaw.)

WESTGARTH, William, *Personal Recollections of Early Melbourne and Victoria*, Melbourne, 1888. (Geelong, Rippleside Press, 1970, facsimile.)

WHITE, Charles, *History of Australian Bushranging*, 2v. Sydney, 1900-6. (Melbourne, Lloyd O'Neil, 1981. Australian Classics.)

WHITE, John, *Journal of a Voyage to New South Wales*, London, 1790, F.97. (New York, Arno Press and the *New York Times*, 1971. Physician Travellers, facsimile.)

WHITE, Myrtle Rose, *No Roads Go By*, Sydney, 1932. (Adelaide, Rigby, 1973.)

WHITE, Patrick, *Voss*, London, 1957. (Melbourne, Penguin, 1960.)

The Tree of Man, London, 1956. (Melbourne, Penguin, 1961.)

WILLIAMS, F. E., *Drama of Orokolo*, Oxford, 1940. (London, Oxford University Press, 1969.)

Orokaiva Society, London, 1930. (London, Oxford University Press, 1969.)

Papuans of the Trans-Fly, Oxford, 1936. (London, Oxford University Press, 1969.)

Orokaiva Magic, London, 1928. (London, Oxford University Press, 1969.)

WITHERS, W. B., *The History of Ballarat*, 2nd edn, Ballarat, 1887. (Melbourne, Queensberry Hill Press, 1980, facsimile.)

WOOD, F. L. W., *A Concise History of Australia*, Sydney, 1935. (Rev. edn, 1944. Reprinted, Sydney, Dymocks, 1957.)

WOOD, G. A., *The Discovery of Australia*, London, 1922. (Rev. edn, Melbourne, Macmillan, 1969. Revised by J. C. Beaglehole, foreword by O. H. K. Spate.)

The Voyage of the "Endeavour", Melbourne, 1926. (Melbourne, Macmillan for the Royal Australian Historical Society, 1970. Foreword by Allen E. Bax.)

INDEX